STATE
PUBLICATIONS
AND
DEPOSITORY
LIBRARIES

STATE PUBLICATIONS AND DEPOSITORY LIBRARIES

A REFERENCE HANDBOOK

MARGARET T. LANE

Greenwood Press

WESTPORT, CONNECTICUT • LONDON, ENGLAND

Library of Congress Cataloging in Publication Data

Lane, Margaret T
    State publications and depository libraries.

    Bibliography: p.
    Includes index.
1. Libraries—Special collections—Government
publications. 2. Libraries, Depository—United States.
3. United States—Government publications (State
governments). I. Title.
Z688.G6L36   027.5'0973   80-24688
ISBN 0-313-22118-9 (lib. bdg.)

Library of Congress Catalog Card Number: 80-24688
ISBN: 0-313-22118-9

First published in 1981

Greenwood Press
A division of Congressional Information Service, Inc.
88 Post Road West, Westport, Connecticut 06881

Printed in the United States of America

10 9 8 7 6 5 4 3 2 1

Copyright Acknowledgments

Grateful acknowledgment is given for permission to reprint the following:

The sections of codes and statutes listed below by permission of the publisher, West Publishing Co., St. Paul, Minn.

ARIZ. REV. STAT. § 41-1335 (West)

CAL. GOV'T CODE §§ 14868, 14886, 14900-14912 (West)

CONN. GEN. STAT. ANN. §§ 11-9b to 9d (West)

FLA. STAT. ANN. § 257.05; §§ 283.22-24; § 283.28 (West)

ILL. ANN. STAT. ch 128 § 121 (Smith-Hurd)

IOWA CODE ANN. §§ 303A.21 to 303A.24 (West)

LA. REV. STAT. ANN. §§ 25:121-124; 36:209(I) (West)

ME. REV. STAT. ANN. tit. 1, §§ 501, 501-A (West)

MICH. COMP. LAWS §§ 397.55, 397.56, 397.59, 24.20 (West)

MINN. STAT. ANN. §§ 3.195; 3.302; 15.18 (West)

MO. ANN. STAT. §§ 181.100-181.140 (Vernon)

N.J. STAT. ANN. §§ 52:14-25.1 to 25.2 (West)

N.Y. LEGIS. LAW § 47 (McKinney); N.Y. STATE PRINT. & PUB. DOC. LAW § 6 (McKinney); N.Y. EDUC. LAW § 250 (McKinney)

OKLA. STAT. ANN. tit. 65, §§ 113.1 to 115; tit. 74, §§ 3104, 3106.1 (West)

PA. STAT. ANN. tit. 24, §§ 4201, 4425 (Purdon)

For my father the late Archer Taylor
and
my husband Horace Lane

CONTENTS

x   Contents

TABLES AND LISTS

TABLES

LISTS

PATTERNS AND

PREFACE

The opportunity which the preface affords me to write an informal note to the reader is one I cannot let pass. I enjoy writing about state document concerns and over the years have corresponded with state document librarians in many states. Although it seemed appropriate in this text to adopt a more formal and concise writing style, I hope my readers will consider themselves part of a circle of state document friends.

The comparative study that is Part I of the text has been written since my retirement as recorder of documents in Louisiana and is complementary to the materials in the bibliography and the state sections. I administered the document distribution program in Louisiana for more than twenty-five years and during that time collected citations to journal articles and laws relating to state depository programs.

The transformation of these materials into a publication began in January 1978 when I assembled a collection of depository laws for a committee of the State Documents Task Force of the Government Documents Round Table of the American Library Association. The committee encouraged me to make the collection more widely available. At that time, I was fortunate in meeting Arthur Stickney, then an editor with Greenwood Press, who recognized the possibility of expanding the collection into a book. He suggested a text to expand on the statutory language and to permit comparisons among the programs of the various states. The text is based on my own experience and reading in the literature.

I decided not to circulate a questionnaire but rather to assemble materials already available, albeit widely scattered. Although librarians are interested in what other states are doing, this interest is counterbalanced by the feeling that one's own state is unique. This contradiction in approach to the problems which state document librarians face makes it difficult to make valid comparisons or to prescribe a model program. Another self-evident truth that has haunted me in the preparation of this book is that local people know their own state and its laws better than outsiders. Nevertheless, I believe that librarians in the various states can learn from one another and that if maximum availability and use of state documents are to be achieved, the sharing of information on identifying, collecting, and using state publications is essential. Furthermore, as the importance of the information in state documents is recognized and as the public continues to exercise its right of ready access to the publications of its government, some degree of uniformity, some basic safeguards, and some minimum standards are necessary.

Some states already recognize the need to bring *all* the publications of *all* state agencies under bibliographical control, the need to maintain a definitive collection of state documents, and the right of the public to convenient access to the publications. The gathering of the laws supporting these policies should provide encouragement and stimulation in those states where these concerns are not formalized by legislation.

While it is exciting to work in a field where new legislation is being enacted, it is frustrating to attempt to maintain a completely up-to-date collection of the laws. The legislation as reproduced here is current as of mid-1980; thus, for almost all the states, coverage is through 1979. Only a few references to 1980 legislation were available at the time the present compilation was made. The number and frequency of changes in the laws, regulations, and practices in this developing field place the burden on the reader to check local sources for the most up-to-date information. Librarians in the individual states know the latest amendments and also the ways the law is interpreted and the extralegal practices that have arisen.

Administrators of state document distribution programs and librarians attempting to establish depository library programs are among the primary audiences to whom this book is addressed. The concern with words and definitions and the details of administration are included for their benefit. Every librarian, however, uses state documents, at least the state manual, and should understand the role of libraries in making these publications available to the citizens of the state.

Although I am a maker of lists, I have no list of those who have helped me. Such a list would include those with whom I have worked over the years as well as those who in the last year have generously responded to my requests. In a book about fifty states, thanks are due to people in each state, and I trust that those who answered questions related to their own state will accept an anonymous thank you.

Those who helped me with the actual assembling of the book include Nancy Cline, who read the manuscript, made detailed suggestions, and, most important, believed in the need for the book; Agnes Ferruso, who commented on an early draft; Anna Perrault, who looked at the bibliography section; and Elizabeth Martin, who typed parts of the text. My friend Marjorie B. Morgan, formerly at the Louisiana State Library, stood by my side throughout the writing and did whatever was necessary to keep the book moving toward completion, including professional advice and editing, and the more mundane tasks of typing, proofreading, and library errands. I am grateful to her for her constructive encouragement, moral support, and especially for the generous gift of her time. The members of my family have all contributed individually, my husband most of all. I thank you all.

I am grateful to all my friends; I appreciate their help and absolve them of all responsibility for errors and omissions; and I trust that they all join me in the hope that you, the reader, will find this book useful.

PART I Characteristics of Depository Library Legislation

1.

INTRODUCTION

To make freely available to its
inhabitants all state publications
by distribution to libraries throughout
the state

These words from the 1945 California policy statement were the first legislative recognition by a state of its responsibility for making state publications
available to all citizens. Most states had provisions for the distribution of state
publications to libraries, and a few mentioned depository libraries, but these
pre-1945 statutes stopped short of providing by law for availability to the
public. The goal of the earlier statutes was to supply documents to libraries for
preservation and research; many emphasized exchange with out-of-state
libraries. The idea expressed in the 1945 California law that the libraries were
merely the means for making the publications available to the public marks a
turning point in the legislation on state documents for libraries.

As other states followed the California example of stressing public access to
government information, a new body of legislation evolved, popularly called
depository library laws. These laws provided that public libraries, in addition
to college and university libraries, should serve as the access points for the
public. A second feature of this new legislation was the recognition by the
states that a central agency for monitoring the flow of publications to the
libraries could perform many tasks that would make the system more efficient
and more economical. Thus, a requirement was built into these new laws
creating a central distributing agency. Another change was the imposition of a
mandatory duty on the state agencies to supply copies of their publications.
This was a departure from the earlier practice of merely requiring the state
agencies to respond to requests from the libraries.

As the information industry introduced new forms of reproduction, broader
definitions of state documents were adopted and the term ''state publications''
came into use. These terms are used interchangeably throughout this text to
refer to all types of information produced by state governments. In addition to
state agencies, county and municipal agencies were occasionally embraced
within the new laws. The authority of the distribution center was extended to
include microfilming of state publications for the libraries, to provide more

complete distribution, and to alleviate storage problems. A listing of the publications received or reported by state agencies or distributed by the central agency was frequently required.

The foregoing recitation of new elements in legislation for library collections of state documents is an overview of changes that have come about since 1945. Although a pattern can be seen and although states have copied from one another, no single law incorporating all these new concepts has been produced. Even the most recent laws do not incorporate all possible features and are not necessarily the best. Compromise is a part of the legislative process, as is clearly evident in some of the depository legislation that has been enacted.

Even when a depository law provides for the flow of documents from the state agencies to a distribution center and on to depository libraries, such a law may not necessarily be effective, and no depository program may have developed. This is true, for instance, in Tennessee. In other states, the legislation is so loosely worded that it might not be recognized as the basis for a depository program. The New York program, for example, has operated for years without specific mention of depositories in its law.

Depository legislation, although intended for the benefit of the public, is most frequently initiated by librarians. When several libraries in a state recognize and try to meet the needs of the public for state publications, they duplicate each other's efforts if they do not follow a coordinated plan. Planned cooperation includes acquisition, centralized cataloging and bibliographical control, and geographically oriented availability. Librarians have favored these plans, known as depository library programs, because they are designed to bring state publications to the libraries systematically and automatically, to increase the resources available to the citizens of the state, and to ensure easier access to the publications for everyone. A depository library program has been correctly described as the best way to make government publications available to the public.[1]

What is a depository library program? It is a plan, established by law, that governs the flow of state publications from the state agencies, through a distribution center, to designated libraries, for the use of the public.

ESTABLISHED BY LAW

The importance of a legal basis for a depository library program cannot be overemphasized. One of the basic provisions in a depository library law is a clear requirement that state agencies send or furnish copies of their publications for distribution. The library that is dependent upon the benevolence of the state agencies for copies of publications is greatly hampered in its acquisitions program. Although a legal requirement that the state agencies furnish copies of their publications is no guarantee that they will do so, obviously the program is much stronger with such a legal requirement than without one.

STATE AGENCIES

The term "state agencies," as used here, should be understood in the broadest possible sense. (A chart showing possible types of agencies that have been included in a definition of "state agency" is included in Chapter 4.) The interest and cooperation of the state agencies in supplying copies of their publications are essential to a successful depository library program. Whether a state agency should publish, what it should publish, and the details of the printing laws are not within the scope of depository legislation considered here.

Librarians, of course, do have an interest in having state agencies publish their reports and research. In some instances, librarians have served on editorial advisory boards in state government, and they have frequently registered concern over the discontinuance of agency publications which they, as librarians, know have filled useful functions. These matters, however, are usually not an integral part of depository legislation, which is customarily limited to the publications that state agencies have elected to issue. The state section in Part III of this book includes the depository legislation that brings these matters within its provisions; an example is the new Washington legislation which provides for the state librarian as a member of an editorial board.

DISTRIBUTION CENTERS

The distribution center or clearinghouse as the bridge between the state agencies and the depository libraries is one of the important elements of modern depository legislation. Earlier legislation provided for direct distribution by the state agencies to the libraries or for distribution at the request of the libraries. Current depository legislation that provides for a distribution center, as a link between the state agencies and the libraries to regularize and monitor the flow of publications, brings life to the program and makes it work.

Such a center is usually in the state library agency. It may be only a staff position and not a unit of the library structure. The distribution center is located wherever activities related to the depository library program are administered at the state level. The center, sometimes called the clearinghouse, is the agency that receives the publications from the state agencies, lists them, and forwards them to the depository libraries. The performance of these activities has so many ramifications that the chapter on the distribution center (Chapter 6) is the longest in this book. Here again, it is important that the assignment of these duties to the distribution center be made in the legislation, preferably in general terms that will not restrict service to the depository libraries or to the state agencies. If the distribution center is not named in the law, its requests to the state agencies for publications as well as its applications for operating funds will be weakened. It is a well-known fact that it is always more difficult to secure appropriations for programs that are not mandated by the legislature.

DEPOSITORY LIBRARIES

Depository libraries are the recipients of the state agency publications and in most states are limited to libraries within the state. In establishing depository library programs, legislatures have assumed, and have sometimes stated specifically, that only libraries within the state may be participants in the program. Legislators are primarily interested in providing for the libraries that serve their constituents. The Library of Congress and the Center for Research Libraries are notable exceptions; they are usually included even in depository programs that permit no other out-of-state libraries in the system. Out-of-state libraries are specifically identified when they are included in the discussion of depository libraries.

Depository libraries are often thought of as the purpose for which a depository library program exists, and they are indeed an indispensable element of such a program. However, these libraries, because they assume the depository responsibilities of providing free access to the publications they receive through the program and give guidance in the use of the materials, can be more accurately described as the *means* for achieving the goals of the program rather than the purpose of the program.

One caution should be observed in reading the literature about depository libraries. Some writers refer to the library which receives and distributes the publications as the "depository," thus combining the distribution and the use functions. It seems more precise to use the term "distribution center" for the distribution function and to limit the term "depository" to the agency that maintains a collection, even when the two functions are administered in the same library.

No attempt has been made in this book to discuss the organization and maintenance of the collection within the library, except insofar as the depository legislation sets down specific requirements that the libraries must meet. Clearly, certain parallels can be drawn from those handbooks written about the handling of federal documents in libraries, and many practices recommended for federal documents are appropriate for state documents. It can be expected that as more manuals are prepared by state document administrators for individual states, a general handbook of recommended practices for the maintenance of state document collections in libraries may be developed.

THE PUBLIC

A less formal way of describing a depository library program is to think of it as a way for libraries to secure state publications readily and automatically. A library patron might say, "The depository system is the way our library gets state documents." The mention of "our library" indicates awareness of the local availability of the publications. The thought that state publications are deposited in geographically dispersed libraries for easy access by citizens across the state is basic to the concept of a depository program.

It must be admitted that only an astute user, perhaps a library trustee, would be able to answer the question, ''What is a depository library program?'' For the ordinary user, the depository system is a library procedure from which he or she benefits without knowing of its existence. The availability of state documents to answer a user's query may be taken for granted. In fact, the user may not even realize that the publication which the librarian suggests is a state document. Nevertheless, the availability of state publications is basic to good government and a primary reason why depository systems were first established.

A depository program is a plan that provides local availability of state publications and their contents to citizens through libraries. For most citizens the procedure itself is not important; the convenient and guided access to current and retrospective publications of their government is.

ADVANTAGES OF A DEPOSITORY SYSTEM

In a depository library, the publications that arrive on a regular basis in an established pattern are expected and would have to be acquired through individual effort were there no depository program to provide them. The saving in time, staff, and money gained in each local depository library by regular and automatic receipt of state publications can be multiplied by the number of libraries in the system to substantiate a significant saving of tax monies on a statewide basis. At the local level, a depository system is clearly a cost-effective program.

At the state level, the state agencies that contribute their publications to the system also realize savings through a one-time distribution to a number of libraries. In states with a depository program, state agencies can reduce distribution to individuals, thereby saving tax dollars and requiring less stock to supply the public's information needs. In addition to the financial benefits from the depository program, state agencies receive wider and more permanent exposure of the information in their publications. The publications reach a wider audience merely by being in a library.

In addition to providing access to documents in depository libraries throughout the state, a depository library program has two other advantages for the citizens of the state. First, a checklist of publications is usually prepared for the depository libraries. In many states, the depository legislation requires the distribution center to issue such a list. Most states have recognized that this list should not be limited to the documents in the distribution program but should be a comprehensive bibliographical control tool—an ''official list,'' as it is sometimes called. Regardless of the operation of the depository system, the state checklist should be as complete a list as it is possible to produce. Furthermore, some library in the state should maintain a collection of all the items in the checklist—a complete historical collection.

These related concerns are within the province of the distribution center and should be recognized as obligations of the center whether or not they are required by law. The checklist should be the official record of government publications and the means of access to the information produced by the government. The complete collection of publications is the backup collection for all the libraries in the state, the source of last resort for the citizen. Through these services, a depository program makes state publications, which citizens have a right to see and to use, easily and economically accessible to them.

TEXT ARRANGEMENT AND SCOPE

The state-level activities relating to the availability, distribution, and accessibility of state publications within the state are a broad topic. The specific documents that are published and their importance as keys to information and sources of information, multistate collection of documents, and exchanges of documents among the states; and the use, handling, and publicizing of the documents by the local library are all discussed in varying degrees in the existing literature and are beyond the scope of this text.

The framework for this text follows the movement of the state document from the originating state agency to the distribution center, and then to the depository libraries, which make it available to the public. Although the movement of the state document is a direct one from the state agency through the distribution center to the depository library, the duties of these entities toward one another run in both directions. The allocation of a particular activity to chapters five, six, and seven on these parts of the system is governed by the place where the burden of performing a particular activity rests rather than by the agency affected by the activity. Thus, lists of publications prepared by state agencies for the distribution centers are assigned to the state agency chapter (Chapter 5), and the depository contracts between the distribution center and the depository libraries are discussed in the distribution center chapter (Chapter 6). Not all states place the burden in the same place (for example, in some states, the depository libraries must initiate the depository contracts). Hence, the three chapters must be taken as a unit to reveal all the relationships among the parts of the system.

Even when all the duties of the state agencies, distribution centers, and depository libraries are merged, a full picture is not produced. Informal practices in each state have amplified, restricted, and otherwise altered the bare language of the law. The actual program that operates in each state depends on the law, on the way the administrator interprets it, and on the funds available for its implementation. An outsider can report only part of the picture.

There are many kinds of depository programs in the fifty states. A number of states now have legally based programs, augmented in some instances by rules and regulations, and depository contracts. A comparative analysis of the laws of the fifty states is a beginning step in the study of these depository systems. *American Library Laws* identifies laws providing for the distribution and for deposit of state publications.[2] These topics are too broad for a study of depository library systems because such laws may relate to the distribution of a single type of publication (typically the session laws) or to deposit in a single library (often the state library). These laws are often the ones providing for out-of-state exchanges. Depository library program laws, as collected in this text, are limited to those that provide for the distribution of all or almost all state publications to a system of libraries within the state.

AREAS FOR FUTURE STUDIES

A step beyond a report on depository systems is the suggestion by Bernard Fry to "identify the extent to which the various state depository libraries make use of their own depository privileges."[3] Peter Hernon also recommends more study of the depository libraries, particularly their reference services. Another area of research suggested by Hernon is a study of the relationship of state bibliographical control, publications, and collections to those at other levels of government.[4]

All these areas of study require the collection of data from libraries, and other data not assembled at this time. The present study is based on information that exists in the statutes, in the Documents on Documents Collection, or in other published sources. This information is assembled for the convenience of the user in the state section of this book.

THE DOCUMENTS ON DOCUMENTS COLLECTION

In 1973 and 1974, the State Documents Task Force (now the State and Local Documents Task Force) of the Government Documents Round Table of the American Library Association gathered a collection of materials relating to the administration of state depository library systems. Each state was asked to supply copies of its legislation, rules and regulations, brochures, manuals, lists, forms, questionnaires and related tabulations, and a brief commentary on the strengths and weaknesses of the depository law. Five sets of these materials were assembled and made available for interlibrary loan. The library currently maintaining the sets and sending them out in response to interlibrary loan requests is the Louisiana State Library.[5]

This collection, called the Documents on Documents Collection, has expanded from two binders in 1974 to five looseleaf binders per set in 1980. In 1976, the custodian of the collection, Brenda Olds of the Texas Legislative Reference Library, made a major effort to secure new materials. Another major supplementation is expected in 1980. Some of the materials in the state section of this book have been taken from this collection, particularly the comments on the strengths and weaknesses of the laws. Three lists of the materials in the collection have been published.[6] The lists, however, are not a substitute for browsing through the notebooks.

THE 1979 S&LDTF SURVEY

The compilation of a survey of state depository systems was a 1979 project of the State and Local Documents Task Force (S&LDTF). Each state was asked for a report on its distribution and bibliographical control of state documents. Although the format of the reply was specified, each state was asked to fit its local information into the outline without regard to strict conformity to the headings. The committee expressed a hope for unusual or variant answers as distinguished from those that could be compared or tabulated. Some of the information is factual—legal authority, staff, depository libraries, documents distributed, dissemination of cataloging data, microforms, publications, budget—and some is opinion—problems, projects being emphasized, and hopes for the future.[7]

LEGISLATION

A comprehensive report on all depository systems would include the laws and formal documents of the program; the manuals and other publications and articles written to facilitate and publicize the program; the comments of the state agencies that supply copies of their publications, of the administrator of the program, and of the libraries that serve as depositories; and the evaluations of the citizens for whose ultimate benefit the program operates. Only with the full cooperation of several individuals in each state could the data for such a study be collected.

The collection of legislation included in this text was originally assembled as a working tool for librarians interested in enacting depository legislation. The concern of those librarians was to provide by law for the distribution of all publications to depository libraries through a central source. Although in some instances these librarians studied the larger problem of distribution in general, the specific goal was to establish a system of libraries that would automatically receive all the publications. In recent years, many states have enacted depository legislation, but some states are still working toward that goal. For the states in need of depository legislation, for those revising outdated laws, and for those considering amendments to bring their existing law up to date, the collection herein should be a time-saving tool.

PUBLICIZING THE DEPOSITORY SYSTEM

Just as it is important to publicize the state agencies' publications, it is also important to make known to potential users the means by which these publications are made available—the depository library system. Students and scholars in many disciplines, political science and public administration to name a few, are direct beneficiaries of a depository library system when it not only identifies the materials with which they work but also makes them conveniently accessible.

The text presented here compares and comments on the legislation of the individual states and should be a useful handbook for the distribution center staff. The historical and comparative material should serve as a stimulus, and perhaps a justification, for improving the existing system. All the staff in a depository library, particularly the administrators and directors, will find here a glimpse of a little known part of the total library picture. Bert Halcli has forcefully expressed the need for those in positions of authority to understand documents as library resources: "The key people on the library staff should not be permitted to run away [from documents]. Force an understanding on them, whether they like it or not."[8]

Similarly, librarians in nondepository libraries should be aware of the resources of the depository system and of the benefits it offers them through interlibrary loan. In several states, California and Texas for example, the acquisition needs of nondepository libraries are served directly by the distribution center after the needs of the depository libraries are met. All libraries, depository and nondepository, benefit from some of the auxiliary depository activities such as the publication of checklists, authority lists, and manuals.

Students in library schools, although they may have a particular interest in their home state, must concern themselves with the broader picture and must have materials for study and comparison. Trustees who want to become acquainted with the total library scene and the public at large which benefits from this systematic way of making information available need to know about depository library systems.

The place of the state programs in the national library scene has not yet been firmly established. Each state is certainly entitled to pursue its goals in its own way and to have a depository system suited to those objectives. The number of depository libraries in a state, for example, is a matter for local decision. At the same time, individual state preferences on the type of depository library program should be exercised within a national framework of standards and guidelines. The report on documents prepared by Bernard Fry for the National Commission on Libraries and Information Science recommends that "Planning for improved availability and access to state government publications should be carried out and coordinated at both state and national levels."[9] National standards for cataloging and for microreproduction must be followed to ensure maximum use of these valuable information resources.

GUIDELINES

The American Library Asociation (ALA) adopted guidelines for a state document program in 1975. Entitled "Guidelines for Minimum State Servicing of State Documents," this document prescribes the elements of the basic depository program and additional features of a full state program. In addition to provisions for a legally regulated flow of documents from state agencies through a distribution center to depository libraries, the guidelines specify that a comprehensive collection of the documents should be maintained, that out-of-state exchanges should be conducted (or at least that copies of the documents should be available to meet out-of-state requests), and that an authority list of state agencies should be maintained and distributed. Clearly, these added requirements enhance a depository library program.

The ALA Guidelines requirement for maintenance of a collection is found in many of the depository library laws, but provisions for exchanges are included less frequently, and then usually in permissive form. Because exchange laws, particularly those for legal publications (the most usual kind of document subject to exchange), have been omitted from this collection of depository laws, no conclusions should be drawn about the existence or nonexistence of these laws in a particular state. Although it is out of date, the reader is referred to Chapter 21 of the *Manual on the Use of State Publications*, which summarizes both exchange and distribution laws in all the states.[10]

The requirement in the ALA Guidelines for an authority list would, the drafters hoped, operate as a challenge because so few states have prepared such lists. With the increased use of national data bases in cataloging, authority lists have become more and more necessary.

Other guidelines have also been adopted, not by the American Library Association as a whole, but by its Government Documents Round Table and the State Documents Task Force (now the State and Local Documents Task Force). The text of those guidelines is included in the Appendix and is referred to in the appropriate chapters.

Although not essential parts of a depository program, or even enhancements required by the guidelines, there are other activities in a state documents program that are efficiently, effectively, and economically conducted at the state level. Cataloging of state publications, if done by the state library or another designated authority within the state, has the advantage of cataloging "at source," in addition to being a task that can be done once for all libraries. The catalog product must, of course, be complete and must be prepared pursuant to the standard cataloging rules. Likewise, microfilming, whether for preservation or distribution, should only be done once. The microform product must be of high quality, produced in conformity with all relevant national standards. Cataloging, micropublishing, workshops, visits to local libraries, publicity brochures, and related activities can all be part of a complete state program. Although it makes the name "distribution center" a misnomer, all these activities and services fall within the purview of such a center. Depository library programs should do as much as possible with whatever funds and whatever legal authorizations are available.

The recognition of a state-level responsibility for the documents originating within a state encompasses the ideas that citizens have a right to the information collected by their government, that prompt availability goes hand in hand with the right to access, and that the publications of state government should be readily accessible in places other than the offices of the issuing agencies. The efficient and economical discharge of this broad state responsibility can be handled best by libraries, which are the ideal agents because they are institutions dedicated to the dissemination of information. Legislation for a depository library program is the first step toward these goals.

NOTES

1. *Revision of Depository Laws: Hearings Before a Subcommittee of the Committee on House Administration*, 85th Congress, 1st Session, pursuant to H. Res. 128, a resolution authorizing a full study of federally operated printing services and government paperwork in general, October 7, 10, 14, and 17, 1957 (on H.R. 9186), June 19, 1958 (on H.R. 11042) (Washington, D.C.: U.S. Government Printing Office, 1958), (statement of Jerome K. Wilcox), p. 118.

2. *American Library Laws*, 4th ed. (Chicago: American Library Association, 1973); see index entries under "distribution" and "deposit."

3. Bernard M. Fry, et al., *Research Design for a Comprehensive Study of the Use, Bibliographic Control and Distribution of Government Publications, Final Report.* (Bloomington, Ind.: Research Center for Library and Information Science, Indiana University, October 1970), p. 52.

4. Peter Hernon, "State 'Documents to the People'." *Government Publications Review* 3:262 (1976).

5. The Documents on Documents Collection may be borrowed from Grace Moore, Louisiana State Library, P.O. Box 131, Baton Rouge, La. 70821.

6. The listings of the contents of the Documents on Documents Collection are reported in *Documents to the People*: 3, no. 2:23-26 (1974); 3, no. [7]:44 (1975); 5:206-208 (1977).

7. Margaret T. Lane (comp.), *State Publications: Depository Distribution and Bibliographical Programs*, State and Local Documents Task Force, Government Documents Round Table, American Library Association; Texas State Publications Clearinghouse, Documents Monograph Series, no. 2 ([Austin, Tex.]: Texas State Library, 1980).

8. Albert Halcli, "How to Escape from the Documents Ghetto," *Illinois Libraries* 54:414 (June 1972).

9. Bernard M. Fry, *Government Publications: Their Role in the National Program for Library and Information Services* (Washington, D.C.: National Commission on Libraries and Information Science, December 1978), p. 78.

10. American Library Association, Committee on Public Documents, *Manual on the Use of State Publications*, ed. by J. K. Wilcox (Chicago: American Library Association, 1940), pp. 295–331.

2. LIBRARIES AND STATE PUBLICATIONS

Libraries and state publications do not add together to equal depository libraries. The combination, that is, the collecting and use of state publications by libraries, existed before there were depository libraries. Depository libraries as we know them today are a relatively recent phenomenon in most states. (For a chronological table, see Chapter 3, Table 2.)

Some of the differences in state depository libraries today may become clear if one examines the background from which depository libraries emerged. The full study of the relationship between libraries and state publications can best be written by historians, perhaps on a state-by-state basis by individuals who have intimate knowledge of the state. But the landmarks on the national scene, the events and enterprises that involved most or all of the states, should be recalled briefly to indicate how we reached our present status and to prevent "reinventing the wheel."

Also among the significant events of the past are the activities of the library association document committees. During the 1930s, the papers presented at the American Library Association conferences were published in a series titled *Public Documents*. Although these papers would not be overlooked in a literature search inasmuch as they are indexed in *Library Literature*, they are mentioned here as a model.

The reasons why librarians are interested and why indeed they *should* be interested derive from the nature of state documents and of libraries. Robert Leigh explains the role of libraries, saying that libraries are part of the system of communication that makes available "the more serious, more reliable, and more permanent materials of all kinds," and that because they are tax-supported agencies, libraries have a "natural and strategic role to play in the conservation and distribution of information which aids communication between the government and the citizen."[1]

The passage of the Freedom of Information Act by Congress and the enactment of public records and open government acts by state legislatures are signs of the growing interest and awareness of citizens in their government. Such laws acknowledge the rights of citizens to information about their government and to information which that government produces.

In a recent article entitled "The Public's Right to Know," Kathy Schneider lists three essentials of a program of government accountability and sums up the role of the librarian:

First, government officials must be committed to making their reports and studies available for public review and inspection. Second, citizens must express an interest in governmental activities and demand information on day-to-day as well as long-range operations and plans. And, third, there must be an established procedure through which such information is more readily and regularly accessible.

It is our job to work with our patrons and with our government to keep the public aware of and the government accountable for policies and programs which affect us all.[2]

Although one begins with the premise, well-documented in library journal articles, that state publications are important, the thought must quickly be added, important *to individuals*. Librarians sometimes think in terms of building collections, but they must keep in mind that it is the ultimate user for whom the collections are being built. Thus, recognizing the importance of state documents to the individual user, one must first ask whether the user should be served directly by the issuing agency or through a library. Where is the best service likely to be provided?

The answer, of course, is that state documents should be made available through libraries. A 1951 California study on information services, which recognized this principle in one of its four recommendations, considered it necessary to devote only a few lines to explanation:

Free distribution of publications to individuals should be extremely limited. The State should rely on libraries as its documents link with the public.
  Drastic steps should be taken to reduce present free agency mailing lists.
  The inherent wastefulness of distribution to individuals is quite obvious. A publication is perhaps used only once and then discarded. Publications sent to libraries are readily available and may be used many times.[3]

The explanation, appearing in a legislative study committee report, is significant as a statement by a layperson of facts that are well known to librarians.

Libraries have long recognized their responsibility for collecting official publications. In the early part of this century, libraries emphasized the collecting and preserving of collections for researchers and scholars, then and in the future, and the collections were established in university and research libraries. State libraries and state law libraries, which often had multiple copies for exchange purposes, built up large collections of state publications, particularly those from the legislative and judicial branches of state government.

After World War II, changes occurred in both the types of libraries collecting state publications and in the quantity and types of publications. The increase in the number of state publications, as a result of the creation of government agencies in new areas of regulation (for example, environment, social welfare, and occupations), new types of publications (for example, state plans, grant reports, and research surveys), and new formats (such as film, tape, and recordings), led to an effort to make these publications available through public libraries. Today, it is recognized that state publications are not only the so-called legal publications—the legislative journals, the acts, and court reports—but also research studies in agriculture, geology, and many other subjects. A water bulletin issued by a department of natural resources may well be more up to date and more authoritative than any other publication on the subject. The bulletin is also probably inexpensive, although cost is not a primary consideration when information is needed.

STATE DOCUMENTS IN THE LIBRARY

Peter Paulson maintains that government documents are, in the universe of the acquisition librarian, of secondary importance because the documents are not part of the commercial book trade.[4] Books are promoted and sold through bookstores, magazines, subscriptions, memberships, and television programs. Documents, on the other hand, are not, and usually cannot be, handled through these channels. They must be identified, located, perhaps paid for in advance, and, in general, given special attention in the ordering process. Paul Pross calls this "document discovery, the process whereby the librarian ascertains the existence of a document."[5] Since these paragraphs were first written, John Henry Richter has published an article "Documents are a Different Kettle of Fish" in the September 1980 issue of *Documents to the People* that discusses seven distinct characteristics of government publications.

One area of difference between trade books and state documents is that state documents are the official pronouncements of the agencies that issue them. Their purpose is to impart information to the citizen who has paid for the gathering and dissemination of the information through taxes. By publishing the information, the state agency is saying that it needs to be brought to the attention of people outside the agency. It is important to both the state agency and to the citizen that the information be made known and be conveniently available.

Profit is a second area in which government publications differ from trade books and magazines. Many state documents are available without charge. State agencies are not profit-making institutions. Any sales apparatus—bookstores, sales lists, and the like—which a government operates, while expected to "break even," can rely on some subsidy (for example, office space in a government building) to accomplish its mission of making information available, and the sales program can wait for its customers to seek it out rather than the reverse.

A third point of difference arises because the state agencies are not full-time publishers. Some state agencies may issue only one publication every other year, and hence, for such agencies, the issuance of a publication is a peripheral, temporary concern.

In view of these factors which make state publications difficult to discover and to acquire, the availability of state publications through libraries is important because (1) the official nature of government publications requires that the information be available, yet it is not usually available through commercial channels, (2) the existence of the publications is difficult to establish, and (3) the publications go out of print rapidly and are seldom reprinted.

There are several kinds of library collections of state documents: (1) the collections that are carefully assembled with a goal of absolute completeness; (2) the archival collections, maintained by a historical society or an archives and records commission; (3) regional collections, which consist primarily of current materials and are located so that they are easily available to the population of the state; and (4) the depository collections that may overlap any of these types of collections in purpose and in extent.

COMPREHENSIVE COLLECTIONS

Document librarians have long accepted the need for a comprehensive collection in each state of that state's documents. One of the most important statements of this principle in recent years was that in the Standards for state library agencies: "A state agency, preferably the state library, should be a central depository for its own state documents."[6] A similar statement is made in the American Library Association's "Guidelines for Minimum State Servicing of State Documents": "In each state an agency or agencies should be designated by law to act as the depositories for the documents published by the state to maintain a collection . . . ." (See Appendix.)

A comprehensive collection is needed for historical purposes, for convenience in use (going from agency to agency to consult documents is not practical), and because persons with expertise in the use of documents can give more effective service from the documents when all the documents are in one location. The complete collections are called historical collections in some states. Some thought is being given in the Government Documents Round Table of the American Library Association to identifying the most comprehensive collection in each state and encouraging the establishment of such a collection where none is presently known.

IDENTIFICATION OF COMPLETE COLLECTIONS

Identifying the comprehensive state collection in each state saves time, money, and effort. The reasons for identifying a library in each state which will assume responsibility for a complete collection are clear—for on-site research and for interlibrary loan. Usually, there are only one or two such libraries in each state.

Table 1 illustrates the work done in the past in identifying the libraries in each state with responsibilities for local state document collections. Interest in building the definitive, comprehensive collections of state documents in the state of their origin, rather than at a national center, dates back fifty years. One of the goals of the State Document Center Project of the 1930s was to identify these libraries in each state and to encourage the states in their efforts to achieve their goals of comprehensive collections. The list of libraries identified in 1932 by the Social Science Research Council, when compared with the 1966 list prepared by Robert D. Downs listing ''the most complete holdings, state by state'' for the documents originating in each individual state, reveals that in twenty-six states the libraries either remained the same (nine states) or additional libraries were added (seventeen states).[7] In eleven states, one library was dropped; in these states, only three states added libraries to compensate for the withdrawals. In the remaining eleven states (the total number of states in 1932 was forty-eight), a complete change of libraries was made.

Thirty-five years, during which there undoubtedly were changes in the library administration in all the states, elapsed between the time of the two lists. The 1932 list included some libraries that had not yet signed formal agreements to participate in the State Document Center plan, which may account for some changes that occurred. Other changes may have inadvertently been listed as changes when in fact they were only changes in name. (For example, Howard Memorial Library was recognized as the library at Tulane University, but similar situations may not have been noticed.) Another factor which might account for the variances between the two lists is that they were compiled with slightly different objectives. The 1932 list was a list of libraries willing to collect state documents, and the 1966 list was a list of libraries that had developed strong collections.

A list compiled in 1969 is also available for comparison. In her first chart, Casey included a column for ''Agency Responsible for Official File.''[8] She summarizes:

State libraries are responsible for maintaining the official file of state documents in thirty-four of fifty states, though some states, California, Illinois and Virginia, indicate this is by practice, rather than by statutory provision. State archives and history departments are responsible in seven states and share responsibility with state libraries in two states. State historical society libraries have this duty in five states; state law libraries in two states; a state historical library and museum in one, and a university library in one.[9]

Of the agencies which Casey identified as responsible for the official file, fourteen are not in the list compiled by Downs. Ten of these are state libraries: Hawaii, Iowa, Louisiana, Maryland, Missouri, Montana, New Mexico (the state law library), North Dakota, South Carolina, and Utah. She also identified the archival agencies in Kansas, Kentucky, and Utah, and the historical agency

TABLE 1.
COLLECTIONS OF STATE PUBLICATIONS IN THEIR STATE OF ORIGIN

	White	Downs	Casey	Survey	Type of Library
ALABAMA					
State Department of Archives and History	x		x	x	Archival
University of Alabama		x		x	Academic
Auburn University				x	Academic
ALASKA					
State Historical Library		x	x		Historical
Alaska State Library		x			State
ARIZONA					
State Library, Department of Library and Archives	x	x	x		State
State Law and Legislative Reference Library					Law & Legislative
ARKANSAS					
University of Arkansas	x	x	x		Academic
CALIFORNIA					
University of California at Berkeley	x	x			Academic
California State Library		x	x		State
Los Angeles Public Library	x				Public
Casey has note "without authority"					
COLORADO					
Denever Public Library	x	x			Public
University of Colorado Library	x	x			Academic

	Category				
Division of Archives and Public Records	Archival		x	x	
Colorado State Library	State		x	x	
CONNECTICUT					
Connecticut State Library	State	x	x	x	
Yale University Library	Academic	x			
DELAWARE					
University of Delaware Library	Academic	x			
Wilmington Institute Free Library	Public	x			
Delaware State Archives	Archival		x	x	x
FLORIDA					
University of Florida	Academic	x	x	x	
Florida State Library	State		x	x	
GEORGIA					
Georgia State Library	State	x	x	x	x
HAWAII					
University of Hawaii	Academic		x	x	
Hawaii State Library	State			x	x
IDAHO					
University of Idaho	Academic	x	x	x	x
Idaho Historical Society	Historical		x	x	x
Idaho State Library	State				x

Table 1. **COLLECTIONS OF STATE PUBLICATIONS IN THEIR STATE OF ORIGIN** (continued)

	White	Downs	Casey	Survey	Type of Library
ILLINOIS					
Illinois State Library		x	x		State
University of Chicago Libraries	x	x			Academic
University of Illinois Library	x	x			Academic
Casey has note "without authority"					
INDIANA					
Indiana State Library	x	x	x		State
Indiana University		x			Academic
IOWA					
State University of Iowa	x	x		x	Academic
State Historical Society of Iowa Library	x	x			Historical
State Law Library			x		Law
Iowa State Library				x	State
KANSAS					
Kansas Historical Society Library	x	x			Historical
University of Kansas Library	x				Academic
Kansas State Library		x		x	State
Public Records			x		Records
KENTUCKY					
Free Public Library, Louisville	x				Public
University of Kentucky		x			Academic
Archives and Records			x		Archival

LOUISIANA				
Louisiana State University	x			Academic
Tulane University (Howard Memorial)	x			Academic
Louisiana State Library			x	State
MAINE				
Bowdoin College Library	x			Academic
University of Maine		x		Academic
Maine State Library		x	x	State
MARYLAND				
Johns Hopkins University Libraries	x			Academic
Maryland Historical Society Library	x			Historical
Enoch Pratt Free Library		x		Public
Maryland Hall of Records		x		Records
Maryland State Library (?)			x	State
MASSACHUSETTS				
Massachusetts State Library	x	x		State
Harvard University Library	x			Academic
Survey has note "but weak 1940-1960"				
MICHIGAN				
University of Michigan Library	x			Academic
Michigan State Library		x	x	State
Detroit Public Library		x		Public

23

Table 1. **COLLECTIONS OF STATE PUBLICATIONS IN THEIR STATE OF ORIGIN** (continued)

	White	Downs	Casey	Survey	Type of Library
MINNESOTA					
University of Minnesota Library	x				Academic
Minnesota Historical Society Library		x	x		Historical
MISSISSIPPI					
Mississippi State Library	x				State
Mississippi Department of Archives and History		x			Archival
State Historical Society			x		Historical
MISSOURI					
University of Missouri Library	x				Academic
State Historical Society of Missouri Library	x	x			Historical
Missouri State Library			x	x	State
Missouri State Archives				x	Archival
Survey has note ''1971 on'' for Missouri State Library.					
MONTANA					
State University of Montana Library	x			x	Academic
Montana State University		x		x	Academic
Montana Historical Society Library		x		x	Historical
Montana State Library			x	x	State
NEBRASKA					
University of Nebraska Library	x	x			Academic
Nebraska State Library		x	x		State
Nebraska State Historical Society Library		x		x	Historical
Nebraska Publications Clearinghouse				x	State
Survey notes that the Historical Society has a pre-1972 collection; Clearinghouse, post-1972.					

Institution					Type
NEVADA					
Nevada State Library	x				State
University of Nevada		x		x	Academic
NEW HAMPSHIRE					
New Hampshire State Library	x	x			State
New Hampshire Historical Society	x	x			Historical
NEW JERSEY					
New Jersey State Library	x	x	x	x	State
Rutgers University		x			Academic
NEW MEXICO					
University of New Mexico Library, Albuquerque	x	x	x		Academic
University of New Mexico, Los Cruces				x	Academic
Supreme Court Law Library			x		Law
New Mexico State Records Center and Archives				x	Archival
New Mexico State Library				x	State
NEW YORK					
New York State Library	x	x	x	x	State
New York Public Library	x	x			Public
NORTH CAROLINA					
University of North Carolina Library	x	x	x		Academic
North Carolina State Library	x	x			State
NORTH DAKOTA					
University of North Dakota	x	x			Academic
North Dakota State University		x			Academic

Table 1. COLLECTIONS OF STATE PUBLICATIONS IN THEIR STATE OF ORIGIN (continued)

	White	Downs	Casey	Survey	Type of Library
State Historical Society of North Dakota		x			Historical
North Dakota State Library		x	x		State
OHIO					
Ohio State University Library	x				Academic
Ohio State Library		x	x	x	State
Cleveland Public Library		x			Public
Ohio Historical Society				x	Historical
OKLAHOMA					
University of Oklahoma Library	x			x	Academic
Oklahoma State University		x		x	Academic
Oklahoma State Library		x	x		State
Oklahoma Department of Libraries, Clearinghouse				x	State
Oklahoma Department of Libraries Archives & Records				x	Archival
OREGON					
Oregon State Library	x	x	x		State
PENNSYLVANIA					
Pennsylvania State Library	x	x	x	x	State
Carnegie Library of Pittsburgh	x				Public
Free Library of Philadelphia				x	Public
Penn State Library				x	Academic
University of Pittsburgh				x	Academic

26

RHODE ISLAND					
Rhode Island State Library	x		x		State
Rhode Island Historical Society	x		x		Historical
SOUTH CAROLINA					
South Carolina State Library	x		x		State
University of South Carolina Library	x	x	x		Academic
South Carolina Archives Commission		x			Archival
SOUTH DAKOTA					
South Dakota State University			x		Academic
University of South Dakota Library			x		Academic
State Department of History	x		x		Historical
TENNESSEE					
Tennessee State Library & Archives	x		x		State
TEXAS					
University of Texas Library	x		x		Academic
Texas State Library		x	x	x	State
Texas Legislative Reference Library				x	Legislative
UTAH					
University of Utah Library	x				Academic
Utah State Historical Society			x		Historical
Utah State Library		x		x	State
VERMONT					
Vermont State Library (Department of Libraries)	x		x	x	State

Table 1. COLLECTIONS OF STATE PUBLICATIONS IN THEIR STATE OF ORIGIN (continued)

	White	Downs	Casey	Survey	Type of Library
VIRGIN ISLANDS					
Enid M. Baa Library and Archives				x	Territorial
VIRGINIA					
Virginia State Library		x	x	x	State
University of Virginia Library	x	x	x		Academic
Virginia Historical Society		x			Historical
WASHINGTON					
Washington State Library		x	x		State
University of Washington Library	x				Academic
WEST VIRGINIA					
State Department of Archives & History	x		x	x	Archival
West Virginia University Library	x	x			Academic
WISCONSIN					
State Historical Society of Wisconsin	x	x	x	x	Historical
University of Wisconsin Library	x				Academic
Legislative Reference Bureau				x	Legislative

WYOMING

	Academic	State	Archival
University of Wyoming Library	x	x	
Wyoming State Library	x	x	x
Wyoming Archives & Historical Department			x

Sources:

1. Leonard D. White, "State Document Centers," *ALA Bulletin* 26:554-555 (1932).
2. Robert B. Downs, "Government Publications in American Libraries," *Library Trends* 15:187-189 (July 1966).
3. "Legal Structure for Deposit and Distribution of State Documents." *In* Genevieve M. Casey and Edith Phillips, *Management and Use of State Documents in Indiana*, Wayne State University, Office of Urban Library Research, Research Report no. 2 ([Detroit: 1969]).
4. Margaret T. Lane (comp.), *State Publications: Depository Distribution and Bibliographical Programs*, State and Local Documents Task Force, Government Documents Round Table, American Library Association; Texas State Publications Clearinghouse, Documents Monograph Series, no. 2 ([Austin, Tex.]: Texas State Library, 1980).

29

in South Dakota as having official file responsibilities, but none of these is on the Downs list. Many of these state libraries, particularly those in states where depository legislation has been adopted in recent years, have probably begun to assemble complete files of state documents. Of the thirty-seven state libraries identified by Casey, she and Downs have twenty-seven in common. Of these, fourteen are also on the 1932 list, indicating a longstanding commitment to the collecting of state documents. The Indiana law, enacted in 1973 after the study by Casey, embodies the concept of "official file": "The Indiana State Library shall maintain a complete collection of all Indiana public documents. This collection shall be the official file of Indiana state documents."

The history of such designations is relevant today because of the current interest in the designation of a library in each state as a documents center for documents originating in the state. It is disturbing to find that fourteen of the agencies which Casey says are the agencies officially responsible for the definitive collection in the state are not credited by Downs as having the strongest collections. In fact, in most of the fourteen states, there are at least two other libraries with strong collections, an interesting difference to bear in mind. Several factors enter into the explanation of this situation. First, it must be recognized that the Downs survey is no longer up to date. Second, the Casey study, although dating from about the same time as the Downs survey, purports to set out the agencies with official responsibilities and not necessarily those with strong collections.

In selecting a documents center for each state, there are three possibilities: (1) libraries that volunteer, that is, the 1932 plan (remember, however, that in some states an invitation to volunteer was required), (2) libraries with strong collections as determined by the Downs survey or a later one, and (3) libraries with legal responsibilities. The strong emphasis in the Casey study on the state libraries as having official responsibilities might derive from the fact that her questionnaire was sent to state libraries.

ARCHIVAL COLLECTIONS

A second type of collection has received very little attention—the archival collection. The Society of American Archivists standards for state archival agencies provide in the section on the functions of state archival agencies:

RESPONSIBILITY FOR PRINTED GOVERNMENT DOCUMENTS

1. Responsibility for assembling and preserving a complete record set of published state documents normally rests with the state archivist.

Inasmuch as these documents constitute part of the records of state agencies and institutions, the record set should normally be preserved in the state archives together with the unpublished records. This responsibility may be discharged by arrangement with the state library or other appropriate state institution. Also, unless close at hand, complete sets of the laws, legislative proceedings, and other governmental publications should be available in the state archives for the convenience of staff and searchers.

2. If there is no other agency to undertake the task, the state archival agency should prepare and issue annual or biennial lists of all state publications.[10]

Several states provide in the depository laws that the state archives agency shall receive copies of the publications distributed. Posner mentions Delaware, Maryland, and Hawaii as having legislation requiring the deposit of publications in the archives agency. He notes that the Kentucky State Archives and Records Service is designated a depository and publishes a list, and that the departments of history and archives in South Carolina and West Virginia publish checklists of state documents. Posner concludes with the statement that ''the archival agency should make sure that in addition to copies exposed to staff and public use and therefore subject to eventual damage or loss, a complete set of government documents is assembled and kept intact as a record set.''[11] Taking the idea one step further, he cites, in a footnote, a statement by Paul Lewinson that archivists should encourage the preservation in nonarchival collections of those state publications which it is not practical to preserve in an archival collection.[12]

In many states, the archival collection envisioned by Posner is probably the noncirculating reference collection in one of the major libraries of the state. It is very possible that this collection is arranged without regard for *respect des fonds*, particularly if the state documents are not a separate collection but are part of the collection of primary and secondary materials devoted to the individual state.

There is something to be said for an archival collection arranged with respect for the provenance of the materials and stored so that loss and damage are minimized. Likewise, it is appropriate to have the state agency's published records available for use in conjunction with the archival records. The advantage of having the published records available at the same place as the manuscript records is at variance with the idea of a collection which is not used by the staff or the public and remains in pristine condition.

The conflict can be resolved by preparing a microfilm copy that would reinforce the safety of the archival set and at the same time provide a copy for use. The preparation of film copies of records and documents is a traditional function of records centers and archival agencies and is thus a logical solution. Another possibility is that the archival agency might be able to create an extra set of original documents from noncurrent materials weeded from depository libraries and returned to a central agency.

REGIONAL COLLECTIONS

Another kind of collection is the regional collection. Such a collection is one of a number of such collections in a state that are so located as to be conveniently accessible to citizens throughout the state. It is a type of depository library, distinguished from the ordinary depository library by the scope of its collection. The regional centers usually have an extensive basic collection but rely on the comprehensive collection for scarce or unusual publications. The regional center emphasizes current publications. Both the complete collection and the regional center collection receive full distribution from the distribution center. The difference between the two types arises because the complete collection has a priority in the distribution scheme if there are not enough copies for full distribution and also because the complete collection is augmented by the acquisition efforts of its librarians. The Wisconsin proposal outlined by John Kopischke in 1974 provides for regional depositories in addition to historical and regular depositories with different criteria and standards for each level of depository.[13]

PROVISIONS FOR NONDEPOSITORY LIBRARIES

The legislation discussed in this book is limited to that which establishes depository libraries and uses the depository libraries as a means of making state documents available to the public. The major emphasis is on the duties imposed on the state agencies, the distribution centers, and the depository libraries to achieve the goal of public availability of publications. The depository libraries are the key to this public access and availability.

Although the depository libraries are a fundamental part of the distribution program, depository legislation benefits all libraries in a state. The depository legislation of some states includes provisions that directly benefit nondepository libraries. These provisions are similar to those found in library legislation that is unrelated to a depository program. Thus, from these comments on the depository legislation no conclusions should be drawn about the existence or nonexistence of a particular measure in any state.

The most important benefit to nondepository libraries of having a depository library program in the state is the availability of a checklist of state publications. Nondepository libraries use checklists in the same ways as depository libraries use them, and in some additional ways. For both depository and nondepository libraries, the checklists are reference tools that save libraries an enormous amount of time. Of course, the checklists must be indexed and cumulated so that they can be used quickly and easily.

Checklists serve an organizational function in a library by providing a method of arranging the collection, if documents are in a separate collection. They can also be used for inventory. They often give classification numbers and cataloging data and serve as the index to the state document collection. For nondepository libraries, checklists serve as verification tools for interlibrary loan requests. Montana and Nevada laws refer specifically to nondepository libraries in requirements that copies of publications should be deposited at the state library "to provide interlibrary loan service to those libraries without depository status."

Finally, checklists are an acquisition tool for nondepository libraries. They often have addresses of state agencies or tell where addresses can be found, and if they do not have this information, they should have it, according to the Checklist Guidelines (see Appendix).

Connecticut and Oklahoma have mandatory provisions that the checklist be distributed to libraries in the state. In Georgia, the state librarian "may disseminate" copies of the lists. Even in the absence of statutory requirements, the lists, if published, are always available to libraries within the state.

Other tools developed and published in support of the depository program— classification schemes, cataloging aids, manuals, annotated bibliographies, and brochures—can all be acquired and used by nondepository libraries. For example, Allen Sugden reports that the new "Basic List" of California state publications was sent to nondepository libraries to guide them in selection. He says, "By offering assistance to the non-depository libraries the State Documents Committee hopes to foster wider use and acceptance of California State publications as an integral part of library collections."[14] In states that have programs for reproducing their documents in a microformat, this convenient, space-saving format is available to all libraries, although the cost may be an inhibiting factor if the microforms are produced commercially.

The depository legislation in some states refers specifically to nondepository libraries. North Dakota provides for an optional selection program for nondepository libraries. In California, a library stockroom, after making the depository library distribution, distributes "the balance to any library which may write for a copy or copies." A similar provision, requiring nondepository libraries to apply to a central agency for documents they need, is found in the Rhode Island law. Likewise, the Pennsylvania law states that certain libraries are eligible to receive the documents without charge. In Georgia and in Idaho, where depository libraries are not established by the legislation, the publications are to be sent to those who desire to receive them (Georgia) and to libraries and to others "within the discretion of the state librarian" (Idaho). The Oklahoma statutory provision states that the Department of Libraries may send copies of publications to other bodies or persons. The Indiana provision is stronger—"and shall distribute to other libraries copies of those public documents published by the state which are of greatest interest or use and for which a more general distribution is appropriate.''

The situation is reversed in some states (for example, Alaska, Montana, Nebraska, New Mexico, and South Dakota) which have provisions that no general distribution of publications or lists of publications shall be made. The New Mexico provision is qualified by an exception in cases where the state library is operating as a library.

At least a dozen states have exchange provisions benefiting out-of-state libraries which are not part of the depository system. Examples from depository legislation include Connecticut, Florida, Michigan, and Oklahoma. There are, of course, many exchange statutes which are not part of the depository library laws.

Indirect advantages to a nondepository library of having a depository system in the state lie in the reliance that can be placed on the depository library system to meet the needs of the user who starts a search in a nondepository library. Through interlibrary loan, the library needs of any citizen, whether he or she is using a nondepository library or a depository library, can be met. Second, depository librarians and librarians at the distribution center can give advice to the librarian in a nondepository library on any document problem from acquisitions to reference. Workshops conducted by the administrator at the distribution center are often open to all document librarians regardless of whether they are in depository libraries.

LIBRARY OF CONGRESS

The Library of Congress placed particular emphasis on acquiring state documents when, in 1910, it began publication of an accessions list. The publication of the *Monthly Checklist of State Publications* continuously and regularly since 1910 has given librarians a tool that is unparalleled in the state documents field. The retrospective bibliographies of Hasse, Bowker, and others are useful for inventory and for reference, but do not serve as acquisition tools as the *Monthly Checklist* does. For states without checklists, the *Monthly Checklist* is the only listing of their state documents; for states with checklists, it is an additional source. A definite correlation has been observed between the number of documents listed for a state in the *Monthly Checklist* and the issuance of a state checklist. It may be supposed even today, when almost all the states issue a checklist, that cooperation with the Library of Congress by sending documents is closely related to the quality of the local program.

The comments and recommendations relating to the role of the Library of Congress in the state document field can be divided between what the Library of Congress does to fulfill its own mission and what it does to encourage and assist the states. It is an internal/external dichotomy.

The collections of state documents at the Library of Congress and that library's reference service can in no way override or replace the necessity for the states to maintain their own collections and to provide reference service. The Library of Congress cannot maintain complete collections of the documents of all the states and does not add to its collections all the items listed in the *Monthly Checklist of State Publications*. The Library of Congress can, however, play a major leadership role in the area of state documents by encouraging and monitoring the states' efforts in assembling complete collections, by assisting in the development of standards, particularly in the areas of bibliographical control, and by coordinating retention and preservation policies, especially with respect to microfilming projects.

Preservation in microform is another area in which the Library of Congress has great expertise. Whether state publications are filmed by the local archival agency or by a commercial firm, careful planning to assure that standards are observed must precede the implementation of a program. Any states embarking upon such a program should consult with microfilming experts at the federal level, especially in the Library of Congress and the Government Printing Office (GPO). The GPO's experience in preparing microfiche for distribution to depository libraries should be of special interest to states engaged in similar programs.

The Library of Congress has recently begun a project to authenticate the corporate entries for Texas state publications. The project is an outgrowth of a speech by Lucia Rather and others at the 1978 GODORT Annual Program and the resolution adopted by the American Library Association at that conference. The resolution reads:

LIBRARY OF CONGRESS—STATE COOPERATIVE CATALOGING
RESOLUTION

WHEREAS, the Library of Congress has effectively demonstrated the feasibility of cataloging federal documents with the Government Printing Office on a cooperative basis, and

WHEREAS, the Library of Congress has encouraged a library or agency within each state to act as the cataloging authority for publications of their respective states, and

WHEREAS, the Library of Congress has indicated the necessity for standardization of bibliographic records,

THEREFORE BE IT RESOLVED, that the American Library Association encourages the Library of Congress to establish a pilot project for the cooperative cataloging of state publications with several states representing various differences in population and geographical location, and

BE IT FURTHER RESOLVED, that the results of the project be carefully evaluated and documented for implementation on a national level.[15]

NOTES

1. Robert D. Leigh, "Foreword," in James L. McCamy, *Government Publications for the Citizen* (New York: Columbia University Press, 1949), p. x.

2. Kathy Schneider, "The Public's Right to Know: Government Must Give an Account of Itself," *Wisconsin Library Bulletin* 73:29 (January-February 1977).

3. California Legislature, Assembly, Interim Committee on Governmental Reorganization, "Information Services," in *First Partial Report* ([Sacramento]: 1951), p. 117.

4. Peter J. Paulson, "Government Documents and Other Non Trade Publications," *Library Trends* 18:363 (January 1970).

5. A. Paul Pross and Catherine A. Pross, *Government Publishing in the Canadian Provinces* (Toronto: University of Toronto Press, 1972), p. 62.

6. American Association of State Libraries, Standards Revision Committee, *Standards for Library Functions at the State Level*, rev. ed. (Chicago: American Library Association, 1970), p. 16.

7. L. D. White, "State Document Centers," *ALA Bulletin* 26:554-555 (1932).
Robert B. Downs, "Government Publications in American Libraries," *Library Trends* 15:187-189 (July 1966).

8. Genevieve M. Casey and Edith Phillips, *Management and Use of State Documents in Indiana*, Wayne State University, Office of Urban Library Research, Research Report no. 2 (Detroit: 1969), "Chart 1," pp. 15-20.

9. Ibid., p. 21.

10. Ernest Posner, *American State Archives* (Chicago: University of Chicago Press, 1964), p. 358.

11. Ibid., p. 347.

12. Ibid., p. 347n.

13. John Kopischke, "State Document Depositories: Wisconsin Outlines a New Approach," *Wisconsin Library Bulletin* 70:133 (May-June 1974).

14. Allen F. Sugden, "First Aid for California Document Selection," *California Librarian* 16:196 (April 1955).

15. *Documents to the People* 6:207-208 (September 1978).

3. LEGISLATION

Library interest in the distribution of state publications is not new, but in the past thirty years there has been a noticeable shift in emphasis. Since 1945, the states have been enacting a new kind of library legislation that most librarians call depository legislation. These words have not always meant the same thing to all librarians, and even today there is some confusion among librarians about the meaning of the term.

This confusion is understandable. Recent legislation is often enacted as an amendment to earlier legislation that had a different emphasis. In addition, depository legislation (even in the new meaning of the term) is changing as more states are adopting or amending such legislation; and it lacks uniformity, a characteristic common to other library legislation.

"LEGISLATION"

There are few difficulties with the word "legislation." Simply stated, it means laws enacted by the legislature. A few librarians interpret the word as *including* rules and regulations, which, of course, have the effect of laws and for that reason are called quasi-legislation. Because there is a difference between legislation (which is enacted by the legislature) and rules (which are adopted by an agency or board pursuant to legislative authorization), the distinction should be observed and, for present purposes, will be adhered to. (Both legislation and rules are included in the compilation of legal materials in Part III).

Perhaps because only a few state constitutions mention libraries,[1] librarians do not include constitutional provisions in their mental image of the concept of depository legislation. However, a statement that access to state publications is one of the rights of citizenship would not be inappropriate in a state constitution.

"DEPOSITORY"

The confusion over the term "depository" arises because the word was used in the early years of this century to refer to the establishment of a single

depository library (or perhaps two libraries) for state documents. The requirements that these depository collections be maintained and also that multiple
copies of documents be deposited for exchange were sufficient reason to call
this legislation "depository legislation." To add to the confusion, this early
legislation has sometimes been the basis for later depository legislation with a
much broader scope and more far-reaching effects.

The change in meaning in the world "depository" reflects the extension of
library service, in most of the states, to many local libraries. For example, the
number of public libraries in Louisiana has increased from twelve in 1928 (the
year a "depository" law was first enacted) to sixty-four in 1979. Likewise, the
number of depository libraries has increased from one (plus a few unnamed
college and university libraries) in 1928 to forty-three in 1979.[2] These increases in the number of libraries and depositories are a result of the desire on
the part of librarians to make library service more widely available. Obviously,
a statute that establishes a single depository library is different from one that
establishes (or permits the creation of) numerous depositories. It is this latter
type of depository legislation which is the subject of this book. The compilers
of the *1978 Directory of Government Document Collections and Librarians*
recognized this question of the interpretation of the word "depository":
"Also, there is no uniformly accepted and understood definition for the
depository designation as it applies to all types of documents . . . it is possible
that libraries identifying their collections as 'depository' are really only
'collectors' of these documents."[3]

HISTORY

State document legislation and plans are very recent. In 1950, Francis
Waters submitted a Master's thesis on legislation relating to state depository
libraries and cited laws in six states.[4] Because his study devotes a whole
chapter to the then new California legislation and because his outline of the
features of such legislation mentions as one of the characteristics of the
legislation that "other libraries are allowed to contract for service," the
impression arises that he is discussing "modern" depository legislation. His
first sentence, however, reveals his ties to the past. He begins, "This paper
discusses the problem of preserving social science source materials and how
some states have met *this problem of preservation* [italics added] by enacting
'depository' type legislation which provides for the designation of certain
libraries as state depositories." Although modern depository legislation includes the idea of preserving documents (today librarians say "maintaining a
collection for reference"), it places equal emphasis on convenient locations
for the use of state publications, that is, accessibility.

The states included in Waters' study are, in chronological order: Wisconsin (1903), Tennessee (1917), California (1945), Arkansas (1947), Minnesota (1947), and Louisiana (1948).

The Wisconsin law directs the library commission to ascertain and report libraries (public and academic) which could use public documents and to send the list of such depositories to the director of purchases. This Wisconsin legislation was an amendment of a 1903 law and was not new legislation.

The Tennessee law, which Waters describes as "not unlike the recent legislation passed on the problem," provides for three named depositories and others as named by the governor. This law is still in effect.

Waters calls the California law the "model." It provides for a library stock room and a system of libraries based on contracts. The California law has been amended many times.

The Arkansas law designates the General Library of the University of Arkansas as a depository for state and local documents. The section on state documents was amended in 1955 to change the number of copies to be sent and to permit more flexibility in what was sent. This law is still in effect. It was supplemented in 1971 by legislation designating other institutions of higher learning in the state as depositories and in 1979 by a law creating a state and local government publications clearinghouse.

The Minnesota law has two separate sections. The first provides for distribution to three libraries (including the state library, which is to receive exchange copies). This section was amended in 1963 to change the number of copies for one of the libraries and to add new categories of libraries and in 1975 to change "college" to "university." The other section cited by Waters is a requirement that local documents be sent to the historical society, upon request.

The Louisiana law provides for depository libraries and imposes a duty on the secretary of state to supply the depositories. This law was enacted as new legislation, but in fact it was a rewriting of a 1928 law to include public libraries as depositories and to provide for a list of publications. The law is still in effect, although the functions were transferred to the office of the state library in 1977.

Waters places some emphasis on the plan proposed by Kuhlman in the 1930s and revived in 1960 by Ralph Blasingame. Now, forty-five years later, the plan still appears sound. Blasingame's paper, presented at the Second Assembly of State Librarians in 1960, was a tongue-in-cheek presentation of the 1930s State Documents Center Plan as though it were in full operation.[5] He refers to the 1930s plan to "gather, organize, index and service massive collections." The plans were designed to preserve several categories of materials identified by the Social Science Research Council as essential for scholars. One of the categories was state documents. One or two libraries that already had strong collections were identified in each state and were asked to volunteer to assume responsibility for the building of comprehensive collections. The publication of checklists for inventorying the collections was part of the overall program.[6] Stimulation of legislation to require the deposit of publications was encouraged. Blasingame's paper recapitulates the plans outlined by Kuhlman.[7] According to Blasingame:

There are informal State programs (and a few formal ones) for the systematic collection and *distribution* of State and local publications of the types described. New York, California, Louisiana, and perhaps one or two other States have moved far ahead. But as a whole, coordinated picture, the vision has certainly become badly faded. [Italics added] . . . If this group is looking for a program by which it can make a substantial contribution to the improvement of government in general, here is a ready-made one.[8]

Insofar as the 1930s Document Center Plan was limited to collecting, Blasingame's challenge to use the 1930s plan should be augmented by the idea of distributing. His enumeration of the states that have "moved far ahead" (and these are all states that in 1961 had extensive distribution programs) indicates that he was thinking not only of the 1930s concept of collecting, but also of the modern idea of distributing.

This inference is confirmed by comments from the floor and by Blasingame's own statement on the Pennsylvania situation. In reference to that state, he said: "Pennsylvania does not have an adequate checklist either current or retrospective, has no consistent method of distribution, has no adequate legal base for a document program, has no single agency capable of serving in a real sense as a documents center, and has had no consistent policy regarding State documents." He comments that "the situation is no better perhaps in many other states" and as an example cites Irvin's article on Missouri documents.[9]

Other participants at the meeting emphasized distribution as supplementary to maintaining a collection. Charles Gosnell, state librarian of New York, reported that, although the New York law was neither ideal nor self-enforcing, a reasonably good job was being done with a great amount of personal contact and followup. He mentioned the list of depository libraries published in the *Checklist*. Loleta Fyan, state librarian of Michigan, reported on a "not too effective" Michigan preservation plan for older documents (twenty-five years old and older). This author, then Louisiana recorder of documents, reported for Louisiana that "the program of distribution aims at good coverage for a system of depositories within the State." Ralph Hudson, an Oklahoma state librarian, observed that "the system in Oklahoma operates satisfactorily" under a reasonably good law, and although "hard labor" was required, it presented no insuperable problems.[10] Present-day document librarians in Oklahoma explain this optimistic Oklahoma report with the comment that the system was always embryonic.

Blasingame's challenge lay dormant, except for enactment of new laws by the individual states, until 1975, when the Government Documents Round Table, and indeed the American Library Association as a whole, issued a new and broader challenge in the "Guidelines for Minimum State Servicing of State Publications." The association adopted the guidelines at the Council meeting in Chicago, in January 1975.

EARLY LEGISLATION

In hindsight, it is possible to identify some of the weaknesses of the early legislation, recognizing, of course, that this legislation had a different goal from today's depository legislation. One of the principal purposes of early legislation was to build document collections, that is, preserve materials for scholarly research. Laws for the exchange of documents were seen as one method of building collections. That these collections were not only the documents of the local state but also out-of-state documents is indicated in Harriet Skogh's 1936 article "Recent Developments in Publication and Distribution of American State Documents."

The emphasis in the Skogh article is on building state documents collections in state libraries and large public, university, or research libraries, primarily through exchanges. The author keeps returning to the theme of "building documents collections" and clearly indicates that these collections are out-of-state documents. She says: "It must be admitted that there was a purely utilitarian idea back of the legislation establishing the first exchanges, the desire to expand and enlarge the state's own library resources."[11] Incidentally, she cites only one development relating strictly to distribution — a comment on restrictive legislation with reference to distribution outside the state. Other recent developments reported in that article included discontinuance or suspension of important documents, publication in small editions, tendency toward sale of publications, use of "highly perishable mimeograph paper," and no printing whatever of certain reports. Some of these observations are still pertinent today.

The advent of the microform image may have made the need to preserve less critical. If only one copy of a document can be located, that is sufficient to permit copying for distribution to any number of libraries. The need to collect still exists, but the collections can be limited to only a few locations. Some major libraries have discontinued their collections of out-of-state documents and are willing to rely on the Center for Research Libraries in Chicago, on a collection in the state of origin, or on the availability of microforms. Thus, the expensive feature of the early legislation, large quantities of multiple copies for exchange purposes, is no longer necessary in depository legislation.

A summary of the distribution and exchange laws of the individual states is included in Wilcox.[12] Such a summary, if prepared today, very likely would place less stress on exchange laws, except for legal materials. Law libraries have longstanding exchanges for session laws and reports, on either a volume-for-volume or a cost basis. In contrast, the variety of executive department publications does not permit such a precise basis for exchange.

Another feature of the Wilcox survey is its emphasis on the various agencies that have responsibilities for sending publications to libraries. The distributing agencies (which are italicized) average over three agencies per state; the sole exception is Kentucky, which has a single agency involved in distribution. Some states have as many as six or seven different agencies with distribution functions affecting libraries. One objective of modern depository library legislation is to centralize such responsibility in a distribution agency, which is usually a section of the state library.

Many of the acts Wilcox summarized provide for the distribution of legal materials usually designated by title or type: session laws, journals, court reports, and so forth. This kind of legislation not only is frequently limited to publications of the legislative and judicial branches of government, but also fails to include all the publications even of those branches. The wording is not broad enough to include legislative rosters and court rules, which are important reference tools. Because designation by title or category is restrictive, this type of legislation is weak.

''Shall send to [certain libraries] on request,'' a phrase often used in early depository legislation, has a built-in defect because libraries cannot request publications of which they are unaware. An even weaker provision, because it employs a permissive verb, is worded ''libraries may receive on request.'' In order to be effective, any depository legislation must clearly establish that state agencies have a responsibility to supply copies of their publications. The designation of specific libraries by name as depositories, which requires amending legislation to add new libraries to the list, as is done in North Carolina, is also a limiting feature of early legislation. The failure to include public libraries within the depository law is another limitation. Arkansas, which adopted legislation for the University of Arkansas in 1947 and did not enact new legislation to include other institutions of higher learning until 1971, did not have depository legislation for public libraries until 1979.

Lack of an appropriation for the distribution program is a serious deficiency in depository legislation. Whether a state has made an appropriation for its depository program cannot be determined from the compiled statutes (which do not customarily include appropriations), nor from the session laws (which in some states are enabling acts only). The appropriation may be in a separate financial bill. (Available appropriation figures are included in the state section.) Fourteen states have reported budget figures in the 1979 survey.[13]

Finally, the lack of enforcement provisions in all legislation of this type, past and current, is often deplored, but no effective remedy has been found.

This summary is included here as history. The goals of libraries today in the distribution of state publications differ from those in the past. The North Carolina law which Skogh cited with approval in 1936 no longer meets the needs of libraries in that state, and new legislation has been adopted.[14] Another early law, passed in 1928, Skogh called "strong and apparently workable, but not enforced."[15] Very likely this law is Louisiana Act 82 of 1928. The startling thing is that the 1928 act was the basis for a very similar new act in 1948, which became the foundation for the Louisiana depository library program.

Much of this early legislation is still in force. However, it has been supplemented in most states by depository legislation which has the following characteristics: (1) definitions of "state publication," "state agency," and "print," (2) automatic forwarding of publications by the issuing agencies to the distribution center; (3) a system of libraries to serve as depositories; and (4) provision for the issuance of a checklist.

A program embodying the essential elements of a depository program could be set up without legislation. In Nevada, the state library operated a pilot program for three years prior to the adoption of legislation in 1971 to demonstrate to the legislature and to the state agencies the kind of program that the libraries wanted. The state library was necessarily dependent on the voluntary cooperation of the state agencies in supplying copies of their publications to conduct the demonstration.

Legislation is important because it establishes a legal framework for the program and is the basis for budget requests. If an agency or the agency function is not provided for by law, difficulties in funding can easily arise. A statutory basis for the program assures the continuity of the program as long as the legislation is not repealed.

Drafting legislation is like a self-study; it brings issues into focus and identifies the decisions that must be made. Some of the questions that must be answered are easy. If the state library is willing to accept the appropriation and administer the program, a major question is answered. If the governing board of that state library is always the agency which adopts rules and regulations, then another question is answered. Such questions, and many others, must be answered by the librarians who want depository legislation for their state.

When the drafting of depository legislation is the topic of discussion or the subject of an article, the same remark is repeated over and over—as a preliminary step in planning for a depository program, the statutes of all the other states were read and the distribution systems studied. This is a large undertaking. Ron Haselhuhn of Emporia State University states that his library school class worked with all the statutes but confined their comparisons to the statutes of only six states.

SHARING INFORMATION

How have the results of all this effort been shared? Carolyn Kohler, University of Iowa librarian, prepared a survey of depository library systems. Iowa has been trying to get depository legislation for a number of years, and, as each new need for her survey arises, Kohler revises it. Her latest revision was January 1977 and is included in the Documents on Documents Collection.

Another way in which there has been a sharing of information is through the Documents on Documents Collection, which includes the statutes of almost all the states. The collection is kept up to date by requests for new information without any effort to verify whether the materials in the collection are still current. When the last request for new materials was made in June 1976, a number of states responded; but, as Brenda Olds, who was then custodian of the collection, reported, more states asked to borrow the collection than submitted additional materials. For an overview, however, the collection is very convenient. The collection of statutes included in the state section of this book is based on the Documents on Documents Collection. Without the collection, the lack of uniformity in the legislation of the states would have made it difficult to determine what each state considers its "depository legislation."

American Library Laws has two index entries which lead to depository legislation: "deposit of public documents" and "distribution of public documents."[16] The first entry refers to laws imposing a duty on state agencies, usually to deposit specific titles. The second entry includes the depository legislation as well as special distribution statutes, thus supplying more information than is needed when the general depository statutes are being sought. The special distribution statutes included in this book are those which were identified by the states as "depository legislation." In considering depository legislation, librarians need to compare the legislation of all the states and at the same time be fully aware of the history of such legislation in their own state.

Even though modern depository legislation is to be supplementary to existing legislation and does not include the repeal of earlier legislation, those involved in its enactment must study the earlier legislation carefully to coordinate the distribution patterns. Awareness of the existing legislation not only avoids conflicts in the statutes but also prepares one for testifying during the legislative process. The Nebraska and the Oklahoma legislation are examples of depository legislation that amended other sections of the statutes in addition to enacting new legislation. In Nebraska, a computer search of the Nebraska statutes was made to locate all existing legislation on the distribution of individual publications. Amendments to the legislation to include the new clearinghouse in the distribution patterns for each such publication were included in the depository bill. The amending of these fourteen sections served a double purpose: securing the publications for the clearinghouse and making the agencies aware of the program.

While libraries should ideally receive all publications through the depository program, it is possible to exclude legal publications, as the Indiana depository law does, if the libraries are already receiving those publications pursuant to other statutes. A trend, noted in recent Delaware, Oklahoma, and Washington legislation, is the enactment of depository legislation in conjunction with the revision of printing statutes or public information statutes.

MODEL LAWS

In 1909, an American Library Association committee calling itself the Committee on Model Law for the Distribution of State Documents reported at the annual meeting.[17] The committee commented first that it had received some advice "that the legal forms and phrases varied in the different states so much as to make an attempt to draw up a uniform law in concrete form a matter of somewhat uncertain value." Then the committee outlined the main feature which should be included in such a law: the state library or some other library should be designated to distribute the public documents of the state and to receive and care for those of other states. This again is the idea of building a collection of out-of-state documents and engaging in exchanges. The inclusion of a provision that no printing bills be paid without a certification that the library had received its copies was suggested. The report continues with a discussion of the number of copies of publications to be supplied (50 to 250!), the location of depositories (not only in state libraries, but also in commercial and educational centers, and in principal countries of the world), and printing and binding rules. A still pertinent peripheral recommendation was that dates used on the binding of publications be for the period covered by the report and not the date of publication.

In his 1915 treatise Reece has a section called "Suggestions for a Model Law on Printing and Distribution." He favors a central agency with authority over printing and distribution. He says: "It [the central authority] should seek not alone to publish in fitting and permanent form the records of state activities, but should place those publications at once with regard to economy and with the design of rendering them in the highest degree useful."[18]

The model law suggested by the Library of Congress[19] and adopted by the Council of State Governments in its 1971 Suggested Legislation places heavy emphasis, as might be expected, on sending copies of publications to the Library of Congress. It includes a provision for a central collecting and distributing agency and refers to exchanges with other states. The section on distribution to libraries in the state is independent of the one on distribution to the Library of Congress.

Since about 1974, a group in the State Documents Task Force of the Government Documents Round Table of the American Library Association

(ALA GODORT) has been considering state depository legislation. Ron Haselhuhn, who worked with the group, concluded that it was not possible to draft model legislation because of the variances among the states. He prepared a paper on the laws affecting distribution of public documents based on the Documents on Documents Collection and *American Library Laws*. He reported some difficulty in determining the legal citations for the statutes in the Documents on Documents Collection because the title and chapter designations were not always included on the copies he used.[20] The citations to the laws included in this book are in a table in the state section. When this list was published in *Documents to the People*, the author received no corrections, but one addition from the Virgin Islands.[21]

GUIDELINES

The Task Force group then turned its attention from a model law to the drafting of guidelines for depository legislation. These guidelines, adopted by the State Documents Task Force in June 1978 and by the Government Documents Round Table in July 1980, are reproduced in the Appendix. Although the concepts covered by the Task Force Guidelines are discussed more fully in subsequent chapters, some brief comments here will provide an overview.

DEFINITIONS

Definitions are written from the library point of view for the purpose of ensuring that the libraries can acquire copies of everything the state agencies issue. The librarians want to be able to cite the definitions to the state agencies as authority for requiring that all possible publications be included in the depository library program. Because state publications are not in the general stream of publications, those which are not included within the definition are not caught elsewhere. Therefore, the coverage must be as wide as possible. Balancing comprehensive coverage with a limitation on the number of copies furnished will avoid waste and reduce expense, while at the same time ensure bibliographic control and the availability of at least one copy of each publication.

DISTRIBUTION

Automatic distribution parallels one of the ideas behind the federal depository library law that more than a mere ability to purchase or request documents is necessary to make them easily available. Such distribution recognizes the logic of a statewide system and the savings to the individual libraries in eliminating acquisition procedures. The provision for distribution also recognizes the fact that public libraries, while they have no publications to offer in an exchange program, furnish an essential service to the public.

Centralized distribution to the depository libraries, as distinguished from direct mailing by the state agencies, has the advantage of increasing the probability that the depositories will receive the documents they need. The central distribution source assumes responsibility for contacting the state agencies on a regular basis. A librarian is usually appointed to acquaint the state agencies with the needs of libraries, to claim missing documents, and to ascertain the details of the publishing programs of the state agencies. If there is a central distributing agency, a shipping list can be sent to the depository libraries to serve as a record, or invoice, for the depositories.

SYSTEM OF DEPOSITORIES

Modern depository legislation provides for an indeterminate group of libraries to serve as depositories, including academic and public libraries, and in Idaho, special libraries. It often mandates a system or network of libraries. Sometimes the system concept is achieved indirectly through provisions which instruct the state library agency to designate depository libraries in various geographical areas, or according to rules it establishes.

INCLUSION OF ALL STATE PUBLICATIONS

The inclusion of a guideline stressing the deposit of *all* state publications is related to the definitions just discussed. Not only must the definition be broad, but also the publications included in the definition must be available in at least one library. Some legislation for depository programs excludes university publications, or even the publications of the legislative and judicial branches of government. Even though these excluded publications are available elsewhere in the state (university publications at the university, for instance), the degree of accessibility for the general user decreases with every separately established location of the official documents files.

BIBLIOGRAPHICAL CONTROL

An important feature of most current depository legislation is a provision for the issuance of a list of publications. The requirement for the list, which gives bibliographic control of the documents, was implemented in Nebraska before the system of depository libraries was established there. In some states, a list is issued without a specific legal requirement.

INCIDENTAL PROVISIONS

The inclusion of a special effective date for the legislation is not unusual. For example, the new Arkansas law was effective on July 1, 1979 and the

Colorado legislation, on July 1, 1980. An immediate effective date as found in the Oregon amendment adopted in 1979 is, however, noteworthy. The Oregon emergency clause reads, ''This Act being necessary for the immediate preservation of the public peace, health and safety, an emergency is declared to exist, and this Act takes effect on its passage.'' The Oregon act reduced the number of copies required, which may have been a reason for the emergency clause.

Among other less critical provisions found in recent legislation are policy statements, inclusion of local documents within the scope of the program, designation of historical depositories, naming of contact persons or liaisons, provision for partial depositories, substitution of microform copies, distribution of microform copies in lieu of hard copies, furnishing by state agencies of lists of publications and mailing lists, duties of depository libraries, and authorization to the distributing center to issue rules and regulations. All these features of depository legislation are discussed in the appropriate chapters in this book.

OTHER PROPOSALS

Two other statements outlining provisions for depository legislation can be compared to the Task Force Guidelines—the Casey study for Indiana in 1969, which lists five necessary provisions, and the Wisconsin article by Schneider in 1977, which lists seven.[22]

The Wisconsin proposal begins by including two policy statements, one on awareness and accessibility and one on encouraging state agencies to economize by using the depository system. The Guidelines, Casey, and Schneider give the definition of state documents as a requirement. The Guidelines add a definition of state agency.

The provision in the Guidelines for deposit of all state publications at one location comes closest to a requirement that state agencies deposit their publications. In Wisconsin this duty is stated as identifying the basic responsibilities and providing for the accountability of the producers of documents in terms of distribution. Casey provides that state agencies be responsible for depositing all documents with the state library and in a separate item that a sufficient number of copies be supplied.

The Guideline requirement on automatic distribution to a system of libraries is also found in the Wisconsin list, as a requirement for the description of the system, definition of the privileges and responsibilities of the depository libraries, and a limitation on the number of depository libraries. The Casey parallel is merely an authority to the state library to distribute.

Except for the provisions on definitions, on depositing of copies by state agencies, and on distribution by a central source, the lists are not parallel. Casey adds a requirement that a document officer be appointed in every state agency, and in another section of her study she recommends publication of a checklist. Wisconsin, in addition to the policy statements, includes provision for a public documents advisory committee and for the incorporation of all sections related to distribution into a single chapter of the compiled statutes.

Librarians considering legislation may also want to review Cole's elements of an ideal system, Virginia's proposed recommendations for a system, and Carmack's recommendations for action at the end of his report for the study commission. [23]

Cole's statement is the most complete. It recognizes the importance of centralized distribution; suggests responsibilities to be assumed by state agencies, the distribution center, and depository libraries; recommends the Carmack definition of public document; and provides for a complete collection, discretionary distribution, and a checklist. The Virginia proposal is also comprehensive. It includes limitation on distribution beyond that to depository libraries and out-of-state libraries, and provides specifically for partial depositories by categories established by the state library. Cole does not commit himself on the question of partial depositories, but he comments that the full depository requirement is less likely to be abused. Cole recommends a checklist with a cumulative index; Virginia, a quarterly checklist with annual cumulations.

Carmack's proposals for action include an outline of a system of depositories for South Dakota. The system would consist of full and partial depositories, which would receive hard copy publications, microform copies on request, and copies of nonprint material on payment of reproduction costs. A monthly checklist was to be issued, rules and regulations were to be promulgated, and a staff of one professional and two classified personnel were to be added to the state library staff. One important proposal was that for an appropriation to fund the system.

CHRONOLOGY

Modern depository legislation is broader in scope than earlier legislation with respect to the range of publications and more inclusive in the types of libraries in the program. The provision for a checklist is rarely found in pre-1950 legislation.

Because recent depository legislation is sometimes based on older legislation (for example, Louisiana's 1948 act was based on one enacted in 1928), it is difficult to say which state was the first to enact depository legislation. California lays claim to being the first, [24] but Waters disputes this[25] and credits Tennessee with the first law, in 1917. Wisconsin used the word "depository" as early as 1903 in legislation which provided for designation of depositories and distribution to those depositories. [26] The contents table of the state section gives the dates of state depository legislation.

For the same reasons, it is difficult to establish a date for the beginning of the depository program in each state. For example, the date customarily used in Louisiana for the beginning of the program is 1948. However, the 1948 Louisiana law is practically a reenactment of a 1928 law. The active and continuing interest of librarians in the 1948 law, the appointment of a "graduate" librarian to administer the program, the support of the secretary of state, in whose office the service was administered, and a small appropriation were the determining factors in the effectiveness of the Louisiana program under the 1948 law. The fortuitous circumstances which resulted in both the librarian and the secretary of state remaining in office during the first twenty-five years of the program probably were also factors in the survival of the Louisiana program.

A chronological arrangement of depository statutes, while somewhat of an academic exercise, reveals the changes that have been made and are being made in state depository laws. Table 2 gives the date of the original legislation (edited to exclude the earlier exchange statutes) and Table 3, the latest amendments.

AMENDMENTS

There have not been many substantive amendments to depository laws. Some amendments have merely incorporated new agency names that were made necessary by reorganization acts, or changes required by an annual legislative session in lieu of a biennial session. Hence, they do not affect the administration of the programs provided for by the legislation. On the other hand, substantive changes, indicative of the development of the programs provided for in the legislation, are instructive and should be studied by those who follow such legislation. Table 3 shows the effect of the most recent amendments.

The California legislation has been amended numerous times to change the responsibilities of the agencies involved in the administration of the law. A study of these changes is included in the state section under California.

The Washington legislation was not amended until fourteen years after its original enactment in 1963. The 1977 changes were part of a general act relating to the executive management and control of state publications. One of the major changes in the section on the depository program related to the duty of the state agencies to deposit copies of their publications with the state library. Formerly, the section read, "Every state agency *may* upon release deposit . . . "; it was changed to read, "Every state agency *shall* promptly deposit . . . " [Emphasis added in both quotations.] Another significant change affects the number of copies to be deposited. The 1963 law provided for the deposit of three copies and additional copies as required. The 1977 law is

TABLE 2.
DATES OF DEPOSITORY LEGISLATION IN CHRONOLOGICAL ORDER

The date when a state first enacted depository legislation varies according to whether the program was enacted as new, or as amending, legislation. The sources for the early dates are the writings and comments of librarians. The dates should not be taken too literally because some are for distribution or archives laws rather than a full depository program. The arrangement here shows the concentration of this legislation in the last ten years.

1902 Rhode Island	1970 Alaska
1903 Wisconsin	1971 Nevada
1911 Kansas	1971 Pennsylvania
1915 Alabama	1972 Idaho
1917 Tennessee	1972 Nebraska
	1973 Indiana
	1973 New Hampshire
1941 North Carolina	1974 Delaware
1941 Wyoming	1974 South Dakota
1945 California	1975 Georgia
1947 Arkansas	
1947 Minnesota	
1948 Louisiana	1976 Arizona
	1976 Michigan
	1976 Missouri
1953 Oregon	1977 Connecticut
1953 West Virginia	1977 North Dakota
1954 Maine	1977 Virgin Islands
1955 New York	1977 Virginia
1957 New Jersey	1978 Iowa
1957 Ohio	1978 New Mexico
1957 Utah	1978 Oklahoma
1958 Kentucky	
	1980 Colorado
1963 Washington	
1965 Hawaii	
1966 Mississippi	
1967 Florida	
1967 Illinois	
1967 Montana	
1969 Texas	
1969 Vermont	
1969 Model Law	

TABLE 3.

AMENDMENTS TO DEPOSITORY LEGISLATION

Some states have had numerous amendments to their depository legislation. Only the latest amendment is given here in this overview of the kinds of changes that have been made most recently.

1967—New Jersey: New legislation for copies of publications for distribution

1970—Hawaii: Number of copies deposited increased to 15

1971—Arkansas: Publications for libraries of colleges and universities

—Vermont: Designates the Bailey library as a depository

—Wisconsin: Editorial changes

1973—New York: Agencies that produce films, audio-or videotape, or other electronic information required to notify state library; state library to list the programs

1974—Kentucky: Archives and records function transferred to state library

1975—Maine: Reduced number of copies to be delivered to 55

—Mississippi: Depository functions transferred to a library agency

1976—California: Assessment for listing in checklist deleted

—Kansas: New legislation for a depository system

—Minnesota: Checklist for legislators

—South Dakota: Permanent retention by two libraries, microform permitted, libraries added

1977—Florida: Editorial change

—Louisiana: Depository functions transferred to a library agency

—Montana: Two additional entities exempted from depository law

—Virginia: Recodification; no substantive change

—Washington: Major changes in four sections of act

1978—Georgia: State agencies required to report titles published

1979—Alaska: Name of state publications library distribution center changed to state library distribution and access center; definitions broadened to include University of Alaska and to define ''research data''

—Arkansas: Authorized a state and local government publications clearinghouse; provides for depository libraries and a checklist

—Florida: Law library of Nova University added to state legal depositories

—Maryland: Resolution to create a study commission

—Montana: Amendment was part of a bill affecting the legislative branch

—Nebraska: Number of copies to be deposited reduced from 8 to 4; number of copies to Library of Congress and Center for Research Libraries reduced to 1 copy for each institution

TABLE 3 (continued)

—Nevada: Distribution to the division of state, county, and municipal archives eliminated

—North Carolina: Deposit of 5 copies of all publications with the state library; checklist to be published

—North Dakota: State library commission changed to state library

—Ohio: Distribution of pamphlet laws and legislative materials to depository libraries

—Oregon: Number of copies to be deposited standardized at 45; state printer authorized to withhold depository copies from the printing order

—South Dakota: Repeal of section providing that distributions by the governor, secretary of state, and bureau of administration would not be affected by the depository legislation

—Texas: Major new legislation including definitions, duties of the state library; deposit of not more than 75 copies of publications, state agency contact persons, and so on

—Utah: Major new legislation, including definitions, deposit of publications from political subdivisions, micrographics authority for the distribution center, list of publications with access by agency, author, title, subject, and other means

—Virginia: Distribution to Division of Purchases and Supply eliminated

—Wisconsin: Superintendent changed to state superintendent

1980—Wisconsin: Numbers for cross-references changed

general and does not specify a minimum number but only "in quantities as certified by the state librarian as required." An additional part of the section provides for the exemption, in full or in part, of a publication or a class of publications from the requirements of the section.

Another interesting change in the Washington law is the provision for contracts with public out-of-state libraries on a reciprocal basis, and the deletion of the specific mention of the Library of Congress, the Midwest Inter-Library Center (now the Center for Research Libraries), and other state libraries in one of the two 1977 amendments.

CASE HISTORIES

There are many texts on how to lobby and how to approach legislators, and many civics books which detail the steps in the legislative process. This chapter bypasses these traditional areas and concentrates on the special techniques applicable to depository legislation. The case histories and comments outlined here highlight special considerations relating to depository legislation from the time the idea for the legislation is first conceived until it is enacted.

In his 1950 thesis on state legislation relating to state depository libraries, Waters discusses the background of the California legislative effort. A committee of the state library association, under Jerome K. Wilcox, was active in preparing a questionnaire (some of the results are given at pages 9 and 10 of the thesis) and in the introduction of the bill. Waters says that the intent of the authors of this legislation was "to establish in certain libraries absolutely complete collections of every publication being issued by the state of California."[27] Evelyn Huston outlines the background of the California legislative effort and the beginning of the California program.[28]

Dallas Shaffer's article is the most detailed account of the preliminary steps in preparing depository legislation.[29] In studying this article on the Nebraska experience, the reader should notice particularly that it took only a year from the time the first questionnaire was sent out until the law was signed. In Kansas, the promoter of the legislation had "three years of often frustrating experience," before a bill was enacted. Iowa librarians spent over seven years studying and working on legislation.[30] Shaffer said in her article, "I often felt I was working without proper information to guide me,"[31] and recommends the Documents on Documents Collection as a means of filling this information gap. Others have endorsed and followed her suggestion that this collection be borrowed and examined. A study of the collection should be one of the first steps in gathering information.

The Nebraska legislation was prepared before the Documents on Documents Collection was assembled. Therefore, the first step in that state was to prepare and distribute a questionnaire to all the states, which included queries on legislation, checklist production, depository systems, staff, and budgets.[32]

Ron Haselhuhn in his unpublished study on Kansas legislative endeavors emphasizes, first, that someone must provide the leadership and, second, that this person must "seek the help of like-minded people." Haselhuhn, who is a library school faculty member, enlisted the help of his students, who discussed and drafted proposed legislation.[33] In Nebraska, Shaffer, the government services librarian at the Nebraska Library Commission, was assigned, on a part-time basis, the responsibility for drafting and enacting the legislation. In Wisconsin, a new staff position was created, "a librarian whose primary responsibility was government documents and liaison with state agencies."[34] In Indiana, the state library commissioned a survey.[35] In South Dakota, a study commission was established pursuant to an act passed by the legislature. The report of the commission and an article by its chairman on the work of the commission are annotated in the state section.[36]

R. G. Cole has observed that "working out the details of . . . a system is a difficult task that requires statewide effort. Almost invariably in other states this effort has been initiated by the state library associations."[37]

These approaches are not inconsistent and, in fact, should all be adopted. A dedicated librarian and the colleagues whom he has recruited are usually behind any depository legislation. The state library, which in most of the states is the coordinating agency, almost always is involved early in the planning, as are the state library association and its committees. It is important, after the legislation has been drafted and is accepted and understood by the library community, and to the extent feasible by the officers of state government, that the base of support be extended to include civic organizations and other user groups. The need for such support, however, is not unique to state depository legislation.

After the legislation is adopted, the legislator who authored the bill could be invited to the annual banquet of the library association to receive the thanks of the members, as was done in New Mexico.

RECENT LEGISLATION

A full report on recent depository legislation cannot be made without resorting to individual inquiries to many of the states. The session laws and the supplementary services for the statutory compilations are published with varying degrees of promptness after the end of the legislative sessions, and, of course, the sessions end at varying times. Moreover, citations are necessarily only to the bills, which are not readily available. The new 1980 Colorado act is the most recent major legislation included in the state section. The provisions of the most recent legislation are incorporated in the lists but not in all the tables and text discussions.

Bills for complete depository programs introduced in 1979 in Colorado and South Carolina unfortunately failed to pass. The Colorado bill was successful in 1980. On the other hand, it was fortunate that a New Mexico bill to repeal the newly established depository program failed to pass. The document librarian at the New Mexico State Library reported that the sponsor had introduced the bill because he was tired of having his mailbox stuffed with state agency reports, and that the result of rallying the state document librarians to amend the bill was to bring everyone involved in the state document program closer together.

Maryland has a 1979 resolution (Senate Joint Resolution 35) "requesting the governor to create a Task Force to study and evaluate the system of collecting, distributing and making accessible various state and local government publications and reports."

Most of the 1979 legislation was enacted as amendments to existing legislation or programs. The 1979 programs enacted in Arkansas, Texas, and Utah have been described as new legislation, although those states had some deposit and distribution legislation before 1979. Other 1979 amendments are shown in Table 3.

NOTES

1. *American Library Laws*, 4th ed. (Chicago: American Library Association, 1973), p. 1960. Only twelve states are listed under the index heading "Constitutional Provisions."

2. The number of public libraries in Louisiana for 1928 is found in Louisiana, Library Commission, *Second Biennial Report, 1926-28*, p. 20; for 1979, in Louisiana, Office of the State Library, *Public Libraries in Louisiana, Statistical Report, 1978*, p. 4. The number of libraries with document holdings in the 1930s is found in Lucy B. Foote, *Bibliography of the Official Publications of the State of Louisiana, 1803-1934* ([Historical Records Survey] American Imprints Inventory, no. 19), (Baton Rouge, La.: Hill Memorial Library, Louisiana State University, 1942), p. xiii; for 1979, in Louisiana, Office of the State Library, *Public Documents, January-December 1979*, pp. viii-ix.

3. American Library Association, Government Documents Round Table, *1978 Directory of Government Document Collections and Librarians*, 2d ed. (Washington, D.C.: Congressional Information Service, 1978), p. vi.

4. Francis B. Waters, "Analysis of State Legislation Relating to State Depository Libraries" (M.S.L.S. Thesis, Western Reserve University, 1950).

5. Ralph Blasingame, "Public Documents of the States: Their Collection, Listing, Distribution and Value," *Proceedings of the Second Assembly of State Librarians . . .* 1960 (Washington, D.C.: Library of Congress, 1961), pp. 1-6.

6. See listing in Vladimir Palic, *Government Publications: A Guide to Bibliographic Tools*, 4th ed. (Washington, D.C.: Library of Congress, 1975), p. 86, under National Association of State Libraries.

7. A. F. Kuhlman wrote several articles about the state document center plan. See Part II, State Publications - The Literature Section.

8. Blasingame, "Public Documents of the States," pp. 5, 6.

9. Charles E. Irvin, 'The Distribution of Missouri State Documents," *Missouri Library Association Quarterly* 13:109-112 (December 1952).

10. Blasingame, "Public Documents of the States," pp. 7-8.

11. Harriet M. Skogh, "Recent Developments in Publication and Distribution of American State Documents," American Library Association, Committee on Public Documents, *Public Documents, 1936*, p. 141.

12. Jerome K. Wilcox, ed., *Manual on the Use of State Publications* (Chicago: American Library Association, 1940), pp. 295-331.

13. Margaret T. Lane (comp.), *State Publications: Depository Distribution and Bibliographical Programs*, State and Local Documents Task Force, Government Documents Round Table, American Library Association; Texas State Publications Clearinghouse, Documents Monograph Series, no. 2 ([Austin, Tex.]: Texas State Library, 1980).

14. Robert Grey Cole, "North Carolina Needs an Improved Depository System for State Documents," *North Carolina Libraries* 31:35 (1973).

15. Skogh, "Recent Developments," p. 144.

16. *American Library Laws*, pp. 1962, 1963.

17. C. W. Andrews, "A Model Law for the Distribution of State Documents," *ALA Bulletin* 3:327-328 (September 1909).

18. Ernest J. Reece, *State Documents for Libraries, (University of Illinois Bulletin* v. 12, no. 36) (Urbana, Ill.: University of Illinois, 1915), p. 101.

19. See state section, following Wyoming.

20. Ron Haselhuhn, "Laws Affecting Distribution of Public Documents," in Documents on Documents Collection.

21. *Documents to the People* 6:143 (May 1978).

22. Genevieve M. Casey and Edith Phillips, *Management and Use of State Documents in Indiana*, Wayne State University, Office of Urban Library Research, Research Report no. 2 (Detroit: 1969), pp. 51-52.

Kathy Schneider, "New Documents Legislation? A Wisconsin Proposal Would Ease and Speed Document Use," *Wisconsin Library Bulletin* 73:38 (January-February 1977).

23. Cole, "North Carolina Needs an Improved Depository System," p. 37.

"Proposed Recommendations for a State Depository System [in Virginia]," in Documents on Documents Collection.

South Dakota, Interim Public Documents Study Commission, *Report* (Pierre, S.D.: The Commission, 1972), pp. 10-13.

24. Evelyn Huston, "California Solves Documents Distribution: In Face of Opposition, Its Library Association Secured a Bill Which Benefits the State Depositories and Other Exchanges," *Library Journal* 73:7 (January 1, 1948).

25. Waters, "Analysis of State Legislation," p. 8.

26. John Kopischke, "State Document Depositories: Wisconsin Outlines a New Approach," *Wisconsin Library Bulletin* 70:131 (May-June 1974).

27. Waters, "Analysis of State Legislation," pp. 8-13. Cites the Huston and Klausner articles annotated in the state section.

28. Huston, "California Solves Documents Distribution," pp. 8-10.

29. Dallas Shaffer, "State Document Legislation: Nebraska; a Case Study," *Government Publications Review* 1:19-27 (Fall 1973)

30. Carolyn Kohler's first survey was dated March 1971, and the depository library act was signed by the Iowa governor in May 1978.

31. Shaffer, "State Document Legislation," p. 23.

32. A copy of the Oklahoma response is in the Documents on Documents Collection.

33. Haselhuhn, "Laws," p. 1, in Documents on Documents Collection.

34. Kopischke, "State Document Depositories," p. 132.

35. Casey and Phillips, *Management and Use of State Documents*, p. 1.

36. Bob D. Carmack, "South Dakota Public Documents: A Report of a Study," *Government Publications Review* 1:251-256 (1974).

South Dakota, Interim Public Documents Study Commission, *Report*.

37. Cole, "North Carolina Needs an Improved Depository System," p. 38.

4. POLICY STATEMENTS AND DEFINITIONS

The reader, especially one who uses state publications for the information they contain, may question why an entire chapter is devoted to policy statements and definitions. Doesn't everyone know that government-produced information should be readily and easily available to all, and what a government document or a state agency is? Shouldn't it be a simple matter to authorize the distribution and use of the information in government publications? The paradox lies in the fact that even these most generally accepted ideas and frequently used terms may be subject to more than one interpretation. The simplest general statement in a piece of depository legislation may be understood differently by different individuals or agencies unless the intent is carefully spelled out as unambiguously as possible. On the other hand, the whole program for making government materials available and accessible to those who would use them may be thwarted if the language used in the enabling legislation is unduly specific and restrictive.

Anyone working toward enactment of legislation, or administering legislation, soon realizes that a clear statement of the purpose and careful definition of the terms used in the legislation are invaluable. Analysis of definitions and policy statements in the legislation already enacted and in the amendments that have been adopted to accommodate new developments is helpful in drafting new legislation or amending existing laws.[1]

POLICY STATEMENTS

Policy statements are an expression of the intent of the legislature in enacting legislation, generally stating the reason for the legislation and the purpose behind it. They usually specify what group will benefit from the legislation, what action will be taken to achieve the legislative goals, and what agency or entity is required to take action.

The policy statement in the 1945 California law established that law as the first depository legislation. The California statement announces, first, that state publications should be available to the inhabitants of the state, and then continues by stating that this availability should be through libraries. This emphasis on availability to the public was completely new in 1945.

Although in public libraries there may be no distinction between receiving publications in the library and making them available to the public, such a distinction may arise in academic libraries, where the primary clientele is faculty and students, not the general public. In academic libraries, receipt by the library does not *ipso facto* mean availability to the public at large. The California policy statement emphasizes availability to the public.

An example of the change in emphasis found in the 1945 California legislation that illustrates the post-1945 philosophy that the libraries are merely a means to an end is the wording of the legislation enacted in the Virgin Islands in 1977: "To effectuate the territory's public policy to make governmental information available . . . there are established depository libraries." Earlier legislation, although it mentions depository libraries (for example, Wisconsin in 1903 and Tennessee in 1917), is concerned with availability to libraries. The Wisconsin legislation provided for depository libraries, which the legislation identified as those libraries which could "suitably care for and advantageously use the public documents printed at the expense of the state." The Tennessee legislation designated several libraries by name and "other libraries as the governor may at any time name" as depository libraries. The purpose of the legislation in both instances, it may be assumed, was to meet the needs of libraries. This assumption arises because in both Wisconsin and Tennessee the depository libraries are required, first, to "care for" (Wisconsin) and "preserve" (Tennessee), and then to "advantageously use" (Wisconsin) and to lend "to the persons, if any, allowed to take other books from the library" (Tennessee).

Even as late as 1950, Francis Waters in his paper on depository legislation failed to acknowledge that the California policy statement was breaking new ground. He refers to "the policy of the state toward the collection and preservation of state documents" and does not recognize that the California policy statement stresses an additional goal. He credits Tennesee with having the earliest depository legislation, although Wisconsin has a more valid claim to that distinction.[2]

CURRENT POLICY STATEMENTS

Not all states that have enacted depository legislation since 1945 have used policy statements to express a legislative intent to assure the availability of publications to the public. Provisions adding public libraries to those which may become depositories (for example, Louisiana), requiring geographical distribution of the depositories (such as Alaska), and imposing a duty on the depositories to make publications accessible to the public (for example, Texas) have achieved the same objective. This chapter, however, is limited to formal policy statements, identified by such words as "whereas," "it is a policy," or "for the purpose of."

Although Waters credits policy statements with being an essential element of depository legislation, they are not often found in such legislation today. Waters' survey was based on the laws of the six states, and of those six states, Wisconsin and Tennessee had adopted their legislation before the modern California legislation was enacted, and Minnesota and Louisiana did not include policy statements in their legislation. Policy statements, or statements of purpose, are found in the legislation of California, Delaware, Indiana, Michigan, Nevada, Ohio, and the Virgin Islands. (See "Statements and Declarations of Policy in Depository Legislation" at the end of this chapter.) The Arkansas statement is in the preamble to a 1947 act, whereas a separate Senate concurrent resolution expresses the legislative intent of the Oklahoma legislature.

The policy statements quoted and discussed here do not include the duty of the center to "promote the establishment of an orderly depository system." (See Chapter 6, the section on duties of the distribution center.) The Washington provision, which was formerly a duty to promote an orderly depository system, was rewritten in 1977 to read, "The center shall utilize the depository library system to permit citizens economical and convenient access to state publications." This provision is included here because the purpose of the system is articulated. The duty of the center to maintain a collection "to meet the reference and information needs of officers, departments, agencies of state government, and other libraries" in the Ohio law is included in the list at the end of the chapter for the same reason.

Likewise, the definition of depository library in the few states which define this phrase, for example, Connecticut, may include a policy-type statement referring to making the publications available to the general public. Or, as in the Florida legislation and that of many other states, the depository libraries may be required to make the publications accessible to the public. In Oklahoma, the depository library system itself is to be established for the use of the citizens of the state of Oklahoma. None of the statements of this type is included in the compilation of policy statements.

Another purpose, recited in the Indiana act, "in order that selected documents of various other states shall be available for use by the citizens of Indiana," is included here only because the exchange provisions are an integral part of the Indiana depository legislation. The exchange legislation of other states has not been examined but may include similar policy statements.

PARTS OF THE POLICY STATEMENT

The policy statements are usually a sentence stating that some agency shall take some action for a stated purpose for the benefit of some group. (See Table 4.)

TABLE 4.
POLICY STATEMENTS

State or Territory	Agency	Action	Group Affected
Indiana	Act designates state library as depository	To preserve and make available for use	Citizens of the state
Michigan	Act designates state library as depository	To preserve and make available for use	People of the state
California	By distribution to depository libraries*	To make freely available	Its inhabitants
Nevada	By distribution to depository libraries	For use	All inhabitants of the state
	Depository libraries	Keeping readily accessible for use and rendering assistance	Patrons
Virgin Islands	Depository libraries established	To make governmental information available	To governmental agencies and to the general public
Washington	Center shall utilize depository system	To permit economical and convenient access	Citizens
Delaware	State agencies shall deposit	Making accessible	To Delaware and other citizens
Arkansas	University of Arkansas**	Maintain comprehensive collection	Teachers, students and research workers
Ohio	State librarian maintain comprehen-collection	Meet reference and information sive needs	Officers, departments, agencies of state government, and other libraries

*The California statement continues, "subject to the assumption by such libraries of the responsibilities of keeping such documents readily accessible for use, and of rendering assistance in their use to qualified patrons without charge."
**The Arkansas statement recites that the University of Arkansas is a federal depository, and also that it is handicapped in acquiring documents for exchange.

The group that is to receive the benefit is the most uniform element in the statements. The people, the citizens, or the inhabitants of the state are usually the group for whom the policy is enunciated. The law enacted in the Virgin Islands says, ''for governmental agencies and the general public,'' which is more specific in its mention of the governmental agencies and more inclusive in its reference to the general public than the statements found in most state legislation. Almost all the statements refer to individuals in, or of, the state, whereas the ''general public'' in the Virgin Islands legislation is not limited to the individuals in the territory.

The only two statements that do not include all citizens or inhabitants are in the Ohio law, which is not strictly a policy statement, and the Arkansas law, which is an early law (1947) for the benefit of the University of Arkansas. The Ohio statement says, ''officers, departments, agencies of state government and other libraries.'' The Arkansas law says, ''for teachers, students and research workers in the state.''

The stated objective of most statutes is to make the publications available or accessible to the specified groups. The California law says, ''freely available'' and the Nevada law, ''readily accessible.'' The Iowa proposal of 1973 combines both of these sentiments—''freely available and readily accessible''; however, the policy statement was not incorporated in the act that was finally adopted. Washington in a 1977 amendment says, ''economical and convenient access.'' The statement in the law of the Virgin Islands is slightly different because it does not refer to publications or documents being made available or accessible but to the availability of governmental information.

The Ohio provision, perhaps because the group for whom the service is to be rendered is not the public, specifies ''to meet the reference and the information needs of. . . . '' Indiana and Michigan, which have similar statements, add ''to preserve'' to the availability requirement. Both the Indiana and Michigan laws announce the legislative designation of the state library as the agency to bring about the availability of the publications. Several other states and the Virgin Islands provide in their policy statements for multiple depository libraries (California and Nevada), for a system of depository libraries (Washington) to achieve availability. The Washington law says that the center ''shall utilize the depository system'' to reach the legislatively stated objectives.

In Arkansas and Ohio, the policy is the maintenance of a ''comprehensive collection'' rather than the establishment of a depository library or libraries. However, the laws in these two states are borderline depository legislation.

The Delaware law represents a different approach because it places the duty on the state agencies to deposit publications in order that they might be accessible to citizens. The Delaware law does not mention depository libraries; they are provided for in the regulations.

The Oklahoma resolution focuses on getting state publications for the state library agency. Presumably, its purpose was to reinforce and clarify legislation already enacted.

POLICY STATEMENTS IN PROPOSED LEGISLATION

The policy statements taken from drafts of legislation prepared by library committees in Iowa and Kansas were not adopted by the legislatures of those states. Both included the statement that access to public documents was one of the rights of citizenship. This reference to the rights of citizenship is the oft-quoted one by Congressman William S. Moorhead, chairman of the Foreign Operations and Government Information Subcommittee, U.S. House of Representatives, and author of the 1974 Freedom of Information Act amendment.

The Wisconsin legislative proposal announces two policies. One is to make public documents readily available to depository libraries. Although there is no mention of availability to the public, this is presumably covered in the rules of operation which the depository libraries agree to follow. The second policy is to make all documents that are sold available through one sales office. This policy is limited to documents "of general public appeal" and is further qualified by the phrase "whenever possible."

CONCLUSION

Policy statements serve a useful purpose in preventing misinterpretation of other sections of the legislation. They are "something to point to" when restrictions on the implementation of the depository program are threatened. Just as important as the inclusion of a policy statement in the text of the legislation is a complete understanding on the part of librarians, legislators, and citizens of the reasons for depository legislation. Perhaps such an understanding may be fostered more successfully through personal communications and through articles and leaflets than through a single statement in a law few will read.

DEFINITIONS

THE ROLE OF DEFINITIONS

When a law is being drafted, it is common practice to include a section on definitions. This is particularly true in the legislation under consideration in this text, which is limited to laws establishing depository programs. Definitions of technical terms make the meaning of the terms clear and permit the use of the defined terms without qualifications in the remainder of the law. Definitions are a kind of shorthand and serve practical purposes in legislation by eliminating repetition and by establishing the interpretation of the legislative intent more positively.

The need for a definition can arise even before the drafting stage as it did in South Dakota. Carmack, in his report on the work of the South Dakota Document Study Commission, said, "the lack of a unanimously acceptable definition of a public document posed a problem at almost every session of the Commission."[3] Document librarians need to be able to tell legislators precisely what they mean when they say that documents should be accessible to the public through libraries. Librarians need to know which agencies are state agencies and to explain to the personnel at the agencies exactly what publications the agency is being asked to send to the library. Lobbyists must have facts, including definitions, at their fingertips.

"Guidelines for State Publications Depository Legislation" (see Appendix) includes definitions of "state agency" and "state publication" as the first of the required provisions in depository legislation. The existing legislation of many states meets this first guideline, while some states even exceed the guideline requirements for the two definitions and define "print," and a few define "depository library" or other terms. Twenty-four states and the Virgin Islands have definitions for one or more terms. (See Table 5.)

Among document librarians, the word "documents," when used in casual conversation, conveys a clear image. Document librarians "know" what a state document or a state publication is. Neither Wilcox in his *Manual* nor Parish in his recent book found it necessary to define "state publications." Morehead in his text on federal documents explains that he uses the terms "public documents," "government publications," and similar words synonymously to provide variety.[4] This policy of interchangeable use accommodates a terminology that has been changing over the years and that is especially appropriate when discussing the legislation of the different states, which use the various terms without any real distinction in meaning. This practice has been adopted in this text.

A document librarian, being a service-oriented person, uses the word "document" in an all-encompassing sense. In the document department, the librarians have their own jargon and have no need for definitions. But, if you have a document department, than *a priori* there are other departments in the library, and all the librarians in those departments should be involved with the documents. When the entire library staff is involved in the use of documents, then the jargon must be abandoned, or, at least, easily understandable definitions must be known to everyone. The librarian who is not a document specialist needs a definition of "document" so that he or she will know what is in the document room or the document catalog. Morehead says, "The uninitiated may view attempts to define a government publication as an exercise in academic punctilio, but these attempts become necessary in decisions of record-keeping, storage, and general library policy."[5]

A definition of "state document" or "state publication" is even more essential for communication between document librarians and laymen. To laymen, the word "document" often means an instrument like a marriage license or a corporate charter, a use of the word based on the first meaning in Webster's *Dictionary*, "an original or official paper relied on as the basis, proof, or support of something." It is no longer possible to distinguish this

TABLE 5.
DEFINITIONS IN DEPOSITORY LEGISLATION

State or Territory	State Pub.*	State Agcy.	Print	Other Words
Alaska	x	x		Center, municipal(ity), research data
Arkansas	x			
California	x		x	
Connecticut	x	x	x	Depository library
Florida	x			
Hawaii	x	x	x	
Illinois	x			
Iowa	x	x		Depository library
Kansas	x	x		
Kentucky	x			Department, commission
Maine		x		
Minnesota	x			
Missouri	x			
Montana	x	x	x	
Nebraska	x	x	x	Governmental publication
New Hampshire	x		x	
North Dakota	x			
Oklahoma	x	x	x	Governmental publication
Oregon	x			
South Dakota	x	x	x	
Texas	x	x		Depository libraries
Utah	x	x		Commission, political subdivision
Virgin Islands	x	x		See below
Virginia	x	x		
Washington	x	x	x	

*Column also includes definitions of document or state document and other terms equivalent to state publication.

Virgin Islands also defines: Territorial librarian, depository libraries, public funds, publication date, library, and recognized newspaper.

layman's version of the term "document" from the librarian's use of the word simply on the basis of number of copies printed or issued. Since the advent of the office copier, multiple copies are easily produced. Boll, in attempting to discover "What are Wisconsin Documents?" cites two laws defining "documents" in terms of the number of copies issued and by the number of pages contained.[6]

Librarians need a definition of "state document" that excludes the "document" of the layman and also one that differentiates state documents from the ''records'' of the archivist. Paul Pross suggests a definition that does incorporate this distinction: ''a government publication is created when a document prepared by or for an agency of government is reproduced and circulated to individuals and groups other than those advising or negotiating with the government concerning the subject matter of the documents.'' Pross explains his definition further:

Thus, a publication is defined not by the process by which it is reproduced, but by the breadth of circulation afforded it. Its circulation beyond the immediate confines of a government and those advising or doing business with authority removes a document from the status of record, and thus the concern of the records manager and the archivist, to the status of publication, and the purview of the general public and the librarian.[7]

''Publication,'' ''state agency,'' and ''print'' are separately defined in some states. In others, for example, North Dakota, these separate definitions are combined into one with a formula that says that a state publication is a report, book . . . (the list continues), issued in print by any department, board . . . (again a list follows), except correspondence and interoffice memoranda. The pattern is publication, agency, print, and exceptions; all the separate definitions are consolidated into one. Whether separate definitions are used or a composite definition is created is relatively unimportant.

Librarians assisting in the drafting of depository legislation attempt to create as broad a definition of state publications as possible because whatever is not caught in the web created by the definition is lost to libraries. As Boll points out, ''The use of a narrow definition would not decrease the number of items published with public money; it would only decrease the number that reach libraries easily.''[8]

Although not always clearly recognized in the legislation, there are two conflicting goals—first, the need to identify everything that has been published so that it can be brought under bibligraphical control and retrieved as needed, and second, the need to acquire multiple copies of those publications that should have some distribution for convenient use by the public. The exercise of discretion is necessary at some point in the process if both of these objectives are to be met. If the definition is drawn broadly enough so that *all* publications fall within it (the first objective), restrictions must be placed on what the libraries receive in order to avoid wasteful distribution. On the other hand, if the definition encompasses only publications that should have at least minimal distribution throughout the state, then the opportunity for a survey of the complete output of the state agencies is lost.

The state agencies, the distribution center, or the depository libraries can exercise the discretion mentioned above. If the definition places the burden on the *state agency* to send everything, the state agency interpretation of ''everything'' will prevail. The dangers in interpretation by the state agencies lie in the tendency of state agencies to rationalize that "everything" is an unreasonable requirement and, therefore, they will send nothing, or to interpret the wording literally and send a "flood" of forms, releases, and insignificant materials. If the *distribution center* makes the decision, the well-known bureaucratic, paternalistic specter comes into the foreground and selective depositories are denied freedom of choice. Finally, if the *depository libraries* decide what they will receive, the burden shifts to an individual who may not have the training or experience to make a wise decision and who, in most instances, would be required to decide without examining the publication involved. The appointment of an advisory committee, with representation from the state agencies and the library community, is one solution to this dilemma.

Is the definition of "publication" one that will bring all publications into the distribution center or only those that are to be distributed? The answer to this question will govern the wording of the definition.

Legislation intended to bring all publications to a central collection and only selected publications to the depository libraries is not written into the definitions in those terms. However, definitions, such as the Virginia one, which refers to "all unrestricted publications," are based on this philosophy as demonstrated by reading the Virginia definition in conjunction with the next section, which provides that state agencies shall furnish two copies of each publication to the state library. The section continues with a provision that the state library may require delivery of an additional number of copies, thus giving the state library the power to decide whether it will forward copies to other libraries. In fact, the Virginia proposed legislation includes, as part of the definition of state publication, the statement "the State Library shall have the authority to determine which documents meet the criteria set forth in this definition."

Another example is found in the Indiana legislation, which exempts certain categories of publications (publications with other legal distribution requirements, university publications, and university press publications) and at the end of each of the sections enumerating the categories states that the Indiana State Library shall nevertheless receive two copies. There is a seeming inconsistency in the Indiana statute in that the state agency must send fifty copies of each publication to the state library (with the above exceptions), yet the state Library is required to distribute only those of general interest.

This state library first, depository libraries second, philosophy is found in other legislation. For example, Alaska requires state agencies to send four copies first and then additional copies on request. Montana also requires four copies and then additional copies, as required for the depository libraries and interlibrary loan. Other states have legislation with a similar pattern, usually requiring more copies at the time of the initial deposit: for example, Hawaii, fifteen copies; Nebraska, eight copies; and Oklahoma, twenty-five copies.

The second type of legislation, in which the definition encompasses only what is to be distributed to the depository libraries, is illustrated by the Florida and the Kansas laws. In the Florida legislation, the definition limits the publications to those for which over five hundred copies are printed and which may be subject to distribution to the public. The Kansas definition is limited by the wording "provided by a state agency for use by the general public." Here the drafter of a definition must give special attention to the connotations of the words "for use by the general public." The "general public," or even the "public," is an indeterminate group that presumably has rather broad but nonspecific interests. Highly technical publications, of interest only to a highly specialized group, cannot be said to be provided by an agency for use by the general public. Yet, there are libraries in which such publications would receive intensive use and in which they should be available. Availability should be curtailed only by the need for personal privacy, criminal justice, public safety, and similar considerations. Availability to the "public" is not sufficiently broad to meet the needs of all possible users.

"STATE PUBLICATION"

Some states have enacted legislation without including a definition of "state publication" or its equivalent. Words used to refer to state publications in depository legislation without their being specifically defined include:

> Public documents—Indiana
> Public records—Louisiana and Mississippi
> State documents—Tennessee
> Reports of departments—Maine
> Reports, pamphlets, documents or other publications—Ohio
> Documents, reports, surveys—Idaho

The list of definitions of "state publication" quoted at the end of this chapter illustrates the variety of terms referring to state publications or state documents. Table 6 arranges these terms by frequency of use and dates of the legislation. Twenty-one states define "publication" or "state publication"; three (Arkansas, Florida, and Minnesota) and the Virgin Islands define "document" or "state document." Kentucky defines "record"; however, this definition is part of the state records act rather than depository legislation. The statement "made or received in pursuance of the state law or in connection with the transaction of public business" in the Kentucky law indicates the broad scope of the definition. Nebraska defines an additional term, "government publication," and Oklahoma also includes that definition in its 1978 law.

The scope of the definitions varies; provisions that some states include in definitions are relegated to different sections of the law in other states. This chapter is devoted to definitions as such, so that those who are interested in drafting legislation can compare the terms that are defined and the wording of the definitions.

Informally in their writings, librarians have referred to documents as "jewels," "buried treasure," and similarly romantic terms indicative of their value. Their all-too-frequent inaccessibility caused by a lack of indexing and cataloging results in name-calling such as "bugbear," "can of worms," and "the terror of librarians." In attempting to guarantee the availability of and accessibility to this mixed blessing, more prosaic terms of greater exactitude can better serve the purpose.

RECENT LEGISLATION

Thirteen of the twenty-two governments that have enacted depository library programs since 1970 have chosen the term "state publication" or "publication" as the one to be defined, if definitions are included in the legislation at all. Six states have list-type definitions. Three—Alaska (1970), New Hampshire (1973), and South Dakota (1974)—begin their lists in the same way that the Montana and Hawaii laws do; "document, compilation, journal . . ." North Dakota (1977) and Oklahoma (1978) have lists very similar to one another beginning "reports, directories, statistical compendiums." The Utah list is arranged differently than the others and has several unique items. Seven states have brief definitions of "state publication" without lists of the types of publications or the kinds of agencies. Of the seven, Missouri (1976), Iowa (1978), and Texas (1979) follow the Nebraska (1972) pattern using "multiply-produced." Connecticut (1977) has a short, carefully constructed definition. The definition in Nevada (1971) is essentially short and is lengthened only by a list of seven categories of exclusions. The Kansas definition (1976) is the shortest of the six and, according to one of the drafters of the original bill, is a legislative compromise.

The Virgin Islands is an exception to the rule that governments with post-1970 legislation have chosen the word "publication" as the one to be defined, choosing instead to define "public documents." Its definition is brief, without lists, but in a two-sentence format.

One new term, "research data or data," was added by an amendment to the Alaska list of definitions, which already included a definition for "state publication."

Eight of the states with recently enacted legislation did not include definitions. These are Pennsylvania (1971), Idaho (1972), Indiana (1973), Delaware (1974), Maine (1975), Arizona (1976), Michigan (1976), and New Mexico (1978).

PARTS OF THE DEFINITION

The definitions of state publication are usually a single sentence, constructed with a subject, a verb, and then a noun or nouns with modifying clauses. The Connecticut definition follows a typical pattern:

"State publications"	the words being defined
means	the verb
all publications	the general category
printed or purchased for	
distribution	limitation on "distribution"
by a state agency	
or any other agency	limitation on "distribution"
supported wholly or	
in part by state funds	limitation on "agency"

Often the sentence is longer than the example above. The general category may be a long list of words, and there may also be a list of words in the state agency phrase.

The subject of the sentence, that is, the word being defined, is most frequently "publication" or "state publication." Various words are used as the verb: includes, comprises, shall mean, as herein employed, as used, and refer to. Some of these words are more restrictive than others, and if a listing follows the verb, the final item in the list may broaden its scope.

Most definitions use the term "publications" (for example, Arkansas, Connecticut, Iowa, Minnesota, Missouri, Nebraska, Texas, and Virginia) as the general category in which the term being defined is put. The word in the proposed Rhode Island legislation is "media," which, in turn, is defined as "printed or audiovisual forms of communication." North Dakota and Oklahoma use "informational materials," Nevada uses "document," and the Virgin Islands, "public record."

Iowa, Missouri, Nebraska, and Rhode Island (proposed) all refer to "multiply-produced" publications. Arkansas says "printed, mimeographed or other near-print publications," and Virginia, "all unrestricted publications of whatever kind."

The states that give a list of kinds of publications copy one another quite closely. The different items included in these lists and the number of items for each state are shown in Table 6. The Arkansas 1947 definition is not included in the table because the list consists largely of specific titles. Incidentally, that list includes "reports of investigations of impeachment trials," a category of publications not found in the legislation of other states. Table 6 gives the words that the states with post-1970 legislation have added to the lists first used by Washington and Hawaii and indicates the trend toward the addition of new terms.

The words used only by a single state are listed at the bottom of Table 6. North Dakota, Oklahoma, and South Dakota have added words which describe nonprint forms of publications. Oklahoma's inclusion of charts, maps, and surveys is a distinct expansion of the earlier listings. Kentucky includes maps in its definition of records, and South Carolina includes them in its proposed legislation. Hawaii's use of the word "ordinance" is pertinent to its legislation because that legislation includes municipal publications. Other words, such as

TABLE 6.
TERMS USED IN DEFINITIONS OF "STATE PUBLICATION"
(Chronological by state and weighted by terms)

	WA '63	HI '65	CA '67	IL '67	MT '67	AK '70	NH '73	SD '74	ND '77	OK '78	UT '79	
Bulletin									x	x		2
Map										x	x	2
Microphotographic form							x				x	2
Ordinance			x								x	2
State plan									x	x		2
Statistical compendium									x	x		2
Tape or disc recording							x				x	2
Bibliography				x					x	x		3
Brochure				x					x	x		3
Committee minutes or minutes									x	x	x	3
Newsletter				x					x	x		3
Proceedings					x			x			x	3
Rules				x					x	x		3
Bluebook			x		x	x		x			x	5
Memorandum			x		x		x	x			x	5
Resolution			x		x	x		x			x	5
Code			x		x	x	x	x		x		6
Order			x		x	x	x	x			x	6
Register			x		x	x	x	x			x	6
Bill or legislative bill			x		x	x		x	x	x	x	7
Compilation		x	x		x	x	x	x			x	7
Journal		x	x		x	x		x	x		x	7
Law			x		x	x		x	x	x	x	7
Leaflet	x		x		x	x	x	x			x	7
List			x		x	x	x	x	x		x	7
Magazine	x		x		x	x		x	x		x	7
Book	x		x		x	x	x	x	x		x	8
Document		x	x	x	x	x	x	x			x	8
Hearing			x		x	x	x	x	x	x	x	8
Statute		x	x		x	x	x	x		x	x	8
Directory			x	x	x	x	x	x	x	x	x	9
Pamphlet	x		x	x	x	x	x	x		x	x	9
Periodical	x		x	x	x	x	x	x	x	x	x	10
Regulation		x	x	x	x	x	x	x	x	x	x	10

TABLE 6 (continued)

	WA '63	HI '65	CA '67	IL '67	MT '67	AK '70	NH '73	SD '74	ND '77	OK '78	UT '79	
Report	x	x	x	x	x	x	x	x	x	x	x	11
Unique terms		1				1	1		5	5	4	17
TOTALS	6	8	22	10	23	22	17	25	20	28	31	

Unique terms:
Hawaii—Confidential publications
Alaska—Study
New Hampshire—Serial
North Dakota—Audiotapes, videotapes, films, filmstrips, or slides
Oklahoma—Charts, surveys, microfilm, microfiche, and all sale items
Utah—Contract and grant report, monograph, public memorandum, audiovisual material
''Memorandum hearing'' in the New Hampshire law has been tabulated as two terms rather than one.

study (Alaska), serial (New Hampshire), and proceedings (South Dakota), may also have special local significance in those states.

The 1947 Arkansas definition has a catchall at the end, ''and sundry documents.'' Similar statements found at the end of lists of kinds of publications include ''other printed matter'' (North Dakota and Oklahoma), ''other similar written material'' (South Carolina proposed), and the more general ones, ''other materials'' (Kansas and Washington). Another way of providing this type of safeguard is the wording of the Wisconsin proposed legislation, ''but not limited by this enumeration.''

The words ''regardless of format'' are added almost as frequently in definitions of print as in definitions of state publications. States using this phrase include Connecticut, Montana, Nebraska, Oklahoma, and South Dakota.

The method of production or the source of the publication is given as: issued (in print), prepared, purchased, printed, published, paid for, supported by, contracted for, originating in or produced, reproduced, and provided for use. These words are used in various combinations in the different states. The Virgin Islands does not formulate its definition in terms of issuance, preparation, and so on by the agencies but in relationship to the territorial library, and refers to publications ''which [are] designated for deposit pursuant to this section.''

LISTS OF STATE AGENCIES

In some states, the verb is followed by a listing of the agencies that issue, prepare, or otherwise release the publications. Montana's list is typical: ''the state, the legislature, constitutional officers, any state department, committee or other state agency.'' New Hampshire and Minnesota do not include the legislature. New Hampshire inserts ''councils, bureaus, research centers, [and] societies.'' In California, New Hampshire, and Minnesota, the list takes the place of a definition of ''state agency.'' South Carolina's proposed legislation follows this practice but does not include the legislature, constitutional offices, and commissions, and adds colleges and universities. On the other hand, Montana, Nebraska, South Dakota, and Utah include lists of agencies very similar to the lists used by California, New Hampshire, and Minnesota; yet, at the same time, they have a definition of state agency. Colorado's and Virginia's proposed legislation also have lists of types of agencies in both definitions. The comparison of these lists of agencies—one in the definition of state publication and the other in the definition of state agency—reveals duplication in the lists only in the South Dakota legislation. Most states with lists in both definitions include additional terms in the state agency definition. The added words in Montana are office, officer, division, bureau, board, commission, and subdivisions of each. In Nebraska, institutions of higher education are added, and in Utah, specific mention is made of the courts.

The reference to support by state funds in the legislation of Connecticut, Montana, Nebraska, South Dakota, and Washington clearly refers to the support of state *agencies* by those funds. Colorado, in its proposed legislation, also refers to the support of state agencies. These references to support must be clearly distinguished from the use of similar words to refer to the support of state *publications*.

In instances where the state publications are supported by state funds, an entirely different purpose is the objective. The Virginia statement, "published or issued by an agency of the State in full or in part at State expense," is the most unambiguous grammatically. The Iowa statement, "publications of state agencies regardless of format which are supported by public funds," is slightly ambiguous because the "supported by" clause could be interpreted to refer either to "state agency" or to "publications." The placement of the words "regardless of format," which can refer only to "publications," leads one to believe that the "supported by" also refers to "publications." On the other hand, the reference to support in the legislation of so many other states so clearly refers to the support of state agencies that an assumption could be made that such was the intent here.

CONTRACT PUBLICATIONS

California amended its definition of "state publication" or "publication" in 1972 to add the words, "or prepared for the state by private individual or organization and issued in print." The legislature's recognition of the new type of publication resulting from contract work done for a state agency broadened the scope of the definition and presumably has brought this new kind of survey and report under bibliographical control and into the depository distribution channel in California. The Minnesota law, enacted in 1976, has similar language.

The North Dakota legislature in 1977 and the Oklahoma legislature in 1978 enacted definitions of "state publication" encompassing this new type of publication with the wording "the definition incorporates those publications that may or may not be financed by state funds but are released by private bodies such as research and consultant firms under contract with or supervision of any state agency." Utah in 1979 included "contract and grant report" in its long list of types of publications.

CONFIDENTIAL PUBLICATIONS

The states publish far fewer publications of a confidential nature than does the federal government, which must consider the question of national security in classifying documents. Nevertheless, several states do mention confidentiality in their state document legislation. Hawaii specifically provides that confidential publications shall be deposited "in accordance with security regulations to be determined by the issuing agency." On the other hand, Iowa and Illinois exclude confidential publications from the scope of the depository legislation. The Iowa definition of state publication excepts "materials designated by law as confidential." The Illinois law is not as specific in its language; it excepts "confidential publications." The Wisconsin proposed legislation states that its definition of print does not include "privileged information restricted by contract with governing authority."

Delaware, in its regulations, approaches the issue of confidentiality in a different way. The section defining publication concludes with the sentence "Documents protected against disclosure under the 'sunshine' law are not 'publications' because they cannot be circulated to the general public."

PRESS RELEASES AND NEWSLETTERS

A 1977 amendment to the Washington law specifically exempts "news releases sent exclusively to the news media" from the definition of state publication.

The Florida depository legislation does not mention news releases specifically. A 1978 Florida attorney general's opinion held that "issuance and delivery of press releases, by state agencies [was] not promulgation of a public or state document." Two factors inimical to library interests, that is, to a holding that press releases are within the scope of the depository library legislation, may have influenced the opinion. First, the opinion was sought by a state agency that would normally prefer its own distribution procedure and would not be eager for depository library distribution. Second, the question of the need for a statement of cost would, from the agency's standpoint, be more likely resolved in the negative.

Delaware, which defines publication only in its regulations, includes press releases in its listing of publications. The New Jersey contract provides that news releases and press summaries need not be retained and a proposed regulation in Rhode Island has the same provision. Related to this subject is the Nebraska regulation, which requires that only the latest three months of college newspapers need to be kept.

Illinois, North Dakota, and Oklahoma include newsletters in their listing of publications. South Carolina in its proposed legislation includes newsletters. No other states mention newsletters.

AUDIOVISUAL PUBLICATIONS

In the 1930s, when government publications began to be produced by various forms of reproduction other than print, efforts were made to include these materials within the definitions. Now, effort is being expended to include audiovisual materials within the definition.

Because format is one of the distinctive features of the new methods of reproducing materials, several states have used the phrase "regardless of format" to encompass audiovisual materials. Variations include:

regardless of format (Iowa)
regardless of physical form or characteristics (Kentucky)
regardless of format or purpose (Missouri and Vermont)
regardless of format, method of reproduction, or
    source (Oklahoma and North Dakota)

In definitions of print, the phrase uniformly used is "regardless of format or purpose." This phrase is found in the definitions of print in Connecticut, Montana, Nebraska, Oklahoma, and South Dakota. Colorado includes it in its proposed legislation. Oklahoma, it will be noticed, used the phrase in both its definition of state publication and that of print.

The inclusion of audiovisual materials is sometimes explicit in legislative definitions of state publication or of print, in regulations, and in proposed legislation. Mention of these special types of publications in the legislation follows in chronological order:

1974—South Dakota, "including audio-visual materials"
(in the definition of print).
1977—North Dakota, "audio tapes, video tapes, films, filmstrips or slides"
(in definition of state publication).
1977—Virgin Islands, "audiovisual forms of communication and their accompanying technology" (in definition of public document).
1979—Utah, "audiovisual material" (in definition of state publication).

The proposed Rhode Island law contains this sentence in its definition of public documents: " 'Media' is defined as printed or audiovisual forms of communication."

MICROGRAPHICS AND OTHER NONPRINT FORMATS

A few states specifically include publications issued in nonprint formats within the definition of state publication. As early as 1974, the South Dakota law read: "microphotographic form, tape or disc recording." The Oklahoma law included "microfilm" and "microfiche" in its list of types of publications. The 1979 Utah law follows the South Dakota definition in including "microphotographic form and tape or disc recording."

The Nevada regulations, in the definition of print, add this sentence, "This is intended to include publications issued in a microformat."

THE PUBLIC

The specific mention of "the public" in definitions is found in the legislation of Florida ("subject to distribution to the public"), Kansas ("provided for use by the general public"), and Nevada ("which may legally be released for public distribution"). Although mention of the public can be advantageous in policy statements and in reference to the duties of depository libraries, it can be restrictive in a definition of state publications. It can too easily be argued that technical publications are not issued for the general public.

AMENDED DEFINITIONS

Some states have found it necessary to amend their definitions of state publications because imperfections have been revealed by the operation of the law over a period of years. New types of publications, developed since the original enactment of the law, have also been included. The California amendment to its definition to incorporate publications contracted for by state agencies is one notable case that has already been mentioned.

In 1977, Washington, as part of a broad act on state government publications, amended the definitions in its depository library law. The definition of "public document" was eliminated, and the "annual and biennial reports" to which it referred were incorporated into the definition of "state publication," together with an additional type of report, the "special" report. This may have been derived from the Florida law, which reads "annual, biennial, regular or special reports." Another change in the definition was to substitute "all other materials" for the enumeration of types of publications in the original law. The specific exception of "news releases sent exclusively to the news media" from the scope of the definition was also part of the 1977 amendment. No other state specifically excludes news releases in its law.

The Washington definition is amplified in "the Washington guidelines" that the state library sent to all state agencies in June 1978. These guidelines establish categories of publications: full depository publications, selected depository publications, and publications the cost of which prohibits wide distribution.

The full depository publications list is the longest (thirteen types of publications).This list is reduced to eight types of publications for the selective depository publications by omitting (1) research reports, (2) statistical publications, (3) general information issued by an agency about its function or programs, (4) directories listing businesses and licensees, and (5) planning publications. Two types of publications are curtailed: the legislative publications by the omission of bills and audits, and serial publications because they are limited to the types of publications in the list.

The five types of publications excluded from depository status are (1) intra-office information, (2) interoffice memoranda, (3) press releases sent exclusively to the news media, (4) environmental impact statements, unless the plan has statewide impact, and (5) alumni magazines, brochures, and the like from community colleges or from universities.

The Washington guidelines are further qualified by the authority of the state library to except a publication or class of publications from distribution in the interest of economy or efficiency.

In 1979, the three states that made major changes in their depository legislation included definitions in their new laws. Of special interest is the addition of the terms "research data" and "data" in the Alaska definition section. The formulation of a definition comprehensive enough to encompass various technologies must have been an intriguing enterprise. The definition begins, "a representation of facts, concepts or instructions in a formalized manner" and is qualified by a requirement that there be a determination by the state librarian that indexing would be appropriate. The Alaska definition of "state publications" was amended to add at the end of the list of items "determined by the state librarian to be appropriate for retention in the center." The list of items was not changed.

The new Texas definition is a short statement incorporating the words "multiple copies" and including publications produced by the authority of, as well as at the expense of, the state agencies. It replaces a definition that was a cross-reference to the section of the law providing for the acquisition and distribution of documents.

The Utah definition is not an amended definition but is a new one listing many items. It is incorporated in Table 6. "Contract and grant report," "monograph," and "public memorandum" are unique items in this definition. Also on the list is "audiovisual material," which encompasses the "audio tapes, video tapes, films, film strips or slides" of the North Dakota definition.

PROPOSED DEFINITIONS

Although most states have not yet amended their definitions of the term "state publication," some states are considering such amendments. For example, in the Virginia proposed legislation, the definition tracks the Nebraska definition, adding "which may legally be" before the word "distributed" and the sentence "the state library shall have the authority to determine which documents meet the criteria set forth in this definition." This sentence would give the state library powers similar to those exercised by the Washington state librarian, who is to be consulted on what other printed informational matter the term "state publications" might include, and by the Alaska state librarian, who determines what is "appropriate for retention by the center."

The proposed Wisconsin definitions are new rather than amending legislation because Wisconsin presently has no definition in its distribution statute.

The words "public document," "official publication," and "state publication" are defined. The definition of "public document" is similar to the Nebraska definition, although it uses the verb "issued" rather than "printed or purchased" and continues, "for public information, guidance, regulation or general distribution." The recitation of these purposes is unique in definitions of this kind. The definitions of "official publication" and "state publication" are subordinate to the definition of "public document." "Official publications" are those publications required by law to be published, and "state publications" includes all other publications except those specifically exempted.

"STATE AGENCY"

Definitions of "state agency" in depository legislation are invariably a recitation of the entities that are included in the meaning of the phrase (List 3). Table 7 arranges the terms referring to the state agencies by frequency of use. South Dakota and Virginia have catchall phrases at the end of the list: "but is not limited to" and "or other entity." Connecticut uses the adjectives "permanent or temporary."

Four states, Connecticut, Hawaii, Illinois, and Iowa, provide specifically that the agencies of all three branches of government are to be included within the definition. Nevada and South Dakota include the legislature and constitutional officers; Texas includes legislative committees. Another group of states specifically includes state-supported institutions of higher learning in the list of agencies. A phrase common to many of the definitions is "and all subdivisions of each." The definition used by Hawaii includes county agencies as well as state agencies. Alaska and Utah have separate definitions for "municipal and municipality," and for "political subdivisions," thus accomplishing a similar objective.

Unique terms, found only in the legislation of a single state, are "associations" and "corporations" (Alaska), "section" and "service" (Illinois), "society" (Kansas), "sub-state planning district" (Oklahoma), "legislative committee" and "substate planning bureau" (Texas), and "the state" and "hospital, college, university or other instrumentality" (Utah).

The unpublished North Carolina study by John Finning Allison, Jr., cites the definition from the Louisiana proposed legislation as "one of the best" and also cites the Montana and Washington definitions with approval.[9]

The definition in the Louisiana proposal, according to the commentary which accompanies the draft,

was taken largely from R.S. 39:2(1) (which established the Division of Administraton). The committee likes the breadth of the idea of function, rather than of origination or of funding, as the essential criterion of agency. It is felt this definition is broad enough to include the three branches of state government, educational institutions, and bodies with multi-parish jurisdictions.[10]

TABLE 7.
DEFINITIONS OF "STATE AGENCY"

	AK	CT	HI	IL	IA	KS	ME	MT	NE	NV	OK	SD	TX	UT	VI	VA	WA	
Entity																x	x	2
Committee			x	x								x						3
Legislature						x				x				x				3
Unit				x	x									x				3
Authority					x	x			x	x	x		x	x	x			5
Institution				x	x				x		x	x	x	x	x	x		5
Institution Higher Education*	x	x		x		x		x		x	x	x	x			x	x	6
Subdivisions		x	x	x			x	x		x	x	x	x				x	7
Agency	x				x	x	x	x	x	x	x	x	x	x	x	x	x	12
Bureau		x		x	x	x		x	x	x	x	x	x		x	x		12
Officer	x	x	x	x	x	x		x	x	x	x	x				x	x	12
Division	x	x	x	x	x	x		x	x	x	x	x	x		x	x	x	14
Office	x	x	x	x	x	x	x	x	x	x	x	x	x	x	x	x	x	15
Board	x	x	x	x	x	x	x	x	x	x	x	x	x	x	x	x	x	17
Commission	x	x	x	x	x	x	x	x	x	x	x	x	x	x	x	x	x	17
Department	x	x	x	x	x	x	x	x	x	x	x	x	x	x	x	x	x	17
Unique terms**	2	2		2	2	1							2	5				13
Totals	9	9	5	12	9	12	5	9	10	8	14	9	13	12	10	8	9	

*Modifying the term "Institutions of higher education," Connecticut, Nebraska, and Oklahoma say "state-supported"; Iowa adds, "governed by the state board of regents." Texas has "university system or institution of higher education as defined . . . ." Alaska added to its list in 1979 "and the University of Alaska and its affiliated research institutes."

**Alaska—Associations, corporations; Illinois—Section, service; Kansas—Society; Oklahoma—Substate planning district; Texas—Substate planning bureau, legislative committee; Utah—The state, hospital, college, university or other instrumentality.

Other modifying words are:

Connecticut, Hawaii, Illinois, and Iowa—all (three) branches of government

Connecticut—"permanent or temporary"

Hawaii—defines "state and county agency" and includes state, city and county, and county

Illinois—"and which agencies expend appropriations of State funds"

Kansas—"within any . . . other state authority"

Maine—"quasi-independent agency board, commission, authority or institution"

South Dakota—"but is not limited to"

Utah is the first state to include in its definitions a definition for agencies at the local level. It defines "political subdivisions" to include "any county, city, town, school district, public transit district, redevelopment agency, special improvement or taxing district." Other states that encompass publications from local agencies within their program (for example, Alaska, Arkansas, and Nevada) merely refer to municipalities or local agencies without a separate definition.

"PRINT"

Only twelve states have separate definitions of "print." These definitions, in general, indicate an awareness of information produced by the new technologies available for the dissemination of information as illustrated by references to printing or duplicating and by inclusion of the phrase "regardless of format or purpose." Undoubtedly, these words are intended to provide the flexibility necessary to accommodate new methods of duplicating and new formats as they are developed. Microreproduction in its various forms is clearly a duplicating process, as are video recordings. Electronic data transmission is a format for disseminating information that is not usually duplicated (the user accesses the original data base), but if the data base were duplicated, one might suppose that it would be encompassed in the definition.

Most states have used the definition of state publication to encompass various types and formats of publications. Table 6 shows words which North Dakota, Oklahoma, and Utah have added in their recent legislation (audiovisual material, audiotapes, videotapes, films, filmstrips, slides, microfilm, microfiche, microphotographic form, and tape or disc recording). South Dakota mentions audiovisual materials in the definition of "print."

The definitions of "print" are of two kinds. The first says, in substance, "any form of duplicating except by the use of carbon paper." The longer definition refers to printing or duplicating, adds "regardless of format or purpose," and specifically excepts correspondence and interoffice memoranda. The pattern of the definitions is illustrated in Table 8. The Washington definition, before it was amended in 1977, followed that pattern. The 1977 amendment in the Washington laws changed the wording to "all forms of reproducing multiple copies" and modified correspondence with the adjective "typewritten." The South Dakota definition is the only one that mentions audiovisual materials specifically.

OTHER WORDS DEFINED

Other words defined in depository legislation are given in List 4 at the end of this chapter. Colorado and South Dakota have definitions for "center," both of which are the same: "center means the state publications distribution

TABLE 8.
DEFINITIONS OF "PRINT"

	CA	CT	HI	IL	MT	NE	NV	NH	OK	SD	UT	WA	
Duplicating	x			x			x			x	a		4
Printing and duplicating		x	x		x	x	x		x	x^b			7
Regardless of format or purpose		x			x	x			x	x			5
Exceptions:													
Carbon paper			c				x	x			x		3
Correspondence		x			x	x			x	x	x^d		6
Interoffice memoranda	x				x	x			x	x		x	6

a—"includes all forms of reproducing multiple copies"
b—"including audio-visual materials"
c—"except administrative forms"
d— typewritten correspondence"

center." The Alaska definition for "center" was amended in 1979 to "state library distribution and data access center."

Connecticut, Iowa, Texas, and the Virgin Islands have definitions for "depository library." The Connecticut definition refers to the functions of the library—collecting, maintaining, and making available to the general public. The Iowa definition says only that a depository library is one that is designated under the act. The Texas definition, as amended in 1979, names the libraries included as depository libraries: the state library, the legislative reference library, the Library of Congress, the Center for Research Libraries, and other designated libraries. Libraries in state institutions of higher education were formerly included in the definition.

The proposed South Carolina law has three definitions related to depository libraries, which represents more detail than is found in legislation that has actually been enacted. Alaska, because its act includes municipal documents, defines "municipal" and "municipality." This definition was amended in 1979 to include municipalities of a specific statutory type. Utah has a definition of "political subdivision" that encompasses counties, cities, towns, and various other districts.

The Virgin Islands includes six terms in its list of definitions in addition to the definitions for "public document" and "governmental agency." The law defines "territorial librarian" because that librarian administers the depository law. It defines "depository libraries" in terms of the functions of those libraries, including reproducing documents on demand or making them available.

The Virgin Islands law defines "publication date" as the earliest date on which a publication is made available outside the publishing agency. It requires that the agency supply its publications within five weekdays of this date and that distribution be made to the depositories within two calendar weeks thereafter. This provision, which necessitated the definition of "publication date," is unique in depository legislation insofar as it establishes two deadlines in the routine of getting the publications to the depository libraries.

The word "library" is defined in the Virgin Islands legislation because, in addition to the depository libraries mentioned by name in the law, other libraries may be designated as depository libraries by the territorial librarian. "Public funds" is defined because that term is used in the definition of "public document," which is defined as a "public record . . . supported in whole or in part by public funds." The reason for the definition of "recognized newspaper" is not immediately apparent.

"State Document Center" and "Document Depository" as defined in the ANSI Standard Z39.7, 1968 (R 1974), are out of date. "State Document Center" as defined refers to the centers established in the 1930s. "Document Depository" mentions only federal depositories and the now discontinued LC card depositories. There is no mention of state or municipal depository libraries. Both these definitions are the same as those in the *ALA Glossary*.

EXEMPTIONS FROM THE OPERATION OF THE LAW

Five states specifically exclude publications produced by the use of carbon paper. Four of these, California, Nevada, New Hampshire, and South Carolina (proposed legislation), have worded their definition of print to exclude only carbon paper copies. (Nevada has an extra sentence as part of its definition that publications issued in a microformat are included within the definition.) Minnesota excludes carbon paper copies in its definition of "document," saying "issued in print, including all forms of duplicating other than by the use of carbon paper."

An even more common exclusion is correspondence and interoffice memoranda. Colorado, Connecticut, Montana, Nebraska, Oklahoma, South Dakota, Virginia (proposed legislation), and Washington all have this exclusion as part of their definition of "print." Washington says, "typewritten correspondence." Missouri has the same exclusion as part of its definition of "state publication." Other variations are the exclusion of "confidential publications" in the Illinois and Iowa laws, the exclusion of news releases in the Washington law, the mention of only interoffice and intraoffice communications in the proposed South Carolina law and in the Virgin Islands law, and the exemption in the proposed Wisconsin law of a list of eight kinds of publications. Utah in its recently amended law had a significant number of exclusions: "correspondence, internal confidential publications, office memoranda, university press publications, and publications of the state historical society."

Each of the following exclusions is found in one state only:

administrative forms—in definition of print (Hawaii)

administrative or training materials—in definition of state publications (South Dakota)

publications of the university, forms—in definition section of law (California)

revised statutes, reports, statutes, the digest, press items of the university system and other university items, publications with other legally required distribution—in definition of state publication (Nevada)

revised statutes, certain legislative material—in definition of publications (Oregon)

There are other exclusions in the laws of the various states, but these are not part of the definitions in those states. In some instances, the exclusions are included in the definition section of the regulations. The Connecticut regulations include a long list of exceptions:

Business forms

Informal administrative memos and instructions for the internal use of agency personnel

Blueprints

Complimentary, visiting, and business cards

Correspondence

Minutes of meetings

Announcements of lectures, meetings, seminars, and workshops

Doctoral dissertations

Master's theses

The Delaware regulations, in the section defining publication, state that letterheads, forms, internal memoranda, and duplicated procedural materials are not publications. The section continues: "Documents protected against disclosure under the 'sunshine' law are not 'publications' because they cannot be circulated to the general public."

The proposed law in Wisconsin has a subsection in its definition of "public document" reciting items exempted from inclusion in the definition: "directives for internal administration, procurement and operational bulletins, intra and inter-departmental publications, forms, memoranda, correspondence, dated promotional materials and classroom materials."

Although not a part of the definitions, certain types of materials excluded from the requirements of the depository laws of some states are listed here for the sake of comparison:

Legal and historical bureau publications with other legally required distribution, university publications, and publications of state university presses (Indiana)

Appellate division reports or advance sheets, the State Bureau of Investigation. Investigative "Bulletin," or other materials intended for the internal use of a state agency (North Carolina)

CONCLUSION

To determine how particular types of publications and different kinds of state agencies are accommodated in the definitions, all the definitions of a state must be examined together. To determine whether a state has enacted legislation with respect to a particular topic, the entire chapter of the revised statutes must be studied. For example, Oklahoma mentions sale publications in its definitions. The Minnesota law says that the legislative reference library shall receive the publications without cost. The result is substantially the same— free publications—although the Minnesota law is slightly stronger because even shipping charges are avoided.

Definitions can be helpful but must be considered in their relationship to one another and as part of the legislation as a whole. The line between being too specific and not specific enough must be carefully drawn. Safeguards to prevent interpretation by the rule, *inclusio unius est exclusio alterius*, must be included.

LIST 1

STATEMENTS AND DECLARATIONS OF POLICY IN DEPOSITORY LEGISLATION

Arkansas—Whereas, it is desirable that there should be a comprehensive collection of public documents for teachers, students and research workers in the State; and

Whereas, the General Library of the University of Arkansas is a full depository for the documents of the United States Government; and

Whereas, this library is seriously handicapped in acquiring Arkansas State, Municipal and County Documents, and the documents of other States for lack of suitable documents to offer in return, Now, Therefore, . . . 1947 ARK. ACTS NO. 170, PREAMBLE

California—It is the policy of the State of California to make freely available to its inhabitants all state publications by distribution to libraries throughout the state, subject to the assumption by such libraries of the responsibilities of keeping such documents readily accessible for use, and of rendering assistance in their use to qualified patrons without charge. CAL. GOV'T CODE § 14900

Delaware—Every state agency shall provide and deposit with the Department sufficient copies of all publications issued by such agencies for the purpose of making accessible to Delaware and other citizens, resource materials published at the expense of the State. DEL. CODE ANN. tit. 29, § 8610(b)

Indiana—In order that all public documents of the state of Indiana shall be preserved and made available for use of the citizens of the state, the Indiana state library is hereby designated as the depository library for Indiana documents. IND. CODE ANN. § 4-23-7-23.4

Michigan—The state library is designated as the depository library for state documents to preserve the public documents of this state and to make those documents available for use by the people of this state. MICH. COMP. LAWS ANN. § 397.55

Nevada—DECLARATION OF LEGISLATIVE INTENT. It is the intent of the legislature in enacting NRS 378.150 to 378.210 inclusive, that:
1. All state and local government publications be distributed to designated depository libraries for use by all inhabitants of the state; and
2. Designated depository libraries assume the responsibility for keeping such publications readily accessible for use and rendering assistance, without charge, to patrons using them. NEV. REV. STAT. § 378.150

Ohio—The state librarian shall: . . . (F) Maintain a comprehensive collection of official documents and publications of this state and a library collection and reference service to meet the reference and information needs of officers, departments, agencies of state government, and other libraries. OHIO REV. CODE ANN. § 3375.02

Oklahoma—Whereas, the Department of Libraries is the main general source for the storage, accumulation and dissemination of information in all its forms; and
Whereas, to make the Department of Libraries effective for the purpose and functions of its creation, all material published at state expense should be on file in the Department of Libraries; and
Whereas, Section 3-114 of Title 65 of the Oklahoma Statutes provides for distribution of publications to the Department of Libraries. Now, Therefore . . . 1971 OKLA. SESS. LAWS S. C. RES. NO. 18

Virgin Islands—*Statement of policy.* To effectuate the territory's public policy to make governmental information available to governmental agencies and to the general public, there are established depository libraries for specified public documents and for indexes to those public records which are not required to be deposited pursuant to this section. V.I. CODE ANN. tit. 3, § 883(a)

Washington—The center shall utilize the depository system to permit citizens economical and convenient access to state publications. WASH. REV. CODE ANN. § 40.06.020

LIST 2

DEFINITIONS OF "STATE PUBLICATION" IN DEPOSITORY LEGISLATION

Alaska—"State publication" includes any official document, compilation, journal, bill, law, resolution, bluebook, statute, code, register, pamphlet, list, book, report, study, hearing transcript, leaflet, order, regulation, directory, periodical or magazine issued or contracted for by a state agency determined by the state librarian to be appropriate for retention in the center. ALASKA STAT. § 14.56.180(4)

"Research data" or "data" means a representation of facts, concepts or instructions in a formalized manner suitable for communication, interpretation, or processing by humans or by automatic means which was prepared to serve as a basis for reasoning, calculation, discussion or decision and which is determined appropriate for indexing by the state librarian. ALASKA STAT. § 14.56.180(5)

Arkansas—For the purposes of this Act [§ § 6-301—6-307], the expression "State publication" and/or "local publication" shall include any document issued or printed by any State agency or local government which may be released for such distribution, but does not include:

(i.) the bound volumes of the printed Acts of each of the sessions of the General Assembly of the State of Arkansas;

(ii.) the bound volumes of the Arkansas Supreme Court Reports;

(iii.) printed copies of the Arkansas Statutes, 1947, annotated, or pocket part supplements thereto;

(iv.) any other printed document which may be obtained from the office of the Secretary of State upon the payment of a charge or fee therefor;

(v.) correspondence and intraoffice or interoffice or agency communication [communications] or document [documents] which are not of vital interest to the public;

(vi.) publications of State or local agencies intended or designed to be of limited distribution to meet the requirements of educational, cultural, scientific, professional, or similar use of a limited or restricted purpose, and which are not designed for general distribution; and similarly, other publications or printed documents which are prepared to meet the limited distribution requirements of a governmental grant or use, which are not intended for general distribution, shall also be deemed exempt from the provisions of this Act unless funds have been provided for printing of a quantity of such publication [publications] sufficient for distribution, provided, that a depository copy of each such document noted in subsections (i.), (ii.), (iii.), and (vi.) shall be made available to the State Library. ARK. STAT. ANN. § 6-307(a)

California—''State publication'' or ''publication'' as herein employed is defined to include any document, compilation, journal, law, resolution, Blue Book, statute, code, register, pamphlet, list, book, report, memorandum, hearing, legislative bill, leaflet, order, regulation, directory, periodical or magazine issued by the state, the Legislature, constitutional officers, or any department, commission or other agency thereof or prepared for the state by private individual or organization and issued in print, . . . CAL. GOV'T CODE § 14902

Colorado—''State publication'' means any printed or duplicated material, regardless of format or purpose, which is produced, purchased for distribution, or authorized by any state agency, including any document, compilation, journal, law, resolution, bluebook, statute, code, register, contract and grant report, pamphlet, list, microphotographic form, audiovisual material, book, proceedings, report, public memorandum, hearing, legislative bill, leaflet, order, rule, regulation, directory, periodical, magazine, or newsletter, with the exception of correspondence, interoffice memoranda, or those items detailed by section 24-72-204, C.R.S. 1973. COLO. REV. STAT. § 24-90-202(4)

Connecticut—''State publications'' means all publications printed or purchased for distribution by a state agency, or any other agency supported wholly or in part by state funds; CONN. GEN. STAT. ANN. § 11-9b(a)

Florida—A ''public document'' as referred to in this section shall be defined as any annual, biennial, regular or special report or publication of which at least 500 copies are printed and which may be subject to distribution to the public. FLA. STAT. ANN. § 257.05(1)

Hawaii—''Publication'' includes any document, compilation, journal, report, statute, regulation, ordinance issued in print by any state or county agency, and confidential publications which shall be deposited in accordance with security regulations to be determined by the issuing agency. HAWAII REV. STAT. § 93-2(2)

Illinois—''Publications'' means any document, report, directory, bibliography, rule, regulation, newsletter, pamphlet, brochure, periodical or other printed material paid for in whole or in part by funds appropriated by the General Assembly or issued at the request of a State agency, excepting however, correspondence, inter-office memoranda, and confidential publications. ILL. ANN. STAT. ch. 128 § 121(2)

Iowa—''State publications'' means all multiply produced publications of state agencies regardless of format which are supported by public funds, except correspondence and memoranda intended solely for internal use within the agency or between agencies, and materials designated by law as being confidential. IOWA CODE ANN. § 303A.21(2)

Kansas—''Publication'' means any report, pamphlet, book, or other materials provided by a state agency for use by the general public; KAN. STAT. ANN. § 75-2565(a)

Kentucky—''Records'' means all books, papers, maps, photographs, and other documentary materials, regardless of physical form or characteristics, made or received by any agency of the state government in pursuance of the state law or in connection with the transaction of public business and preserved or appropriate for preservation by that agency or its legitimate successor as evidence of the organization, functions, policies, decisions, procedures, operations, or other activities of the government or because of the informational value of data contained therein. KY. REV. STAT. ANN. § 171.410(1)

Minnesota—As used in this chapter, ''document'' shall include any publication issued by the state, constitutional officers, departments, commissions, councils, bureaus, research centers, societies, or other agencies supported by state funds, or any publication prepared for the state by private individuals or organizations and issued in print, including all forms of duplicating other than by the use of carbon paper, considered to be of interest or value to the legislative reference library. Intraoffice or interoffice memos and forms and information concerning only the internal operation of an agency are not included. MINN. STAT. ANN. § 3.302(3)

Missouri—''State publications'' shall include all multiple-produced publications of state agencies, regardless of format or purpose, with the exception of correspondence and interoffice memoranda. MO. ANN. STAT. § 181.100

Montana—''State publication'' includes any document, compilation, journal, law, resolution, bluebook, statute, code, register, pamphlet, list, book, proceedings, report, memorandum, hearing, legislative bill, leaflet, order, regulation, directory, periodical or magazine issued in print, or purchased for distribution by the state, the legislature, constitutional officers, any state department, committee or other state agency supported wholly or in part by state funds. MONT. CODE ANN. § 22-1-211(2)

Nebraska—State publications shall include any multiply-produced publications printed or purchased for distribution, by the state, the Legislature, constitutional officers, any state department, committee or other state agency supported wholly or in part by state funds; NEB. REV. STAT. § 51-411(2)

Governmental publications shall include any publications of associations, regional organizations, intergovernmental bodies, federal agencies, boards and commissions, or other publications that may contribute supplementary materials to support the work of the state Legislature and state agencies. NEB. REV. STAT. § 51-411(4)

Nevada—"State publication" includes any document issued in print by any state agency and which may legally be released for public distribution, but does not include:

(a) Nevada Revised Statutes;

(b) Nevada Reports;

(c) Bound volumes of the Statutes of Nevada;

(d) The Nevada Digest or Annotations to Nevada Revised Statutes prepared by the legislative counsel;

(e) Press items of the University of Nevada System which are not in the nature of public and other university items not designed for external distribution; or

(f) Correspondence and intraoffice or interoffice communications which are not of vital interest to the public.

(g) Publications from established agencies which are required by federal and state law to be distributed to depositories which duplicate those under NRS 378.200. NEV. REV. STAT. § 378.160(3)

New Hampshire—"State publication" or "publication" includes any document, compilation, code, register, pamphlet, list, book, report, memorandum[,] hearing, leaflet, order, regulation, directory[,] periodical or serial issued by state constitutional officers, or any department, division, commission or other agency of the state in print. N.H. REV. STAT. ANN. § 202-B:3(I)

North Dakota—State publications refer to any informational materials regardless of format, method of reproduction, or source, originating in or produced with the imprint of, by the authority of, or at the total or partial expense of, any state agency. The definition incorporates those publications that may or may not be financed by state funds but are released by private bodies such as research and consultant firms under contract with or supervision of any state agency. . . . State publications are specifically defined as public documents appearing as reports, directories, statistical compendiums, bibliographies, laws or bills, rules, regulations, newsletters, bulletins, state plans, brochures, periodicals, committee minutes, transcripts of public hearings, other printed matter, audio tapes, video tapes, films, filmstrips, or slides, but not those administrative or training materials used only within the issuing agency. N.D. CENT. CODE. § 54-24-09

Oklahoma—"State publication" means any informational materials regardless of format, method of reproduction, or source, originating in or produced with the imprint of, by the authority of, or at the total or partial expense of, or purchased for distribution by, the state, the Legislature, constitutional officers, any state department, committee, sub-state planning district, or other state agency supported wholly or in part by state funds. The definition incorporates those publications that may or may not be financed by state funds but are released by private bodies such as research and consultant firms under a contract with and/or the supervision of any state agency; and specifically includes public documents appearing as reports, directories, statistical compendiums, bibliographies, laws or bills, rules, regulations, newsletters, bulletins, state plans, brochures, periodicals or magazines, committee minutes, transcripts of public hearings, journals, statutes, codes, pamphlets, lists, books, charts, maps, surveys, other printed matter, microfilm, microfiche and all sale items. OKLA. STAT. ANN. tit. 65, § 3-113.2(4)

"Governmental publications" means any publication of associations, regional organizations, intergovernmental bodies, federal agencies, boards and commissions, or other publishers that may contribute supplementary materials to support the work of the State Legislature, state officers and state agencies; OKLA. STAT. ANN. tit. 65, § 3-113.2(2)

Oregon—The term "publication," as used in this section, does not include:

(a) Oregon Revised Statutes or any edition thereof.

(b) Legislative bills, calendars and interim committee reports made available under ORS 171.215.

(c) Reports and publications of the Oregon Supreme Court, Oregon Court of Appeals and the Oregon Tax Court. OR. REV. STAT. § 182.070(2)

South Dakota—"State publication," any document, compilation, journal, law, resolution, bluebook, statute, code, register, pamphlet, list, microphotographic form, tape or disc recording, book, proceedings, report, memorandum, hearing, legislative bill, leaflet, order, regulation, directory, periodical or magazine published, issued, in print, or purchased for distribution, by the state, the Legislature, constitutional officers, any state department, committee or other state agency supported wholly or in part by public funds. S.D. COMPILED LAWS ANN. § 14-1A-1(2)

Texas— "State publication" means printed matter that is produced in multiple copies by the authority of or at the total or partial expense of a state agency. The term includes publications sponsored by or purchased for distribution by a state agency and publications released by private institutions, such as research and consulting firms, under contract with a state agency, but does not include correspondence, interoffice memoranda, or routine forms. TEX. REV. CIV. STAT. ANN. art. 5542a § 1(1)

Utah—"State publication" means any blue book, book, compilation, directory, document, contract and grant report, hearing memorandum, journal, law, leaflet, legislative bill, list, magazine, map, minutes, monograph, order ordinance, pamphlet, periodical, proceeding, public memorandum, resolution, register, regulation, report, statute, audiovisual material, microphotographic form and tape or disc recording regardless of format or method of reproduction, issued or published by any state agency or political subdivision for distribution, not including correspondence, internal confidential publications, office memoranda, university press publications, and publications of the state historical society. UTAH CODE ANN. § 35-5-1(1)

Virgin Islands—"Public document" means any public record, regardless of format or purpose, supported in whole or in part by public funds, for distribution by any territorial governmental agency, and which is designated for deposit pursuant to this section, but does not mean inter-office and intra-office memoranda. "Public records" includes printed or audio-visual forms of communication and their accompanying technology. V.I. CODE ANN. tit. 3, § 883(b)(4)

Virginia—"Publication" includes all unrestricted publications of whatever kind which are printed or reproduced in any way, published or issued by an agency of the State in full or in part at State expense. VA. CODE § 2.1-467.1

Washington—"State publication" includes annual, biennial, and special reports, state periodicals and magazines, books, pamphlets, leaflets, and all other materials, other than news releases sent exclusively to the news media, typewritten correspondence and interoffice memoranda, issued in print by the state, the legislature, constitutional officers, or any state department, committee, or other state agency supported wholly or in part by state funds. WASH. REV. CODE ANN. § 40.06.010(3)

DEFINITIONS OF "STATE PUBLICATION" IN REGULATIONS

Connecticut—A "state government publication" is any document produced by or purchased for an agency of state government in multiple copies at government expense, with the exception of:

A. Business forms
B. Informal administrative memos and instructions for the internal use of agency personnel
C. Blueprints
D. Complimentary, visiting and business cards
E. Correspondence
F. Minutes of meetings
G. Announcements of lectures, meetings, seminars, and workshops
H. Doctoral dissertations
I. Master's theses

Delaware—A "publication" for purposes of deposit is any book, map, pamphlet, press release, report, or other document intended for circulation outside the originating agency. Certain internal documents may be considered to be publications if they are of general interest. Letterheads, forms, internal memoranda, and duplicated procedural materials, are not publications. Documents protected against disclosure under the "sunshine" law are not "publications" because they cannot be circulated to the general public.

Illinois—Definition is word for word as it appears in the law.

Kentucky—Reports and publications as used in this regulation shall be construed in the broadest sense to include typed, printed, mimeographed, and multilithed publications.

Nevada—Definition is the same as that in the law, with the insertion, before the list of exclusions, of the sentence: "This includes everything from lengthy technical reports to brief printed or mimeographed leaflets."

Pennsylvania—*Publication.* Any printed or otherwise reproduced item prepared for distribution to the public, or used within any state agency as a regulatory instrument, including but not limited to documents, pamphlets, studies, brochures, books, annual reports, codes, regulations, journals, periodicals or magazines printed by or for the Commonwealth, its legislature, its courts, its constitutional offices, or any authority, board, commission, department or other state governmental agency or issued in conjunction with, or under contract with, the Federal government, local units of government, private individuals, institutions or corporations.

DEFINITIONS OF "STATE PUBLICATION" IN PROPOSED LEGISLATION

Colorado—"State publication" includes any document, compilation, journal, law, resolution, bluebook, statute, code, register, pamphlet, list, microphotographic form, tape or disc recording, book, proceedings, report, public memorandum, hearing, legislative bill, leaflet, order, rule, regulation, directory, periodical, magazine or newsletter published, issued, in print, or purchased for distribution, by the state, the legislature, constitutional officers, any state department, committee or other state agency supported wholly or in part by state funds. PROPOSED COLORADO LAW [1978]

South Carolina—"State publication" means any document, compilation, journal, resolution, statute, register, book, act, pamphlet, report, map, leaflet, order, regulation, directory, periodical, magazine or other similar written material excluding interoffice and intraoffice communications issued in print by the State, any State agency or department or any State-supported college or university for the use or regulation of any person; S.C. SENATE BILL 2-203, 1972, § 1.

DEFINITIONS OF "STATE PUBLICATION," "GOVERNMENT PUBLICATION," AND RELATED TERMS IN OTHER SOURCES

From "Checklist Commentary" *Documents to the People* 5:68 (1977)—the following definitions have been adopted and are to be used in all State Documents Task Force guidelines.... State Documents/Publication. Information produced by or for a state agency in any format.

From Albert Halcli's "Comments on the Guidelines for Minimum State Servicing of State Documents," *Documents to the People* 3, no. 7:33-34 (September 1975)—State Documents or Publications. The term "publications" means any printed material paid for in whole or in part by funds appropriated by the state legislative body or issued at the request of or under the direction of a state agency. Publications include any documents, report, directory, statistical compendium, bibliography, law or bill, rule, regulation, newsletter, pamphlet, brochure, periodical, or other printed matter but do not include administrative material intended for internal use only. Printed material means publications duplicated by any and all methods of duplication. The term includes publications issued by private bodies, such as consultant or research firms, even though they may not have been financed by any state funds, when the publications have been issued under contract with and/or supervision of a state agency.

From *Checklist of United States Public Documents 1789-1909*, 3d ed., 1911, p. vii—... any publication printed at government expense or published by authority of Congress or any government publishing office, or of which an edition has been bought by Congress or any government office for division among members of Congress or distribution to government officials or the public,
    Referred to as "the official one." *Oklahoma Librarian* 16:80 (1966).

From 44 *United States Code Annotated* 1901 (1969) the federal definition— "Government publication" as used in this chapter, means informational matter which is published as an individual document at Government expense, or as required by law.

From the ALA *Glossary*—"Government Publication. Any printed or processed paper, book, periodical, pamphlet, or map, originating in, or printed with the imprint of, or at the expense and by the authority of, any office of a legally organized government. Often called Document, Government Document, and Public Document." (p. 65, column 1)

    "State Publication. Any printed or processed paper, book, periodical, pamphlet, or map, originating in, or printed with the imprint of, or at the expense and by the authority of, any office of a state government. Often called State Documents." (p. 134, column 1)
    The American National Standards Institute definition, the "ANSI" definition of government document, uses the words, "bearing a government imprint." (ANSI Z39.7 [1968] p. 13)

From *Handbook on Exchange*—By the Brussels Convention of 1886, "official publications" are defined as "official documents, parliamentary and administrative, which are published in the country of their origin; works executed by the order and at the expense of the governments." In Convention B is added "official journals, public parliamentary annuals and documents."

LIST 3

DEFINITIONS OF "STATE AGENCY" IN DEPOSITORY LEGISLATION

Alaska—"State agency" includes state departments, divisions, agencies, boards, associations, commissions, corporations and offices, and the University of Alaska and its affiliated research institutes; ALASKA STAT. § 14.56.180(2)

Colorado—"State agency" means every state office, whether legislative, executive, or judicial, and all of its respective officers, departments, divisions, bureaus, boards, commissions, and committees, all state-supported colleges and universities which are defined as state institutions of higher education, and other agencies which expend state-appropriated funds. COLO. REV. STAT. § 24-90-202(4)

Connecticut—"State agency" means every state office, officer, department, division, bureau, board and commission, permanent or temporary in nature, whether legislative, executive or judicial, and any subdivisions of each, including state-supported institutions of higher education; CONN. GEN. STAT. ANN. § 11-9b(c)

Hawaii—"State and county agency" includes every state, city and county and county office, officer, department, board, commission, and agency, whether in the legislative, executive or judicial branch. HAWAII REV. STAT. § 93-2(1)

Illinois—"State agencies" means every State office, officer, department, division, section, unit, service, bureau, board, commission, committee, and subdivision thereof of all branches of the State government and which agencies expend appropriations of State funds. ILL. ANN. STAT. ch 128 § 121(1)

Iowa—"State agency" means a legislative, executive, or judicial office of the state and all of its respective officers, departments, divisions, bureaus, boards, commissions, committees, and state institutions of higher education governed by the state board of regents. IOWA CODE ANN. § 303A.21(1)

Kansas —"State agency" means any state office or officer, department, board, commission, institution, bureau, society or any agency, division or unit within any state office, department, board, commission or other state authority. KAN. STAT. ANN. § 75-2565(b)

Maine—"Agency" shall mean a state department, agency, office, board, commission; or quasi-independent agency, board, commission, authority or institution. ME. REV. STAT. ANN. tit. 1, § 501

Montana—"State agency" includes every state office, officer, department, division, bureau, board, commission and agency of the state and, where applicable, all subdivisions of each. MONT. CODE ANN. § 22-1-211(3)

Nebraska—State agency shall include every state office, officer, department, division, bureau, board, commission and agency of the state, and where applicable, all subdivisions of each including state institutions of higher education, defined as all state-supported colleges, universities, junior colleges, and vocational technical colleges. NEB. REV. STAT. § 51-411(3)

Nevada—"State agency" includes the legislature, constitutional officers or any department, division, bureau, board, commission or agency of the State of Nevada. NEV. REV. STAT. § 378.160(2)

Oklahoma—"Agency" means any state office, officer, department, division or unit, bureau, board, commission, authority, institution, sub-state planning district, and agency of the state, and, where applicable, all subdivisions of each, including state institutions of higher education, defined as all state-supported colleges, universities, junior colleges and vocational-technical schools. OKLA. STAT. ANN. tit. 65, § 3-113.2(1)

South Dakota—"State agency," includes, but is not limited to, the Legislature, constitutional officers, and any department, division, bureau, board, commission, committee, or agency of the state of South Dakota; S.D. COMPILED LAWS ANN. § 14-1A-1(3)

Texas—"State agency" means any state office, officer, department, division, bureau, board, commission, legislative committee, authority, institution, sub-state planning bureau, university system or institution of higher education as defined by Section 61.003, Texas Education Code, as amended, or any of their subdivisions. TEX. REV. CIV. STAT. ANN. art. 5442a § 1(2)

Utah—"State agency" means the state, any office, department, agency, authority, commission, board, institution, hospital, college, university or other instrumentality of the state. UTAH CODE ANN. § 37-5-1(3)

Virgin Islands—"Governmental agency" includes the Legislature, any governmental entity, board, bureau, commission, department, agency, division, authority, office, or agent, or semi-private governmental entity receiving governmental funds for its operation in whole or in part, or any entity having bonding authority under the Virgin Islands Government in whole or in part. V.I. CODE ANN. tit. 3, § 883(b)(3)

Virginia—"Agency" includes every agency, board, commission, office, department, division, institution or other entity of any branch of the State government. VA. CODE § 2.1-467.1

Washington—"State agency" includes every state office, officer, department, division, bureau, board, commission and agency of the state, and, where applicable, all subdivisions of each. WASH. REV. CODE ANN. § 40.06.010(2)

DEFINITIONS OF "STATE AGENCY" IN REGULATIONS

Illinois—The legal definition is repeated word for word.

Nevada—The legal definition is repeated word for word.

DEFINITIONS OF "STATE AGENCY" IN PROPOSED LEGISLATION

Colorado—"State agency" includes every state office, officer, department, division, section, unit, service, bureau, board, commission, committee, and subdivision thereof of all branches of the state government and which agencies expend appropriation of state funds. PROPOSED COLORADO LAW [1978]

LIST 4

DEFINITIONS OF "PRINT" AND OTHER WORDS IN DEPOSITORY LEGISLATION

California —"Print" is defined to include all forms of duplicating other than by the use of carbon paper. CAL. GOV'T CODE § 14902

Connecticut—"Printed" means all forms of printing and duplicating, regardless of format or purpose, with the exception of correspondence and interoffice memoranda. CONN. GEN. STAT. ANN. § 11-9b(b)

Hawaii—"Print" includes all forms of printing and duplications, except administrative forms. HAWAII REV. STAT. § 93-2(3)

Illinois—"Printed material" means publications duplicated by any and all methods of duplication. ILL. ANN. STAT. ch 128 § 121(3)

Montana—"Print" includes all forms of printing and duplicating, regardless of format or purpose, with the exception of correspondence and interoffice memoranda. MONT. CODE ANN. § 22-1-211(1)

Nebraska—Print shall include all forms of printing and duplicating, regardless of format or purpose, with the exception of correspondence and interoffice memoranda. NEB. REV. STAT. § 51-411(1)

Nevada—"Print" means all forms of printing and duplicating other than by use of carbon paper. NEV. REV. STAT. § 378.160(1)

New Hampshire—"Print" includes all forms of duplicating other than by the use of carbon paper. N.H. REV. STAT. ANN. § 202-B:3(II)

Oklahoma—''Print'' means any form of printing and duplication, regardless of format or purpose, with the exception of correspondence and interoffice memoranda. OKLA. STAT. ANN. tit. 65, § 3-113.2

South Dakota—''Print,'' all forms of printing and duplicating, including audio-visual materials, regardless of format or purpose, with the exception of correspondence and interoffice memoranda. S.D. COMPILED LAWS ANN. § 14-1A-1(1)

Washington—''Print'' includes all forms of reproducing multiple copies, with the exception of typewritten correspondence and interoffice memoranda. WASH. REV. CODE ANN. § 40.06.010(1)

DEFINITIONS OF ''PRINT'' IN REGULATIONS

Illinois—The legal definition is repeated word for word.

Nevada—The legal definition is repeated word for word in the regulations. This sentence is added: ''This is intended to include publications issued in a microformat.''

DEFINITIONS OF ''PRINT'' IN PROPOSED LEGISLATION

Colorado—''Print'' includes all forms of printing and duplicating, including audio-visual materials, regardless of format or purpose, with the exception of correspondence and interoffice memoranda. PROPOSED COLORADO LAW [1978]

South Carolina—''Print'' means all forms of duplicating other than by the use of carbon paper. S.C. SENATE BILL 2-203 (1972) § 1.

DEFINITIONS OF OTHER WORDS IN LEGISLATION

Alaska—''Center'' means the state library distribution and data access center. ALASKA STAT.§ 14.56.180(1)
   ''Municipal'' and ''municipality'' includes cities and organized boroughs of every class, including municipalities unified under AS 29.68.240—29.68.440. ALASKA STAT. §14.56.180(3)

Colorado—''Center'' means the state publications depository and distribution center. COLO. REV. STAT. § 24-90-202(1)
   ''Depository library'' means a library designated to collect, maintain, and make available to the general public state agency publications. COLO. REV. STAT. § 24-90-202(2)

Connecticut—"Depository library" means the designated library for collecting, maintaining and making available to the general public Connecticut state agency publications. CONN. GEN. STAT. ANN. § 11-9b(d)

Iowa—"Depository library" means a library designated for the deposit of state publications under the provisions of this Act. IOWA CODE ANN. § 303A.21(3)

Kentucky—"Department" means the department of library and archives. KY. REV. STAT. ANN. § 171.410(2)
"Commission" means the state archives and records commission. KY. REV. STAT. ANN. § 171.410(3)

South Dakota—"Center," the state publications library distribution center. S.D. COMPILED LAWS ANN. § 14-1A-1(4)

Texas—"Depository libraries" means the Texas State Library, the Texas Legislative Reference Library, the Library of Congress, the Center for Research Libraries, and other libraries that the Texas Library and Historical Commission designates as depository libraries. TEXAS REV. CIV. STAT. ANN. art. 5442a § 1(3)

Utah—"Commission" means the state library commission established under section 37-4-3. UTAH CODE ANN. § 37-5-1(1)
"Political subdivision" means any county, city, town, school district, public transit district, redevelopment agency, special improvement or taxing district. UTAH CODE ANN. §37-5-1(2)

Virgin Islands—"Territorial Librarian" means the Director of the Bureau of Libraries and Museums.
"Depository libraries" means those libraries where, pursuant to this section, public documents and indexes shall be deposited, retained and reproduced upon demand, or made available to the general public and governmental agencies.
"Public funds" includes cash, checks, bills, notes, drafts, stocks, bonds and all similar media of exchange which are received or disbursed under law by a governmental agency.
"Publication date" means the earliest date when a copy or copies of the first publication, including preliminary drafts, advance copies, unofficial editions and confidential publications, were placed on sale, donated or exchanged, or made available to any entity outside the publishing governmental agency.
"Library" means any public or private institution which maintains a media of communication collection for loan, internally or externally, including all college or university libraries, public, private or parochial school libraries.

"Recognized newspaper" means any newspaper or publication accepting paid advertisements whose copies are offered for sale, by public subscription or by the copy, or whose copies are distributed without cost to the general public, issued at regular intervals, not to exceed one week. V.I. CODE ANN. tit. 3, § 883(b)(1, 2, 5-8)

DEFINITIONS OF OTHER WORDS IN REGULATIONS

Pennsylvania—Depository Collection. A gathering of official Commonwealth publications in a formally organized library organized either for public use under The Library Code, (24 P.S. § 4101 *et seq.*), or for academic use in a state accredited institution of higher education. 22 PA. CODE § 143.1.

DEFINITIONS OF OTHER WORDS IN PROPOSED LEGISLATION

Colorado—"Center" [means] the state publications depository distribution center. PROPOSED COLORADO LAW [1978]

South Carolina—"Complete depository" is a place, usually a library, that receives at least one copy of all State publications;
    "Selective Depository" is a place, usually a library, that from time to time requests and receives copies of State publications;
    "Depository System" is a system in which copies of all State publications are deposited in one central depository or library and copies are sent to other designated depositories or libraries; S.C. SENATE BILL 2-203 (1972) § 1.

RELATED DEFINITIONS FROM OTHER SOURCES

"State Document Center. A library that assumes the responsibility of collecting, organizing, and preserving as complete a file as possible of the public documents of the state in which it is located." (ALA *Glossary*) The ANSI Z39.7 (1968) definition is the same.
"Documents Depository. A library legally designated to receive without charge copies of all or selected U.S. government publications; or a library designated to receive without charge a full set of Library of Congress printed cards." (ALA *Glossary*) The ANSI Z39.7 definition is the same.

NOTES

1. Citations are not given for each section of the law mentioned in the text. Lists of sections relating to the chapter are included at the end of each chapter. As an alternative, the reader may refer to the full depository law for each state as included in the state section.

2. Francis B. Waters, "Analysis of State Legislation Relating to State Depository Libraries" (M.S.L.S. Thesis, Western Reserve University, 1950).

3. Bob D. Carmack, "South Dakota Public Documents: Report of a Study," *Government Publications Review* 1:252 (Spring 1974).

4. Joe Morehead, *Introduction to United States Public Documents* (Littleton, Colo.: Libraries Unlimited, 1975), p. xxv. Childs, in his article in the *Encyclopedia of Library and Information Science*, uses the words "Government Publications (Documents)" as his subject.

5. Morehead, *U. S. Public Documents*, p. xxv.

6. John J. Boll, "Tame the Terror for Its Use: Or, What are Wisconsin Documents?" *Wisconsin Library Bulletin* 70:79 (March 1974).

7. A. Paul Pross and Catherine A. Pross, *Government Publishing in the Canadian Provinces: A Prescriptive Study* (Toronto: University of Toronto Press, 1972), p. 17.

8. Boll, "Tame the Terror," p. 80.

9. John Finning Allison, Jr., "A Distribution System for North Carolina State Publications: A Proposal" (M.S.L.S. Thesis, University of North Carolina, Chapel Hill, 1978).

10. Proposed Louisiana law, 1976, in Documents on Documents Collection.

5. STATE AGENCIES

The various agencies of state government, the departments, divisions, offices, commissions, and committees, are the foundation of a state documents program. It is their publications that are being made available and their cooperation that makes a depository library program truly effective. The state agencies are the starting point for the distribution process. State publications are issued by state agencies, sent to the distribution center, forwarded to depository libraries, and finally made available to the public. A depository program begins with the state agencies.

Although a depository program begins outside the library field, it becomes essentially a library undertaking. A library distribution center acquires and forwards the publications; the depository libraries organize the publications, publicize them, and make them accessible to the public.

Among documents librarians, the phrase "state agency" is used as a general term to refer to all state governmental units as a group. This informal usage includes units in all branches of government and all state institutions. In some states (for example, South Dakota and Virginia) formal definitions of the term "state agency" confirm this interpretation. It is in this broad sense that the term is used in this chapter.

There are many state agencies in even the less populous states, and huge numbers of them in the larger states.[1] Those who have worked with state documents over a period of years recognize that the governmental structure in the individual states is ever-changing. Charles Wolfe, a Michigan law librarian, expresses these thoughts well with the words, "the bigness of state government" and "a never satisfied passion to reorganize and reshuffle governmental units."[2]

Most of the larger, more permanent state agencies issue publications. Little has been written on the number of state agencies that issue publications. A writer some time ago observed that it could be argued that the number of state publications should not vary appreciably from state to state because all the states exercise the same functions.[3] Some agencies never publish (a state plumbing board, for example), and perhaps never will, but contact should be maintained on the chance that the agency will change. In Louisiana, for example, contact is maintained with twice as many agencies as report issuing any publications. State agencies issue publications for a variety of reasons: (1) legal mandate (annual reports are often in this category), (2) dissemination of research (Geological Survey studies), (3) guidance of the public (rules and regulations such as driver's license requirements), (4) public information (tourist leaflets, cooperative extension service bulletins), and (5) current information on activities (newsletters and press releases).

Librarians have informally commented on the fact that state agencies do not appreciate the importance of their own publications to an audience wider than the one the agency is accustomed to serving.[4] Many state agencies feel that they know the distribution that ought to be made of their publications. Yet, one of the areas in which librarians have wide experience is in evaluating and selecting publications for users of all kinds and ages. John Boll, a library school professor in Wisconsin, wrote: "in the past, selection by public relations offices has been practiced and found ineffective. It must be done by people who see the material from a subject point of view."[5]

An Idaho librarian, Gar Elison, makes the same point, stating that agency officials tend to look at the format of publications and do not consider the less formal publications appropriate for library distribution. He explains, "the efforts [of the distribution center administrator in going to the state capitol to locate and collect state publications] did point out a fact that the governor and the legislature still haven't recognized—i.e., State agencies seem to be least able to judge the value of their own publications." Elison also comments that state agencies do not prepare bibliographies of their publications.[6] Librarians have a unique role to play in advising state agencies on the value of state publications to users in general.

The duty of the state agency to furnish its publications is, seemingly, one that runs contrary to the interest of the state agency, because it is required to supply multiple copies of publications for which it has paid through its own appropriation. Some states avoid this issue. Pennsylvania requires deposit of those publications "remaining after regular distribution according to existing allocations." In Montana, the distribution center reimburses the state agencies for additional copies under certain conditions. Nevada includes a statement in the law requiring that copies be supplied, "if sufficient funds are available."

The 1979 Arkansas legislation recognizes the financial impact of furnishing publications for the libraries and has several qualifying provisions designed to lessen the financial burden on the state agencies. The distribution is required only if sufficient funds are appropriated for the printing of the materials by the agencies and for the distribution thereof by the state library. Another subsection provides that if the agency does not have sufficient funds to furnish fifty copies, it may notify the state library and deliver three copies. In still another part of the law, publications prepared to meet governmental grant requirements are excluded from the program unless printing funds are sufficient to provide copies for distribution.

In most states, however, the law merely provides that the state agencies shall deposit their publications with the distribution center. Significantly, there are usually no penalties for noncompliance.[7]

In 1967, Indiana Senate Enrolled Act 61, which had a section providing that "Any person who fails to comply with the provisions of this act shall be guilty of a misdemeanor and upon conviction shall be liable to a fine not exceeding one hundred dollars ($100)," was held unconstitutional by the attorney general and was vetoed by the governor.[8]

The 1978 Oklahoma law provides for an enforcement procedure, a writ of mandamus, which is probably little used but effective merely because it is in the law. This provision strengthens the earlier provision that the attorney general should "immediately initiate appropriate action" in a case of non-compliance by a state agency. The new law sets up a procedure requiring notice.

Indirect enforcement procedures are found in the Arkansas and Texas laws. The 1947 Arkansas law provides for an affidavit certifying to delivery to the library before accounts for printing may be approved. Likewise, the Texas law, in an article that was repealed in 1979, required a receipt from the librarian. This Texas provision was carried into the new law, for agency printing done by contract. The 1979 Texas section reads:

If a state agency's printing is done by contract, an account for the printing may not be approved and a warrant for the printing may not be issued unless the agency first furnishes to the State Board of Control a receipt from the state librarian for the publication or a written waiver from the state librarian exempting the publication from the requirements of this Act.

In this connection, it must be remembered that the number of copies required for the depository program is frequently so small in proportion to the total number of copies printed that there is little, if any, impact on the agency budget. Twenty-five or fifty copies out of a printing of thousands of copies cannot have an appreciable impact on the agency budget. On the other hand, a request for even twenty-five copies from the small mimeographed runs of less than one hundred or the very expensive consultant reports produced in limited number (often as few as twenty-five or fifty) does produce an economic burden. If the distribution center can be realistic in these latter instances, then the state agencies should be cooperative in supplying multiple copies of their larger printings.

The distribution center's main reason for being is the building of contacts with state agencies that will enable the center to acquire the publications for distribution. The primary function of the distribution center is the acquisition one. Distributing the publications, because it is essentially a routine function, is secondary.

The relationship between the state agencies and the distribution center must be created through communication between persons in unrelated fields of endeavor. Working together is advantageous to both the state agencies and the library community. It is essential that a sound working relationship be established and that it be maintained and nurtured.

The distribution center must assume the responsibility for creating the lines of communication with the state agencies and must make sure that continuing cooperation is maintained. The relationship of the distribution center with the state agencies is one of education, persuasion, and constant vigilance. The first step is to be sure that the state agencies are aware of the law. A second step is to ensure that the state agencies understand the purpose of the law. This understanding should extend to an appreciation by the state agencies of the advantages of compliance with the law. The next steps are all the same—maintaining the awareness and understanding.

Additional areas in which the distribution center might counsel or advise the state agencies could be added here—considerations of appropriate printing and binding (title pages, indexes), bibliographic details (issuing agency and date of publication on each publication), the effects of restrictions on distribution, and the purging of mailing lists—but these are not basic to the depository program.

DISTRIBUTION METHODS

The distribution of documents by state agencies can be made directly to the public, to libraries, or to a distribution center. A state agency's first distribution of a new publication is almost always to the group for which it was prepared. This group may be designated by statute, or the group may be a mailing list that the agency has created to include those individuals and organizations concerned with and interested in the agency's work.

Direct distribution to the public has public relations value to the distributing agency, a factor particularly important to an elected official. However, it is often a wasteful form of distribution because the use of the publication is usually for current information only and is limited to a single individual.[9]

The mere addition of the names of libraries to the mailing lists of state agencies is a practice that should be approached with caution. State agencies are usually generous with their publications and cooperative in adding libraries to their mailing lists. However, the state agency may not understand that a library wants all publications from the agency, that it wants to be on all mailing lists, and that it wants to remain on the mailing lists indefinitely. The mailing list may be scrapped when the official who created it leaves office, or when a successor agency replaces or absorbs an existing agency. Constant vigilance is required to remain on a state agency mailing list.

ADVANTAGES AND COST-BENEFITS OF DEPOSITORY DISTRIBUTION

Distribution to libraries permits use by the general public in a situation where related materials can be provided and also preserves the publications for future use. Prompt distribution to the distribution center makes possible the bibliographical control of publications, if not "at the source," at least very close to it. The distribution center can catalog and list the publications at a time when it is still possible to consult the author or the issuing agency if additional bibliographical information is needed to supplement that in the publications.

The operation of a depository system includes the following advantages for a state agency: (1) the elimination of the handling of individual, perhaps incomplete, requests for information; (2) the ability to refer users to the library when the state agency stock of a publication is exhausted; and (3) the existence of a security file of the agency's publications.

A security file is important because of the inevitable changes that occur in state government structure and personnel. In several instances in Louisiana, for example, state agencies admitted either that they did not have back files of their own publications or that the files were not conveniently accessible. A similar situation exists in New Mexico, and probably in other states as well, where the library has received many requests from current state employees for publications no longer available at the state agency and unfortunately not available at the state library.[10]

For state agencies, distribution through libraries is cost-effective. Fewer copies need to be printed if individual distribution is curtailed in favor of distribution to libraries. Likewise, the number of names maintained on a state agency mailing list can be reduced if, for example, forty copies are sent to one distribution center in lieu of forty individual libraries. A saving results from routine bulk handling for depository distribution as opposed to individual handling. Finally, if the regulations that some states (for example, Alaska, Montana, and Washington) have adopted requiring that all depository libraries deal with state agencies only indirectly through the distribution center are enforced, the expense to the agency of handling inquiries and telephone calls from libraries is reduced.

DUTY TO SEND COPIES FOR DISTRIBUTION

The statutory duty of state agencies to furnish copies of their publications for distribution to depository libraries is the foundation of a depository system. (See List 5.) Ideally, the state agencies should send the publications to a distribution center, as opposed to direct distribution to the depository libraries. The duty of the distribution center to forward the publications to the libraries is secondary and is not as critical to the successful operation of the law as the duty imposed on the state agencies. The current attitudes of the distribution centers in recognizing the importance of state documents to all citizens and in accepting the responsibilities of distribution and bibliographic control of state publications contribute toward this finding.

Under depository legislation, the principal duty of the state agencies is to send copies of their publications to the appropriate place for distribution. If the state agencies were to perform this function faithfully, on a comprehensive basis, they would need assume no other obligations for the state to have a successful depository program. If the state agencies supplied all their publications, regularly, and in sufficient quantity, any deficiencies in the program would not be attributable to the state agencies.

Louis Coatney, documents librarian at the state library in Alaska, has a pertinent comment on the attitude of the state agencies toward their duty:

It is felt that *forcing* State agencies to comply with our requests for depository quotas of their publications (by strengthening those State statutes concerned with the depository program) would be counterproductive. By far, most of the problem with collecting depository quotas stems from honest ignorance of the program largely caused by a typically heavy clerical turnover. Generally, the agencies' cooperation seems to be improving as they come to understand the cost-effective potential of the depository program. Our annual "dragnets" for unreceived publications have met with steadily increasing responsiveness and success." [Italics in the original.][11]

Most modern laws mandate that the state agencies supply copies of the publications for distribution. Typically, the statutes use the word "shall"; sometimes, "have a duty" (Idaho), followed by such words as "deposit," "furnish," "file," "send," and "supply." The Washington statute that for many years said "may promptly deposit" was amended in 1977 to read "shall promptly deposit." The 1953 Oregon statute that reads "shall make available to the State Librarian" is weaker because no active duty is placed on the state agencies. The Oregon law was amended in 1979 to permit the state printer to withhold the depository copies and forward them to the state librarian. One purpose of the North Carolina legislation in 1979 was to establish the duty on the part of the state agencies to supply copies of their publications, at least to the Division of State Libraries. The existing North Carolina legislation which requires the other libraries in the state to make requests for the state agencies' publications remains in effect.

WHEN TO SEND COPIES FOR DISTRIBUTION

In some states, the statutes continue with statements on when the copies shall be furnished to the distribution center. For several reasons, the time when the publications shall be sent is set as near the time of publication as possible. First, the libraries need the publications when they are current. If the issuing agency has made newspaper announcements of the release of a publication, libraries throughout the state will receive requests for it. Second, libraries need to receive the publications in an even flow, not *en masse* once a year, although day by day distribution, as is possible with federal publications, should not be expected. The small volume of state publications does not make daily mailing from the distribution center feasible as a routine procedure. Weekly or monthly mailings are the general practice, supplemented by additional mailings whenever justified by the volume of materials ready for mailing.

Special mailings of very timely or intensively used publications are sometimes made. The distribution center is the best judge of the importance of such special handling and can make suitable arrangements for prompt distribution if the state agencies cooperate by forwarding their publications immediately after issuance. Examples include the daily mailing of bills and daily legislative journals, and separate mailing for heavily used publications, such as the state manual or the statistical abstract.

Another important reason for prompt and regular delivery of copies to the distribution center is that state publications go out of print very rapidly. As a stock of copies at the state agency dwindles, the likelihood of having the number of copies on hand needed for the depository libraries diminishes.

Typical statements are "upon release" (Alaska, Missouri, Nevada, and South Dakota); "at the time of publication, or as soon thereafter as practicable" (Florida); "upon issuance" (Iowa); "immediately" (Oklahoma); and "immediately upon release" (Hawaii). The law in the Virgin Islands says "within five weekdays from the publication date" and defines publication date as the earliest date when a copy is "made available to any entity outside the publishing governmental agency." The South Carolina proposed legislation says "within fifteen days after such printing."

COPIES SENT FOR DISTRIBUTION

Because the state agencies must send multiple copies of each publication to the distribution center, it is important that the agencies understand the purpose for which they are supplying copies. The state agencies must not think of the state library (if it serves as the distribution center) as a depository library that needs multiple copies. The state library *as a depository* generally needs only two or three copies for its reference and circulating collections. If the state library is also the distribution center, it needs many more copies in order to supply the other depositories. The two purposes are separate, and if they can be understood as such by the state agencies, greater cooperation can be expected from them.

The state agencies must be encouraged to support the state library collections as well as wider distribution to depository libraries throughout the state. The "depository copies" which the state agencies supply are not "deposited" in the state library (except for the very few copies that are added to the state library's collections) but are forwarded to "depository libraries" of which there are several in different areas of the state.

Although it seems pedantic to distinguish between the two roles of the state library when those roles are combined, as they often are, the difficulty caused by referring to the state library as the "depository library" arises because the impression it creates is that the state library needs many, many copies of the publications. In fact, it is not the state library which needs the copies, but individual libraries all over the state.

The same confusion prompted a recommendation in the California management study for "changes to the State Administrative Manual to spell out the difference in nature between the State Library and other libraries" with respect to the distribution of state publications. The confusion in California did not affect the understanding of the state agencies as to the number of copies required. Rather, it affected their lack of understanding that the state library needed copies for its own collection of those publications that did not receive distribution to the depository libraries.

A slightly different situation exists in New Mexico, where the state library receives copies of most publications under the Rules Act, which was in operation for about ten years before the depository program was enacted to make publications available to the other libraries in the state. The sending of publications pursuant to two different acts permits a double check on their receipt at the state library.

In many of the recent statutes, the number of copies which an agency must supply has been stated as "sufficient copies." Other wording used to achieve the same result is "in such quantity as shall be specified" (Kansas), or "in quantities as certified by the state librarian" (Washington).

Many states stipulate that a fixed number of copies be supplied. The range for the number of copies to be supplied is large—from 4 in Alaska to 350 in California.[12] In California, not all the copies are distributed to depository libraries; a large number remain in the library stockroom to fill requests from individual libraries. A common requirement is that additional copies be supplied on the request of the distribution center, as in the Alaska legislation. Of course, there is a direct correlation between the number of copies to be furnished and the number of depositories in the state.

When the requirement is that fewer than twenty-five copies be supplied, there is a close relationship between the number of copies required and the number of depository libraries, but usually a margin or surplus is built into the law. Such a surplus permits the addition of new depository libraries to the system, changes in the selections made by libraries, the replacement of defective or lost copies, or the distribution of additional copies, all without reapplying to the state agencies for more copies. For these same reasons, a small surplus should be incorporated into the number of copies requested in those states in which the distribution center specifies the number of copies required.

A requirement that a large number of copies be sent can be detrimental to the program if the agency reasons that, because it cannot supply so many copies, it will not send any at all. The Maine legislature enacted amendments to the depository law to reduce the number of copies from 175 to 80 in 1955, and then to 55 copies in 1975. New Jersey introduced legislation in 1976 to reduce the number of copies required for distribution from seventy-five to twenty-five, but the measure died in committee. In Oregon, 1979 legislation changed the number of copies from twenty-five copies of technical publications and seventy-five copies of all other publications to forty-five of all publications.

In Texas, the attorney general recently ruled,

Since the ''quantity specified in article 5442'' is 150 or more, in our opinion, the clear words of the Legislature require the printing of a minimum of 150 copies for the State Library, where the State Librarian requisitions a document from the Board of Control.[13]

The result was that when the state librarian needed copies, both he and the state agency were bound by the number 150, even though both recognized that a smaller number of copies would be in their best interests. Legislation to correct this situation was adopted in 1979.

WHERE COPIES ARE TO BE SENT

In general, the state agencies send, forward, or furnish the copies to the distribution center. Variances from this practice are of special interest. In Nevada, the statute reads, ''to be collected by the state publications distribution center.'' In Washington, a special provision reads, ''Upon consent of the issuing state agency such state publications as are printed by the public printer shall be delivered directly to the center.'' This is a very practical procedure, which could be implemented by supplying ''consent'' forms to the state agencies. The procedure could even be adopted through informal agreements in the absence of statutory authorization. The 1979 Oregon amendment permits the state printer to withhold the depository copies.

ADDITIONAL DUTIES

The additional duties sometimes incorporated in the legislation—appointing a liaison, supplying lists of publications—are included as insurance because the agencies cannot always comply fully with their duty to send publications regularly. Such additional duties are a check on the operation of the system. They are a recognition of the value of personal contacts through the liaison and of the benefits of a routine in sending a list of publications.

The appointment of a liaison and the preparation of a list of publications, although duties imposed on the state agency, differ from the primary duty to supply publications in that they do not represent a direct cost to the state agency. In most states, the issuing agencies absorb the cost of the extra copies of the publications which the state agencies forward to the distribution center.

Appointment of a person to undertake the minimal duties of a liaison, or the preparation of a list, on the other hand, does not have a direct impact on a state agency's budget.

The distribution center can more readily urge a state agency to undertake these ancillary duties than it can tell the state agency that it must supply copies of its publications. Yet, the former is a step toward the latter. It is not really the liaison activities or the list of publications that the distribution center needs, but the publications themselves. The liaison and the list are a means to an end.

The California management study on the Library Distribution Act (LDA), although it made an unfortunate recommendation that the state agencies should be charged for the listing of the titles of their publications in the state checklist, had other recommendations. The goal of the recommendations was "to make the Library Distribution Act important to the participants by intertwining a series of 'automatic' and constant reminders into the current production procedures."[14] Among these were including an instruction box on the printing and duplicating requisitions forms to indicate whether the publication should be distributed to the depository libraries, sending the checklist to the department liaisons, putting a note of LDA distribution on the title page of every publication distributed to the depositories, and requiring annual confirmation of the name, address, and telephone number of the departmental liaisons.

THE DEPARTMENTAL LIAISON

Personal contact is particularly important in dealing with state agencies because of the changing personnel in state government. A liaison, sometimes called the publications representative, is the person in a state agency assigned to work with the distribution center. The liaison can alert the distribution center when changes in personnel, or changes in policy, occur within the state agency. If the liaison changes, the distribution center is immediately aware of the need to start again at the beginning to acquaint a new person with the obligations of the state agency and the advantages of the depository program.

California uses this wording to describe the duties of the departmental liaison: "The designated person shall develop and apply procedures to assure a distribution of . . . publications . . . , which are in harmony with [the Act]." The California management study includes as one of the exhibits a section to provide illustrative data on the job titles of the liaisons, their review of departmental publications, and so forth. Significantly, the institution of the management study itself resulted in the appointment of eleven liaisons.[15]

The liaison is responsible for preparing the list of the agency's publications if the act requires such a list, monitoring the regular shipments to the distribution center, and filling claims from and responding to queries from the center.

Both Alaska and Texas in their recent amendments to their depository program legislation included requirements for the appointment of liaisons.

LIST OF PUBLICATIONS

The routine forwarding by an agency of a list of publications is a help to the distribution center in two ways. The list tells the distribution center about the publications of the agency—what the agency considers the title of a publication to be, its date of issuance, and possibly its frequency—and it alerts the center to publications that have not yet been supplied.

It is almost as important for the distribution center to know that an agency has not issued any publications as to know the titles of those it has issued. Especially for regularly issued publications, any skips or cessations need to be reported by the state agencies and recorded by the depository libraries. For example, in Louisiana the annual "Strawberry Marketing Report" is not issued if the crop fails. If this fact is reported by the distribution center to the depository libraries, none of the depositories need claim the report for that year.

The agency's list of publications also acquaints the distribution center with titles that are not within the distribution requirements so that they can be included in the checklist, thus achieving more comprehensive bibliographical control.

Six states, Alaska, Connecticut, Montana, Nebraska, South Dakota, and Washington, require that state agencies file a list of publications, using the wording "a complete list of current publications." The use of the word "current" should be avoided because it does not necessarily include publications issued during the year but no longer in print at the time the list is compiled. Moreover, if an agency keeps a publication in print at all times, titles might be repeated unnecessarily, and new editions might not be noticed if the agency is not careful about including the date of publication. Finally, if the agency has a long list of titles that remain in print, it might feel that submitting the list each time was repetitious and a waste of time and effort. It is difficult enough to get the agencies to list their serials with volumes and dates each time, and any simplification of the list which can be advocated, without depriving the distribution center of the information it needs, should be adopted.

Kansas uses similar, but better, wording: "a complete list of publications for the previous year." The words "for the previous year" would include not only the publications that were "current" at the time the list was prepared but also those that had been issued but were available for only a few months of the year. Louisiana and Mississippi have the same kind of provision. The Mississippi statute reads, "a list of all its publications issued for public distribution." The Louisiana provision modified "publications" with the words "printed and mimeographed." California has a different approach, requiring state agencies to "supply information . . . for the preparation of the monthly or quarterly lists and the annual cumulation." The New York provision is limited to film, audio- or videotape, or other information programs, and requires "written notification of the program completion." This notification would be on a title-by-title basis, it would seem, but of course the number of titles issued in nonprint form is more limited than the number issued in print. The notification is to "include title, author, and the terms of distribution."

Some states have publications lists designed for distribution to the general public and supplemental to the official checklist. The Virginia State Library issues *Virginia State Publications in Print*, for which a list of current publications from each agency is essential. In Minnesota, the sales agency prepares a list of available publications; thus, the assembling of information is not dependent on information supplied by the state agencies but derived from the actual publications. In addition, Maryland and Minnesota have lists that are prepared at the legislative reference library for the use of legislators in requesting publications and are designed to serve as a substitute for distribution of publications to the members of the legislature.

Even when the state agencies have a statutory duty to supply a list, it is appropriate and expedient as a practical matter for the distribution center to furnish the form on which the list is to be submitted. This not only encourages uniformity of data and of presentation, but also serves as an excellent opportunity for the distribution center to remind the state agencies of their duty under the law. Once, in Louisiana in the early years of the program, when no form was distributed, only four of some two hundred agencies submitted the legally required list.

The time when the list is to be submitted varies from "on request" (Alaska, Montana, Nebraska, South Dakota, and Washington) through specified intervals: monthly (Texas), semiannually (Louisiana and Mississippi), annually (Kansas) to "upon completion of the program" (New York; this refers to the nonprint materials). The Connecticut law says "annually or upon request."

The disposition of the list is mentioned specifically in the legislation of four states. The Texas statute formerly provided that "this list be reproduced and distributed to all depository libraries and to such other agencies and institutions which request this list." The 1979 Texas provision is for a list of all publications that the library has received; that is, a list originating in the state library rather than in the state agencies. Louisiana and Mississippi have identical provisions, which are similar to the earlier Texas statute, and read, "shall make and furnish to each depository a duplicate copy of the same [that is, the lists from the agencies]." This provision caused serious difficulty in Louisiana when a legislator, intent on eliminating unnecessary state publications, wanted literally to take the lists from the state agencies, reproduce them, and limit the distribution to the depository libraries, thus precluding the possibility of editing or augmenting the agency lists and drastically restricting the number of copies produced. It is only with extensive editing and the addition of items not listed by the agencies that the state agency lists are put into a form that meets the needs of the libraries. The Kansas statute provides for a better use of the agency lists: "which the state librarian shall use to maintain a permanent record of publications.'' Thus, in Kansas the lists can be ''used'' rather than unrealistically ''reproduced.''

MAILING LISTS

Other provisions sometimes included in depository legislation relating to the duties of the state agencies serve different purposes. The duty to supply mailing or exchange lists, or the duty to confer with the distribution center when the full quota of copies cannot be supplied, is part of the larger picture of document distribution in general and serves to keep the distribution within bounds and to avoid waste. Inclusion of such provisions in legislation drafted by librarians is evidence that the librarians appreciate their responsibilities to society and that they know the need for economy in government. One of the arguments in favor of a depository program is that it is a cost-effective method of making state publications available to the public. Any economies that can be written into the program without jeopardizing the availability of the publications should be encouraged.

The duty of supplying mailing and exchange lists, found in the South Dakota legislation (or mailing and/or exchange lists, as found in the Montana and Washington legislation, or one or the other as in Alaska), arises only upon the distribution center's request. No states require the automatic turning over of a mailing list. Some diplomacy is needed in handling the problem that arises when a state agency has a depository library on its mailing list and prefers that the distribution center delete the library from *its* list. The depository library will receive the publication regardless of whether the state agency or the distribution center mails it. The distribution center's administrator, who has a duty to know exactly what the depository libraries receive, can explain this duty to the state agency, can point out the saving in postage by mailing in a package with other materials, and can indicate that it is convenient for the depository libraries to receive depository material with a depository label on it, so that the materials can be checked on the monthly list and handled in accordance with procedures established for documents. The exercise of judgment and tact will reveal when exceptions should be made and an agency permitted to withhold the depository copies for direct mailing.

The aids and reminders that the distribution centers provide to the state agencies to encourage and assist them in the performance of their duties are discussed in the next chapter.

CITY AND COUNTY DOCUMENTS

A few states include county and municipal documents in the state depository legislation. Hawaii is the only state that treats the local publications in exactly the same manner as the state publications. The statute defines ''state and county agency'' and begins the depository requirement, ''Every state and county agency shall. . . .''

Alaska, Nevada, Arkansas, and Utah all have slightly less onerous requirements for the deposit of local documents than for state documents. Alaska requires the deposit of the same number of copies of the publications from both state and municipal agencies but in the case of the municipal agencies does not provide that additional copies may be requested as is provided with respect to the state publications. Alaska includes a definition of ''municipal'' and ''municipality.''

The Nevada provisions are similar to those of Alaska in that only one copy of the city, county, and regional publications is to be deposited (and ''a specified number of copies,'' of the state publications). The Nevada statute begins with a declaration of legislative intent that opens with the words ''All state and local government publications. . . .''

Arkansas has had legislation since 1947 providing for the deposit of publications with the University of Arkansas. One section of the act provides for twenty copies of state publications to be sent to the university, and another section of the same act states that two copies of county and municipal publications should be sent. The new 1979 Arkansas legislation also encompasses local publications. It makes no distinction between state and local publications as to the particular publications to be furnished or the number of copies to be supplied. In the subsection on the list of publications, the list is called ''a list of State publications'' and is to be distributed to state agencies and contracting libraries. This variance did not occur in Hawaii because that law does not provide for the publication of a documents list.

Utah law provides for the deposit of only two copies of each publication issued by a political subdivision. As mentioned in Chapter 4, the Utah definition of ''political subdivision'' is comprehensive.

Municipal and local depository legislation in other states is not identified here because it is not part of the state's depository legislation. The Maryland legislation is included because the state has no legislation for a depository system but does have code sections on the deposit of state publications, county codes, and municipal documents. The Maryland legislation provides for the deposit of single copies in a few named libraries and agencies.

Other mention of city and county documents in depository legislation includes the provision of the Nebraska legislation that defines ''governmental publications'' to include regional organizations and intergovernmental bodies which, of course, could include some agencies below the state level. Another provision of the Nebraska statute that is relevant to a discussion of city and county documents is the section stating that the Nebraska Publications Clearinghouse shall provide access to local governmental publications.

Mention of municipal libraries as being eligible to become depositories is found in the statutes of some states but is not significant here because the more widely used term ''public libraries'' is broader and encompasses municipal libraries. The chapter on depository libraries (Chapter 7) lists the types of libraries that may be designated as depository libraries.

LIST 5

DUTIES OF STATE AGENCIES

Alabama— . . . the state printer or other person printing such report or document shall print two hundred and fifty additional copies for the use of the department of archives and history. ALA. CODE § 41-6-12

Alaska—(a)Each state agency shall deposit, upon release, at least four copies of each of its state publications in the center. Additional copies of each publication may be requested by the center for deposit in quantities necessary to meet the needs of the depository library system and to provide inter-library service to those libraries not having depository status.

(b) Each state agency shall notify the center of the creation of all data published or compiled by or for it at public expense and provide for its accessibility through the center, unless the data is protected by the constitutional right to privacy or is of a type stated by law to be confidential or the agency is otherwise prohibited by law from doing so.

(c) The center is also a depository for publications of municipalities and regional educational attendance areas, including surveys and studies produced by a municipality or regional educational attendance area or produced for it on contract. Four copies of each publication produced for a municipality or regional educational attendance area may be deposited with the center for record and distribution purposes.

(d) Each municipality or regional attendance area may notify the center of the creation of all data published or compiled by or for it at public expense and provide for its accessibility through the center, unless the data is protected by the constitutional right to privacy or is of a type stated by law to be confidential or the municipality or regional educational attendance area is otherwise prohibited by law from doing so.

(e) When a research project or study is conducted for a person by a state agency, a municipality, or a regional educational attendance area, even though no state funding is involved, the state agency, municipality or regional educational attendance area shall request that person for permission to make copies of its final report available to the center under AS 14.56.090—14.56.180. If permission is granted, the report shall be deposited with the center. ALASKA STAT. § 14.56.120

Each state agency shall and each municipality and regional educational attendance area may designate one of its employees to be responsible for depositing the materials and information specified in AS 14.56.120.ALASKA STAT. § 14.56.123

Upon notification of the creation of data under AS 14.56.120, a state agency shall and a municipality or regional educational attendance area may prepare an abstract or summary of it. ALASKA STAT. § 14.56.125 (a)

Upon the request of the center, a state agency shall furnish the center with a complete list of its current state publications, data published or compiled by or for it at public expense, and a copy of its mailing or exchange lists. However, data which is protected by the constitutional right to privacy or is of a type stated by law to be confidential or which the agency is otherwise prohibited by law from distributing may not be furnished to the center. ALASKA STAT. § 14.56.130

Arizona— . . . the department [of libraries] shall make requisition upon the secretary of state, the heads of departments and all officers and agents of the state for the number of copies of official publications the department needs for the depository system and any exchange programs established pursuant to this subsection and it shall be the duty of the officers to supply them. ARIZ. REV. STAT. § 41-1335

Arkansas—All State agencies, including the General Assembly . . . , and all local governments, . . . shall furnish to the State Library, upon release, a specified number of copies of each of its State or local publications, to enable the State Publications Clearinghouse to meet the needs of the Depository Library System and to provide library loan services to those libraries without depository status. Such distribution will be required only if sufficient funds are appropriated for the printing of these materials by the agencies, boards, and commissions, and for the distribution thereof by the Arkansas State Library to depository libraries . . . ARK. STAT. ANN. § 6-307 (a)

(d) Each State and local agency printing or duplicating publications of the type which are to be made available to the State Publications Clearinghouse shall, if sufficient funds are available therefor, print or duplicate fifty (50) additional copies or such lesser number as may be requested by the State Library, for deposit with the State Publications Clearinghouse of the State Library for distribution to established depository libraries or interstate library exchange. Provided, however, that if a State agency or a local governmental agency does not have sufficient funds or resources available to furnish said fifty [50] copies to the State Publications Clearinghouse of the State Library, they shall notify the State Library and deliver to the State Publications Clearinghouse three (3) copies of each publication to be maintained in the State Library, to be indexed and made available on loan to participating libraries through the interlibrary loan services of the State Library. ARK. STAT. ANN. § 6-307 (d)

California— . . . of publications not printed by the State Printer, the department, commission or other agency concerned shall print one hundred (100) copies for such distribution. CAL. GOV'T CODE § 14901

Publications not printed by the State Printer shall be distributed by the issuing department, commission or other agency as soon as practicable after printing, first to all "complete depositories," and second to "selective depositories," designated by the Department of General Services. CAL. GOV'T CODE § 14904

All state departments, commissions and other agencies shall, upon request, supply information to the State Library for the preparation of the monthly or quarterly lists and the annual cumulative lists. CAL. GOV'T CODE § 14910

Whenever any state agency maintains a mailing list of public officials or other persons to whom publications or other printed matter is sent without charge, the state agency shall correct its mailing list and verify its accuracy at least once each year. [The section continues with procedural details.] CAL. GOV'T CODE § 14911

Colorado—Every state agency shall, upon publication, deposit at least four copies of each of its state publications (with the exception of audiovisual materials) with the center. One copy of each such audiovisual material shall be deposited with the center. The center may require additional copies of certain state publications to be deposited when designated by the state librarian as being required to fulfill the purposes of this part 2. COLO. REV. STAT. § 24-90-204

Upon request by the state librarian, each state agency shall furnish the center with a complete list of its current state publications. COLO. REV. STAT. § 24-90-205

Connecticut—Designated staff in each state agency shall be responsible for supplying the publications of that agency to the state library. Each such agency shall notify the state library of the identity of such designated staff within thirty days after October 1, 1977, and upon any change of personnel. Said staff shall supply the state library annually or upon request with a complete list of the agency's current publications.

Every state agency shall, upon publication, deposit a sufficient number of copies of each of its publications with the state library to meet the needs of the depository library system. CONN. GEN. STAT. ANN. § 11-9d

Delaware—Every state agency shall provide and deposit with the Department sufficient copies of all publications issued by such agencies for the purpose of making accessible to Delaware and other citizens, resource materials published at the expense of the State. DEL. CODE ANN. tit. 29, § 8610 (8) (b)

Florida—(2) Each and every state official, state department, state board, state court or state agency of any kind, issuing public documents shall furnish the division of library services of the department of state twenty-five copies of each of those public documents, as issued, for deposit in and distribution by the division. However, if the division shall so request, as many as twenty-five additional copies of each public document shall be supplied to it. . . . (4) The division shall also be furnished by any state official, department or agency having charge of their distribution, as issued, bound journals of each house of the legislature; acts of the legislature, both local or special and general; annotated acts of the legislature, and revisions and compilations of the Laws of Florida. The number of copies furnished shall be determined by requests of the division, which number in no case shall exceed twenty-five copies of the particular publication and, in the case of legislative acts, annotated legislative acts, and revisions and compilations of the laws, not more than two copies. (5) In any case in which any state official, state department, state board, state court, or state agency of any class or kind has more than ten copies of any one kind of publication from time to time heretofore issued, he or it shall, upon request of the division, supply said division with one copy of each such publication for deposit in the state library. FLA. STAT. ANN. § 257.05

[Agencies are empowered to distribute publications to the general library of institutions in the university system (§ 283.22), state legal depositories (§ 283.23), and the Library of Congress (§ 283.24).]

At the time of publication, or as soon thereafter as practicable, each agency, pursuant to subsection (1)(d), shall forward not less than the number of copies required in s.257.05 F. S. of each of its publications to the State Library of the Division of Library Services of the Department of State. FLA. STAT. ANN. § 283.28

Georgia—The Governor and all of the officers who are, or may be, required to make reports to the General Assembly, shall furnish the librarian with at least three copies of each of said reports. . . . GA. CODE ANN. § 101-210

Each department and institution within the executive branch of State government shall make a report on or before December 1 of each year to the State Librarian containing a list by title of all public documents published or issued by such department or institution during the preceding State of Georgia fiscal year. The report shall also contain a statement noting the frequency of publication of each such public document. GA. CODE ANN. § 101-203

Hawaii—Every state and county agency shall immediately upon release of a publication, deposit fifteen copies with the state publications distribution center and one copy each with the state archives and the University of Hawaii. Additional copies of the publications shall be deposited with the publications distribution center upon request of the state librarian so long as copies are available. HAWAII REV. STAT. § 93-3

Idaho—It shall be the duty of the head of every agency, board, bureau, commission or department of the state of Idaho, including all state supported institutions of higher education in Idaho, to deposit with the librarian of the Idaho state library for use and distribution to the academic, regional public, special libraries of Idaho, the Library of Congress, and to others within the discretion of the state librarian twenty (20) copies of all documents, reports, surveys, monographs, serial publications, compilations, pamphlets, bulletins, leaflets, circulars, maps, charts or broadsides of a public nature which it prints, mimeographs or otherwise reproduces for public distribution. IDAHO CODE § 33-2510

Illinois—All State agencies shall provide and deposit with the Illinois State Library sufficient copies of all publications issued by such State agencies for its collection and for exchange purposes. ILL. ANN. STAT. ch 128 § 121

Indiana—Each and every state official, state department, state board, state commission or state agency of any kind, which issues public documents shall furnish the state library fifty (50) copies of all publications issued by them whether printed, mimeographed, or duplicated in any way, which are not issued solely for use within the issuing agency. However, if the library requests, as many as twenty-five (25) additional copies of each public document shall be supplied. [Exemptions: publications for which other provision is made by law (but 2 copies shall go to the State Library), publications of units of the state universities (but 2 copies shall go to the state library), and publications of university presses, directives for internal administration, etc.] IND. CODE ANN. § 4-23-7-23.5

Iowa—Upon issuance of a state publication a state agency shall deposit with the depository library center at no cost to the center, seventy-five copies of the publication, or a lesser amount if specified by the depository librarian. IOWA CODE ANN. § 303A.24

Kansas—Each state agency shall deposit with the Kansas state library copies of any publication issued by such state agency in such quantity as shall be specified by the state librarian. KAN. STAT. ANN. § 75-2566

Annually each state agency shall furnish to the state library a complete list of their publications for the previous year which the state librarian shall use to maintain a permanent record of publications. KAN. STAT. ANN. § 75-2567

Every state agency that prints or otherwise reproduces more than fifty (50) copies of any publication, except through the director of printing or the central duplicating service, shall make two additional copies of each publication it reproduces and shall deliver such additional copies to the state library for its use, unless the same are confidential. KAN. STAT. ANN. § 75-3048c

Kentucky—It shall be the duty of all departments, boards, commissions, officers or other agencies of the Commonwealth to supply to the central depository copies of each of their reports and publications issued for general public distribution after July 1, 1958, in the number and in the manner prescribed by rule or regulation promulgated by the department pursuant to KRS 171.450. KY. REV. STAT. ANN. § 171.500

Louisiana—All agencies of state government shall furnish to the secretary of state sufficient copies of each record mentioned in R. S. 25:121. . . . LA. REV. STAT. ANN. § 25:122

Each agency of state government shall furnish to the secretary of state semiannually a list of all its printed and mimeographed publications issued for public distribution. . . . LA. REV. STAT. ANN § 25:123

Maine—At least 18 copies of all other publications, including periodicals, bulletins, pamphlets, leaflets and special reports issued by any agency or by any legislative committee shall be delivered to the State Librarian. The agency or committee preparing a publication shall have the authority to determine the date on which a publication may be released, except as may be otherwise provided by law. ME. REV. STAT. ANN. tit. 1, § 501-A

Maryland [Agencies file copies of publications with certain named libraries.]

Massachusetts—Every state agency receiving, issuing, or distributing a publication as defined below shall provide the State Librarian with no less than eight copies of each such publication. . . .

Each issuing agency shall take full cognizance of this requirement when contracting for the number of copies to be produced of any publication.

The required copies shall be forwarded to the State Librarian no later than five working days after they are received by the agency from the printer or contractor. ADMINISTRATIVE BULLETIN 76-5 (May 12, 1976)

Michigan—Each state official, state department, state board, state commission, and state agency which issues or publishes a public document shall furnish to the state library a minimum of 75 copies of each document issued in printed, mimeographed, or other duplicated form, which is not issued solely for use within the issuing agency. Additional copies of each public document shall be supplied upon the request of the state librarian [Exemptions: Publications of the units of the state universities (except that 2 copies shall be deposited in the state library), and publications of university presses, directives for internal administration, etc.] MICH. COMP. LAWS ANN. § 397.56

Minnesota—Except as provided in sections 5.08, 16.02, and 648.39, when any department, agency, or official of the state issues for public distribution any book, document, journal, map, pamphlet, or report, copies thereof shall be delivered immediately as follows: [libraries and groups of libraries are named and provision is made for additional copies.] MINN. STAT. ANN. § 15.18

Mississippi—All agencies of state government shall furnish to the director of the Mississippi Library Commission sufficient copies of each public document printed. . . . MISS. CODE ANN. § 25-51-3

Each agency of state government shall furnish to the director of the Mississippi Library Commission semiannually a list of all its publications issued for public distribution. . . . MISS. CODE ANN. § 25-51-5

Missouri—Every state agency, as enumerated in section 181.100, shall, upon release, deposit with the state library sufficient copies of each of its publications to meet the purposes of section 181.100 to 181.140, and sections 182.140 and 182.291, RSMo. MO. ANN. STAT. § 181.140

Montana—Every state agency shall deposit upon release at least four copies of each of its state publications with the state library for record and depository purposes. Additional copies shall also be deposited in quantities certified to the agencies by the state library as required to meet the needs of the depository library system and to provide interlibrary loan service to those libraries without depository status. [Additional copies of sale copies shall be furnished only upon reimbursement of the full cost. If additional copies necessitate additional printing or other expense, that expense shall be reimbursed also.] MONT. CODE ANN. § 22-1-213

Upon request by the center, issuing state agencies shall furnish the center with a complete list of their current state publications and a copy of their mailing and/or exchange lists. MONT. CODE ANN. § 22-1-216

Nebraska—Every state agency head or his appointed records officer shall notify the Nebraska Publications Clearinghouse of his identity. The records officer shall upon release of a state publication deposit eight copies and a short summary including author, title, and subject of each of its state publications with the Nebraska Publications Clearinghouse for record purposes. . . . Additional copies shall also be deposited in the Nebraska Publications Clearinghouse in quantities certified to the agencies by the clearinghouse as required to meet the needs of the Nebraska publications depository system. NEB. REV. STAT. § 51-413

Upon request by the Nebraska Publications Clearinghouse, records officers of state agencies shall furnish the clearinghouse with a complete list of their current state publications. NEB. REV STAT. § 51-416

Nevada—Every state agency shall, upon release, deposit a specified number of copies of each of its state publications with the state publications distribution center to meet the needs of the depository library system and to provide interlibrary loan service to those libraries without depository status. This distribution shall be required only if sufficient funds are appropriated for the printing of these materials. NEV. REV. STAT. § 378.180

New Humpshire—Each state agency shall print 25 copies of their publications for deposit with the state librarian. N.H. REV. STAT. ANN. § 202-B:2

New Jersey—[See §§ 52:14-25.1 and 25.2, which provide for filing of 75 copies of annual or special reports, and if typewritten, one copy (25.1); and 75 copies of serial or other publications, and if typewritten, one copy (25.2).]

New Mexico—Unless otherwise directed by the state librarian, every state agency shall deposit twenty-five copies of all its publications intended for public distribution, when issued, with the state library depository for depository and distribution purposes, excluding those publications issued strictly for internal use and those intended for public sale. N.M. STAT. ANN. § 18-2-4.1

New York—Every state officer, department, commission, institution and board shall, as soon as any report thereby is printed, deliver two hundred copies thereof to the state library. N.Y. STATE PRINT. & PUB. DOC. LAW § 6

. . . the regents shall maintain a duplicate department to which each state department, bureau, board or commission shall send not less than five copies of each of its publications when issued, and after completing its distribution, any remaining copies which it no longer requires. N.Y. EDUC. LAW § 250

North Carolina—Every State official and every head of a State department, institution or agency issuing any printed report, bulletin, map, or other publication, shall, on request, furnish copies of such reports, bulletins, maps or other publications to the following institutions in the number set out below: [15 institutions are named.] N.C. GEN. STAT. § 147-50

Every State official and every head of a State department, institution, or agency issuing any document, report, directory, statistical compendium, bibliography, map, rule, regulation, newsletter, pamphlet, brochure, periodical, or other publications shall deposit five copies with the Division of State Library of the Department of Cultural Resources. N.C. GEN. STAT. § 147-50.1

North Dakota—The state purchasing and printing agent shall arrange to deposit with the state library commission eight copies of all publications issued by all executive, legislative, and judicial agencies of state government intended for general public distribution. These publications shall be provided to the state library commission without charge. Should expense and limited supply of state publications, particularly audiovisual items, make strict compliance with the depository requirement impossible, the state library commission shall accept as many copies as an agency can afford to provide. However, no less than two copies shall be provided to the state library commission by each agency . . . . In circumstances not directly involving the state purchasing and printing agent, a state agency shall comply with the depository requirement by arranging with the necessary parties for the printing and deposit of eight copies of any state publication issued. N.D. CENT. CODE § 54-24-09

Ohio—Any department, division, bureau, board, or commission of the state government issuing a report, pamphlet, document, or other publication intended for general public use and distribution, which publication is reproduced by duplicating processes such as mimeograph, multigraph, planograph, rotaprint, or multilith, shall cause to be delivered to the state library one hundred and fifty copies of such publication, subject to the provisions of section 125.42 of the Revised Code. OHIO REV. CODE ANN. § 149.11

Oklahoma—Every agency, authority, department, commission, board, institution, office or officer of the state, except institutions of higher education but specifically including any board of regents for higher education, who issue or publish, at state expense, regardless of form, any book, chart, document, facsimile, map, paper, periodical, report, serial, survey or any other type of publication, including statutes, statute supplements and sessions laws, shall immediately deposit a minimum of twenty-five (25) copies with the Publications Clearinghouse of the Department.

[Upon failure of an agency to comply with the section, a procedure for notice and mandamus proceedings is established.] OKLA. STAT. ANN. tit. 65, § 3-114

[Tit. 74, § 3106.1 provides in detail for records officers of state agencies and their duties.]

Oregon—[Person responsible for distribution shall make available to state librarian 50 copies of each bill and daily calendar and 125 copies of each legislative interim report.] OR. REV. STAT. § 171.215

[Person responsible for distribution shall make available to the state librarian copies of all publications. The state printer may withhold the prescribed number of copies from each printing order and forward them to the state librarian.] OR. REV. STAT. § 182.070

Pennsylvania—The Department of Property and Supplies shall direct each such department, board, commission or agency to supply it with the number of copies, if any, of each publication remaining after regular distribution according to existing allocations, but in no case to exceed two hundred fifty copies. . . . PA. STAT. ANN. tit. 24, § 4425

Rhode Island—It shall be the duty of each state officer and director, upon the requisition of the state librarian to supply the state library with a sufficient number of each publication issued from his department to enable him to carry into effect the provisions of chapters 1 and 2 of this title. R.I. GEN. LAWS § 29-1-7

South Dakota—Every state agency shall upon release, deposit at least fourteen copies of each of its state publications, with the state library for record and depository system purposes, with the exception of audio-visual materials. At least two copies of audio-visual materials shall be deposited with the state library for record and depository system purposes. S.D. COMPILED LAWS ANN. § 14-1A-3

Upon request by the center, each issuing state agency shall furnish the center with a complete list of its current state publications and a copy of its mailing and exchange lists. S.D. COMPILED LAWS ANN. § 14-1A-4

Tennessee—It shall be the duty of every officer of this state making any publication or in charge of the printing of any document for the state to notify the secretary of state of their publication and to send to the secretary of state such number of copies as he shall demand in accordance with the provisions of § 12-607—12-612. TENN. CODE ANN. § 12-609

Texas—(a) Each state agency shall furnish to the Texas State Library its state publications in the quantity specified by the rules of the Texas Library and Historical Commission. The commission may not require more than 75 copies of a state publication.

(b) On the printing of or the awarding of a contract for the printing of a publication, a state agency shall arrange for the required number of copies to be deposited with the Texas State Library. TEX. REV. CIV. STAT. ANN. art. 5442a(3)

Each state agency shall designate one or more staff persons as the agency's publications contact person and shall notify the Texas State Library of the identity of each person selected. A state agency's contact person shall furnish to the Texas State Library each month a list of all of the agency's state publications that were produced during the preceding month. TEX. REV. CIV. STAT. ANN. art. 5442a(5)

If a state agency's printing is done by contract, an account for the printing may not be approved and a warrant for the printing may not be issued unless the agency first furnishes to the State Board of Control a receipt from the state librarian for the publication or a written waiver from the state librarian exempting the publication from the requirements of this Act. TEX. REV. CIV. STAT. ANN. art. 5442a(6)

Utah—Each state agency shall deposit with the commission copies of each state publication issued by it in such number as shall be specified by the state librarian. UTAH CODE ANN. § 37-5-3(1)

Each political subdivision shall deposit with the commission two copies of each state publication issued by it. UTAH CODE ANN. § 37-5-3(2)

Each state agency shall deposit with the commission two copies of audio-visual materials, and tape or disc recordings issued by it for bibliographic listing and retention in the state library collection. Materials not deemed by the commission to be of major public interest will be listed but no copies will be required for deposit. UTAH CODE ANN. § 37-5-3(5)

Virgin Islands—Each governmental agency shall be responsible for supplying the Territorial Librarian with at least two copies of each public document designated for deposit for each depository library, within five weekdays from the publication date of said public document. V.I. CODE ANN. tit. 3, § 883(c)(1)

Virginia—Every agency shall furnish two copies of each of its publications at the time of issue to the Virginia State Library and shall deliver one copy to the Division of Purchases and Supply at the same time. The State Librarian may require an agency to deliver to the State Library not exceeding one hundred additional copies of any publication delivered to him under this section. VA. CODE § 2.1-467.2

Washington—Every state agency shall promptly deposit copies of each of its state publications with the state library in quantities as certified by the state librarian as required to meet the needs of the depository library system. Upon consent of the issuing state agency such state publications as are printed by the public printer shall be delivered directly to the center.

In the interest of economy and efficiency, the state librarian may specifically or by general rule exempt a given state publication or class of publications from the requirements of this section in full or in part. WASH. REV. CODE ANN. § 40.06.030

Upon request by the center, issuing state agencies shall furnish the center with a complete list of its current state publications and a copy of its mailing and/or exchange lists. WASH. REV. CODE ANN. § 40.06.060

Wisconsin—Three copies of all printed, mimeographed, or otherwise reproduced state publications, reports, releases and other matter published at the expense of the state shall be sent to the historical society by the department of administration in accordance with s. 35.85(7). In those instances where a given publication is not distributed by the department of administration, 3 copies shall be sent to the historical society by the department, commission or agency of origin. WIS. STAT. ANN. § 44.06

Wyoming—Each and every state officer, commission, commissioner or board of a state institution shall deposit in the state library, for its permanent file, four (4) copies of every publication which they issue. WYO. STAT. § 9-1-109

Each and every state officer, commission, commissioner or board of a state institution shall deposit in the university library at Laramie at least one (1) copy of every publication and report which they issue. WYO. STAT. § 9-1-110

NOTES

1. Some unsubstantiated estimates are: Texas—1,000, California—500, and Louisiana and North Carolina—250 or 300. Texas counts planning districts and other substate agencies. This practice is commendable because that many more publications are being monitored by the state documents clearinghouse and are being brought to the attention of the public.

2. Charles Wolfe, "Current Problems Facing Law Libraries," *Law Library Journal* 71:112 (February 1978).

3. LeRoy C. Merritt, "Municipal and State Document Collecting in the Rocky Mountain Region, with Indications of Important Documents," American Library Association, Committee on Public Documents, *Public Documents*, 1938, p. 177n.

4. Rosita LoRusso and Linda Kennedy, "The Crisis in the California State Documents Distribution System" (1973?), p. 12, in Documents on Documents Collection.

5. John J. Boll, "Tame the Terror for Its Use; or, What are Wisconsin Documents?" *Wisconsin Library Bulletin* 70:82 (March 1974).

6. Gar T. Elison, "The Problem of Government Publications in Idaho," *Pacific Northwest Library Association Quarterly* 34:16 (October 1969).

7. Genevieve M. Casey and Edith Phillips, *Management and Use of State Documents in Indiana*, Wayne State University, Office of Urban Library Research, Research Report no. 2 (Detroit, Mich.:1969), p. 7.

8. Ibid., pp. 68-69.

9. California Legislature, Assembly, Interim Committee on Governmental Reorganization, "Information Services," *First Partial Report* (Sacramento: 1951), p. 117.

10. Letter to author from Sandra K. Faull, Documents Librarian, New Mexico State Library, March 1979.

11. Louis Coatney, "Questions and Answers: Alaska State Publications," *Sourdough* 13:4 (May 1976).

12. Casey and Phillips, *Management and Use of State Documents in Indiana*, pp. 15-20. At p. 21, Casey says variance is from 1 to 500. She includes, it seems evident, copies deposited for exchange as well as for depository distribution.

13. 1977 Tex. Att'y Gen. OP. 4356 (H-1061, September 17, 1977).

14. California Department of General Services, "Library Distribution Act Procedures and Definitions, M-698" (1973), p. i.

15. Ibid., Exhibit H, p. [1].

6. THE DISTRIBUTION CENTER

The distribution statutes in the individual states were summarized in 1940 in the *Manual on the Use of State Publications*.[1] The italicized names of the officers and entities that had distribution duties called attention to the fact that almost every state had three or four agencies with such duties. Many of these statutes are still in force, particularly those on the distribution of legal materials, such as court reports and session laws. However, in most states these statutes have been supplemented by modern depository legislation which provides that a single agency shall distribute to the libraries in the state. This single agency, usually the state library agency, acts as an intermediary between the state agencies which produce the publications and the libraries which make them available to the public. Because of the functions, both statutory and voluntary, performed by these intermediate agencies, the availability and usefulness of state documents in the libraries in the individual states have improved noticeably since 1940. A survey of these functions reveals the changes which the new depository laws have made.

The duties and responsibilities of the intermediate agencies are both more varied and more numerous than those imposed by legislation on the state agencies or on the depository libraries. Only through the diligent exercise of its responsibilities by the distribution center can the success of a depository program be achieved. Distribution centers have taken seriously the mandate to administer a depository program and have exercised their prerogative to issue rules and regulations when so authorized. In order to get a full picture of a depository system from the point of view of the administering agency, the statutes, the regulations, and the informally assumed duties must all be examined.

Of course, no two states are alike. What is mandated by statute in one state is governed by a regulation in another state and may be performed informally in a third state. No table of statutory sections outlining the duties of the distribution centers has been prepared because these sections are less identifiable than those on the duties of the state agencies or the depository libraries. Some states provide only that the center shall distribute the publications, and in another section of their laws include a provision for a checklist. Other states follow the 1963 Washington example, "shall promote the establishment of an orderly depository system," and leave the duties of the center to the administrator's imagination. Since the adoption of the "Guidelines for State Distribution Center Activities" by the Government Documents Round Table in July 1980, no administrator should be at a loss for ideas to enhance the local program. (The Guidelines are reproduced in the Appendix.)

In recent years, some depository laws have included a separate section on distribution center duties. Florida (1967) lists three specific duties; Michigan (1976) and Iowa (1978), five; Texas (1979), six; Connecticut (1977), nine; and Oklahoma (1978), ten.

The statutory duties most often found include: (1) establish, supervise, and administer a depository program, (2) receive and distribute publications, (3) designate and contract with depository libraries, (4) maintain a collection of state publications of the home state, and (5) publish an official list of state publications.

DUTY TO ESTABLISH A DEPOSITORY PROGRAM

This basic, general duty is included in legislation, with variations, in sixteen states. Interestingly, the Washington legislature changed the state's 1963 statement in 1977 to read "utilize the depository library system to permit citizens access to state publications." Variations include:

Alaska—promote the establishment of an orderly depository library system (also Montana and South Dakota)

Connecticut—administer a depository library system

Indiana—establish a state document depository system

Iowa—administer the depository library center *and* establish and operate a depository library system

Kansas—establish, maintain, and operate a depository system

Kentucky—establish procedures for collection and distribution by the central depository

Louisiana—administer [the statutory provisions] (also Mississippi)

Nebraska—establish and operate a depository system

North Dakota—develop an optional selection program

Washington—utilize the depository library system to permit citizens access to state publications

Wisconsin—administer the depository library program

One reason for including a specific authorization for the administration of the depository library program in the legislation is the trend, on the part of appropriating units and budget officers, to fund only legislatively approved programs. Another reason is that difficulties, such as those experienced in California when the administration of the program was fragmented, may arise.[2]

DUTY TO RECEIVE PUBLICATIONS FROM THE STATE AGENCIES

Receiving and distributing state publications are the primary functions of the intermediate agency. In fact, in states where a separate division or section has been created by statute, this separate unit is often called a distribution center. In Nebraska and Texas, the name used is clearinghouse, a word that carries the dictionary meaning, "a central agency for collection, classification and distribution."

The receiving of publications from the state agencies is never entirely automatic. At the very least, state agencies need reminders and encouragement to do their duty.

Some publications are easier to secure than others, the easiest kinds being those most frequently published. In the case of a weekly publication, setting up a control scheme to assure that a failure to receive an issue will immediately be noticed is not a complicated procedure. A point to be remembered is that state publications are largely serial in nature, with the percentage varying between 60 and 80 percent.

For any serial title already being received, clerks should be trained to observe gaps and to follow up with a telephone call or postcard claiming the missing number. The mention of telephone calls brings to mind the fact that most distribution centers, being part of the state library, are located in the state capital. Telephoning and even visiting nearby state agencies, which are logical functions to be conducted at the state level, can be conveniently done under these conditions.

Next, a "date-expected file" can be created for serials. For dailies, weeklies, and monthlies, a list of titles is perhaps sufficient as a guide for a periodic check to determine that none has ceased publication. If Kardex files are used, color-coding can reveal the titles to be checked. For semi-annual and annual publications, the date-expected file can be arranged by month and used both in the distribution center for checking and as a mail-out item to state agencies to alert them that the center will be expecting their publications. These sheets might be mailed quarterly to every agency on the list, with the agency name highlighted or checked before insertion in the envelope. The date-expected file is a time-consuming procedure, involving preparing the list, canceling items as the publications are received, and carrying forward the items that are late, but if computer time is available, the results can easily justify the time invested.

An accurate record of the date on which an issue of a publication is received is necessary for the preparation of a publications-expected list. The record of date received is also helpful in claiming missing numbers because it reveals whether or not the issues are published in numerical order. It also provides a clue when straightening out misnumbering problems.

All of the foregoing discussion will be familiar to serials librarians. The differences, when dealing with state documents, are (1) the universe of titles is smaller and can be given more individual attention, (2) the records on receipt should be given more attention because all the depository libraries are dependent on the distribution center's securing multiple copies before the publication goes out of print, (3) the depository libraries are dependent on the distribution center for "negative information"—reports on misnumbering, ceased publication, and other notes, (4) claiming can often be done by telephone because the distribution center is in the state capital, and (5) claiming—and alerting about expected publications, and so on—can often be done by "messenger service" mail which, of course, is "free."

RECEIVING MONOGRAPHS AND NEW SERIALS

The real problems in receiving publications arise when a monograph is issued or a new serial started. There are various ways of learning about new publications issued by agencies with which contact has already been established. The procedure is called "discovery" and Paul Pross defines it as "the process by which the existence of a document is ascertained."[3] The enterprising receiver/distributor must do all, or many of the following things.

First, scan the newsletters and monthlies of the state agencies. Check through the annual reports for lists of publications issued and look at the inside covers of monographic serials for other titles issued in the series.

Second, read the state newspapers, particularly the ones published at the state capital. This is often an ideal source for noting the release of new reports and studies.

Develop personal contacts with officers and employees in other agencies. Visit the legislature when it is in session and observe the publications being distributed to the legislators. Because several states (such as Maryland and Minnesota) have recently enacted laws prohibiting indiscriminate distribution to legislators, this suggestion may be less useful in the future. In the past, it was recommended that the librarian visit the legislative chambers on the day after adjournment when the janitors were cleaning out the legislators' desks. Oregon mentions a similar activity, "going through agency discard boxes, if available."[4]

Encourage the depository librarians to report titles they have managed to procure for their own library and titles they have not received but have seen listed.

In some states, the state agencies have a duty to appoint a liaison or records officer (Nebraska, for example) from whom the distribution center receives publications. This relationship can be enhanced by personal visits which will make the followup easier and will acquaint the state agencies with the needs of the depository libraries.

Missouri, Kansas, and Texas have prepared handbooks on their depository programs for use by the state agencies. These handbooks include an informal statement on the purpose of the depository library law, the law itself, rules and regulations, lists of the depository libraries, and other background information to enhance state agency participation in the program. The Missouri handbook even advises the state agencies that pickup services are available. The forms used in the acquisition procedures in the three states can serve as examples for administrators in other states.

The Nevada practice of collecting the publications from the department of state printing, provided for in the Nevada statute, is an alternative for those states that have a state printer.

Oregon amended its law in 1979 to provide that "the State Printer may withhold the prescribed number of copies from each printing order and forward them to the State Librarian. . . ."

Thus, receiving publications includes claiming missing issues, requesting new titles, and maintaining contacts with the state agencies. However, there is more to receiving than these regular routines.

RECEIVING PUBLICATIONS FROM NEWLY CREATED AGENCIES

Awareness of the creation of a new state agency and the issuance of its first publications must also be part of the acquisitions program. The terminology changes here from "receiving" to "acquiring" because the responsibility of the documents administrator changes and becomes more exacting. A state agency cannot realistically be expected to send publications to the distribution center until it has been made aware of the distribution program. Even though the laws in most states place the burden on the state agencies to send their publications, the agencies, especially new agencies, need to have the law brought to their attention. The administrator of the distribution center must actively attempt to acquire the publications of new agencies. A special letter, perhaps accompanied by an eye-catching brochure, should be prepared and sent to new state agencies. A personal visit may also be feasible and may be even more effective.

LIST OF AGENCIES

How does a documents administrator find out about the existence of a new state agency so that it can be brought into the program? Sources for information include session laws, legislative resolutions, executive orders, state telephone directories, bluebooks or rosters, newspapers, and any other lists of state agencies.

The distribution center should compile a list of agencies based on all these sources so that no agency that might publish is overlooked. The list should include not only newly created agencies, but also those that were merged, changed their names, or were abolished. The newspaper is a source for popular names of agencies, which should also be included. Cross-references should be made for the popular names, for all variant forms of the agency names, and for the key words in the agency names. All levee boards, hospitals, marketing boards, and so on, will thus be grouped by means of these cross-references.

AUTHORITY FILE

The authority file, if carefully prepared with notes on the statute or order creating, changing, or abolishing the agency, could become an authority list for catalogers and reference librarians, as well as a tool for the acquisition function of the distribution center. Some states already have a retrospective authority file which the documents administrator can use as a starting point. In states that do not have such a list, the documents administrator should start with a current list, based on a roster, bluebook, or telephone book. This current list can be kept up to date through the session laws and other sources cited, and, as time permits, can be expanded to include discontinued and merged agencies. An authority record for both past and future agencies provides a history record for each agency if the entries are cumulated. The computer-produced files of today make cumulations a mechanical process, thus eliminating the problems of yesterday when an updated record included only the new information.

The "Guidelines for Minimum State Servicing of State Documents" require that the state authority list be available for distribution. Publication of the list, either separately or as part of the state checklist, is strongly recommended because of its usefulness for cataloging and reference purposes in all types of libraries.

LIST OF CURRENT AGENCIES

As a byproduct of the authority list compiled from the session laws and executive orders, a list of current agencies should be prepared. Such a list would omit all agencies that have ceased, merged, or acquired new names. Essentially, it would be the mailing list of the documents administrator. For each agency currently in existence, the list should give name, address, and telephone number. Other useful information that could be incorporated includes (1) name of agency liaison, if the depository law requires that the state agencies appoint a liaison, (2) classification numbers, if the library uses a classification scheme based on agency names, (3) Anglo-American Cataloging Rules (AACR) headings, if different from the name used by the agency, and (4) records of reports of "no publications issued," if the law requires such reports. The list would be a complete record of all current information about an agency except its publications.

As was suggested for the authority file, it is recommended that the current list be published and distributed also. It would be useful for the depository libraries to be assured that the distribution center has all agencies on its mailing list. It would be invaluable to the nondepository libraries in the state, which must, in most states, request each publication individually from each agency. In this connection, the inclusion of the classification numbers in the list would be helpful because they would identify the agencies that have published. Lack of a classification number would be a sign that the agency need not be contacted. (Of course, the documents administrator should contact all agencies, whether or not they publish, so that no publications will be overlooked.)

The current list described above does not take the form of a separate list in all states. In Nebraska, it is a list, titled "Guide to Nebraska State Agencies," which is a supplement to the checklist. The Nebraska Guide is "designed for use in ordering publications from State agencies," and includes address and telephone number, agency classification number, and information on recent name or structural changes. In Nevada, addresses are added to the checklist. With more states changing to computer-produced checklists, adding addresses presents new problems, which perhaps will be solved by the publication of separate lists like the Nebraska one. In North Carolina, *The Docket* has a list of "Resource Persons in State Offices" that serves somewhat the same purpose.[5] Although no state seems to have a complete, published record of all the current information about each agency at this time, the author is working on one for Louisiana.

DUTY TO DISTRIBUTE PUBLICATIONS TO DEPOSITORY LIBRARIES

The distribution of publications, the other half of the receiving and distribution function, is an apparently simple function. Again, as is true of the duty to receive publications, appearances are deceiving. If all the depository libraries receive the same publications and if there are enough copies to go around, distribution problems are minimized. The distribution patterns and the quantity of publications available for distribution are the major problems.

Minor distribution problems arise when the publications have an unusual format, when postal rates change, when sorting and wrapping space are inadequate, and so forth. These problems are not the subject of legislation or regulations and must be solved on an administrative, or even clerical, level.

Obviously, adequate working space is a necessity. Because the functions involve large numbers of copies of publications, more space is needed than in library operations which involve only paper work or the handling of a few books. The operation is an in-and-out one, and proximity to the mailing facilities of the library is a distinct advantage. In Missouri, "the State Library has contracted with the Library Services Center for the distribution of documents."[6]

Those states with established distribution centers or clearinghouses do not always impose a duty to distribute, but do specify that contracts which provide for distribution shall be made with the depository libraries. States that specifically impose duties to distribute use such words as "send," "distribute," "furnish," or "deliver."

Distribution to depository libraries under modern depository legislation is automatic. That is, after a library has been designated as a depository library, state publications arrive at the library without further acquisition effort on the part of the depository librarian. It is this automatic distribution, as distinguished from the "on request" provisions of earlier legislation, which makes the depository program so valuable to librarians. North Carolina, although it amended its law to provide for one library in the state, still has "on request" legislation for the other libraries in the state.

One characteristic of distribution to depository libraries, its predictability, makes it a very satisfying activity for the distribution center. The mailing list is constant, and the addresses of the depository libraries do not change often. Although there are exceptions—new depositories are added, sometimes depositories withdraw, and libraries occasionally change their address—the mailings are generally the same month after month.

The physical task of distribution can be handled by assigning a bin or a specific spot on a shelf to each library and piling up publications until a sufficient quantity has accumulated to make a package.

Very few states specify in their legislation when the distribution to the depository libraries should be made. The California law says, "as soon as practicable after deposit in the library stockroom." In Ohio, because the law provides that undistributed copies should be returned to the issuing agencies after ninety days, the distribution must necessarily be made within ninety days. Missouri distributes weekly. The law in the Virgin Islands states that the distribution center is responsible for the subsequent distribution to the depository libraries within two calendar weeks from the date of receipt of said documents. In Maine, the date of release of a publication is determined by the agency or committee preparing the publication.

It is recommended that a supply of labels be addressed in advance for each library so that the labels are ready when it is time to mail. These preaddressed labels can be kept in a holder in the corner of the bin so that the label and the publications that are ready for mailing can be moved to the wrapping table in one step. A different procedure is followed in California, where all the packages in the shipment are identical because the printer always supplies sufficient copies and the selective depositories all receive the same publications, making it simple to run off a complete set of labels whenever a mailing is scheduled.

Some states (Louisiana, Mississippi, Nebraska, and Texas) have adopted special mailing labels for the depository program. Such a special label is a distinct advantage to the depository libraries because it immediately identifies the package as one containing depository items. If a special label is not used, it is recommended that a special code be included in the address so that the publications can be identified as depository materials. For example, in Missouri the packages are addressed to "Mo. Depository Docs. Libn," while the U.S. Government Printing Office uses the depository number as its code. Even in states where the mailing is done by the state's central distributing agency (Pennsylvania and Wisconsin), the address could include a code number. Especially in states which provide that depository items remain the property of the state, or of the state library agency, such coding should be used.

In connection with mailing, the 1977 provision in the Washington law, while not directly applicable to depository libraries or state agencies, states that any publication distributed to the public and the legislature shall be mailed at the lowest available postal rate.

The distribution to depository libraries by the state's central distributing agency (in California, the library stockroom and in Wisconsin, the Department of Administration) has little relationship to direct shipment by the state agencies to the libraries. In California, where the state printer supplies copies to the library stockroom, the statement of legislative intent, the definition of state publication, and the duties of the state librarian in determining the number of copies to be printed combine to give the state library agency a definite influence on the distribution. In Wisconsin, the state library agency furnishes the mailing lists for the publications which are to be distributed. These distributions by central distributing agencies accomplish the goals of a modern depository program.

On the other hand, direct distribution (as in North Carolina, for example, where the state agencies send copies on request to the libraries named in the statute) creates a separate distribution relationship for every library with every state agency. Fifteen libraries and perhaps a hundred state agencies which issue publications could result in fifteen hundred lines of communication, as contrasted with the situation in a state with centralized distribution, where the depository libraries each have only one line of communication for receiving publications.

In Montana, selective depository status is set up by arranging for the library's name to be added to the mailing lists of the appropriate state agencies.

RESTRICTIONS ON DISTRIBUTION

Missouri includes in its new (1976) legislation the restriction "No publications shall be distributed to any libraries unless a request is made therefor." The section might have been included to reassure legislators that the distribution would not be haphazard. However, the administrator of the Missouri program has stated that the provision was included to permit selective depositories. The language, which requires that the libraries select the publications they need, parallels that used in the 1922 amendment to the federal depository law to create the selective depository system.[7]

Rhode Island provides for distribution of state publications to libraries within the state, "except for such as are distributed by public law."

Several states have a restriction against "general public distribution." This provision is found first in the Montana legislation (1967), and then in Alaska (1970), Nebraska (1972), and South Dakota (1974). In the 1978 New Mexico law, the restriction against engaging in general distribution is qualified by "except in those cases where the state library does so in the course of operating as a library or a state extension service."

In New Hampshire, a provision on the distribution of legislative publications, judicial publications, and intraoffice and interoffice publications and forms is stated in the form of a restriction: "The state librarian shall not distribute copies of. . . ." The same result is accomplished in other states by statements that the distribution act shall not apply to certain publications, or, by excluding specified publications from the definition of state publications, as in Illinois, Minnesota, Missouri, Nevada, and Oregon.

DISTRIBUTION TO NATIONAL LIBRARIES

Other provisions concerning the libraries to which publications are to be distributed include the special provisions for distribution to the Library of Congress and the Center for Research Libraries in Chicago. Eleven states have such provisions in the statutes which are reproduced in this book. Connecticut, Indiana, Iowa, Kansas, Nevada, North Carolina, Ohio, Oklahoma, and South Dakota provide for two copies for the Library of Congress. Indiana adds, "excluding those where other provisions are made by law," and South Dakota's wording is, "shall assure that the Library of Congress shall receive two copies." Nebraska (since 1979 when the requirement was reduced from two copies) and Utah distribute one copy to the Library of Congress by law. Montana has a duty to enter into a depository contract with the Library of Congress, and Alaska may enter into such a contract. Texas names the Library of Congress and the Center for Research Libraries as depositories. Very often provisions for sending to the Library of Congress are included in the statutes for the distribution of session laws and statutory materials, or statutes governing the distribution of the court reports, which are not included in this compilation.

The model law published in the *Monthly Checklist of State Publications* (December 1969) was drafted as a guide for states that want to include the Library of Congress in their document distribution. The same model law provisions are included in the Council of State Governments' *1971 Suggested Legislation*.

The states that have made special provision for distribution to the Center for Research Libraries are Kansas, Montana, South Dakota, and Texas. The Connecticut law reads, "one copy to an additional national or regional research library." The state document librarian at the Center for Research Libraries has said that the center prefers being named specifically in the law, even though the center is, at the present time, the primary national research library specializing in the collection of state documents.

NUMBER OF COPIES DISTRIBUTED

In most states, only one copy of each publication is forwarded to each depository library. This undocumented assertion is derived from discussions with state document librarians who apparently had never envisioned the distribution of more than one copy, and corresponds to the practice of the federal depository system.

The laws of California, Hawaii, Ohio, and Pennsylvania specify one copy or a copy directly, and the North Dakota law does so by matching the number of copies to be furnished with the number of depository libraries. In California, certain libraries receive multiple copies which may be used for exchange.

The laws in Louisiana, Nevada, and Tennessee say two copies, and in Mississippi, "as many as two copies." The Arkansas law providing for the institutions of higher learning permits ordering of copies, "not to exceed three."

The Connecticut law says, "in accordance with the terms of their depository contracts"; that of Florida, "the number of copies desired" for libraries in the university system; and in Missouri, "such numbers of copies of such publications as [the state library] deems necessary."

LESS THAN FULL DISTRIBUTION

When the distribution center does not receive enough copies for full distribution, one or more copies are deposited in the state library collection. Usually, the publication is listed in the checklist, and distribution of the remaining copies to the depository libraries is made in accordance with established priorities. This ranking of the libraries usually takes into account the same factors that were considered when the depositories were designated. In addition, the number of items the library normally receives and the length of time the library has been in the program will influence the ranking.

The ratio of the documents distributed to the total listed in the state checklist is given in chart form in a 1978 Texas study. For the first five years of the distribution program (1970-1974), the percentage decreased from 52 to 48. In

1975, the percentage dropped to 35 and, in 1976, to 25. Because the total number of documents received at the state library increased almost fourfold during the years 1970-1976, from 1,048 to over 3,500, the quantity of the publications that the depository libraries actually received increased rather than decreased.

Other figures on the percent of known documents distributed are given in the State and Local Documents Task Force survey:[8]

Alaska—75 percent	New Hampshire—100 percent
California—Most	New Mexico—60 percent
Indiana—1/3	New York—13 percent
Kansas—44 percent	Oklahoma—75 percent
Maine—60 percent	Pennsylvania—25 percent
Massachusetts—41 percent	Rhode Island—20 percent
Mississippi—100 percent	Texas—20 percent
Missouri—Try to include	Utah—75 percent
Nebraska—All, on fiche	Washington—60 percent
Nevada—85 percent	

An awareness of the waste in distributing publications that will not be used is shown by two related Utah provisions. A provision permitting the distribution of additional copies "on the basis of demonstrated need, as determined by the state library" and a parallel provision that the state library commission "may omit from such distribution such official publications as it shall find and determine are of such limited public interest that such distribution will serve no reasonable public purpose" give considerable discretion to the state library commission. The permission to omit publications from distribution was added to the Utah law in 1963 when the section dealing with distribution to libraries was rewritten. When the Utah law was revised in 1979, the concept that agencies should not be required to supply more copies than were needed was stated, "Materials not deemed by the commission to be of major public interest will be listed but no copies will be required for deposit." Similarly, Arkansas excludes communications or documents "which are not of vital interest to the public."

COSTS AND SAVINGS IN DISTRIBUTION

Other elements of costs and savings in the distribution programs involve the charges, if any, for forwarding the documents to the depositories. The statutes which specifically state that such forwarding shall be done without cost are Arkansas ("without charge or cost") and Tennessee ("at the expense of the state"). On the other hand, the Florida statute provides that libraries in junior colleges shall be designated depositories for the Florida statutes and supplements, and may receive one copy of each volume on request without charge except for payment of shipping costs.

TEXAS DISTRIBUTION PLANS

"Standard distribution" in Texas includes (1) automatic distribution to the fifty-one depository libraries, (2) automatic distribution to twenty-four unofficial depositories, and (3) special orders from the 265 libraries that receive the monthly checklist. The difference between the official and the unofficial depositories is that the official depositories have been designated as such and the others have merely requested that they receive copies of everything that is "open for distribution." The official depositories receive more publications than the unofficial. The third group of libraries places special orders rather than blanket orders. The duty of California's state printer to fill requests from other libraries after the complete and selective depositories have received their copies is comparable to the Texas special orders.

Texas also has "clearinghouse distribution," which is the handling of distribution, correspondence, claims, and so forth for a particular publication on behalf of a state agency. A third type of distribution in Texas is designated "special requests" and refers to distribution in response to claims for back issues and noncurrent publications. The fourth type is "periodical distribution" which is a standing order plan for periodicals that are available on an annual basis to the 265 libraries that select from the checklist.

The Texas plan is very liberal since it does not limit the distribution to depository libraries. The plan permits libraries that do not have a depository designation either to receive state publications automatically or to select publications individually by title, with special provisions for periodicals. In its special request service, the plan has adopted the functions of a gift and exchange department.[9]

DISTRIBUTION IN MICROFORMAT

Texas began an extensive microfiche program in 1980. Nebraska and Utah are also distributing in fiche. Nevada is evaluating a trial program conducted in 1977. The North Dakota law adopted in 1977 provides that the state library commission shall arrange for the conversion of the state publications to microfilm and shall make the same available for distribution to the designated depository libraries. The new Oklahoma law gives more latitude for the exercise of discretion by the distribution center in its requirement that the clearinghouse determine the necessity for conversion. The unstated assumption seems to be that the finding will be positive because the law continues with a requirement for a system of distribution to the depositories. Utah in its 1979 legislation provides that "The Commission may use micrographics or other copying or transmission techniques to meet the needs of the depository system." The South Dakota law provides, "Permanent retention may be encompassed through the use of microforms"; thus, the filming burden is shifted to the two libraries required to retain the documents permanently, a university library and the historical resource center.

Some states are carrying out their own programs, designating which publications are to be filmed and distributed, developing bibliographical control requirements, and publishing finding aids. The micrographics program may be handled by a state governmental agency (Nebraska and Utah are examples), or it may be contracted out to a commercial firm (for example, New York). Current commercial microfilming projects, except those limited to a single state, do not encompass comprehensive collections for the individual states, but tend to focus on regular series and special subjects. Retrospective commercial plans are unrelated to problems of current distribution.

Whether or not a commercial micrographics program is selected, the distribution center, on behalf of the depository libraries, should require adherence to standards for quality microform products. If the microfiche are supplied directly by various state agencies, the distribution center should advise, counsel, and recommend guidelines so that the depository libraries—and ultimately the users—are assured a good, readable product. Microfilm technology offers the appeal of saving money in publishing and distribution, but it should not be undertaken carelessly or casually.

DESIGNATION OF DEPOSITORY LIBRARIES

The duties of designating the depository libraries or entering into contracts with the libraries and adopting or observing rules or standards in designating or contracting are sometimes assigned to policymaking library agencies as distinguished from the distribution centers that handle the day-by-day receiving and distributing functions.

WHO DESIGNATES DEPOSITORY LIBRARIES?

The state library or the state library board designates depositories in Florida, Indiana, Missouri, New Hampshire, Ohio, Oregon, Pennsylvania, Vermont, and Wisconsin. In Indiana, certain libraries are named as depositories in the statutes, and others are named as secondary depositories by the state library. In Tennessee, the governor may name depository libraries. Today the governor cannot be expected to designate depository libraries (remember that the Tennessee act dates from 1917); moreover, the designations should not be political. The formal designation should be made at a high level in the library hierarchy with, perhaps, an appeal. The Washington regulations provide for a committee of arbitration in the event of a disagreement.

STANDARDS FOR DESIGNATION

The statutes of some states cite specific criteria that must be taken into consideration in the designation of depository libraries: geographical distribution (Connecticut, Hawaii—one in each county), geographical distribution so that publications will be accessible in all areas of the state (Nebraska, Nevada, Ohio), readily accessible for use (Indiana), ability to preserve and make available for public use (Nebraska, Nevada), ability to preserve (Ohio), suitably care for and advantageously use (Wisconsin), render assistance to qualified patrons without charge (Indiana), and type of library (Nebraska, Nevada). The 1979 Arkansas law combines all these elements and itemizes them in three categories: (1) type of library, (2) preserve and make available, and (3) geographical location to assure accessibility. In all these states, except Hawaii, the law continues with a provision for the adoption of rules, which presumably could include other criteria.

In other states, the law merely provides that the requirements for eligibility to contract shall be established by a policymaking official or body (Alaska, Missouri, Montana, Pennsylvania, South Dakota, and Washington), without detailing what the rules must include.

In some states, the distribution center has a further duty, after the designation of the depository libraries, to adopt additional rules for the operation of the libraries. Three states where the law provides for the adoption of such rules are: Connecticut, develop and maintain standards for depository libraries; Oregon, prescribe the conditions for use of state documents in depository libraries; and Wisconsin, libraries to serve as public documents depositories in accordance with published rules. Other states have prescribed rules for their depository libraries under their general authority to adopt rules, or informally under their duty to administer a system.

CONTRACTS OR AGREEMENTS

Fourteen states have specific provisions for depository contracts or agreements. Six states (Colorado, Connecticut, Iowa, Montana, South Dakota, and Wisconsin) use the wording "shall enter into" or "shall contract"; the other states with such provisions (Alaska, Arizona, Hawaii, Missouri, Nebraska, Nevada, Texas, and Washington) use "may enter into." Utah provides that a library *must* contract with the commission in order to be designated as a depository library. Only four states (Arkansas, Hawaii, Missouri, Nevada) use the word "agreements"; the other states use "depository contract," except Arizona, which refers to "contracts to establish a system." The contracts or agreements are to be entered into with specific types of libraries and, in Hawaii, with "educational, historical, or scientific institutions" in addition to libraries.

DUTY TO ESTABLISH A COLLECTION

Development of a collection of state documents by the state library agency is one of the guidelines for servicing state documents adopted by the American Library Association. This function is included in the depository legislation of eleven states.

In some states, there is a positive duty to establish a collection and in others, merely a recognition of the right to retain copies. Pennsylvania provides that the state library shall receive state publications "in order to maintain a definitive and organized collection." The Ohio law imposes a duty to "maintain a comprehensive collection of official documents and publications . . . to meet the reference and information needs of officers, departments, agencies of state government and other libraries." Nebraska, one of the states with a duty to establish a collection, also has a duty to provide access to government publications to state agencies and legislators.

In the states authorized to retain copies, the number of copies to be retained varies from one or two (Indiana, Nevada) to "sufficient" (Oklahoma, Connecticut, Nevada). Connecticut, Kansas, and Nevada made the duty to retain more definite by the use of the words "preserve" and "permanently." Connecticut specifically mentions retention for interlibrary loan; Nebraska imposes interlibrary loan obligations towards citizens of the state; and Nevada requires lending to those libraries without depository status.

While it might seem unnecessary to tell a state library that it should collect the documents of its own state, there are valid reasons for such a collection and for including such a requirement in depository legislation.

First, budgetary support for a program is easier to justify if the program is mandated by the legislature. Incidentally, this observation is true also with respect to the issuance of publications, particularly the checklist.

Second, one of the traditional functions of a state library agency is to serve as a backup for the resources of the state's libraries. It is even more important that the state library agency exercise its support functions in an area where it has better possibilities of acquiring the publications than most libraries and in an area in which comprehensiveness can be a realistic goal. State library agencies are often one of the central nodes of a library network and as such should have the most complete collection.

Third, more use of the state publications at the state library, where the legislature and state agencies have ready access, than at other libraries in the state can be expected because of the secondary materials which such libraries usually collect and because the state is more likely to have micrographic equipment available for preserving its collection. Nebraska specifically imposes a duty on the clearinghouse to make not only state, but also local, federal, and other government publications available to legislators and state agencies.

Another reason for the state library agency to have a complete collection of state publications is that in some states (in New Hampshire, North Dakota, and Texas by statute, and in Missouri by regulation) the state library agency catalogs not only for its own collection but also for other libraries in the state. Related to the cataloging of state publications is the preparation of authority lists, which according to the guidelines should be undertaken by a single agency in each state. The preparation of classification schemes is usually done at the state level also. Iowa is required by statute to adopt a classification scheme. All of these state-level activities are predicated on the availability of a strong state publications collection. This collection should have statutory authority for its existence.

CHECKLIST DUTIES

Twenty-seven states have a statutory duty to prepare a checklist. In some instances, the statute continues with provisions on the required distribution. The wording of the statutory provisions for checklists is shown in List 6 at the end of this chapter.

THE LIST

In drafting a provision for a checklist, several variations can be considered. Most states refer to a list, but Virginia uses the word "catalog," Florida, "bibliography," and Alaska, "index." Should the list consist of publications received (Illinois and Texas are examples), of available publications (Montana, South Dakota, and Washington), or of documents issued or printed (California, Indiana, Michigan, and Virginia)? Although the states that copied the 1963 Washington law did not add the words "on file," as Alaska did in 1970, it is probable that available is intended to mean only availability in a library and not from the issuing agency. The Alaska index provided for in the new 1979 legislation includes publications as well as data abstracts or summaries.

FREQUENCY

The frequency of the lists is almost always stated in the law:

annual—Virginia
quarterly—Indiana, Iowa, Michigan
quarterly or more often—Arkansas, Virgin Islands

monthly—Connecticut, Minnesota (legislators' list), Missouri, New York
monthly or quarterly—California
regularly—Alaska, Montana, Nebraska, South Dakota, Washington
    from time to time—Delaware, Illinois
a periodic list—Florida, Kansas, Nevada, Texas, Utah, Wisconsin

Exceptions are:

Georgia, Louisiana, Mississippi, and Texas— lists are reproduced from reports filed by state agencies at varying times and presumably issued when the agency reports are received.
Oklahoma—as specified in the rules and regulations
Ohio—no mention of frequency

INDEXING AND CUMULATING

Indexing and cumulating stipulations for the checklists are found in the legislation of nine states:

California—cumulated at the end of the calendar year
Connecticut—annual cumulative index
Indiana—cumulated and printed annually
Iowa—cumulated index *and* decennial cumulative indexes
Kansas—at least an annual cumulation
Michigan—cumulated at the end of each calendar year
Nebraska—annual cumulation
Utah—at least an annual cumulation; access by author, title, subject, and other means
Virginia—indexed by subject, author, and issuing agency

SPECIAL FEATURES INCLUDED IN LISTS

Special features are as follows:

Kansas—a record of each agency's publications showing author, title, major subject content, and other appropriate catalogue information
Nebraska—a record of each agency's publishing and author, agency, title, and subject approaches
Oklahoma—name of publishing agency, name of the publisher, and title and subject matter
Virginia—date of publication; note if only library copies are available; price and where and how to obtain
Wisconsin—shall publish this list in such form and with such notes as to show the scope and purpose of such publication

DISTRIBUTION

Seventeen states make provision in the statutes for the distribution of the list:

Alaska—distribute to contracting libraries and to other libraries on request

Arkansas—distribute to all state agencies and contracting libraries

Connecticut—distribute to libraries in Connecticut, other state libraries, the legislature, state agencies, and libraries, upon request

Indiana—distribute to state departments and agencies and to public and college libraries within the state

Iowa—distribute without charge to depository libraries and upon request to other libraries, or by subscription

Kansas—distribute to complete depository libraries, selective depository libraries, state agencies, state officers, and members of the legislature

Louisiana—furnish to each depository

Michigan—distribute to state departments, legislature, and public and college libraries within the state

Minnesota—distribute to legislators

Mississippi—furnish to each depository

Montana—distribute to contracting depository libraries and other libraries on request

Nebraska—distribute to contracting depository libraries, other libraries, state agencies, and legislators

Nevada—distribute to all state agencies and contracting depository libraries.

Oklahoma—distribute to all contracting depository libraries, other libraries within the state, and every state agency

South Dakota—distribute to all contracting depository libraries and other libraries upon request

Texas—issue to all depository libraries and to other libraries on request

Utah—distribute to depository libraries, state agencies, state officers, members of the legislature, and other libraries selected by the commission

Virgin Islands—automatically mailed or distributed free of charge to depository libraries and to any other individual, institution, firm, library, or other entity who shall request checklists, either on a single copy or subscription basis. Territorial librarian must fill requests within a reasonable time.

Virginia—made available without cost; out-of-state by exchange or at price sufficient to equal unit cost; complimentary copies from the state librarian

SPECIAL PROVISIONS

In California the state library, which issues the checklist, may request information from the state agencies for the preparation of the lists.

The Oklahoma law provides that rules and regulations will set out the requirements pertaining to the list.

The Washington distribution center "may publish and distribute such other descriptive printed matter as will facilitate the distribution of state publications."

The New York law, although it has no statutory provision requiring publication of a checklist, recognizes the checklist that the state library issues by providing that a listing of films, audio- and videotapes, and other electronic information be listed in the monthly and annual checklists.

The Alaska index includes not only publications but also abstracts or summaries of research data. The center is referred to as a recordkeeping agency and is required to coordinate its activities with those of other such state agencies.

RULES AND REGULATIONS

In many states, rules and regulations supplement the statutes. These are of various types: (1) general rules and regulations to carry out the purposes of the act, including the duties of the distribution center (for example, Nebraska), (2) rules for designating the depository libraries (for example, Pennsylvania), (3) rules directed toward the state agencies—what publications shall be made available for the depository libraries (for example, Washington "Guidelines") and the number of copies to be deposited (Illinois and Kansas), and (4) rules for the depository libraries (Connecticut, Iowa, Oregon, and Wisconsin).

EXCHANGES

Legal provisions for exchanges are not always included in depository library laws, and when included they are often permissive. Arizona, California, Delaware, Oklahoma, Oregon, Texas, and Washington have permissive provisions. In the laws of Connecticut, Indiana, Nevada, Ohio, and Utah, the publications, sometimes limited to the remaining copies (for example, Nevada), are to be used "in accordance with exchange agreements," or simply "in exchange."

The question of exchanges is not always considered when depository legislation is enacted because satisfactory exchange arrangements may already exist and the legislation on which they are based should not be disturbed. Exchange provisions are found in various, scattered sections of the law, and although each state document librarian must be familiar with the exchange laws of his own state, they are not, in a narrow sense, depository legislation. *American Library Laws* is recommended as a current source for locating provisions on exchanges.

A different approach to exchanges of state publications is that taken in the Montana law which provides that the center may enter into depository contracts with other state libraries and in Nebraska, which provides for contracts with out-of-state research libraries.

Whether out-of-state libraries should be exchange libraries, which implies reciprocity, or depository libraries, which does not, is a question each state must decide. There is a good argument that state publications should be shared with other states regardless of reciprocity. The 1915 Wisconsin statement of this philosophy is eloquent.[10] At the same time, the decline in the number of libraries that are building large collections of out-of-state documents reduces the number of copies needed for exchange purposes. The American Library Association Guidelines requirement that "the appropriate state agency should be prepared to exchange documents" does not necessarily mean that exchanges must be part of the depository legislation, or a responsibility of the distribution center. In some states, the university library handles exchanges.

OTHER STATUTORY DUTIES OF THE DISTRIBUTION CENTER

In two states, Connecticut and Iowa, a statutory duty is imposed on the distribution center to advise the state agencies annually concerning the number of copies of publications needed for distribution.

Arkansas and Tennessee provide for the preparation of the checklist that is sent to the libraries for ordering purposes.

The new Iowa law, adopted in 1978, provides that the distribution center (the law uses the term "depository librarian") shall "establish a record of the number and manner of distribution" of the state publications. In the proposed law, the wording was "shall devise and maintain an itemization scheme for their distribution." The word "itemization" may be derived from the "item books" used by the U.S. Superintendent of Documents to record the distribution patterns for the "items" (that is, classes of publications) available for distribution.

Oklahoma has a duty to "compile and maintain a permanent record of all state publications caused to be published from and after the effective date of this act." This requirement is similar to that in Kansas where the state librarian is required to use the reports from state agencies "to maintain a permanent record of publications." Although these records are in separate sections from those requiring the checklist and are not described as published records, it would seem that the checklist could be designated as the permanent record.

NONSTATUTORY DUTIES

It is not possible, nor is it desirable, to specify in the law all the duties that the distribution center and its administrator should assume. A service-minded librarian will seize every opportunity to adapt the depository program to the needs of the depository libraries, within the constraints of the budget. One of the premises of state depository programs is that it is more economical for a central source to identify, acquire, and distribute state publications. Other activities relating to state publications are also more economically performed at the state level on a one-time basis for the benefit of many who would otherwise duplicate each other's efforts. Some of the nonstatutory activities of the distribution center are for the benefit of the state agencies, and others are for the benefit of the depository libraries. A provision like the one in the Louisiana law, that the administrator shall be preferably a graduate librarian, can be interpreted to mean that the administrator should be a person who can fulfill all the functions that good library practice require.

SERVICES TO STATE AGENCIES

For example, a graduate librarian would recognize that, if the law requires state agencies to appoint liaisons or contact persons, the logical agency to provide training and advice to these liaisons is the distribution center. Eaton, in her oft-cited "70%" article, lists as one of the suggestions for alleviating the problem of acquiring state publications "better and continuing training of personnel responsible for sending the [distribution center] copies." The emphasis on continuing is deliberate, as Eaton says, because "Many of these people do not stay with the job for long and the Library's yearly reminder memo may never have been seen by the person in the agency publications job."[11] A legal requirement that the distribution center be notified of personnel changes in the liaison position is a partial solution to this problem.

No formal training programs for state agency liaisons have been outlined or discussed in the library literature. Remarks, such as those of Elison in his 1969 Idaho article, that librarians must educate the state agencies, are not elaborated on.[12]

The 1975 Nevada report includes a recommendation that agency visits be made at the completion of the book catalog to check on titles omitted, explain service, and establish or reaffirm channels. The report also emphasizes the need for a "concerted campaign to reeducate the state agencies."[13]

The administrator of the New Mexico program reported the following:

training sessions for liaison officers of state agencies were held [about six weeks after the depository libraries were established and shipments of documents begun]. Almost 100 people attended. An increase in material deposited was noticed immediately. A manual for state agency liaison officers was developed and distributed.[14]

The literature more commonly reports contacts with state agencies during the planning stages for new legislation than after the legislation is enacted.

In Nebraska, the gathering of information prior to bill drafting began with an examination of the state budget and of the accounting records on funds spent by each agency for publications. The appropriation for printing and the amounts given to each agency were found, but no agency records were available on how those amounts were spent. The figures were "a persuasive point in documenting the lack of accountability." In addition, fifty-five mailing lists from forty-four state agencies were examined, revealing "that only 12 Nebraska libraries were on two or more mailing lists, while 27 out-of-state libraries were on two or more lists." Shaffer concluded that "State information simply was not reaching those for whom it was designed."

Shaffer notes that, after the Nebraska legislative bill was drafted, the governor's office supported it "since the months of working with them had resulted in their gaining a clear understanding of what the Library Commission wished to accomplish."[15]

In Wisconsin, Schneider reports that the first draft of legislation prepared by the documents advisory committee was submitted to the heads of major publishing agencies for comment. The committee also held a meeting with the agency printing people which "was very successful and the input received both improved the proposal and provided a wider base of support for its passage."[16]

STATE AGENCY HANDBOOKS

The publication in 1977 in Missouri of a *State Agency Handbook* is a first. This twenty-six page booklet has introductory paragraphs on the nature of the depository program and its advantages for state agencies:

The depository library system offers your agency the opportunity to place its publications in a variety of geographical locations with a minimum of effort. When the number of copies of a publication available for distribution is limited, the depository system makes sure that these copies will be made available to the largest possible number of people, rather than scattered on a "first-come, first-serve" basis.

If you provide the copies . . . we'll do the rest.[17]

The New Mexico handbook follows the arrangement and the wording of the Missouri booklet but puts special emphasis on the filing of publications under the State Rules Act. The Texas manual, published in 1980, was designed primarily for use by the contact persons designated under the recently amended Texas law. It includes detailed guidelines on the types of publications to be deposited and examples of publications that are exempt from deposit requirements and those for which a reduced number of copies may be substituted for the full quota.

BROCHURES AND LEAFLETS FOR STATE AGENCIES

Leaflets have been prepared in other states to remind the state agencies of their obligations under the depository program.[18] Ohio's "It's the Law" was the first to use the theme: "If you'll do one thing, we'll do three." The one thing that the state agencies are asked to do is, of course, send copies of their publications. The three things that the distribution center agrees to do are to put a copy in the state library collection, distribute to the depository libraries, and list the publication in the checklist. Alaska's publication has the same title as

Ohio's and follows it very closely. The Pennsylvania publication has the title "Act 150 is the Law" and lists five things that the state library will do, including exchanging with other libraries and general mailing to libraries. The Nevada leaflet has the locally appropriate title "Three Four One," with the words tumbling like dice on the cover. Nevada concludes with "everyone wins," instead of "and everyone benefits," as do the leaflets of the other states. Nevada includes a footnote defining "state publication." On the back of the leaflet is a map showing the locations of the depository libraries.

The Indiana brochure, entitled "Deposit Your Documents with the Indiana State Library and . . . ," has a map on the front cover and a list of depositories on the back cover. It, too, follows the slogan one thing for three, and everyone profits.

The brochure used in Louisiana, and copied in Minnesota, is entitled "The Case of the Missing Documents" and seeks the cooperation of the state agencies in supplying their "missing" documents so that they can be distributed. Both brochures call attention to the law, raising the possibility that the agencies may have overlooked it. The Louisiana brochure ends with "Here's why your publications are needed," and the Minnesota one with "Your help will serve a two-fold purpose."

An early Kansas brochure has a reproduction of the 1971 law relating to publications produced by Central Duplicating or by the state agencies. It provides space for the agencies to list the publications sent to the state library.

OTHER SERVICES TO STATE AGENCIES

The distribution center's preparation of forms for the use of the state agencies, although a convenience for the state agencies, is of distinct benefit to the distribution center as well. Packing slips, self-addressed labels, and report forms for listing publications or for identifying liaisons all make the work of the distribution center flow more smoothly. Although forms of this type are useful in their own right—packing slips as an invoice to tell the center what the agency thinks the titles are, address labels to ensure more accurate delivery, and report forms to secure all the necessary information—they have another purpose. Their distribution to state agencies affords the distribution center an indirect method of reminding the agencies of their duties under the law. The distribution center needs the cooperation of the state agencies, and if voluntary cooperation can be gained without the awkwardness of having to tell the state agencies directly that they should comply with the law, the relationship will be more harmonious.

SERVICES TO THE DEPOSITORY LIBRARIES

The distribution centers have provided more extra services to libraries than to state agencies. Perhaps this is because the state agencies perform only a one-time function with respect to each publication—that of sending it to the distribution center. The depository libraries' handling of the publications involves not only entering them in the library records, cataloging, and perhaps binding them, but also retrieving them for repeated use and circulation. Consequently, the distribution center can perform more services for the libraries than for the state agencies.

The distribution center can prepare shipping lists; it can catalog the documents, classify them, and reproduce them in a microformat; and it can prepare promotional materials. When the Nebraska depository librarians met in May 1977, they asked "that they receive extra copies of the Clearinghouse brochures on state documents for distribution, and that the Clearinghouse prepare spot radio announcements, new brochures, a decal, information on the loan policies of the depositories, and a handbook for depositories."[19]

SHIPPING LISTS

The preparation of a shipping list is one of the more important voluntary duties of a distribution center. The shipping list serves as an invoice for the depository libraries and permits them to claim any missing items promptly. It may also include cataloging data, OCLC numbers, and state classification numbers. (The OCLC, formerly the Ohio College Library Center, is a bibliographical utility now incorporated under its acronym.) The Kansas shipping list, sent in the package with the documents, includes title, Kansas documents classification number, OCLC number, and recommended Dewey classification number. Because it is produced from the OCLC tapes the state library receives monthly, the shipping list is presumably produced monthly and the packages mailed monthly.

INSPECTIONS

No state depository legislation includes a requirement that personnel from the distribution center inspect or visit the depository libraries. The law governing federal depositories has such a provision, "make first hand investigations," and indeed, a comprehensive inspection program has been followed in the past few years.

The Nebraska rules, however, state that the clearinghouse staff will conduct visitations, not more often than once a year, and, if violations are found, followup inspections will ensue.

The first issue of *Public Documents Highlights for Texas* reported that twenty-nine state and federal depositories had been visited by Texas State Library staff members and that another forty-seven visits were scheduled. The news note said,

[T]he TSL representatives have gained a much better perspective of the problems and concerns of each individual library. Unlike larger group meetings where emphasis is placed on trends in the documents area, the depository visits provide an opportunity for each individual librarian to discuss specific problems concerning that particular documents collection and to voice any criticism or suggestions concerning the State Library documents programming.[20]

PROMOTIONAL MATERIALS

Brochures, spot radio announcements, and decals are all aids and tools that can be prepared at the state level. If the distribution center is located in the state library, it is likely that both talented personnel and reproduction equipment would be more readily available than in the individual depository libraries. Centralized preparation of publicity materials is particularly helpful to the small depository libraries. Such materials enable the individual depository libraries to publicize their state document resource in an effective, non-amateurish way with a minimum of effort. The Nebraska rules require a depository library to "take measures to publicize its state documents collection. . . ."

Examples of spot radio announcements and decals prepared by state distribution centers, when completed, should be shared through the Documents on Documents Collection. By way of comparison, the U.S. Government Printing Office has prepared a decal, in both glass door and solid wall versions, for the federal depository libraries.

Several states have prepared brochures. Examples in the Documents on Documents Collection include:

> Louisiana and Mississippi—"There's No End of Valuable Information Available Through the State Documents in [Louisiana's or Mississippi's] Depository Libraries"
> Nebraska—"What's Up Doc? How to Obtain a Public Document from the Nebraska Publications Clearinghouse." Covers U.S. documents also and gives examples of materials on drug abuse.
> Ohio—"Looking for Information." Includes map and list of depository libraries.
> Texas—"Texas Documents." Includes map and list of depositories.
> Wisconsin—"Do You Know What Your Government Is Doing?" Includes list of depositories.

NEWSLETTERS

Recently, some state distribution centers have begun publication of document newsletters. Nebraska, New Mexico, and Texas are examples. All these newsletters include federal documents news as well as state documents news.

Oklahoma had a newsletter in the early 1950s, but it was discontinued, as was the Oklahoma checklist. For a while, the monthly Kentucky state documents checklist had news notes on the first page.

In some states, such as California and Illinois, the newsletter is a publication of the state documents round table or the state documents committee. These newsletters also include both state and federal coverage. In Missouri, a regular column on documents is included in the state library bulletin, *Show-Me Libraries*. This column is usually federal but gives good coverage of state documents activities.

Newsletters are being collected by the American Library Association's Government Documents Round Table liaison to state and local groups. The preliminary compilation is included in the bibliography chapter in Part II.

WORKSHOPS

The Nebraska rules require that each depository library ''send a representative from their staff to attend Clearinghouse meetings on the depository program'' no less than once each year. This is, of course, another way of saying that the clearinghouse has a duty to hold meetings. The reports of the first and second meetings of the depository librarians, on November 18, 1976 and May 11, 1977, are included in the *DOCumentor*.[21] The suggestions made by the depository librarians are indicative of the ideas that can result from workshops:

1. Number changes should be indicated on the shipping lists.
2. The clearinghouse should give extra copies of brochures about state documents to depositories for them to distribute to patrons and staff.
3. The clearinghouse should work on developing spot radio announcements about state documents, new brochures, and a decal for state document depositories (similar to the one the Government Printing Office developed for federal depositories).
4. The clearinghouse should compile information on the loan policies of the various depositories.
5. The clearinghouse should work on a depository handbook for use by depositories in training staff and for utilization by new depositories.

Other states have held workshops, sponsored generally by the state library association or its documents committee. In 1963, California held workshops at three different locations to acquaint California librarians with California documents and the depository program. Speakers from the state library, the state printing office, and four public libraries participated. The proceedings for this workshop and another held in 1965 on California legislative publications were published in *News Notes of California Libraries*.

Other major state documents workshops include the North Carolina meeting in 1964; Oregon, 1965; Illinois, 1972; Pennsylvania, 1973; New York, 1976; and the Southwestern Library Association/Mountain Plains Library Association (SWLA/MPLA) Pre-Conference in 1976, for which the ''State of State Documents'' was prepared.

DEPOSITORY LIBRARY HANDBOOKS

Most of the services provided by the distribution center to the depository libraries are continuing activities. A new shipping list, for example, is needed every week or every month; inspections and workshops should be conducted annually; and newsletters, in addition to being serial by nature, must be as current as possible.

The preparation of a handbook for the depository libraries, though usually a one-time undertaking, is one of the most important services that the distribution center can provide for the depository libraries. The handbook serves two purposes and is directed toward two groups of librarians, being both a training tool for librarians new to state document work and a handy compendium of information on the depository program for experienced librarians.

The handbook collects the basic data on the program—the law, the names and addresses of the depository libraries, and sometimes a map with the locations of the libraries; the rules established by the center for the libraries; suggestions on handling the state documents after they are received at the library; and recommended reference tools. The contents of the California manual are listed in detail here in the state section. Less well known because they are more recently published are manuals issued by Kansas, Louisiana, Missouri, Pennsylvania, and Wisconsin. These manuals and others are available for examination in the Documents on Documents Collection.

The preparation of a manual, because it includes not only instructions from the distribution center but also suggestions on the handling and reference use of the documents, can be a cooperative project between the distribution center and document librarians in the state. After the initial preparation of a handbook, revision and reissuance should be scheduled as needed.

GUIDELINES

The duties and activities of the distribution center are summarized in the "Guidelines for State Distribution Center Activities," prepared by the State and Local Documents Task Force in January 1979. These guidelines are supplementary to the other guidelines and do not include such major duties as issuing the checklist or coordinating the inputting of state documents into a data base.

Although the list seems long, it should be noted that some of the activities are one-time functions. Setting up the system so that all areas of the state are served, preparing standards for the depository libraries, and publishing manuals and brochures are all part of getting the program established rather than continuing duties. Many of the other activities, such as contacting the state agencies and holding workshops for the state agencies and for the depository librarians, fall into a pattern after the first few times.

The duties and activities of the distribution center should be supervised by a professional librarian who will continually seek new, more effective, and more efficient methods of operating the program and who will keep the program current with developments in library practices in general. Using the computer effectively in a bibliographical control program and taking advantage of microformatting possibilities are the two areas that are currently being explored by state documents librarians and distribution centers.

Computers are widely used in the large research libraries today. Their use in state documents programs must conform to the standards being followed by the national library community. This means that cataloging must be in the MARC format, for example. State documents librarians must be aware of the possibility of including the local classification number in one of the available fields, must consider the need for additional indexing points, and must decide whether the data should be so tagged that an appropriate program can be used to produce a checklist. The GODORT cataloging manual for documents, to be published in 1981 and edited by Sue Ellen Sloca for the American Library Association, will be an aid to catalogers in applying the *AACR 2* to state documents and should be used as a guide.

The Texas State Library uses two independent computer programs in the processing of state documents. The cataloging department prepares an on-line bibliographic record for all Texas documents in the AMIGOS data base. The individual records in this file are standard cataloging records in MARC format. The authority file for the corporate names in the catalog file is in a separate record in the same data base. The new entries for the authority file are authenticated by the Library of Congress before being incorporated in the file and thus become part of the national name authority file. This cooperative project between the Library of Congress and the Texas State Library is being conducted as a pilot project that will, it is hoped, be expanded to include other states.

Another computer program in the Texas State Library is conducted in its documents division for the production of the documents checklist and a detailed subject index for the state documents. The index analyzes the content of the documents and stresses geographical areas, which are used only indirectly in the Library of Congress subject heading list and cannot be used for searching the MARC records. The documents department data base is used to produce the checklist and, as programs are developed, will be used for (1) serial records tasks, such as claiming, binding, and making date-expected reports, (2) distribution records, such as the selection lists of the depository libraries, the ranking of libraries for distribution of scarce items, and the record of distribution to the depositories, (3) union lists of depository items and of serials, (4) statistics on the operation of the clearinghouse, and other applications as appropriate.

In other states (Washington, New York, Kansas, and Utah), a single data base is used to maintain the cataloging record and to produce the document checklist.

ADVISORY COUNCILS

The chapter on legislation (Chapter 3) emphasizes that the establishment of a depository program is a cooperative effort. The legislative effort is usually a committee undertaking.

The Wisconsin proposed legislation includes the establishment of a public documents advisory council. Membership would be comprised of representatives from the State Historical Society, Legislative Reference Bureau, Document Sales, State Printing Section, Wisconsin Library Association, regional depository libraries, selective depository libraries, the University of Wisconsin System, and one other major state department.

Georgia also adopted the advisory council idea in 1967 and provided for membership as follows: one member of the Senate, one member of the House of Representatives, the secretary of state, the state auditor, the legislative counsel, and the state librarian. The president of the Georgia Library Association was added to the membership by a 1972 amendment. Since the functions of the council were transferred to the Department of Administration in the Executive Reorganization Act of 1972, the council has been inactive.

It is appropriate to have a council such as those in Wisconsin or Georgia that includes state officials in addition to librarians. In the formulation of policy, advice from those who *produce* state documents and those who *use* them, as well as from librarians, should be sought.

Another type of advisory council can also serve a useful purpose. An organization composed of the depository librarians can be a real help to the distribution center in identifying problem areas and proposing changes. The daily operation of the depository system would be the concern of such a group, as contrasted with the broader policy interest of the advisory councils that include nonlibrarians. In Nebraska, there are regular meetings of the depository librarians, although they may not consider themselves an organized group.

The two kinds of councils differ in their membership, their method of appointment, their term of office, and their functions. The council of depository librarians might be called a conference or consortium, if there are many depository librarians, and might have an executive board to act as its spokesman.

STAFFING OF THE DISTRIBUTION CENTER

The staffing of the distribution center is not provided for by statute in most states. The Louisiana statute has a provision that a person "who shall be preferably a graduate librarian" shall administer the program under the supervision of the secretary of state. The Mississippi law, which was modeled on the Louisiana law, formerly had the same provision, but the phrase quoted above was deleted when the law was amended in 1975 to transfer the distribution center functions from the secretary of state's office to the Mississippi Library

Commission. The Louisiana and Mississippi provisions were justified at a time when the depository functions were the only library functions administered in the secretary of state's office of those states.

The staff of the distribution center and that of the library which is host to the center is usually the same, and the duties overlap. The staff has responsibility for both the distribution program and the reference service for the local library collection. In several states, Nebraska and Texas, for example, the functions of the staff also embrace federal document responsibilities. These factors, in addition to the lack of published data, make comparisons difficult. For those libraries that are adding the distribution and checklist functions to a department which administers the state document collection, the Louisiana staffing pattern might be a guide. In Louisiana, the distribution and the checklist functions, which were not administered in the library agency, were staffed by a half-time professional person and a full-time secretary with intermittent student help. Recently, the professional position was converted to a full-time one, and the functions were transferred to the Louisiana State Library. (For current information, consult the State and Local Documents Task Force survey heading on ''staff.'')[22]

ALTERNATIVES AND MICROFORMS

To simplify a depository library program when budgetary considerations make this necessary, the administrator might explore the possibility of adopting a system concept for the depository libraries, if depositories were originally established without a plan. A reduction in the number of depository libraries by including only system resource centers immediately reduces the number of copies of publications required as well as handling time and records at the distribution center. However, this approach is politically difficult if libraries have been serving as depositories for a number of years because depository status is often prized as a status symbol.

A second possible economy is to screen the distribution patterns and only attempt to furnish a full set of publications to a minimum number of libraries. This change, too, is difficult to inaugurate in a long-established system. The Indiana system operates on this principle, distributing those documents which the state library considers ''of general interest or use.'' In Washington, the standards provide for the partial depositories to receive ''general interest publications deemed essential to the public interest.'' In both of these states, the state library determines what the depository libraries will receive.

MICROFORMATS

Offering publications in a microformat not only provides full distribution to the depository libraries but also eliminates handling, wrapping, and postage for hard copy publications. For the depositories, an added advantage is that in most cases a more complete collection is possible, and less space and processing time are required. For the state agencies, the use of microforms in the depository program means that supplying fewer copies of the publications may fulfill their obligations.

In considering a microformat, several factors beyond the ordinary objectives of space-saving and preservation must be weighed. The first question is whether the primary purpose of the microform program is distribution or preservation. If the microform is to replace the distribution function, it must be available *promptly*. One of the particular values of state documents is that they are often more current than federal documents and are useful in the interim when federal statistics are being collected.[23] The information in state newsletters and journals is most useful at the time of publication. Any delay caused by the filming process diminishes access to the publications when they are most needed.

Another factor to be remembered is that not all state documents can be suitably put into microformat, and even those that can be filmed present problems. State documents have relatively few pages, and in the filming process repeated adjustments must be made to set the exposure and to accommodate the different type sizes. Color, fine lines, extremely small type, charts, and maps all present filming difficulties that cannot always be overcome.

Because state documents are often brief—the average number of pages in a newsletter is four, and in a monthly publication, about twenty—the usual practice of filming one document per microfiche would be wasteful. The South Dakota study commission report says, "Publications of less than ten pages will not be prepared in microform."[24] If the fiche is "packed," that is, several related titles filmed on a single fiche, then a key or finding aid is needed to determine what it contains. If the monthly list is used as the key, that arrangement of items presents the problem of varying exposures just mentioned.

Some states (Nebraska is an example) film for distribution and then film again at the end of the year to put a year's issues of a particular title on a single fiche. South Dakota planned to film complete volumes of periodicals, in lieu of binding, and to make distribution annually.

The *use* of the state documents must also be considered. Some are reference materials in daily use in a library. The bluebook, the statistical abstract, the state telephone book, and the checklist itself are reference tools that are used in conjunction with other materials and are used more conveniently in hard copy.

Another consideration is that, in order to achieve equitable geographical access to state publications, smaller public libraries have undertaken depository responsibilities for their area of the state. These smaller libraries are not as well equipped with reading equipment to provide service through microforms as are the large research libraries, and neither the library staff nor the readers are accustomed to the use of nonprint formats.

The planning of a microform program must take into consideration the physical format of the state documents, the necessity for timely distribution, the key for access to the collection (perhaps the checklist), and the needs of the persons who will use the documents.

Planning for a micrographics program must include recognition of accepted standards in the area that apply to all publications whether state documents or not. The standards for the physical quality of the film, for the headers, for the film envelopes, the packing for shipment, the storage facilities for the master film and for the copies of the film in the libraries, and other considerations are the same for documents on film as for other materials and should not be neglected in the planning of a program. The Government Printing Office program for the procurement of source documents in microfiche, "(154-S)"[25] might be examined and should be helpful if specifications are to be drawn for a commercial firm to do the microformatting. Planning and adherence to established standards are essential.

COPYRIGHT

Copyright is another area that must be given attention when one is reproducing state documents. Many people believe that government publications cannot be copyrighted; this has been true of most federal publications. The statute reads, "Copyright protection under this title is not available for any work of the *United States* Government . . . " [Italics added].[26] States can, and sometimes do, copyright their publications. For example, Oklahoma has copyrighted its session laws since 1963; Louisiana and Nebraska, their revised statutes; California, its water atlas; and Texas, an annual report. Brenda Olds reported in *Public Documents Highlights for Texas* that "an increasing number of Texas documents are being copyrighted," and that a legislative study has been started.[27]

Items under copyright must either be omitted from the microform collection, or permission to reproduce the material must be secured. If the microformatting is being done by a state agency, permission to copy the publication of another state agency might be granted as a courtesy and should be requested so that the microform collection can be complete.

Whether state publications should be copyrighted or whether they should be left in the public domain is a policy decision for the legislators of each state. The position of librarians is stated in an American Library Association resolution endorsing "The principle that publications produced with public monies remain free of copyright constraints."[28]

ANNUAL REPORT

Finally, the administrator of the distribution center, after spurring the state agencies on to full compliance with the law; running an effective and economical distribution center with complete and accurate records; and serving the depository libraries, collectively through all services that are most appropriately performed at the state level and individually as needed to meet local circumstances, should prepare an annual report. This report would thank the state agencies for their cooperation, summarize accomplishments to encourage the staff and the administration of the distribution center, and remind the depository libraries of their responsibilities. Programs that are just starting can follow the example set in New Mexico and prepare a report on the first year of their operation. Others can, perhaps, recall enough from their early years of operation to present a historical sketch and continue that with annual reports.

LIST 6

DUTY TO ISSUE LIST OF PUBLICATIONS

Alaska—(b) The center shall prepare and keep current an index of all publications and data abstracts or summaries on file and shall publish and distribute that index regularly to contracting depository libraries and to other Alaska libraries upon request. ALASKA STAT. § 14.56.125

Arkansas—The State Publications Clearinghouse of the State Library shall publish, at least quarterly and more frequently if funds are available, and upon request, distribute to all State agencies and contracting depository libraries a list of State publications. ARK. STAT. ANN. § 6-307(e)

California—To facilitate the distribution of state publications, the State Library shall issue monthly or quarterly a complete list of state publications issued during the immediately preceding month or quarter, such lists to be cumulated and printed at the end of each calendar year. All state departments, commissions and other agencies shall, upon request, supply information to the State Library for the preparation of the monthly or quarterly lists and the annual cumulative lists. CAL. GOV'T CODE § 14910

Colorado—The center shall quarterly publish an index to state publications and distribute it to depository libraries and certain other libraries and state agencies as designated by the state librarian. COLO. REV. STAT. § 24-90-207

Connecticut—The state library shall . . .(9) publish at least monthly and distribute to depository and other libraries in Connecticut, other state libraries, to state legislators and state agencies and libraries, upon request, an official indexed list of Connecticut state publications with an annual cumulated index. CONN. GEN. STAT. ANN. § 11-9c

Delaware—From time to time listing of such documents received under the terms of this section shall be published. DEL. CODE ANN. § 8610(8)(b)

Florida—It shall be the duty of the division to . . .(c) Publish a periodic bibliography of the publications of the state. FLA. STAT. ANN. § 257.05(3)(c)

Georgia—The State Librarian may disseminate copies of the lists [supplied by state agencies], of such parts thereof, in such form as the State Librarian, in his or her discretion, deems shall best serve the public interest. GA. CODE ANN. § 101-203

Illinois—The State Librarian shall from time to time publish a listing of the publications received by him under this Act. ILL. ANN. STAT. ch 128 § 121(b)

Indiana—It shall be the duty of the Indiana state library to . . . (d) Prepare and issue quarterly, complete lists of state issued documents, which were issued during the immediately preceding quarter. These lists shall be cumulated and printed annually, at the end of each calendar year. Copies of these lists shall be distributed by the Indiana state library to state departments and agencies, and to public and college libraries within the state. IND. CODE ANN. § 4-23-7-23.6

Iowa—The depository librarian shall . . . 4. Prepare, publish, and distribute on a quarterly basis without charge to depository libraries, and upon the request of other libraries or by subscription, a list of state publications which lists shall include a cumulated index. The depository library center established in section 303A.22 of this chapter shall also prepare and publish decennial cumulative indexes. IOWA CODE ANN. § 303A.23

Kansas—The state librarian shall periodically publish and distribute to complete depository libraries, selective depository libraries, state agencies, state officers and members of the Kansas legislature, an official list of state publications with at least an annual cumulation. Said official list shall provide a record of each agency's publications and shall show, in addition, the author, title, major subject content and other appropriate catalogue information for any such publication. KAN. STAT. ANN. § 75-2567(a)

Louisiana—The secretary of state shall make and furnish to each depository a duplicate copy of the same [i.e., the lists furnished by the state agencies.] LA. REV. STAT. ANN. § 25:123

Michigan—The state library shall . . . (d) Prepare and issue quarterly, a complete list of public documents issued or published by the state during the immediately preceding quarter. The lists shall be cumulated and printed at the end of each calendar year. Copies shall be distributed by the state library to state departments, legislators, and to public and college libraries within the state. MICH. COMP. LAWS ANN. § 397.59(d)

Minnesota—The legislative reference library shall monthly publish and distribute to legislators a checklist of state documents. MINN. STAT. ANN. § 3.195

Mississippi—The director of the Mississippi Library Commission shall make and furnish to each depository a duplicate copy of the same [i.e., the lists furnished by the state agencies.] MISS. CODE ANN. § 25-51-5

Missouri—The state library shall, under the direction of the coordinating board for higher education, publish monthly an official indexed list of all printed publications of all state offices, departments, divisions, boards and commissions, whether legislative, executive or judicial, and any subdivisions of each, including state-supported institutions of higher education. MO. ANN. STAT. §181.110

Montana—The center shall publish and distribute regularly to contracting depository libraries and other libraries upon request a list of available state publications. MONT. CODE ANN. § 22-1-215

Nebraska—The Nebraska Publications Clearinghouse shall publish and distribute regularly to contracting depository libraries, other libraries, state agencies and legislators, an official list of state publications with an annual cumulation. The official list shall provide a record of each agency's publishing and show author, agency, title and subject approaches. NEB. REV. STAT. § 51-415

Nevada—The state publications distribution center shall periodically publish, and, upon request, distribute to all state agencies and contracting depository libraries a list of state publications. NEV. REV. STAT. § 378.210

New York—The state gift and exchange section of the state library shall be responsible for: (I) listing the programs [film, audio- or videotape, or other electronic information program] on the monthly and annual check lists; N.Y. STATE PRINT. & PUB. DOC. LAW § 6(3-a)

North Carolina—The Division of State Library shall publish a checklist of publications received from State agencies and shall distribute the checklist without charge to all requesting libraries. N.C. GEN. STAT. § 147-50.1

Ohio—The state librarian shall . . . (G) Issue official lists of publications of the state, and other bibliographical and informational publications as appropriate. OHIO REV. CODE ANN. § 3375.02

Oklahoma—The Publications Clearinghouse shall have the following duties . . . 5. To prepare and publish official lists of all state publications and to distribute them to all contracting depository libraries, other libraries within the state, and every state agency, as required by the rules and regulations. The official list shall include the name of the publishing agency, the name of the publisher, and the title and subject matter of each publication. OKLA. STAT. ANN. tit. 65, § 3-113.3

South Dakota—The center shall publish and distribute regularly to contracting depository libraries and other libraries upon request a list of available state publications. S.D. COMPILED LAWS ANN. § 14-1A-7

Texas—Periodically issue a list of all state publications that it has received to all depository libraries and to other libraries on request. TEX. REV. CIV. STAT. ANN. art. 5442a §4(4)

Utah—The commission shall publish a list of each state agency's state publications, which shall provide access by agency, author, title, subject and such other means as the commission may provide. The list shall be published periodically and distributed to depository libraries, state agencies, state officers, members of the legislature and other libraries selected by the commission, with at least an annual cumulation. UTAH CODE ANN. § 37-5-4

Virgin Islands—The Territorial Librarian shall issue, each fiscal year quarter, a checklist of the documents that have been sent to the depository libraries in the preceding quarter, according to the following schedule;

Period	*Issue Date*
July 1 to September 30	October 31
October 1 to December 31	January 31
January 1 to March 31	April 30
April 1 to June 30	July 31

Checklists shall be issued more often if needed, in the discretion of the Territorial Librarian.

Quarterly checklists shall be automatically mailed or distributed free of charge to depository libraries and to any other individual, institution, firm, library or other entity who shall request checklists, either on a single copy or subscription basis. It shall be the responsibility of the Territorial Librarian to fill such requests within a reasonable length of time. V. I. CODE ANN. tit. 3, § 883(e)

Virginia—The State Librarian shall prepare, publish and make available annually a catalog of publications printed by State agencies. Each such publication shall be indexed by subject, author and issuing agency. The date of publication of each listed publication shall be noted in the catalog together with information showing, in appropriate cases, that library copies only are available. To the extent such information is available, the catalog shall set forth the price charged, if any, of each publication and how and where the same may be obtained. VA. CODE § 2.1-467.7

The catalog shall be made available without cost to persons indicating a continuing interest in such catalog. Copies sent out of state shall be on an exchange basis or at a price sufficient to equal the unit cost of printing and mailing; complimentary copies may be made available by the State Librarian. VA. CODE § 2.1-456.8 (VA. CODE §§ 2.1-301 and 302 are identical, except for an introductory phrase, "On and after June twenty-sixth, nineteen hundred sixty-four.")

Washington—The center shall publish and distribute regularly a list of available state publications, and may publish and distribute such other descriptive printed matter as will facilitate the distribution of state publications. WASH. REV. CODE ANN. § 40.06.050

Wisconsin—The historical society shall prepare a periodic checklist of public documents issued by the state, including all reports, circulars, bulletins and releases issued by the various state departments, boards, commissions and agencies and shall publish this list in such form and with such notes as to show the scope and purpose of such publication. WIS. STAT. ANN. § 44.06(5)

NOTES

1. American Library Association, Committee on Public Documents, *Manual on the Use of State Publications*, Chapter 21, "The Exchange and Distribution of American State Documents; A Summary of Legal Provisions," pp. 295-331.

2. California, Department of Finance, Organization and Cost Control Division, "Management Survey for the Department of Finance: Depository Library System" (Sacramento, 1959).

3. A. Paul Pross and Catherine A. Pross, "Canadian Provincial Government Publishing: Recent Developments," *Government Publications Review* 1:258 and footnote (1974).

4. Katherine G. Eaton, "The Missing 70%: The Availability of Oregon State Documents to Libraries," *Pacific Northwest Library Association Quarterly* 33:11 (October 1968).

5. *The Docket: Newsletter of the Documents Librarians of North Carolina* 6, no. 3:4-8 (June 1979).

6. Missouri State Library, Government Documents Division, "Depository Library Handbook" (The Library, 1979), p. 16.

7. Anne M. Boyd, *United States Government Publications*, 3d ed. by Rae E. Rips (New York: H. W. Wilson, 1949), p. 31n.

8. Margaret T. Lane (comp.), *State Publications: Depository Distribution and Bibliographical Programs*, State and Local Documents Task Force, Government Documents Round Table, American Library Association; Texas State Publications Clearinghouse, Documents Monograph Series, no. 2 ([Austin, Tex.]: Texas State Library, 1980).

9. Dale Propp and Robert Walton, *Texas State Documents: The Development of a Program*, rev. (Austin, Tex.: Texas State Publications Clearinghouse, Texas State Library, 1978), pp. 17-20.

10. 1915 Wis. Att'y Gen. Op. 459.

11. Eaton, "The Missing 70%," p. 12.

12. Gar T. Elison, "The Problem of Government Publications in Idaho," *Pacific Northwest Library Association Quarterly* 33:18 (October 1969).

13. Nevada, Statewide Coordination of Collection Development Committee, Documents Subcommittee, *Government Documents in Nevada: A Report*, rev. (Carson City, Nev.: Nevada State Library, 1975), Part III, p. 4 and Part II, p.2.

14. Sandy Faull, "Report from the Clearinghouse," *New Mexico Documents Express* 1, no. 1:4 (April 1979).

15. Dallas Shaffer, "State Document Legislation: Nebraska, a Case Study," *Government Publications Review* 1:21, 22 (Fall 1973).

16. Kathy Schneider, "New Documents Legislation? A Wisconsin Proposal Would Ease and Speed Documents Use," *Wisconsin Library Bulletin* 73:38 (January-February 1977).

17. Missouri State Library, Government Documents Division, "State Agency Handbook," prepared by Maggie Johnson, rev. (The Library, 1979), p. 2.

18. Samples of leaflets on state publications programs can be seen in the Documents on Documents Collection, available on interlibrary loan from Grace Moore, Recorder of Documents, Louisiana State Library, P.O. Box 131, Baton Rouge, La. 70821.

19. *The DOCumentor: A Government Documents Newsletter for Depository Libraries in Nebraska*, 4:4 (October 1977).

20. "T.S.L. Representatives Visit US/Texas Depositories," *Public Documents Highlights for Texas* 1:1 (Fall 1978).

21. *DOCumentor* 2:5 (December 1976) and no. 4:3-4 (October 1977).

22. Lane (comp.), *State Publications: Depository Distribution*.

23. Kenneth D. Sell, "Sources of State Vital Statistics Reports," *RQ* 16:45 (Fall 1976).

24. South Dakota, Interim Public Documents Study Commission, *Report* (The Commission, 1972), p. 11.

25. U.S. Government Printing Office, "General Terms, Conditions, and Specifications for the Procurement of Source Document Microfiche" (Program 154-S) (Washington, D. C.: U.S. Government Printing Office, 1978?).

26. 17 U.S.C.A. 105.

27. Brenda Olds, "Documented by the Legislative Reference Library," *Texas Public Documents Highlights* 1:6 (Fall 1978).

28. "ALA Position on Copyright of Government Publications," *Documents to the People* 4, no. 5:13-14 (September 1976).

7. DEPOSITORY LIBRARIES

A depository library is a library that has been officially designated to collect state publications and make them available to the public. It is the place where the state publications, issued by the state agencies and forwarded by the distribution center, actually reach the public. The state agencies and the distribution centers have been cited as principal parts of a depository program, but it is not until the publications arrive at the depository library that the public has ready access to them. Thus, the depository libraries join the producers of the publications and the distributors of them as a vital part of programs for bringing "documents to the people."

In the federal depository system, there is little confusion about which libraries are depository libraries. Depository status is conferred by statute either directly or by a member of Congress. The superintendent of documents, who administers the program, recognizes a new depository by assigning it a depository number.

At the state level, depository status is not as well delineated. A library which is merely a collector of state documents may describe itself as a depository, and a true depository may fail to claim its status. For example, in the Louisiana section of the 1978 *Directory of Document Collections and Librarians*, although there are no libraries claiming state depository status without being so designated, there are four libraries that fail to report their status as state depository libraries.[1] Paul Pross, who surveyed Canadian provincial libraries, found libraries in both categories: five claiming depository status without official designation and four with designations but failing to list them. Pross described and defined a "depository library," deciding that "designation is certainly essential, since deposition is a privilege that entails obligations and consequently some authoritative body has to accord the privilege and ensure that the obligations are being duly observed." He added thereto the ingredients of automatic receipt and broad range of documents to construct his definition:

[A] depository library can be defined as a library designated as a depository by the relevant publishing government and, consequently, entitled to receive automatically all publications, pamphlets, or circulars issued or released by a department or agency of the government for general or limited public distribution.[2]

Only in states that have a depository distribution program do the libraries feel any confidence in their ability to assemble complete collections of state publications and to maintain bibliographical control of them. And even in such states, the large research libraries do not rely totally on the depository program but supplement their collections by all the traditional current awareness plans. For such libraries, the depository distribution program is merely one way, albeit a good way, of securing state publications.

Not only do libraries need to know that their collections are as complete as possible and to have bibliographical access to their collections, but because this is highly specialized material, they also need to receive it automatically. Skogh says, "Any library which can and will organize for effective use the heterogeneous mass of material emanating from the various states, particularly in the executive and administrative branches, should have the pathway made reasonably easy up to that point at least."[3] Her remarks are equally true with respect to the publications of state agencies of an individual state. She explains:

What is really wanted by those libraries which are trying to build up adequate and effective state documents collections is some one agency, or at least only a few agencies, in each state, from which would come automatically, and on a continuing mailing list, a complete file of the publications of that state without further effort on the part of the recipient. A desirable ideal, which for its realization assumes a permanence of policy and personnel which may exist in the majority of states, but certainly does not exist in all states at present.[4]

The automatic nature of the receipt is more important than free receipt.[5] There is a strong argument that state publications should be free to libraries which are publicly supported because these materials are paid for by tax monies and should be freely available to taxpayers. Ensuring this availability through libraries is much more economical than random distribution to individuals. There are advantages to the taxpayer in the use of libraries in making the state publications available and advantages to the libraries in having an automatic, systematic distribution—a distribution that will ensure, as far as possible, that the publications will be available when needed.

In this connection, the provision in the Kentucky regulations that the depository libraries must desist from all direct contact with the state agencies upon penalty of losing their depository status seems unduly harsh. Alaska has a similar provision in its depository contract: "The Depository agrees that all inquiries and special requests concerning state documents for libraries will be channelled through the Center." The Washington rules include the same provision. In addition, Washington libraries "should send to the state library names of every department on whose mailing list they are currently listed." This last provision is a companion one to the provision in the Washington law that the state agencies should, upon request, supply copies of their mailing lists. The South Dakota law also imposes this duty on state agencies.

Serving as the point of contact between the public and the publications of state government is the primary function of a depository library. Connecticut in its definition of "depository library" conveys this idea, using the words "making available to the general public." The Wisconsin *Manual*, prepared as an agreement between the Division for Library Services and the document depository libraries, states this duty clearly: "Designation as a document depository carries a specific responsibility to the state and a commitment to the goals of the depository program. It should never be looked upon as a mere acquisition technique."[6]

Libraries are mentioned in depository legislation in several ways: kinds of libraries that may be depositories, number of depositories, standards libraries must meet to be established as depositories, rules that must be observed to maintain depository status, and kinds of publications depositories are entitled to receive.

Most states do not detail all these specifications in their legislation on the theory that maximum flexibility in the operation of the law will be achieved if such provisions are in rules and regulations and depository contracts.

The first question, "What libraries may be depository libraries?" includes location of depository libraries, kinds of libraries that may be depositories, the types and numbers of depositories in the state, and who determines what libraries may be depositories.

LOCATION

In the few policy statements found in depository legislation, the intent expressed is to make the documents available *in the state*. Arkansas, California, and Nevada use the word "inhabitants," and Indiana refers to "citizens."

Not surprisingly, the legislatures in many states specifically limit the depository privilege to libraries *in the state*, because state legislation is customarily enacted for the benefit and welfare of citizens and institutions of the state. Louisiana, Mississippi, Oregon, and Pennsylvania are examples of legislation specifying "in the state." To the researcher incorporating the Louisiana legislation into the revised statutes it was "evident that the college and public libraries contemplated are those located in the state." The Idaho legislation, which does not refer to the libraries as depositories, says "in Idaho."

Limitation of depository status to libraries within the state, when not specifically limited by statute, is often effected by the interpretation of the statutes, as evidenced by the lists of depository libraries in several of the states. On the other hand, the Hawaii legislation specifies "within or without the State." This phrase, coupled with the use of the terms "private and public" and "institutions or libraries," makes the Hawaii statutory provisions the most liberal of any of the states. The only omission in the Hawaii law might be Alaska's "public library associations." The reference by Hawaii and Georgia to institutions and by Alaska to library associations are the only references to entities other than libraries.

A few states make references to out-of-state libraries more specifically than Hawaii does: state library agencies (Alaska), out-of-state research libraries (Arizona), Library of Congress, Midwest Interlibrary Center, and other state libraries (Montana).

Many states provide for distribution to the Library of Congress and the Center for Research Libraries (formerly the Midwest Interlibrary Center) without designating these libraries as depositories.

IDEAL LOCATIONS

In establishing a new depository system, it is possible to locate depository libraries according to a pattern if the designation of depositories is made pursuant to regulation rather than by the statute. Casey suggests this possibility, saying, "A plan of distribution could be based on 1) a concept of regional reference centers, bringing documents within driving distance of all users in the state. . . ." Wisconsin, in its proposed legislation, is thinking in terms of regional depositories.

A study of the possibilities of a plan for regional distribution was made in Iowa preliminary to the drafting of new legislation. In that study, the population center of each county and the total population of the county were entered into the computer. The distance traveled was measured from the population center of each county to the nearest population center which might house a state depository. The study concludes,

[T]he "best" solution, providing the greatest good with the least number of depositories (least cost) was: 30 centers; average distance traveled, 10 miles; maximum distance traveled, 35 miles. From that point it takes a sharp increase in the number of depositories to make a slight decrease in the maximum distance traveled.[7]

The Iowa study determines not only which locations, but how many locations (that is, how many depository libraries) constitute the optimum number.

TYPES OF LIBRARIES

After the question of where the depositories are located comes the question of the kinds of libraries that are or may be designated as depository libraries. (See List 7, at the end of this chapter.) Historically, the state libraries and the academic libraries have collected state documents. State libraries often handled exchange and distribution of state publications in the early part of the century, particularly for publications of the legislative and judicial branches of government, and thus built substantial collections. That academic libraries also have a long history of collecting in this area is shown by the number of such libraries identified as state documents centers in the 1930s. In the 1966 survey made by Downs, just over one-half of the states list an academic library as having a strong collection of state documents. The only public libraries identified by Downs in the same survey are: Denver Public, Enoch Pratt, New York Public, Cleveland Public, and Detroit Public.[8]

In several states, distribution is, or was at one time, limited to academic institutions. For example, in Arkansas the 1947 and 1971 legislation applies to the University of Arkansas and to state-supported institutions of higher learning. The Louisiana law, until it was amended in 1948, referred to "the library of every college and university in the state." In 1972, Alphonse F. Trezza, then director of the Illinois State Library, wrote in a letter to state agencies in which he was requesting additional copies of state publications, that in the past state-supported universities were the prime recipients in the depository program and that now public libraries should be given access to these publications.[9]

Other types of libraries mentioned as depository libraries in depository legislation include:

    law school libraries (California, Florida, Oregon)
    libraries that are depositories for federal documents (Wisconsin)
    public library associations (Alaska)
    such libraries as can suitably care for and advantageously use . . . (Wisconsin)
    libraries in cities of the first class (Minnesota)
    municipal libraries (Alaska, Arizona)
    county libraries, county free libraries (Arizona, Montana)
    regional public libraries (Arizona, Idaho)
    public junior college libraries (Missouri)
    community college libraries (Alaska)
    state-supported college and university libraries.

This last group of libraries is sometimes broadened to include selected academic libraries in the Commonwealth (Pennsylvania) or even academic libraries in the state (Idaho).

LAW LIBRARIES

In connection with law libraries, Dan Henke, law librarian at the University of California at Berkeley, has said: "Some states have depository programs that meet the needs of law libraries. Others do not. Let us take California as an example. . . . Under the present system, the needs of the Law School and County Law Libraries are woefully neglected."[10]

It was not until 1965 that the California law was amended to provide that law libraries might contract as selective or complete depository libraries. This law provided that proximity to another depository should be disregarded and that law libraries did not need to receive the basic general documents, but only the basic legal documents. The basic legal documents listed in the statute include ''legislative bills, legislative committee hearings and reports, legislative journals, statutes, administrative reports, California Administrative Code and Register, annual reports of state agencies and other legal material published by the state where obtainable through the agency preparing the same.''

Florida also has special provisions for law libraries as depositories. There the law libraries of five universities are specifically designated as state legal depositories to receive, on request and on payment of shipping costs, legal publications not to exceed a stated number of copies (varying from one copy to forty-five copies).

In Oregon, the trustees of the Oregon State Library in designating certain libraries in the state as depository libraries are required to include in that group the library of every nationally accredited law school in the state.

KINDS OF DEPOSITORIES

A number of states have only one kind of depository library; every depository receives all publications that are distributed. These depositories are commonly called ''complete depositories.'' This practice of full distribution follows the federal depository program as it existed until 1922. At least fifteen states have depository systems in which all libraries are full depositories. However, in some instances, the libraries are under no obligation to keep the publications forwarded to them, so the collections in these libraries cannot be described as complete. In such states, full distribution does not necessarily result in complete collections.

The concept of selective depositories for the federal depository system was established in 1922 with the statement ''No part of the sum [appropriated to the Government Printing Office] shall be used to supply depository libraries any documents, books or other printed matter not requested by them.''[11] This change was adopted at the request of librarians who felt burdened by the quantity of publications being distributed and were unable to use all the different publications in their local situation. Boyd and Rips have commented on selective depositories:

The selective plan has been beneficial to many libraries and has checked much waste in government publications, but it has not proved as successful as was hoped, nor has it solved the problem of an equitable distribution so that all the public might have access to all government publications. Many libraries have failed to assume their full responsibility as a designated depository and at the same time, by retaining the privilege, have deprived other libraries from giving a needed and legally provided service to the public.[12]

Missouri, in its recent legislation, has adopted the federal approach: "No publications shall be distributed to any libraries unless a request is made therefor." The Mississippi provision, which was a 1975 amendment to the law, is similar: "as many as two copies of each document requested." However, a recent report from Mississippi says that all depository libraries in that state are full depositories;[13] it must therefore be assumed that the idea of requesting only the publications needed is not used to permit selective depositories in Mississippi. Connecticut has a slightly different way of stating the law to provide for selective depositories: "copies to depository libraries in accordance with the depository contracts."

R. G. Cole, in contrasting the systems that permit selective depositories with those that do not, says: "Both systems have their strengths and weaknesses. A selective system allows smaller libraries to participate in the system, but the full depository requirement guarantees citizenry access to all state publications and is least likely to be abused."[14]

Another type of depository is the historical depository. California first established this type of depository in 1954, designating two libraries as "retaining a historical collection of California state publications beyond that required for complete depositories." Louisiana followed suit in 1963, also designating two libraries, these being (as in California) the state library and a university library. The Louisiana designation followed an attorney general's opinion that no preservation was necessary after six years. Because of this sweeping ruling, the Louisiana recorder of documents secured voluntary commitments from two libraries to assure historical preservation of the state publications received by those libraries.

Other states have "archival" depositories which serve the same function, although they are not in the department of archives and are not arranged by archival principles. The proposed Iowa law used the term "archival depository." Under that proposal, the state library, the University of Iowa, and a library in the western part of the state were to be the archival depositories and to receive two copies of each publication and to retain them permanently. One copy was to be held for research purposes and was not to be removed from the library, and the other copy was to be loaned to other libraries. In the law as enacted, although the State Library Commission and the University of Iowa are to receive and retain permanently two copies of each publication, the term "archival library" was dropped.

In 1973, Wisconsin, which has had depository libraries since 1903, began a study of the existing depositories. The plan that was developed involved a hierarchy of depositories: the historical depository, ten regional depositories which would be full depositories, and the "regular" depositories. Criteria and standards for each level of depository were to be established and the document distribution patterns appropriately adjusted.[15]

NUMBER OF DEPOSITORIES

The total number of depository libraries within each state varies widely. The most current source for determining the number of depositories in each state is the survey compiled in 1979 by the State and Local Documents Task Force of GODORT:[16]

Alaska	20	New Hampshire	18
California	146	New Jersey	62
Connecticut	14	New Mexico	16
Florida	24	New York	186
Hawaii	8	North Carolina	17
Idaho	18	Ohio	86
Indiana	23	Oklahoma	21
Iowa	37	Pennsylvania	82
Kansas	20	Tennessee	5
Louisiana	43	Texas	52
Maine	13	Utah	15
Maryland	29	Vermont	4
Massachusetts	6	Virgin Islands	5
Mississippi	38	Virginia	9
Missouri	27	Washington	58
Montana	17	West Virginia	1
Nebraska	12	Wisconsin	58
Nevada	8		

Because some states do not list the Library of Congress and the Center for Research Libraries as depositories, even though they regularly send publications to those libraries, and also because out-of-state libraries, if any, suggest a different and more far-reaching program, the totals are not strictly comparable.

The only state specifically restricting the number of depositories by a numerical limit is New Hampshire: "no more than 25 public or academic libraries." It is more common to limit the number of depositories by providing for the eligibility of categories of libraries. The most usual groups are public libraries, and college and university libraries.

Lists of depository libraries in each state are not available in collected form. Often the list of depository libraries is included in the state checklist or in a depository manual, if one has been issued. Sometimes a list is prepared as a separate publication; there are examples in the Documents on Documents Collection.

Factors that influence the number of depository libraries are governed first by the philosophy behind the depository legislation. Was the purpose to make state publications freely and widely available with little or no consideration of cost? Although this philosophy may have prevailed in the past—it is implied in the Wisconsin provision that the documents shall be sent to those libraries that can advantageously use them, and perhaps in legislation like that of Louisiana that says merely "large public libraries"—this attitude is becoming difficult to defend in these days of zero-based budgeting and general fiscal caution. Free and openhanded distribution without a plan is recognized as wasteful.

Another theory, suggested by Casey, is to send "all or a selection of documents only to those libraries needing them for their own constituency, with the rest of the libraries receiving rapid service from the state library collection."[17] The Nebraska plan might be cited as an extension of Casey's proposal because in that state the checklist was established first and the libraries out in the state were dependent on interlibrary loan from the state library. Recently, Nebraska has begun distribution to depository libraries through microfiche, as an alternative to hard copy distribution.

The number of depository libraries in a state depends first on the number of appropriate locations for depository collections. Two factors governing the location of federal depositories mentioned by Wilcox are population figures and metropolitan areas.[18] For state depositories there is more correlation between population figures or the number of educational institutions and the number of depositories than between the area of the state and the number of depositories. For example, California with the largest population and the second largest number of educational institutions has the most in-state depositories. Nevada is at the other end of the scale with a small population, six institutions of higher learning, and five depository libraries. Both California and Nevada are among the largest states in area.

ESTABLISHING DEPOSITORY LIBRARIES

Size of book collection is a criterion for a federal depository, but state legislation has not usually followed the federal legislation in this respect. Florida has a provision that public libraries must have book collections larger than 250,000 volumes in order to be designated as depository libraries, but this requirement is in the regulations rather than the law.

Another prerequisite for designation, that the state documents collection be administered by a professionally trained librarian, is also usually found in the rules rather than the law. Florida makes such a requirement, "a professionally trained full-time documents librarian," for private four-year colleges. Other states with such a provision not only do not specify "full-time" but also say "This librarian need not spend full time on state publications" (for example, Alaska and Montana).

The most definitive, and an almost obsolete, way of becoming a depository for state publications is by direct designation in the law. In Tennessee and North Carolina, the depository libraries are named in the statute. Wyoming has two statutory sections, one for the state library and one for the university library. Another type of statute provides that all libraries in a certain category shall be considered depositories. For example, in Arkansas provision is made for libraries in all institutions of higher learning to become depositories. The statute that lists categories of eligible libraries may be almost as specific as the one that names the libraries directly. In Minnesota, one category is "cities of the first class," which in 1974 included three cities.[19]

Some states have statutory provisions that combine designation of certain libraries by name with provision for additional designations. Idaho, North Dakota, Tennessee, and the Virgin Islands have such provisions. In Tennessee, it is the governor who has the authority to name the additional depository libraries. Such authority is usually vested in a library officer or board.

Another way in which libraries become depositories is by contracting with the state library agency. (These contracts or agreements have already been discussed in Chapter 6.) In all states except California, Kansas, and Utah, the burden is on the state library agency to initiate the contract. These three states shift the burden to the individual library and provide that the library desiring depository status must contract with the distribution center. The phrasing in the California and Kansas legislation is "to be placed on the mailing list as a 'complete depository'." In Utah, the law reads, "Upon application, a library may be designated . . ." and then, "a library must contract. . . ."

An even less formal way for a library to become a depository is the procedure indicated in the Louisiana and Mississippi laws, "upon written application." In both these states, a form is supplied on which such an application can be made.

If a library is designated a depository by statute, it can be assumed that the library initiated the request for the designation. Likewise, if a library enters into a contract or makes a written application, it must actively desire depository status. In several states, however, the decision as to which libraries will be depositories is made, not by individual libraries, but at the state level. For example, in Florida and Wisconsin the Division of Library Services designates the depository libraries; in New Hampshire, the state librarian; and in Ohio and Oregon, the state library board.

In some states, the designation is made by the distribution center under its statutory authority to establish and operate a depository library system. The Alaska law, for example, provides in one section for the establishment of the system and in another for contracts with libraries.

DUTIES OF DEPOSITORY LIBRARIES

The arrival of the documents at the depository libraries is not the end of their journey. The whole purpose of the depository library program is to make the publications available and accessible *to the public*. How the library accomplishes this depends on the requirements of the depository law, the rules and regulations adopted pursuant to the law, the depository contract, and the enthusiasm and zeal of the library staff. Once the publications have arrived at the library, it is the duty of the library to assure their accessibility.

Fourteen states have legislative pronouncements on the duties of the depository libraries. (See List 8 at the end of this chapter.) New Hampshire and Tennessee have formal sections of the law devoted to such duties. Connecticut has perhaps the least formal statement, found in its definition of the term "depository library": "the designated library for collecting, maintaining and making available to the general public Connecticut state agency publications." The Arkansas provision, "copies . . . shall remain . . . in the General Library . . . accessible to the public," is an indirect or passive statement of a duty.

The duties of the depository libraries are not usually the subject of a separate section in the law, but are included in sections providing for the establishment of the depository libraries or in sections on the purpose of the law. Whether or not one notices the lack of a separate section on duties of depositories depends on whether one thinks of depository legislation as a means of getting publications to the libraries or as a means of getting publications to the users. If getting publications to the libraries is the ultimate goal, then no duties need be imposed on the libraries. However, if the intent is to make the publications available to the public, then a duty is often stated. As a practical matter, the lack of a statement of duties is not critical because all librarians today know that libraries exist to serve the user.

The legal provisions on duties of the depository libraries are, with only a few exceptions, very general, basic requirements. The Kansas law recognizes the general nature of its provisions by the words "agreeing *at a minimum* to provide" (Italics added). New Hampshire is an exception to the rule in its requirement that the libraries catalog the documents.

The themes common to almost all the states are the ideas of availability of the publications in the depository library, and of service to the public without charge. A restatement of the provisions generally included in the statutes, with variations interspersed, is provided here for those drafting a section on the duties of the depository libraries.

Depository libraries ASSUME THE RESPONSIBILITY (provide, be a condition of the depository privilege, agree to receive, shall receive one copy of every publication, give receipt for) TO PROVIDE ADEQUATE FACILITIES FOR THE STORAGE (carefully preserve, remain on permanent deposit, retain permanently, and maintain its full collection indefinitely, not to dispose of any such publication without prior approval; permanent retention may be encompassed through the use of microforms) AND USE (free use) IN CONVENIENT FORM (accessible for use, shall catalogue the publications in an acceptable fashion) ACCESSIBLE (readily accessible, available) TO THE PUBLIC (the general public, patrons, qualified patrons, any person) AND TO RENDER SERVICE (services, reasonable service, assistance) WITHOUT CHARGE (free).

A table on the duties of the depository libraries identifies the states that have legal provisions, those that have administrative or contractual provisions, and those that have both.

PROVISIONS ON DUTIES OF DEPOSITORY LIBRARIES

	Legal	Administrative	Both
Alaska		x	
Arkansas	x		
California	x	x	x
Connecticut	x	x	x
Florida	x	x	x
Indiana		x	
Kansas	x	x	x
Louisiana	x		
Mississippi	x		
Missouri	x	x	x
Montana		x	
Nebraska		x	
Nevada	x		
New Hampshire	x		
New Mexico		x	
Ohio		x	
Oklahoma	x		
Pennsylvania		x	
South Dakota	x	x	x
Tennessee	x		
Utah	x		
Washington		x	
TOTALS	14	14	6

The duties required of depository libraries that are made part of a depository contract, or are outlined in rules and regulations, are more varied and more specific than those provided for in legislation. Although properly adopted rules have the force of law, they are more easily changed than legislative enactments. Laws, adopted by legislative authorities, are more permanent and usually more general in their wording, so that they can be both permanent and flexible. Rules and regulations have more details, and because of their specificity are more varied from state to state.

States that have both rules and contracts have sometimes incorporated the same provisions in both. Sometimes the regulations provide a little more detail than the contract for some of the requirements. Consideration of the duties imposed on the depository libraries, whether by rule or by contract, is of greater interest here than the reporting of the instrument in which the provisions are recorded.

No study has been published on rules and regulations adopted in the states, nor on the contracts between the distribution centers and the depository libraries. The Documents on Documents Collection provides examples but does not compare them. The practice among documents librarians seeking to draft rules has been to find a set of rules that seems reasonably comprehensive and to modify it to fit local needs. Eight states, Alaska, California, Connecticut, Kansas, Missouri, Montana, New Mexico, and Washington, which have rules and contracts that are quite similar to one another, are evidence of this practice.

Missouri, although having substantially the same provisions as these eight states, reverses the order of the list of duties so that reference service is at the beginning of the list. Thus, the state recognizes the appropriate priorities.

ACCESSIBILITY—SERVICES

A depository library that looks upon acceptance of the depository designation as an opportunity to give more service to its patrons would not feel burdened by requirements to publicize the collection or to inform the public frequently of the availability of the publications. Free public reference and information service, lending or circulating the publications, and interlibrary loan service are required in one or more states. In the recently adopted New Mexico regulations, the agreement to provide availability for public use includes provision of adequate equipment for viewing microforms. Some states specify that the publications must be available when the library is open. Hours (forty-five or fifty per week) and days (weekends or Saturday or Sunday) when the publications must be available are required in Connecticut and South Dakota. Missouri has a more general provision, requiring only that the publications be available for use any hours that the library is open. Colorado provides that "No rule or regulation shall deny public access during normal working hours to the state publications enumerated in this part. . . ."

ACCESSIBILITY—RETENTION AND DISPOSAL

To insure that the publications which have been distributed are truly accessible, almost all the states include a statement in the regulations or contracts that the publications can be disposed of only with the permission of the distribution center. Most states require that the documents be kept for five years. Offering publications to the state library before disposal is sometimes required. Nebraska permits discarding of documents that are no longer of value to the library's collection, but suggests a minimum one-year retention of all documents. California's disposal policies, printed in the annual issue of *California State Publications*, are referred to in the California contract. Specific provisions for disposing of the publications upon termination of depository status are written into the New Mexico regulations and are part of the New Mexico contract.

DEPOSITORY STATUS

Termination of the depository status is usually permitted on six months' written notice. Connecticut requires only three months' notice. Pennsylvania has sections on both voluntary and involuntary termination. Florida has two relevant sections in its regulations: one providing for an appeal by a library if an application is rejected and another requiring an annual application for designation.

OWNERSHIP OF PUBLICATIONS

The question of ownership of the publications is related to the topics of disposing of depository publications and termination of depository status. When a statement on ownership of the publications is made, it is either that they are the property of the state or the property of the state library agency.

RESPONSIBILITIES TO THE DISTRIBUTION CENTER

The depository libraries must asssume certain responsibilities in their relationship with the distribution center. Such duties include complying with all rules adopted by the center (Connecticut and Montana), supplying information required by the center (California and Kansas), agreeing to inspection by the center (Connecticut, Kansas, and South Dakota), keeping the center informed on the number of copies needed (Montana), appointing a liaison to the center (South Dakota), sending someone to take training at the center or to attend meetings at the center (Nebraska and New Mexico), sending the center the name of every state agency from which the depository is receiving publications (Montana and Washington), forwarding patrons' requests to the interlibrary loan network (New Mexico), and channeling all inquiries and special requests concerning state documents for libraries through the center (Alaska, Montana, and Washington).

This last requirement can be viewed from two positions. For the state agency, it means that all requests from libraries will be handled by one library and the state agency will not be inconvenienced by repeated requests from many different libraries. On the other hand, however, it means that the depository libraries are dependent on the state library for action on their requests, even though the state library might be remiss in the performance of its duty. Making the depository libraries dependent on the state library's diligence is a restraint on their acquisition activities and increases the response time for the end user.

The requirement that the depository libraries respond promptly to any request by the center for information on the storage and use of the publications is a reasonable requirement that should be useful to the center in compiling data on the program. Bernard Fry in his plan for a study on distribution, use, and bibliographical control points up the need for information from the depository libraries: "One of the many things that need to be done is to identify the extent to which the various state depository libraries make use of their own depository privileges."[20]

RESPONSIBILITIES IN THE LOCAL LIBRARIES

The obligations which depository libraries assume require some adjustments in the local library. First, the library must have enough space to house the documents. The typical regulations say, "provide (suitable), (shelf) space to house the collections," sometimes adding "in an approved manner," and usually continuing, "with adequate provisions for expansion." In some states, the regulations explain that vertical file storage is acceptable. Likewise, a statement is sometimes made that a separate collection for the state publications is not necessary. The New Mexico requirement for microform equipment, mentioned above as a service to readers, bears repeating here as an element of the physical facilities.

In a number of states, the depository library must provide an orderly, systematic record of receipt and, in most states, must process and shelve all publications within thirty days. Connecticut changes the thirty-day requirement to a "reasonable period." California requires indexing or cataloging, and subject reference cards in the general card catalog if the publications are cataloged in a reference room card catalog.

RESPONSIBILITIES AS MEMBERS OF THE DEPOSITORY SYSTEM

In Wisconsin, the depository libraries have a responsibility that, although it may be recognized in other states, is not stated specifically, if at all. The Wisconsin manual, which serves as the agreement between the distribution center and the depository libraries in the absence of more formal arrangements, states:

All depository libraries share a responsibility for the total effectiveness of the depository system. They are encouraged to sustain open communication with one another, and to disseminate information, ideas and problems that may bring about common improvement to the whole state system.[21]

This cooperation between the depository libraries is an extension of the cooperation between regional depository libraries and other depositories within the region. Smaller depository libraries are encouraged to communicate with depository libraries outside their region, which may have similar characteristics and, therefore, similar problems. A council of depository librarians, mentioned in Chapter 6, is one way of acquainting depository librarians with one another for the exchange of ideas.

PARTIAL DEPOSITORIES

The regulations sometimes outline the differences between the complete depository and the partial depository, and indicate what the partial depository must receive. California introduced the idea of a basic collection, first as a suggested list and then as a mandatory requirement. In Connecticut and Montana, regulations provide that the partial depository must receive the core or basic collection. Missouri also has a core collection that is required for the partial depository, to which the partial depository must also add its choice of the publications of a department or other logical grouping of publications as assembled by the state library. In Kansas, the partial depository must accept at least 20 percent of all available item numbers. In Florida, Montana, New Jersey, and New Mexico, all depository libraries must agree to accept all documents sent to them. These four states are not the only ones that have full distribution to all depositories; they are the ones that, by regulation or contract, require the acceptance of all documents distributed.

The requirement that a depository library accept all publications distributed or all publications in a core collection recognizes the basic philosophy underlying a depository library system. The system is created to serve the public; therefore, the publications in the depository libraries should be those that *the public* needs or might need as contrasted with the publications that the library needs for its own constituency. Even a small library, if it accepts depository status, should have all the basic state publications. Every depository library should have a copy of the state constitution, the state roster, the checklist of state publications, and other standard reference tools.

The Wisconsin manual carries this idea a step further in its section on interlibrary loan: "Depositories should provide access to all Wisconsin public documents, not merely those held in the individual depository collection. Document interloan is thus an integral depository function."[22]

PERSONNEL IN THE DEPOSITORY LIBRARY

A requirement for professionally trained personnel to render satisfactory service to the public is found in the regulations of many states. Missouri requires, in addition, adequate support staff. Connecticut requires that the responsibility for the state document collection be assigned to a department headed by a professionally trained librarian. South Dakota requires that the library be administered by a librarian with a Master's degree in library science or have such a librarian on its staff to administer the depository program.

Three states stipulate the further training of the librarian in charge of the document collection. Nebraska and South Dakota require the appointment of a liaison to the distribution center, and Nebraska further provides that a representative be sent to clearinghouse meetings. New Mexico goes even beyond this and provides that the document librarian must take training at the distribution center within nine months of appointment and must also take any advanced training offered. The first such training session, held recently in Santa Fe, was reported in *New Mexico Documents Express*:

Seventeen people attended the first state documents depository training session. The training session included an hour of discussion on the current program, a tour of the depository Clearinghouse, and a practical exercise in answering reference questions with state documents. Each of the attendees received a certificate for successful completion of the basic training in state documents.

The reference questions and the annotated bibliography of state documents were mailed out to those depository librarians who couldn't attend the April 30 meeting.[23]

Although many details have been given in this chapter on the depository libraries in order to illustrate the various methods followed in the different states for achieving a sound depository program, the basic purpose of such programs is *service to the public*. Cole gives us his idea of the role of depository libraries and sums up their duties:

In an ideal depository system the depository libraries would be required to furnish the space and staff necessary for the proper maintenance of the collection. They would make the documents accessible to the general public and would circulate them through interlibrary loan. The depository libraries would be required to hold all the publications for a specified amount of time or they would be required to get the approval of the central depository agency before disposing of any documents.[24]

LIST 7

TYPES OF LIBRARIES WHICH MAY BE DEPOSITORIES

Alaska—Municipal, regional educational attendance area, university or community college libraries, public library associations, state library agencies and the Library of Congress, and other state and federal library systems. ALASKA STAT. § 14.56.150

Arizona—Any municipal, county or regional public library, state college or state university library and out-of-state research libraries. ARIZ. REV. STAT. § 41-1335 B

Arkansas—Any city, county, district, regional, town, school, college, or university library in this State. ARK. STAT. ANN. § 6-307(c)

Colorado—Any state agency or public library or . . .out-of-state libraries, and other state libraries. COLO. REV. STAT. § 24-90-206

Georgia—State institutions, public libraries and public schools, and such other institutions of learning as maintain libraries. GA. CODE ANN. § 101-202

Hawaii—Private and public educational, historical, or scientific institutions or libraries, within or without the State . . .at least one in each county. HAWAII REV. STAT. § 93-3

Idaho—Academic, regional public, special libraries of Idaho (but not referred to as depositories). IDAHO CODE § 33-2510

Louisiana—Libraries of colleges or universities and public libraries located in the state. LA. REV. STAT. ANN. § 25:121

Minnesota—Public library of any city of the first class; library of each state university as defined in Minnesota Statutes (but not referred to as depositories). MINN. STAT. ANN. § 15.18

Mississippi—Libraries of state agencies, public junior colleges, colleges, public universities and public libraries located in the state. MISS. CODE ANN. § 25-51-1

Missouri—Public libraries and college and university libraries. MO. ANN. STAT. § 181.130.

Montana—Any municipal or county free library, state college or state university library, the library of congress and the midwest inter-library center, and other state libraries. MONT. CODE ANN. § 22-1-214

New Hampshire—No more than 25 public and academic libraries. N.H. REV. STAT. ANN. § 202-B:1

Oregon—Certain libraries within the state, including the library of every nationally accredited law school. OR. REV. STAT. § 357.015.

Pennsylvania—Selected academic or public libraries within the Common-wealth. PA. STAT. ANN. tit. 24 § 4201 (4)

Tennessee—Named libraries and such other libraries as the governor may at any time name. TENN. CODE ANN. § 12-607

Texas—The Texas State Library, the Texas Legislative Reference Library, the Library of Congress, the Center for Research Libraries, and other libraries that the Texas Library and Historical Commission designates as depository libraries. TEX. REV. CIV. STAT. ANN. art. 5442a § 1 (3)

Wisconsin—Such libraries as can suitably care for and advantageously use copies of the public documents . . . and all libraries designated as depositories for federal documents. WIS. STAT. ANN. § 43. 05 (7)

LIST 8

SECTIONS ON DUTIES AND PRIVILEGES OF DEPOSITORY LIBRARIES

Arkansas—Copies required for public use shall remain on permanent deposit in the General Library of the University of Arkansas in convenient form accessible to the public. ARK. STAT. ANN. § 14-429

California—To be placed on the mailing list as [a depository], a library must contract with the Department of General Services to provide adequate facilities for the storage and use of the publications, and must agree to render reasonable service without charge to qualified patrons in the use of the publications. CAL. GOV'T CODE § 14905

Connecticut—None, except as implied in the definition of depository library: the designated library for collecting, maintaining and making available to the general public Connecticut state agency publications. CONN. GEN. STAT. ANN. § 11-9b(d)

Florida—Depositories receiving public documents under this section shall keep them in a convenient form accessible to the public. FLA. STAT. ANN. § 257.05 (3)
    —It is made the duty of the library to keep public documents in convenient form accessible to the public. FLA. STAT. ANN. § 283.22 and § 283.23(3)

Kansas—To be designated as a complete depository library . . . must contract with the state librarian agreeing at a minimum to provide adequate facilities for the storage and use of any such publications and to maintain its full collection of such publications indefinitely subject to disposal upon approval by the state librarian. KAN. STAT. ANN. § 75-2576(b)

Louisiana—These records shall be made accessible by the depository receiving them to any person desiring to examine the same. LA. REV. STAT. ANN. § 25:122

Mississippi—These records shall be made accessible by the depository receiving them to any person desiring to examine the same. MISS. CODE ANN. § 25-51-3

Missouri— . . .shall serve as depositories for making available to the public such publications. MO. ANN. STAT. § 181.100

Nevada—Designated depository libraries assume the responsibility for keeping such publications readily accessible for use and rendering assistance, without charge, to patrons using them. NEV. REV. STAT. § 278. 150(2)

New Hampshire—Duties of Depository Libraries. Depository libraries shall provide adequate facilities for the storage and use of the publications. They shall render reasonable service without charge to qualified patrons who desire to use the publications. They shall catalogue the publications in an acceptable fashion. N.H. REV. STAT. ANN. § 202-B:5

Oklahoma—[T]he contracting library agrees to receive and maintain the full and complete collection of such publications and not to dispose of any such publication without prior approval of the Publications Clearinghouse, to provide adequate facilities for the storage and use of such publications and to provide free services to its patrons in the use of such publications. OKLA. STAT. ANN. tit. 65, § 3-113.3(3)

South Dakota—The university of South Dakota at Vermillion and the historical resource center shall each retain permanently at least one copy of each document distributed by the center for the purpose of historical research. Permanent retention may be encompassed through use of microforms. S.D. COMPILED LAWS ANN. § 14-1A-5

Tennessee—Care of depository copies. It shall be the duty of the librarian or other person in charge of each depository to give receipt for and carefully preserve all state documents and publications so received. One of the two (2) copies shall be lendable on application, to the persons, if any, allowed to take other books from the library of the depository. The other copy shall not be allowed to be taken from the premises of the depository. TENN. CODE ANN. § 12-612

Utah A library must contract with the commission to provide adequate facilities for the storage and use of state publications, to render reasonable service without charge to patrons and reasonable access to state publications. UTAH CODE ANN. § 37-5-6

NOTES

1. American Library Association, Government Documents Round Table, *1978 Directory of Government Document Collections and Librarians*, 2d ed. (Washington, D. C.: Congressional Information Service, 1978), pp. 81-85.

2. A. Paul Pross and Catherine A. Pross, *Government Publishing in the Canadian Provinces* (Toronto: University of Toronto Press, 1972), p. 53.

3. Harriet M. Skogh, "Recent Developments in Publication and Distribution of American State Documents," American Library Association, Committee on Public Documents, *Public Documents, 1936*, p. 142.

4. Ibid., p. 140.

5. John J. Boll, "Tame the Terror for its Use; or, What Are Wisconsin Documents?" *Wisconsin Library Bulletin* 70:81 (March-April 1974).

6. Wisconsin Division of Library Services, "Manual for Wisconsin Document Depositories" (Madison, Wis.: Wisconsin Division for Library Services, 1975), p. [1].

7. Carolyn W. Kohler, "Results, Computerized Search for Ideal Locations, Iowa State Documents Depositories, " June 1974, in Documents on Documents Collection.

8. Robert B. Downs, "Government Publications in American Libraries," *Library Trends* 15: 187-189 (July 1966).

9. [Form letter to state agencies from Alphonse F. Trezza, Director, Illinois State Library, August 11, 1972], in Documents on Documents Collection.

10. Dan Henke, ["The State Legal Publications Field"], "Government Documents and Publications: A Panel," *Law Library Journal* 53:333 (November 1960).

11. 42 *Stat.* 436.

12. Anne M. Boyd, *United States Government Publications*, 3d ed. by Rae E. Rips (New York: H. W. Wilson, 1949), p. 31.

13. Margaret T. Lane (comp.), *State Publications: Depository Distribution and Bibliographical Programs*, State and Local Documents Task Force, Government Documents Round Table, American Library Association; Texas State Publications Clearinghouse, Documents Monograph Series, no. 2 ([Austin, Tex.]: Texas State Library, 1980).

14. Robert Grey Cole, "North Carolina Needs an Improved Depository System for State Documents," *North Carolina Libraries* 31:38 (1973).

15. John Kopischke, "State Document Depositories: Wisconsin Outlines a New Approach," *Wisconsin Library Bulletin* 70:133 (May-June 1974).

16. Lane (comp.), *State Publications: Depository Distribution*.

17. Genevieve M. Casey and Edith Phillips, *Management and Use of State Documents in Indiana*, Wayne State University, Office of Urban Library Research, Research Report no. 2 (Detroit: 1969), p. 44.

18. Jerome K. Wilcox, "Proposed Survey of Federal Depository Libraries," American Library Association, Committee on Public Documents, *Public Documents, 1938*, pp. 26-27.

19. Shawn Duffy [Statement in state section under Minnesota], in Documents on Documents Collection.

20. Bernard M. Fry, et al., *Research Design for a Comprehensive Study of the Use, Bibliographic Control and Distribution of Government Publications, Final Report* (Bloomington, Ind.: Research Center for Library and Information Science, Indiana University, October 1970), p. 52.

21. "Manual for Wisconsin Document Depositories: Guidelines for Standards and Procedures of the Wisconsin Document Depository Program" (Madison, Wis.: Wisconsin Division for Library Services, January 1975), p. 4.

22. Ibid., p. 6.

23. *New Mexico Documents Express* 1, no. 2:3 (June 1979).

24. Cole, "North Carolina Needs an Improved Depository System," p. 38.

Part I Appendix

GUIDELINES FOR MINIMUM STATE SERVICING OF STATE DOCUMENTS

1. In each state an agency or agencies should be designated by law to act as the depositories for the documents published by the state to maintain a collection of and to distribute copies of such documents within the state and to exchange copies with other states. The functions of such depository should be adequately defined and determined in legislation.

2. The appropriate state agency should maintain a list of in-state depositories to which it regularly sends some or all state documents, and should receive a sufficient number of copies to serve those depositories.

3. The appropriate state agency should be prepared to exchange documents with other states, or at least to have an adequate supply of copies available to meet out-of-state requests. What is an adequate supply will depend on the nature of the documents and its potential interest to persons in other states.

4. The appropriate state agency should compile and distribute a checklist and/or shipping list of its state publications.

4a. Such lists should appear at least quarterly.

5. The appropriate state agency should deposit at least one copy of all its state publications with the Library of Congress, and send at least one copy to an additional designated national depository, if and when one is created.

6. The appropriate state agency should maintain and have available for distribution an authority list of state agencies.

7. In the appropriate state agency at least one professional person (full time or equivalent) should be assigned to the state documents function, and that person should have adequate supportive staff.

Approved by Government Documents Round Table, Association of State Library Agencies (ASLA), Resources and Technical Services Division (RTSD), and the Interdivisional Committee on Public Documents, July 1974. Approved by Reference and Adult Services Division (RASD), American Library Association (ALA) Executive Board and ALA Council, January 1975.

GUIDELINES FOR STATE DOCUMENTS CHECKLISTS

WHEREAS, the ALA has adopted "Guidelines for Minimum State Servicing of State Documents" which states: (4) The appropriate state agency should compile and distribute a checklist and/or shipping list of its state publications. Such lists should appear at least quarterly; and

WHEREAS, the Library of Congress *Monthly Checklist of State Publications* is selective and does not purport to be a comprehensive state bibliographic tool; and

WHEREAS, the checklists of state publications are necessary for bibliographic control; now, therefore be it

RESOLVED that each state must assume primary responsibility for bibliographic control of its own publications in order to provide access to state documents, and, be it further

RESOLVED that Guidelines for checklists of state publications are hereby promulgated.

1. *Legality.* A checklist of state documents should be required statutorily.

2. *Scope.* This official state document checklist should provide the most complete listing of the state's documents as is possible.

3. *Format.* The checklist publication should follow the American National Standards Institute, Inc. *American National Standard for Periodicals: Format and Arrangement.* 1967 (11 p.) (ANSI Z39.1-1967)

4. *Frequency.*
   A. The checklist should be published at least quarterly (ALA Guidelines for Minimum State Servicing of State Documents, 4a)
   B. A cumulative index should appear at least annually.

5. *Distribution.* Adequate in-state and appropriate out-of-state distribution should be provided.

6. *Preparation.* Preparation of the checklist should be by, or supervised by, professional library personnel.

7. *Checklist Content.*
   A. Full statement of the scope of the checklist:
      1. Policy statement developed by the responsible agency.
         a. Agencies & types of publications excluded from the list.
         b. Period covered (publication date or receipt date of publications listed)
         c. Inclusion policy for "older" publications.
         d. Treatment of periodicals (listed each issue, semi-annual, annual, etc.)
   B. Information on how to obtain copies of listed publications.
   C. Cross-references.

8. *Bibliographical Content of Entries*.
   A. Issuing agency
   B. Full title
   C. Author(s)
   D. Holding statement for each edition
   E. Imprint (including copyright if applicable)
   F. Collation
   G. Series
   H. Price
   I. Restrictions on distribution and availability
   J. Other identifiable information such as ISSN, ISBN and stock numbers

9. *Mailing Addresses*. Mailing address of agency should appear either as an adjunct to the entry, or at the end of the checklist.

10. *Mailing Lists*. Prior to updating the mailing list notification should appear in the checklist to alert recipients.

11. *New Agencies*. When the first publication of a new agency is listed, the legal authority for the agency's creation and a brief history should be included.

> Approved by State Documents Task Force, February 1, 1977; approved by Government Documents Round Table, June 21, 1977; approved by Association of State Library Agencies, June 24, 1978; approved by Reference and Adult Services Division, June 26, 1978; approved by Library and Information Technology Association, June 26, 1978. Amended by State and Local Documents Task Force, June 26, 1979.

GUIDELINES FOR INPUTTING STATE DOCUMENTS INTO DATA BASES

The purpose of this document is to establish policies for the creation of state bibliographic records which are compatible with the developing national bibliographic networks.

1. A single institution within each state should have sole responsibility for coordinating input of state documents into the data bases (e.g. OCLC, RLIN, WASHINGTON, etc.). State documents should be considered as any information produced by or for a state agency in any format (*Guidelines for State Documents Checklists, Checklist Commentary*, p. 1, in *DttP*, volume 5, no. 2, March 1977, p. 68). State supported college and university publications will be considered as state publications with the exception of copyrighted university press publications. Cataloging role assignments may be made in selected areas.

2. The institutions will input full original cataloging in MARC format.

3. The coordinating institution should compile, publish and maintain an authority file of state agencies citing the name of the agency as it is to be used for cataloging.

    A. The authority file should be based on the latest edition of *AACR*.

    B. A history of each agency, its position in the government structure and any necessary cross references should be included in the authority file.

Approved by Government Documents Round Table, January 26, 1978; approved by Association of State Library Agencies, June 24, 1978; approved by Reference and Adult Services Division, June 26, 1978; approved by Library and Information Technology Association, June 26, 1978. Amended by State and Local Documents Task Force, June 26, 1979.

GUIDELINES FOR STATE PUBLICATIONS DEPOSITORY LEGISLATION

WHEREAS, The ALA has adopted "Guidelines for Minimum State Servicing of State Documents" and

WHEREAS, each state must assume primary responsibility for acquiring, distributing and bibliographic control of its own publications in order to provide access to state documents, and, be it further

RESOLVED, that Guidelines for state publications depository legislation are hereby promulgated.

State publications depository legislation should provide for:

1. Definitions of a "state agency" and "state publication." The definitions in *Guidelines for State Documents Checklists, Checklist Commentary* (*DttP*, v. 5, no. 2, March 1977, p. 68) should be followed.

2. A specific administering agency designated by law to carry out depository legislation. Authorization to the administering agency to adopt rules and regulations.

3. A requirement that state agencies must supply sufficient copies of all their publications to meet distribution requirements.

4. Authorization for the administering agency to use micrographics or other means of reproduction to meet the needs of depository distribution.

5. Systematic and automatic distribution of state publications from the administering agency.

6. Distribution to a system of designated depository libraries—to insure easy availability to the public. Such a system should include full and partial depository libraries. Distribution should include the Center for Research Libraries and the Library of Congress.

7. A provision for the maintenance of a complete, permanent historical collection.

8. Bibliographic control of state publications compatible with national developments and preparation of a checklist in accordance with *Guidelines for State Documents Checklists* (*DttP*, v. 5, no. 2, March 1977, p. 68.)

Approved by State and Local Documents Task Force, January 22, 1980; approved by Government Documents Round Table, July 2, 1980.

GUIDELINES FOR STATE DISTRIBUTION CENTER ACTIVITIES

These Guidelines supplement and expand the Guidelines on servicing, checklists, data bases, and legislation already adopted by S&LDTF. Items relating to the distribution centers which are outlined in the existing Guidelines are not repeated, e.g., the duty to issue a checklist, to provide for out-of-state libraries, etc.

The state distribution center should:

1. Coordinate state agency efforts to comply with the law, and educate and advise state agencies on library and user needs through training sessions, manuals and brochures, and personal contacts.

2. Follow an intensive, systematic program of document identification and acquisition and encourage libraries throughout the state to assist in identifying documents to be acquired.

3. Encourage the acceptance of depository library responsibilities in all appropriate areas of the state.

4. Prepare and promulgate standards for depository libraries.

5. Send documents promptly to the depository libraries, with shipments at least once a month.

6. Prepare a shipping list for the depository library packages.

7. Make available to the depository libraries a manual containing legal and administrative documents related to the depository program and recommendations on the handling of documents in various kinds of libraries.

8. Insure through provision of variant formats and through appropriate duplication processes that sufficient copies of publications are available to meet the needs of the depository system.

9. Consider the establishment of a microform program by the distribution center to satisfy the storage needs of depository libraries.

10. Maintain records on the distribution to the depository libraries.

11. Visit and inspect depository libraries on a regular basis.

12. Hold workshops and training sessions for depository librarians.

13. If state has a statewide classification scheme, maintain the scheme, supplying new numbers as required.

14. Prepare and distribute a current list of state agencies with addresses, telephone numbers, contact persons, etc.

15. Prepare brochures, posters, news releases, radio spots and other publicity that can be used throughout the state.

16. Promote state documents as reference and information sources through annotated bibliographies, workshops, etc. for depository and non-depository libraries.

17. Administer an exchange program or a warehouse for duplicates and encourage state agencies to list or deposit their surplus publications with the program.

18. Consider establishing a depository library council with a representative from each depository library.

19. Consider establishing an advisory board with membership from publishing agencies, the legislature, the budget office, depository and other libraries.

Approved by State and Local Documents Task Force, July 1, 1980; approved by Government Documents Round Table, July 2, 1980.

PART II State Publications— The Literature

PART II

8. SURVEYING THE LITERATURE OF STATE PUBLICATIONS

Countless librarians have selected, acquired, processed, and publicized state documents in their individual libraries. The state document collections assembled over the years are one evidence of their work. Another is the literature produced in the field of state documents. Books and articles set forth the reasons why libraries value documents and why they compile bibliographies, guides, and tools for their acquisition, handling, and use, thus sharing and making available to others the results of investigations, compilation, and research.

The background reading which a conscientious state document librarian should do begins with the literature of one's own state. Because in many states only a few articles and tools relating solely to state documents have appeared, this first step is often a small one and should not delay the reader from progressing immediately to the examination of those materials that are comprehensive in scope and cover all fifty states. These are largely bibliographical aids and tools. Comparative analyses of state document activities and discussions of problems common to many states are considered less frequently

Next, one should turn to the publications reporting on the individual states in order to compare these to the literature of one's own state. This large undertaking is best approached by examining the most recent publications first. Finally, the state document librarian must read the literature about documents on all different levels of government because many situations parallel one another in the documents issued by different jurisdictions, both in the documents themselves and in their processing and use. Much of the literature relating to federal documents is relevant for the state document librarian.

LISTS OF BIBLIOGRAPHIC ITEMS

Supplementing the present discussion of the literature is a bibliography of state documents literature. References in this discussion to items in the bibliography are given in a short form, consisting of the author's last name or the first few words of the title. This "name dropping" technique is used solely to reduce the number of footnotes and does not imply disrespect or familiarity.

Footnotes are given for works not included in the bibliography. Thus, references to works on documents in general which are cited for comparative purposes or to note a section on state documents are not part of the bibliography and are in the footnotes. The bibliography does include some items on federal documents that have been cited as "state," in order to allow comment on the extent of state coverage.

The major listing of state document articles before 1945 was that in the *Manual* compiled by Wilcox. Chapter 9 in the *Manual* is a bibliography prepared by Edith M. Coulter's class in government documents at the University of California in 1938. Of the eighty-eight articles in that list, about one-third have been cited in later lists and are thus included here, though some are not annotated because they have not been seen by this author.

The present bibliography is a single alphabetical listing of titles selected from several sources. *Library Literature*,[1] the principal current listing of published information on state documents, was the first source searched. Over four hundred entries have appeared in *Library Literature* under the heading "State Publications." Some of these are duplications because entries are repeated under the name of the state when appropriate.

The major listing devoted solely to articles on documents is Schorr's *Government Documents in the Library Literature*.[2] Schorr performs a valuable service by consolidating entries for lists which appeared as regular features in library bulletins with a note "See issues of . . ." and by associating reprints and reviews with the works to which they relate. Because his list covers documents at all levels of government, general articles are not repeated in his state section. Schorr groups the 248 publications titles listed into four categories, with each title in only one category. For example, articles about checklists are included with the articles which are, in themselves, checklists. Only about thirty titles from *Library Literature* are not included in Schorr. These are largely both state and federal in scope, and some are on archives and records.

Another, much more selective list is that in Fry's *Research Design for a Comprehensive Study of the Use, Bibliographic Control and Distribution of Government Publications*. It was compiled in 1969 and includes eleven titles designated as "state," all of which are included here.

Supplementing Fry is the list by a group of library school students at Simmons College, referred to here simply as Sachs, the name of the first author.[3] With slight modifications, the list follows the grid pattern established by Fry and cites fifty-five titles under "state," although a number of these have very little state information. They have been included here with a note on the extent of the state coverage as a guide to the reader. Although the Sachs team consulted a number of library indexes which Peter Hernon, in his review of Schorr, mentioned as not having been used in that work, they did not say how many new titles were discovered in the more general sources.

In 1979, Lovgren continued the Fry-Sachs series by listing monographs[4] and also used the convenient grid pattern. She lists thirty-five titles under "state," only seventeen of which are exclusively state. Most of the seventeen titles are major bibliographies included by Lovgren for practicing librarians and are frequently listed elsewhere. The only monographs relating solely to state documents published since 1945 are Parish (1974), Jenkins (four titles), and the Council of State Governments (three titles). The 1915 work by Reece, as the first comparative study of the types of state documents and their subject matter, should not be permitted to fall into oblivion, and thus is included in the bibliography.

Another source checked for titles of articles on state documents is the bibliography in Parish's *State Government Reference Publications*. Parish, pubished in 1974, lists fifty-four titles, of which fifteen have brief annotations. Again, discretion has been exercised in the selection of titles from this list.

The "Bibliography for State Documents Syllabus,"[5] compiled by the State Documents Task Force Education Committee, was scanned for relevant titles that do not appear in other lists.

Some of the features of a citation index are provided in the present bibliography by references to the sources consulted in compiling it. For those accustomed to keeping up to date in the field by using *Library Literature*, it will be a simple matter to skim through the list for the titles not cited therein. Likewise, the articles most widely cited can be identified.

KEEPING UP TO DATE

Peter Hernon discusses the task of keeping up to date in his article "State Documents to the People'." He mentions *Documents to the People, Government Publications Review*, and *Microform Review* [6] as good sources for current information. Since Hernon's article was written, *Microform Review* has begun an annual "government documents issue." To these should be added *Jurisdocs* [7] and the state documents newsletter of one's own state. Among these newsletters are some which are from the document interest groups of state library associations and some from state library agencies. Others are cooperative projects (for example, Virginia's *Shipping List*, prepared by the staff of the Public Documents Section of the University of Virginia Library in association with the Public Documents Forum of Virginia).

DOCUMENTS NEWSLETTERS

CALIFORNIA
    California Library Association,
    Government Publications Chapter, *Newsletter*.

v. 1, no. 1- [March 1976-   ] Bimonthly, January,
March, May, July, September, & November
Latest issue seen: v. 4, no. 2, March 1979
Combined issue v. 3, no. 5-6, November 1978
Subscription included in dues: CLA members $2.00
                                        Nonmembers $5.00
Editor: Janet Casebier, Millikan Library 1-32,
California Institute of Technology, Pasadena,
California 91125

ILLINOIS

ILA-GODORT Newsletter
v. 1, no. 1- March 1976-   Irregular
Latest issue seen: v. 3, no. 3, December 1978
Issues reported:
> v. 1, no. 1, March 1976
> v. 1, no. 2, August 1976
> v.2, no. 1, August 1977
> v.3, no. 1, April 1978
> v.3, no. 2, August 1978
> v.3, no. 3, December 1978

Editor: Ann Glascoff, Library, Governors State
University, Park Forest South, Illinois 60466

IOWA

Iowa Library Association, Government Documents
Section, *Interim Newsletter*.
[v. 1, no. 1?-] March/April 1978
Latest issue seen: March/April 1978
Editor (i.e., return address on March/April 1978 issue:
Government Documents Section, Iowa Library
Association, c/o Mary McInroy, University of Iowa
Library, Government Documents Department, Iowa City, Iowa
52242)

KANSAS

KLA GODORT Newsletter
Pilot issues [no. 1]-2, October 1977-April 1978//
Editor: Mac Reed, Forsyth Library, Fort Hays State
University, Hays, Kansas 67601

KENTUCKY

Let's Talk Documents (News about documents for
Kentucky libraries, rotated around depository
libraries in state)
no. 1- July 1977-   Irregular
Not seen

Issues reported:

no. 1, July 1977	no. 5, April 1978
no. 2, January 1978	no. 6, August 1978
no. 4, February 1978	no. 6, October 1978

MICHIGAN
Red Tape
no. 1- January/February 1979-
Latest number seen: no. 3, May/June 1979
Editor: Paul Thurston, Sociology & Economics
Department, Detroit Public Library, 5201 Woodward Avenue,
Detroit, Michigan 48202

NEBRASKA
The DOCumentor (A Government Publications Newsletter for Nebraska Libraries)
no. 1- September 1976- Irregular
Latest number seen: no. 6, August 1978
Issues reported:

no. 1, September 1976	no. 4, October 1977
no. 2, December 1976	no. 5, January 1978
no. 3, April 1977	no. 6, August 1978

Distributed free by: Nebraska Publications Clearinghouse,
Nebraska Library Commission, 1420 P. Street, Lincoln, Nebraska 68508

NEW ENGLAND
Infodocs, Newsletter of the NELINET Government
Documents Task Force
v. 1, no. 1? Irregular
Latest issue seen: v. 5, no. 3, August 1978 (Misdated 1977)
Infodocs Reviews
v. 1, no. 1- early Fall 1978- Quarterly
Available at $6 per year from: New England Library
Information Network, 40 Grove Street, Wellesley, Massachusetts 02181

NEW JERSEY
Government Documents Association of New Jersey,
Newsletter
no. 1- Irregular
Issues reported:
    no. 11, April 1978
    no. 13, November 1978
    no. 15, June 1979
Editor: Jaia Heymann, Drew University Library,
Madison, New Jersey 07940

NEW MEXICO
New Mexico Documents Express
v. 1, no. 1- April 1979- Irregular

Latest issue seen: v. 1, no. 2, June 1979
Distributed free by: State Documents Clearinghouse,
New Mexico State Library, P.O. Box 1629,
Santa Fe, New Mexico 85703

NORTH CAROLINA
*The Docket: Newsletter of the Documents Librarians of
North Carolina*
v. 1, no. 1- ??   Quarterly
Latest issue seen: v. 6, no. 3, June 1979
Available on request.
Editor: Elaine Lengle, Hunter Library, Western
Carolina University, Cullowhee, North Carolina 28723

PENNSYLVANIA
Documents to Pennsylvania (Newsletter of the
P.L.A. Government Documents Round Table)
Only issue seen: December 1977
Editor: ?? Suggested contact: Kathy Warkentin, Chairperson,
PLA GODORT, Library, Shippensburg State
College, Shippensburg, Pennsylvania 17257

TEXAS
Public Documents Highlights for Texas
v. 1, no. 1-   Fall 1978-   Quarterly
Latest number seen: v. 1, no. 3, Spring 1979
Available free from: Bob Walton, Editor, Texas
State Publications Clearinghouse, Texas State
Library, Box 12927 Capitol Station, Austin, Texas 78711

VIRGINIA
The Shipping List
v. 1, no. 1-   [1971-   ]   Quarterly
Suspended publication for ''almost two years, 1975-77.''
Latest issue seen: v. 5, no. 2, October 1977
Editor: The Staff of the Public Documents Section
Library, University of Virginia. Address: SHIPPING
LIST, c/o Public Documents, Alderman Library,
University of Virginia, Charlottesville, Virginia 22901

(See also Patrick J. Wilkinson, ''Directory of Documents Newsletters,''
Documents to the People 8: 209+ [September 1980].)

A collection of these newsletters is in the hands of the GODORT Liaison to
State and Local Groups, who shares information extracted from them through
articles in *Documents to the People*. Available newsletters were scanned for
state news, which has been noted in the state section.

Another way to keep up to date is through the regular columns in other library journals. *RQ* started including information about state documents beginning with the Fall 1976 issue (v. 16, no. 1) in its government documents column.

Articles in this bibliography are annotated, with the exception of articles published before 1945, theses, separately issued publications not seen by the compiler, and bibliographic tools for which the title is clearly descriptive. Publications and articles relating to a single state are annotated in the state section, where they are arranged appropriately for each state, usually chronologically to provide historical background (California is the best example), to keep the papers from workshops together (Illinois and Pennsylvania are examples), or to group the articles produced to set the climate for legislation (see North Carolina and Wisconsin). All the articles in the state section are included in the master list, with a *see*-reference to the state section. News notes from library bulletins and documents newsletters are included in the state section without being listed in the master list, if titles are not significant or the information is ephemeral in nature.

The grouping of articles by state serves the convenience of the reader interested in a particular state and identifies the articles from a state which have been included in the literature indexes. From this starting point, a more complete listing of all articles and publications relating to a particular state could be compiled, including the publications of the distribution center, such as manuals for depository libraries (the California one is listed because it has been cited in the library indexing tools, but there are others in Kansas, Louisiana, Nevada, and Pennsylvania) and state agency manuals (Missouri was the first state to issue one and New Mexico has one now); stories from local newspapers; and other sources not known outside the particular state.

A few state library and state documents committee publications that are in the Documents on Documents Collection are listed, including a special report written for the state library development committee (Nevada), a handbook on state documents information (Louisiana), the Texas primer (Olds), two major Texas studies (Propp and Walton), and the annual report issued in New Mexico (another "first," at least in out-of-state distribution and a commendable idea that gives needed visibility to the program). A thorough analysis of the Documents on Documents Collection with annotations would give state document librarians a valuable tool for identifying publications that might be useful as examples for local application.

Although a literature study should begin by focusing on one's own state, a bibliographic essay logically starts with the more general publications dealing with documents at all levels of government.

Books on documents in general which have a section on state documents include Brown, Markley, and Schmeckebier.[8] It is much more difficult to identify general articles that have specific coverage of state documents. Some such articles have been cited as "state" and thus are included in the bibliography with notes on the extent of state coverage.

Because much more has been written about federal documents than about state documents, state document librarians have always relied on that literature for discussion of the problems in document handling and for examples of useful tools. Two librarians have compared the state and federal depository programs. Carma Zimmerman outlines the parallels between the California and the federal program, and Kopischke, more briefly, comments on the differences between the Wisconsin program and the federal one. White has published a comparative study on federal and New York publications. This work was adapted and used for the multistate comparisons in the *State of State Documents*.

For purposes of comparison, the study by Pross, which covers the publishing of the Canadian provinces, is excellent.[9] American librarians would indeed be fortunate if they had a "Pross" for the fifty states. Pross deals with ten Canadian provinces in detail which is not possible for fifty states. He queried the Queen's printer in each province (which would be complicated in the United States, where most states do not have an official printer) and surveyed eighty libraries with documents holdings (likewise a difficult task in the United States where there are, for example, seven out-of-state libraries that collect Alaskan state documents).[10] Nevertheless, for his listing and discussion of the problems in acquiring, distributing, and using governmental publications issued by jurisdictions below the national level, and for comparative purposes, this work is invaluable.

Pross identifies five central problems in his study: (1) to define provincial government publication, (2) to rationalize the structure for processing and distribution, (3) to establish procedures for discovery, (4) to create an effective depository system, and (5) to devise and introduce workable library procedures for handling provincial publications, including arrangements for reporting and locating documents and for retrieving the information they contain.[11] American librarians will identify with these problems. In his concluding chapter, "Summary of Recommendations," Pross gives his recommendations in priority order. He suggests that "depository status be sought early in the campaign (and that the attendant rationalization of collections be carried out), since although few libraries will derive much immediate benefit, it should provide them with an incentive to make the designation meaningful."[12]

The serious student will appreciate this study. Fortunately, there has been a definite increase in the number of articles about state documents in the last ten years. Yet, in passing, it might be noted that two recent anthologies of library literature have, according to a reading of the titles included, no articles on documents, except from the archival point of view.[13]

BIBLIOGRAPHIC TOOLS—CHECKLISTS

Palic is the source for state-by-state listings of bibliographic works on state documents.[14] Although this bibliography closes with 1971, Palic includes "a number of works published later." The entries for each state are divided into "current" and "retrospective." Some citations to Palic have been included in the bibliography here as a clue to the reader that the listed title is a bibliographic tool.

The word "current," as Palic uses it, refers to the checklists. Palic begins with the *Monthly Checklist of State Publications*,[15] which is known to all state documents librarians and is the first state document tool a library should acquire after its own state checklist. A general checklist that is too recent to have been included in Palic is the Information Handling Services' *State Publications Index*, (formerly *Checklist of State Publications*) that began publication with its 1975-76 volume.[16]

For the checklist entries in Palic, a more up-to-date listing is Nelson's "Current Checklists of State Publications." Nelson's list supersedes lists published in 1951 (Hardin), 1962 (Tennessee), 1966 (Lane), 1968 (Current . . .), and 1972 (Littlewood). The *Monthly Checklist of State Publications* includes checklists (identified with an asterisk) in its semiannual periodical issues.

For the retrospective state document lists, Palic is at this time the most up-to-date source, superseding the Loftus survey of states in the Northwest in 1935, the Wilcox list in Chapter 6 of the *Manual*, the Lloyd supplement, the Wilcox supplemental lists (cited by Lloyd, p. 149n), and Childs' list in *Library Trends* in 1966. Tanselle's *Guide to the Study of United States Imprints* should not be considered to have been superseded because the arrangement therein is chronological. The document section in Tanselle is limited strictly to documents lists and does not include the author heading lists found in Palic.[17]

Richard Korman, specialist in government publications bibliography, is preparing a new edition of the Palic bibliography at the Library of Congress. No formal systematic mechanism exists for the publication of a listing of newly issued publications for the period after the publication of Palic, although Korman is happy to receive notes on new titles. A regular listing in *Documents to the People*, arranged in the traditional state format, would be useful. An added feature for such a supplemental listing would be reports on delays in the publication of regularly issued serials as a service for those who maintain an up-to-date collection of checklists.

The articles on the preparation and functions of checklists are all out of date except Woolley (published in *Documents to the People*). Lathrop's 1940 article mentions the checklists of the individual states only in passing and emphasizes the publications of the National Association of State Libraries, the old *State Law Index*,[18] and other lists covering all the states.

Lloyd (1948) gives a full history of state bibliographies and checklists, both those covering all or some of the states, and those limited to the publications of a single state. This historical account, along with that by Tanselle, is recommended.

Hardin's 1951 paper established that only nineteen states were then issuing checklists and recommended that efforts be concentrated on improving the

Monthy Checklist of State Publications. A chart tabulated five characteristics of the checklists.

The 1957 Wisconsin study contains several tables on the features of the checklists and a still pertinent section on the user's problems. Casey also includes a table on checklists that is more up to date (1969) than the Wisconsin study and has four categories of data. The most recent tabulation of checklist features is that by Hordusky, included in *The State of State Documents*, for eleven southwestern and mountain plains states. Details, even on the content of the bibliographic entry, are given in twenty major categories. The Hordusky tabulation was a working paper for the GODORT State Documents Task Force committee which drafted the Checklist Guidelines (see Appendix).

This author's 1966 article on checklists discusses those checklists issued at that time, their content and editing, and presents a plea for the preparation of a checklist as a means of getting bibliographic records on state documents in order.

Woolley (1977) suggests that checklists be "a reflection of bibliographic control rather than carry that charge as their primary role." He recommends producing checklists from cataloging data bases to reduce duplication of effort.

The titles of individual state checklists are not included in the master list except for those included in lists of the literature. Citations to Palic identify these as tools.

BIBLIOGRAPHIC TOOLS—STATE MANUALS

A number of librarians have recognized the usefulness of state manuals and have prepared works about them. Two theses, one a checklist (Farrier, 1957) and the other a comparative study (Lowenberg, 1962), are probably too old to be helpful. Among those works that have been superseded are the listing in the *Book of the States* (included until 1948-1949),[19] Hotaling (1948, 1953, 1963), Press (1962, although this may still be useful for the publications on election results), and Cook (1971). Clarke's 1972 article is not a list, but rather a recommendation that the value of manuals be recognized. All of these have been superseded by the more inclusive lists by Hernon and Parish.

Hernon in his 1972 and 1974 lists includes not only manuals, but also checklists, statistical abstracts, directories, and so on. Hernon has sent out a survey in preparation for the issuance of a new list. Parish lists, with annotations, the same type of tools listed by Hernon and also includes representative documents for each state. That author, too, is planning a new edition of his work.

LAWS AND DEPOSITORY PROGRAMS

Articles on state documents laws and depository programs tend to be limited to a discussion of the situation in a single state. Articles on legislation which are exceptions to this generalization are the 1909 Andrews committee report on model legislation, the 1950 thesis by Waters on the legislation of six states, the chapter in Casey's 1969 study, the survey by Gaines in 1978, and the author's list of citations published in 1978. The ALA "Guidelines for Minimum State Servicing of State Documents" (see Appendix), which are applicable to all the states, have not received critical comment in the literature.

Articles on laws and programs in the states usually date from a year or two before the enactment of legislation to a few years thereafter. In Missouri, however, two articles in the early 1950s (Hylton and Irvin, both 1952), setting forth the need for attention to state documents and for legislation, antedated by some twenty-four years the enactment of depository legislation in 1976.

Examples of articles appearing before the enactment of legislation and designed to alert librarians to the need for such legislation and to explain legislative proposals include Atterberry (Missouri), McGuire (New Mexico), Owen (Louisiana), and a series of Wisconsin articles. Major studies that preceded legislation include the Casey study (Indiana) and the South Dakota report, which was the official report of a legislatively established commission.

After the enactment of the South Dakota legislation, Carmack, author of the report of the study commission, published an article describing the work of the commission. Other reports on the enactment of legislation include Shaffer's classic study on the Nebraska experience, the reports by Mundkur (Connecticut, 1977) and McClure (Oklahoma, 1978). Shorter reports, which served primarily to inform the library community of the new legislation, include "Louisiana Depository . . ." (1948), "Legislature Establishes . . ." (Mississippi, 1966), and "State Documents. . . ." (New Mexico, 1978).

Articles and notes on legislation and depository programs have been published for the following states and are summarized in the state section:

Alaska	Mississippi	Oklahoma
California	Missouri	Oregon
Connecticut	Montana	Pennsylvania
Florida	Nebraska	South Dakota
Idaho	Nevada	Texas
Illinois	New York	Wisconsin
Louisiana	North Carolina	

The articles about the state depository systems are customarily written by the administrators of those systems. For a contrasting view, see the New York article by Yun, the article by Henke on depository service to law libraries, Shepard's comment on the Alaska system, LoRusso's reaction to the California management study, and the plaintive remark by Welch, "we believe . . . we qualify for state depository status."

Of particular interest are articles on the depository library program written for state officials and others who are not librarians and published in nonlibrary journals. An example is Kerschner's article in *Nevada Government Today*.

THE DOCUMENTS AS SUCH

Articles about the state documents themselves are the most usual kind. These vary from the ones listing all official state publications for a certain period (and thus serving as a substitute for an independently issued checklist) to selected lists limited by subject matter, audience, or type of document.

Comprehensive lists of documents include those for Idaho and Indiana. Lists that appear more or less regularly in library bulletins are included in Schorr with the note "see issues of. . . ." In some instances, the time span Schorr gives for repeatedly issued lists is not as long as that given in Palic for the same title, presumably because the indexing of the journal began after the checklist began to appear. This is true for Idaho, Indiana, and Maryland.

Selected lists are too numerous to mention by name (there are at least twenty-five in the bibliography). Moreover, they tend to go out of date quickly, especially if they are limited to recent or new publications.

LISTS—BY BRANCH OF GOVERNMENT

Before listing the discussions and articles limited to the documents of a single branch of government, the works covering all the states should be cited. Retrospective lists for statutes, session laws, and other legal publications are found in Pimsleur, a looseleaf service kept up to date by periodic releases. A supplementary service giving the latest volume or number issued has been published as section 3 of *Current Publications in Legal and Related Fields*, titled "Checklist of Current State, Federal and Canadian Publications," since 1968.[20] (For a complete listing of works covering all the states, see Palic, pp. 84-87.)

Tseng's list of state administrative rules and regulations is useful for its ordering information, although administrative codes and registers of regulations are also included in section 3 of *Current Publications*. . . .

Another source with information on all the states is Epstein's legislative article. Driscoll's 1956 thesis is a comparative study of the legislative journals for a two-year period.

Works limited to a single state include:

Statutory, adminstrative, or executive publication articles:

   Tennessee, Cheney, 1940
   Wisconsin, Marshall, 1942
   Minnesota, Hennen, 1977
   Pennsylvania, Oller, 1970, and Crowers, 1972
   Texas, "Texas Register. . . ." 1975

Legislative publications:

   California, California State Library, 1976
   Illinois, Adams, 1972

Mississippi, Raymond, 1955
Pennsylvania, Hirschman, 1970
West Virginia, Goff, 1976.

LISTS—SPECIAL SUBJECTS

Education is the most popular subject for which lists have been compiled. The bibliographical essay by Lester in 1971 probably supersedes all the earlier compilations. Barron has had a continuing column on curriculum and media since 1969. The most recent educational item is that by Woodbury on California sources for educational legislation.

Serials and statistics are the other areas in which more than one person has shown an interest in publications on a special subject or appropriate for certain groups of people.

For statistics, a specialized but useful list is that by Sell on sources for vital statistics. Two general articles on statistics, cited because they include some mention of state documents, are Yun (1973) and Weintraub (1974). On serials, there are articles by Alleman (State Experiment Station serials), Stewart (Pennsylvania union list), and White (California serials).

In addition to Alleman on agricultural publications, there is a note of agricultural interest by Schmidt on the "Memorandum of Understanding," which has been entered into by many states, providing for preservation within the home state of Agricultural Experiment Station and related publications.

Other subjects include the Negro (Staten), children (Wood), and home and garden (Taylor). Special audiences include the businessman (Sawyer), small and medium-sized libraries (Sullivan), and a medium-large public library (Welch).

LIBRARY HOLDINGS AND UNION LISTS

Downs in 1966 listed library holdings for state documents, first a state-by-state list of the strongest state collections which, not surprisingly, are in the state of origin, and second, the multistate collections. Pullen describes the North Carolina out-of-state collection. The Louisiana Documents Committee, Tomberlin for Oklahoma, and Hummel for Virginia report on local holdings. Pennsylvania's union list of serials (Stewart) is the only known union list in this field, although in states that have comprehensive distribution of periodicals, current holdings are in the depository libraries.

DOCUMENTS IN THE LIBRARY

Handling the documents within the library has been a perennial topic in the literature. Some of the works have been tools, for example, author heading or authority lists and classification schemes, and others, discussion of procedures with examples. Rosenkoetter's article is based on a comprehensive survey of library practices and is probably still valid.

AUTHORITY LISTS

Markley has a list of the author heading lists issued prior to 1951. This list, supplemented by those compilations issued since then and a 1915 article included as an indication of early interest in this topic, is as follows:

Alabama, Markley, 1948
Arizona, Pitts, 1951 (Thesis)
Colorado, Dorzweiler, 1953 (Thesis)
Connecticut, Winkler, 1951
Kansas, Wilder, 1956
Louisiana, Foote, 1948
Nevada, Poulton, 1964
New Jersey, Oellrich, 1951 (Thesis)
Ohio, Reddy, 1958 (Thesis), and Gillon, 1959 (Thesis)
Oklahoma, Tomberlin, 1977
Pennsylvania, Holt, 1941
Texas, Vaught, 1955 (Thesis)
Washington, Tucker, 1950
Wisconsin, Hayes, 1915, and Jackson, 1954
Wyoming, Fisher, 1951

All such lists were compiled before the adoption of the *Anglo-American Cataloging Rules*, when the cataloger looked to the legal name of the agency in establishing the entry. Today, under the *AACR*, catalogers look at the name provided on the piece, and the lists of names they subsequently compile are referred to as name authority lists. (See Sternlicht and the articles about Texas.) Bibliographical citations to the more recent lists are not given here because they are not readily available outside the state of origin and because they are often maintained on cards or in a computer data base rather than in printed format.

An American Library Association committee report and an article by Tucker about the author heading project of the 1940s and 1950s have been superseded by the standards and the procedure set out in the Alabama author heading list by Markley.

CATALOGING AND CLASSIFICATION

The other type of tool prepared for the convenience of librarians is the classification scheme. General classification schemes applicable to documents issued by different levels of government are not usually indexed under state.

Mina Pease's "Plain J" and the Guelph system, commonly called CODOC, come readily to mind.[21]

Classification schemes prepared for use in a multistate collection include the well-known one by Swank, Jackson's notation scheme, and Glidden, which is abstracted in the *Documents to the People* article (Classification . . .). More recent schemes are described in Gronbeck (1971) and Gavryck (1972). Heenan (1974) also has a scheme which is based on the home city but expands to include other localities.

Hartman's bibliography with its supplement is a recent guide to individual classification schemes for various states. The "Classification Abstracts . . ." published for five schemes give full and detailed explanations.

Dale's 1969 article discusses the history of and reasons for the archival-type classification schemes based on the principle of provenance. Other discussions on the nature of classification schemes are by Alderman and Henrich.

Classification schemes for individual states that have been listed in the library literature and perhaps for that reason are more readily available are:

Illinois (Nakata)
Ohio (Houk, and another by Lester)
South Dakota (Helgeson)
Texas (Cook)

Explanations of state schemes, as distinguished from those above which are the complete classification scheme, are

Florida (Newsome)
Illinois (Anderson)
Louisiana (Tilger)
Maine (Kirkwood)
Pennsylvania (Bordner)
Wisconsin (Alderman)

Journal articles describe key word in context (KWIC) and key word out of context (KWOC) indexes as used in Mississippi (Carson), New York (Sternlicht), South Dakota (entered under South Dakota), and Wisconsin (Schwarz). The Mississippi KWIC system is designed to interface with the microform of the documents.

Articles with less emphasis on classification and more on cataloging include Akers (1925), Spinney (1948—English), Moody (1960), Keefer (1962—this is the "Oregon" plan), Lane (1963), Clarke (1966), Jackson (1966), and Carter (1970). Announcements of the Library of Congress/Texas joint project on Texas state names have appeared, and readers should be alert for progress reports. If time permits the reading of only one article, Carter is recommended for its style and its coverage of a broad range of problems relative to state documents, from the question of integrating versus segregating to the changes made by the then-new *Anglo-American Cataloging Rules*.

MICROFORMS

The *Microform Review* is the place to start searching for articles in this relatively new area. Janet Lyons prepared a bibliography of state documents titles reviewed in that journal. Kerschner wrote an article on recent programs that helps bring Railsback's study up to date. Cohen explains the Information Handling Services program that provides microfiche for many state documents. Carson has written about the Mississippi program, and Lane has summarized the Delaware plan briefly.

WRITERS OF THE PAST

The librarian new to the literature of state documents should read some of the articles of the past. Names and projects that are prominent in the journal articles are Childs, Kuhlman, Wilcox, Jenkins, and Macdonald. The projects that have distinctive names are the State Document Center Plan, the State Document Microfilming Project, and the State Document Clearing House.

James Bennett Childs, to whom we are indebted for his listing of the bibliographical tools for state publications and for his insistence on the importance of an understanding of the structure of government, is best known for his three editions of *Government Document Bibliography*.[22] Vladimir Palic produced the fourth edition of this work. Childs authored numerous articles, most of which covered documents at all levels of government. Although his area of interest was worldwide, he was concerned about U.S. documents on the state and local levels as well, and his lists of state bibliographic tools were the standard ones. When writing on author headings, or other cataloging problems, his examples included those from the various states.[23]

An observation Childs made in his article in the *Encyclopedia of Library and Information Science*, [24] that documents constitute a borderland area between libraries and archives, is thought-provoking for state document librarians. Because state institutions are smaller and the borders less distinct than those in the federal government, the possibilities of cooperation might well be better.

Augustus Frederick Kuhlman was chairman of the American Library Association Documents Committee when the Social Science Research Council turned over to it the project for the preservation of primary source materials. This project was called the State Document Center Plan. In a 1933 article, Kuhlman stated that ''the preservation of public documents stands as the original and most important objective of this movement.'' There were nine or ten categories of materials that the documents centers were to collect, beginning with public documents and continuing with other materials that ''do not find their way into libraries automatically through copyright or the book marketing procedure.'' Ten possible state programs were suggested, including issuance of a checklist of state publications and introduction of legislation to make official depository libraries. The goal of this legislation was preservation in the depository libraries rather than the current one of using the depository libraries as convenient centers for citizen access to the documents. Kuhlman's article in the *American Library Association Bulletin* is recommended, partly because it is printed immediately following that of Leonard White listing the state documents centers, which the reader can check for his own state. The aricle by Kuhlman in *Illinois Libraries* is much the same. Kuhlman's article in *Library Quarterly* in 1935 further develops an idea first explored in *Public Documents, 1933*. The 1933 article has a good discussion of the scope and subject matter of the available bibliographical tools. The 1935 article presents a comprehensive plan, with a set of rules for compilation of state checklists.

In 1934 Kuhlman presented a paper on regional planning for state document collections. The major emphasis was on the geographical approach, but the conclusion mentions a subject approach, such as transportation, education, church history, and social work.

Kuhlman edited the first volumes of the *Public Documents* series published in the 1930s. This American Library Association publication printed the speeches from the Association's conventions and was devoted entirely to documents for a number of years, after which it was enlarged in scope to include archives. A number of articles from this work are cited in the bibliography.

Jerome K. Wilcox, who took over the chairmanship of the American Library Association Documents Committee from Kuhlman and also edited the Public Documents series, was chairman of the Documents Committee when the *Manual on the Use of State Publications* was compiled. State document librarians know him best for his editorship of the *Manual*, which is popularly called Wilcox. He published lists of supplementary document tools, including those for state documents, in *Special Libraries* for a number of years following the publication of the *Manual*.[25] His ''Publications of New State Agencies . . .'' was an important contribution to state document bibliography at that time. His report on the State Document Center Plan is the last contemporary report on that plan.

A reading of the Calfornia articles reveals that Wilcox was in California at the time depository legislation was being considered for that state and was one of the leaders in securing that legislation.

William S. Jenkins, University of North Carolina, established a joint project with the Library of Congress to film the early state documents, and his *Guide* (U.S. Library of Congress) is the key to this collection. A good explanation of the project is his article in *Illinois Libraries* or in his 1960 monograph. The State Records Microfilm Project, as it was called, filmed early state records up to the begining date (in the second half of the nineteenth century) of the collections at the University of North Carolina. Adelaide Hasse served as bibliographer.

A final name that might attract attention is that of Grace MacDonald. MacDonald worked for the Public Document Clearing House in Providence, Rhode Island, a committee of the National Association of State Libraries, housed at the Rhode Island State Library. The references in the literature to the "MacDonald lists" are to those that Palic enters under National Association of State Libraries. The clearinghouse not only prepared checklists of the session laws, statutes, and legislative journals, but also arranged exchanges of state documents.

NOTES

1. *Library Literature, 1909-* (New York: H. W. Wilson).

2. Alan Edward Schorr, *Government Documents in the Library Literature, 1909-1974* (Ann Arbor, Mich.: Pierian Press, 1976). Reviewed by Peter Hernon in *Government Publications Review* 4, no. 4:360-361 (1977).

3. Vivian Sachs, et al., "Periodical Literature for Government Documents Librarians: A Selected Classified Bibliography, 1970-Mid 1976," *Government Publications Review* 4:215-230 (1977).

4. Amy Lovgren, "Major Monographic Literature for Government Documents Librarians: A Selected Classified Bibliography 1900-Mid 1978," *Government Publications Review* 6:37-45 (1979).

5. "Bibliography for State Documents Syllabus," *Documents to the People*, 6:54-63 (January 1978).

6. *Documents to the People*, v. 1-, September, 1972- (Chicago: American Library Association, Government Documents Round Table), bimonthly ("The official publication of the Government Documents Round Table, American Library Association.")

Government Publications Review, v. 1-, Fall 1973- (Elmsford, N.Y.: Pergamon Press), quarterly ("An international journal covering the field of documents production, distribution, library handling and use of documents at all levels of government: federal, state and municipal, UN and international agencies and all countries.")

Microform Review, v. 1-, January 1972- (Westport, Conn.: Microform Review), quarterly.

7. *Jurisdocs*, v. 1-, September 1978- (Available from Susan Thevenet, Dow, Lohnes and Albertson, 1125 Connecticut Avenue, NW #500, Washington, D.C. 20036. $5 payable to AALL/GDSIS). (Newsletter of the Government Documents Special Interest Section, American Association of Law Libraries.)

8. Everett S. Brown, *Manual of Government Publications, United States and Foreign* (New York: Appleton-Century-Crofts, 1950), pp. 45-51.

Anne Ethelyn Markley, *Library Records for Government Publications* (Berkeley: University of California Press, 1951), pp. 40-45.

Laurence F. Schmeckebier and Roy B. Eastin, *Government Publications and Their Use* (Washington, D.C.: Brookings Institution, 1969); see index entries under "states".

9. A. Paul Pross and Catherine A. Pross, *Government Publishing in the Canadian Provinces: A Prescriptive Study* (Toronto: University of Toronto Press, 1972).

10. American Library Association, Government Documents Round Table, *1978 Directory of Government Document Collections and Libraries*, 2d ed. (Washington, D.C.: Congressional Information Service, 1978), p. 342.

11. Pross, *Government Publishing*, p. 10.

12. Ibid., p. 157.

13. Dianne J. Ellsworth and Norman D. Stevens, eds., *Landmarks of Library Literature, 1876-1976* (Metuchen, N. J.: Scarecrow Press, 1976).

Library Literature: The Best, 1970- (Metuchen, N. J.: Scarecrow Press, 1971-).

14. Vladimir M. Palic, *Government Publications: A Guide to Bibliographic Tools*, 4th ed. (Washington, D.C.: Library of Congress, 1975).

15. U.S. Library of Congress, Exchange and Gift Division, *Monthly Checklist of State Publications*, v. 1-, 1910- (Washington, D.C.: U.S. Government Printing Office, 1910-).

16. *State Publications Index*, v. 1- 1975/1976- (Englewood, Colo.: Information Handling Services), quarterly. (Formerly *Checklist of State Publications*).

17. G. Thomas Tanselle, *Guide to the Study of United States Imprints* (Cambridge, Mass.: Belknap Press of Harvard University Press, 1971), v. 1, pp. 89-108.

18. *State Law Index*, v. 1-12, 1925/1926-1947/1948 (Washington, D.C.: U.S. Government Printing Office), biennial.

19. *The Book of the States*, v. 1-, 1935- (Chicago: Council of State Governments), biennial.

20. Meira G. Pimsleur, *Checklists of Basic American Legal Publications*, AALL Publications Series, nos. 4 and 4A, (South Hackensack, N.J.: Published for American Association of Law Libraries by F. B. Rothman, 1962-), looseleaf.

"Checklist of Current State, Federal and Canadian Publications," *Current Publications in Legal and Related Fields*, section 3 (South Hackensack, N.J.: Rothman).

21. Mina Pease, " 'Plain J': A Document Classification System," *Library Resources and Technical Services* 16:315-325 (Summer 1972).

Margaret Beckman, et al., *The Guelph Document System, with a Manual of Procedures*, University of Guelph Library Report 3 (Guelph, Ontario: 1973).

22. Editions of 1927 and 1930, by J. B. Childs, published under title: An account of government document bibliography in the United States and elsewhere. Third ed., by J. B. Childs, published in 1942 under title: Government document bibliography in the United States and elsewhere.

23. James B. Childs, "The Author Entry for Government Publications," American Library Association, Committee on Public Documents, *Public Documents, 1934*, p. 107.

24. *Sub verbo*, "Government Publications (Documents)," v. 10, p. 42.

25. Palic lists Wilcox's works on unemployment relief agencies (p. 79), new guides and tools, 1953-1956 (p. 83), and official defense publications (p. 87). The compilations by Wilcox on new guides and aids to public documents use in *Special Libraries* are: 40:371-377 (November 1949) and 40:406-412 (December 1949) for 1945-1948; 45:29-36 (January 1954) for 1949-1952; and in *SLA Bulletin*, no. 2 (1957) for 1953-1956.

BIBLIOGRAPHY

"Access to State Documents Improved by New Programs." *Texas Libraries* 37:180-181 (Winter 1975).
   Lib. Lit.   *See* Texas.

Adams, Stanley E. "Illinois Legislative Documents and Services." *Illinois Libraries* 54:420-423 (June 1972).
                                                                                    See Illinois.

Akers, Susan Grey. "Simple Cataloging of Popular State Documents." *Wisconsin Library Bulletin* 22:3-6 (1926) (Summary appeared in *ALA Bulletin* 19:289 [1925]).
   Schorr 1038.
Author's talk at a library conference has an informal tone. It is directed to small libraries and recommends pamphlet boxes or vertical files in lieu of cataloging, or if cataloging is done, it should, for example, pick out that part of the title which is common to the series for the title, use "Pub. by the state" as imprint, and make subject analytic cards for special articles. The basic premise is that documents should be handled like any other book and that they should be used.

Alderman, Alice. "Classifying State Documents." *Documents to the People* 4:58-63 (May 1976).
   Sachs.   *See* Wisconsin.

Alderman, Alice. *Organizing Wisconsin Public Documents: Cataloging and Classification of Documents at the State Historical Society Library*. Madison, Wis.: Wisconsin Department of Public Instruction, Division for Library Services, Bureau of Reference and Loan Services, 1974. 62 p. (Bulletin no. 5075.)
   Parish.   *See* Wisconsin.
Parish lists this with title beginning, "Procedures for Cataloging and Classifying . . . ."

Alleman, Mrs. W. M. "New Serial Publications of the United States Department of Agriculture and the State Experiment Stations." *Special Libraries* 44:66-69 (February 1953).
   Lib. Lit.
A list, eight state documents included. "Recent trends in government publishing in the field of agriculture are to publish more readable and popular publications; to further separate the technical material from the popular; and to achieve greater artistic variety and attractiveness in format and size" (p. 69).

American Association of Law Libraries, Special Committee to Study Cooperative
Purchasing of Law Books. "Report." *Law Library Journal* 32:294-303 (Sep-
tember 1939).
Lib. Lit.

Annotation in *Library Literature* says in part, "[D]iscusses the cost of state reports,
state session laws, and revisions of statutes and compilations. State publications are
often sold at different prices inside and outside the state."

American Library Association, Catalog Section, Committee on State Author Headings.
"Report of a Survey on Standards for State Author Heading Lists." *ALA
Cataloging and Classification Yearbook* 9:38-43 (1940). (Appeared abridged in
ALA Bulletin 34:85-87 [August 1940].)

The committee was appointed in January 1939. A total of 112 circulars were sent out;
96 were returned. Five standards were presented, and discussion of pros and cons
followed. *See also* Tucker and Markley.

American Library Association, Council. "Guidelines for Minimum State Servicing of
State Documents." *Documents to the People* 3, no. 7:32-34 (September 1975).
(Same in *ALA President's Newsletter* 5:8 [May 1975]; *Government Publica-
tions Review* 2:389-390 [1975]; and *RQ* 15:36 [Fall 1975].)
Lib. Lit.   *See* Appendix.

Sachs cites under title.

American Library Association, Government Publications Round Table. *1978 Directory
of Government Document Collections and Librarians*, by Nancy Cline and Jaia
Heymann. 2d ed. Washington, D.C.: Congressional Information Service, 1978.

Depositories for libraries' "home" state are indicated by a star. State collections for
other than the "home" state are indexed by state in the Special Collections Index. A
supplemental leaflet, "State Document Authorities," includes ALA/GODORT affili-
ates and chairpersons of state documents committees in addition to the state authorities.

Anderson, P. G. "Classification Scheme for State Documents." *Illinois Libraries* 54:
426-429 (June 1972).
Lib. Lit., Schorr 1040, Sachs, Parish with annotation.   *See* Illinois.

Andrews, C. W. "A Model Law for the Distribution of State Documents." *ALA
Bulletin* 3:327-328 (September 1909).
Waters.

The author, the chairman of a committee to draft a uniform law, finds the task almost
impossible. He offers to have a law drafted according to the laws of a single state.

Atterberry, Meryl. "Missouri Documents to the People." *Show-Me Libraries* 27:11-14
(January 1976).
                                                                See Missouri.

Atterberry, Meryl. "Missouri State Depository Documents Update." *Documents to the
People* 6:24-25 (January 1978). (Reprinted from *Show-Me Libraries* 29:20
[October 1977].)
                                                                See Missouri.

Atterberry, Meryl. "Update: Missouri State Depository Law." *Documents to the People* 5:235, 237 (November 1977). (Reprinted from *Show-Me Libraries* 28:20-21 [August 1977].)

See Missouri.

Bailey, Dorothy. "Service to You Through the Illinois Documents Unit." *Illinois Libraries* 37:34-35 (February 1955).
Schorr 905.   *See* Illinois.

Barron, R. E. (comp.). "Publications in Curriculum and Media." *Bookmark* 29:67-73 (November 1969). Also in later issues.
Lib. Lit., Schorr 953-955.

Blake, T. "Journey's End." *Dartmouth College Library Bulletin* 15:90-91 (April 1975).   *See* New Hampshire.

Blanchard, Marion L. "Documents for California." *California Librarian* 19:111-112 (April 1958).
Lib. Lit., Schorr 831.   *See* California.

Blasingame, Ralph. "Public Documents of the States: Their Collection, Listing, Distribution and Value." *Proceedings of the Second Assembly of State Librarians . . . 1960*. Washington, D.C.: Library of Congress, 1961. pp. 1-8.
Lib. Lit., Schorr 832, Parish.
The author, then Pennsylvania state librarian, presented the activities of the documents librarians of 1930 as though they were currently taking place and concluded that little progress had been made since then.

Boggess, C. A. "The Present Worth of Some Records." *Virginia Libraries* 4:22-28 (1931).
Lib. Lit., Schorr 833.

Boll, John J. "Tame the Terror for Its Use: Or, What Are Wisconsin Documents?" *Wisconsin Library Bulletin* 70:79-82 (March 1974).
Lib. Lit., Schorr 834.   *See* Wisconsin.

Bordner, George W. "Certification Program for Documents Distribution." *Pennsylvania Library Association Bulletin* 25:84-85 (March 1970).
Lib. Lit., Schorr 906.   *See* Pennsylvania.
Paper from Workshop (entry under Stewart).

Bordner, George W. "Classification Scheme: Pennsylvania State Publications." *Documents to the People* 4, no. 4:15-17 (June 1976).

See Pennsylvania.

Bostick, Mary. "South Carolina State Documents." *South Carolina Librarian* 15:23 (Fall 1970).
Lib. Lit.   *See* South Carolina.

Bowker, Richard Rogers. *State Publications: A Provisional Checklist of the Official Publications of the Several States of the United States from Their Organization.* New York: Publishers Weekly, 1908. 1031 p.
Parish with annotation.
The standard list for the period covered.

Brackett, T. "New Hampshire Documents." *Bulletin, New Hampshire Public Library* 33:121-127 (September 1937).
Lib. Lit.

Brees, M. A. "Texas Documents Collection of the Legislative Reference Library." *Texas Library Journal* 49:259-261+ (December 1973).
Lib. Lit   *See* Texas.

Brigham, H. O. "Cooperative Want List and Duplicate List of State Documents." *ALA Bulletin* 22:498-500 (1928).
Lib. Lit., Schorr 907.

Brigham, H.O. "Public Document Clearing House and Its Activities." American Library Association, Committee on Public Documents. *Public Documents, 1936.* pp. 146-149. (Also appeared in National Association of State Libraries, *Proceedings and Papers* 39:25-27 [1936].)
Lib. Lit. annotated.
"A check list of session laws has been completed, a check list of house and senate journals is in compilation and similar bibliographical projects are planned for future dates. The Clearing House is also preparing a complete analysis of want and offer holdings for exchanges."

Britten, Christine. "What Do You Do with Them? Put Your Documents Where Their Service Is." *Wisconsin Library Bulletin* 73:32-33 (January-February 1977).
Lib. Lit.   *See* Wisconsin.

Brown, D. C. "Distribution of State Documents." *ALA Bulletin* 18:259-260 (1924).
Lib. Lit., Schorr 908.

Brown, E. "Seattle Solves Problem of Standards and Specifications." *Library Journal* 82:33-35 (January 1, 1957).
Schorr 909.
This is federal only.

Brunner, J. Terrence. "Freedom of Information at the Local Level." *Illinois Libraries* 57:271-277 (April 1975).
Sachs.
A talk by the executive director of the Better Government Association, a citizens' watchdog association working exclusively with the media. The association's position is that the public doesn't have an adequate right of access to records. Examples are given. The association urges passage of a general right of access statute.

Bryan, Vivian. "Materials Relating to Vermont at the Vermont Department of Libraries Law and Documents Unit." (Guides to Major Vermont History Collections, a Bicentennial Series, no. 3.) *Vermont Libraries* 5:15-18 (January 1976).
Lib. Lit.

Bryan, Vivian. "Vermont State Publications." *Vermont Libraries* 2:33-35 (February 1972). Also in later issues.
Lib. Lit., Schorr 957-959.

Buber, E. J. "Pennsylvania Bureau of Publications."*Pennsylvania Library Association Bulletin* 25:82-83 (March 1970).
Lib. Lit., Schorr 910.   *See* Pennsylvania.
Paper from Workshop (entry under Stewart).

Butt, Cecilia. "Creating an Arkansas Documents Collection." *Arkansas Libraries* 34:15-17 (June 1977).
Lib. Lit.   *See* Arkansas.

California, Department of General Services. *Library Distribution Act Procedures and Definitions, M-698.* 1973. 11 p., exhibits.

California Library Association, Documents Committee. *California State Publications: Manual for Acquisition, Processing, Use.* The Association, 1957.
Lib. Lit., Schorr 911.
See 2d edition under California, State Library.

California, State Library, Sacramento. *California State Publications: Manual for Processing, Use.* 2d ed. rev. Department of Finance, Organization and Cost Control Division, 1961.
Lib. Lit., Schorr 1041, Fry, Parish.   *See* California.

California, State Library, Sacramento. Government Publications Section. *California Legislative Publications Charts.* 3d ed. rev. by Richard H. Nicoles and Mary Schell. The Library, 1976. 24 p. (GPS Publication 3.)
Lib. Lit., Schorr 835.   *See* California.
Schorr lists 2d ed., which was by Ruth Elwonger and Mary Schell, 1968, 27 p.

Campbell, Ruth. "Selected List of Recent Louisiana State Documents." *Louisiana Library Association Bulletin* 9:90-93 (March 1946).
Lib. Lit., Schorr 960.   *See* Louisiana.

Carmack, Bob D. "South Dakota Public Documents: Report of a Study." *Government Publications Review* 1:251-256 (1974).
Sachs.   *See* South Dakota.

Carroll, Marian. "A Profile of Illinois Libraries Collecting State Documents." *Illinois Libraries* 54: 434-439 (June 1972).
                                                        See Illinois.

Carson, Calvin S., and Read, D. E. ''Computer/Microform System for State Documents.'' *Mississippi Library News* 41:131-132 (September 1977).

See Mississippi.

Carter, Catherine. ''Cataloging and Classification of State Documents.'' *Pennsylvania Library Association Bulletin* 25:86-97 (March 1970).

Lib. Lit., Schorr 1042, Sachs, Parish annotated.   *See* Pennsylvania.

Paper from workshop (entry under Stewart).

Casey, Genevieve M., and Phillips, Edith. *Management and Use of State Documents in Indiana*. Detroit: Office of Urban Library Research, Wayne State University, 1969. 75 p. (Research Report no. 2.) Also published as Indiana Library Studies Report 17 (Bloomington, Ind.): Indiana University, Bloomington. Graduate Library School, 1970. 68 p. ERIC ED 046 473.

Lib. Lit., Schorr 912, Fry, Parish.   *See* Indiana.

Charts analyzing legislation from all states have been copied and quoted from in other studies (Carmack, Fry). Parish cites as 1970, 97 p. Schorr cites as 1970, 63 p. Fry cites as 1969.

Chamberlin, Edgar W. ''Do You Receive U.S. and Missouri Documents?'' *Missouri Library Association Quarterly* 16:48-51 (June 1955).

Lib. Lit., Schorr 913.   *See* Missouri.

Chamberlin, Richard. ''Introduction to United States Government, United Nations, Massachusetts State Documents.'' *Bay State Librarian* 56:9-11 (April 1966).

Fry.   *See* Massachusetts.

''Checklist of Idaho Publications, 1969- .'' See issues of *Idaho Librarian* 1970-

Lib. Lit., Schorr 961, Palic, p. 99.

Lib. Lit. enters under ''State of Idaho . . .''

Cheney, F. N. ''Historical and Bibliographical Study of the Administrative Departments of the State of Tennessee.'' M.S. Thesis , Columbia University, 1940. 245 p.

Schorr 836.

Childs, James Bennett. ''Bibliographic Control of Federal, State and Local Documents.'' *Library Trends* 15:6-26 (July 1966).

Fry.

Includes a state-by-state report on current and retrospective coverage. Superseded by Palic except for informal remarks on ''gaps'' needing attention and on possible manuscripts (for example, Hasse for South Carolina).

Childs, James Bennett. ''Trends in State Publications.'' *Library Journal* 53:697-700 (1928). (Extract appeared in *ALA Bulletin* 22:451 [1928].)

Lib. Lit., Schorr 837.

''Some recent trends in state publications may be attributed either to state advertising and publicity or to the movement for efficiency and economy.'' Advertising and publicity are primarily to attract tourists and investors. The movement for efficiency and economy has been directed toward reorganization of state governments and better edited state publications. Many examples from the documents of various states are given. One of a series of four articles; others are by Lesem, Sawyer, and Sullivan.

Clarke, J. A. "State Manuals." *RQ* 12:186-188 (Winter 1972).
    Lib. Lit., Schorr 838, Sachs.
Browsing in state manuals reveals a wide range of information—political, biographical, and historical—for a variety of readers. Clarke cites Cook's article in *Special Libraries* (February 1971) and Hernon's in *Library Journal* (April 15, 1972).

Clarke, Norman F. "Cataloging, Classification and Storage of Government Publications When Incorporated into the General Library Collection." *Library Trends* 15:58-71 (July 1966).
    Pages 65-66 cited by Parish with variant title.
Even when cataloged, documents are not cataloged as fully as other collections in the library. Clarke says, "The format in libraries today is that of limited cataloging of government publications and the use of bibliographies, indexes, and printed lists as a means of reducing the quantity of entries in the catalog." He refers to the Oregon plan (citing Keefer) and to Ruth Hardin's comments on the indexing situation for state documents.

[Classification abstracts in *Documents to the People*]:
    Glidden, Nebraska, New York (Milne Library) 3:36-43 (May 1975).
    Pennsylvania 4:15-17 (June 1976) Also listed under Bordner.
    Texas 4:28 (November 1976).

"Classification and Shelving Devices in Current Use in California Libraries." *News Notes of California Libraries* 56:409-410 (Fall 1961).
    Schorr 1043.
U.S. documents only. Follows Ruth Elwonger's article on U.S. depositories in California.

Coatney, Louis. "Questions and Answers: Alaska State Publications."
    Sourdough 13:4 (May 1976).
    Lib. Lit.   *See* Alaska.

Cohen, Herbert C. "An Immodest Proposal: State Publications When and Where You Want Them (Almost)." *Illinois Libraries* 58:200-204 (March 1976).
    Lib. Lit., Sachs.
A full explanation of the Information Handling Services system program by the editorial director, including the checklist and the microfiche. Short list of reference sources from Bowker and Hasse to Wilcox and *Monthly Checklist of State Publications*.

Cole, A. H. "Public Documents as Source Material for Graduate Students in Professional Schools." National Association of State Libraries. *Proceedings* 44:6-8 (1941).
    Lib. Lit., Schorr 839.
Speech as panelist at joint meeting of National Association of State Libraries (NASL) and American Library Association Public Documents Committee. Cole, librarian at the Harvard School of Business Administration, explains types of state documents in his library and reasons for their use. Title given is title of panel. Other speakers, Eldon R. James, Elmer M. Grieder (both from Harvard), and Violet A. Cabeen (Columbia), say less about state documents, and Cabeen, nothing at all. Cabeen states that catalogers help researchers with (1) list of agency names, (2) list of subject headings, and (3) shelf list (that is, classification schemes).

Cole, Robert Grey. "North Carolina Needs an Improved Depository System for State Documents." *North Carolina Libraries* 31, no. 4:35-38 (1973).
    Lib. Lit., Schorr 914.   *See* North Carolina.

Colorado, University, Library. *Classification for State, County, and Municipal Documents. See* Swank.

Columbia University, Teachers College, Library. *State and Municipal Education Documents.* (Library consultant, no. 11.) (mimeographed.) The Library, 1936.
    Lib. Lit., Schorr 962.

Cook. A. F. "Texas State Documents: A Classification Scheme." Denton, Tex.: 1975. 44 p. (Texas Woman's University, School of Library Science, Occasional Paper no. 5.)

Cook, Frederick G. "State Manual Procurement Guide." *Special Libraries* 62:88-93 (February 1971). Same *Illinois Libraries* 54:430-434 (June 1972).
    Lib. Lit., Schorr 915-916, Sachs, Parish annotated.
This is the latest revision of Hotaling's list and is essentially the same as Hotaling's. Cook says, "For up-to-date information on state manuals check under 'Directories' in PAIS Bulletin, or under 'State Government' in the 'Research Reports' section of Legislative Research Checklist."
    The annotation for the article reads, "State manuals published by official state agencies or by commercial publishers are useful and important reference tools, and a majority of them are available for the asking, or at low prices any library can afford. A checklist of current state manuals is provided, with specific information on how to obtain them." *See also* Hernon's *Library Journal* articles.

Corson, J. J. "Virginia Publishes Many Documents of Importance." *Virginia Libraries* 2:73-77 (1930).
    Lib. Lit., Schorr 963.

Council of State Governments. *State Bluebooks and Reference Publications (a Selected Bibliography)*. Rev. and annotated ed. Lexington, Ky.: The Council, 1974. 86 p. *Lib. Lit.*

A standard guide, arranged by state. Schorr 964 lists 1972 ed., 70 p.

Cramer, Rose Fulton. *Author Headings for the Official Publications of the State of Oklahoma*. Rev. by Carolyn C. Mohr. Chicago: American Library Association, 1954.

Crane, Elizabeth R. "Privilege vs. Responsibility: Document Depositories Are Meant to Serve Library Users." *Wisconsin Library Bulletin* 73:30-31 (January-February 1977).

See Wisconsin.

Crowers, Clifford P. "It's Great! Three Parts of the Federal Register System." *Pennsylvania Library Association Bulletin* 27:303-309 (November 1972).

Sachs.   *See* Pennsylvania.

Federal; includes mention that Pennsylvania follows the federal model.

"Current Checklists of State Publications." *Bookmark* 27:201-203 (February 1968). *Lib. Lit.*, Schorr 965.

A list, arranged by state, of the checklists issued. *See* entry under Nelson for later lists.

Dale, Doris Cruger. "The Development of Classification Systems for Government Publications." *Library Resources and Technical Services* 13:471-483 (Fall 1969).

Sachs.

"It was not until the principle of provenance was adopted for the classification of documents that order was given to this material. . . . In general, the translation of the complete symbol of a document should be read backward: A/PV. 1122 Verbatim Record of the 1122nd Plenary Meeting of the General Assembly, September 18, 1962." Cites Swank and Jackson. Gives five advantages of a classification scheme based on principle of provenance: (1) simple, easy to understand, and expandable, (2) economical because already assigned by U.S. and U.N., (3) works well as shelf location device, (4) full advantage can be taken of indexing in *Monthly Catalog* and *UN Document Index*, and (5) separate collection requires specialized librarians who in turn can provide better reference service. Main disadvantage is that subjects for different jurisdictions are not together on the shelf. "In conclusion, it may be stated that collections of government publications, whether of the UN, US, or other jurisdictions, are most easily accessible to the student and the scholar if they are classified on the basis of the archival principle of organizational structure. This statement is especially valid if these documents can be coordinated with analytical subject indexes."

Dale, Doris Cruger. "Manual Retrieval of Government Publications." *Bookmark* 29:106-110 (December 1969).

Sachs.

Very limited state information. One sentence mentioning *Monthly Checklist* and mention of Ellen Jackson and Swank for classifying.

Dalton, P. I., et al., "Government and Foundation Publishing." *Library Trends* 7: 116-133 (July 1958).
   Schorr 966.
Information on the states and state publications is presented as each topic is discussed: "financial backing, decisions of what shall be published and editorial and financial control over the physical presentation of the material," methods of distribution and of sales and advertising and sales promotion, and so on. Statistics are given, but states are not named.

Demorest, R. "Pennsylvania Government Documents." *Pennsylvania Library Association Bulletin* 9:3-4 (May 1953).
   Lib. Lit., Schorr 840.   *See* Pennsylvania.

"Depository Libraries Announced." *Pennsylvania Library Association Bulletin* 27: 298-299 (September 1972).
   Lib. Lit.   *See* Pennsylvania.

"Depository Libraries for Illinois State Documents; Addresses of Libraries to Which the Illinois State Library Regularly Sends All Illinois Publications Deposited with Its Documents Branch as of November 1971." *Illinois Libraries* 54:446 (June 1972).
   Schorr 841.   *See* Illinois.

"Directory of Government Document Dealers and Jobbers." *Documents to the People* 3:40-43 (September 1975). Later one is 5:209-212 (September 1977).
   Sachs.
Includes about a dozen dealers who offer state documents. Since most dealers offer several kinds of documents, there is only a single list.

"Distribution and Acquisition of Pennsylvania State Publications." *Pennsylvania Library Association Bulletin* 25:81 (March 1970).
                                                             See Pennsylvania.

"District Depository Libraries in Illinois." *Illinois Libraries* 53:443-446 (June 1971).
   Schorr 842.
These are federal depositories.

"Documents." *Nebraska Library Quarterly* 6:20-23 (Spring 1975).
                                                             See Nebraska.

"Documents News: State Documents Received by the Indiana State Library." *See* issues of *Library Occurrent* beginning August 1976.
   Lib. Lit.

"Documents Useful in Small Public and School Libraries." *Library Occurrent* 7:223-230 (1925).
   Lib. Lit., Schorr 967.

Dorzweiler, A. N. "Author Headings for the Official Publications of the State of Colorado." M.A. Thesis, University of Denver, 1953. 160 p.
Schorr 1045.

Douglas, Mrs. I. D. "New York State Documents for the Reference Librarian." *Grosvenor Library Bulletin* 21:38-48 (December 1938-March 1939).
Lib. Lit., Schorr 843.

Downs, Robert B. "Government Publications in American Libraries." *Library Trends* 15:178-194 (July 1966).
Lib. Lit., Parish.
A state-by-state list of the most complete library holdings of state documents in the state of origin and another list (twenty-five states only) of substantial collections beyond state borders. The summary mentions the extensive collections at the Library of Congress, the New York Public Library, and the Center for Research Libraries.

Driscoll, E. A. "State Legislative Journals for the Period 1952-1953, a Comparative Analysis." M.S.L.S. Thesis, University of North Carolina, 1956. 88 p.
Lib. Lit., Schorr 844.

Eaton, K. G. "The Missing 70%: The Availability of Oregon State Documents to Libraries." *Pacific Northwest Library Association Quarterly* 33:10-14 (October 1968).
Lib. Lit., Schorr 917, Fry.   *See* Oregon.
One of a series of three articles; others by Elison (Idaho) and Speer (Montana).

Ebbin, Arthur. "Access to N. Y. S. Publications: Summary of a Questionnaire Survey." 1975. 14 p. ERIC ED 119 739.

Elison, Gar T. "The Problem of Government Publications in Idaho." *Pacific Northwest Library Association Quarterly* 33:13-19 (October 1969).
Lib. Lit., Schorr 918.   *See* Idaho.
One of a series of three articles; others by Eaton (Oregon) and Speer (Montana).

Ellis, E. G., and Stewart, R. C. *List of Basic Pennsylvania Publications for Depository Libraries.* Prelim. ed. Harrisburg, Pa.: Pennsylvania State Library, 1967. 25 p. mimeo.
Lib. Lit., Schorr 968.   *See* Pennsylvania.

Ellis, E. G. "State Publications: Problems in Effective Use." *Drexel Library Quarterly* 1:42-46+ (October 1965).
Lib. Lit., Schorr 845, Parish.
A quick look at problems of acquiring, cataloging, and using state documents, followed by a selective bibliography.

Elwonger, Ruth. *California State Documents Maze: A Practical Approach on How to Get California Documents and Information.* California State Library, 1973, 11 p.

(Available from the author, 1733 Sherwood Avenue, Sacramento, California 95822.)
Lib. Lit., Schorr 846.   *See* California.

Elwonger, Ruth. *California State Information Sources Today (1970)*. California State Library, Government Publications Section, 1971. 7 p. (GPS publication 7.)
Lib. Lit., Schorr 847.   *See* California.

Elwonger, Ruth. *Introduction to State Information Sources*. California State Library, Government Publications Section, 1966. 11 p. (GPS publication 1.)
                                                                   See California.

Elwonger, Ruth, et al. "Documents Workshops in 1963." *News Notes of California Libraries* 58:373-386 (Fall 1963).
Lib. Lit., Schorr 848.   *See* California.

Enoch Pratt Free Library, Maryland Department. "Maryland State Documents Mid 1953-Mid 1954." *Between Librarians* 21:13-16 (Winter 1954-1955).
Lib. Lit., Schorr 969.   *See* Maryland.

Epstein, J. F. "Early Warning System for Monitoring State Legislation." *Special Libraries* 65:161-168 (April 1974).
Lib. Lit., Schorr 970, Sachs.
Industries need to know about pending legislation in all states. The Government Affairs Information Center in Washington, D.C., forwards legislation to units of industry that are concerned with a particular topic. No indexing is done because bills change too much. Bills can go through a state legislature in one week. For a letter commenting on the article and criticizing the "sources" for Washington state, see Chalfant, M. E., *Special Libraries* 65:6A (October-November 1974).

Farrier, G. B. "Official State Manuals: A Checklist." M.S.L.S. Thesis, University of North Carolina, 1957. 103 p.
Lib. Lit., Schorr 971.

"Federal Documents Regional Workshop: Conference Proceedings, Kansas City, Missouri, April 13-14, 1973." *Government Publications Review* 1:173-232 (Winter 1973); 303-315 (Spring 1974).
Sachs.
Although Sachs lists as "State," speakers did not discuss state documents as such.

Ferruso, Agnes. "Library of Congress Monthy Checklist. State Documents Section. *Illinois Libraries* 54:403-405 (June 1972).
Parish with annotation.   *See* Illinois.
An account of the production, coverage, and purpose of the *Monthly Checklist* and the activities of the State Documents Section at the Library of Congress.

Ferruso, Agnes. "Monthly Checklist of State Publications." Washington, D.C.: Library of Congress, 1974. 10 p. ERIC ED 095 891.
Paper presented at American Library Association Annual Conference, New York, New York, July 6-13, 1974.

Finn, Geneva. "Bibliography on Government Publications in Microform." *Illinois Libraries* 58:227-229 (March 1976).
    Sachs.
An annotated bibliography. The only reference to state documents is to the Railsback article in *Documents to the People*.

Finn, Geneva. "Publishing and Acquisitions of Illinois Documents." *Illinois Libraries* 54: 410-411 (June 1972).

See Illinois.

Fisher, Hail. *Author Headings for the Official Publications of the State of Wyoming*. Chicago: American Library Association, 1951. 60 p.
    Palic, p. 137.

Fleischer, Mary Beth. "State Documents Source for Varied Information." *Texas Libraries* 37:182-188 (Winter 1975).
    Lib. Lit.   *See* Texas.

Fleming, T. P. "Exchange and Distribution of Duplicate State Documents." American Library Association, Committee on Public Documents. *Public Documents, ·1936*. pp. 150-155.
    Lib. Lit., Schorr 919.
Emphasis on exchange of duplicates rather than exchange of publications of one's own institution. Procedures and recordkeeping in Minnesota are explained. Fleming noticed recent (1934) surge of interest compared with 1927.

Fleming, T. P., and Hegland, M. "Regional State Document Exchange Depositories and Regional State Document Centers." American Library Association, Committee on Public Documents. *Public Documents, 1937*. pp. 44-53.
    Lib. Lit., Schorr 920.
Advocates establishing ten or twelve regional document centers to supplement the state documents centers, to handle exchanges, and to act as clearinghouses for duplicates. These regional centers would collect all the documents, municipal, county, and state, for their region. An especially apt sentence is "It cannot be denied that state documents demand an exasperating amount of time and attention because of the vagaries of the officials who publish them."

Floersch, M. "Government Newsletter: A Selective Bibliography." *Illinois Libraries* 54:444-445 (June 1972).
    Lib. Lit.   *See* Illinois.
A listing of government newsletters. Only nine are state (of these five are under heading "government"). Seven are municipal.

Floersch, M. ''Illinois State Publications: A Selected Bibliography.'' *Illinois Libraries*
54:442-443 (June 1972).
Lib. Lit., Schorr 972.   *See* Illinois.

Florida Library and Historical Commission. ''Library Commission Adopts Criteria for
Depository Libraries.'' *Florida State Library Newsletter* 15:15 (November
1967).
Schorr 849, Fry.   *See* Florida.

Foote, Lucy B. *Author Headings for the Official Publications of the State of Louisiana.*
Chicago: American Library Association, 1948. 125 p.

Fry, Bernard M.; Libbey, Miles A.; Kósa, Géza A.; and Meredith, Joseph C. *Research
Design for a Comprehensive Study of the Use, Bibliographic Control and
Distribution of Government Publications, Final Report.* Bloomington, Ind.:
Research Center for Library and Information Science, Indiana University,
October 1970. ERIC ED 050 796.
Sachs.
The state section relies on Casey's study and proposes a considerably expanded version
of her table on checklists. Fry says that the extent to which depository libraries make use
of their depository privileges should be identified and that a more efficient distribution
system is required. Bibliography lists eleven titles under ''state.''

Furer, Shiela. ''Conference Report: Documents Depository Workshop.'' *Sourdough*
16:18 (March 1979).
                                                                                      See Alaska.

Gaines, Robert F. ''North Carolina State Documents Depository System: An Update.''
North Carolina Libraries 36:21-23 (Spring 1978).
                                                                                      See North Carolina.

Gaines, Robert F. ''Recent Developments in Depository Systems for State Government
Documents.'' *Documents to the People* 6:229-230 (November 1978).
Gaines notes an increase from between twenty and twenty-five states with depository
programs before 1970 to thirty-two in 1978, and an additional seven states with limited
programs. Gaines used Documents on Documents and information from articles and
newsletters as sources of information. The status of the program in each state is noted
briefly. The use of microforms (Utah, Nebraska, Kentucky, Massachusetts, New York,
and Information Handling Services [IHS]) and computerized bibliographical control
(Utah, Mississippi, North Dakota, Texas, Missouri, New York, and Kansas) are
discussed.

Gardner, Jack. ''Nevada State Publications Distribution.'' University of Nevada,
Bureau of Governmental Research. *Governmental Research Newsletter*, 7:[1]-8
(November 1968).
                                                                                      See Nevada.

Gavryck, Jacquelyn, and Knapp, Sara. "State Secrets Made Public: The Albany Plan." *Library Resources and Technical Services* 17:82-92 (Winter 1973).
   Lib. Lit., Schorr 1046, Sachs, Parish.

See New York

Gehringer, Michael E. "American Association of Law Librarians State Documents Workshop." *Documents to the People* 4, no. 6:36 (November 1976).
Summaries of the eight reports made in the two panel discussions. Emphasis was placed on methods of acquiring documents, acquisitions tools, and the problems encountered in securing documents. Some of the speakers were from depository libraries. One speaker described basic legal materials published by the states.
   The same report is found in *LC Information Bulletin* 35:503-504, Appendix II (August 27, 1976).

Gharst, Willie Dee. "Mississippi Government Publications: A Survey of Depositories." *Mississippi Library News* 38:16-17 (March 1975).

See Mississippi.

Gillon, E. H. "Author Headings for the Official Publications of the State of Ohio, 1803-1900." M.A.L.S. Thesis, Kent State University, 1959. 67 p.
   Schorr 1047.

Goff, Karen E. "Bibliographic Control and Acquisition of State Documents." *West Virginia Libraries* 27:23 (Spring 1974).
   Lib. Lit., Schorr 921.   *See* West Virginia.

Goff, Karen E. "Legislative Information." *West Virginia Libraries* 29:12 (Spring 1976).
   Lib. Lit.   *See* West Virginia.

Goff, Karen E. "State and State-Related Publications." *West Virginia Libraries* 26:16-17 (Fall-Winter 1973).
   Lib. Lit., Schorr 973.   *See* West Virginia.

"Government Documents." *Pennsylvania Library Association Bulletin* 15:65-66 (Winter 1960).

See Pennsylvania.

"Government Documents." *Wisconsin Library Bulletin* 73:29-38 (January 1977).
   Lib. Lit.   *See* Wisconsin.
A series of seven articles by Schneider (two articles), Crane, Britten, Schultz, and Lueck. Article by Waidelich on municipal documents not included here. Title taken from *Library Literature*.

"Government Documents for Small Libraries in Virginia." *Virginia Libraries* 3:57-62 (1930).
   Lib. Lit.

"Government Documents in Nevada: A Report to the Nevada Statewide Coordination of Collection Committee." Rev. June 1975. Various paging.

See Nevada.

"Governor of Mississippi Signed into Law House Bill 'H 125—Establish Depository for Public Documents in Research and Development Center Library and Provide for Recorder of Documents in Secretary of State's Office'." *Southeastern Librarian* 16:188 (Fall 1966).
Schorr 851. *See* Mississippi.

Graham, Jamie R. "Document Processing and Bibliography."*Special Libraries* 53:492 (October 1962).
Schorr 1048.
Example is U.S.; no specific reference is made to state documents. A "call number" is created using the year, a letter for the month (for example, July is "G"), and an agency accession number. Subject cards are removed from the catalog periodically, photocopied and assigned a "Biblio"number, and replaced by a single card referring to the Biblio.

Graves, W. B. "Present Status of Governmental Reporting in the American States." American Library Association, Committee on Public Documents. *Public Documents, 1936.* pp. 156-175. (Also appeared in National Association of State Librarians *Proceedings* 39:27-35 [1936].)
Lib. Lit., Schorr 852.

Gronbeck, Nancy. "Organizing a State Documents Collection." *Southeastern Librarian* 21: 169-171 (Fall 1971).
Lib. Lit., Schorr 1049, Sachs.
The author was documents librarian at Murray State University at Murray, Kentucky. A classification scheme covering all the states is explained. "Basically all that is required is a list of the numbers assigned to each state and a Cutter table." Using the scheme, one person cataloged 2,000 to 3,000 Kentucky documents in four weeks full time—that is, creating call number, marking the document, and making shelflist card with author, title, and holdings.

"Guidelines for Minimum State Servicing of State Documents." *See* American Library Association, Council.

Halcli, Albert. "Census Data: From Magnetic Tape to Microfiche." *Illinois Libraries* 56:279-282 (April 1974).
Sachs.
No state publications are mentioned.

Halcli, Albert. "How to Escape from the Documents Ghetto." *Illinois Libraries* 54:412-415 (June 1972).
Sachs. *See* Illinois.

Hale, Mrs. C. L. "Sources of Current Information on State Government Functions."
    M.A. Thesis, University of California, 1939. 113 p.
    Lib. Lit., Schorr 853.

Hall, W. L. "Bibliography of Virginia Documents: Scope and Methods." *Virginia
    Libraries* 3:43-56 (1930). (Appeared abridged in *ALA Bulletin* 24:457-458
    [1930].)
    Lib. Lit., Schorr 974.

Hall, W. L. "Some 'Lost' Virginia Documents of the Civil War Period." *Virginia
    Libraries* 3:21-23 (1930).
    Lib. Lit., Schorr 854.

Hamelin, Kristine. "Faculty Use Patterns of Government Documents." Albany, N.Y.:
    1973. 46 p.
    Parish.
Parish says, "This master's thesis studies use patterns for both U.S. and state documents in a college library."

Hammer, D. P. "Pennsylvania Government Publications." *Pennsylvania Library
    Association Bulletin* 10:8-10 (Spring 1955); 11:2-4 (Fall 1955).
    Lib. Lit., Schorr 922-923.   *See* Pennsylvania.

Hardin, A. R. "Selected, Annotated List of Illinois Official Publications for Use in the
    Five State Teachers' Colleges of Illinois." M.S. Thesis, University of Illinois,
    1942. 143 p.
    Lib. Lit., Schorr 975.

Hardin, A. R. "United States State Publications." *College and Research Libraries*
    12:160-163 (April 1951).
    Lib. Lit., Schorr 976.
This work is cited in Schorr with the title "Official checklists and indexes versus
cataloging of government publications; a symposium" because it is one of a series of
papers on U.S., state, and foreign checklists.
    Hardin poses the question: "To what extent can checklists take the place of detailed
analytics in the card catalog?" She says, "There has been practically no literature on
this subject."
    A chart shows the nineteen states issuing checklists, with frequency, cumulation,
index, bibliographic detail, and form. A second chart, compiled at the California State
Library, gives figures for fifteen states on items in the state checklist, mimeographed
items listed, items in *Monthly Checklist*, LC mimeographed items, and time lag.
    Hardin's summary of the state situation is: (1) incomplete coverage of the states, (2)
unequal value of the lists issued because of scanty bibliographical detail, (3) infre-
quency of cumulation of issues and indexes, (4) gaps in the historical coverage of a
state, and (5) issuance in such impermanent form that there is no definite assurance of
their continuance over a long period.

Libraries use checklists (1) to identify a title, (2) to establish a corporate entry, and (3) to order publications. Requests for state publications are usually by subject. *Agricultural Index, PAIS*, and *Education Index* are more satisfactory for that approach than the brief state checklists.

In order to improve the use of state publications, Hardin recommends concentrating on expanding and improving the *Monthly Checklist* by (1) more complete coverage in collecting items from all states, (2) indexing the monthly issues, (3) a more detailed annual index, and (4) assigning each item a number for more ready reference.

Harrison, Amalia. "Of Perennial Interest: The Capital Annuals." *Alabama Librarian* 29:11-13 (November-December 1977).
   Lib. Lit.   *See* Alabama.

Harrison, Rose. "Connecticut Statistical Sources: A Guide to Materials in the Connecticut State Library Collection." *Connecticut State Library Document News Letter* no. 7, November 1973. 11 p.

Hartman, Ruth D. (comp.). "Bibliography of Classification Schemes Used for State Documents Collections." *Documents to the People* 3:23-25 (March 1975). "Supplement No. 1." *Documents to the People* 4:23 (September 1976).
   Sachs.
Some annotations; notes on person to contact for further information.

Hawaii, State Library System, Honolulu. *Classification Scheme for Hawaii Documents*. The Library, 1970. 24 p.
   Lib. Lit., Schorr 1050.   *See* Hawaii.

Hays, F. C. "Author Headings for Current Wisconsin State Publications." *Wisconsin Library Bulletin* 11:140-142 (May 1915).

Hazard, Marjorie. "State Documents—Their Use and Value." *Michigan Library Bulletin* 21:177-178 (1930).
   Lib. Lit., Schorr 855.

Hazelton, Philip A. "New Hampshire State Publications." *North Country Libraries* 8, no. 3:5 (May-June 1965).
                                                          See New Hampshire.

Hebert, Elise S. "How Accessible Are the Records in Government Records Centers." *Journalism Quarterly* 52:23-29+ (Spring 1975).
   Sachs.
Archival records and records centers. Name misspelled as Herbert in Sachs.

Heenan, Thomas. "Classification of Local Publications." *Special Libraries* 65:73-76 (February 1974).
   Lib. Lit., Sachs.

Primary departmental units are indicated by a capital letter, and secondary divisions, by a whole number assigned on a sequential basis. A capital letter designates type of publication. The example is a municipal document.

Helgeson, E. H. "Classification System for South Dakota State Publications." *South Dakota Library Bulletin* 57:185-190 (April-June 1971).
Lib. Lit., Schorr 1051, Parish.   *See* South Dakota.

Helgeson, E. H. "South Dakota State Documents." *South Dakota Library Bulletin* 55:51-108 (April 1969).
Schorr 978.   *See* South Dakota.

Parts cited separately as:
  (1)"Check List of South Dakota State Publications, revised, August 1, 1969." *South Dakota Library Bulletin* 55:65-102 (April 1969).
      Lib. Lit., Schorr 977, Palic, p. 128.
  (2)"Printing and Distribution of South Dakota State Documents." *South Dakota Library Bulletin* 55:55-61 (April 1969).
      Lib. Lit., Schorr 924.

Henke, Dan. [The State Legal Publications Field.] "Government Documents and Publications: A Panel." *Law Library Journal* 53:332-337 (November 1960).
Henke, law librarian at the University of California, Berkeley, favors a depository system for the distribution of documents, but believes that not all presently established systems meet the needs of law libraries. He recommends the drafting of a model act because that would simplify the task of seeing the legislation through the legislative process. He concludes that if lawyers are well served and become the allies of librarians, legislation for a library program is easier to achieve.

Hennen, Thomas J., Jr. "Using Minnesota Statutes, the Minnesota Code of Agency Rules and the State Register." *Minnesota Libraries* 25:180-184 (Summer 1977).
                                                         See Minnesota.

Henrich, Fredrick K., and Martino, Elizabeth. "A Modified Archival Classification for New York State Government Publications." State University of New York at Buffalo, 1973. 3 p.
Parish.   *See* New York.

Hernon, Peter. "The Academic Reference Librarian as Documents Specialist and Promoter." *Pennsylvania Library Association Bulletin* 30:27-28 (March 1975).
Sachs.
Reference librarians should collect state checklists, retrospective checklists, bibliographies, bluebooks, and statistical abstracts. Acquisitions guides include *Monthly Checklist*, Hernon's *Library Journal* article, Council of State Government's *State Bluebooks and Reference Publications*, and state checklists.

Hernon, Peter. "Municipal Publications: A Bibliographic Guide to Library Litera-
    ture." *Government Publications Review* 5:445-453 (1978).
An annotated list of ninety-nine publications on municipal documents.

Hernon, Peter. "The Role of Academic Reference Librarians Concerning Government
    Publications, with Special Emphasis Given to Municipal Publications." *Gov-
    ernment Publications Review* 2:351-355 (1975).
    Sachs.
Reference librarians need to acquire, use, and make known government publications at
more than just the federal level. Problems in carrying out these roles are discussed.

Hernon, Peter. "State 'Documents to the People'."*Government Publications Review*
    3:255-266 (1976).
    Lib. Lit., Sachs.
Hernon states that the primary reference value of state documents is (1) current
statistics, (2) information of governmental structure, activities, and personnel, (3)
reports of agencies whose activities are not reported elsewhere, and (4) other published
information.
    Under "Recent Developments," he discusses the bibliographic guides, microforms,
and the inputting of state documents into network data bases. He recommends as ways
to keep abreast of developments in the state documents field: *Documents to the People*,
Government Publications Review, and *Microform Review*.
    Hernon's third major topic, "Reference Service and Collections," includes sugges-
tions for positive, aggressive reference service, including referral to other sources.
Suggestions for creating reference statistics are given.
    Hernon reports that the literature on "Outreach Programs" is sparse and that research
is needed. He cites articles by Reynolds and Grossman and a list, "Suggestions . . ." in
Government Publications Review.
    The "Areas in Need of Research" which Hernon identifies can be broadly grouped:
(1) local projects, such as filming, creating new tools (he gives examples), or studying
the relationship of the state to other levels of government; (2) use studies and reference
service studies; and (3) awareness devices, such as sharing knowledge of research in
progress and collecting guides to libraries.
    The final section, "Cooperative Relationship Between Documents and Reference
Librarians," includes a recommendation that documents be included in the discussions
at library conventions and in continuing education programs. Hernon thinks that the
working relationship should be strengthened between librarians and these groups—
researchers, students, faculty, legislators, and the public.
    Hernon's conclusion is that "the area of state publications is rich with research and
publishing opportunities."

Hernon, Peter. "State Publications: A Bibliographic Guide for Academic (and Other)
    Reference Collections." *Library Journal* 97:1393-1398 (April 15, 1972).
    "Addendum." *Library Journal* 97:2321 (July 1972).
    Lib. Lit., Schorr 979-980, Sachs, Parish.
Brought up to date in 1974.

Hernon, Peter. "State Publications: A Bibliographic Guide for Reference Collections." *Library Journal* 99:2810-2819 (November 1, 1974).
    Lib. Lit., Schorr 981, Sachs.
Expands 1972 article. Lists bluebooks, documents checklists, statistical abstracts, directories, and so on, with ordering information. For a letter commenting on "misinformation" in the article, see Westergard, Marjorie D., *Library Journal* 100:348 (February 15, 1975). Hernon's reply was that his Wisconsin information had been checked in Wisconsin.

Hernon, Peter, and Aluri, Rao. "Municipal Publications: A Selective Bibliographic Guide to 153 Cities." *Government Publications Review* 2:127-165 (Spring 1975).
    Sachs.
Strictly municipal, with the addition of "appropriate state non-governmental publications."

Hesseltine, W. B. "Return of Louisiana Documents." *Library Quarterly* 23:284-286 (October 1953).
    Schorr 856.
Records, not publications.

Hill, O. W. "Public Records Division." *Vermont Libraries* 1:11-14 (December 1970).
    Schorr 857.
Archival records, state records center, and central microfilming.

Hirschmann, Agnes, and Ellis, Elizabeth G. "Reference Use of Legislative Publications." *Pennsylvania Library Association Bulletin* 25:98-106 (March 1970).
    See Pennsylvania.

Historical Records Survey. *Bibliography of the Official Publications of Louisiana, 1803-1934.* Compiled by Lucy B. Foote. New Orleans: The Survey, 1942. (American Imprints Inventory, no. 19.)
    Schorr 982, Palic, p. 106.
Palic enters this under: Foote.

Hobson, J. W. *Damned Information: Acquiring and Using Public Information to Force Social Change; Legal Discussion and Analysis of the Federal Freedom of Information Act and Similar Laws in 50 States.* Washington Institute for Quality Education. 1971. 68 p.
    Lib. Lit.

Hodnefield, Jacob. "Minnesota Public Documents." *Minnesota Libraries Notes and News* 9:9-11 (1928).
    Lib. Lit., Schorr 858.

Hoffman, J. L. "Recent Government Publications for High Schools." *Library Journal* 83:1260-1262 (April 15, 1958). (Also appeared in *Junior Librarian* 4:20-22 [April 1958].)

Schorr 983.
Cites only federal documents. Cited in Lester's paper.

Holbrook, F. K. (comp.). "Checklist of Current State, Federal, and Canadian Publications." *Law Library Journal* 60:128-145 (February 1967). Also in earlier and later issues.
Schorr 984-985.
The checklist is currently published in *Current Publications in Legal and Related Fields*, Sec. III.

Holt, Olive S. "Pennsylvania Author Headings." State College, Pa.: Library, Pennsylvania State College, 1941. 54 p. (Pennsylvania State College Library studies, no. 3.) An issue of the Pennsylvania State College *Bulletin* 35, no. 39.
Palic, p. 125.

Hotaling, D. O. "State Manual Procurement Guide." *Special Libraries* 54:206-209 (April 1963).
Lib. Lit., Schorr 925-927. Parish cites April 1963 list.
Earlier lists appeared in *The Book of the States* (until the 1948-1949 edition) and in *Special Libraries* (July-August 1948 and July-August 1953).

Houk, J. A. *Classification System for Ohio State Documents.* Columbus, Ohio: State Library, 1962. 27 p.
Schorr 1052, Parish.

"How to Obtain Massachusetts State Documents." *Massachusetts LC Bul* 19:15 (1929).
Lib. Lit., Schorr 928.

Hughes, M. E. "Collected Documents of the Southeastern States." *Southeasten Librarian* 13:165-172 (Fall 1963).
Lib. Lit., Schorr 859.
A general introduction and the conclusion give an overview of the Collected Documents series. The great disadvantage in the use of these sets is the lack of indexing. The sets for the southeastern states are discussed in detail.

Hughes, M. E. "Collected Documents of the States of the United States: An Analysis of the Form and Content." M.S.L.S. Thesis, University of North Carolina, 1956. 104 p.
Lib. Lit., Schorr 860.

Hummel, Ray O., Jr. "State Library Collections: Past, Present, Future." *Southeastern Librarian* 18:25-31 (Spring 1968).
State libraries usually have good collections of state and local documents. In the last twenty years, acquisition of the documents of other states has become more selective, and thousands of documents have been "returned to their state of origin—or at least offers of return were made . . . . Part of this change in policy was due to regional storage

plans, such as the Center for Research Libraries in Chicago, but in most cases the libraries simply had found that the material was not being used."

Huston, Evelyn. "California Solves Documents Distribution." *Library Journal* 73:7-14 (January 1, 1948).
    Lib. Lit., Schorr 929.   *See* California.

Hylton, P. H. "Missouri State Publications Need Attention." *Missouri Library Association Quarterly* 13:13-16 (March 1952).
    Lib. Lit., Schorr 861.   *See* Missouri.

"Idaho to Distribute State Publications." *Library Journal* 60:299 (April 1, 1935).
    Lib. Lit., Schorr 930.   *See* Idaho.

"Illinois State Documents Received by the State Library." *See* issues of *Illinois Libraries*, 1970.
    Lib. Lit., Schorr 986.

"Illinois State Documents Workshop, January 20-21, 1972." *Illinois Libraries* 54:401-452 (June 1972).
    Lib. Lit., Schorr 862.   *See* Illinois.

Ilnicki, H., (comp.) "Official New York State Publications." *See* issues of *Bookmark* 1970-1971.
    Lib. Lit., Schorr 987.

Indiana State Library, Indianapolis. "Indiana Documents." *See* issues of *Library Occurrent*, 1968-1976.
    Lib. Lit., Schorr 988.

Innes-Taylor, Cathie. "Report on State Documents Depository System." *Sourdough* 14:7 (May 1977).
                                                  See Alaska.

"Institutions to Receive Illinois State Documents Through the Illinois State Library Depository and Exchange Program, December 1972." *Illinois Libraries* 55:225-226 (March 1973).
    Schorr 931.   *See* Illinois.

"Instructions to Depository Libraries for Illinois State Documents." *Illinois Libraries* 55:224 (March 1973).
    Schorr 932.   *See* Illinois.

Irvin, C. E. "Distribution of Missouri State Documents." *Missouri Library Association Quarterly* 13:109-112 (December 1952).
    Lib. Lit., Schorr 933.   *See* Missouri.

Jackson, Ellen. "Cataloging, Classification and Storage in a Separate Documents Collection." *Library Trends* 15:50-57 (July 1966).
    Parish.
The author refers the reader to the section on classification schemes in the California State Library *Manual*. She also mentions the appendix in the *Manual* on "Binding, Covers, and Pamphlet Boxes: Description, Sources and Use," a subject which she characterizes as a "tribulation of documents librarians" and which she says has not been the subject of a major study.

Jackson, Ellen. *A Notation for a Public Documents Classification*. Stillwater, Okla.: Oklahoma Agricultural and Mechanical College, 1946.

Jackson, Ruth L.W. *Author Headings for the Official Publications of the State of Wisconsin*. Chicago: American Library Association, 1954. 211 p.

Jacobs, Katharine. "State Publications: The Cataloguers' Viewpoint." *Agricultural Library Notes* 11:287-289 (May 1936).
    Schorr 1053, Parish.
Discusses the confusion that results from the cataloger's inability to determine which of several cooperating agencies issued a publication. Difficulty in ordering a publication arises and a further problem may occur when an incorrect entry causes the "loss" of a publication in the bibliographic file. Several examples are given.

Jenkins, William S. *Collecting and Using the Records of the States of the U. S.: 25 Years of Retrospection*. Chapel Hill, N.C.: University of North Carolina, 1960. 102 p.
    Fry, Parish.
A detailed account of the State Records Microfilm Project (an undertaking of the Library of Congress and the University of North Carolina, Chapel Hill), with historical background on collecting and preserving state publications. The Bureau of Public Records Collection and Research at the university, an agency for utilizing the resource, is explained.
    For the *Guide, see* entry under U. S. Library of Congress.

Jenkins, William S. "Legislative Documents Microfilm Project." *Illinois Libraries* 30:466-470 (November 1948).
    Lib. Lit., Schorr 863.
Covers the purpose, the structure, the libraries that will benefit, and the kinds of materials included in the program.

Jenkins, William S. "State Documents Microfilms as Research Resources for Law Libraries." *Law Library Journal* 41:77-87 (May 1948).
    Lib. Lit., Schorr 864.
The Legislative Journals Microfilms Project began in the summer of 1941, with the Library of Congress and the University of North Carolina cooperating. After suspension during the war, it expanded into the Legislative Documents Microfilms Project and then into the State Documents Microfilm Project. "The over-all aim of the project is to

assemble in orderly fashion on microfilm a compendium of the official records of the states. . . . [T]erminal dates [correspond] to the rarity of holdings in law libraries.'' Jenkins discusses in detail the different types of materials included from session laws through constitutional conventions, to record books of the Indian nations and records of the organized mining districts of the West.

Jerabek, E. (comp.). *Check List of Minnesota State Documents, 1858-1923*. Minnesota Historical Society, 1972. 216 p.
    Lib. Lit., Schorr 989, Palic, p. 113.

Johnson, Everett. [Government Documents Round Table Program (Conference, Chicago, 1978).] *Library of Congress Information Bulletin* 37:476-477 (August 11, 1978).
Speakers from the National Commission on Libraries and Information Science, the Government Printing Office, and the Library of Congress discuss a network of state agencies for bibliographic control of state publications and the need for authority files.

''Kansas.'' *Documents to the People* 6:105 (March 1978).

                                                                              See Kansas.

''Kansas State Publications.'' *See* issues of *Kansas Library Bulletin*, 1947-1953.
    Lib. Lit., Schorr 990, Palic, p. 104.

Keefer, Mary. ''Simplified Cataloging of Federal and State Documents.'' *Library Resources and Technical Services* 6:262-264 (Summer 1962).

                                                                              See Oregon.

Keith, M. ''Arizona in Documents, 1950.'' *Arizona Librarian* 8:16-20 (April 1951).
    Lib. Lit., Schorr 991.

Kerschner, Joan. ''Documents at Her Fingertips.'' *Nevada Government Today*, p. 7 (Winter 1974).

                                                                              See Nevada.

Kerschner, Joan. ''State and Local Documents Microfilming Programs.'' *Microform Review* 7:268-270 (September-October 1978).
Commercial programs discussed in detail are Greenwood's Urbandoc and the Information Handling Services' program for state publications. Projects mentioned are session laws, bluebooks, Minnesota and Wisconsin collected sets, Colorado, Utah, and Nevada current documents, Illinois selected series and in-house program, and New York and Massachusetts current commercial filming. The Nevada filming program is described in detail.

Kessler, R. R. ''State Documents, an Expanding Resource.'' *Southeastern Librarian* 21:172-175 (Fall 1971).
    Lib. Lit., Schorr 865, Sachs, Parish with annotation.
A general article on the role state documents can play in a library. Not many libraries collect state documents beyond their own boundaries.

Proliferation of publications is attributable to (1) growth in bureaucracy, (2) more money for research, and (3) individuals publishing to justify their existence.

"The scope and range of state documents is staggering and sobering." The social sciences and particularly matters of social conscience, environmental issues, planning, and education all require use of state documents.

Selection depends on the individual library. Basic tools are the *Monthly Checklist*, *Legislative Research Checklist*, and Childs' list of checklists in *Library Trends*.

More has been written about classification than about use. Use can mean sending to departmental libraries. Kessler includes a paragraph on how documents are handled at his library (University of North Carolina at Chapel Hill).

Kessler's conclusion is that state documents "often are hard to locate, hard to acquire, and difficult to work with; but they can be worth the effort."

Kirkwood, R. E. "Suggestion for Classifying Official Maine Publications." *Maine Library Association Bulletin* 27:3-4 (August 1966).
  Lib. Lit., Schorr 1054, Fry, Parish.   *See* Maine.

Klausner, M. M "California Documents, 1949." *California Library Bulletin* 11:15-16+ (September 1949).
  Lib. Lit., Schorr 866.   *See* California.

Kling, Susan. "Nebraska State Documents." *Documents to the People* 6:25 (January 1978). Reprinted from *DOCumentor* 4:1-2 (October 1977).
                                                                        See Nebraska.

Kopischke, John. "State Document Depositories: Wisconsin Outlines a New Approach." *Wisconsin Library Bulletin* 70:131-133 (May 1974).
  Lib. Lit., Schorr 876.   *See* Wisconsin.

Krueger, R. C. "South Dakota State Publications." M.A. Thesis, University of Illinois, 1936. 180 p.
  Lib. Lit., Schorr 992.

Kuhlman, A. F. "Exchange and Distribution of State Publications." *ALA Bulletin* 27:837-851 (December 15, 1933).
  Lib. Lit., Schorr 934.

Kuhlman, A. F. "A Movement to Preserve Social Science Source Materials." *American Journal of Sociology* 39:49-62 (July 1933).

Kuhlman, A. F. "Need for a Checklist-Bibliography of State Publications." In American Library Association, Committee on Public Documents. *Public Documents, 1933*. pp. 65-79 [i.e., p. 80].
  Lib. Lit., Schorr 993.

Kuhlman, A. F. "Need for a Comprehensive Check-list Bibliography of American State Publications." *Library Quarterly* 5:31-58 (January 1935).
  Lib. Lit., Schorr 994.

Kuhlman, A. F. "Next Steps in the Organization of State Document Centers." *ALA Bulletin* 26:555-558 (1932).
    Schorr 868.

Kuhlman, A. F. "The Preservation of Primary Source Materials for the Social Sciences in Illinois." *Illinois Libraries* 14:142-149 (1932).
    Lib. Lit., Schorr 869.

Kuhlman, A. F. "Proposal to Modify the System of Exchange and Distribution of State Publications in Certain States." American Library Association, Committee on Public Documents. *Public Documents, 1934.* pp. 59-68.
    Lib. Lit., Schorr 935.

"LC and Texas State Library Test Joint Cataloging Project." *American Libraries* 10:217-218 (April 1979).

                                                                    See Texas.

Lane, Margaret T. "Acquisition of State Documents." *Law Library Journal* 63:92-99 (February 1970).
    Lib. Lit., Schorr 936, Sachs, Parish.
Emphasis on legal publications. List of state checklists.

Lane, Margaret T. "Cards with Documents." *Louisiana Library Association Bulletin* 26:59-60 (Summer 1963).
    Lib. Lit., Schorr 1055, Parish.   *See* Louisiana.

Lane, Margaret T. "Delaware Regulates State Documents." *Documents to the People* 6:171-172 (June 1978).

                                                                See Delaware.

Lane, Margaret T. "List of Current State Documents Checklists." *Library Resources and Technical Services* 10:504-506 (Fall 1966).
An updating of the list by Tennessee State Library and Archives (*Library Resources and Technical Services*, Fall 1962). Arranged by state. Gives title, frequency, and latest issue.

Lane, Margaret T. "State Documents Checklists." *Library Trends* 15:117-134 (July 1966).
    Lib. Lit., Schorr 996, Fry.
Discusses "the maintenance of a collection of state checklists, the characteristics of the checklists, and the compilation of the lists."

Lane, Margaret T. "State Publications Depository Legislation." *Documents to the People* 6:143 (May 1978).
A list of citations to the codes or revised statutes for the depository legislation of all the states.

Lapp, J. A. ''The Public Documents on Indiana.'' *Library Occurrent* 2:108-111, 130-133 (1910).
    Lib. Lit., Schorr 870.

Lathrop, O. C. ''Federal and State Check Lists.'' *Law Library Journal* 33:289-293 (September 1940).
    Lib. Lit.
A paper presented at a meeting of the American Association of Law Libraries. A thorough coverage, but too old and too much legal emphasis to be generally helpful. Includes an interesting paragraph on the origin of the now defunct *State Law Index*.

''Legislature Establishes Depository for Public Documents, Provides for Document Recorder.'' *Mississippi Library News* 30:94 (September 1966).
    Lib. Lit., Schorr 940.   *See* Mississippi.
Listed in *Lib. Lit.* and Schorr under Mississippi.

Lesem, Josephine. ''State Documents for School Use.'' *Library Journal* 53:1043-1045 (1928).
    Lib. Lit., Schorr 871.
A supplement to Lesem's earlier paper, *Library Journal* 53:747, a list.

Lesem, Josephine. ''State Documents in the Schools.'' *Library Journal* 53:747-750 (1928). Extract appeared in *ALA Bulletin* 22:451-452 (1928).
    Lib. Lit., Schorr 872.
One of a series of four articles; others by Childs, Sawyer, and Sullivan.

LeSourd, Margaret. ''Pennsylvania Documents: A Valuable Resource.'' *Pennsylvania Library Association Bulletin* 32:4 5+ (January 1977).
    Lib. Lit.   *See* Pennsylvania.

Lester, M. A. ''Federal and State Government Publications of Professional Interest to the School Librarian: A Bibliographic Essay.'' University of Illinois, Graduate School of Library Science, Occasional Papers no. 100 (Champaign, Ill., 1971). 31 p. ERIC ED 056 717.
175 publications, of which about 125 are state, from 1963 to 1969. Essay provides subject approach. (*See also* Lesem and Woodbury).

Lester, M. A. *State Documents Classification: Ohio Edition.* Government Documents Department, Bowling Green State University, 1969.
    Lib. Lit., Schorr 1056, Parish.

Levy, Grace. ''Cuttering the Corporate Entry.'' *Special Libraries* 60:657-658 (December 1969).
    Sachs.
A classification scheme—Cutter the corporate author and interfile with personal authors. (1) Use ALA rules, (2) maintain authority file, and (3) be consistent.

Libbey, Miles A. ''Development of a Research Design for a Comprehensive Study of
    Government Publications.'' *Illinois Libraries* 53: 412-425 (June 1971).
    Sachs.
A report at a workshop on federal documents by one of the editors of the *Research
Design*. (See entry under Fry.) Libbey said that the objective of the study project was to
create a blueprint, detailed enough for immediate implementation, for a system of
bibliographical control and distribution of all levels of government documents and that
the *Research Design* concluded that a comprehensive study was needed. He expressed his
surprise that the work on this project had ''hooked'' him on government publications.

''Librarians' Choice of California State Publications.'' *See* issues of *News Notes of
    California Libraries*, 1952-1955.
    Lib. Lit., Schorr 997.

''Library Commission Adopts Criteria for Depository Libraries.'' *See* Florida Library
    and Historical Commission.

Litsinger, Elizabeth. ''Collecting Maryland State Documents.'' *Between Librarians*
    10:9-11 (October 1943).
    Lib. Lit., Schorr 937.   *See* Maryland.

Litsinger, Elizabeth, (comp.). ''Maryland State Documents of 1950 and 1951; a
    Selected List.'' *Between Librarians* 19:13-15 (Spring 1952).
    Lib. Lit., Schorr 998.   *See* Maryland.

Littlewood, J. M. ''Current Checklists of State Publications.'' *Illinois Libraries*
    54:439-442 (June 1972).
    Lib. Lit., Schorr 999, Sachs.
Arranged by state. Gives issuing agency, title, beginning date, frequency, and some
additional notes.

Lloyd, D. G. ''Official Publications of Florida, 1821-1941.'' M.A. Thesis, University
    of Illinois, 1943. 537 p.
    Lib. Lit., Schorr 1000.

Lloyd, D. G. ''Status of State Document Bibliography.'' *Library Quarterly* 18:192-199
    (July 1948).
    Lib. Lit., Schorr 1001.
Historical background. Supplement, 1940-1947, to list in Chapter 6 of Wilcox. Superseded by Palic.

Loftus, M. L. ''Compilation of Document Check-lists.'' *Pacific Northwest Library
    Association Proceedings* 26:63-65 (1935).
    Lib. Lit., Schorr 1002.
Reports status of document bibliography in Oregon, Montana, Utah, Idaho, and Washington. Recommends Kuhlman's rules.

LoRusso, Rosita, and Kennedy, Linda. "The Crisis in California State Documents Distribution System." (1973?)

    See California.

"Louisiana Depository Libraries." *Louisiana Library Association Bulletin* 12:13 (November 1948).
    Lib. Lit., Schorr 938.   *See* Louisiana.

Louisiana Library Association, Documents Committee. *Documents in Louisiana: People, Places, Publications.* [Baton Rouge, La.: 1975?] 72 p.

    See Louisiana.

Lowenberg, P. C. "Comparative Survey of State Manuals from 1938 to 1957." M.S.L.S. Thesis, University of North Carolina, 1962. 82 p.
    Lib. Lit., Schorr 873.

Lu, Joseph K. "Government Publications, A Highly Unusual Resource." *Idaho Librarian* 26:43-47 (April 1974).
    Sachs.
Covers U.S. documents only.

Lueck, Barbara A. "Quick—A Document Please!" *Wisconsin Library Bulletin* 73:34 (January-February 1977).

    See Wisconsin.

Lusk, Karen. "Nebraska State Documents Depository System." *Documents to the People* 5:121 (May 1977). From: *DOCumentor* no. 1 (September 1976).

    See Nebraska.

Lyons, Janet. "Documents in Microform: A Selective Bibliography." *Illinois Libraries* 58:229-232 (March 1976).
    Sachs.
A bibliography of reviews of documents in microform. Nine state titles, all reviewed in *Microform Review.*

McClure, Charles R. "The State of Oklahoma State Documents." *Documents to the People* 6:231-232 (November 1978).

    See Oklahoma.

McDowell, E. R. "The Selection and Arrangement of State Documents." *Pacific Northwest Library Association Proceedings* 17:78-84 (1926).
    Lib. Lit., Schorr 939.
Selection for Seattle Public Library of documents of all states. Recommends New York and Massachusetts, in addition to western states.

McGuire, Laura. "Upcoming State Publications Legislation." *New Mexico Libraries Newsletter* 3:4 (January 1975).

    See New Mexico.

Markley, Anne Ethelyn. *Author Headings for the Official Publications of the State of Alabama*. Chicago: American Library Association, 1948. 123 p.
Schorr 1057.
The first list in this series. *See* Introduction for "A guide for compilers of state author heading lists" and "Suggested method of procedure." Schorr lists the University of Illinois thesis, 1944.

Markley, Anne Ethelyn. *Library Records for Government Publications*. Berkeley, Calif.: University of California Press, 1951. pp. 40-45.
Includes a "General" list, which is annotated, and "Sources of information for entering state publications." The latter section is arranged by state and lists principally the author heading publications and the state imprints publications.

Marshall, P. G. "Wisconsin Statutory Materials." *Law Library Journal* 35:316-324 (September 1942).
Lib. Lit., Schorr 1003. *See* Wisconsin.

Martin, Wade O., Jr. (comp.). "New State Publications." *Louisiana Library Association Bulletin* 15:44-46 (Spring 1952).
Lib. Lit., Schorr 1004. *See* Louisiana.

"Maryland State Documents; a Selected List." *See* issues of *Maryland Libraries*, 1965-1969.
Lib. Lit., Schorr 1005.

Matkovic, P. "Docs Law Aids Collection." *Focus* 31:6 (July 1977).
Lib. Lit. *See* Indiana.

Merritt, LeRoy C. "Municipal and State Document Collecting in the Rocky Mountain Region, with Indications of Important Documents." American Library Association, Committee on Public Documents. *Public Documents, 1938*. pp. 175-233.
Lib. Lit.
Discussion of types of documents and of library holdings. Listing of 462 state titles for eight states, all published since 1935.

Meyer, Sandra M. "State Documents in an Anglo-American Law Collection." *Illinois Libraries* 54:417-420 (June 1972).
See Illinois.

"Microforms and State Documents: The Texas Experience." (1975?) 4 p.
See Texas.

Miele, Anthony W. "Technical Services Department." *Illinois Libraries* 53:298-309 (April-May 1971).
See Illinois.

Mills, Lois P. "Illinois State Documents at Western Illinois University." *Illinois Libraries* 54: 415-416 (June 1972).
Lib. Lit., Schorr 874.   *See* Illinois.

"Mississippi." *Documents to the People* 6:105-106 (March 1978).
See Mississippi.

"Mississippi Legislature Establishes . . ." *See* "Legislature Establishes . . ."

Moberg, Barbara. "Oregon's Documents Depository Laws and Policies: Past and Present." Oregon State Library, 1965. 9 p.
See Oregon.

Monical, Carol. "State Documents Review." *Government Publications Review* 2:49-51 (Winter 1975).
Sachs.
An annotated list with ordering information.

"Montana State Publications." *Montana Libraries* 22:18-23 (January 1969).
Lib. Lit., Schorr 1006.   *See* Montana.

Moody, Margaret. [Cataloging of State Documents.] "Government Documents and Publications: A Panel." *Law Library Journal* 53:342-343 (November 1960).
The reference is to the pages where state documents are discussed. Moody says the problems are the same as those with federal documents, but more challenging because no uniformly adequate checklists exist. She says that many of the state documents are self-classifying and self-cataloging, and recommends that specialized treatment be given only to the documents of the home state and perhaps to those of neighboring states. The main advantage of using "Jackson" or "Swank" is "the hold-over value of similarity of arrangement in federal and state documents . . . . This hold-over value is equally useful to staff and patrons."

Mundkur, Mohini. "Connecticut State Depository Act." *Documents to the People* 5:233-235 (November 1977).
See Connecticut.

Mundkur, Mohini. "Some Selection and Acquisition Aids for Current State Documents." *Documents to the People* 6:107-109 (March 1978).
Well annotated. Ordering information. Based on reports from eighty librarians throughout the United States on tools used for acquiring both in-state and out-of-state documents.

Mustonen, Karlo K. "Utah Publications Retrieval System (UPRS)." *Agricultural Libraries Information Notes* 3:6 (September 1977).
See Utah.

Nakata, Yuri, and Strange, M. *Classification Scheme for Illinois State Publications as Applied to the Documents Collection at the Library, University of Illinois at Chicago Circle.* University of Illinois, Graduate School of Library Science. Occasional Papers, no. 116. (Champaign, Ill.: 1974). 39 p.
Lib. Lit.

National Association of State Libraries, Public Documents Clearing House Committee. *Check-list of Legislative Journals of States of the United States of America,* comp. by G. E. Macdonald. Providence, R. I.: Public Documents Clearing House, 1938.
Lib. Lit., Schorr 1007, Palic, p. 86.

"Nebraska State Document Depository System."*Documents to the People* 6:25-26 (January 1978). Reprinted from the *DOCumentor* 4:2, 4 (October 1977).
See Nebraska.

Nelson, Barbara W. "Acquisition and Publishing Patterns of the Council of State Governments." *Illinois Libraries* 54:405-410 (June 1972).
Sachs.   *See* Illinois.
Speech at Illinois workshop.

Nelson, Barbara W. (comp.). "Currrent Checklists of State Publications." *Government Publications Review* 2:83-90 (Winter 1975).
Lib. Lit., Schorr 1008, Parish.
Earlier lists by Nelson in the same *Review* at 1:109-115 (Fall 1973) and 1:295-301 (Spring 1974). (The page reference at the beginning of Nelson's first article is "pp. 109-116," but p. 116 is an advertisement.) Earlier similar lists are New York (1957), Tennessee (1962), Lane (1966), "Current Checklists ..." (1968), and Littlewood (1972). Hernon includes checklists in his *Library Journal* articles. For later information, *see* items with asterisks in periodical section of June and December issues of *Monthly Checklist of State Publications.*

Nelson, William N. "Government Documents of Florida: Acquisition, Organization and Use." *Southeastern Librarian* 27:157-162 (Fall 1977).
See Florida.

New Hampshire, State Library, Concord. "Checklist of New Hampshire's State Departments Publications." Suppl. of Biennial Report ... 1948-1950. The Library.
Lib. Lit., Schorr 1009, Palic, p. 117.

"New Mexico Depository Library Law Passes." *Documents to the People* 6:143 (May 1978).
See New Mexico.

Newsome, W. L., and Sanders, Nancy P. "Florida Public Document Classification in the Florida Atlantic University Library." *Florida Libraries* 21:27-29 (March 1970).
   Lib. Lit., Schorr 1058, Parish.   *See* Florida.

"1922 State Publications of Interest to Librarians." *Illinois Libraries* 5:10 (1923).
   Lib. Lit., Schorr 1010.

North Dakota, State Library Commission, Bismarck. *Keyword Index to Publications of the State of North Dakota Received by the State Library during the Years 1965-1974.* The Library, 1975. 2 v.
   Lib. Lit.

North Dakota, State Library Commission, Bismarck. "Publications of the State Library Commission, January 1965-September 1973." *North Dakota Library Notes* 4, no. 5 (October 1973).

Norton, M. C. (comp.). "Illinois Documents: A Checklist, 1812-1850." *Illinois Libraries* 32:592-600 (October 1950); 32:634-640 (November 1950); 32:669-675 (December 1950).
   Lib. Lit., Schorr 1012-1014, Palic, p. 101.

Oellrich, G. "New Jersey State Author Headings; a Preliminary Analysis." M.A. Thesis, Columbia University, 1951. 57 p.
   Lib. Lit., Schorr 1059.

"Official State Depository Libraries for Texas State Documents." Texas, State Library, Austin. *Texas Public Library Statistics for 1972.* The Library, 1973. pp. 118-119.
   Schorr 1015.   *See* Texas.

Ohio, State Library. *Ohio Documents Classification Scheme.* Prepared by Joanne E.M. Tortoriello, Susan M. Correa, and Jean M. Sears. Columbus, 1975.
   Cited in Bibliography for State Documents Syllabus.

Olds, Brenda Shelton. "Texas State Documents Classification and Almost Compleat List of Texas State Agencies from Statehood to the Present." Austin, Tex.: Legislative Reference Library, 1976. (Reference series no. 7.) Abstracted in *Documents to the People* 4:28 (November 1976).
                                                                     See Texas.

Olds, Brenda Shelton. *Texas State Documents: A Primer for Librarians.* Austin, Tex.: Legislative Reference Library, 1975. (Reference series no. 1.)
                                                                     See Texas.

Olds, Brenda Shelton. "Texas State Documents: Survey Results." *Texas Library Journal* 50:185-191 (October 1974).
   Sachs.   *See* Texas.

Oller, Kathryn, and Stewart, R. C. "Reference Use of Executive Publications."
  Pennsylvania Library Association Bulletin 25:112-120 (March 1970).
  Lib. Lit., Schorr 875.   *See* Pennsylvania.

Owen, Delores. "Revision of State Documents Depository Law Proposed." *Louisiana
  Library Association Bulletin* 38:87-90 (Winter 1976).
  Lib. Lit.   *See* Louisiana.

Packard, H. "State Document Notation System." *Library Journal* 62:581 (August
  1937).
  Lib. Lit., Schorr 1060, Parish.
Markley notes that this is "A description of a scheme used in the Technology Department of the Toledo Public Library."

Parish, David W. "Selection Guide to High Interest Government Publications; State
  Government." *Government Publications Review* 3:305-314 (1976) and alternate issues thereafter.
An annotated list with ordering information; a regular section in this journal.

Parish, David W. *State Government Reference Publications: An Annotated Bibliography*. Littleton, Colo.: Libraries Unlimited, 1974. 236 p.
A state-by-state guide to useful and typical state publications, with brief annotations.
Suggested readings (54 titles, some annotated.)
Reviews by:
  Hernon, Peter. *Government Publications Review* 2:55-56 (Winter 1975).
  Hernon, Peter. *RQ* 14:266 (Spring 1975).
  Hernon, Peter. *Special Libraries* 66:556 (November 1975).
  Schumaker, Earl. *College and Research Libraries* 36:159 (March 1975).
  Choice 12:50 (March 1975).

Parsley, G. M. (comp.). "Are You Using Your State Publications? A Selected List of
  Recent Titles." *Tennessee Libraries* 7:34-35 (January 1955).
  Lib. Lit., Schorr 1016.   *See* Tennessee.

Paulson, Peter J. "Government Documents and Other Non Trade Publications."
  Library Trends 18:363-372 (January 1970).
  Sachs.
Thirty-six states issue checklists; the *Monthly Checklist* includes 60 percent of current state publications; *PAIS* is even more selective. An increasing number of states have established depository systems, but not all offer a full range of government publications, and some are able to designate depositories only within the state. About twenty-two state libraries offer documents on exchange. Historically, the collected documents are useful; Massachusetts is distributing its printed collected documents in microcopy, and the *Legislative Research Checklist* publications are available. A national program for bibliographical control and dissemination of state publications is becoming increasingly important.

Paulson, Peter J. ''Materials and Services Available from the Gift and Exchange Section, New York State Library.'' Law Library Association of Greater New York. *Proceedings, Third Annual Institute on Law Librarianship*, April 29-30, 1960, pp. 16-22.

See New York.

Paulson, Peter J. ''What New York State Documents Offer Libraries.'' *Bookmark* 41:33-36 (November 1961).
Lib. Lit., Schorr 876.   *See* New York.

Peck, E. R. ''Arrangement, or Disposition in a Library of Pamphlets, Documents, and Bulletins for Ready Reference.'' *Library Occurrent* 6:106-107 (1921).

''Pennsylvania State Government and Its Publications: Selected References.'' *Pennsylvania Library Association Bulletin* 25:121-123 (March 1970).
Lib. Lit., Schorr 1017.   *See* Pennsylvania.

''Pennsylvania State Library Arrangement Scheme for Pennsylvania State Documents.'' *Pennsylvania Library Notes* 14:592-604 (July 1935).

Peterson, Irene H. ''Value of Federal and State Documents.'' *Illinois Libraries* 41:350-354 (May 1959).
Fry.
Very general article acquainting librarians with documents. Mentions both U.S. and Illinois documents. Out-of-date.

Pimsleur, Meira G. (ed.). *Checklists of Basic American Legal Publications*. AALL Publications Series, nos. 4 and 4a. South Hackensack, N.J.: Pub. for American Association of Law Libraries by F. B. Rothman, 1962-. (looseleaf).
Brings up to date and supersedes the Macdonald checklists for session laws, statutes . . .

Pitts, P. D. Author Headings for the Official Publications of Arizona.'' M.S.L.S. Thesis, University of Illinois, 1951. 166 p.
Schorr 1062.

Poulton, Helen J. *Nevada State Agencies: From Territory Through Statehood*. [Reno, Nev.], University of Nevada Press [1964]. 97 p. (University of Nevada Press. Bibliographical series, no.5.)
''Author headings for the official publications of the state of Nevada'' (Palic, p. 116).

Powers, W. H. ''Classification Scheme for Government and State Publications.'' *Agricultural Library Notes* 2:137-138 (1927).
Lib. Lit., Parish.
Explanation of a classification scheme designed to integrate documents into the Dewey scheme. ''A'' for agriculture, subdivided by numbers assigned to each state, and by letters for type of agency, and so on, would shelve after Dewey's ''639.''

Press, Charles, and Williams, Oliver. *State Manuals, Blue Books, and Election Results*. Berkeley, Calif.: Institute of Governmental Studies, University of California, 1962. 101 p.
Parish.
For later compilations, see entries under Hotaling, Cook, and Hernon. Still useful for identifying election publications and the type of information they contain.

Propp, Dale, and Walton, Robert. *Texas State Documents: The Development of a Program*. Rev. Austin, Tex.: Texas State Publications Clearinghouse, Texas State Library, 1978. 61 p.

See Texas.

Pullen, William R. "State Document Resources of the University of North Carolina Library." *North Carolina Libraries* 13:79-82 (March 1955).
Lib. Lit., Schorr 877.   *See* North Carolina.

"RPI (Research Publications, Inc.) Microfilms State Documents." *Government Publications Review* 2:296 (1975).
Lib. Lit.
Announcement of filming of New York, Illinois, and Massachusetts documents.

Railsback, Beverly. "State Documents Microfilming Projects Survey." *Government Publications Review* 2:345-350 (1975).
Lib. Lit., Sachs.
The abstract reads, in part:
Nineteen of 45 states replied that some program was planned or in progress. The microforms used varied widely. The low positive response rate and tentative nature of the positive replies leads to the conclusion that such projects are currently in their infancy.
A brief report of the unupdated survey appeared in *Documents to the People*, Volume 2, Number 1, October 1973, p. 8-10.
Railsback says that these programs are mostly selective programs run by state or other noncommercial agencies. She expresses the hope that her article "will encourage the development of guidelines for the microfilming of state documents."

Railsback, Beverly, and Kennedy, Linda. "State Documents Microfilming Projects." *Documents to the People* 2:8-10 (October 1973).
Part 1, "State Documents Filmed by States," by Railsback is the tabulation of a survey on what state agencies are doing in regard to microfilming state documents. (This part was expanded by Railsback into a longer article in *Government Publications Review*.)
Part 2 by Kennedy is entitled "State Documents Filmed by Micropublishers." The publications, and the publishing plans, of six publishers are reported.

Rankin, E. P. "First Current Checklist of Alabama State Publications." *Alabama Librarian* 28:10-12 (May 1977).
Lib. Lit.   *See* Alabama.

Raymond, A.L.M. "Publications of the Mississippi Legislature, 1789-1951."
    M.S.L.S. Thesis, Atlanta University, 1955. 123 p.
    Lib. Lit., Schorr 1018.
Reddy, J. N. "List of Author Headings for the Official Publications of the State of
    Ohio, 1900-1957; with History, Subdivisions of Departments and Cross Refer-
    ences. M.A. Thesis, Kent State University, 1958. 61 p.
    Schorr 1063.

Reece, Ernest J. *State Documents for Libraries*. Urbana, Ill.: University of Illinois,
    1915. (University of Illinois Bulletin 12, no. 36.)
The forerunner of the 1940 *Manual* compiled by Wilcox. A comparative study of types
of publications and subjects common to all the states. Comprehensive, annotated lists of
bibliographic tools.

Reeder, C. W. "Popularizing State Documents." *ALA Bulletin* 11:368-375 (July
    1917).
    Parish.
Cited by Parish as "Pioneering effort in promoting the use of state documents."

"Registration of the Illinois State Library Workshop." *Illinois Libraries* 54:447-452
    (June 1972).
                                                                    See Illinois.

"Rep. Malry Successful in Passage of Documents Bill." *New Mexico Library News-
    letter* 6:1 (March 1978).   *See* New Mexico.

Richardson, J. V. "Kentucky Publishes More Documents of Importance." *Kentucky
    Library Association Bulletin* 38:5-8 (Spring 1974).
    Lib. Lit., Schorr 1019.
Schorr's citation to v. 8 is incorrect.   *See* Kentucky.

"Right-to-Know Symposium and Resolution." *New Jersey Libraries* 10:20 (Novem-
    ber 1977).
                                                                 See New Jersey.

Robinson, M. P. "Suitable Materials for Public Records of Virginia." *Virginia Li-
    braries* 3:8-18 (1930).
    Lib. Lit., Schorr 879.

Rogan, O. F. "Texas State Documents." *Texas Library Association News Notes* 8, no.
    4:3-6 (1932).
    Schorr 880.

Rollins, A. "Documents Course: Trying to Find Something for Everyone." *Sourdough*
    13:3 (May 1976).
    Lib. Lit.

Rosenkoetter, Paula. "Treatment of State Documents in Libraries." *Government Publications Review* 1:117-134 (Winter 1973).
    Sachs.

Examines cataloging, classification, and other means of access for state documents in 125 libraries that responded to questionnaire. Librarian satisfaction with various methods of handling was tabulated. "[F]or highest satisfaction, all documents should be found in the main public catalog. Printed checklists or bibliographies are helpful but should not be the sole means of access. . . . The one unbreakable rule is: be consistent."

Rucker, L. and Meinders, M. "Government Publications in Oklahoma Public Libraries." *Oklahoma Librarian* 16:80-82 (July 1966).
    Schorr 881.

Covers U.S. only.

"Rules and Regulations for Deposit of Publications by State Agencies." *Illinois Libraries* 55:226-227 (March 1973).
    Schorr 941.   *See* Illinois.

"SDTF Takes Position on AACR." *Government Publications Review* 2:390 (1975).

Recommendations made at time of ALA discussions on AACR II.

Santen, V. B. "New York State Inventory Project." *American Archivist* 20:357-367 (October 1957).
    Lib. Lit., Schorr 882.   *See* New York.

Sawyer, R. A. "State Documents from the Business Man's Point of View." *Library Journal* 53:701-703 (1928). Extract appeared in *ALA Bulletin* 22:451 (1928).
    Lib. Lit., Schorr 883.

Sawyer, chief of the Economics Division of the New York Public Library, believed that the businessman does not have any point of view at all on state documents. The businessman wants information. Moreover, state documents do not have distinctive titles by which he would remember them. Sawyer discussed state documents that relate to business—industrial directories and documents dealing with corporations, banking, and insurance, the bulletins of the agricultural experiment stations for the monographs on production and marketing, and the journals and reports published by the schools of business administration. He suggested that those schools compile statistical abstracts. This is one of a series of four articles; others are by Childs, Lesem, and Sullivan.

Saylor, C. E. "Official Publications of the State of Missouri." M.S. Thesis, University of Illinois, 1941. 375 p.
    Lib. Lit., Schorr 1020.

Schell, Mary E. "Acquisition, Handling and Servicing in State Libraries." *Library Trends* 15:135-142 (July 1966).
    Lib. Lit., Parish.

Pages 137-138 give a good summary of state library collecting activities for the documents of their own state and of other states. Twenty-three of the thirty-nine checklists are compiled by state libraries.

School Library Association of California, Northern Section, Senior High School Committee. "California State Publications." *School Library Association California Bulletin* 10:3-8 (March 1939).
Schorr 1021.

Schmidt, Fred. "State Agricultural Documents." *Documents to the People* 2:15, 20 (October 1973).
The proposed "Memorandum of Understanding" of 1973 is to be entered into between the National Agricultural Library and the libraries in state land-grant colleges and universities. The agreements would cover the collecting and maintaining of the major serial publications of state agricultural experiment stations, extension service, and colleges of agriculture at the local level. The full memorandum is included with Schmidt's outline of its provisions.

Schneider, Kathy. "Do You Know What Government Is Doing?" *Wisconsin Library Bulletin* 72:45 (January-February 1976).
Lib. Lit.   *See* Wisconsin.

Schneider, Kathy. "New Documents Legislation? A Wisconsin Proposal Would Ease and Speed Documents Use." *Wisconsin Library Bulletin* 73:37-38 (January-February 1977).
See Wisconsin.

Schneider, Kathy. "The Public's Right to Know: Government Must Give an Account of Itself." *Wisconsin Library Bulletin* 73:29 (January-February 1977).
See Wisconsin.

Schneider, Kathy. "Wisconsin State Printing." *Wisconsin Library Bulletin* 73:142 (May 1977).
Lib. Lit.   *See* Wisconsin.

Schultz, Carol J. "Research and Archives Plan." *Wisconsin Library Bulletin* 73:33-34 (January-February 1977).
See Wisconsin.

Schwarz, Philip. "Key-Word Indexing of Wisconsin Public Documents." *Documents to the People* 2:14 (February 1974).
See Wisconsin.

Schwarz, Philip J. "State and Local Document Retrieval: KWOC Solution." *RQ* 11:250-252 (Spring 1972).
Schorr 884, Sachs, Parish.
Schwarz details the procedure for creating a KWOC (Key Word Out of Context) index for state documents by using a computer. Nineteen columns were devoted to the call number and sixty to the title. The title was established by the serials librarian. Only one card was punched for each item, except for the few instances when a second title was developed.

Seal, Charles. "State Documents." *RQ* 10:49-52 (Fall 1970).
     Lib. Lit., Schorr 885, Sachs, Parish.
A discussion of possible places to begin a document collection. Two beginning points are bluebooks and state documents in microform. Hotaling's checklist, 1963, is recommended.

   Microforms discussed include (1) the State Records Microfilm Project, (2) the collection of the Genealogical Society of the Church of Jesus Christ of the Latter-Day Saints (not exclusively state documents but many early state records and documents), and (3) the microform of the documents listed in the *Legislative Research Checklist.* Special mention is made of the fact that the numbering system of the fiche does not correspond to the order in the *Checklist.*

Sell, K. D. "Sources of State Vital Statistics Reports." *RQ* 16:45-54 (Fall 1976).
     Lib. Lit.
The author is chairperson, Department of Sociology, Catawba College, North Carolina. A state-by-state list, giving title of report, address for obtaining, latest edition available, cost and LC entry with LC card number. Time lag is three to five years for U.S. vital statistics summaries; therefore, state reports are useful.

Shaffer, Dallas. "Clearinghouse." *Nebraska Library Association Quarterly* 3:4 (Summer 1972).
     Lib. Lit., Schorr 942.   *See* Nebraska.

Shaffer, Dallas. "State Document Legislation: Nebraska; a Case Study." *Government Publications Review* 1:19-27 (Fall 1973).
     Lib. Lit., Schorr 886, Sachs.   *See* Nebraska.
"Must reading" for anyone thinking about legislation.

Shannon, Michael O. "For the Control of Municipal Documents." *Special Libraries* 61:127-130 (March 1970).
     Sachs.
Of particular interest in Shannon's article is the section titled "Lists of state publications covering more than one state." It includes fifteen titles, all currently published. Some are not listed elsewhere, for example, *Best in Documents* from the Michigan State Library.

Shaw, Thomas S. (ed.). "Distribution and Acquisition." *Library Trends* 15:37-49 (July 1966).
Does not cover state documents, but refers to articles by Schell and Lane in the same issue.

Shaw, Thomas S. (ed.). "Federal, State and Local Government Publications." *Library Trends* 15:3-194 (July 1966).
The individual articles are listed separately in this list by author: Childs, Buckley, Shaw, Jackson, Clarke, Scott, Darling, Mahler, Sims, Lane, Schell, Heinritz, Shaw, and Downs.

Shepard, M. L. "Alaska State Document Depository Program." *Sourdough* 15:7 (January 1978).

> *See* Alaska.

Skogh, Harriet M. "Recent Developments in Publication and Distribution of American State Documents." American Library Association, Committee on Public Documents. *Public Documents, 1936*, pp. 129-145. Also appeared in National Association of State Libraries. *Proceedings* 39:19-25 (1936).
Lib. Lit., Schorr 943.

Of the six developments, most relate to changes in publishing patterns. The distribution developments include restrictive legislation for distribution outside the state and a tendency toward the adoption of a sale basis for many publications. Publication in limited quantities also affects distribution.

Skogh, H. M. "Recent Government Publications Selected for Library Service." *Illinois Libraries* 7:103-107 (1925).
Lib. Lit., Schorr 1022.

Smiley, G. L. "Study of Problems Presented by Author Headings of Official Publications of the District of Columbia." M.S.L.S. Thesis, Catholic University of America, 1952. 121 p.
Schorr 1064.

Smiley, W. W. "Official Publications of South Carolina." M.A. Thesis, University of Illinois, 1939. 78 p.
Lib. Lit., Schorr 1023.

Smith, Jessalyn. "Acquisition from Office of State Printing." *News Notes of California Libraries* 58:376-377 (Fall 1963).

> *See* California.

Smith, Joshua I. "Documents Processing at ERIC/CLIS." *Illinois Libraries* 56:266-268 (April 1974).
Sachs.

No specific state information.

Snyder, M. E. "Arizona in Documents, 1949." *Arizona Librarian* 7:14-16 (January 1950).
Lib. Lit., Schorr 1024.

South Dakota, Interim Public Documents Study Commission. *Guidelines for Printing and Publishing South Dakota Public Documents*. The Commission, 1972. (Available from B. Carmack, University of South Dakota, Vermillion, South Dakota 57069). Prelim. ed. in ERIC ED 072 791.
Lib. Lit., Schorr 887.   *See* South Dakota.

South Dakota, Interim Public Documents Study Commission. *Report*. The Commission, 1972. 29 p. (Available from B. Carmack, University of South Dakota, Vermillion, South Dakota 57069.) ERIC ED 072 790.
　　Lib. Lit., Parish with annotation.　　　　　　　　　　*See* South Dakota.

''South Dakota Law.'' *American Libraries* 3:336 (April 1972).
　　Lib. Lit., Schorr 888.　　　　　　　　　　　　　　*See* South Dakota.

Speer, L. ''Progress in Availability of Montana State Documents.'' *Pacific Northwest Library Association Quarterly* 33:17-23 (July 1969).
　　Lib. Lit., Schorr 944.　　　　　　　　　　　　　　　　*See* Montana.
One of a series of three articles; others by Eaton (Oregon) and Elison (Idaho).

Spinney, G. H. ''Cataloging Official Publications.'' *State Librarian* 1:[2-3] (August 1948).
　　Schorr 1065.
The author, from the British Museum, addressing a British audience, said, ''Government documents are far more likely to be of real significance than the general run of commercial literature. . . . [A]ny work worthy of shelf room is also worthy of adequate cataloguing, so long as there is staff for the task.'' The problem has two parts: coping with the publications of our own government, and second, with those of foreign governments. To make more efficient use of staff, have (1) a central cataloging service and (2) cooperative cataloging. ''[T]he special difficulties which attend the cataloguing of government publications make it undesirable that the work involved should be unnecessarily duplicated, and . . . the centralisation of publication in the Stationary Office would make it particularly easy for the Cataloguing Service to clear up doubtful points.''

''State and Local Documents in a University Library: A Symposium.'' *Library Journal* 61:445-447 (June 1, 1936); 61:478-480 (June 15, 1936).
　　Lib. Lit., Schorr 889-890.
Listed inWilcox under Hollingsworth.

''State Depositories: The Connecticut State Library Has Designated 12 Public and College Libraries as Depositories for State Publications.'' *New England Library Association Newsletter* 10:[2] (October 1978).
　　　　　　　　　　　　　　　　　　　　　　　　See Connecticut.

''State Documents.'' *See* issues of *Wisconsin Library Bulletin*, 1970-1973.
　　Lib. Lit., Schorr 1026.

''State Documents Act Passes.'' *New Mexico Library Association Newsletter* 6:1, 10 (March 1978).
　　　　　　　　　　　　　　　　　　　　　　　　See New Mexico.

''State Documents Program Serves Agencies and Libraries.'' *Texas Libraries* 34:38-42 (Spring 1972).
　　Lib. Lit., Schorr 891.　　　　　　　　　　　　　　　*See* Texas.

"State of Idaho Publications Checklist . . ." *See* "Checklist . . ."

The State of State Documents: Past, Present, Future. Edited by Brenda F. Shelton Olds.
  Austin, Tex.: Legislative Reference Library, November 1976. ERIC ED 142
  174.
This booklet was prepared by the Planning Committee of the Pre-Conference on State
Documents, Albuquerque, New Mexico, November 10, 1976. The Table of Contents
lists: Nationwide Programs: Center for Research Libraries (CRL), Council of State
Governments (CSG), Information Handling Services (IHS), and Library of Congress
(LC); "Guidelines for Minimum State Servicing of State Documents"; Statement of
American Association of State Libraries (AASL) on State Documents; State Reports:
from the Southwestern Library Association (SWLA) and the Mountain Plains Library
Association (MPLA) states; Selection and Acquisition Aids; Selected Reference Sources
—Comparative Chart of Federal/State Sources (SWLA and MPLA states); Revised
Standards for State Author Heading Lists; Checklists (Guidelines, current lists, New
York tabulation, and so on); Hordusky Questionnaire on State Document Checklists;
Depository Legislation; Model Legislation—State Publications to Library of Congress.

"State Publications Library Distribution Center." *Montana Libraries* 21:19-20 (January 1968).
  Schorr 945, Fry.   *See* Montana.

"State Pubs." *Sourdough* 8:9 (July 1971).
  Lib. Lit., Schorr 1025.   *See* Alaska.

Staten, C. M. "State Publications on the American Negro, 1930-1950." M.S.L.S.
  Thesis, Atlanta University, 1956. 72 p.
  Lib. Lit., Schorr 1027.

Sternlicht, Dorothy. "How to Control a Runaway State Documents Collection."
  Special Libraries 64:561-565 (December 1973).
  Lib. Lit., Schorr 1028, Sachs, Parish.   *See* New York.

Stewart, H. "Iowa State Publications." M.A. Thesis, University of Illinois, 1937. 360 p.
  Lib. Lit., Schorr 1029.

Stewart, R. C. (ed.). "Pennsylvania State Publications: Papers from a Workshop
  Sponsored by the Pennsylvania State Library." *Pennsylvania Library Associ-
  ation Bulletin* 25:79-123 (March 1970).
  Lib. Lit., Schorr 893.   *See* Pennsylvania.

Stewart, R. C. "Research Resources Among Pennsylvania State Publications." *Pennsylvania Library Association Bulletin* 23:232-242 (May 1968).
  Lib. Lit., Schorr 892.   *See* Pennsylvania.

Stewart, R. C. "Selected Pennsylvania Publications." *See* issues of *Pennsylvania
  Library Association Bulletin*, 1967-1969.
  Lib. Lit., Schorr 1030.

Stewart, R. C. *Union List of Selected Pennsylvania Serial Documents in the Pennsylvania Libraries*. Pennsylvania Library Association, 1971. 68 p.
    Lib. Lit., Schorr 1031.

Stutsman, E. B. ''Historical Development from 1792 to 1936 in the Printed Documents of Kentucky, with a View to Their Cataloging.'' M.S. Thesis, Columbia University, 1944. 94 p.
    Lib. Lit., Schorr 1066.

Sugden, Allen F. ''First Aid for California Documents Selection.'' *California Librarian* 16:175-177+ (April 1955).
    Lib. Lit., Schorr 946.   *See* California.

Sullivan, M. D. ''How the Public Library Uses Documents.'' *Library Journal* 53:704-705 (1928). Extract appeared in *ALA Bulletin* 22:451 (1928).
    Lib. Lit., Schorr 894, Parish.
Written from the point of view of the small or medium-sized library by a librarian from the El Paso Public Library. Texas state documents are sent monthly to forty-nine libraries in the state and 104 libraries out of state. ''Documents are doubly appreciated because they are either free or very inexpensive.'' They are ''a veritable mine of interesting and valuable information.'' Numerous titles are cited as examples. This is one of a series of four articles; others are by Childs, Lesem, and Sawyer.

Summers, F. William. ''The State Documents Depository Program.'' *Florida Libraries* 19:157-158 (December 1968).
    Lib. Lit., Schorr 947.   *See* Florida.
The title, ''Florida State Documents Depository Program,'' sometimes cited, is incorrect.

Swank, Raynard. ''A Classification for State, County, and Municipal Documents.'' *Special Libraries* 35:116-120 (April 1944).
    Schorr 1044, Parish.
Shorr cites, under the heading, ''Colorado. University,'' an unpublished manuscript by Swank which is essentially the same as the *Special Libraries* article. Dale also cited this unpublished manuscript in December 1969. The exact title of the manuscript is ''An Experimental Classification for State, County, and Municipal Documents''; it has 14 pages.
    One of the standard, and perhaps the best known, classification schemes for state documents. Accommodates all the states as well as local governments. Classification by jurisdiction and issuing office. *See also* Jackson, Ellen.

Taylor, M. D. ''State Publication Aids for the Homemaker and Garden Lover.'' *Wilson Library Bulletin* 5:510-514 (1931).
    Lib. Lit., Schorr 895.

Tennessee, State Library and Archives, Nashville (comp.). ''Current Checklists of State Publications, as of May, 1962.'' *Library Resources and Technical Services* 6:357-359 (Fall 1962).

Lib. Lit., Schorr 1032.
A list. *See* entry under Nelson for later information.

"Texas Register to Provide Weekly Update on State." *Texas Libraries* 37:189-191
   (Winter 1975).
   Lib. Lit.   *See* Texas.

Thomas, M. E. "California State Documents Distribution." *California Librarian*
   12:101-103+ (December 1950).
   Lib. Lit., Schorr 948.   *See* California.

Thornton, M. L. "North Carolina State Publications." *North Carolina Library Bulletin*
   4:173-178 (1921).
   Lib. Lit., Schorr 1033.

Thorp, L. W. "Lending of State Publications by Certain Rocky Mountain and Pacific
   Northwest State-Sponsored Libraries." *Pacific Northwest Library Association
   Quarterly* 17:145 (July 1953).
   Lib. Lit., Schorr 896.
Because of a shortage of shelving space, the University of Idaho Library circulated a
questionnaire "to determine to what extent it would be possible to depend upon
borrowing state publications in occasional demand, instead of collecting as many such
publications as could be secured by gift and exchange."

Tilger, Ellen R. "Louisiana Documents: They're Free—and Easy." *Louisiana Library
   Association Bulletin* 20:123-126 (Summer 1957).
   Lib. Lit., Schorr 949.   *See* Louisiana.

Toll, Henry W. "Public Reporting and Printing: A Field for Research." American
   Library Association. Committee on Public Documents. *Public Documents,
   1933.* pp. 48-65.
   Lib. Lit., Schorr 897.
Emphasizes the differences from state to state, using legislative documents as examples. A study of legislative printing, proposed by the American Legislators' Association, was to be expanded at the suggestion of the Committee on Public Documents of the
American Library Association to include the entire field of state reporting and printing.
   Listed in Wilcox, p. 112, with title "American State Documents . . .," which is the
title of the section, and as ending on p. 64. Other articles in the section are by Kuhlman
and Brigham.

Tomberlin, Irma. *Official Headings for Oklahoma State Publications.* Dallas, AMIGOS
   Bibliographic Council for the Oklahoma Department of Libraries, 1977. (Reprinted by Oklahoma Department of Libraries.) 24 p.
                                                                  See Oklahoma.

Tomberlin, Irma. *State Documents Collections in Oklahoma.* For the AMIGOS Bibliographic Council. November 1977. [25 p.]
                                                                  See Oklahoma.

Tseng, Henry P., and Pedersen, Donald B. "Acquisition of State Administrative Rules and Regulations." *Administrative Law Journal* 28:277-298 (Spring 1976).
Rules and regulations should be collected because they have the force of law. Effective legal research demands their availability. State-by-state list with ordering information.

Tucker, Lena L. *Author Headings for the Official Publications of the State of Washington.* Seattle, Wash.: University of Washington Press, 1950. 75 p.

Tucker, Lena L. "Revised Standards for State Author Heading Lists." *ALA Cataloging and Classification Yearbook* 10:66-67 (1941).
    Schorr 1067.
The American Library Association Committee on State Author Headings suggests seven rules and gives ten procedural steps to follow. *See* Markley.

Turgeon, L. J. "Vermont State Documents." *North Country Libraries* 8:3-5 (May 1965).
    Lib. Lit.   *See* Vermont.

U.S. Library of Congress. *A Guide to the Microfilm Collection of Early State Records,* prepared by the Library of Congress in association with the University of North Carolina. Collected and compiled under the direction of William S. Jenkins; edited by Lillian A. Hamrick. [Washington, D.C.] Library of Congress, Photoduplication Service, 1950. 1 v.

——— *Supplement.* [Washington, D.C.:] Library of Congress, Photoduplication Service, 1951. xxiii, 130 p.

Van Horne, E. R. "State Documents: Their Acquisition and Use." *Kentucky Library Association Bulletin* 31:9-15 (April 1967). Appeared without checklist in *Library Occurrent* 22:161-163 (August 1967).
    Lib. Lit., Schorr 950, Parish.
Van Horne lists reasons why state documents are valuable: (1) they are free, (2) they are valid or authoritative, (3) they are issued regularly, (4) they provide information on a variety of subjects, and (5) they are expendable. She comments on the state checklists (those issued annually are often too late to serve as acquisitions tools) and the *Monthly Checklist of State Publications,* both of which she characterizes as incomplete. She recommends shelving by state and then subject, or by subject, regardless of state, but stresses that, in any event, the handling procedure should be kept simple. Publicizing can be done through the newspaper, library bulletins, or "the old reliable 'display'."

Vaught, K. J. "Author Headings for the Official Publications of Texas, 1824-1846." M.L.S. Thesis, University of Texas, 1955. 75 p.
    Schorr 1068.

"Virginia." *Documents to the People* 6:106 (March 1978).
                                                                See Virginia.

Virginia Library Association, Committee on Virginia Documents. "The Printing and Distribution of Virginia State Publications." *Virginia Libraries* 2:68-73 (1930). *Lib. Lit.*, Schorr 899.

Walton, Bob. "Texas State Documents Survey." *Documents to the People* 6:26 (January 1978).

See Texas.

Walton, R., and Propp, D. *Texas State Documents Depository Survey, 1977: Findings and Results.* Austin, Tex.: Texas State Publications Clearinghouse, Texas State Library, 1978. 46 p., charts (Documents Monograph Series, no. 1).

See Texas.

Washington State Publications Received at Washington State Library. *See* issues of *Library News Bulletin.*

Waters, Francis B. "Analysis of State Legislation Relating to State Depository Libraries." M.S.L.S. Thesis, Western Reserve University, 1950. 28 p.
Lib. Lit., Schorr 951.
Depository legislation provides for the designation of certain libraries as state depositories. Laws included are Arkansas, California, Louisiana, Minnesota, Tennessee, and Wisconsin. The bibliography cites Andrews, Fleming, Huston, Klausner, Kuhlman, and White.

Weech, T. L. "Characteristics of State Government Publications, 1919-1969." *Government Publications Review* 1:29-51 (Fall 1973).
Lib. Lit., Schorr 900, Sachs, Parish.
"[S]tate government publications are probably among the least utilized of available information resources. Part of the lack of utilization may well be related to their lack of visibility and the limited access potential users have." Weech examines some of the characteristics of state publications, using LeRoy Merritt's study of federal publications as a model. He compares the publications listed in the *Monthly Checklist* in seven different time periods (1910, 1919, 1929, 1939, etc.) by subject classification and by functional characteristics. Weech begins with a brief review of bibliographic tools for state publications.
Note: Page reference at beginning of article cites p. 29-52, but p. 52 is blank.

Weech, Terry Laverne. "State Governments as Publishers: An Analytic Study of State Government Publications." Ph.D. dissertation, University of Illinois at Urbana-Champaign, 1972. 242 p.

Weintraub, D. Kathryn. "Use of Statistical Publications as Resources for Librarians." *Government Publications Review* 1:317-342 (Fall 1974).
Sachs.
"Nature and reference value of U.S. Government statistical data" are discussed. The three U.S. Bureau of the Census directories of statistics on federal statistics for local areas (1966), federal statistics for states (1967) and nonfederal statistics for states and local areas (1969) are listed.

Welch, Ingrid. ''State Documents in the Oak Park Public Library.'' *Illinois Libraries*
54:423-425 (June 1972).
Sachs.   *See* Illinois.

Welsh, Harry E. ''An Acquisitions Up-date for Government Publications.'' *Microform
Review* 6:285-298 (September 1977).
A series of developments in the past five years has affected methods of acquiring
government publications: (1) publication of comprehensive bibliographies, (2) influence of library associations on governments for improved information dissemination,
(3) legal requirements for ''openness'' in public bureaucracy, (4) increased access to
official publications through bibliographical networking, and (5) the role of the private
sector in public information. The Acquisitions Guide includes guides (Parish, Council
of State Governments), sources (Information Handling Services, *Legislative Research
Checklist*, and *Monthly Checklist*), and addresses (*National Directory of State Agencies*).

''What Do You Do with Them . . . .'' *See* Britten.

''What's in the State Library; or, Mining Florida's Underground Resources.'' *Florida
State Library Newsletter* 15:2 (November 1967).
                                                                               See Florida.

White, Amelia M. ''California State Periodicals, a Hidden Asset.'' *News Notes of
California Libraries* 51:353-358 (April 1956).
Lib. Lit., Schorr 901.   *See* California.

White, L. D. ''State Document Centers.'' *ALA Bulletin* 26:553-555 (1932).
Schorr 902.

White, Marilyn Domas. ''Drawing Analogies Between State and Federal Documents:
A Method for Increasing Access to State Publications.'' *Government Publica-
tions Review* 2:111-125 (Spring 1975).
Sachs.
The abstract reads:
> As a means of expanding information about useful state documents, the author
> suggests drawing analogies between the more widely used federal publications and
> commercial publications providing access to federal information and the relevant
> state publications where counterparts exist. The article is accompanied by an
> illustrative bibliography of New York State documents which have counterparts in
> federal documentation. The bibliography emphasizes serial publications which
> should constitute a part of any major collection of New York State documents.
This suggestion was followed in *The State of State Documents*. The chart there gives
comparable documents for the states in the southwestern and mountain plains areas of
the United States. Also included in the chart are publications covering all the states,
which the editor labels ''collective.'' The types of documents compared are not the
same as those in White.

Whitlock, R. L. "Author Headings for the Official Publications of the State of Wisconsin." M.A. Thesis, University of Illinois, 1941. 364 p.
Schorr 1069.

Wilcox, Jerome K. "History Behind the Manual." *Special Libraries* 31:330-331 (September 1940).
Lib. Lit., Schorr 903.
Wilcox credits Ernest J. Reece with the conception of the idea of a manual. Kuhlman wrote the first outline when he was chairman of the American Library Association Committee on Public Documents. Wilcox became chairman of the committee and was responsible for the actual publication of the *Manual*. The outline was revised, expanded, and modified, and chapters were assigned to competent individuals. The American Library Association published the *Manual*.

Wilcox, Jerome K. (ed.). *Manual on the Use of State Publications*. Chicago: American Library Association, 1940. 342 p.
Lib. Lit., Schorr 824, Parish.
The classic text; compiled by the chairman of the American Library Association Documents Committee. Primarily a reference tool with many chapters on types of documents and on subject lists of documents. List of checklists; list of periodical articles; summaries of state printing laws and exchange and distribution laws, and so on.
    Reviews by:
        Cabeen, Violet A. *College and Research Libraries* 1:370-371 (September 1940).
        Faison, Georgia H. *Social Forces* 19:292 (December 1940).
        Hollingsworth, Josephine B. *Library Journal* 65:696 (September 1, 1940).
        Norton, Margaret C. *ALA Bulletin* 34:292-293 (April 1940).
        Paape, Charles W. *American Archivist* 3:201 (July 1940).
        Wyer, James I. *Library Quarterly* 10:607-608 (October 1940).
        Schorr 825-830.
Several reviews mentioned the contributors to this composite work. *See also* the article on the history behind the *Manual* by Wilcox. Available from University Microfilms.

Wilcox, Jerome K. "Publications of New State Agencies and Sources of Information Concerning These New State Functions." American Library Association, Committee on Public Documents. *Public Documents, 1937*. pp. 54-139.
Lib. Lit., Schorr 1034.

Wilcox, Jerome K. "State Document Center Plan: Report and Recommendations." American Library Association, Committee on Public Documents. *Public Documents, 1938*. pp. 234-242.
Lib. Lit., Schorr 952.

Wilcox, Jerome K. (comp.). *Unemployment Relief Documents; Guide to the Official Publications and Releases of F. E. R. A. and the 48 State Relief Agencies*. New York: H. W. Wilson, 1936. 95 p.

Wilder, B. E. *Author Headings for the Official Publications of the State of Kansas.* Chicago: American Library Association, 1956. 136 p.

Winkler, Paul W. "Author Headings for the Official Publications of Connecticut, 1818-1947." M.S.L.S. Thesis, University of Illinois, 1949. 247 p.
Schorr 1071.

Wire, G. E. "Shelf Arrangement of State Reports." *Law Library Journal* 17:26-31 (1924).
Lib. Lit., Schorr 1072, Parish.

Wisconsin Legislative Reference Library. "The Preparation and Distribution of Periodic Lists of Official State Publications." Informational Bulletin, no. 167. Madison, Wis.: 1957.
A government which professes to be efficient should know the scope of its publication program, the proportion of its assets which are set aside for this purpose, and whether its publications are reaching those for whom they are intended.
The study is based on questionnaire responses from forty-six states. Tables included are:
(1) By Whom Prepared, Frequency of Compilation, and Price
(2) Materials Included in the Checklist
(3) Statement of Inclusions and Exclusions
(4) Completeness of the Checklists
The booklet continues with "Mechanics of the Checklist" and "Problems of the User." The user problems include: incompleteness as a deterrent to full reliance, exclusions that are not clear, time element (annual publication is too infrequent), failure to assure that copies will be available, and lack of price and availability data.

Wohlson, T. O. "Selected Connecticut State Publications." *See* issues of *Connecticut Libraries*, 1972-   .
Lib. Lit., Schorr 1035.

Wood, H. A. "Children's Charter: A Bibliography of Minnesota Publications." *Minnesota Library Notes and News* 10:73-74 (1931).
Lib. Lit., Schorr 1036.

Woodbury, M. "Keeping Up with Educational Legislation: State Sources." *California School Libraries* 45:28-33 (Spring 1974).
Lib. Lit., Schorr 1037.   *See* California.

Woolley, Robert D. "State Documents Checklists: Implications for Future Development." *Documents to the People* 5:236-237 (November 1977).
Woolley's paper is based on these premises: "State checklists have traditionally been 'the' bibliographic control vehicle for publications of state government agencies. . . . Checklists seem to serve far better as access, current awareness and selection tools, than as the primary vehicle for bibliographic control. . . . Checklists ought to be a reflection of bibliographic control, rather than carry that charge as their primary role."

Woolley deplores duplication of effort and believes that checklists should be a byproduct from the entering of the documents into a data base. He mentions the importance of developing and sharing state authority files, and of providing access to publications, possibly through a microform program. Librarians should "organize within [the] state to insure that the bibliographic net is tight and secure."

Woolley says, "In all probability a good checklist will provide creative modes of access and be just a bit more than a 'laundry list' of state agencies and their publications." He envisions "a highly usable and reliable checklist, no longer the primary 'bibliographic control' document of the past, but a reflection of the bibliographic control exercised by your state as part of a much larger effort."

"Workshops on California Legislative Publications: Proceedings." *News Notes of California Libraries* 60:335-392 (Summer 1965).
    Schorr 904.   *See* California.

Wyer, J. I. *U.S. Government Documents*. Rev. Chicago: American Library Association, 1922. pp. 32-35. (Manual of Library Economy, 23).
    Lib. Lit.
See later edition.

Wyer, J. I. *U.S. Government Documents: Federal, State and City*. Rev. Chicago: American Library Association, 1933. pp. 39-44.
The chapter on state documents is divided into "Printing and Distribution," "Check-Lists and Indexes," and "Value to Libraries."

"Any change in, or reform of, document printing or distribution in any state should be grounded upon a careful study of its present laws regulating these matters and an intimate acquaintance with the practice, often extra-legal, which has grown up."

"The reasons [for lack of centralized distribution], not far to seek, are the reluctance of members of the legislature to part with this attractive perquisite [generous quotas of publications for distribution], and the natural feeling of issuing departments that they can distribute their own publications better than anyone else can do it for them."

The checklist section cites Bowker, Childs, Hasse, *Monthly Checklist of State Publications*, and Reece.

"[E]very library, even the smallest, will find use for some of the documents of its own state. . . ." Two paragraphs are devoted to explaining the State Document Center Plan.

Yun, Jai L. "New York State Government Documents: Their Distribution and Information Retrieval." *Government Publications Review* 3:267-270 (Winter 1976).
    Lib. Lit.   *See* New York.

Yun, Jai Liong. "Statistics and Government Documents." *RQ* 13:124-125 (Winter 1973).
    Sachs.
Very brief mention of state statistical sources. Quality and publication patterns for statistics of state governments have not been well developed. Only comprehensive guide is *Directory of Non-Federal Statistics for States and Local Areas*. New York

(1967), Utah (1971), and Missouri (1971) have guides. An "ASI" for state and local government documents is needed.

Zimmerman, Carma R. "Comparison of Depository Systems for United States and California State Publications."*Revision of Depository Library Laws: Hearings Before a Subcommittee of the Committee on House Administration, House of Representatives, Eighty-fifth Congress, First Session, pursuant to H. Res. 128, A Resolution Authorizing a Full Study of Federally Operated Printing Services and Government Paper Work in General, October 7, 10, 14, and 17, 1957 (on H. R. 9186), June 19, 1958 (on H. R. 11042).* Washington, D. C.: U.S. Government Printing Office, 1958. pp. 185-186.

See California.

PART III   The States

THE STATES: GENERAL INFORMATION

	Orig. Law	Last Am.	St. Com.	Ed. Com.	Rules	Contract	A. G.	Bibl.	Misc.
Alabama	'15		x				1	x	
Alaska	'70	'79	x	x	x	x		x	
Arizona	'76		x					x	
Arkansas	'47	'79	x	x				x	
California	'45	'76	x	x	x	x		x	
Colorado	'80		x	x				x	
Connecticut	'77		x	x	x	x		x	
Delaware	'74			x	x			x	
Florida	'67	'79	x	x	x	x	4	x	
Georgia	'75	'78		x					
Hawaii	'65	'70	x	x				x	
Idaho	'72		x					x	
Illinois	'67		x		x			x	
Indiana	'73		x		x		1	x	
Iowa	'78			x	x			x	
Kansas	'11	'76	x		x	x		x	
Kentucky	'58	'74	x	x	x			x	
Louisiana	'48	'77	x	x		x	3	x	
Maine	'54	'75	x	x				x	
Maryland		'79	x	x				x	S. J. R. 1979
Massachusetts								x	Admin. Bull. 1976
Michigan	'76		x	x					
Minnesota	'47	'76	x	x				x	
Mississippi	'66	'75				x		x	

274

State	Year							Notes
Missouri	'76				x		x	
Montana	'67 '79		x	x	x		x	
Nebraska	'72 '79		x	x			x	
Nevada	'71 '79		x	x	x		x	
New Hampshire	'73		x	x			x	
New Jersey	'57 '57		x	x	x		x	
New Mexico	'78		x	x	x		x	
New York	'55 '73		x	x			x	
North Carolina	'41 '79	3	x				x	
North Dakota	'77 '79		x				x	
Ohio	'57 '79		x	x			x	
Oklahoma	'78		x	x	x		x	S. C. R. 1971
Oregon	'53 '73		x	x			x	
Pennsylvania	'71			x	x		x	
Rhode Island	'02		x	x				
South Carolina			x	x	x		x	Senate Bill, 1972
South Dakota	'74 '79		x	x	x		x	1972 Laws, ch. 118
Tennessee	'17		x	x			x	
Texas	'69 '79	1	x	x	x		x	
Utah	'57 '79		x	x			x	
Vermont	'69 '71		x	x				
Virgin Islands	'77			x				
Virginia	'77 '79		x	x	x		x	
Washington	'63 '77		x	x	x			
West Virginia	'53		x	x			x	
Wisconsin	'03 '80	1	x	x			x	
Wyoming	'41		x				x	
Model Law	'69		x					

Key: For Column Headings

Orig. Law = The date of the original depository legislation in the state, sometimes established from journal articles or informal comments. The date should not be taken literally because it does not always indicate the enactment of an effective law or the establishment of a depository program.

Last Am. = The date of the last legislative change. See Table 3 in Chapter 3 for a brief statement on the nature of the change.

St. Com. = The comments are from Documents on Documents, and thus are often out of date. In some instances, recent comment has been substituted.

Ed. Com. = Editorial comment on the legislative history of the sections.

Rules = Rules, regulations, guidelines, and other documents amplifying the law. Includes both formal and informal documents.

Contract = Contracts and agreements.

A.G. = Attorney generals' opinions; the number of opinions is shown.

Bibl. = Bibliography.

Misc. = Miscellaneous, includes bills, resolutions, and other legal items in the state section.

CITATIONS TO DEPOSITORY LEGISLATION

(Citation authority: *A Uniform System of Citation*, 12th ed.)

ALABAMA CODE § 41-6-12 (1975)

ALASKA STATUTES §§ 14.56.090-180 (1979)

ARIZONA REVISED STATUTES § 41-1335 (West Supp. 1979-1980)

ARKANSAS STATUTES ANNOTATED § 6-307 (Supp. 1979); §§ 14-428 to 14-432; 14-440 to 14-442 (1979)

CALIFORNIA GOVERNMENT CODE §§ 14686, 14886, 14900-14912 (West Supp. 1963-1979)

Colorado, House Bill 1199 [1980], § 1 (to be codified as 24-90-201 to 208)

CONNECTICUT GENERAL STATUTES ANNOTATED §§ 11-9b to 9d (West Supp. 1980)

DELAWARE CODE ANNOTATED tit. 29, § 507 (Michie 1974); tit. 29, § 8610 (Michie 1979)

FLORIDA STATUTES ANNOTATED § 257.05 (West 1975); §§ 283.22-24 (West 1975 & Supp. 1980); § 283.28 (West Supp. 1980)

GEORGIA CODE ANNOTATED §§ 101-201 to 101 204 (Supp. 1979)

HAWAII REVISED STATUTES §§ 93-1 to 93-5 (1976)

IDAHO CODE § 33-2510 (Supp. 1979)

ILLINOIS ANNOTATED STATUTES ch. 128 § 121 (Smith-Hurd Supp. 1979)

INDIANA CODE ANNOTATED §§ 4-23-7-23.4 to 23.6 (Burns 1974)

IOWA CODE ANNOTATED §§ 303A.21 to 303A.24 (West Supp. 1980-1981)

KANSAS STATUTES ANNOTATED §§ 75-1023; 75-2565 to 75-2568; 75-3048a to 3048c (Vernon 1977)

KENTUCKY REVISED STATUTES ANNOTATED §§ 171.410; 171.450; 171.500 (Baldwin 1977)

LOUISIANA REVISED STATUTES ANNOTATED §§ 25:121-124 (West 1975); 36:209I (West Spec. Pam. 1980)

MAINE REVISED STATUTES ANNOTATED tit. 1, §§ 501, 501-A (West Supp. 1978)

MARYLAND ANNOTATED CODE art. 23A, § 9A; art. 25, § 32A (Michie Supp. 1979); art. 40, §§ 51, 53 (Michie 1978 & Supp. 1979)

Massachusetts Administrative Bulletin 76-5

MICHIGAN COMPILED LAWS §§ 397.55, 397.56, 397.59 (West Supp. 1980-1981); § 24.20 (West 1967)

MINNESOTA STATUTES ANNOTATED §§ 3.195; 3.302; 15.18 (West 1977)

MISSISSIPPI CODE ANNOTATED §§ 25-51-1 to 7 (Supp. 1979)

MISSOURI ANNOTATED STATUTES §§ 181.100-181.140 (Vernon Supp. 1980)

MONTANA CODE ANNOTATED §§ 22-1-211 to 22-1-218 (1979)

NEBRASKA REVISED STATUTES §§ 51-411 to 51-418 (1980)

NEVADA REVISED STATUTES §§ 378-150 to 210 (1979)

NEW HAMPSHIRE REVISED STATUTES ANNOTATED §§ 202-B:1 to 5 (1977)

NEW JERSEY STATUTES ANNOTATED §§ 52:14-25.1 to 25.2 (West 1970)

NEW MEXICO STATUTES ANNOTATED §§ 18-2-4, 18-2-4.1, 18-2-7.1 (Supp. 1979)

NEW YORK LEGISLATIVE LAW § 47 (McKinney Supp. 1979-1980); NEW YORK STATE PRINTING AND PUBLIC DOCUMENTS LAW § 6 (McKinney Supp. 1979-1980); NEW YORK EDUCATION LAW § 250 (McKinney 1969)

NORTH CAROLINA GENERAL STATUTES §§ 147-50 to 147-50.1 (Supp. 1979)

NORTH DAKOTA CENTURY CODE § 54-24-09 (Supp. 1979)

OHIO REVISED CODE ANNOTATED §§ 149.09, 149.11-12 (Anderson 1978 & Supp. 1979), § 3375.02 (Anderson 1980)

OKLAHOMA STATUTES ANNOTATED tit. 65, §§ 3-113.1 to 115; tit. 74, §§ 3104, 3106.1 (West Supp. 1979-1980)

OREGON REVISED STATUTES §§ 171.215, 182.070, 357.005(j), 357.015 (6) (1979)

PENNSYLVANIA STATUTES ANNOTATED tit. 24, §§ 4201, 4425 (Purdon Supp. 1980-1981)

RHODE ISLAND GENERAL LAWS §§ 29-1-5; 25-1-8 (1968)

South Carolina, Proposed Law, 1972

SOUTH DAKOTA COMPILED LAWS ANNOTATED §§ 14-1A-1 to 14-1A-9 (1975 & Supp. 1979)

TENNESSEE CODE ANNOTATED §§ 12-6-107 to 12-6-112 (1980)

TEXAS REVISED CIVIL STATUTES ANNOTATED art. 5442a (Vernon Supp. 1980)

UTAH CODE ANNOTATED §§ 37-5-1 to 37-5-8 (Supp. 1979)

VERMONT STATUTES ANNOTATED tit. 22, §§ 603, 605 (1978)

VIRGIN ISLANDS CODE ANNOTATED tit. 3, § 883 (Supp. 1979)

VIRGINIA CODE §§ 2.1-467.1 to 467.2, 467.7 to 467.8 (1979)

WASHINGTON REVISED CODE ANNOTATED §§ 40.06.010-.900 (1972 & Supp. 1980-81)

West Virginia   none located

WISCONSIN STATUTES ANNOTATED §§ 35.85(2)(b), (6), (7); 43.05(5) and 44.06 (West 1980)

WYOMING STATUTES §§ 9-1-109 to 9-1-110 (1977)

MODEL LAW *Monthly Checklist of State Publications*, December 1969, p. iv.

SOURCE MATERIALS FOR THE STUDY OF THE DEPOSITORY LEGISLATION OF THE FIFTY STATES

In any text with a fifty-state orientation, the reader naturally turns first to the part on his own state. The reader can indulge that impulse in this section. For those who are unfamiliar with the depository legislation of their own state, this state section provides a background of basic documents and facts; for others, it presents a convenient collection of materials already known but not assembled elsewhere. Experts in the field may find misinterpretations and omissions, particularly in the materials on their home state, but will appreciate the value of the collection as a whole.

Two other compilations of related materials will also be found useful. *American Library Laws* and its supplements include the depository laws through 1978, under the heading "Distribution of State Documents." This set includes more statutory provisions than have been included in the present section, especially statutes providing for the distribution of particular legal titles, and some provisions are omitted (for example, the New York sections from the Printing and Public Documents Law). For the reader who needs all the distribution, exchange, and printing laws of a state, that is, anyone seriously interested in promoting depository legislation, *American Library Laws* is a good starting point for locating the laws.[1]

The Documents on Documents Collection[2] contains the statutes for most of the states, but they are not necessarily up to date, they are from varying sources (often not indicated on the excerpt), and they are not marked to show the relevant sections. The Documents on Documents Collection contains much material related to depository programs not included here. The forms, brochures, manuals, and reports, all part of the collection, illustrate physical format as well as content. Material of a temporary nature, workshop announcements, posters, and preliminary studies, are also part of the collection. Again, the serious reader will extend his research by examining this collection.

The state section contains for each state, as appropriate, the depository library law, comment on the law from librarians in the state taken from the Documents on Documents Collection and other written sources, editorial comment, depository rules and regulations, depository contracts, opinions of attorney generals, and annotated bibliographies. In only a few instances has the length of a document or its extensive copying from another document necessitated some editorial deletions.

The sections of the law chosen for inclusion have been identified primarily by librarians in each state. The author's collection of statutes, supplemented by contributions from colleagues and by laws included in the Documents on Documents Collection, is the basis of the statutory part of this section.

Only those sections relating specifically to document distribution to depository libraries have been copied. As a result, coverage is uneven because in some states exchange provisions are an integral part of the depository law (for example, Connecticut and Ohio), while in others such provisions are in separate statutory sections. Likewise, purging of the mailing lists, which is part of the California law, for example, is not included if the provisions are not usually cited as part of the depository law, even though this topic may be dealt with in other sections of the statutes.

Because any extensive search of the statutes must necessarily be done in a law library, the citations familiar to law librarians have been used. They follow the rules in *A Uniform System of Citation*, a standard legal tool.[3] Inasmuch as the abbreviations may be unfamiliar to readers unaccustomed to legal citations, the names of the codes are written out in full in a table at the beginning of this section. The citation does not include the traditional imprint. The reader is cautioned that the date is not the year in which the depository legislation was enacted. The *Uniform System of Citation* rule is: "the year that appears on the spine of the volume, the year that appears on the title page, or the latest copyright year—in that order of preference." For "replacement" volumes, the date of the replacement volume is used. The date when the legislation was enacted is given in a history or source note at the end of each section. Tables 2 and 3 in Chapter 3 give the date of the original enactment of the depository legislation for each state and the date of the latest amendment.

The text of the laws has been reproduced in the revised statute or code format, thus eliminating all the titles, appropriations, repealing clauses, and separability clauses of the session laws, as well as provisions unrelated to the depository programs.

The search through the revised statutes was made on the basis of the legislation on hand. Thus, amendments to the legislation were located, but completely new legislation that did not amend the earlier statutes may have been overlooked. The search for amendments ended with the legislation available in the summer of 1980, which for most states includes the 1979 legislation. Reports on legislation for 1979 that did not pass which have come to the author's attention are included under the comments sections for New Mexico and South Carolina.

For a few states, nonstatutory materials have been included. For South Carolina, a bill as introduced in the legislature is included. Both Colorado and South Carolina introduced bills in 1979 and were unsuccessful in securing passage. The Colorado legislation passed in 1980, with an appropriation of

$80,000. For Massachusetts an administrative bulletin is copied, and for West Virginia, some repealed legislation is included for reference.

A recent survey conducted by the State and Local Documents Task Force, Government Documents Round Table, American Library Association, published as a Texas Documents Monograph,[4] brings the information in this section up to date. Although the survey does not reproduce the law, rules and regulations, contracts, and other documents relating to the depository library program, it cites the laws and provides current statements on the depository programs. The laws cited by the states in the survey are the ones reproduced here with only minor variations. Oklahoma and Rhode Island listed more sections than are included.

State comments are the next major part of the state section. The comments come primarily from the Documents on Documents Collection which, when the original request was made for publications, asked for ''a brief commentary on your state's depository library legislation indicating strengths, weaknesses, proposed amendments, etc.'' The statements varied in content and in formality. The formal statements are included in their entirety; the others are edited to eliminate transmittal and nonpertinent remarks. No editing was done to bring the comment up to date, except for a few changes suggested by recent communications.

Additional commentary comes from letters written in 1976 when a big revision of the Documents on Documents Collection was undertaken, and for the southwestern and mountain plains states, from *The State of State Documents*, a manual prepared for a pre-conference on state documents held by the regional library associations for those states.

The editorial comment unit for each state attempts to answer questions raised by the legislation. It traces amendments to the law and explains references to other sections of the codes. Notes on the session laws include the title of the session law if meaningful, whether or not an appropriation was included, and sections not codified as part of the depository library law. The editorial comment also notes changes in the numbering of the statutory sections and bill numbers for sections and bills referred to in other documents and the literature.

The opinions of attorney generals relating to depository library laws are reproduced in a separate unit.

The next part of the state section is on rules and regulations. Twenty states have adopted rules. Some were adopted pursuant to statutory authority granted in the depository legislation, and some were adopted in accordance with an administrative procedure act. Such acts often require notice of intent to promulgate rules, public hearings, and publication prior to the effective date. For some states (Hawaii, for example), although statutory authority for adopting rules exists, no rules have yet been adopted. In other states, the rules have been adopted without statutory authority and are merely operational guidelines.

Contracts are another legal instrument employed in a depository library program. The contracts for eleven states are reproduced in the state section. A contract is required by the depository law in some states; in others, a contract is entered into without specific authorization. For Louisiana and Mississippi, the designation form is included in the contract section, although this form is not a true contract.

The final part of the state section is the summary of journal articles relating to each state. Although these articles are listed in the master bibliography, they are included here in an arrangement and in the detail deemed appropriate for each state. For California and Louisiana, a chronological arrangement of the articles provides an overview of the two depository systems with the longest histories. For other states, the most recent article is given first. For some states, some notes taken from state document newsletters are included.

Following the listing for the states, the model law proposed by the Library of Congress and adopted by the Council of State Governments is reproduced.

NOTES

1. *American Library Laws*, 4th ed. (Chicago: American Library Association, 1973); *First Supplement, 1973-1974* (Chicago: American Library Association, 1975); *Second Supplement, 1975-1976* (Chicago: American Library Association, 1977); *Third Supplement, 1977-1978* (Chicago: American Library Association, 1979).

2. The Documents on Documents Collection was assembled by a committee of the State Documents Task Force, Government Documents Round Table, American Library Association. It is administered by and available on interlibrary loan from Grace Moore, Recorder of Documents, Louisiana State Library, P.O. Box 131, Baton Rouge, Louisiana 70821.

3. *A Uniform System of Citation*, 12th ed. (Cambridge, Mass.: Harvard Law Review Association, 1976).

4. Margaret T. Lane (comp.), *State Publications: Depository Distribution and Bibliographical Programs*, State and Local Documents Task Force, Government Documents Round Table, American Library Association; Texas State Publications Clearinghouse, Documents Monograph Series, no. 2 ([Austin, Tex.]: Texas State Library, 1980).

ALABAMA

ALA. CODE § 41-6-12 (1975)

§ 41-6-12. Provision of official publications, etc., of commissions, bureaus, boards, etc., to department; disposition of same by department. In addition to the number of copies of any report or other official publications of any executive office, department, commission, bureau, board and state institution, now or which may hereafter be authorized by law, except the reports of the supreme court, the court of civil appeals, the court of criminal appeals and the acts and journals of the legislature, the state printer or other person printing such report or document shall print two hundred and fifty additional copies for the use of the department of archives and history, to be held for free distribution and exchange with state libraries, public libraries, institutions and individuals in Alabama and elsewhere. (Acts 1915, No. 679, p. 738; Code 1923, § 1408; Code 1940, T. 55, § 265.)

STATE COMMENT (1980)

Distribution of state documents has never been funded nor has there ever been any organization for the systematic distribution of them. They have been distributed on request to libraries, agencies and individuals. In 1978 a comprehensive survey of state documents was made by the Alabama Department of Archives and History and the Alabama Government Documents Round Table, and a workshop on depositories was held at Archives and History. A state-wide Advisory Committee on Depositories is being appointed to work out the details of a depository system. A quarterly Accessions List will be compiled and distributed by the Alabama Department of Archives and History at the end of the first quarter of 1980. (Letter of Milo B. Howard, Jr., Director, Department of Archives and History, Montgomery, Alabama, January 8, 1980.)

ATTORNEY GENERAL OPINION

1928-1930 ALA. ATT'Y GEN. REP. 893

August 26, 1930

Hon. C.A. Moffett,
    President, Board of Administration,
        CAPITOL.
        Alabama Historical Quarterly is not a report or other official publication within the meaning of Section 1408, Code of Alabama, 1923.
        Opinion by Assistant Attorney General Evans.

Dear Sir:

I have your letter of August 21, 1930. You make the following statement of facts:

The Department of Archives and History has ordered one thousand copies of the Alabama Historical Quarterly.

You ask my opinion if, under the facts above stated, two hundred and fifty copies of such Quarterly, in addition to the one thousand ordered, must be printed in order to comply with Section 1408 of the Code of Alabama, 1923.

In reply to your inquiry will say that, in my opinion, Section 1408 has no application in the case stated.

It is my opinion that the Alabama Historical Quarterly is not a report or other official publication of any executive office, department, commission, bureau, board or state institution within the meaning and intent of said Section.

                Yours truly,
                CHARLIE C. McCALL,
                Attorney General.

BIBLIOGRAPHY

Markley, Anne Ethelyn. "Author Headings for the Official Publications of the State of Alabama." Chicago: American Library Association, 1948. 123 p.
Schorr 1057 lists the University of Illinois thesis, 1944.
    This is the first list in this series. See her Introduction for "A guide for compilers of state author heading lists" and "Suggested method of procedure."

Rankin, Eugenia Patton. "First 'Current' Checklist of Alabama State Publications."
    Alabama Librarian 28:10-12 (May-June 1977).
Includes much of the information from the Foreword to the 1973 *Checklist*. Mentions
retrospective Alabama bibliographical sources and explains decision to issue a current
list. Concludes with the hope that state publications will soon be available through
regional depositories and an appeal for copies of titles not included in the Alabama
Department of Archives and History collection.

Harrison, Amalia. "Of Perennial Interest: The Capital Annuals." *Alabama Librarian*
    29:11-13 (November-December 1977).
"There are a great number of specialized publications that can be of immense help in the
search for the latest Alabama fact, statistic or name. These are published yearly . . ."
Annotated list of about fifteen titles.

ALASKA

ALASKA STAT. §§ 14.56.090-180 (1979)

ARTICLE 2. State Library Distribution and Data Access Center.

Sec. 14.56.090. State library distribution and data access center established. There is established in the state library the state library distribution and data access center. (§ 1 ch 2 SLA 1970; am § 2 ch 27 SLA 1979)

Sec. 14.56.100. Duties of center. The center shall, in cooperation with federal, municipal, and private data collection and research efforts, promote the establishment of an orderly depository library and data index distribution and access system. (§ 1 ch 2 SLA 1970; am § 3 ch 27 SLA 1979)

Sec. 14.56.120. Deposit of publications and research data. (a) Each state agency shall deposit, upon release, at least four copies of each of its state publications in the center. Additional copies of each publication may be requested by the center for deposit in quantities necessary to meet the needs of the depository library system and to provide inter-library service to those libraries not having depository status.

(b) Each state agency shall notify the center of the creation of all data published or compiled by or for it at public expense and provide for its accessibility through the center, unless the data is protected by the constitutional right to privacy or is of a type stated by law to be confidential or the agency is otherwise prohibited by law from doing so.

(c) The center is also a depository for publications of municipalities and regional educational attendance areas, including surveys and studies produced by a municipality or regional educational attendance area or produced for it on contract. Four copies of each publication produced for a municipality or regional educational attendance area may be deposited with the center for record and distribution purposes.

(d) Each municipality or regional educational attendance area may notify the center of the creation of all data published or compiled by or for it at public expense and provide for its accessibility through the center, unless the data is protected by the constitutional right to privacy or is of a type stated by law to be confidential or the municipality or regional educational attendance area is otherwise prohibited by law from doing so.

(e) When a research project or study is conducted for a person by a state agency, a municipality, or a regional educational attendance area, even though no state funding is involved, the state agency, municipality or regional educational attendance area shall request that person for permission to make copies of its final report available to the center under AS 14.56.090—14.56.180. If permission is granted, the report shall be deposited with the center. (§ 1 ch 2 SLA 1970; am § 4 ch 27 SLA 1979)

Sec. 14.56.123. Liaison with center. Each state agency shall and each municipality and regional educational attendance area may designate one of its employees to be responsible for depositing the materials and information specified in AS 14.56.120. (§ 5 ch 27 SLA 1979)

Sec. 14.56.125. Summaries and indices. (a) Upon notification of the creation of data under AS 14.56.120, a state agency shall and a municipality or regional educational attendance area may prepare an abstract or summary of it.

(b) The center shall prepare and keep current an index of all publications and data abstracts or summaries on file and shall publish and distribute that index regularly to contracting depository libraries and to other Alaska libraries upon request. (§ 5 ch 27 SLA 1979)

Sec. 14.56.130. Other documents required of state agencies.. Upon the request of the center, a state agency shall furnish the center with a complete list of its current state publications, data published or compiled by or for it at public expense, and a copy of its mailing or exchange lists. However, data which is protected by the constitutional right to privacy or is of a type stated by law to be confidential or which the agency is otherwise prohibited by law from distributing may not be furnished to the center. (§ 1 ch 2 SLA 1970; am § 6 ch 27 SLA 1979)

Sec. 14.56.135. Efficiency and computerization. The center shall, to the extent practicable, avoid duplication, coordinate its activities with other state agencies charged with record-keeping functions, and employ computerization to compile or organize research data and other materials. (§ 7 ch 27 SLA 1979)

Sec. 14.56.150. Depository library contracts. The center may enter into depository contracts with municipal, regional educational attendance area, university or community college libraries, public library associations, state library agencies, the Library of Congress, and other state and federal library systems. The requirements for eligibility to contract as a depository library shall be established by the Department of Education upon the recommendation of the state librarian and shall include and take into consideration the type of library, its ability to preserve publications or data and to make them available for public use, and the geographical location of the library for ease of access to residents in all areas of the state. (§ 1 ch 2 SLA 1970; am § 8 ch 27 SLA 1979)

Sec. 14.56.170. Distribution of state publications and research data. The center may not engage in general public distribution of either (1) state publications or lists of publications or (2) the index of publications and research data. However, unless expressly prohibited by law, the center shall make available to any person, upon request and under procedures established by it, publications, summaries, research data, indices, and other materials in its possession. Reasonable fees for reproduction or printing costs and for mailing and distribution of materials may be charged by the center. (§ 1 ch 2 SLA 1970; am § 9 ch 27 SLA 1979)

Sec. 14.56.180. Definitions. In AS 14.56.090—14.56.180, unless the context otherwise requires,

(1) "center" means the state library distribution and data access center;

(2) "state agency" includes state departments, divisions, agencies, boards, association, commissions, corporations and offices, and the University of Alaska and its affiliated research institutes;

(3) "municipal" and "municipality" includes cities and organized boroughs of every class, including municipalities unified under AS 29.68.240—29.68.440;

(4) "state publication" includes any official document, compilation, journal, bill, law, resolution, bluebook, statute, code, register, pamphlet, list, book, report, study, hearing transcript, leaflet, order, regulation, directory, periodical or magazine issued or contracted for by a state agency determined by the state librarian to be appropriate for retention in the center;

(5) "research data" or "data" means a representation of facts, concepts or instructions in a formalized manner suitable for communication, interpretation, or processing by humans or by automatic means which was prepared to serve as a basis for reasoning, calculation, discussion or decision and which is determined appropriate for indexing by the state librarian. (§ 1 ch 2 SLA 1970; am § 10 ch 27 SLA 1979)

STATE COMMENT (1978)

Our Division of State Libraries and Museums has no formal in-house rules and regulations concerning our State publication depository system, other than the depository contract and standards for service. However, our working procedures conform to the above and to the word and intent of the authorizing statutes, of course. (Letter from Louis R. Coatney, Documents Librarian, Division of State Libraries and Museums, Juneau, Alaska, dated January 2, 1980.)

EDITORIAL COMMENT

The extensive 1979 amendments to the Alaska legislation are reflected in the change of name from "state publications library distribution center" to "state library distribution and access center." A new definition, for "research data or data,'' was added. The former list of publications was changed to an ''index of publications and research data.'' Emphasis is placed on the deposit of publications of and data from municipalities and educational attendance areas, although this deposit and the notification of the creation of data are referred to permissively, ''may be deposited'' and ''may notify.'' The University of Alaska and its affiliated research institutes were added to the definition of ''state agency.'' In the definitions of both ''state publication'' and ''research data or data,'' a requirement for a determination by the state librarian is added.

RULES AND REGULATIONS

STATE PUBLICATIONS LIBRARY DISTRIBUTION CENTER

STANDARDS

1. There will be only two classes of Depository Libraries in Alaska. These will be complete and selective depositories. Any other library in the state may request specific state documents from the State Library, and these will be furnished whenever available. A complete depository shall be sent one copy of every state publication. A selective depository shall be sent one copy of every publication from the specific State agencies it designates.

2. Any municipal, college or university library, any public library association, state library agencies, and the Library of Congress, may be designated as a depository provided that all other qualifications are met.

3. Any library designated as a depository, shall agree to the following conditions, with the understanding that failure to comply with any one condition is sufficient ground for cancellation of the contract between the State and the library:

a. Provide space to house the publications with adequate provisions for expansion. State publications do not need to be maintained in a separate collection unless the receiving library prefers to do so. Housing in a vertical file rather than on shelves is acceptable for appropriate pamphlet-type materials.

b. Provide an orderly, systematic recording of receipt of the documents.

c. Process and shelve all state publications within 30 days after receipt of the material.

d. Provide trained personnel to render satisfactory service without charge to qualified patrons in the use of such publications. This librarian need not spend full time on state publications.

e. Dispose of publications only with permission of the State Librarian.

f. Accept and maintain all publications unless specified as discardable.

g. Library rules must assure that the documents are available for public use and circulations, unless for some unusual reason it becomes necessary to restrict use.

4. The State Library will take into consideration the geographical location of the applying library for ease of access to residents in all areas of the state.

CONTRACT

ALASKA DEPOSITORY LIBRARY CONTRACT

This agreement made this _____ day of _____ 19____, by and between the State Publications Library Distribution Center of the Alaska State Library hereinafter called the "Center", and the _____ Library, hereinafter called the "Depository".

WITNESSETH: WHEREAS, the legislature of the State of Alaska in 1970 enacted legislation as Chapter 2, SLA creating a State Publications Library Distribution Center within the State Library and

WHEREAS, under that law the Center is authorized to enter into depository contracts with any municipal, college or university library, any public library association, state library agencies, and the Library of Congress; and

WHEREAS; the _____ Library is desirous of entering into such a contract;

NOW, THEREFORE, IT IS MUTUALLY AGREED AND UNDERSTOOD, that,

(1) The Center shall publish an annual list of documents.

(2) The Center shall send documents on permanent deposit to the Depository in monthly shipments.

(3) The Depository shall provide space to adequately house the publications in a manner approved by the Center.

(4) The Depository shall provide an orderly systematic record of receipt of all documents from the Center and all state publications shall be processed and shelved within thirty days after receipt.

(5) A Depository shall provide trained personnel to provide service to patrons of the depository in the use of such publications.

(6) The Depository agrees to make the documents readily available for public use.

(7) The Depository agrees to accept and maintain all publications received and dispose of publications only with the permission of the Center.

(8) The Depository agrees that all inquiries and special requests concerning state documents for libraries will be channelled through the Center.

(9) The Depository agrees to send to the Center the name of every state agency from which it is currently receiving publications.

(10) The Depository agrees to comply with all of the rules, regulations and standards adopted by the Alaska State Library for depository libraries.

The contract may be terminated by either party upon six (6) months written notice to the other party that said contract is to be terminated. Upon termination of the contract the Depository shall ship all documents to the Center or to such other Depositories as may be specified by the Center.

    In signing this contract the _____ Library makes application to become a _____

                                                                 (Selective, Complete)

Depository of Alaska State Publications.

        Dated this _____ day of _____, 19_____.

By: _____

       Librarian

       _____

       Library

       _____

       Address

Approved for _____ Depository

By: _____   _____

Director, Division of State Libraries   Date

BIBLIOGRAPHY

"State Pubs." *Sourdough* 8:9 (July 1971).
Announces the new depository law effective May 3, 1970 and outlines standards enacted by the Department of Education to facilitate the program. Seven complete depositories (including the Washington State Library) and one selective library elected to participate. Article says that library rules must assure that the documents are available for public use and circulation. Several regional libraries throughout the United States have been contacted to join in the program.

Rollins, A. "Documents Course: Trying to Find Something for Everyone." *Sourdough* 13:3 (May 1976).
Reports on the credit course on documents offered at the annual conference of the Alaska Library Association. The course moved back and forth from federal to state publications. Some confusion about the scope of the course caused some dissatisfaction. The documents librarian at the state library in Juneau was the resource person.

Coatney, Louis. "Questions and Answers: Alaska State Publications." *Sourdough* 13:4 (May 1976).
Responses to questions raised during the annual conference of the Alaska Library Association and at the documents course. (1) The state library cannot undertake the general distribution of the shipping lists, but will add names to its quarterly *Information Center* mailing list. (2-4) Reports on the status of the annual checklist. (5) A comment that "*forcing*" state agencies to deposit publications would be counterproductive and that the annual "dragnets" had met with steadily increasing responsiveness and success (italics in the original).

Innes-Taylor, Cathie. "Report on State Documents Depository System." *Sourdough*
    14:7 (May 1977).
Report on a special meeting held to answer questions on the depository library system:
how documents are arranged at the state library, arrangement of the shipping list, and
what happens when a library is newly designated as a depository (answer—it gets boxes
of documents!).

Shepard, Martha. "Alaska State Depository Program." *Sourdough* 15:7 (January
    1978).
Shepard reports that for the depository libraries the advantages of the program "are
myriad; including having cataloging for the documents in hand when they arrive,
receiving automatically instead of asking each agency individually, and being able to
acquire a good cross section of Alaska materials."
    The article continues by reporting that not all problems have been solved, the most
harassing being lack of cooperation by the state agencies.
    An editor's note at the end comments that the University of Alaska has a similar
program for university publications and that, in additon, the university participates in
the State Documents Program.

Furer, Shiela. "Conference Report: Documents Depository Workshop." *Sourdough*
    16:18 (March 1979).
"Nearly all Alaska Depository Libraries were represented at the meeting, and each
person had a chance to air specific problems and give occasional murmurs of appreciation for the depository program. One thing is certain: NO ONE wants to return to the
days when every library tried to stay abreast of state documents, and every acquisitions
department librarian was wringing hands in frustration."
    "Topics for future discussion by this group could include: Recommended guidelines
for arranging documents; weeding; record keeping; and promotion of government
documents to the general public."

ARIZONA

ARIZ. REV. STAT. § 41-1335 (West Supp. 1979-1980)

Sec. 41-1335. Powers and duties of director of library, archives and public records.
****

B. The director of the department of library, archives and public records may enter into contracts to establish a depository system and an exchange program with any municipal, county or regional public library, state college or state university library and out-of-state research libraries. Except for statutes and official supplements of the statutes which shall be purchased directly by the department and distributed, the department shall make requisition upon the secretary of state, the heads of departments and all officers and agents of the state for the number of copies of official publications the department needs for the depository system and any exchange programs established pursuant to this subsection and it shall be the duty of the officers to supply them. Added Laws 1976, Ch. 104, § 6.

STATE COMMENT (1976)

We have not established a depository system. However, we do, in the near future plan to implement a statewide depository program by authority of A.R.S. 41-1335 (1976 Leg., Ch. 104), effective September 23, 1976. . . .

The Department is responsible for distributing the documents; listing them on the checklist; housing them; making them available through interlibrary loan. (Report by Marguerite B. Cooley, Director, Department of Library, Archives & Public Records, Phoenix, Arizona 85007. *In* The State of State Documents: Past, Present, Future. Texas Legislative Reference Library, 1976 at p. 9.)

BIBLIOGRAPHY

Snyder, M. E. ''Arizona in Documents, 1949.'' *Arizona Librarian* 7:14-16 (January 1950). (Not seen.)

Keith, M. ''Arizona in Documents, 1950.'' *Arizona Librarian* 8:16-20 (April 1951). (Not seen.)

Pitts, P. D. ''Author Headings for the Official Publications of Arizona.'' M.S.L.S. Thesis, University of Illinois, 1951. 166 p. (Not seen.)

ARKANSAS

ARK. STAT. ANN. §§ 6-307 (Supp. 1979); 14-428 to 14-432; 14-440 to 14-442 (1979)

6-307. Federal documents depository—State and local publications clearinghouse—Definitions. (a) The Arkansas State Library shall serve as the State's regional depository library for federal documents and shall become the official depository for State and local documents. The Arkansas State Library shall create and maintain a State and Local Government Publications Clearinghouse. All State agencies, including the General Assembly and its committees, constitutional officers, and any department, division, bureau, board, commission, or agency of the State of Arkansas, and all local governments, including cities of the first and second class and incorporated towns, and counties, and all boards, commissions or agencies thereof, shall furnish to the State Library, upon release, a specified number of copies of each of its State or local publications, to enable the State Publications Clearinghouse to meet the needs of the Depository Library System and to provide library loan services to those libraries without depository status. Such distribution will be required only if sufficient funds are appropriated for the printing of these materials by the agencies, boards, and commissions, and for the distribution thereof by the Arkansas State Library to depository libraries.

For the purposes of this Act [§§ 6-301—6-307], the expression "State publication" and/or "local publication" shall include any document issued or printed by any State agency or local government which may be released for such distribution, but does not include:

(i.) the bound volumes of the printed Acts of each of the sessions of the General Assembly of the State of Arkansas;

(ii.) the bound volumes of the Arkansas Supreme Court Reports;

(iii.) printed copies of the Arkansas Statutes, 1947, annotated, or pocket part supplements thereto;

(iv.) any other printed document which may be obtained from the office of the Secretary of State upon the payment of a charge or fee therefor;

(v.) correspondence and intraoffice or interoffice or agency communication [communications] or document [documents] which are not of vital interest to the public;

(vi.) publications of State or local agencies intended or designed to be of limited distribution to meet the requirements of educational, cultural, scientific, professional, or similar use of a limited or restricted purpose, and which are not designed for general distribution; and similarly, other publications or printed documents which are prepared to meet the limited distribution requirements of a governmental grant or use, which are not intended for general distribution, shall also be deemed exempt from the provisions of this Act unless funds have been provided for printing of a quantity of such publication [publications] sufficient for distribution, provided, that a depository copy of each such document noted in subsections (i.), (ii.), (iii.), and (vi.) shall be made available to the State Library.

(b) The State Library shall make rules and regulations as may be necessary to carry out the purposes of the State Publications Clearinghouse.

(c) The Arkansas State Library may enter into depository agreements with any city, county, district, region, town, school, college, or university library in this State. The State Library shall establish standards for eligibility as a depository library under this Section. Such standards may include and take into account:

(i.) the type of library;

(ii.) its ability to preserve such publications and to make them available for public use; and

(iii.) its geographical location, in order to assure that the publications are conveniently accessible to residents in all areas of the State.

(d) Each State and local agency printing or duplicating publications of the type which are to be made available to the State Publications Clearinghouse shall, if sufficient funds are available therefor, print or duplicate fifty (50) additional copies or such lesser number as may be requested by the State Library, for deposit with the State Publications Clearinghouse of the State Library for distribution to established depository libraries or interstate library exchange. Provided, however, that if a State agency or a local governmental agency does not have sufficient funds or resources available to furnish said fifty [50] copies to the State Publications Clearinghouse of the State Library, they shall notify the State Library and deliver to the State Publications Clearinghouse three (3) copies of each publication to be maintained in the State Library, to be indexed and made available on loan to participating libraries through the interlibrary loan services of the State Library.

(e) The State Publications Clearinghouse of the State Library shall publish, at least quarterly and more frequently if funds are available, and upon request, distribute to all State agencies and contracting depository libraries a list of State publications.

(f) Nothing in this Act shall be construed to repeal, amend, modify, or affect the status of the General Library of the University of Arkansas at Fayetteville as a depository of State, city, and county documents under the provisions of

Act 170 of 1947 [§§ 14-431, 14-432], nor shall this Act repeal, amend, modify, or affect the powers of the General Library of the University of Arkansas at Fayetteville, or the library of each of the State-supported institutions of higher learning to be a selective or partial depository of State, city, and county documents under the provisions of Act 163 of 1971 [§§ 14-440—14-442]. Provided, however, that the State Library is hereby authorized to enter into contracts or agreements with the General Library of the University of Arkansas at Fayetteville and the library of each of the State supported institutions of higher learning in this State to provide through the State Publications Clearinghouse any of the clearinghouse, exchange, depository or selective or partial depository duties or functions of any of said libraries, or to provide depository library services in behalf of any of said libraries that may be mutually agreed to by the State Library and the General Library of the University of Arkansas at Fayetteville or one of the several institutions of higher learning of this State.

All powers, functions, and duties to be performed by the Secretary of State under the provisions of Act 163 of 1971 [§§ 14-440—14-442] are hereby transferred to, and shall hereafter be performed by, the Arkansas State Library. [Acts 1979, No. 489, § 8, p.—.]

14-428. General library of University of Arkansas designated as state depository. The General Library of the University of Arkansas [shall] be designated as an official state depository of all public documents published by or under the authority of the State or any division thereof. (Acts 1947, No. 170, § 1, p. 398.)

14-429. Publications furnished to library of University of Arkansas— Exchange of documents. Each department or division of the State under whose jurisdiction any document is issued is hereby authorized and directed to send to the General Library of the University of Arkansas at Fayetteville twenty [20] copies of all such documents or publications, provided that this requirement may be waived or the number of copies required reduced upon instructions of the University Librarian to the state printing clerk and the state agency issuing the publication. These documents shall comprise all printed, mimeographed or other near-print publications, including proceedings of constitutional conventions, Senate and House Journals, Acts of the General Assembly, Revised statutes, Constitutions, Statutes at Large, Digests, Codes, Supreme Court Reports, of all department reports of the State government, publications of all state supported institutions, miscellaneous publications, reports of investigations of impeachment trials, and sundry documents. Copies required for public use shall remain on permanent deposit in the General Library of the University of Arkansas in convenient form accessible to the public. Copies not required by the University libraries may be used by the University Librarian for exchange for needed publications of other states.

Provided, that only three [3] copies of all mimeographed or near-print publications, other than annual or biennial reports, shall be sent to the University Library unless other copies are specifically requested by the Librarian. (Acts 1947, No. 170, § 2, p. 398; 1955, No. 379, § 1, p. 924.)

14-430. Affidavit showing delivery to library required before printing account paid. No account for printing of any documents as provided for in Section 2 [§ 14-429] shall be approved and no warrants or voucher checks shall be issued therefor until the Auditor's State Printing Clerk is furnished by the disbursing officer with an affidavit certifying to delivery to said library of copies of publications as provided for. (Acts 1947, No. 170, § 3, p. 398.)

14-431. County and municipal governments to send copies of publications to university. Each department or division of government of municipalities and counties under whose jurisdiction any printed or processed book, pamphlet or report or other publication is issued at the expense of a municipal corporation or of a county, or of a county and city, is hereby directed to send two [2] copies of each such publication to the General Library of the University of Arkansas for inclusion in said depository. (Acts 1947, No. 170, § 4, p. 398.)

14-432. Act cumulative. This act [§§ 14-428—14-432] is cumulative to and shall not repeal Sections 12236 to 12242 [§§ 6-201—6-204, 6-207, 6-208], inclusive of Pope's Digest of the Statutes of Arkansas. (Acts 1947, No. 170, § 5, p. 398.)

14-440. Publications of state and its subdivisions furnished to libraries of institutions of higher learning—Designated as depositories. In addition to the General Library of the University of Arkansas at Fayetteville, which was designated as a depository of all State, city and county documents under the provisions of Act 170 [§ 14-428] of 1947, as amended, the library of each of the State supported institutions of higher learning in this State is hereby designated as a selective or partial depository of State, city and county documents. Each department or division of the State, city and county which is directed to furnish copies of publications to the General Library of the University of Arkansas, is hereby authorized and directed to send to the Secretary of State a list of all publications published by such department or division during the preceding quarter. The Secretary of State shall prepare a check-list of all publications published by all county, city and all departments and agencies of this State, and shall furnish quarterly a copy of such check-list to each of the institutions of higher learning in this State. (Acts 1971, No. 163, § 1, p. 405.)

14-441. Publications of state and its subdivisions furnished to libraries of institutions of higher learning—Procedure. Any institution of higher learning desiring to obtain copies of any publication contained in such check-list, shall order the number of copies, not to exceed three [3] copies of any one [1] report or publication, desired from the Secretary of State. The Secretary of State shall collect such orders and shall periodically obtain from State agencies and departments, and from the various cities and counties, a sufficient number of copies and documents and publications to fill such order. The Secretary of State shall furnish all such institutions of higher learning copies of any documents and publications so ordered without charge or cost. (Acts 1971, No. 163, § 2, p. 405.)

14-442. Publications of state departments and divisions furnished to secretary of state. Each department or division of the State, cities or counties under whose jurisdiction any printed or processed book, pamphlet or report or other publication is issued at the expense of a municipal corporation or of a county, or of a county and city, or of the State, is hereby directed to furnish, without charge, to the Secretary of State such number of copies of such publications as the Secretary of State may order. (Acts 1971, No. 163, § 3, p. 405.)

STATE COMMENT (1976)

Under Act 163 of 1971 (*Acts of Arkansas*, 1971, pp. 405-7) each department or division of the state, city and county is required to send to the Secretary of State a list of all of its publications quarterly. (1947-1971, the publications were sent to the General Library of the University of Arkansas at Fayetteville.) From the information received, the Secretary of State is required to publish a checklist of publications to be mailed to all Arkansas Libraries of institutions of higher education (each being eligible to become a selective or partial depository). The libraries are to forward their requests for publications to the Secretary of State who is directed to acquire the publications and fill the orders. Legislation specifies that publications be furnished without charge to the Secretary of State and academic libraries. All other libraries should request documents from the issuing agency.

The 1971 law became a reality through the efforts of academic and reference librarians working through the Arkansas Library Association and with members of The Arkansas General Assembly.

Arkansas Statutes designate the Secretary of State as Librarian for the State Library and give him the responsibility of maintaining files of some publications of historical and legal significance, including the *Acts of the General Assembly*. (Arkansas Statutes Annotated, 1947: 12-414.)

Since its establishment in 1911, The Arkansas History Commission has been charged with the preservation of state documents and, in the beginning, was designated a depository for exchange of documents. In 1963, the Commission was relieved of its responsibility to collect 60 copies of each state document for exchange purposes. Now, the Commission receives two copies for preservation. The History Commission microfilms state records and some state publi-

cations. Inquiries should be addressed to the Arkansas History Commission, 300 West Markham, Little Rock, AR 72201.
****

The challenge to Arkansas librarians is to help make Act 163 of 1971 effective. There is still a problem in knowing what is published. (Report by Gladys Sachse, Assistant Librarian, Torreyson Library, University of Central Arkansas, Conway, Arkansas 72032. *In* The State of State Documents: Past, Present, Future. Texas Legislative Reference Library, 1976, at p. 10.)

EDITORIAL COMMENT

The 1979 legislation is supplementary to that enacted in 1947 and 1971 affecting the University of Arkansas and the institutions of higher learning. It is part of an act providing "for the creation and establishment of the Arkansas State Library." The title of the act does not mention the new clearinghouse that is provided for in section (a). The Arkansas State Library is authorized to provide through the new State Publications Clearinghouse for any duties, functions, or services relating to the depository activities of the university or the institutions of higher learning that may be mutually agreed to by the state library and the university or one of the institutions of higher learning.

The new Arkansas legislation has several qualifying clauses designed to avoid undue financial hardship on the state agencies. If the agency does not have sufficient funds to furnish fifty copies of its publications, it may notify the state library and deliver three copies. The distribution is required only if sufficient funds are appropriated for the printing of the material by the agencies and for the distribution by the Arkansas State Library. The requirement that the checklist be published quarterly is augmented by the clause "and more frequently if funds are available."

The preamble to 1947 Arkansas Acts, No. 170, reads:
"Whereas, it is desirable that there should be a comprehensive collection of public documents for teachers, students and research workers in the State; and
"Whereas, the General Library of the University of Arkansas is a full depository for the documents of the United States government; and
"Whereas, this library is seriously handicapped in acquiring Arkansas State, Municipal and County Documents, and the documents of other States for lack of suitable documents to offer in return, Now, Therefore, . . ."

The 1955 amendment to 14-429 made these changes: (1) in the first sentence, reduced the number of copies to be sent from *thirty* to *twenty* and added the clause "provided that this requirement may be waived or the number of copies required reduced upon instructions of the University Librarian to . . ." (2) substituted "Copies required for public use" for "two copies of all documents . . .'' and also substituted ''Copies not required by the University libraries . . .'' for ''Other copies shall be used . . .'' and (3) in the last sentence, increased the number of copies of all mimeographed or near-print publications from *two* to *three*.

Sections 14-440 to 14-442 were emergency legislation, effective February 26, 1971. (1971 Ark. Acts, No. 163, § 6.)

BIBLIOGRAPHY

Butt, Cecelia. ''Creating an Arkansas Documents Collection.'' *Arkansas Libraries*
    34:15-17 (June 1977).
Fayetteville Public Library wanted to be able to channel documents into a planned acquisitions program and to catalog the documents so that they would be accessible. They used agency name as author on the catalog cards, made cross-references, and devleloped a subject authority file. Butt concludes with three wishes: (1) a complete list of state agencies, (2) a list of documents and availability of documents from a central source, and (3) a central cataloging system.

CALIFORNIA

CAL. GOV'T CODE §§ 14868, 14886, 14900-14912
(West Supp. 1963-1979)

§ **14868. Costs necessitated by section 14901.** Charges for printing publications, including legislative printing, shall include the cost of printing and distributing copies thereof to libraries as required by Section 14901. (Added by 1965, c. 371, p. 1560, § 179. Amended by Stats. 1976, c. 1038, p. 4648, § 1, operative July 1, 1977.)

§ **14886. State blue book; distribution; sale; publication with similar title; penalty.** The volumes shall be distributed as follows: . . . and copies as provided in Section 14901 of this code.
****

(Added by Stats. 1965, c. 371, p. 1562, § 179. Amended by Stats. 1967, c. 17, p. 837, § 40; Stats. 1973, c. 7, p. 13, § 25, urgency, eff. March 13, 1973.)

ARTICLE 6. DISTRIBUTION OF STATE PUBLICATIONS

§ **14900. State policy; distribution of state publications to libraries.** It is the policy of the State of California to make freely available to its inhabitants all state publications by distribution to libraries throughout the state, subject to the assumption by such libraries of the responsibilities of keeping such documents readily accessible for use, and of rendering assistance in their use to qualified patrons without charge. (Added Stats. 1965, c. 371, p. 1563, § 179.)

§ **14901. Library stock room; copies for state archivist; disposition of remaining copies.** To the end that the policy specified in Section 14900 may be effectively carried out, the State Printer shall print a sufficient number of copies of each state publication as determined by the State Librarian in accordance with Sections 14901, 14903, 14904, 14905.1, and 14907, not to exceed three hundred fifty (350), unless the Department of General Services with the advice of the State Librarian determines that a greater number is necessary in order to meet the requirements for deposit in a "library stockroom" (to be maintained by the State Printer for that purpose) for distribution to libraries as hereinafter provided, except that of legislative bills, daily journals, and daily or weekly histories, not more than one hundred fifty (150) copies shall be printed for such deposit and distribution, and of publications not printed by the State Printer, the department, commission or other agency concerned shall print one hundred (100) copies for such distribution. An additional two (2) copies of each state publication as selected by the State Archivist shall be printed and delivered to the State Archivist by the State Printer or the department, commission, or other agency concerned, and all remaining copies in excess of two (2) copies heretofore received shall be distributed to interested parties without charge or destroyed. The cost of printing, publishing, and distributing such copies shall be fixed and charged pursuant to Section 14866. (Added by Stats. 1965, c. 371, p. 1563, § 179. Amended by Stats. 1965, c. 1825, p. 4214, § 1; Stats. 1972, c. 616, p. 1085, §1; Stats. 1976, c. 1038, p. 4648, § 2, operative July 1, 1977.)

§ **14902. Definitions.** "State publication" or "publication" as herein employed is defined to include any document, compilation, journal, law, resolution, Blue Book, statute, code, register, pamphlet, list, book, report, memorandum, hearing, legislative bill, leaflet, order, regulation, directory, periodical or magazine issued by the state, the Legislature, constitutional officers, or any department, commission or other agency thereof or prepared for the state by private individual or organization and issued in print, and "print" is defined to include all forms of duplicating other than by the use of carbon paper. The publications of the University of California, however, and intraoffice or interoffice publications and forms shall not be included. (Added by Stats. 1965, c. 371, p. 1564, § 179. Amended by Stats. 1972, c. 616, p. 1085, § 2.)

§ **14903. Forwarding to state and university libraries; exchange copies.** As soon as practicable after deposit of the copies in the library stockroom, the State Printer shall forward of each publication other than the legislative bills, daily journals and daily or weekly histories, fifty (50) copies to the State Library at Sacramento, twenty-five (25) copies each to the University of California libraries at Berkeley and Los Angeles, and fifty (50) copies to the California State Colleges, to be allocated among the libraries thereof as directed by the Trustees of the California State Colleges. Such copies in excess of the number required for the institutions themselves, may be used for exchanges with other institutions or with agencies of other states and countries. (Added Stats. 1965, c. 371, p. 1654, § 179; as amended Stats. 1965, c. 1825, p. 4214, § 2.)

§ **14904. Distribution to complete and selective depositories; distribution to other libraries on request.** The copies remaining in the library stockroom, including the legislative bills, daily journals, and daily or weekly histories, shall be distributed as soon as practicable by the State Printer first one copy each to the libraries which are on his mailing list as "complete depositories," second one copy each to the libraries which are on his mailing list as "selective depositories," and third the balance to any libraries which may write for a copy or copies. Publications not printed by the State Printer shall be distributed by the issuing department, commission or other agency as soon as practicable after printing, first to all "complete depositories," and second to "selective depositories," designated by the Department of General Services. (Added Stats. 1965, c. 371, p. 1564, § 179.)

§ 14905. **Designation of libraries as complete or selective depositories; conditions.** To be placed on the mailing list as a "complete depository" or as a "selective depository," a library must contract with the Department of General Services to provide adequate facilities for the storage and use of the publications, and must agree to render reasonable service without charge to qualified patrons in the use of the publications. A library designated as a "complete depository" shall be sent one copy of every state publication, while a library designated as a "selective depository" shall be sent one copy of each publication of the type or issuing agency it selects. (Added Stats. 1965, c. 371, p. 1564, § 179.)

§ 14905.1. **Exchange of publications.** The California State Library may enter into agreements with the appropriate state agencies of each of the 49 other states of the United States of America, to establish a program for the exchange of publications of legislative service agencies, other than publications of the Joint Legislative Audit Committee and of the Joint Legislative Budget Committee. The California legislative reports to be exchanged shall be selected by the State Librarian after consultation with, and subject to the approval of, the Joint Committee on Legislative Organization. The legislative research reports received from other states in exchange shall be made available by the California State Library to the California Legislature.

Prior to designation as an exchange agency, the state agency shall agree to provide adequate facilities for the storage and use of the publications, and must agree to render reasonable service in the use of the publications without charge to the legislature of that state and other qualified patrons.

The California State Library shall notify the appropriate state agency of each of the other states of the provisions of this section.

The additional number of copies of publications, not to exceed 100, needed to implement the program shall be printed or otherwise duplicated. The State Printer and the state legislative agencies upon notification of the need shall provide the designated number of publications. (Added Stats. 1965, c. 1232, p. 3085, § 2.)

§ 14906. **Designation of libraries as complete or selective depositories; eligibility; consideration of applications.** Any municipal or county free library, any state college or state university library, the library of any incorporated college or university in this state, and the State Library, may contract as above provided. Applications are to be considered in the order of their receipt by the Department of General Services. (Added Stats. 1965, c. 371, p. 1565, § 179.)

§ **14907. Law libraries; designation as complete or selective depositories.** Upon application, county law libraries, the law libraries of any law school approved by the State Bar of California, the Supreme Court Library, and the law libraries of the Department of Justice and the law library of the Continuing Education of the Bar of the University of California Extension may contract as provided in Section 14905 to become a selective or complete depository library. (Added Stats. 1965, c. 371, p. 1565, § 179.)

§ **14908. Disregard of proximity to another depository in selection of law library as depository.** Because of the specialized service rendered the citizens of this state through assistance in the administration of justice, proximity to another depository library shall be disregarded in the selection of a law library as a depository of legal materials. (Added Stats. 1965, c. 371, p. 1565, § 179.)

§ **14909. Basic documents.** Maintenance of basic general documents shall not be required of law library depositories, but basic legal documents shall be maintained by them. Such basic legal documents shall include legislative bills, legislative committee hearings and reports, legislative journals, statutes, administrative reports, California Administrative Code and Register, annual reports of state agencies and other legal materials published by the state, where obtainable through the agency preparing same. (Added Stats. 1965, c. 371, p. 1565, § 179.)

§ **14910. Monthly or quarterly lists of publications; annual cumulative list.** To facilitate the distribution of state publications, the State Library shall issue monthly or quarterly a complete list of state publications issued during the immediately preceding month or quarter, such lists to be cumulated and printed at the end of each calendar year. All state departments, commissions and other agencies shall, upon request, supply information to the State Library for the preparation of the monthly or quarterly lists and the annual cumulative lists. (Added by Stats. 1965, c. 371, p. 1565, § 179. Amended by Stats. 1976, c. 1038, p. 4649, § 3, operative July 1, 1977.)

§ **14911. Mailing lists; annual correction.** Whenever any state agency maintains a mailing list of public officials or other persons to whom publications or other printed matter is sent without charge, the state agency shall correct its mailing list and verify its accuracy at least once each year. This shall be done by addressing an appropriate post card or letter to each person on the mailing list. The name of any person who does not respond to such letter or post card, or who indicates that he does not desire to receive such publications or printed matter, shall be removed from the mailing lists. The responses of those desiring to be on the mailing list shall be retained by these agencies for one year. (Added Stats. 1965, c. 371, p. 1565, § 179.)

§ **14912. Number of copies of statutes.** Notwithstanding any other provision of this article, the number of copies of statutes distributed to an authorized recipient shall not exceed the number requested by such recipient, or the number authorized by this article, whichever is the lesser. (Added by Stats. 1970, c. 72, p. 86, § 2, urgency, eff. April 30, 1970.)

STATE COMMENT (1973)

The great weakness has proved to be the lack of any single over-all responsible agency *with funding* to carry out the program, or as an alternative, a legislative committee responsible for the funding of the program. The State Library (Dept. of Education), the State Office of Printing (Dept. of General Services) and all the State agencies share responsibility of the program although theoretically the State Library has administrative responsibility.

As the result of a recent management survey, it was recommended that State agencies be charged $20 approximately for each title listed in CALIFORNIA STATE PUBLICATIONS by the State Printer to defray the cost of publishing the list and of the free copies distributed to libraries under the program. Obviously agencies are going to choose to list a minimum number of their publications, so that consequently the list will be greatly reduced in size.

Also, the management survey put the responsibility of determining what is "LDA" in the hands of each agency of which there are more than 500. Prior to this time, we have been listing in CALIFORNIA STATE PUBLICATIONS all the relevant publications received at the State Library, within the limitations of our staff time.

Another problem is that the classification developed for use with our extremely large collection of California documents is becoming very difficult to use. Rapid and continual changes in the organization of California State government make an agency classification difficult to keep current. (Letter from Ruth Elwonger, California State Publications Librarian, California State Library, dated June 29, 1973. *In* Documents on Documents Collection.)

STATE COMMENT (1976)

Assembly Bill 3539 . . . makes changes in the Library Distribution Act (California Government Code sections 14900-14912). The importance of the $41,000 appropriation is that the costs of issuing the monthly checklist CALIFORNIA STATE PUBLICATIONS will no longer be apportioned among the agencies whose publications are listed. The present system is counterproductive because agencies are discouraged from submitting publications to the State Library for listing. The bill cleared the Assembly on June 18, 1976, and is presently in the Senate awaiting assignment to a policy committee. (Letter from Richard H. Nicoles, California State Publications Librarian,

Government Publications Section, California State Library, dated June 24, 1976. *In* Documents on Documents Collection.)

STATE COMMENT (1979)

In 1976 Assembly Bill 3539 was introduced and passed (Chap. 1038, Stats. 1976). Its final effect was to give the State Library full control and authority over the publishing of the monthly checklist CALIFORNIA STATE PUBLI-CATIONS. That was not the bill's original intent, however, and the background is interesting.

Prior to AB3539, the State Printer met the costs of producing and distributing *CSP* by assessing the agencies a fixed charge per listing. For printed publications, this charge was simply added to the printing bill where it caused little comment. However, agencies which reproduced their own publications had to be separately billed annually. Out in the naked light of day, as it were, this listing charge (it rose as high as fifty dollars per title) caused quite a stir. AB3539, then, was an attempt by the Legislature (whose reports and hearing transcripts are not printed) to avoid this charge by simply excusing itself from the listing requirement of LDA [Library Distribution Act]. Such a move, had it succeeded, would have been a serious blow to the bibliographic control of California documents.

Fortunately, the State Library, well aware of the inequities and paperwork caused by the charge back system (we had tried to amend the law a year or two earlier but were unable to win the support of the Dept. of Finance), knew what sort of changes it would like to see and was able with the support of documents librarians from all over California to amend the bill into its final form. It is our feeling that ending the listing charge back has encouraged agencies to submit more of their publications for listing and to be added to our collection. (Letter from Richard H. Nicoles, California State Library, dated August 10, 1979.)

RULES AND REGULATIONS

STATE ADMINISTRATIVE MANUAL
PUBLICATIONS AND DOCUMENTS

LIBRARY DISTRIBUTION ACT (Revised 11/65)   **3120**

The Library Distribution Act establishes a system to distribute state agency publications to libraries in order to make such publications widely available to residents of the State. In order to make this program fully effective, state agency cooperation is needed in distributing publications as required by law. Refer to Government Code Sections: 14900-14911.

DEFINITION OF PUBLICATIONS; STANDARDS DEFINED (New 5/73)   3121.1

Publication means anything produced in multiple copies (Government Code Section 14902). The intent of the following statements are [sic] twofold: (1) to give each Publications Representative some rules by which he can formulate his department's procedures, and (2) to give each Publications Representative an established policy so that questions of LDA applicability will be easier to resolve at the departmental level.

All publications not prohibited by law or elsewhere in SAM [State Administrative Manual] shall fall under the Library Distribution Act. These publications may be:

1. Of lasting interest and use to the public, or
2. Of general interest, or
3. Of special interest when such interest is geographically dispersed, or
4. Of special interest when the State is the monopolistic custodian of data which can be used for other legitimate ends, or
5. Annual compilations of periodicals not qualifying for LDA distribution but, because of the annualization, the data becomes important.

All forms, letters, memorandums, exclusive use documents, legally restricted items, organizational and procedural manuals, and interoffice and intraoffice publications for use within the state administration shall not qualify for distribution under LDA.

A department may elect to qualify local interest circulars and publications; specialized publications of primary utility to a select group; reports on minor reorganizations and policy changes dealing with state administration; and market reports and weeklies that are dated to critical tolerances if it so chooses.

DEFINITION OF STANDARD CERTIFICATION AND ASSISTANCE (New 5/73) 3121.2

The Government Publications Section of the State Library shall review and approve the LDA guidelines and changes in guidelines of all departments, boards, and commissions. The Government Publications Section shall act as counselor to departments, commissions, and boards requesting assistance in determining LDA applicability of specific documents.

EXCEPTION TO THE DEFINITION (New 5/73)   3121.3

Since the State Library is generally expected to be a complete loaning depository of state documents to other public libraries; and since the State Library offers a unique service to state employees, each publication of note produced by an authority in the state administrative structure ought to be available through the Government Publications Section. Therefore, at least one copy of all state publications otherwise not falling under LDA, or excluded by SAM Section 3121.1 above, shall be sent to the State Library, Government Publications Section.

DISTRIBUTION OF PUBLICATIONS PRODUCED BY STATE PRINTING PLANT
(Revised 9/77) 3122.1

The Office of State Printing shall distribute all Library Distribution Act material produced at its facilities to all Complete Depository Libraries, all Selective Depository Libraries, the State Archivist, the Library of Congress, and the Council of State Governments. The State Printer may authorize the director of a department, board, or commission to distribute its own publications reproduced by the Office of State Printing if a written and specific request by the director of the organization is submitted.

The charge to agencies for printing includes the cost of producing the additional copies required by the Library Distribution Act. An additional flat charge is made for the cost of distribution.

DISTRIBUTION OF PUBLICATIONS PRODUCED BY DUPLICATING PROCESS
(Revised 9/77) 3122.2

Each agency, except the University of California, is responsible for distributing publications which are produced by its own facilities or produced for them by the central duplicating service. Agencies are to prepare 100 extra copies of such publications and are responsible for distributing these 100 copies as follows:

1. State Library, Government Publications Section: *three* copies of each publication except that only *two* copies are required of serials (periodicals and annual reports). These are needed as soon as possible so that the monthly listing of state publications can be prepared without delay.

2. One copy each to the other Complete Depository Libraries listed in the annual edition of "California State Publications."

3. One copy to each Selective Depository Library requesting the publication. Mailing lists are to be maintained by the agency for the purpose of distributing publications to interested Selective Depository Libraries and others.

4. Two copies to the State Archivist.

5. Two copies to Exchange and Gift Division, Monthly Checklist Section, Library of Congress, Washington, D.C. 20540.

6. One copy to Research Librarian, Council of State Governments, Iron Works Pike, Lexington, Kentucky 40505.

7. Copies to any other libraries which may request them, until the supply of remaining copies is exhausted. If demand for a publication exceeds supply, Selective Depositories are to receive first consideration. These copies, if not distributed, shall be retained for a period of one year.

DISTRIBUTION OF PUBLICATIONS PRODUCED UNDER CONTRACT WITH INDIVIDUAL OR FIRM **(New 5/73)** 3122.3

Agencies which let reproduction contracts for Library Distribution Act qualified publications, whether the material to be reproduced is a part of a consulting contract or not, are responsible for distributing the 100 copies as outlined in SAM Section 3122.2 above. Such reproduction contracts should have provision for the additional copies included at time of acceptance of the bid.

PUBLICATIONS REPRESENTATIVES (Revised 5/73)   3123

Each department, board, or commission shall designate one person as their Publications Representative. Documents and Publications of the Office of Procurement and the Librarian (LDA) at the Government Publications Section, State Library, shall be notified as to the name, mailing address, and telephone number of the Publications Representative each December 1.

The designated person shall develop and apply suitable procedures to assure a distribution of departmental, board, or commission publications, both printed and processed, which are in harmony with the provisions of the Library Distribution Act.

When a publication is to be distributed pursuant to the Library Distribution Act, the department, board, or commission shall include this information on the Printing Requisition—Invoice, Std. Form 67, or the Duplicating Order, Std. Form 68.

INTERDEPARTMENTAL COORDINATION (Revised and Renumbered 1/1/63)   3124

The Government Publications Section of the State Library is responsible for coordinating the distribution of both printed and processed state publications, and for the preparation of periodic lists of state publications. They will advise agency Publications Representatives on questions arising as to the operation of the library distribution system. It is recognized that it is not always easy to determine whether or not a publication should be distributed or comes within the "intraoffice or interoffice" category. In order that a consistent policy may be applied, particularly in the case of similar publications issued by different agencies, agency publications representatives are urged to consult with the State Library as questions arise.

EDITORIAL COMMENT

The 1977 amendments to the State Administrative Manual deleted the references to the flat fee charged publishers for listing their publications in the state checklist.

STANDARDS FOR DEPOSITORIES

STANDARDS FOR DEPOSITORY LOCATION

1. At least one depository shall be established in each library district.
2. In districts with a population density of 1-499 persons per square mile,

one depository may be established for each 200,000 persons or major fraction thereof.

3. In districts with a population density of 500-999 persons per square mile, one depository may be established for each 300,000 persons or major fraction thereof.

4. In districts with a population density of 1,000 or more persons per square mile, one depository may be established for each 500,000 persons or major portion thereof.

5. In districts with a population density in excess of 500 persons per square mile, depositories shall be dispersed throughout the district in such a manner that the greatest number of persons may have reasonably ready access to the library.

6. In districts with a population density less than 500 persons per square mile, depositories shall be located in a county seat, one of the largest cities in the district, or in a major marketing area. Also, in these areas, each depository shall be located at least 50 miles from any other depository and shall serve a minimum of 25,000 persons.

7. As a general rule, not more than one depository may be located in any place, community, town, or city.

8. Under certain conditions approved by the State Librarian, one additional depository in excess of the maximum number may be established in districts with a minimum population of 150,000 persons. Designating a library as a depository under this exception will be permitted only if all other conditions are met and if the library is located a minimum of 100 miles from any other existing depository.

9. Because of their specialized and limited clientele, the number of college and university libraries which are granted depository status shall be limited to 25 percent of the total number of depositories authorized, but may be located without regard for the foregoing rules.

PERFORMANCE STANDARDS FOR DEPOSITORY LIBRARIES

1. Any municipal or county free library, any state college or state university, the library of any incorporated college or university in this state, and the State Library may be designated as a depository, either complete or selective, provided that all other qualifications are met.

2. Any library designated as a depository, either complete or selective, shall agree to the following conditions, with the understanding that failure to comply with any one condition is sufficient grounds for cancellation of the contract between the State and the library:

a. Provide space to house the publications in an approved manner with adequate provisions for expansion. State publications do not need to be maintained in a separate collection unless the library prefers to do so.

Housing in a vertical file rather than on shelves is acceptable for appropriate pamphlet-type materials.

b. Catalog, record, or organize state publications in an approved manner. It is expected that state publications will be fully cataloged or, if of a serial nature, will be be fully recorded. Pamphlet materials, however, may be organized in a vertical file under appropriate subject headings without card records. If publications are cataloged in a reference room card catalog, subject reference cards also shall be located in the general card catalog. The purpose of this requirement is to bring automatically to the attention of the library patron the existence of government publications on the subject of his interest in case the patron does not know there is a special catalog elsewhere in the library. These subject references may be general, covering a broad subject field and need not refer to specific titles. Example: FLAGS For material on this subject see also Government Publications Department.

c. Process and shelve all state publications within 30 days after receipt of the material.

d. Provide a professionally trained librarian to render satisfactory service without charge to qualified patrons in the use of such publications. This librarian need not spend full time on state publications.

e. Dispose of publications only in accordance with disposal policies established by the State Librarian.

f. Accept and maintain all publications specified as "basic items."

CONTRACT

CONTRACT FOR DISTRIBUTION OF STATE PUBLICATIONS TO LIBRARIES

THIS AGREEMENT, made and entered into this _____ day of _____, 197____, at Sacramento, California, by and between the STATE OF CALIFORNIA, acting by and through its duly appointed, qualified, and acting Director of General Services, with the approval of the State Librarian, hereinafter called "State", and the _____, hereinafter called "Library";

WITNESSETH:

WHEREAS, pursuant to Chapter 371, Statutes of 1965, (Sections 14900 to 14911, inclusive, Government Code of the State of California) the Legislature has declared it to be the policy of the State of California to freely make available to its inhabitants all State publications by distributing said publications to libraries throughout the State, subject to the assumption by such libraries of the responsibility of keeping such publications readily accessible for use, and of rendering assistance in the use of said publications to qualified patrons without charge; and

WHEREAS, said Chapter authorizes, among others, any municipality or county free library to contract with State and to assume the responsibilities hereinabove mentioned in order to be placed on the mailing list of State as a ''complete depository'' or as a ''selective depository'' to which copies of all such State publications are to be distributed; and

WHEREAS, Library desires to become a ''selective depository'' pursuant to the provisions of said Chapter;

NOW, THEREFORE, Library hereby requests that it be placed on the mailing list of State as a selective depository for the purpose of having distributed to it State publications in accordance with and as defined in Chapter 371, Statutes of 1965.

State agrees to place Library on said mailing list for distribution of such State publications as Library is entitled to receive under said Act as a ''selective depository'' subject to observance by Library of its responsibilities under this agreement.

Until changed by written notice, Library's address to which copies of all such State publications are to be sent is _____.

In consideration of the distribution to Library of State Publications as aforesaid, Library hereby agrees throughout the term of this agreement to perform the following:

1. Provide suitable shelf space in order to house the said publications in an approved manner with adequate provision for expansion.

2. Index or catalog all State publications in an approved manner. If publications are cataloged in a reference room card catalog, subject reference cards shall also be filed in the General Card Catalog.

3. Process and shelve all State publications within thirty (30) days after receipt of said publications.

4. Provide a professionally trained librarian to render satisfactory service and assistance without charge to qualified patrons in the use of such publications.

5. Dispose of publications only in accordance with disposal policies established by the State Librarian. Details of disposal policies for selective and complete depositories are given in the Annual Listing of *California State Publications*.

6. Libraries are encouraged to circulate California state publications in their collections.

Library agrees that State may at any reasonable time inspect the facilities provided by Library for the storage and use of all State publications distributed to it under this agreement, and that it will promptly supply any information which may be requested by State in connection with the storage and use of such publications.

This agreement may be terminated or amended by mutual consent in writing, and unless so terminated shall remain in effect until terminated by either party upon giving thirty (30) days' written notice to the other party.

IN WITNESS WHEREOF, this contract has been executed by the parties hereto on the date first above written.

STATE OF CALIFORNIA
DEPARTMENT OF GENERAL SERVICES
_____ DIRECTOR

BY _____

_____

BY_____

BIBLIOGRAPHY

The California experience with its depository library law is well documented in the library literature. Articles and other publications relating to state documents in California are listed in chronological order.

Huston, Evelyn. "California Solves Documents Distribution: In Face of Opposition, Its Library Association Secured a Bill Which Benefits the State Depositories and Other Exchanges." *Library Journal* 73:7-14 (January 1, 1948).
The author, head of the California State Library's Government Document Section, credits California with being the "first state in the United States to set up a comprehensive distribution system for its official publications." Huston outlines the California distribution statutes prior to 1945 and comments on the lack of a checklist. The list in *News Notes of California Libraries* was limited to documents received at the California State Library and had a publication lag.

Huston records the activities of the California Library Association Committee, chaired by Jerome K. Wilcox, which recognized the opportunity presented by the creation of a legislative investigating committee with a $100 appropriation. The Wilcox committee prepared a questionnaire to determine whether libraries would participate in a depository system and the publications which they would need. Huston reports the introduction of SB 1003 by the chairman of the Interim Committee on the Printing and Distribution of Documents and outlines its provisions. She mentions that the committee had hoped to have all distribution made from the library stockroom but had to compromise and leave the distribution of nonprint material with the issuing agencies. The bill repealed conflicting sections, effecting a saving of $11,475, and appropriated $46,830 for a two-year period. The effective date was September 15, 1945.

Huston outlines the establishment of the depository system. The California Library Association Committee, chaired by Edith M. Coulter after Wilcox left California, monitored the operation of the law and in 1946 surveyed all the complete depositories, most of which reported that they were receiving all the publications printed by the state printer.

Early problems encountered included the need to reduce the number of copies to the keeper of the Archives from twenty-five to five (an act to accomplish this was enacted in 1947), difficulties caused by restrictive interpretations of "intraoffice and interoffice publications and forms," and the lack of a trained bibliographer to prepare the checklist. A special position was created to meet this last-named need and was filled by Martin E. Thomas, who became the first supervisor of documents distribution.

The benefits of the system to California librarians are stated as: (1) part of the State Department of Finance appropriation is earmarked to pay for the distribution of printed publications, (2) nondepository libraries may request publications from the library stockroom, and (3) complete depositories automatically receive mimeographed publications from the issuing agencies. Benefits to librarians outside California include (1) availability of exchange copies and (2) a comprehensive checklist.

Klausner, Margaret. "California Documents, 1949." *California Library Bulletin* 11:15-16, 22 (September 1949).

A report by the then current chairman of the State Documents Committee to the California Library Association on the four years' operation of the Library Distribution Act. A questionnaire was sent to all state depositories (and a response received from all but one) "to check on the operation of the law to determine the effectiveness of the method of distribution, and ascertain how libraries are handling the material."

Of the sixty libraries, thirty-nine increased the man-hours devoted to California documents work (averaging eighteen man-hours a week for processing and ten for reference). Other statistics are given. "One of the surprising finds is that 18 libraries are using a system of notation for classifying materials—and that 13 of these have evolved their own notation."

The *Quarterly Listing* was considered "fine" but tardy. A monthly supplement was suggested, as was the inclusion of the sale price of the documents. Other recommendations included marking of the documents with division, bureau, and date of issue; distribution of bound journals; and immediate distribution of legislative bills.

Replies to the questionnaire "revealed a lack of information and understanding relating to the depository act, and suggested the need for an institute and workshop on public documents." The committee was planning a meeting for 1950.

Thomas, Martin E. "California State Documents Distribution." *California Librarian* 12: 101-103+ (December 1950).

This article, written after the distribution program had been operating for five years, raised the question, "Are California librarians taking full advantage of the documents distribution service for which the state appropriates about $35,000 each year?" Thomas, who was supervisor of publications distribution, State Printing Plant, and compiler of the first fifteen lists of *California State Publications*, emphasizes that just as librarians influenced the adoption of the legislation for depository libraries, they can and should make their needs known with respect to the administration of the law. He states that selective depositories have had two opportunities to select publications, comments in detail on the selection patterns in the most recent list, and raises the question of a basic list which all the selective depositories would be required to receive. The article concludes with seven recommendations on the administration of the program and an admonition to California librarians to read and follow the law. The basic lists postulated by Thomas became a reality as "1954 Basic List of California State Publications."

California Legislature, Assembly, Interim Committee on Governmental Reorganization. "Information Services." (In its *First Partial Report*. ([Sacramento], 1951), pp. 114-132.)

The study is restricted, insofar as possible, to "organizational implications on performing presently authorized central information functions." It stresses two ideas: (1) information facilitates the democratic process (quoting Justice Felix Frankfurter and commenting on the Hoover Commission report), and (2) information encourages cooperation and compliance.

The two recommendations relating to libraries are (1) free distribution to individuals should be limited, and (2) the state should rely on the libraries as its documents link with the public. The comment says: "The inherent wastefulness of distribution to individuals is quite obvious. A publication is perhaps used only once and then discarded. Publications sent to libraries are readily available and may be used many times.''

The three assets of the libraries as a distributing agency for publications are:

> 1. It is the most accessible source of books in the Nation, especially so for government publications which are not stocked in commercial bookstores.
> 2. It has the educational function of leading interested readers to sources of information. . . .
> 3. The public library is an agency of government, and therefore can be expected to be concerned with the function of communication between government and the citizens.

The costs under the Library Distribution Act are difficult to determine. The results should be studied, particularly (1) how many people are using state documents, and (2) how are libraries living up to their part of the contract.

California Legislature, Senate, Interim Committee on Governmental Reorganization. ''Publication Distribution.'' (In its *Second Partial Report*. [Sacramento, 1951], pp. 101-117.)
''Governmental reporting in a democracy has become even more important in recent years with the growth in government participation in social and economic affairs.'' Six purposes which publications serve are identified and reasons for publishing are given. The evaluation of the present program covers three points. (1) Departmental compliance—many departments were not distributing processed materials, and the interpretation of the definition of ''publication'' has been difficult. (2) Library complaints—most complete depositories say they are getting too many documents, some libraries are receiving documents that are too specialized, and some needed documents are not being received. (3) Library compliance—libraries are not cataloging the documents, and libraries cannot always find the documents they have received.

Twelve recommendations include reduction of the number of depositories, standards for the depositories, inspections of the libraries, a more complete checklist for selection of items, a subject approach for *California State Publications*, and a redefinition of ''publications.''

Sugden, Allen F. ''First Aid for California Document Selection.'' *California Librarian* 16:175-177, 196 (April 1955).
Sugden discusses the ''Basic List,'' mentioning that ''during the last seven years in which the Library Distribution Program was in operation a number of surveys and examinations were conducted to determine whether or not the libraries were living up to the provisions of their depository contracts . . . '' He reports that the Division of Finance feels that ''while it is true that selection should be based on the needs of the individual library, it is equally true that the contracting libraries have an obligation to the state and to the citizens of the library community to provide, maintain and make usable a basic reference collection of documents which will tell the story of the State Government.'' The Division of Finance asked the State Documents Committee to revise its 1949 ''Basic List'' (which was a guide to recommended titles). How the ''1954 List'' became a mandatory depository contract requirement, and its distribution to both selective

depository libraries and to nondepository libraries are explained in detail. (It is mentioned that the appropriation was $47,000.)

White, Amelia. "California State Periodicals: A Hidden Asset." *News Notes of California Libraries*. 51:353-358 (April 1956).
An annotated list of thirteen periodicals with ordering data and list of addresses. White (Government Publications Section, California State Library) recommends government periodicals to libraries because they are timely and have "the advantages of low cost and authenticity of information." She says that state agency periodicals "while highly specialized individually, as a group cover the fields of interest of the greatest public and individual concern. . . . "

Blanchard, Marvin L. "Documents for California." *California Librarian* 19:111-112 (April 1958).
Blanchard, from the State Department of Finance, addresses the Documents Committee expressing the belief that the "growing pains" of the first twelve years of the depository system were overcome and acknowledging the indebtedness of the Department to the Committee for (1) the basic list for selective depositories, (2) the educational work with the profession, and (3) the recently issued manual. Blanchard mentions that since 1953, the Department had avoided establishing new depositories but promised to give serious consideration to new requests in the face of the "exploding population problem." (The cost of the program was $60,000 annually.)

Zimmerman, Carma R. "Comparison of Depository Systems for United States and California State Publications." U.S. Congress, House of Representatives, Committee on House Administration. *Revision of Depository Library Laws: Hearings . . . October 7, 10, 14, and 17, 1957 (on H. R. 9186), June 19, 1958 (on H. R. 11042)*. Washington, D.C.: U.S. Government Printing Office, 1958, pp. 185-186.
The items compared are: Manner of selection of depositories, requirements, types of depositories, publications available, list of publications available, sample publications, complete list of government publications, disposal policies for depository libraries, and inspection of depository libraries.
In her testimony, Zimmerman (California state librarian) said:

> In the distribution of publications to depositories, the Federal Government is somewhat ahead of the State of California insofar as procedures are concerned, notably in having the classified list of available publications on cards and in making daily mailings with a shipping list in each package. The California system is superior in the manner of selecting new depositories and in the percentage of total output of publications covered by the program.

California Department of Finance, Organization and Cost Control Division. "Management Survey for the Department of Finance: Depository Library System." [Sacramento, 1959], 19 p.
The responsibility for administration of the system is in the Department of Finance, with no provision for control and liaison functions needed for effective operation of the

system. Thus, (1) location of depository libraries is not based on standards, (2) some depositories are not providing adequate service, (3) all publications have not been distributed on a uniform basis, and (4) many state agencies are uninformed about their obligations to depository libraries.

Among the fifteen proposed improvements are (1) transfer of administration to the state library, (2) establish librarian (LDA) and verityper positions, (3) adopt standards for locations of depositories, cancel some contracts, and establish some new depositories, (4) adopt standards for depository libraries, (5) have committee to select depository items, (6) revise the compilation and printing of *California State Publications*, (7) revise selection list, (8) consider supplying cataloging data, and (9) advocate legislation to require that state agencies prepare enough processed publications for each depository.

Standards and job descriptions are included.

California State Library, Sacramento. *California State Publications: Manual for Acquisition, Processing, Use.* 2d ed., rev. [Sacramento], 1961. Various paging. Distributed by California, Department of Finance, Organization and Cost Control Division. "The first edition of the manual, published in 1957, was compiled by the Documents Committee of the California Library Association, at the request of the State Department of Finance." The new edition brings the first edition up to date, "but no major changes have been made. . . . the description of the California State Library classification scheme has been expanded."

The Table of Contents lists the following sections and appendices:

Section 0, "Introduction." The purpose is to assist both depository and nondepository libraries, particularly the former. It is intended both for experienced reference librarians and for orientation of new staff members.

Section 1, "Depository System." A summary of the Library Distribution Act. References at the end to legislative committee reports, the 1959 management survey, and the articles by Huston, Klausner and Thomas.

Section 2, "Acquisition." Covers distribution to depositories, acquisition by other libraries, purchases, special kinds of publications—University of California, legislative, out-of-print.

Section 3, "Organization and Arrangement." Integrated versus separate collections; arrangement and classification schemes.

Section 4, "Records and Preparation for the Shelves." Types of records with sample forms. (Cataloging how-to is not covered, but selecting documents for cataloging is.) References cited are : Akers, Jackson, Markley, and Osborn.

Section 5, "Reference Tools." An annotated list of California items (except for Bowker, Hasse, Wilcox, LC's *Monthly Checklist*, and so on), arranged by type of publication. Includes some commercial publications.

Section 6, "Lending." Interlibrary loan requirements and information on borrowing from the state library and the two historical depositories.

Appendix A, "Library Distribution Act, as Amended."
Appendix B, "Contract for Distribution of State Publications to Libraries."
Appendix C, "Standards for Depository Libraries."
Appendix D, "Basic List of California State Publications." 104 publications from 62 departments and divisions, not including codes, laws, and statutes also on the list.

Appendix E, ''Disposal Policies.'' 18 titles or categories.

Appendix F, ''Classification Schemes.'' Schemes from California State Library (in full), Glidden, Claremont Colleges (unpublished), Jackson, Miller, Oakland Public Library (unpublished), Swank. All with sample classification numbers for a Bureau of Mines publication.

Appendix G, ''Binding, Covers, and Pamphlet Boxes: Description, Sources, Use.'' Includes dealers and addresses.

Appendix H, ''Complete Depositories.'' 9, including 3 historical depositories; library names and addresses.

Appendix I, ''Selective Depositories.'' 49 selective depositories; names and addresses.

Index. Subjects and titles.

Elwonger, Ruth, et al. ''Documents Workshops in 1963.'' *News Notes of California Libraries* 58:373-386 (Fall 1963).
The workshops were held at the Los Angeles Public Library, the Fresno County Library, and the State Library, Sacramento, and were attended by more than two hundred librarians. ''The major purposes were : (1) to acquaint librarians with current California documents, and methods of acquiring and processing them; (2) to give the who-what-when-why-where of the depository collections in the State.''

Changes in the Library Distribution Act are discussed. The 1961 statutes extended the law to include law libraries and provided for twenty-five additional copies for this purpose. A 1959 study of the program resulted in the transfer of administration of the program to the state library. In 1963, revised location and performance standards for contracting libraries were set up. An urgent unmet need is that of state colleges and state university libraries, which are limited by the 1959 standards to 25 percent of the total number of depositories ''because of their specialized and limited clientele.''

''Acquisition from the Office of State Printing'' by Jessalyn Smith describes distribution to depositories, filling of requests from nondepositories, and purchasing after the library stockroom supply is exhausted.

Talks on the handling of state documents in four different public libraries provide examples of ways to process, shelve, and use documents. Two of the librarians explained simplified classification schemes developed for their libraries. Procedures for ordering copies for branch libraries are explained.

''Workshops on California Legislative Publications.'' *News Notes of California Libraries* 60:335-392 (Summer 1965).
The workshops, sponsored by the Government Publications Section of the California State Library, were held in northern and southern California to ''acquaint librarians with basic information about California legislative publications.'' Acquisition and other information about the publications is available in chart form. The latest edition of these charts was published in 1976 by the California State Library.

The sessions began with a general lecture on ''Standards and Documents Collections'' and continued with group meetings that discussed the legislative process, legislative publications, publications about the Legislature, bill room services, and the like.

Elwonger, Ruth. "The California State Documents Maze: A Practical Approach on How to Get California Documents and Information." Sacramento: n.p., 1973. 11 p., chart. Available from the author, 1733 Sherwood Avenue, Sacramento, California 95822.

Discusses (1) how to know who handles publications and (2) how to find out who knows the subject. Begins with the organization of state government and stresses that only the *latest* directory or publications list should be used. The formal sources of state government documents (the Documents Section, the Legislative Bill Room, and the issuing agency) are described. The state library publication, *California State Publications*, is the only overall listing. Its limitations are outlined.

The second section of the paper discusses informal sources of state government legislation, including research and states sections, data processing centers (the individual agency involved must be contacted, not the center), and information sources in the legislature. Guides to which agency to contact begin with the *State of California Telephone Directory*. It is suggested that you know the organization of your state government and build up a list of resource people. Source and announcement media for both printed and processed documents are given in a chart.

Elwonger, Ruth. "Introduction to State Information Sources." (GPS Publication 1.) California State Library, Government Publications Section, 1966. 11 p.

Speech at Special Libraries Association meeting on unpublished state materials—how much, what does it include, how to learn about it, and availability. List of tools to assist in identifying California state government information sources.

Elwonger, Ruth. *California State Information Sources Today (1970)*. (GPS Publication 7.) California State Library, Government Publications Section, 1971. 7 p.

Updates 1966 paper based on additional interviews. Changes since 1966 are (1) increased rate of change in the organization of California state government, (2) emphasis on efficient handling of information by processing, rather than research, and (3) growing quantities of unpublished data.

California Department of General Services. *Library Distribution Act Procedures and Definitions*, M-698. 1973. 11 p., exhibits.

An *ad hoc* advisory committee of the Management Assistance Division, Department of General Services, "had three roles: first, it provided information on the state of the program, second, it offered specific suggestions for improvements, and third, it was a sounding board for recommendations."

The major recommendations were to spread the cost of the Library Distribution Act (LDA) among all applicable titles, to amend regulations to define LDA responsibilities, to provide rudimentary mechanisms to streamline the administration of LDA, and to offer a plan to state agencies so that they can construct internal LDA procedures. "The goal of the report recommendations is to make the Library Distribution Act important to the participants by intertwining a series of 'automatic' and constant reminders into current reproduction procedures."

There are sixteen specific recommendations, with reasons, and appendices with forms, flowcharts, cost comparisons, and lists of publications representatives and depository libraries. Some of the details recommended are: putting an LDA instruction box on requisition forms, sending the checklist to agencies and the legislature, putting LDA on each publication, including cumulative total of titles by agency in checklist, directing publications representatives to report their name annually, and requiring agencies to include provision for LDA copies in their contracts with consultants or private printers.

Lo Russo, Rosita, and Kennedy, Linda. "The Crisis in California State Documents Distribution System." (1973?) (Unpublished.)
"In May of 1973 revisions were made to the California State Administrative Manual which drastically affect the distribution of state publications; as a result of these revisions, the content of the July 1973 list (and also all forthcoming lists) of *California State Publications* was critically reduced."

The California law (the Library Distribution Act, or LDA) was largely the work of the State Documents Committee of the California Library Association. The law is basically the same as when it was first adopted, except for a substantive change in 1955 which made the cost of printing and distributing the LDA publications and of preparing the checklist a charge against the issuing agencies. The practice of allowing the LDA publications to carry the cost of publishing the entire bibliographical listing helped lead to the present situation.

In January 1973, the Management Assistance Division of the Department of General Services published a report of the LDA. An *ad hoc* advisory committee (from various state agencies, including the Office of State Printing and the state library) provided information, offered suggestions, and served as a sounding board.

"While the recommendations that were offered were directed toward managerial solutions to the difficulties of administering the LDA, some of the actions taken by the Department of General Services—namely, the revisions in the State Administrative Manual—and the state library in its new policy of listing only LDA publications in *California State Publications*—actually curtailed public access to state publications. The recommendations and changes actually hampered the free distribution of publications by providing more loopholes by which publications would be declared ineligible for LDA and reducing bibliographic control.

"In analyzing the report in detail, it appears that the primary concern of the committee was the difficulty the various state agencies apparently had in administering the LDA."

Although the LDA defines "publications" and excludes only University of California publications and inter- intraoffice documents, the State Administrative Manual (SAM) provides that all publications "not prohibited by law or elsewhere in SAM shall fall under LDA." Lo Russo and Kennedy pose the question, "On what basis can SAM prohibit certain publications from falling under LDA if the Government Code does not exclude them?"

Another section of the SAM provides that the state library should receive at least one copy of all publications that do not fall under LDA, because that library is "generally expected to be a complete loaning depository" and because of its "unique services to state employees." The authors observe that the LDA does not make a distinction between the state library and the complete depositories. In addition, they make the point that the SAM provision refers to "publication(s) of note" being sent to the state library, and, if this phrase means "worthy of note," the publications should be listed in

California State Publications and should be made available through the complete depositories. The report concludes,

> It has become apparent to librarians who work in depository libraries that many people working in state agencies have no realization of the public interest in the work of their agency, no real understanding of the role of the library in getting this information to the public, nor any understanding of the importance of bibliographic control. These factors, combined with the fact that assessing LDA charges against the departments in the manner proposed will give them a strong monetary motive for not cooperating, may well result in an LDA program that is only a shadow of the admittedly imperfect one we have had.
>
> In the interests of economy and expediency, many publications of great interest will fail to be listed in *California State Publications* and never be utilized, greatly injuring both the public's right to know and its right to have the results of its tax dollar used to the fullest extent. The fact that these deplorable changes in the procedures for distribution and bibliographic control of state publications were probably done in ignorance of their implications is our only hope in our attempts to rectify the tragic situation before too much damage has been done.

Woodbury, M. "Keeping Up with Educational Legislation: State Sources." *California School Libraries* 45:28-33 (Spring 1974).
"The bulk of this article is an informal directory of some relatively convenient official and unofficial sources for keeping up with state legislative information at various stages in the legislative process."

California State Library, Sacramento, Government Publications Section. *California Legislative Publications Charts.* (GPS Publication 3.) 3d ed. rev. by Richard H. Nicoles and Mary Schell. The Library, 1976. 24 p.
The charts outline the legislative process and show the publications produced at each step with sources for acquiring and notes on the state library's resources.

NOTES FROM THE NEWSLETTER:

In September 1977, a short article by Mary Schell, "California State Library Government Publications Section," reported under the heading "state documents" that the state library is a complete depository, acquires many nondepository publications, and publishes a monthly list, *California State Publications*.

The January 1978 issue has a brief summary of a talk on reports of the offices of Research and the Senate and the Assembly and the amazement of the director of the Senate office and the Senate president *pro tem* that libraries would be interested in reports.

The March 1978 article, "California State Publications Automates," by Richard Nicoles, reports on the production of the checklist from cataloging data keyed into BALLOTS. Checklist has $41,000 approximately. The goal is speedy delivery to users. It is disappointing that agency addresses had to be dropped.

COLORADO

COLORADO, HOUSE BILL 1199 [1980] § 1 (to be codified as 24-90-201 to 208)

PART 2
STATE PUBLICATIONS DEPOSITORY
AND DISTRIBUTION CENTER

24-90-201. Establishment of a state publications depository and distribution center. There is hereby established a state publications depository and distribution center. Such center shall be a section of the state library. Its operation is declared to be an essential administrative function of the state government.

24-90-202. Definitions. As used in this part 2, unless the context otherwise requires:

(1) "Center" means the state publications depository and distribution center.

(2) "Depository library" means a library designated to collect, maintain, and make available to the general public state agency publications.

(3) "State agency" means every state office, whether legislative, executive, or judicial, and all of its respective officers, departments, divisions, bureaus, boards, commissions, and committees, all state-supported colleges and universities which are defined as state institutions of higher education, and other agencies which expend state-appropriated funds.

(4) "State publication" means any printed or duplicated material, regardless of format or purpose, which is produced, purchased for distribution, or authorized by any state agency, including any document, compilation, journal, law, resolution, bluebook, statute, code, register, contract and grant report, pamphlet, list, microphotographic form, audiovisual material, book, proceedings, report, public memorandum, hearing, legislative bill, leaflet, order, rule, regulation, directory, periodical, magazine, or newsletter, with the exception of correspondence, interoffice memoranda, or those items detailed by section 24-72-204, C.R.S. 1973.

24-90-203. Purposes—direction—rules and regulations.

(1) The purposes of the center are to collect, distribute, and make available

to the public state publications. Public access to such publications may be accomplished by use of depository library facilities throughout the state.

(2) The center shall be under the direction of the state librarian.

(3) Adoption of such rules and regulations as are necessary or appropriate to accomplish the provisions of this part 2 shall be the responsibility of the state board of education after such rules are submitted to and approved by the committee on legal services. No rule or regulation shall deny public access during normal working hours to the state publications enumerated in this part 2.

24-90-204. Deposits of state publications. Every state agency shall, upon publication, deposit at least four copies of each of its state publications (with the exception of audiovisual materials) with the center. One copy of each such audiovisual material shall be deposited with the center. The center may require additional copies of certain state publications to be deposited when designated by the state librarian as being required to fulfill the purposes of this part 2.

24-90-205. Publication lists to be furnished by state agencies. Upon request by the state librarian, each state agency shall furnish the center with a complete list of its current state publications.

24-90-206. Depository library agreements—requirements. The center may enter into depository agreements with any state agency or public library or with out-of-state research libraries, and other state libraries. The number of depository libraries shall not exceed thirty. The requirements for eligibility to become and continue as a depository shall be established by the state library. The standards shall include and take into consideration population, the type of library or agency, ability to preserve such publications and to make them available for public use, and such geographic locations as will make the publications conveniently accessible to residents in all areas of the state.

24-90-207. Index of state publications. The center shall quarterly publish an index to state publications and distribute it to depository libraries and certain other libraries and state agencies as designated by the state librarian.

24-90-208. State publications distribution. The center shall distribute state publications, in microfiche, paper copy, or other format where appropriate, to depository libraries. The state librarian may make additional distributions in accordance with agreements with appropriate state agencies.

STATE COMMENT (1973)

The State Library has prepared *no* publication on our state document program, but this does not mean we are unconcerned about it. The Colorado Council for Library Development has established a Documents Committee which is devising and recommending legislation concerning the documents depository system for the state government of Colorado. It also has discussed

the forming of a document roundtable within the Colorado Library Association
to better inform libraries and librarians about the problems involved in both
federal and state documents libraries and depositories. (Letter from Esther B.
Snyder, Supervisor, Library Services, Colorado State Library, Denver, Colorado 80203, dated June 6, 1973. *In* Documents on Documents Collection.)

STATE COMMENT (1976)

Colorado has no state documents depository program. Now that the checklist is started we have the basis for initiating one. (Report by Kurt Keeley,
Supervisor, Library Services, Colorado State Library. *In* The State of State
Documents: Past, Present, Future. Texas Legislative Reference Library,
1976, at p. 10.)

EDITORIAL COMMENT

H. B. 1261 was introduced in 1979 but did not pass. The "Bill Summary"
reads:

Creates a state publications and distribution center as a section of the state library.
Provides for collection and distribution of and public access to state publications.
Makes numerous "housekeeping" amendments to the "1947 Library Law" to accommodate creation of a new part to article 90 of title 24. Makes an appropriation to allow
creation and operation of the center.

The amount of the appropriation is left blank in the bill.

Special features of the bill are, first, a statement that the operation of the
newly established state publications and distribution center " is declared to be
an essential administrative function of the state." The definition of "state
publication" includes micrographic forms, audiovisual material, legislative
publications, and contract and grant reports. "State agency" includes state-
supported colleges and universities. Four copies of publications are to be
deposited (one copy of audiovisual materials); additional copies may be required by the center. The center shall publish an annual index to state publications. The center shall distribute state publications "in microfiche, paper
copy, or other format where appropriate."

The legislation adopted in 1980 is similar to the bill introduced in 1979. The
new legislation is effective July 1, 1980. An appropriation of $80,302 was
included in the act.

BIBLIOGRAPHY

Dorzweiler, A. N. ''Author Headings for the Official Publications of the State of Colorado.'' M.A. Thesis, University of Denver, 1953. 160 p. (Not seen.)

CONNECTICUT

CONN. GEN. STAT. ANN. §§ 11-9b to 9d (West Supp. 1980)

§ 11-9b. Definitions. As used in this section and sections 11-9c and 11-9d:

(a) "State publications" means all publications printed or purchased for distribution by a state agency, or any other agency supported wholly or in part by state funds;

(b) "Printed" means all forms of printing and duplicating, regardless of format or purpose, with the exception of correspondence and interoffice memoranda;

(c) "State agency" means every state office, officer, department, division, bureau, board and commission, permanent or temporary in nature, whether legislative, executive or judicial, and any subdivisions of each, including state-supported institutions of higher education;

(d) "Depository library" means the designated library for collecting, maintaining, and making available to the general public Connecticut state agency publications. (1977, P. A. 77-561, § 1.)

§ 11-9c. Administration of state publications collection and depository library system. The state library shall administer a Connecticut state publications collection and a depository library system. The state library shall: (1) Establish and administer, with the approval of the state library board, such rules and regulations as may be deemed necessary to carry out the provisions of sections 11-9b to 11-9d, inclusive; (2) develop and maintain standards for depository libraries, including ascertaining their geographical distribution, with the approval of the state library board; (3) enter into depository contracts with libraries that meet the standards for eligibility established by the state library; (4) annually advise designated staff in each agency, required by section 11-9d, of the number of copies of publications needed for distribution; (5) receive from state agencies on or about publication date the specified number of copies of each publication; (6) retain sufficient copies in the Connecticut state library for preservation, reference and interlibrary loan purposes; (7) distribute two copies of each publication to the Library of Congress and one copy to an additional national or regional research library designated by the state library; (8) distribute copies of publications to depository libraries within the state in accordance with the terms of their depository contracts and to libraries outside the state in accordance with any agreements entered into for the exchange of state publications and (9) publish at least monthly and distribute to depository and other libraries in Connecticut, other state libraries, to state legislators and state agencies and libraries, upon request, an official indexed list of Connecticut state publications with an annual cumulated index. (1977, P. A. 77-561, § 2.)

§ **11-9d. State agencies to supply publications to state library; designation of staff**.

(a) Designated staff in each state agency shall be responsible for supplying the publications of that agency to the state library. Each such agency shall notify the state library of the identity of such designated staff within thirty days after October 1, 1977, and upon any change of personnel. Said staff shall supply the state library annually or upon request with a complete list of the agency's current publications.

(b) Every state agency shall, upon publication, deposit a sufficient number of copies of each of its publications with the state library to meet the needs of the depository library system. (1977 P. A. 77-561, § 3.)

Approved July 5, 1977.

STATE COMMENT (1980)

Connecticut now has a working depository system, consisting of twelve college and public libraries in Connecticut, the Library of Congress, the Center for Research Libraries and the Connecticut State Library. In accordance with 11 C.G.S. 9d(a), designated staff have been appointed for nearly all agencies. The State Library, as administrator for the program, receives and distributes about 12,000 documents a year. The depository program began in September, 1978 and has an annual budget of about $35,000. *The Checklist of Publications of Connecticut State Agencies* is prepared monthly, with an annual cumulative index, but difficulties in printing have delayed publication.

The State Library also operates a Gifts and Exchanges Program for selected publications. All other publications are distributed solely by the issuing agency.

Due to excellent cooperation from state agencies and depository libraries, no regulations have been issued concerning the depository system. (Letter from Betsy Berry, State Documents Librarian, Connecticut State Library, Hartford, Connecticut, dated January 17, 1980.)

EDITORIAL COMMENT

The 1977 act establishing the depository program appropriated $25,000 to the state library for the year ending June 30, 1978.

RULES AND REGULATIONS

CRITERIA FOR SELECTION OF
DEPOSITORY LIBRARIES

1. Any public library; any special library; any community college, state college, or state university library; the library of any incorporated college or university may be designated as a depository provided that all other qualifications are met. Geographical distribution will be considered.

2. In order to be designated as a depository, a library shall agree to the following conditions, with the understanding that failure to comply with any one condition is sufficient ground for cancellation of the contract between the State and the library.

    (a) Provide space to house the documents. State documents need not be maintained in a separate collection unless the receiving library prefers to do so.

    (b) Maintain orderly, systematic records of receipt of the documents.

    (c) Process and make available all state documents within a reasonable period.

    (d) Assign the responsibility for the state documents collection to a department headed by a professionally-trained librarian.

    (e) Dispose of documents only in accordance with disposal policies established by the State Library.

    (f) Accept and maintain the core collection specified by the State Library.

    (g) Provide that the documents be available for public use at least 45 hours per week and be available during weekend or evening hours, unless for some unusual reason it becomes necessary to restrict use. College, university and special libraries that are depositories must be willing to lend through interlibrary loan and to permit public access to the documents within the library. Public libraries are encouraged to lend documents through Connecticard and interlibrary loan.

    (h) Agree to permit the State Librarian, or his representative to inspect the document collection periodically.

A "state government publication" is any document produced by or purchased for an agency of state government in multiple copies at government expense, with the exception of:

A. Business forms
B. Informal administrative memos and instructions for the internal use of agency personnel
C. Blueprints
D. Complimentary, visiting and business cards

E. Correspondence
F. Minutes of meetings
G. Announcements of lectures, meetings, seminars, and workshops
H. Doctoral dissertations
I. Master's theses

STATE COMMENT ON REGULATIONS

Item 2(d) was amended by the State Library Board. The Committee is asking that it be changed to the original form: "Designate a professionally trained librarian to be responsible for the state documents depository collection."

CONTRACT

STATE DOCUMENTS DEPOSITORY CONTRACT

In accordance with the provisions of Public Act 77-561, the _____
_____ Library hereby makes application as a depository library for state documents. In signing this contract, the library agrees to meet and maintain the *Criteria for Depository Libraries* established by the State Library and approved by the State Library Board, and any amendments thereto.

This contract may be terminated by either party upon 3 months written notice to the other.

_____   _____
Date   Librarian responsible for state documents

                               _____
                               Head Librarian

                               _____
                               Library

                               _____
                               Address

RETENTION AND DISPOSAL OF DOCUMENTS

The Depository must keep all documents (except superseded items) for a minimum of 5 years. When weeding State Documents, the Depository shall offer the State Library the opportunity to claim the unneeded documents for use in the State Library or other depository libraries.

Superseded items may simply be discarded by all depositories. Examples of superseded items are: any publication cumulated in later issues after the later cumulation is received; any revised publication after the revised publication is received, separates upon receipt of final bound volumes.

(The above RETENTION . . . statement is stapled to the contract.)

BIBLIOGRAPHY

Winkler, P. W. "Author Headings for the Official Publications of Connecticut, 1818-1947." M.S.L.S. Thesis, University of Illinois, 1949. 247 p.

Wohlson, T. O. "Selected Connecticut State Publications." *See* issues of *Connecticut Libraries* 1972-.

Mundkur, Mohini. "Connecticut State Depository Act." *Documents to the People* 5:233-235 (November 1977).
Connecticut has just adopted depository legislation for state documents, Public Act 77-561. The "initial spadework" involved "study of existing problems in the printing and distribution of official state publications," interviews with key state officials, drafting the bill by librarians, checking the Documents on Documents file, advice from state documents librarians, and reading Shaffer's article on the Nebraska experience.

It was decided to focus on distribution patterns alone. After the bill was introduced, a bill watch was instituted. "After all this planning and preparation, the end was blissfully anticlimactic." The reasons for success were (1) the impetus provided by public pressure for open government which made it easy to present the depository legislation as a corollary of the Connecticut Freedom of Information Act, (2) support from highly respected legislators, (3) the cooperative lobbying efforts of library and nonlibrary groups, and (4) the singleminded determination of one individual who coordinated the project.

"State Depositories: The Connecticut State Library Has Designated 12 Public and College Libraries as Depositories for State Publications." *New England Library Association Newsletter* 10:(2) (October 1978).
Short news note announcing that this new service would begin and that each library would receive at least 120 serial publications annually.

Harrison, Rose. "Connecticut Statistical Sources: A Guide to Materials in the Connecticut State Library Collection." *Connecticut State Library Document News Letter*, no. 7, November 1973. 11 p. (Not seen.)

DELAWARE

DEL. CODE ANN. tit. 29, § 507 (Michie 1974);
tit. 29, § 8610 (Michie 1979)

§ **507. Acquisition of public documents**. All agencies, departments, boards or commissions of this State or of any county or incorporated municipality thereof shall deposit with the Department of State 2 copies of the best edition of each publication issued. These publications are to be retained for reference and research purposes.

The Department of State shall have the authority to determine whether or not any of said publications lack sufficient information for retention as research materials, and it may request the publishing agency to discontinue depositing such publications with the Department. (29 Del. C. 1953, § 3309; 51 Del. Laws, c. 207; 57 Del. Laws, c. 608, §§ 1B, 1E, 1F.)

§ **8610. Powers and duties of the Department relating to library services**.

(a) The powers and duties of the Department relating to library services, shall be:

****

(8) To provide access to a complete collection of current documents published by state government and a comprehensive collection of current local, state and federal documents of interest to the state:

****

(b) Every state agency shall provide and deposit with the Department sufficient copies of all publications issued by such agencies for the purpose of making accessible to Delaware and other citizens resource materials published at the expense of the State. The Administrator of Libraries shall recommend the number of copies required for deposit, consistent with state interests. From time to time listing of such documents received under the terms of this section shall be published. (29 Del. C. 1953, § 8610; 57 Del. Laws, c. 583, § 1; 59 Del. Laws, c. 480, § 4.)

EDITORIAL COMMENT

Section 8610 is new legislation enacted in 1974 (59 Del. Laws, c. 480, § 4). The former section 8610 was part of a reorganization act, and merely specified that the new Division of Libraries should carry out the duties of the old Library Commission. Those duties were general and did not mention state documents.

RULES AND REGULATIONS

Delaware Department of State, Department of Administrative Services. "Printing, Publishing, and Micropublishing: Manual and Regulations." December 1977. pp. 15, 18.

SUBMISSION OF COPIES

Every state, county, and municipal agency is required by Title 29, section 507, Delaware Code, to deposit two copies of the best edition of each publication with the Bureau of Archives and Records of the Division of Historical and Cultural Affairs.

In addition, every state agency is required by Title 29, section 8610 to make copies of its publication available to the Division of Libraries on demand for distribution to the libraries of Delaware.

Executive Order 38 permits microfiche copies to be submitted to the Division of Libraries in lieu of the printed originals. The microfiche copies will be made by the Division of Historical and Cultural Affairs. Therefore, agencies need not stock additional copies of their printed publications to meet the demands of libraries.

The following regulations govern the deposit of state publications in the Archives. Agency record officers are responsible for seeing that deposit requirements are met.

1. A "publication" for purposes of deposit is any book, map, pamphlet, press release, report, or other document intended for circulation outside the originating agency. Certain internal documents may be considered to be publications if they are of general interest. Letterheads, forms, internal memoranda, and duplicated procedural materials, are not publications. Documents protected against disclosure under the "sunshine" law are not "publications" because they cannot be circulated to the general public.

2. Publications may be issued in microfiche only. In such cases, there obviously is no need to deposit copies with the Division of Historical and Cultural Affairs.

3. At the end of each quarter, the Division of Historical and Cultural Affairs issues its publication, DELAWARE DOCUMENTATION, which lists all the state, local, and county publications deposited in the Archives,

    3.1 Each publication will be listed with its document control number.

    3.2 The document control number will be the reference number for the microfiche of the publication.

3.3 The cost of making microfiche originals and copying them as required under Title 29, section 8610, for libraries, will be billed to the originating agency. Generally, the cost of making and distributing a microfiche (up to about 75 pages) is less than $2.

HOW TO MICROPUBLISH

Beginning with publications issued after January 1, 1977, all state publications will be micropublished. Every agency that issues printed matter for public consumption will be a micropublisher.

When micropublishing begins, agencies should reduce the quantities printed. Requests for copies will generally be handled by the Bureau of Archives and Records. Because micropublishing is part of the new printing and publishing system, there is very little effort required of the originating agency. Here are the steps that will be followed:

1. The agency publishes its document. Each document to be micropublished carries the document control number and the following notice:

This publication is available in microfiche from the Bureau of Archives and Records, Hall of Records, P. O. Box 1401, Dover, Delaware 19901.

2. At the end of the month, each agency record officer will submit two copies of the best edition of each publication, together with the monthly document log, to the Bureau of Archives and Records.

3. All the publications logged during a particular month will be microfilmed and converted into jacketed microfiche masters.

4. Available publications, and their document control numbers, will be listed in the quarterly DELAWARE DOCUMENTATION.

5. Libraries will be permitted to obtain copies of the listed publications through the Division of Libraries, free of charge.

6. Others will pay 10¢ per fiche for copies ordered at the time of publication. Fiche produced from stock, on demand, will cost 20¢ per copy.

7. Each originating agency will be billed $1 per fiche for publication cost, plus the cost of copies produced for libraries under Title 29, section 8610.

BIBLIOGRAPHY

Lane, Margaret T. "Delaware Regulates State Documents." *Documents to the People* 6:171-172 (June 1978).
Summarizes and quotes from a Delaware regulation entitled "Printing, Publishing, and Micropublishing: Manual and Regulations," which makes the state publications available on microfiche. All publications are to be numbered, listed in *Delaware Documentation*, and available to libraries free of charge through the Division of Libraries.

FLORIDA

FLA. STAT. ANN. § 257.05 (West 1975); §§ 283.22-24
(West 1975 and Supp. 1980); § 283.28 (West Supp. 1980)

257.05. Copies of reports of state departments furnished division.

(1) A "public document" as referred to in this section shall be defined as any annual, biennial, regular or special report or publication of which at least 500 copies are printed and which may be subject to distribution to the public.

(2) Each and every state official, state department, state board, state court or state agency of any kind, issuing public documents shall furnish the division of library services of the department of state twenty-five copies of each of those public documents, as issued, for deposit in and distribution by the division. However, if the division shall so request, as many as twenty-five additional copies of each public document shall be supplied to it.

(3) It shall be the duty of the division to:

(a) Designate university, college and public libraries as depositories for public documents;

(b) Provide a system of distribution of the copies furnished to it under sub-section (2) to such depositories;

(c) Publish a periodic bibliography of the publications of the state.

The division is authorized to exchange copies of public documents for those of other states, territories and countries. Depositories receiving public documents under this section shall keep them in a convenient form accessible to the public.

(4) The division shall also be furnished by any state official, department or agency having charge of their distribution, as issued, bound journals of each house of the legislature; acts of the legislature, both local or special and general; annotated acts of the legislature; and revisions and compilations of the Laws of Florida. The number of copies furnished shall be determined by requests of the division, which number in no case shall exceed twenty-five copies of the particular publication and, in the case of legislative acts, annotated legislative acts, and revisions and compilations of the laws, not more than two copies.

(5) In any case in which any state official, state department, state board, state court, or state agency of any class or kind has more than ten copies of any one kind of publication from time to time heretofore issued, he or it shall, upon

request of the division, supply said division with one copy of each such publication for deposit in the state library. (Amended by Laws, 1963, c. 63-39 § 4, eff. Oct. 1, 1963; Laws 1967, c. 67-223, § 1, eff. Sept. 1, 1967; Laws 1969, c. 69-106, §§ 10, 35, eff. July 1, 1969; Laws 1969, c. 69-353, § 21, eff. July 5, 1969; Laws 1973, c. 73-305, § 1, eff. Aug. 5, 1973.)

283.22. Public documents; university libraries. The general library of each institution in the university system shall be entitled to receive copies of reports of state officials, departments, institutions and all other state documents published by the state. Each officer of the state empowered by law to distribute such public documents is hereby authorized to transmit without charge, except for payment of shipping costs, the number of copies of each public document desired upon requisition from the librarian. It is made the duty of the library to keep public documents in convenient form accessible to the public. The library under rules formulated by the board of regents is authorized to exchange documents for those of other states, territories and countries. (As amended by Laws 1963, c. 63-141, § 1; Laws 1963, c. 63-204, § 2; Laws 1967, c. 67-223, § 2, eff. Sept. 1, 1967.)

283.23. Law libraries of certain colleges designated as state legal depositories.

(1) The law libraries of the University of Florida, Florida State University, Stetson University, Nova University, and University of Miami are designated as state legal depositories. (Amended by Laws 1979, c. 79-313, § 1, eff. June 29, 1979.)

(2) Each officer of the state empowered by law to distribute legal publications is authorized to transmit, upon payment of shipping costs or cash on delivery, to the state legal depositories copies of such publications as requested. However, the number of copies of each of the general and special laws shall be limited to eight copies to each of the state legal depositories; the number of each of the volumes of the Florida Statutes and supplements shall be up to a maximum computed on the basis of one set for every ten students enrolled during the school year, based upon the average enrollment as certified by the registrar; and the number of house and senate journals shall be limited to one copy of each to each state legal depository.

(3) It is made the duty of the librarian of any depository to keep all public documents in convenient form accessible to the public.

(4) The libraries of all community colleges approved by the state board of education under § 230.752, Florida Statutes, shall be designated as state depositories for Florida Statutes and supplements published by or under the authority of the state; provided that these depositories may each receive one copy of each volume upon request, without charge except for payment of shipping costs. (As amended by Laws 1967, c. 67-223, § 3, eff. Sept. 1, 1967.)

283.24. Public printing; copies to Library of Congress. Any state official or state agency, board, commission or institution having charge of publications hereinafter named, is hereby authorized and directed to furnish the

Library of Congress in Washington, D.C., upon requisition from the Library of Congress, not to exceed three copies of the journals of both houses of the legislature, volumes of the supreme court reports, volumes of periodic reports of cabinet officers, and copies of reports, studies, maps or other publications by official boards or institutions of Florida, from time to time, as such are published and are available for public distribution. (Amended by Laws 1969, c. 69-183, § 2, eff. June 27, 1969, and Laws 1973, c. 73-305, § 1.)

283.28.   Public documents; purging of publication mailing lists; copies to State Library.

(1)****

(d) The provisions of this section shall apply to any agency of the state, except an agency of state government whose mailing list shall consist only of those registered with the agency and whose registration fee shall include payment by the registrants as subscribers for the publication of the agency.

(2) At the time of publication, or as soon thereafter as practicable, each agency, pursuant to subsection (1)(d), shall forward not less than the number of copies required in s. 257.05 F. S. of each of its publications to the State Library of the Division of Library Services of the Department of State. (Added by Laws 1975, c. 75-84, § 1, eff. July 1, 1975. Amended by Laws 1976, c. 76-97, § 1, eff. June 11, 1976 and Laws 1977, c. 77-174, § 1, eff. Aug. 2, 1977.)

EDITORIAL COMMENT

The current Florida legislation in § 257.05 was enacted in 1967, based on earlier legislation which provided for exchange copies for the state library. In 1969, an amendment (1969 Fla. Laws, ch 69-106, §§ 10 & 35) was made by the Government Reorganization Act, and another amendment (1969 Fla. Laws, ch 69-353, § 21) was made by an act to correct errors. In 1973, an amendment (1973 Fla. Laws, ch 73-305, § 1) was made by an act on annual legislative sessions.

Section 283.22 was first enacted in 1941. It was amended in 1949, 1955, twice in 1963, and in 1967. The 1949 act was a major revision that reenacted §§ 283.22 through 283.24.

The 1941 law enacting 283.22 designated the general library of the University of Florida and the Florida State College for Women as depositories and required that state agencies deposit publications with those libraries. The libraries were to keep the documents in convenient form accessible to the public and, subject to rules, to exchange them. The general library of the University of Florida was instructed to furnish copies of reports and session laws to the Law Library of the University of Florida. Section 283.22 was rewritten in 1949. Deleted were the provisions on the law library, which were put into a new section, as well as the designation "as a state depository." The right to receive publications was retained but was changed from fifty copies to the number "desired." A 1955 amendment extended the application of the law to another institution, and the 1963 amendment changed the designation to "each institution in the university system." Another 1963 amendment changed "board of control" to "board of regents." A 1967 amendment changed "depository" to "library," and a 1972 amendment changed "junior colleges" to "community colleges."

Section 283.23 was originally enacted in 1941 and designated the law libraries of the University of Miami, Stetson University, and the University of Tampa as state depositories. In 1949, the section was rewritten to include the Law Library of the University of Florida, to designate the libraries as state legal depositories, and to change the materials they were to receive from "the reports of departments . . . and all other state documents" to "legal publications." A 1955 act extended the application of the law to the Florida A. & M. University for Negroes. In 1959, junior colleges were added, and in 1972, "community colleges" was substituted for "junior colleges." In 1967, § 283.23(1) was repealed by an act (67-50 relating to history, archives, and public records) and amended by an act (67-223 relating to the state library and historical commission) which also amended 283.22, 283.23, and 257.05. In 1973, a reviser's bill deleted obsolete language and reflected the termination of the law library at Florida A. & M. University. In 1979, the law library at Nova University was added as a state legal depository.

Section 283.24 was originally enacted in 1943. It was rewritten in 1949, changing the number of copies to be furnished for the different titles. In 1969, the reference to the acts of the legislature was deleted, and in 1973, the section was amended to reflect the change to annual sessions of the legislature.

For distribution of session laws, see § 283.25, which was recently amended in 1977 (1977 Fla. Laws ch 77-102).

The 1976 amendment to § 283.28 substantially rewrote and expanded this section. The 1977 amendment made an editorial insertion for clarity.

RULES AND REGULATIONS

FLORIDA STATE LIBRARY
GUIDELINES FOR DESIGNATION OF LIBRARIES
AS DEPOSITORIES OF STATE PUBLICATIONS

1. Only libraries agreeing to accept all publications received for deposit will be eligible. Depository libraries will agree to retain all publications received for a period of five years and thereafter publications will either be retained by the library or disposed of under instructions received from the State Library.

2. All State universities under the jurisdiction of the Board of Regents and any public library system with a book collection larger than 250,000 volumes will be designated as depositories and will receive two copies of each document available for deposit. In addition to the requirements contained in Chapter 257.05, Florida Statutes, relating to public access, these libraries will agree to make the second copy of each document received available for interlibrary loan.

3. Any private four-year university or college which provides a professionally trained full-time documents librarian may be designated a depository under the conditions outlined in 2 above.

4. In the discretion of the State Librarian, dependent upon the availability of sufficient copies, additional depositories may be designated so as to provide:

    a. In the various areas of the state: one depository for each 150,000 people or one for each 200,000 people in areas of more than 500,000 people.

    b. In single counties with less than 500,000 people there will be one depository.

5. Libraries whose applications are rejected by the State Librarian may appeal for a hearing before the Florida Library and Historical Commission.

6. Depositories must annually reapply for designation.

INSTRUCTIONS FOR WEEDING STATE DOCUMENTS DEPOSITORY COLLECTIONS

I. Any depository library may dispose of Florida state documents at least five years old, and still maintain its eligibility as a depository, provided that one copy of the following is permanently retained:

    1. Annual or biennial reports of agencies or subagencies, or any publication fulfilling the purpose of such a report whether or not it is so designated.

    2. Session laws and statutes.

    3. Legislative journals.

    4. Statistical publications covering a period of at least one year, calendar or fiscal.

    5. Series publications having monographic titles. *Exceptions:* only the bulletin series of the Agricultural Experiment Stations and the Agricultural Cooperative Extension Service need be retained; and the Department of Education Bulletins may be retained on a selective basis.

II. In addition to the five categories designated above, monographs and special publications should be retained if, in the judgment of the professional staff member responsible for state documents, they have permanent value. Substantial periodicals, such as *Florida Schools* and *Florida Wildlife*, should also be seriously considered for retention. *Florida Health Notes* falls under number 5 above.

III. No duplicate copies need be retained if single copies will be available for interlibrary loan.

IV Unwanted duplicates in the five categories listed in paragraph I, and documents described in paragraph II not retained by a depository, should be returned to the Florida State Library.

CONTRACT

*APPLICATION AND AGREEMENT FOR DESIGNATION AS A
DEPOSITORY FOR STATE PUBLICATIONS*

The _ _____
            (Name of Library)

_____

            (Mailing Address)

hereby applies and agrees to become a depository to receive and retain the publications of the various departments, divisions, bureaus, boards, commissions and other agencies of the State of Florida in accordance with Section 257.05, Florida Statutes and the resulting guidelines for depository libraries promulgated by the Florida Library and Historical Commission

        The _ __ ___ _____ ___ hereby certifies that the facilities of the library are adequate to house and maintain publications received in reasonable order and to insure that they will be made conveniently accessible to those residents of the state desiring to use them and if more than one copy of a publication is received, to make the second copy available for interlibrary loan.

        The individual who will be responsible for receiving publications for this library and to whom correspondence should be addressed is: _____ ,
                                                    (Name of Individual)

_____ .

                            _____
                                        (Signature)

                            _____
                                        (Title)

_____
            (Date)

ATTORNEY GENERAL OPINIONS

Four Florida attorney general opinions were located. Because they are quite long, only excerpts are included.

1947 FLA. ATT'Y GEN. ANNUAL REP. 373 (July 24, 1947.—047-221)

In answer to a query from the state superintendent of public instruction, the opinion said:

It would be very difficult indeed, if not impossible, to define the phrases "public documents" and "state documents" as used in [§§ 283.22 and 283.23] of the statutes with any great degree of exactness. In general, the phrases cover annual or biennial reports of state agencies, boards and institutions, their studies and surveys, or other valuable data and information assembled by them as a part of their official functions.

Study guides in elementary arithmetic or secondary school agriculture would not, in my opinion, be included in "public documents" or "state documents" as used in the foregoing sections of the statutes.

I have no doubt whatever that the book "Florida: Wealth or Waste?" which I have examined with much interest, would be a welcome addition to any library as a book of general information, as well as for reference; assembling, as it does, in easy and simple form, a great mass of information about this state and its resources. It is my opinion that a text book for use in the schools would not be included in the meaning of the phrases "public documents" or "state documents" as used in sections 283.22 and 283.23.

1973 FLA. ATT'Y GEN. ANNUAL REP. 235 (073-147—May 8, 1973)

In answer to a question from the executive director of the Department of Revenue on the need for a statement of costs for an instruction manual, the attorney general held that the manual was not a document subject to public distribution as defined in § 257.05(1). Section 283(1), which requires the statement of costs, refers to the definition of public document in § 257.05(1). The opinion notes the purpose of the section on the cost statement:

This provision is apparently directed at control of potential diversion of public resources or printing facilities to uses other than required in the public interest. The statute gives notice to each recipient of the unit cost and stated purpose of the document promulgated so that the propriety and scope of general public distribution may be evaluated.

The opinion then considers the purpose of the instruction manual—"to instruct and assist taxing officials in the administration of property taxes." It points out that the statute expressly designates tax assessors and other officials connected with the administration of property taxes as the intended recipients of the manual. This language would apparently rebut any intent that the manual be distributed to the public. Inasmuch as general public distribution of the manual would be inconsistent with the prescribed statutory purpose for its promulgation, it does not appear to be a "public document . . . subject to distribution to the public" as defined in § 257.05(1), *supra*. It follows that the cost and purpose data requirement of § 283.27(1), *supra*, does not apply to the manual.

It may be pertinent to add that the technical nature and purpose of the manual of instructions probably renders it only remotely susceptible to the abuses which 283.27(1), *supra*, is designed to prevent.

1976 FLA. ATT'Y GEN. ANNUAL REP. 136 (076-76—April 6, 1976)

In 1976, in answer to a question from the commissioner of education, an attorney general's opinion discussed the meaning of the term "public" as used in § 283.28 which requires agencies to purge their mailing lists annually. The ruling was that the "public" does not include "subordinate or functionally related or connected governmental agencies and officials," The opinion summarized a number of authorities from other jurisdictions: Barkin *v.* Board of Optometry, 269 C.A.2d 714, 75 Cal. Rptr. 337 (Ct. App. 1969); People *v.* A.A.A. Dental Laboratories, 47 N.E.2d 371 (Ill. 1943); Iowa State Commerce Commission *v.* Northern Natural Gas Co., 161 N.W.2d 111 (Ia. 1968); Griffith *v.* New Mexico Public Service Commission, 520 P.2d 269 (N. M. 1974); and Gary Pickford Co. *v.* Bagley Bros., Inc., 86 P.2d 102 (Cal. 1939). The conclusion from the discussion of these cases was that "There appears to be no clear-cut point from which to determine that a distribution of printed material is 'to the public'." The opinion continues:

The term "public" and each distribution of printed material must be considered in light of the statutory context in which such term is used and the above definitions and judicial constructions of similar terms. Section 283.28, F. S., does provide at least a modicum of guidance in that it requires "their mailing lists" to be purged and that "each subscriber" be required by the affected agency to "reply affirmatively that he wishes to continue receiving" any printed material that he had in fact been receiving. It would seem to follow that those persons on an agency's mailing list to whom printed material is being or has been distributed on a periodic basis without charge would, at least, come within the purview of the phrase "to the public" as used in s. 283.28. It should be noted that the statute does not purport to regulate the distribution of printed material, nor does it seek to inhibit or restrict such distribution without charge on a periodic basis to the public as distinguished from distributions to governmental entities and officials; but it operates on the state agency's mail list or list of subscribers, i.e., those persons to whom the free periodic distributions are being made, and it is those lists which the statute requires to be purged annually. Thus it appears that the term "public" as used in s. 283.28 has reference to those entities and persons other than governmental entities and

officials whose names appear on any one or more mailing or subscribers' lists kept and maintained by the agency to be used by it in making the periodic distributions of printed material without charge to such entities and persons.
****

Although s. 283.28, F. S., is not limited to such printed material, it includes or operates upon the public documents defined in s. 257.05(1), F. S., and regulated by s. 283.27 F. S., but does not appear to include any printed materials or distribution of printed materials for which a charge to the recipient is made by the affected state agency or any printed materials which are not regularly distributed on some periodic basis—recurring at fixed intervals or regularly recurring intervals. *See* Black's Law Dictionary (Rev'd 4th Ed.), at p. 1297, and 70 C.J.S. *Periodic*, at p. 453. The act, in its peculiar context, would not appear to apply to subordinate or functionally related or connected governmental agencies and officials.

The opinion concludes with a reference to the 1973 opinion on the instruction manual.

1978 FLA. ATT'Y GEN. OP. (078-13 January 26, 1978)

In 1978, the attorney general again ruled on the requirement in § 283.27 for the statement of costs. The question came from the director of the Florida Game and Fresh Water Fish Commission and was specifically about press releases. The ruling was that a press release was not a "periodic or special report or publication of a state agency within the meaning of Section 257.05(1), F. S."

Selected quotations from the long opinion are given without the citations. The sources cited included dictionaries, a legal encyclopedia, and cases.

This definition [in § 257.05(1)] in its statutory context and history necessarily is concerned with and limited to state documents and publications issued and published by the state through its officers, departments, boards, courts or other agencies of the state. It may also be noted that §§ 283.22, 283.23, F. S., respectively relating to general libraries of institutions in the state university system and to certain law libraries, refers [*sic*] to "each officer of the state empowered by law to distribute such public documents" or "legal publications," respectively, in authorizing such state officers to transmit copies of such documents and publications to such libraries and state legal depositories. All such documents and publications are, of course, by necessary implication required to be published by or under the authority of the state, i.e., under the authority of the duly enacted acts of the state legislature. [Citations omitted.]

In view of the foregoing, it would appear that the public or state documents which are the subject of § 283.27, F. S., and defined in § 257.05(1), F. S., mean those state documents and publications issued and published by the state through its officers and its agencies, institutions and instrumentalities under and in accordance with the statutory law and reports of officers and agencies of the state authorized or required by state laws, and which are distributed or may be subject to distribution to the public and to those state agencies, institutions, instrumentalities and depositories designated in and provided for by Chapters 257 and 283, F.S., respectively. Cf., AGO 073-147 holding among other things that a manual of instructions for tax assessors (property appraisers) required by statute for a specific purpose and not intended for distribution to anyone other than state and local officials connected with the administration of property taxes was not subject to distribution to the public and therefore was not a public document within the meaning of or for the purposes of § 283.27(1), F. S.

To fall within the requirements of § 283.27(1), F.S., a state department agency must *promulgate* public documents. The word "promulgate" generally means "to publish." [Citations omitted.]

Carrying this definition further, the word "publish" generally means to give to the public . . . . While the meaning of the term "publish" may depend on the subject with which it is connected, it has been said that the word is usually associated with printing by book, circular, pamphlet or newspaper or the like. . . . Equating "publish" with the term "promulgate" appears to be in keeping with the context of § 257.05 and Ch. 283, F. S., generally and § 283.27(1), F. S., in particular which goes on to require that cost and purpose data "be *printed* on *the publication* adjacent to the identification of the agency responsible for *publication* . . . (e.s.) The definition of "publication" lends further support for this construction. [Underlining in the original; citations omitted at ellipses; discussion of definitions of publication omitted.]

Press releases do not readily fall within any such definitions. Courts have generally characterized press releases in the nature of announcements, and not publications or public documents. [Citations omitted.]
****

These statutes [other sections of Chapter 283 and § 257.05(1)] indicate a legislative concern to preserve and distribute state documents of informational and historical significance to the state, to state government and to the public. In this context, it does not appear under the usual and customary definition of the terms, that the announcement or delivery of a press release rises to the level of a "promulgation" of a public document as contemplated by § 283 27(1), F. S.

The opinion continues with a discussion of the definition of "public document" in § 257.05(1) with comments on the meaning of "annual," "biennial," and "regular," citing a legal encyclopedia and examples of reports required by the legislature. The opinion says, "a press release is not characterized by issuance on a periodic or uniform basis, but instead is inherently bound to the particular news event it announces." The opinion finds that press releases are not "special" publications because they "have not been characterized as unusual, uncommon, extraordinary or noteworthy functions of government, but as normal informational techniques of government." [Citation omitted.] The discussion concludes: "In light of the accepted use and functions of press releases, there is no basis to construe such announcements as special or extraordinary in nature."

The opinion then turns to the question "whether distribution to news media is equivalent to distribution to the public under the statutes." After referring to the earlier attorney general opinions (AGO 076-76 and AGO 073-147), the opinion continues:

In the same manner, the press release itself is actually intended for distribution to the news media, which may or may not publish or broadcast the information contained therein. Therefore, while the information contained in a press release may ultimately be disseminated or distributed to the public, distribution to the public is within the discretion of the news media, and the press release itself is intended for the news media, and the transfer of the press release is to the news media. Indeed, by the time information, or any portion thereof, contained in the press release is reproduced by the news media, it is the product and property of the particular news media. [Citation omitted.] Accordingly, in final form, the information distributed to the public is subject to journalistic license which, depending on the individual news account, makes it difficult and unwarranted to characterize a press release as being directly distributed to the public.

BIBLIOGRAPHY

"What's in the State Library, or Mining Florida's Underground Resources." *Florida State Library Newsletter* 15:2 (November 1967).
This general article on the library collection at the state library reports, "Much of the strength of [the Floridiana] collection derives from the state publications which have been acquired over the years. The Florida collection contains . . . 9,235 publications of state agencies. With the exception of items in fragile condition, all of this material is available for interlibrary loan."

Florida, Library and Historical Commission. "Library Commission Adopts Criteria for Depository Libraries." *Florida State Library Newsletter* 15:15 (1967).
An announcement of the criteria adopted by the Florida Library and Historical Commission for the designation of depository libraries. Libraries to be designated will receive an application form. Rejected depositories are entitled to a hearing. Libraries must reapply annually.

Summers, F. William. "The State Documents Depository Program." *Florida Libraries* 19:157-158 (December 1968).
The passage of depository legislation in 1967 is lauded as the "first major step since 1943 when Gwendolyn Lloyd wrote her thesis, *Official Publications of Florida, 1821-1941.*" The University of Florida's *Short-title Checklist* only partially filled the need for a program with a centralized listing of documents.
    The new depository law was initiated by the Florida Library Association and is administered by the state library. Designation of twenty-one depository libraries was possible. Only two eligible libraries declined. Depository libraries receive two copies, one of which is for interlibrary loan. Some state agencies cooperate well, and others have dragged their feet. The reasons why cooperation by agencies benefits an agency are (1) agencies can save storage space, staff time, and postage by not ordering copies to

fill future requests from individuals, and (2) agencies have the option of referring requests to depository libraries instead of making direct distribution. The conclusion is that ''the depository library program is intended for the mutual use and benefit of the public, state agencies and the libraries. . . . ''

Newsome, Walter L., and Sanders, Nancy P. ''Florida Public Document Classification in the Florida Atlantic University Library.'' *Florida Libraries* 21:27-29 (March 1970).
Interest in the classification scheme was created by the publication of the *Keyword-in-Context Index to Florida Public Documents in the Florida Atlantic University Library*. The article explains the classification scheme and gives a full list of Florida agencies.

Lloyd, D.G. ''Official Publications of Florida, 1821-1941.'' M.A. Thesis, University of Illinois, 1943. 537 p. (Not seen.)

GEORGIA

GA. CODE ANN. §§ 101-201 to 101-204 (Supp. 1979)

101-201. Reports of certain officers to be filed with librarian. The Governor and all of the officers who are, or may be, required to make reports to the General Assembly, shall furnish the librarian with at least three copies of each of said reports, and he shall have one copy of each report bound and preserved in the library for public use, the remaining copies to be held in reserve. (Acts 1975, pp. 741, 745.)

101-202. State institutions, public libraries, and public schools to be supplied. Such of the State institutions, public libraries and public schools of Georgia, and such other institutions of learning as maintain libraries and desire to receive them, shall be supplied free of charge by the librarian with copies of public documents when available. (Acts 1975, pp. 741, 745.)

101-203. Librarian as exchange officer. The librarian shall be the exchange officer of Georgia for the purpose of a regular exchange between this and other states of public documents, and the several state departments and institutions are required to deposit with the librarian for that purpose at least 50 copies of each of their public documents. The Attorney General, at his discretion, may order the librarian to exchange copies of public documents, court reports, journals of the House and of the Senate, and Georgia session laws with the proper authorities of foreign governments on whatever basis he deems advisable and in the public interest.

Each department and institution within the executive branch of State government shall make a report on or before December 1 of each year to the State Librarian containing a list by title of all public documents published or issued by such department or institution during the preceding State of Georgia fiscal year. The report shall also contain a statement noting the frequency of publication of each such public document. The State Librarian may disseminate copies of the lists, of such parts thereof, in such form as the State Librarian, in his or her discretion, deems shall best serve the public interest. (Acts 1975, pp. 741, 745; 1978, pp. 2288, 2289, eff. April 11, 1978.)

101-204. Exchange of court reports with other States. The librarian shall establish and maintain with other States, through the proper authorities, the exchange of copies of reports for the reports of their appellate tribunals. (Acts 1975, pp. 741, 746.)

101-205. Distribution and sale of copies of laws and journals; procedures in connection therewith. (Section not reproduced.)

EDITORIAL COMMENT

In 1978, the second paragraph of § 101-203 was added by Acts 1978, pp. 2288, 2289.

Georgia has earlier legislation, enacted in 1967 (1968 Ga. Laws, No. 1119, p. 1186), which attempted to promote the distribution of documents by setting up an advisory commission. A 1971 law (1971 Ga. Laws, No. 84, p. 216), known as "The Georgia Government Documents Act," and codified in GA. CODE ANN. §§ 90-301 to 90-307, repealed the 1967 law. Dr. William Pullen (Georgia State University), one of the sponsors of the legislation, hoped that it would be the first step toward a full documents program for Georgia. The title of the 1967 act was:

An Act to provide for a system of officially designated Georgia Government Documents in order to obtain maximum efficiency, economy, and usefulness in the publication, compilation, distribution and preservation of the written materials defined as government documents; to constitute an Advisory Council to the Legislative Services Committee to establish, maintain and oversee such system; to prescribe the authority of the Advisory Council; to repeal conflicting laws; and for other purposes.

The title of the 1971 Act was almost the same, except that the council was named "Advisory Council on Georgia Government Documents."

The 1971 Act is presently inoperative because the Advisory Council which it created no longer exists. All the functions of the Advisory Council were transferred to the Department of Administrative Services in 1972 by Acts 1972, p. 1015, a reorganization act.

The changes in 1971 included the addition of the president of the Georgia Library Association to the council, a more definite statement on the limits of the authority of the council, and other substantive changes.

HAWAII

HAWAII REV. STAT. §§ 93-1 to 93-5 (1976)

CHAPTER 93. GOVERNMENT PUBLICATIONS

PART 1. STATE PUBLICATIONS DISTRIBUTION CENTER

§ 93-1. Establishment of state publications distribution center. There shall be established within the department of education and under the direction of the state librarian a state publications distribution center for depositing and distributing government publications and for promoting an orderly depository library system for state and county publications. (L 1965, c 175, pt of § 2(b); Supp, § 13-20.)

§ 93-2. Definitions. (1) "State and county agency" includes every state, city and county, and county office, officer, department, board, commission, and agency, whether in the legislative, executive, or judicial branch.

(2) "Publication" includes any document, compilation, journal, report, statute, regulation, ordinance issued in print by any state or county agency, and confidential publications which shall be deposited in accordance with security regulations to be determined by the issuing agency.

(3) "Print" includes all forms of printing and duplications, except administrative forms. (L 1965, c 175, pt of § 2(b); Supp, § 13-21.)

§ 93-3. Deposit of publications. Every state and county agency shall immediately upon release of a publication, deposit fifteen copies with the state publications distribution center and one copy each with the state archives and the University of Hawaii. Additional copies of the publications shall be deposited with the publications distribution center upon request of the state librarian so long as copies are available.

The state librarian may enter into depository agreements with private and public educational, historical, or scientific institutions or other libraries, within or without the State in order to achieve the objectives sought under this part. (L 1965, c 175, pt of § 2(b); Supp, § 13-22; HRS § 93-3, am L 1970, c 121, § 1.)

§ 93-4. Depository library system. The state librarian shall designate at least one government publications depository in each county and shall distribute to each depository one copy of each publication, as defined in this part. (L 1965, c 175, pt of § 2(b); Supp, § 13-23.)

§ 93-5. Rules and regulations. The department of education may make such rules and regulations as are necessary to carry out the purposes of this part. (L 1965, c 175, pt of § 2(b); Supp, § 13-24.)

STATE COMMENT (1978)

The Department of Education has not issued any rules and regulations pursuant to section 93-5 of the Hawaii Revised Statutes. (Letter from Mrs. Proserfina Strona, Librarian, Hawaii and Pacific Unit, Department of Education, State Library Branch, Honolulu, Hawaii 96813, dated April 6, 1978.)

EDITORIAL COMMENT

§ 93-3 was amended in 1970 to increase the number of copies to be deposited from eight to fifteen.

BIBLIOGRAPHY

Hawaii, State Library System, Honolulu. *Classification Scheme for Hawaii Documents*. The Library, 1970. 24 p.
    Based on Ellen Jackson scheme. Classification is keyed to agency names only and does not provide for types of publications. Includes county agencies.

IDAHO

IDAHO CODE § 33-2510 (Supp. 1979)

33-2510. State librarian—Depository for public documents—Distribution. It shall be the duty of the head of every agency, board, bureau, commission or department of the state of Idaho, including all state supported institutions of higher education in Idaho, to deposit with the librarian of the Idaho state library for use and distribution to the academic, regional public, special libraries of Idaho, the Library of Congress, and to others within the discretion of the state librarian twenty (20) copies of all documents, reports, surveys, monographs, serial publications, compilations, pamphlets, bulletins, leaflets, circulars, maps, charts or broadsides of a public nature which it prints, mimeographs or otherwise reproduces for public distribution. (1972, ch. 165, § 1, p. 413.) Eff. date, July 1, 1972.

STATE COMMENT (1980)

State documents are sent to 18 public, academic, and special libraries in Idaho and to the Library of Congress.

There is an understanding with all depository libraries that items that are no longer desired will be returned to the State Historical Society for inclusion in the duplicate document storage. This is designed to be of aid to emerging libraries and to fill gaps in the collections of existing libraries.

****

Problems include: reminding agencies of their legal obligation to supply copies and receiving sufficient copies of federal/state and private/state publications. No solution has been found for this latter problem. If an agency works with, and is funded by, a private organization on a particular study, seldom are depository copies budgeted for. Often, though they carry the bibliographic information of a state document, they are, by definition, not a state document. This same problem arises with university presses.

Response from the depository libraries and from users has been favorable. (Letter from M. Gary Bettis, Idaho State Library, Boise, Idaho 83702, dated January 2, 1980.)

BIBLIOGRAPHY

··Idaho to Distribute State Publications'' *Library Journal* 60:299 (April 1, 1935).
Legislation, described as ··very progressive,'' regarding the distribution of state publications to the Library of Congress. Final section of act states that the preceding provisions of the act are in recognition of benefits received by federal documents depositories in Idaho.

Elison, Gar T. ··The Problem of Government Publications in Idaho'' *Pacific Northwest Library Association Quarterly* 34:13-19 (October 1969).
Bibliographical control of state publications in Idaho is a ··long-standing'' problem. State agencies cannot judge the value of their own publications and often do not consider near-print publications worthy of being called publications. Also, state agencies do not maintain bibliographies. Agencies do not always have the money to print, or they print so few that the supply is quickly exhausted and the agencies have no facilities to make copies.
    The first step is to meet the problem of definition—state agencies must learn the value of the facts and statistics which they collect and prepare. Elison expresses hope that increased demand will result in more publishing by agencies and in sufficient quantities.
    Librarians must educate both the state agencies and the public. In addition, the bibliographies now prepared (in *Idaho Librarian*) must be improved through better cooperation with the state and the Library of Congress. ··We cannot wait another twenty years to find a solution.''

··Checklist of Idaho Publications, 1969-.'' *See* issues of *Idaho Librarian* 1970-.

ILLINOIS

ILL. ANN. STAT. ch 128 § 121 (Smith-Hurd Supp. 1979)

§ 121. Publications and lists—Deposits by state agencies.
(a) All State agencies shall provide and deposit with the Illinois State Library sufficient copies of all publications issued by such State agencies for its collection and for exchange purposes. The State Librarian shall by rule or regulation specify the number of copies required and the publications that must be deposited.

For the purposes of this section: (1) "State agencies" means every State office, officer, department, division, section, unit, service, bureau, board, commission, committee, and subdivision thereof of all branches of the State government and which agencies expend appropriations of State funds.

(2) "Publications" means any document, report, directory, bibliography, rule, regulation, newsletter, pamphlet, brochure, periodical or other printed material paid for in whole or in part by funds appropriated by the General Assembly or issued at the request of a State agency, excepting however, correspondence, inter-office memoranda, and confidential publications.

(3) "Printed material" means publications duplicated by any and all methods of duplication.

(b) The State Librarian shall from time to time publish a listing of the publications received by him under this Act. (1939, July 13, Laws 1939, p. 697, § 18. Renumbered § 21 and amended by P. A. 77-1690, § 1, eff. Jan. 1, 1972.)

STATE COMMENT

[T]he legislation ... is loosely worded so that the number of copies, depositories, etc. can be changed without further legislation. (Note by Geneva Finn, May 2, 1973. *In* Documents on Documents Collection.)

EDITORIAL COMMENT

Enacted in 1967 as § 18 of a general state library act (1967 Ill. Laws, p. 2786). The 1967 Act included a $20,000 appropriation "for the administration of this amendatory Act of 1967" and was effective January 1, 1968.

The 1971 amendment (Public Act 77-1690, eff. Jan. 1, 1972) renumbered the section and amended it by capitalizing the word "State" and by substituting "State Librarian" for "Librarian."

RULES AND REGULATIONS

SECRETARY OF STATE
RULES AND REGULATIONS FOR:
DEPOSIT OF PUBLICATIONS BY STATE AGENCIES

WHEREAS the 75th General Assembly has enacted into law, House Bill 1972, Act 1031, approved by the Governor and effective January 1, 1968, as amended by House Bill 2769, Public Act 77-1690, 77th General Assembly, approved by the Governor and effective January 1, 1972, such laws enacting Section 21 to "The State Library Act" (S.H.A., Chapter 128, Section 121); and

WHEREAS, the Secretary of State is designated by law as the State Librarian and thus the administrator of this law; and

WHEREAS this law requires that the State Librarian shall by rule or regulation specify the number of copies to be required and the publications to be deposited.

NOW THEREFORE, pursuant to the provisions of the aforesaid law, the Honorable John W. Lewis, Secretary of State of the State of Illinois and State Librarian, does hereby promulgate the following revised Rules and Regulations governing the Deposit of Publications by State Agencies.

RULE 12.18-1: DEFINITIONS

For the purposes hereof, the words and phrases used herein shall have the meanings ascribed to them in "The State Library Act", unless the context dictates otherwise.

The term "State Agency" means every state office, officer, department, division, section, unit, service, bureau, board, commission, committee, and subdivision thereof of all branches of the state government and which agencies expend appropriations of state funds.

The term "Publications" means any document, report, directory, bibliography, rule, regulation, newsletter, pamphlet, brochure, periodical or other printed material paid for in whole or in part by funds appropriated by the General Assembly or issued at the request of a state agency, excepting however, correspondence, interoffice memoranda, and confidential publications.

The term "Printed Material" means publications duplicated by any and all methods of duplication.

RULE 12.18-2: NON-PRICED PUBLICATIONS

A. Within two weeks of their release forty copies of all non-priced publications shall be sent to the Illinois Documents Unit, Illinois State Library, by the issuing state agency.

B. In a few specialized instances state agencies may make arrangements with the Illinois Documents Unit, Illinois State Library, to do their own mailing of specific titles. In these cases an agreed number of copies of each item shall be sent to the Illinois Documents Unit. The Illinois Documents Unit shall provide the issuing agency with a mailing list for the remaining number of copies.

C. The State universities are excepted from this regulation. (See Rule 12.18-4.)

RULE 21.8-3: PRICED PUBLICATIONS

A. Within two weeks of their distribution three copies of all priced publications shall be deposited with the Illiniois Documents Unit, Illinois State Library, by the issuing state agency. Information on the price and address of the selling agency shall be sent to the Illinois Documents Unit, Illinois State Library, with the three priced publications so that it can be included in the list of State of Illinois Publications issued by the State Library.

B. The State universities are excepted from this regulation. (See Rule 12.18-4.)

RULE 12.18-4: STATE UNIVERSITY PUBLICATIONS

Within two weeks of their distribution three copies of all State university publications, priced and non-priced, and two copies of books published by the university presses, shall be deposited with the Illinois Documents Unit, Illinois State Library.

RULE 12.18-5: ARRANGEMENTS FOR COPIES

Nothing in these regulations shall preclude the Illinois Documents Unit, Illinois State Library, from making special arrangements to obtain and exchange more than forty copies of certain publications of State agencies.

RULE 12.18-6: ADMINISTRATOR OF STATE AGENCY

Each state agency shall inform the Illinois Documents Unit, Illinois State Library, of the person, persons, or positions responsible for distribution of publications of that agency.

RULE 12.18-7: FORMS AND LISTING

The State Librarian shall prepare the necessary forms implementing these rules, and shall further prepare and publish, from time to time, a listing of the publications received by him.

RULE 12.18-8: DESIGNATION OF DEPOSITORIES

The Director of the Illinois State Library shall designate the institutions that will be the depositories or exchange libraries for Illinois State Documents.

RULE 12.18-9: OWNERSHIP OF DEPOSITORY DOCUMENTS

The Illinois State Library shall retain ownership of Illinois documents deposited in libraries within the State of Illinois.

RULE 12.18-10: INSPECTION OF DEPOSITORIES

The Director of the Illinois State Library, or his representative, shall from time to time visit and inspect the depositories for Illinois State Documents and receive written reports from them.

RULE 12.18-11: EFFECTIVE DATE

These Rules and Regulations shall take effect pursuant to law.
Amended October 20, 1972.

"INSTRUCTION TO DEPOSITORY LIBRARIES FOR ILLINOIS STATE DOCUMENTS, AUGUST 1972." ILLINOIS LIBRARIES 55:224 *(March 1973)*.

GENERAL INFORMATION

Your status as a depository for Illinois state documents is determined by the Director of the Illinois State Library. In accepting the privilege of being a depository you have agreed to abide by the laws, the rules and regulations and these instructions governing officially designated depositories. The Illinois documents you have received in the past through the depository program administered by the Illinois State Library come within the scope of these regulations.

RETENTION AND DISPOSAL OF DOCUMENTS

The Illinois State Library remains owner of the documents which are deposited. The depository must keep all documents received for five years. At the end of that time you may return a list of unneeded documents to the Documents/Serials Branch, Illinois State Library, Centennial Building, Springfield, Illinois 62756, which will circulate the list to other libraries in a manner similar to the method used by regional depositories in weeding federal documents. If other libraries request the documents on the list, the discarding library will forward the documents to them, otherwise they may be destroyed or otherwise disposed of. The Reference and Research Centers, which includes the Illinois State Library, shall keep all depository documents indefinitely, except for superseded items.

Superseded items may simply be discarded by all depositories. Examples are: any publication cumulated in later issues after the later cumulation is received; any revised publication after the revised edition is received; separates, upon receipt of final bound volumes; compilations of laws and regulations upon receipt of new editions.

Replacement copies of lost and worn-out documents can be requested from the Illinois State Library at the discretion of the depository. These will be supplied in hard copy if possible, otherwise in microform.

REFERENCE USE

In order to make the state documents easily accessible cataloging at least in brief form is required. In addition reasonable reference service must be available not only to the library's primary users but to all Illinois citizens.

CIRCULATION

Circulation of Illinois documents is encouraged. It is not necessary to hold Illinois documents as a separate collection. Universities and special libraries that are depositories must be willing to lend to library systems and to permit all Illinois citizens access to the documents within the library. Public libraries and library systems must be willing to lend to all Illinois citizens through the use of reciprocal borrowing.

INSPECTION

The Director of the Illinois State Library, or his representative, shall from time to time visit and inspect the depositories and receive written reports from the libraries on their administration of the depositories. These reports will be made on forms supplied by the Illinois State Library. Reports will not be required more than once a year nor less than once every three years.

TERMINATION

A depository has the right to terminate its status as a depository by a letter to the Director of the Illinois State Library. The Director of the Illinois State Library may terminate the status of a library as a depository upon proof of unsatisfactory administration or use of the depository or if statewide considerations make revision of the list of depositories necessary. At termination the library will request instructions from the Illinois State Library about disposition of the depository publications on hand.

BIBLIOGRAPHY

Bailey, Dorothy. "Service to You Through the Illinois Documents Unit." *Illinois Libraries* 37:34-35 (February 1955).
The author, head of the Illinois Documents Unit at the Illinois State Library, describes the collection that was set up as a unit in 1941. The unit does classification and cataloging, exchange work, and reference. The exchanges are with other state libraries and several university and public libraries. One copy is sent to the Library of Congress.

Miele, Anthony W. "Technical Services Department." *Illinois Libraries* 53:298-309 (April/May 1971).
The part of Miele's article on the Illinois Documents Section (at pp. 308-309) states that the section has a collection of over 63,000 items. The section provides acquisitions, cataloging, and public service functions. Since 1967, when legislation was enacted to require state agencies to deposit copies of their publications for the state library collection and for exchange, the Illinois documents librarian has handled the disposition of the publications. A shipping list accompanies each shipment. A future project is to expand the number of libraries to which publications are distributed to include the eighteen systems and other state libraries.

The June 1972 issue (v. 54, no. 5) of *Illinois Libraries* devotes almost fifty pages to the papers from a State Documents Workshop held in Springfield on January 20-21, 1972. The workshop had as its objectives (1) to discuss mutual problems of documents librarians, (2) to point the way toward solutions for problem areas, (3) to publish proceedings, and (4) to continue to develop cooperation between the state library and documents librarians.

The first day featured a speech by Agnes Ferruso on the *Monthly Checklist of State Publications*. Other speakers were Barbara Nelson on the Council of State Governments and Geneva Finn on the publishing of Illinois documents. The discussion groups focused on (1) acquisition and collection of state publications, and (2) classification and bibliographical control.

On the second day the discussions were summarized, and Mills, Meyer, Adams, and Welch presented a panel on public service use of state documents.

Agnes Ferruso commented on "the general movement toward establishing depository library systems within the states" and said,

> In some states where there is neither a depository system or a specific distribution law, it is known that state libraries find it difficult to obtain copies of all the publications issued by all the agencies of their own state government.

Her paper gives a full account of the acquisition of state documents at the Library of Congress, the preparation of the *Monthly Checklist*, and the library's acquisition policy on state documents for its permanent collections.

Nelson's paper is on the Council of State Governments library, which in its origin and development, was closely related to the National Legislative Conference. The selection policies and procedures of the library include (1) material from legislative service agencies, (2) checklists from the states, (3) bibliographies, indexes, etc., (4) exchanges, (5) feedback from staff, and (6) professional journals and booklists.

Finn reported that the Illinois documents program was currently being revised. In the past, twenty-five copies of publications for distribution were required; the revisions may mean that thirty-five copies will be needed. She cautions acquisitions librarians to watch the newspaper for announcements of new publications because if a really important or unusual publication is released, a state agency may quite often set up a special distribution.

Halcli's summary of the previous day's discussion notes two problems: (1) integration versus segregation, and (2) *Anglo-American Cataloging Rules* (AACR) for establishing main entry. He lists eleven specific recommendations and suggestions that were made: (1) putting older documents on microfilm, (2) microfilming the Illinois section of the University of Illinois catalog, (3) exchanging catalog cards between the state library and the University of Illinois, (4) exchanging classification schemes, (5) need for list of state commissions and commission reports, (6) need for state library to get more copies of the *Directory of State Officials*, (7) need for libraries in the state to support the documents program, (8) subject index for the state checklist, (9) up-to-date list of addresses of state agencies, (10) need for public library system to accept larger role in promoting documents, and (11) statewide committee. He concludes with a plea to bring documents and documents librarians into the mainstream by involving everyone in the library, not forgetting the key people in the library, and by thinking of documents as "treasures," and not as something "free."

Mills describes the situation in her library: arrangement by agency, then by series, no subject approach.

Meyer reports that government documents, in official and nonofficial editions, constitute a large portion of legal literature. Her library must have the latest information, slip laws, and so on. She uses the telephone for administrative regulations, judicial statistics, the latest court decisions, and bill status.

Adams discusses official and unofficial legislative publications and their availability and distribution.

Welch, reporting on state documents collecting and use in her "medium-large public library," which is also a system library serving fifty-six smaller libraries, has 2,500 separate state items and in one month answered twenty-nine state documents' reference questions and in another month, seventeen questions.

Anderson explains a classification scheme for a public library, using letters and numbers. "[A]ccessibility by subject to the documents collection is a retentive memory on the part of the documents librarian."

Cook's paper on state manual procurement is a state-by-state listing with ordering information.

Carroll's paper is based on sixty-two questionnaires, of which thirty-eight were returned. Questions were asked on personnel, holdings, acquisitions tools used, separate versus integrated collection, classification system, use statistics, and discussion topics for the upcoming workshop. Thirty-three possible discussion topics were suggested.

Littlewood's list of checklists includes issuing agency, title, beginning date, frequency, and some additional notes.

Floersch's bibliography on the Illinois government and its publications includes eighteen general publications and sixteen Illinois state publications. Her second paper on newsletters lists mostly federal titles. Only nine titles are Illinois documents. Some Chicago publications are included.

The listing of "Depository Libraries for Illinois State Documents" includes seventeen Illinois libraries, the Center for Research Libraries, the Library of Congress, and the British Museum.

The special section of this issue of *Illinois Libraries* concludes with a list of the registrants for the workshop. There were 105 attendees.

In the March 1973 issue of *Illinois Libraries* (55:224-227) are printed:

> "Instruction to Depository Libraries for Illinois State Documents, August, 1972." (Reproduced above under Illinois rules and regulations.)
>
> "Institutions to Receive Illinois State Documents Through the Illinois State Library Depository and Exchange Program, December 1972." (Includes twenty-seven libraries, all of which receive one copy, except for the Illinois State Library which receives three copies and the Library of Congress which receives two copies. Out-of-state libraries include the Library of Congress, California State Library, New York State Library, and the British Museum.)
>
> "Rules and Regulations for Deposit of Publications by State Agencies (dated October 4, 1972)." (Reproduced above under Illinois rules and regulations.)

Other Illinois publications serving as bibliographic tools, and not seen, are:

Hardin, A.R. "Selected, Annotated List of Illinois Official Publications for Use in the Five State Teachers' Colleges of Illinois." M.S. Thesis, University of Illinois, 1942. 143 p.

Norton, M. C. (comp.). "Illinois Documents: A Checklist, 1812-50." *Illinois Libraries* 32:592-600 (October 1950); 32:634-640 (November 1950); 32:669-675 (December 1950).

Nakata, Mrs. Y., and Strange, M. "Classification Scheme for Illinois State Publications as Applied to the Documents Collection at the Library, University of Illinois at Chicago Circle, Chicago, Illinois." University of Illinois, Graduate School of Library Science, 1974. 39 p.

INDIANA

IND. CODE ANN. §§ 4-23-7-23.4 to 23.6 (Burns 1974)

4-23-7-23.4 [63-807a]. State library designated depository for public documents. In order that all public documents of the state of Indiana shall be preserved and made available for use of the citizens of the state, the Indiana state library is hereby designated as the depository library for Indiana documents. The Indiana state library shall maintain a complete collection of all Indiana public documents. This collection shall be the official file of Indiana state documents. The Indiana state library shall establish a state document depository system by which copies of all those public documents published by the state which are of general interest or use shall be deposited in designated depository libraries, and shall distribute to other libraries copies of those public documents published by the state which are of greatest interest or use and for which a more general distribution is appropriate. (IC 1971, 4-23-7-23.4, as added by Acts 1973, P. L. 27, § 1, p. 126.)

4-23-7-23.5 [63-807b]. Documents to be deposited with state library—Exemptions. (a) Each and every state official, state department, state board, state commission or state agency of any kind, which issues public documents shall furnish the state library fifty (50) copies of all publications issued by them whether printed, mimeographed, or duplicated in any way, which are not issued solely for use within the issuing office. However, if the library requests, as many as twenty-five (25) additional copies of each public document shall be supplied.

(b) If other provision is made by law for the distribution of the session laws of the general assembly, the journals of the house and senate of the general assembly, the Supreme Court and Court of Appeals reports or the publications of the Indiana historical bureau, any of those for which distribution is provided for are exempted from the depository requirements of subsection (a) of this section. However, two (2) copies of each document exempted under this subsection from the general depository requirements shall be deposited with the Indiana state library.

(c) Publications of the various schools, colleges, divisions and departments of the state universities and their regional campuses are exempt from the depository requirements of subsection (a) of this section, but two (2) copies of each publication of these divisions shall be deposited in the Indiana state library.

(d) Publications of state university presses, directives for internal administration, intra-office and inter-office publications and forms are completely exempt from all depository requirements.

(e) A state officer or agency which complies with subsection (a) of this section shall be exempt from the requirements of IC 1971, 4-23-7-8. (IC 1971, 4-23-7-23.5, as added by Acts 1973, P. L. 27, § 2, p. 126.)

4-23-7-23.6 [63-807c]. Permanent retention—Library of Congress—Secondary depository libraries—Exchange system. It shall be the duty of the Indiana state library to:

(a) Keep at least two (2) copies of each Indiana state document as permanent reference copies;

(b) Send two (2) copies of each Indiana state document to the Library of Congress excluding those where other provisions for distribution are made by law;

(c) Designate the four (4) state university libraries and certain selected Indiana public, school and college libraries in the several geographical sections of the state as secondary depository libraries to receive one (1) copy of those Indiana state documents which are of general interest. Selection of secondary depository libraries shall be made by the Indiana state library, based on a determination that the libraries selected will keep the documents readily accessible for use, and will render assistance for their use to qualified patrons without charge.

(d) Prepare and issue quarterly, complete lists of state issued documents, which were issued during the immediately preceding quarter. These lists shall be cumulated and printed annually, at the end of each calendar year. Copies of these lists shall be distributed by the Indiana state library to state departments and agencies, and to public and college libraries within the state.

(e) Set up a document exchange system with agencies in other states, in order that selected documents of various other states shall be available for use by the citizens of Indiana. (IC 1971, 4-23-7-23.6, as added by Acts 1973, P. L. 27, § 3, p. 126.)

STATE COMMENT

Although the Documents Depository Law (Public Law 27) stipulates that up to 75 copies of state documents should be supplied by Indiana state agencies, in reality, the State Library only requests 20 copies of each publication. Visits are made to the Printing Board weekly to check through invoices for Indiana documents. Contact is maintained with public information officers and division heads of state agencies to obtain new publications.

The State Library keeps 2-3 copies of state documents and distributes the remainder to the Indiana document depository libraries, which correspond to the 14 Area Library Services Authority regions in the state. In 1974 the Indiana Library and Historical Board established regulations for the Indiana depository libraries which govern the selection, retention and disposal of state documents.

A separate checklist of state publications entitled *Checklist of Indiana State Documents* is published quarterly with an annual cumulation which includes a subject index. The list of documents which appeared quarterly in the *Library Occurrent* has been replaced by a brief description of new state documents entitled "Document News."

RULES AND REGULATIONS

IND. ADMIN. RULES AND REGULATIONS ANN. (4-23-7-23.6)-1 TO 7 (Burns 1976)
4-23-7-23.6. PERMANENT RETENTION—LIBRARY OF CONGRESS— SECONDARY DEPOSITORY LIBRARIES—EXCHANGE SYSTEM

(4-23-7-23.6)-1. Selection of depository documents. Selection of documents to be sent to depository libraries shall be made by the Indiana state library and shall be determined by the availability and general interest of the document. [Library and Historical Bd., Rule 3, § A.1, adopted Nov. 4, 1974, filed Dec. 16, 1974.]

(4-23-7-23.6)-2. Exemptions from the depository program. Documents available only through purchase must be obtained directly from the agency of publication by the depository library, if it desires the publication. [Library and Historical Bd., Rule 3, § A.2, adopted Nov. 4, 1974, filed Dec. 16, 1974.]

(4-23-7-23.6)-3. Required services. Depository libraries must provide inter-library loan and reference service in connection with Indiana state documents to the libraries and to citizens in their respective regions, and make every effort to see that depository documents are available to the general public and to promote their reference use. [Library and Historical Bd., Rule 3, § B, adopted Nov. 4, 1974, filed Dec. 16, 1974.]

(4-23-7-23.6)-4. Retention of documents. All depository documents must be retained at least five [5] years by the depository library. [Library and Historical Bd., Rule 3, § C, adopted Nov. 4, 1974, filed Dec. 16, 1974.]

(4-23-7-23.6)-5. Disposal of documents by the four state university depository libraries. The four [4] state university depository libraries must request the approval of the state library before disposing of depository documents retained five [5] years or longer. [Library and Historical Bd., Rule 3, § D.1, adopted Nov. 4, 1974, filed Dec. 16, 1974.]

(4-23-7-23.6)-6. Disposal of documents by secondary depository libraries. Secondary depository libraries may, at their own discretion, dispose of documents retained five [5] years or longer, unless the state library has given advance notice that certain documents are needed for the state library's collection. [Library and Historical Bd., Rule 3, § D.2, adopted Nov. 4, 1974, filed Dec. 16, 1974.]

(4-23-7-23.6)-7. Termination as a depository library. Any depository library has the right to relinquish its privilege at any time by addressing a letter to the director of the Indiana state library stating that the library no longer wishes to be a depository for Indiana state documents.

The privilege may also be taken away by the director of the Indiana state library for failure of the library to adhere to the regulations for Indiana document depository libraries.

Upon termination of the depository privilege, either by request or for cause, the library shall request of the director of the Indiana state library instructions concerning disposition to be made of the depository publications of the library. [Library and Historical Bd., Rule 3, § E, adopted Nov. 4, 1974, filed Dec. 16, 1974.]

ATTORNEY GENERAL OPINION

March 7, 1967

Honorable Roger D. Branigan
Governor of Indiana
206 State House
Indianapolis, Indiana 46204

Dear Governor Branigan:

I have examined Senate Enrolled Act No. 61 and find the same to be unconstitutional in that it violates Art. 10, Sec. 3 of the Indiana Constitution.

SENATE ENROLLED ACT NO. 61

This Act, by giving all inclusive definitions, requires every department of Indiana government, state and local (with some minor exceptions), to provide up to 160 copies of all publications to the Indiana State Library. The Act does not appropriate any funds enabling the official or agency to publish these documents. It purports to provide for appropriations for the Library, but does not indicate how much is to be appropriated, nor how this figure may be determined. In view of the fact that the legislature has attempted to provide appropriations for the Library, but not for the publishing official, or agency, it follows under the maxim of *"expressio unius, exclusio alterius;"* that they intended no appropriations for those officials and agencies. *Highland Sales Corp. v. Vance* (1962), 244 Ind. 20, 186 N.E. 2d 682.

Section 3 of Article 10 of the Indiana Constitution provides:

> "No money shall be drawn from the treasury but in pursuance of appropriations made by law."

The office has stated,

> "No one may create an obligation on behalf of the state, either legal or moral, unless there has first been an appropriation." 1954 O.A.G. No. 65, at 67.

A situation similar to the one at hand was at issue in *Book v. State Office Building Commission* (1958), 238 Ind. 120, 149 N.E. 2d 273. In that case plaintiff contended that the statute creating the Commission violated Art. 10, Sec. 3, because it did not provide for any appropriation to enable state agencies to pay for the use of the building. The Court held the statute constitutional, however, on the ground that "It is anticipated that the legislature will make proper appropriations for the use and occupancy of the proposed building. . . ."

This Act goes further, however, by making it a misdemeanor for the person charged with the duty not to comply. Thus the public official is faced with this dilemma, spend public money not appropriated for the purpose outlined in the Act or commit a misdemeanor. If the penal sanction was not present then as in the *Book* case, *supra*, the public official could decline to follow the mandate of the act until an appropriation for compliance is forthcoming. Since the Act does not allow this alternative it must fall as unconstitutional when read against Art. 10, Sec. 3 of the Indiana Constitution.

A statute granting an appropriation must contain the sum to be expended or a method of determining the appropriation, a person or persons authorized to expend the sum, and the purpose for which it is to be expended. 1958 O.A.G., p. 22; 1953 O.A.G., p. 422; and if there is any real doubt as to whether the legislature has exercised its function to appropriate, the officers should not take the money from the treasury. *Ristine v. State* (1863), 20 Ind. 328; 1945 O.A.G., pp. 499, 509; *State ex rel Martin v. Porter* (1883), 89 Ind. 260.

Respectfully submitted,
/s/ John J. Dillon
JOHN J. DILLON
Attorney General of Indiana

BIBLIOGRAPHY

Casey, Genevieve M., and Phillips, Edith. *The Management and Use of State Documents in Indiana.* Detroit: Office of Urban Library Research, Wayne State University, 1969. 75 p. (Research Report, no. 2.) (ERIC ED 046 473.)

This extensive study was undertaken at the request of the Indiana State Library. The chapter on management of state documents in other states discusses the information tabulated in four charts: (1) legal structure for deposit and distribution of state documents, (2) distribution of state documents, (3) organization of documents within state libraries, and (4) state documents checklists. Indiana document librarians will find background materials on their law and charts on practices in Indiana public and academic libraries. The report has eleven recommendations, covering new legislation, an interim executive order, a checklist, designation of depositories, a workshop, and a new staff position.

Matkovic, P. "Docs Law Aids Collection." *Focus* 31:6 (July 1977).
An 1841 law is cited as the forerunner of the 1973 depository law. The author, state documents librarian at the Indiana State Library, believes that the program based on the 1973 law has been successful. She reports that the number of documents received at the state library has doubled, and the number sent to the depository libraries has tripled, thus benefiting the state agencies, the libraries, the citizens, and the state library.

Lapp, J. A. "The Public Documents of Indiana." *Library Occurrent* 2:108-111, 130-133 (1910). (Not seen.)

IOWA

IOWA CODE ANN. §§ 303A.21 to 303A.24 (West Supp. 1980-81)

DEPOSITORY LIBRARY CENTER

303A.21. Definitions. As used in this division unless the context otherwise requires:

1. ''State agency'' means a legislative, executive, or judicial office of the state and all of its respective officers, departments, divisions, bureaus, boards, commissions, committees, and state institutions of higher education governed by the state board of regents.

2. ''State publications'' means all multiply produced publications of state agencies regardless of format which are supported by public funds, except correspondence and memoranda intended solely for internal use within the agency or between agencies, and materials designated by law as being confidential.

3. ''Depository library'' means a library designated for the deposit of state publications under the provisions of this division. (Acts 1978 [67 G. A.] ch. 1105, § 1.)

303A.22. Depository library center. There is created within the Iowa library department a depository library center. The state librarian shall appoint a depository librarian who shall administer the depository library center. The depository library center shall be the central agency for the collection and distribution of state publications to depository libraries. (Acts 1978 [67 G.A.] ch. 1105, § 2.)

303A.23. Duties of the depository librarian. The depository librarian shall:

1. Enter into agreements according to rules promulgated by the depository librarian pursuant to chapter 17A with libraries for the deposit of state publications in the libraries. Rules shall provide for the classification of the libraries into depository libraries which, for a specified period of time, maintain either a full collection of state publications or a selected core of state publications. The state library commission and the state University of Iowa shall each permanently maintain two copies of each state publication. One copy shall not be removed from the library and the other copy may be loaned.

2. Adopt a classification scheme for state publications and establish a record of the number and manner of distribution.

3. Annually advise state agencies of the number of copies of each class of publication needed for distribution.

4. Prepare, publish, and distribute on a quarterly basis without charge to depository libraries, and upon the request of other libraries or by subscription, a list of state publications which shall include a cumulated index. The depository library center established in section 303A.22 of this chapter shall also prepare and publish decennial cumulative indexes.

5. Provide to the library of Congress two copies of each state publication collected. (Acts 1978 [67 G. A.] ch. 1105, § 3.)

303A.24. Deposits by each state agency. Upon issuance of a state publication a state agency shall deposit with the depository library center at no cost to the center, seventy-five copies of the publication, or a lesser amount if specified by the depository librarian. (Acts 1978 [67 G. A.] ch. 1105, § 4.)

EDITORIAL COMMENT

The 1978 Act was titled: "An Act relating to the establishment of a depository library center within the Iowa library department." The act did not carry an appropriation.

RULES AND REGULATIONS

IOWA ADMINISTRATIVE CODE

DEPOSITORY LIBRARY CENTER

560—1.12(303A). Definitions. 1.12(1) *"State agency"* means a legislative, executive, or judicial office of the state and all of its respective officers, departments, divisions, bureaus, boards, commissions, committees, and state institutions of higher education governed by the state board of regents.

1.12(2) *"State publications"* means all multiply produced publications of state agencies regardless of format which are supported by public funds, except correspondence and memoranda intended solely for internal use within the agency or between agencies, and materials designated by law as being confidential.

1.12(3) *"Depository library"* means a library designated for the deposit of state publications under the provisions of this Act.

1.12(4) Depository librarian shall be appointed by the state librarian and shall administer the depository library center.

1.12(5) The depository library center shall be the central agency for the collection and distribution of state publications to depository libraries and shall be referred to as depository library center.

1.12(6) The state library commission and the state university of Iowa shall each permanently maintain two copies of each state publication.

1.12(7) *"Full depository"* shall be a library receiving everything collected by the depository library center.

1.12(8) *"Selective depository"* shall be a library receiving only those publications selected by it.

1.12(9) *"Core list library"* shall receive only those publications found on the periodically compiled core list.

1.12(10) *"Core list"* of Iowa state documents is a selected list intended to meet the basic document needs of libraries.

1.12(11) A library may be designated as either a full depository or as a selective depository under the program. Depositories may receive materials on the ''core list''.

This rule implements section 303A.21 of the Code.

560—1.13(303A). Administration of depository program. 1.13(1) Depository status shall be determined by the state library commission upon written application by the library. Upon approval of the application, a contract between the depository library center and the depository library shall be completed.

1.13(2) A nine member advisory council shall be organized to advise the Iowa library department regarding this program. The advisory council may be composed of members of state agencies, representatives of depository and nondepository libraries, and the general public appointed by the commission.

1.13(3) The document depository program shall be administered by the depository librarian under the direction of the state librarian.

a. The depository librarian shall make a regular inspection of each depository library and shall submit a written evaluation to the depository library at the conclusion of the visit.

b. The depository library center shall compile the core list after consultation with interested parties.

1.13(4) All nondepository libraries may contact the agency or the state printer for material on a first-come, first-served basis.

1.13(5) Materials missing from the depository shipments must be claimed from the depository library center within one month of receipt of the shipment. After that time, requests should be made directly to the issuing agency or the state printer.

This rule implements section 303A.22 of the Code.

560—1.14(303A). Depositories. 1.14(1) The state university of Iowa and the Iowa library department shall be considered as depositories in addition to those mentioned in the subrules.

1.14(2) Depositories shall meet the following minimum requirements:

a. All publications received under this program will be retained for a minimum of three years unless a lesser retention period is designated for an item or items by the depository center.

b. The depository agrees to make the documents available for free public use. Every effort should be made by the depository library to make as few restrictions on circulation as possible.

c. Space for depository operations should be of the same quality as for other operations of the library. If documents are maintained in a separate division of the library, the space provided should be conveniently located to encourage use of the materials.

1.14(3) Depository libraries may be selected on the basis of one or more of the following criteria:

a. Geographic location consistent with a policy of distributing depositories so as to minimize the distance a user would need to travel.

b. Demonstrated ability to handle the receipts desired based on size of collection, identified need of the library's clientele, and the availability of space and staff.

c. Present federal depository status.

1.14(4) The program will be implemented as rapidly as funds, staff, and publications are available. Thirty libraries will be designated in the initial program.

560—1.15(303A). Withdrawal of a library from the program. 1.15(1) A core list library may withdraw from this program by sending written notice to the depository center.

1.15(2) A depository library may withdraw from this program by sending written notice to the document depository center sixty days prior to such withdrawal.

1.15(3) A library's depository designation may be withdrawn for failure to conform to the terms of the contract. The state librarian shall give written notification to the depository. Within thirty days after the receipt of such notice, the depository library and the state library shall hold a meeting to review the stated inadequacies. If inadequacies are not corrected or a written plan of action has not been submitted within thiry days, the state library shall withdraw the library's depository designation.

1.15(4) Upon termination of the contract the depository documents become the property of the depository library center and must be returned to the center or to such other depositories as may be specified by the center.

1.16 to 1.19 Reserved.

BIBLIOGRAPHY

Stewart, H. "Iowa State Publications." M.A. Thesis, University of Illinois, 1937. 360 p. (Not seen.)

KANSAS

KAN. STAT. ANN. §§ 75-1023; 75-2565 to 2568; 75-3048a to 3048c (Vernon 1977)

75-1023. Extra copies of certain publications; distribution, notification of secretary of historical society. Whenever the division of printing prints any of the publications of the state and of its societies and institutions, there shall be printed extra copies thereof as shall be necessary to deliver such number of copies thereof to the state historical society as the secretary of said society shall request but not exceeding thirty (30) copies, thirty-five (35) copies to the state library, to be used by said historical society and said state library in making exchanges with other states, libraries, societies and institutions for similar publications, and two (2) copies thereof to each of the following named libraries, to wit:

The library of the university of Kansas, the library of Kansas state university of agriculture and applied science, the library of Wichita state university, the libraries of Fort Hays state university, Pittsburg state university and Emporia state university. In case any publication is issued in both bound and unbound form, bound copies shall be supplied. This section shall not apply to the reports of the supreme court of the state of Kansas, or to the statutes or session laws.

The director of printing shall notify the secretary of the state historical society of the printings of all publications so that said secretary may make proper requests for copies of such publications. (R. S. 1923, 75-1023; L. 1943, ch. 269, § 21; L. 1961, ch. 407, § 1; L. 1967, ch. 440, § 1; L. 1968. ch. 364, § 1; (L. 1976, ch. 373, § 9; March 2.)

Source or prior law: L. 1911, ch. 304, § 1; L. 1913, ch. 308, § 1.

75-2565. Definitions. As used in this act, the following terms and phrases shall have the meanings respectively ascribed thereto in this section:

(a) "Publication" means any report, pamphlet, book, or other materials provided by a state agency for use by the general public;

(b) "state agency" means any state office or officer, department, board, commission, institution, bureau, society or any agency, division or unit within any state office, department, board, commission or other state authority. L. 1976, ch. 358, § 1; July 1.)

75-2566. Establishment and operation of publication collection and depository system; duties of state agencies and the state librarian. (a) The state librarian is hereby authorized and directed to establish, operate and maintain a publication collection and depository system as provided in this act.

(b) Each state agency shall deposit with the Kansas state library copies of any publication issued by such state agency in such quantity as shall be specified by the state librarian.

(c) The state librarian shall forward two (2) copies of all such publications to the library of congress, one copy to the state historical society, one copy to the center for research libraries and one copy shall be retained permanently in the Kansas state library. Additional copies, as may be prescribed by rule and regulation, may be required for the depository system. (L. 1976, ch. 358, § 2; July 1.)

75-2567. Same; power and duties of state librarian; designation of libraries as complete or selective depositories. (a) The state librarian shall periodically publish and distribute to complete depository libraries, selective depository libraries, state agencies, state officers and members of the Kansas legislature, an official list of state publications with at least an annual cumulation. Said official list shall provide a record of each agency's publications and shall show, in addition, the author, title, major subject content and other appropriate catalogue information for any such publication. Annually each state agency shall furnish to the state library a complete list of their publications for the previous year which the state librarian shall use to maintain a permanent record of publications.

(b) To be designated as a complete depository library any Kansas resource library, regional public library, libraries in institutions of higher education or other libraries must contract with the state librarian agreeing at a minimum to provide adequate facilities for the storage and use of any such publication and to render reasonable service without charge to qualified patrons in the use of such publications and to maintain its full collection of such publications indefinitely subject to disposal upon approval by the state librarian. Any library designated as a complete depository shall receive one copy of every state publication deposited with the Kansas state library. Any library designated as a selective depository shall receive only copies of publications which such library requests. (L. 1976, ch. 358, § 3; July 1.)

75-2568. Same; rules and regulations. The state librarian is hereby authorized to adopt rules and regulations necessary to implement and administer the provisions of this act. (L. 1976, ch. 358, § 4; July 1.)

75-3048a. Reports of state agencies; "publication" defined. As used in this act "publication" means any report or document which is intended to be made available to the public and which is originated by a state agency. (L. 1972, ch. 316, § 1; July 1.)

75-3048b. Same; central duplicating to provide library with copies of certain publications. The central duplicating service of the state department of administration shall make two additional copies of each publication that it reproduces in more than fifty (50) copies and shall deliver such additional copies to the state library for its use, except that no such additional copies shall be so made or delivered in the event that they are of a confidential class of material or if central duplicating is advised that they are of a confidential nature. (L. 1972, ch. 316, § 2; July 1.)

75-3048c. Same; agency to provide library with copies of certain publications. Every state agency that prints or otherwise reproduces more than fifty (50) copies of any publication, except through the director of printing or the central duplicating service, shall make two additional copies of each publication it reproduces and shall deliver such additional copies to the state library for its use, unless the same are confidential. (L. 1972, ch. 316, § 3; July 1.)

RULES AND REGULATIONS

Kansas Administrative Regulations 54-2-1 to 54-2-7.
Article 2.—ESTABLISHING A PUBLICATION COLLECTION AND DEPOSITORY SYSTEM

54-2-1. Deposit by state agency. The state librarian shall determine the number of copies to be supplied by each state agency in accordance with the needs of the depository system, and shall inform each state agency on a quarterly basis as to any change in the number of copies needed. (Authorized by K.S.A. 1976 Supp. 75-2568; effective Feb. 15, 1977.)

54-2-2. Distribution of publications. The state library shall forward one (1) copy to each complete depository, and one (1) copy of each publication requested by each selective depository. (Authorized by K.S.A. 1976 Supp. 75-2568; effective Feb. 15, 1977.)

54-2-3. Complete depository library defined. Complete depository library as employed here shall mean any Kansas resource library, regional public library, libraries in institutions of higher education or other libraries that have contracted with the state librarian having agreed to receive one (1) copy of all publications, and agreeing to provide adequate facilities for the storage and use of any such publication, and agreeing to render reasonable service without charge to qualified patrons in the use of such publications, and agreeing to maintain that full collection of publications subject to disposal only upon approval by the state librarian, and agreeing to abide by other such provisions of the contract as stipulated by the state librarian. (Authorized by K.S.A. 1976 Supp. 75-2568; effective Feb. 15, 1977.)

54-2-4. Selective depository library defined. Selective depository library as here employed shall mean any Kansas resource library, regional public library, libraries in institutions of higher education or other libraries that have been designated by the state librarian as a selective depository, and have contracted with the state librarian agreeing to receive one (1) copy of all publications requested and agreeing to provide adequate facilities for storage and use of any such publications, and agreeing to render reasonable service without charge to qualified patrons in the use of such publications, and agreeing to maintain that collection subject to disposal upon approval by the state librarian, and agreeing to abide by such other provisions of the contract as stipulated by the state librarian. (Authorized by K.S.A. 1976 Supp. 75-2568; effective Feb. 15, 1977.)

54-2-5. Selection of publication by selective depositories. Request for publications by selective depositories shall be submitted in writing to the state librarian, and on proper forms provided by the state librarian. The written request for publication(s) must state the item number(s) of the publication(s) to be received by the selective depositories. (Authorized by K.S.A. 1976 Supp. 75-2568; effective Feb. 15, 1977.)

54-2-6. Item number. The state librarian shall assign each publication or group of publications a specific item number, and shall provide a list of such item numbers and the publication to which they correspond to each complete and selective depository library. Said list shall be revised on an annual basis. (Authorized by K.S.A. 1976 Supp. 75-2568; effective Feb. 15, 1977.)

54-2-7. Agency list of publications. Each state agency shall furnish to the state library a complete list of its publications for the previous year. (Authorized by K.S.A. 1976 Supp. 75-2568; effective Feb. 15, 1977.)

CONTRACT

CONTRACT # 1

THIS AGREEMENT, made and entered into this ___ _____ day of _____ _____, 19_____, at Topeka, Kansas, by and between the Kansas State Library and ___ _____ , an agency authorized to contract on behalf of _____
            (Name of Library)

WHEREAS, K.S.A. *75-2568*, authorized the State Library to contract with libraries seeking to be designated as select depositories.

NOW THEREFORE, _____
                                  (Name of Library)
hereby requests designation as a select depository and asks to be placed on the mailing list for publications requested by said library and distributed by the State Library.

In consideration of the distribution to ___ _____
                                                      (Name of Library)

of state publications as aforesaid library agrees throughout the term of this agreement to:

(1) Provide shelf space to house the collection in an approved manner with adequate provisions for expansion.

(2) Process and shelve all state publications within 30 days after receipt of the material.

(3) Provide a professionally trained librarian to render satisfactory service without charge to qualified patrons in the use of such publications.

(4) Dispose of publications only upon approval by the State Librarian.

(5) Permit the State Library to, at any reasonable time, inspect the facilities provided by the library for the storage and use of all state publications distributed to it under this agreement and that it will promptly apply any information which may be requested by the State Library in connection with the storage and use of such publications.

(6) Select at least 20% of all available item numbers.

This agreement may be terminated or amended by mutual consent in writing by both parties.

Publications received by _____

(Name of Library)

remain the property of the state of Kansas and upon termination of this contract the State Library will issue disposal instructions.

IN WITNESS WHEREOF, the parties have here unto set their hands the day and year first above written.

Kansas State Library
Director
By _____

_____ Library
By _____

EDITORIAL COMMENT

Contract #2, not reproduced, is the same as Contract #1, except for the substitution of the word "complete" for "select" and the omission of the requirement that 20 percent of all available items be selected.

BIBLIOGRAPHY

A news note in *Documents to the People* 6:105 (March 1978) lists future KLA-GODORT projects: (1) a directory of documents resources and collections in Kansas, (2) a Union List of documents microform holdings, and (3) a list of depository items received in depository libraries in Kansas.

The *KLA-GODORT Newsletter* in its pilot issue, October 1977, carried a five-page article by Marc Galbraith, Kansas Documents Librarian, titled "Kansas Documents System: Legislation and Implementation." Galbraith outlines the provisions of the

1976 law and related statutes. The article continues with notes on the nine depository libraries (all complete depositories), the compilation of a manual for depository libraries by a university class in state documents attended by most of the new depository librarians, the distribution procedure (some serials are to be sent directly from state agencies), and a description of the new *State Documents of Kansas Catalog* and *State Documents of Kansas Catalog Index.*

"Kansas State Publications." *See* issues of *Kansas Library Bulletin* 1947-1953. Palic, p. 104, says 1936 to 1952.

Wilder, B. E. "Author Headings for the Official Publications of the State of Kansas." Chicago: American Library Association, 1956. 136 p.

KENTUCKY

KY. REV. STAT. ANN. §§ 171.410, 171.450, 171.500 (Baldwin 1977)

STATE ARCHIVES AND RECORDS

171.410. Definitions for KRS 171.410 to 171.740. As used in KRS 171.410 to 171.740:

(1) "Records" means all books, papers, maps, photgraphs, and other documentary materials, regardless of physical form or characteristics, made or received by any agency of the state government in pursuance of the state law or in connection with the transaction of public business and preserved or appropriate for preservation by that agency or its legitimate successor as evidence of the organization, functions, policies, decisions, procedures, operations, or other activities of the government or because of the informational value of data contained therein.

(2) "Department" means the department of library and archives.

(3) "Commission" means the state archives and records commission. (HISTORY: 1974, S 112, Art VIII, B, § 2, eff. 6-21-74; 1970 S 153, § 32; 1966 c 255, § 159; 1962 c 106, Art V § 2; 1958 c 49, § 1.)

171.450. Department procedures and regulations.

(1) The department shall establish:
****

(d) Procedures for collection and distribution by the central depository of all reports and publications, except the Kentucky Revised Statutes editions, issued by any department, board, commission, officer or other agency of the Commonwealth for general public distribution after July 1, 1958.

(2) The department shall enforce the provisions of KRS 171.410 to 171.740 by appropriate rules and regulations.

(3) The department shall make copies of such rules and regulations available to all officials affected by KRS 171.410 to 171.740 subject to the provisions of KRS Chapter 13.

(4) It is intended that such rules and regulations be drawn in cooperation with the various state agencies and subdivisions. Such rules and regulations when

approved by the department shall be binding on all state and local agencies, subject to the provisions of KRS Chapter 13. The department shall perform any acts deemed necessary, legal and proper to carry out the duties and responsibilities imposed upon it pursuant to the authority granted herein. (HISTORY: 1970 S 153 § 34, eff. 6-18-70; 1958, c 49, § 5.)

171.500. Central depository. The department is hereby constituted the central depository for public records. It shall be the duty of all departments, boards, commissions, officers or other agencies of the Commonwealth to supply to the central depository copies of each of their reports and publications issued for general public distribution after July 1, 1958, in the number and in the manner prescribed by rule or regulation promulgated by the department pursuant to KRS 171.450. College, university, and public libraries may be constituted depository libraries by written order of the department. The central depository shall supply copies to such depository libraries in the number and in the manner prescribed by rule or regulation promulgated by the department pursuant to KRS 171.450. (HISTORY: 1970 S 153, § 38, eff. 6-18-70; 1958 c 49, § 10.)

STATE COMMENT (January 1973)

Please note 171.450 (d), 171.500, Rules and Regulations ARC-PD-1 and ARC-RPR-1 5a as pertains to the deposit of records.

The State Archives and Records Commission has requested the Records Management Advisory Committee to meet with Library representatives of each of the State Universities to try to reach a solution to the problem of publications distribution to each of the records depositories. Hopefully they can make a recommendation that will be workable and satisfactory.

Our present method is not working as well as we would like, since many of the State Agencies do not deposit their publications with us unless requested and we have no way of knowing that we are getting all of their publications.

We are presently having all of the State Publications each year microfilmed at the University of Kentucky and the microfilm copy of these documents can be purchased from the University of Kentucky for approximately $8.00 per reel. This would probably be the best solution for most Universities to purchase the microfilm rather than obtain the hard copies if space is a problem.

I hope the above information will be helpful to you and we welcome any suggestions you might have on the distribution of State documents. We will be glad to give you when available a copy of the Records Management Committee recommendations and based on their recommendations we will probably amend our present Rules and Regulations to our Statutes. (Letter from Howard T. Goodpaster, Director, Division of Archives and Records, Department of Finance, Frankfort, Kentucky 40601, dated January 4, 1973. *In* Documents on Documents Collection.)

STATE COMMENT (December 1973)

I am enclosing a copy of the recommendations of the Records Management Advisory Committee on the distribution of State Documents. We have held in abeyance our putting these recommendations in the form of revised Rules and Regulations to KRS 171.500 pending final action by the Legislature on State Reorganization. We were formerly under the Department of Finance and we are now under the Department of Libraries by Executive Order of the Governor, pending final approval by the legislature.

I will send you a copy of the Rules and Regulations to KRS 171.500 which will implement most of the recommendations of the Records Management Advisory Committee to the State Archives and Records Commission. (Letter from Howard T. Goodpaster, Director, Division of Archives and Records, Department of Libraries, Frankfort, Kentucky 40601, dated December 11, 1973. *In* Documents on Documents Collection.)

EDITORIAL COMMENT

In 1958, an act relating to state archives and records was adopted (1958, ch. 49) and a commission established. The sections of particular interest are § 1 (which became 171.410 and defined ''records''), § 5 (which became 171.450 and mandated the establishment of a procedure for the collection and distribution of all reports and publications), and § 10 (which became 171.500 and required the state agencies to deposit copies of their publications, the creation of depository libraries, and supplying of copies of the publications to the depository libraries as prescribed by a rule to be promulgated).

In 1962, the functions of the State Archives and Records Service were assigned to the Department of Finance (1962, ch. 106, Art. V, § 1).

In 1966, an act to revise and correct the Kentucky Revised Statutes (1966, ch. 255, § 159) made minor editorial changes. This act restated the provisions of the 1962 Act for 171.410(2).

In 1970 (1970 ch. 92, § 32), a definition for ''Commission'' was added to 171.410 as subsection 3. In the same act, ''Commission'' was changed to ''Department'' in 171.450, and ''Archives and Records Service'' was changed to ''Department'' in 171.500, and so on.

In 1974, a reorganization act (1974, ch. 74, p. 76) transferred the archives and records functions to the Department of Libraries and redesignated that agency as ''Department of Library and Archives.''

RULES AND REGULATIONS

725 KAR 1:040. COLLECTION AND DISTRIBUTION OF REPORTS AND PUBLICATIONS.
RELATES TO KRS 171.500
PURSUANT TO: KRS 171.450

NECESSITY AND FUNCTION: KRS 171.450 requires the department to establish procedures for collection and distribution by the central depository of all reports and publications issued by any department, board, commission, officer or other agency of the Commonwealth for general public distribution.

Section 1. The designated records officer of each agency or department of state government is responsible for depositing each month with the Department of Library and Archives, Division of Archives and Records, three (3) copies of all reports and publications issued by his agency for general public distribution. Reports and publications as used in this regulation shall be construed in the broadest sense to include typed, printed, mimeographed, and multilithed publications. In case of doubt by any records officer as to whether a particular publication or report constitutes a publication or report, the records officer should consult with the Director, Division of Archives and Records, and work out a mutual agreement.

Section 2. For purposes of retrieval, each specific edition of each publication title included in a specific edition of the Checklist of Kentucky State Publications shall have a number assigned by the Department of Libraries and Archives, to be called the official number of the publication, consisting of the last two (2) digits of the year of inclusion of that publication in that checklist followed by the publication's assigned number within that checklist. (2 Ky. R. 536; eff. 6-2-76.)

BIBLIOGRAPHY

Three articles by Kentuckians were located. Two, those by Gronbeck and by Van Horne, (annotated in the general bibliography), are about state documents in general and are not limited to Kentucky documents. The 1974 article by Richardson deals with Kentucky documents only. An old thesis (Stutsman, E. B. "Historical Development from 1792 to 1936 in the Printed Document of Kentucky, with a View to Their Cataloging," M.S. Thesis, Columbia University, 1944, 94p. (not seen) is listed in *Library Literature*.

Richardson, John V., Jr. "Kentucky Publishes More Documents of Importance."
    Kentucky Library Association Bulletin 38:5-8 (Spring 1974).
"... state publications are a unique source for matters of public record...." Richardson discusses about a dozen of the "most useful" documents in an entertaining, enthusiastic, and helpful way.

LOUISIANA

LA. REV. STAT. ANN. §§ 25:121-124 (West 1975), 36: 209(I)
(West Spec. Pam. 1980)

CHAPTER 2. DEPOSITORIES FOR PUBLIC DOCUMENTS

§ **121. State and other libraries as depositories of public records**. The Louisiana State Library shall be the depository for the printed or mimeographed public records issued by any government agency for public distribution. The libraries of colleges or universities and public libraries located in the state may also become depositories of these records when designated as such by the secretary of state upon their written request to this effect. (Source: Acts 1948, No. 493, § 1.)

§ **122. Distribution of records to depositories; public inspection**. All agencies of state government shall furnish to the secretary of state sufficient copies of each record mentioned in R. S. 25:121 and the secretary of state shall deliver to each depository two copies of the same. These records shall be made accessible by the depository receiving them to any person desiring to examine the same. (Source: Acts 1948, No. 493, § 1.)

§ **123. List of publications; distribution to depositories**. Each agency of state government shall furnish to the secretary of state semiannually a list of all its printed and mimeographed publications issued for public distribution, and the secretary of state shall make and furnish to each depository a duplicate copy of the same. (Source: Acts 1948, No. 493, § 2.)

§ **124. Recorder of documents; appointment; duties**. A recorder of documents shall be appointed by the secretary of state in his office, who shall be preferably a graduate librarian and whose functions shall be to administer the provisions of R. S. 25:122 and 25:123 under the supervision of the secretary of state. (Source: Acts 1948, No. 493, § 3, 4.)

36:209. Transfer of boards, commissions, departments, and agencies to Department of Culture, Recreation and Tourism
****

I. The functions of the secretary of state related to the deposit and distribution of public documents as provided in R. S. 25:121 through R. S. 25:124 are transferred to the secretary of the Department of Culture, Recreation and Tourism and hereafter shall be exercised and performed through the office of the state library as provided in Part II of Chapter 22 of this Title and other applicable provisions of law. (Acts 1976, No. 513, § 1. Amended by Acts 1977, No. 83, § 1, effective June 22, 1977).

STATE COMMENT (1973)

Special features of the Louisiana law:

1) The original act, Act 493 of 1948, included an appropriation. For many years, until 1968, the appropriation was carried as a separate line item in the General Appropriations Act.

2) The provision requiring the state agencies to furnish copies of their publications is flexible and specifics "sufficient copies."

3) The requirement that the state agencies furnish semi-annually a list of their publications is helpful because it results in regular contact with each state agency. The Recorder sends out a report form to be returned.

4) The list of documents is required by the law. Lucy B. Foote, to whom Louisiana is indebted for its 1803-1948 bibliographic record, was particularly gratified to know that her work would continue. The legal requirement for the list is an important safeguard.

Amendments which should be considered:

1) Out-of-state exchange libraries. We do not have out-of-state depositories now except for the Library of Congress and the Center for Research Libraries. The establishment of exchange libraries rather than depository libraries in other states and provision for wider out-of-state distribution are desirable. At least the law should be amended to eliminate the "in the state" as it applies to depositories, particularly since this phrase was added when the act was incorporated in the Revised Statutes.

2) Selective depositories. We have had selective depositories for many years because it is wasteful to send publications which cannot be used in the libraries. The law could be amended to specify "as many as two copies, as required by the library."

3) Number of copies for each library. Consideration should be given to the advisability of continuing to distribute two copies of each publication to the libraries. Perhaps the needs of the libraries would be met if only the historical depositories were entitled to receive two copies.

4) Historical collection depositories. We do not have any regulations for weeding and the establishment of historical collection depositories is a safeguard. The Secretary of State has designated two historical depositories, but their status is not recognized in the law.

5) "Issued for public distribution." This phrase has always been interpreted to mean public, as distinguished from inter-office, or confidential, distribution. It has been suggested that it might be interpreted restrictively to include only publications issued for distribution to the public at large; that is, publications issued for the purpose of public distribution. Such an interpretation would exclude publications which are available to the public on request, such as the *Rules* of the Senate. Perhaps a definition of "state publication" should be included in the law in lieu of this phrase. (Commentary from Margaret T. Lane, Recorder of Documents, Secretary of State's Office, Baton Rouge, Louisiana. *In* Documents on Documents Collection.)

STATE COMMENT (1976)

The depository library system for state documents in Louisiana was established by Act 493 of 1948, the result of legislative interest by librarians in the Louisiana Library Association, and the support of then Secretary of State Wade O. Martin, Jr. Thus in the Revised Statutes (Title 25, sections 121-124), for the first time systematic distribution of documents was provided. (Ed. note. New legislation introduced in 1976, which would permit formal out-of-state distribution, did not pass.) (Report by Patricia Foster, Recorder of Documents, Baton Rouge, Louisiana. *In* The State of State Documents: Past, Present, Future. Texas Legislative Reference Library, 1976, at p. 12.)

EDITORIAL COMMENT

The reporter's notes on the revision of the Louisiana statutes in 1950 provide background information on the Louisiana depository law. The reporter's summaries are on deposit at the law school libraries at Tulane, Loyola, and Louisiana State University.

The first summary was done on the basis of the law as it existed prior to the 1948 legislative session and was based on Act 82 of 1928. In reference to the first section, the reporter said, "This provision supersedes Section 2184 of the Revised Statutes of 1870 . . . under which all books and documents of every description belonging to the State were required to be deposited with the old State Library at New Orleans." He made no changes in the 1928 law except to substitute the new name of the Louisiana State Library, which was formerly named the Louisiana Library Commission.

The sections were revised after the adoption of the 1948 depository law. The reporter's notes say:

In this Chapter was originally included Act 82 of 1928 (R. S. 26:121-26:123) which constituted as depositories of public records the Louisiana Library Commission (Louisiana State Library) and the library of every state college and university in Louisiana.

This Act has been impliedly repealed by Act 493 of 1948 which designates as the depository of public records, the Louisiana State Library, and permits other libraries to become such upon request being made to the Secretary of State.The provisions of Act 493 of 1948 will, therefore, be incorporated in place of the previous statute.

NOTE: Act 493 of 1948 has been re-drafted for editorial reasons. It was originally in the following language. [Omitted.]

The rewritten version of the foregoing statute follows:

121. STATE AND OTHER LIBRARIES AS DEPOSITORIES OF PUBLIC RECORDS. [Text of section and source note omitted.]

NOTE: It is evident that the Act is limited to apply to those printed or mimeographed materials which are issued by state agencies for public distribution and that it does not include any other public record or document. It is also evident that the college and public libraries contemplated are those located in the State, and that they may request to be constituted depositories, but shall not become such until so designated by the Secretary of State.

122. DISTRIBUTION OF RECORDS TO DEPOSITORIES: PUBLIC INSPECTION. [Text of section and source note omitted.]

NOTE: It is clear that the duty to make these records accessible to persons interested in them rests with the depository, after these records have been received. It is unnecessary to limit the application of the statute to the records after August 1, 1948.

The provisions requiring replacement of records lost in transit become unnecessary if the duty of the Secretary of State is to deliver rather than to furnish.

123. LISTS OF PUBLICATIONS: DISTRIBUTION TO DEPOSITORIES. [Text of section and source note omitted.]

NOTE: The Secretary of State cannot be charged with the duty of delivering copies of these lists to the depositories until he has received an original list from the state agencies. Since he only receives one copy from the State agencies, and he has to furnish two copies to each depository, it necessary [sic] follows that he must make these copies for delivery.

124. RECORDER OF DOCUMENTS: APPOINTMENT; DUTIES. [Text of section and source note omitted.]

NOTE: It is clear that the administrative duties conferred on the recorder pertain only to the duties imposed upon the Secretary of State by R. S. 26:122 and 123, respectively. The Appropriation measure in Section 4 of the original Act has been omitted as executed; it does not fix the compensation of the Recorder but merely requires that the money be spent to pay the salary of the Recorder and to defray the expense of distribution, etc. Since no salary provisions are found in the Act, none was inserted.

CONTRACT

DESIGNATION OF DEPOSITORY FOR PUBLIC DOCUMENTS

December _____, 1948

Hon. Wade O. Martin, Jr.
Secretary of State
Baton Rouge, Louisiana
Dear Mr. Martin:
The Library designated hereunder, through its duly constituted Librarian, hereby requests that said library be constituted a Depository for Public Documents in accordance with the provisions of Act No. 493 of the Regular Session of 1948 in order that it might receive the documents contemplated by said act.

_____
Library
By: _____
Librarian

EDITORIAL COMMENT

The form is in duplicate on an 8½ × 11'' page.

ATTORNEY GENERAL OPINIONS

1946 LA. ATT'Y GEN. OP. AND REP. 768
PUBLIC RECORDS

Libraries of all colleges and universities of the state maintained by public funds are depositories of public documents under Act 82 of 1928.

May 2, 1946

Mr. Eugene P. Watson, Librarian,
Northwestern State College,
Natchitoches, Louisiana.

Your letter of May 1, addressed to the Attorney General, with reference to the introduction into the Legislature of a bill establishing certain libraries of the state as depositories of public records, has been referred to the writer for attention.

Act 82 of 1928 presently establishes the Louisiana Library Commission and the library of every college and university of the state maintained by taxation as depositories of public documents, section 1 and 3 of that act providing as follows:

> The policy of collecting, preserving, and making accessible to students, and others interested in public records, all printed matter and source material relating to the governmental functions of the state, throughout its history, is hereby declared a public duty, the performance of which requires the establishment of depositories for the acquisition, custody, and administration of these archives. To accomplish this purpose the Louisiana library commission and the library of every college and university in the state, maintained by taxation, are hereby constituted depositories for the public documents printed and distributed by any officer, board, department, court, or other agency of government, in the state of Louisiana, and it is hereby made the duty of the librarian in charge of every library, functioning as a depository of public documents under the provisions of this act, to acquire therefor the records and printed matter herein provided for.
>
> It shall be the duty of every department, board, officer, or other public agency in this state responsible for the printing and distribution of the laws, decisions, reports, ordinances, or other public documents, included in the purpose of this act to supply each library, hereby made a depository of public documents, with two copies of every printed document issued thereby and to replace any losses or miscarriages in the transportation of such documents.

There could be no objection whatever to amending this act so as to make all libraries maintained by public funds as depositories, and we see no particular objection of conferring similar rights upon Tulane University. While that institution is not maintained by public funds, it does to some extent have the quasi public standing, its services being generally available to the public.

As a matter of fact, under Article 2194 of the Revised Statutes, Article 4476 of Dart's Louisiana General Statutes, the Fisk Free Library, Howard Memorial Library and other public libraries in Louisiana are authorized to receive copies of the acts of the legislature. Under Revised Statutes 2197, Dart's Louisiana General Statutes 4479, the Secretary of State is authorized to make exchanges of various public documents with the governors of other states.

We might suggest that before preparing any legislation you examine Act 82 of 1928, since it is possible that an amendment of section 1 of that act so as to include additional libraries may be sufficient to accomplish the results desired.

ROBERT R. REID

1956/58 LA. ATT'Y GEN. REP. AND OP. 682
PUBLIC RECORDS

Only public libraries designated by the Secretary of State as official depositories must retain public records received by them from the Secretary of State or his Recorder of Documents.

April 3, 1957

Miss Essae Martha Culver
State Librarian
Louisiana State Library
Post Office Box 131
Baton Rouge, Louisiana

Receipt of your letter dated March 26, 1957, requesting an opinion in regard to the responsibilities of parish libraries under R. S. 25:121-124 to retain documents which are forwarded thereto by the Recorder of Documents and Office of the Secretary of State, is hereby acknowledged.

Under R. S. 25:121, any public library within the State may become a depository of public records when designated as such by the Secretary of State upon its written request to be so designated.

Should a parish library become a depository of public records through the procedure above stated, it becomes the responsibility of that library to retain all documents forwarded thereto by the Secretary of State or his Recorder of Documents in order that these public records can be made accessible to the public. (R. S. 25:122-123).

If a parish library has not become a depository under the procedure as above stated, it is not under a duty to act in that capacity and may dispose of documents forwarded thereto by the Secretary of State or his Recorder of Documents, within its discretion.

Jack P. F. Gremillion

1962 LA. ATT'Y GEN. OP. October 8, 1962, (unpublished)

October 8, 1962

Mr. Eugene P. Watson
Librarian
Northwestern State College of Louisiana
Natchitoches, Louisiana

Dear Mr. Watson:

Your letter dated September 27, 1962, addressed to the Attorney General has been referred to me for attention and answer. Also, I spoke with you on October 4th, relative to the contents of your letter and other matters concerning the application of RS25:121 through 125.

From your letter and our subsequent conversation, you posed the following question for answer by this office:

May a public depository destroy certain public records that have been forwarded to them by the Recorder of Documents, where such destruction is necessary for the conservation of space and other economical reasons.

Under the provisions of R. S. 25:122, a library having been designated as a depository, must make the public records so deposited accessible to any person desiring to examine them.

R. S. 34:36 provides that all persons having custody or control of any public records other than conveyances, probates, mortgages, or other permanent records, required by existing law, to be kept for all time, shall preserve such public record for at least six (6) years from the date on which the public record was made. In view of this provision, this office is of the opinion that you must preserve the public records on deposit in your library, for at least a period of six years. After that period of time has elapsed, you may destroy any public record other than those designated above, which are required to be kept for all time.

This office, in an opinion under the date of June 19, 1962, addressed to the Honorable Raymond H. Downs, had occasion to examine the statutes providing for microfilming of public records. Upon reading and following the expressions contained in that opinion, if such equipment is available to you, this, in itself, will enable you to conserve much storage space. A copy of the opinion is enclosed for your information.

We trust that the above satisfactorily answers your question; however, if any further problem remains, please do not hesitate to address same to our attention.

Sincerely,
Thomas W. McFerrin
Special Counsel

BIBLIOGRAPHY

Historical Records Survey. *Bibliography of the Official Publications of Louisiana, 1803-1934.* Compiled by Lucy B. Foote. New Orleans, The Survey, 1942. (American Imprints Inventory, no. 19.)

Campbell, Ruth. "Selected List of Recent Louisiana State Documents." *Louisiana Library Bulletin* 9:90-93 (March 1946).
An annotated list.

Foote, Lucy B. *Author Headings for the Official Publications of the State of Louisiana.* Chicago: American Library Association, 1948. 125 p.
Supplemented by lists in: Louisiana. Department of State. *Public Documents.*

"Louisiana Depository Libraries." *Louisiana Library Association Bulletin* 12:13 (November 1948).
A very brief announcement of the passage of the depository library act (Act 493, 1948). Libraries desiring depository status should send a formal request to the Secretary of State. All depository libraries will be complete, as no provision can be made for selective depositories. A semiannual list will be issued.

Martin, W. O., Jr. "New State Publications." *Louisiana Library Association Bulletin* 15:44-46 (Spring 1952).
A list.

Hesseltine, W. B. "Return of Louisiana Documents." *Library Quarterly* 23:284-286 (October 1953).
Records, not publications.

Tilger, Ellen R. "Louisiana Documents: They're Free—and Easy." *Bulletin of the Louisiana Library Association* 20:123-126 (Summer 1957).

"[I]t should be a matter of professional pride that we live and work in one of the two states with organized state depository libraries, the other state being California." A complete depository receives 350 pieces per month. Preparation time is sixteen to twenty hours per month—stamping, assigning shelving symbol, marking the piece, entering symbol on monthly list, posting the shelf list, and shelving. A classification scheme, based on the principles of the superintendent of documents scheme, is outlined.

Lane, Margaret T. "Cards with Documents." *Louisiana Library Association Bulletin* 26:59-60 (Summer 1963).

Describes an experimental card distribution service for depository libraries. The final report on this program is found in *Louisiana Library Association Bulletin* 27:31 (Spring 1964), with the comment that the service was supplanted by the distribution of LC cards.

A further expansion of the LC card distribution program was reported in the *Louisiana Library Association Bulletin* 30:79 (Summer 1967) when a plan for ordering pre-1964 cards for 534 document titles on a wholesale basis was announced.

Louisiana Library Association, Documents Committee. *Documents in Louisiana: People, Places, Publications.* [Baton Rouge, La., 1975?] 72 p.

Both U.S. and state data; some international, foreign, and local data. Includes lists of depository libraries, documents resources by library and by subject, tools prepared in Louisiana and, for nine tools prepared at the national level, the Louisiana libraries that owned them (or were or were not ordering them), documents committee members, and so on.

Owen, Delores. "Revision of State Documents Depository Law Proposed." *Louisiana Library Association Bulletin* 38:87-90 (Winter 1976).

Gives a brief history of the adoption of the 1948 law, the reasons for seeking a revision of the law, and the provisions of the committee draft.

"The proposed revision would be intended to establish a firm base for the continuance of the procedures [for administering the law] as they have evolved and would include provisions for partial depositories, and wide distribution of the documents." The recommendations of the "Guidelines for Minimum State Servicing of State Documents" have long been followed in Louisiana, except for service to out-of-state users, and that service along with all the others mentioned in the "Guidelines" is incorporated in the committee's proposal.

The committee's draft begins with a policy statement and definitions. The duties of state agencies remain the same, except for a requirement that additional copies be furnished to provide for out-of-state distribution. New authority and new duties are outlined for the recorder—the obligation to make rules and regulations, and to provide bibliographical and practical assistance to the depositories. Authorization is given to maintain a working collection, to provide documents in microformat, and to request copies of publications for exchange programs.

The requirement for a list of publications is continued, but the list is designated the "Official List" and is to include order information.

The historical depositories are provided for in the proposed law, as is a new type of depository which will receive a preselected group of publications.

MAINE

ME. REV. STAT. ANN. tit. 1, §§ 501, 501-A (West Supp. 1978)

§ **501. State agency defined.** As used in this subchapter, the word "agency" shall mean a state department, agency, office, board, commission; or quasi-independent agency, board, commission, authority or institution. (1975, c. 436, § 1.)

§ **501-A. Publications of state agencies.** The publications of all agencies and the University of Maine and the Maine Maritime Academy may be printed, bound and distributed, subject to Title 5, sections 43 through 46. The State Purchasing Agent may determine the style in which such publications may be printed and bound, with the approval of the Governor. At least 55 copies of any annual or biennial report not included in the Maine State Government Annual Report provided for in Title 5, sections 43 through 46, shall be delivered to the State Librarian, immediately upon receipt by the State Purchasing Agent for exchange and library use; the balance of the number of each such report shall be delivered by the State Purchasing Agent to the agency preparing the report. At least 18 copies of all other publications, including periodicals, bulletins, pamphlets, leaflets and special reports issued by any agency or by any legislative committee shall be delivered to the State Librarian. The agency or committee preparing a publication shall have the authority to determine the date on which a publication may be released, except as may be otherwise provided by law. (1975, c. 436, § 2; 1975, c. 746, § 1, effective April 12, 1976.)

STATE COMMENT

We have no regulations for our depository libraries in the State. (Letter from Sharon Hanley, Documents Librarian, Maine State Library, Augusta, Maine 04330, dated December 31, 1979.)

EDITORIAL COMMENT

Section 501 in the 1954 R. S. had substantially the provisions that are now in § 501-A. A 1955 amendment to § 501 (1955 Me. Acts, c. 185) amended the fourth sentence to reduce the number of copies from 175 to 80. § 501 was repealed in 1975 and replaced by a new section 501, which defines "agency." § 501-A was enacted in 1975 (c. 436). An act of the same legislative session (1975, c. 746) substituted "55" for "80" in the third sentence.

The new § 501-A retains the provision of the old § 501 for copies of annual reports to be delivered to the state librarian but eliminates "general distribution" after "exchange and library use." The new 501-A also retains the sentence requiring delivery of "all other publications" and increases the number of copies from 10 to 18.

Thus, the number of copies of reports to be delivered to the state librarian was reduced from 175 in 1954 to 80 in 1955, and then to 55 in 1975. The number of copies of all other publications was increased from 10 in 1954 to 18 in 1975.

The 1975 law (1975 Me. Acts, c. 436), in addition to enacting sections 501 and 501-A, repealed and reenacted tit. 5, § 43 (annual reports of state agencies) and provided for 55 copies to be delivered to the state librarian.

BIBLIOGRAPHY

Kirkwood, Richard E. "Suggestions for Classifying Official Maine Publications." *Maine Library Association Bulletin* 27:3-4 (August 1966).
The scheme is similar to that of the superintendent of documents.

MARYLAND

MD. ANN. CODE art. 23A, § 9A; art. 25, § 32A (Michie Supp. 1979); art. 40, §§ 51, 53 (Michie 1978 & Supp. 1979)

Art. 23A, § 9A. Deposit with State agencies. (a) *Documents to be deposited with State agencies.*—Whenever the mayor and city council, by whatever name known, of any municipal corporation in this State (as defined in § 9(a) of this article) causes, or is required to cause any of the following documents to be created, implemented or otherwise established, the respective documents shall be deposited with the State agencies, and in the manner, as prescribed by subsection (b) of this section.

(1) A code or compilation containing all or a portion of the municipal charter. . . .

(2) A charter amendment. . . .

(3) A complete list of the measures which enact, amend, or repeal sections in the municipal charter. . . .

(4) A charter amendment, ordinance, referendum or any other device by which the corporate boundaries of the municipality are enlarged or otherwise changed. . . .

(5) A unified charter providing for the merger of two or more municipal corporations. . . .

(6) A charter providing for the creation of a new municipal corporation. . . .

(7) A charter amendment providing for the entire repeal of the charter of a municipal corporation. . . .

(8) In addition to the document and referenda enumerated elsewhere in this subsection, a statement on the results of any referendum on any proposed charter amendment held during the year, and any referendum pending, actually or potentially, but not yet held, at the end of the year; as provided for in § 17A(d) of this article.

(b) *Agencies to which copies to be sent by registered mail.*—The mayor or other chief executive officer, by whatever name known, of each municipal corporation shall send, or cause to be sent, separately by registered mail one copy of each of the documents, as appropriate, enumerated in subsection (a) of this section to the Department of Legislative Reference, to the Secretary of State of Maryland, to the Hall of Records Commission and to the State Law Library.

(c) *Documents ineffective until registered.*—Unless the penalty for failure to comply with the provisions of this subtitle is contained elsewhere in this article, a document or other material required to be filed by this article is not effective, and may not be applied or considered as in effect, unless and until it has been registered as provided by this subtitle. (1976, ch. 628, § 2; 1979, ch. 619.)

Art. 25, § 32A. Deposit of copies with State agencies. Whenever the board of county commissioners or county council of any county in this State publishes or issues in printed, mimeographed or similar duplicated form a code or compilation containing all or a portion of the public local laws, of the county, the board or council shall deposit copies free of charge with the following State agencies: Hall of Records Commission, one copy; State Law Library, one copy; State Department of Legislative Reference, five copies. (1960, ch. 96, § 2; 1966, ch. 571, § 5; 1979, ch. 619.)

Art. 40, § 51. Enumeration of Director's duties; current list of Public Local Laws; distribution of laws and journals; reports and publications of State agencies and officials.

****

(c) The Department [of Legislative Reference] shall distribute bound copies of the laws and journals of the General Assembly. The distribution shall include one copy of the laws and journals to each public circulating library or library association which applies therefor, if at the time of application there are more than 25 copies of the particular volume in the Department's supply. The distribution also may include sale or exchange of the laws and journals.

(d) Each State agency or official shall provide to the Department of Legislative Reference a list of all reports and publications issued by them which are either required by law or intended by them for distribution to the General Assembly. The Department shall compile and maintain a list of all these reports and publications and shall periodically forward these lists to the members of the General Assembly for the purpose of furnishing them a reference source from which they may request reports and publications from the Department of Legislative Reference. In addition, the Department shall preserve, catalogue, and index all reports and publications filed with or submitted to the Department by the various State agencies and officials in compliance with either the requirement of § 53 of this article or the requirements of numerous sections elsewhere in the Code; and may select, preserve, catalogue, and index other reports and publications it deems necessary.

(e) The Department of Legislative Reference shall accept requests for reports and publications from members of the General Assembly and shall obtain those materials from the appropriate agency and distribute them to the members.

****

(An. Code, 1951, art. 41, § 119; 1939, art. 41, § 101; 1924, art. 41, § 65; 1916, ch. 474, § 1; 1966, ch. 571, §§ 1, 7; 1969, ch. 543; 1975, ch. 95, § 2; 1977, ch. 689.)

Art. 40, § 53. Copies of reports and other publications filed with Director, certain libraries, Hall of Records, county agencies and Baltimore department of legislative reference. It is the duty of every officer, board, institution and commission of the State, including special or temporary officers, boards and commissions, to file with the Department of Legislative Reference two copies of every regular or special report, bulletin, periodical, catalog and other publication issued by him or it, whether the report is in printed or other form, and also to file with the State Law Library, the Hall of Records, the McKeldin Library of the University of Maryland, the Enoch Pratt Free Library (central branch), an agency of the respective counties designated by their governing bodies, and the department of legislative reference of Baltimore City, at least one copy of the report or other publication. (An. Code, 1951, art. 41, § 121; 1939, art. 41, § 103; 1924, art. 41, § 67; 1924, ch. 377; 1935, ch. 150; 1947, ch. 7, § 103; ch. 651; 1966, ch. 571, § 7; 1968, ch. 174; 1972, ch. 582; 1973, ch. 340; 1979, ch. 619.)

STATE COMMENT

There is currently no central distribution system for publications issued by the various Maryland agencies, departments, commissions, etc. There is, however, a very ineffective law, Article 40, sec. 53 of the Annotated Code of Maryland, which provides that each agency will file, with a number of designated libraries, copies of their publications. A number of the depository libraries and the State Archives currently issue periodic checklists of publications received from the agencies, but no one library is acting as the central repository and therefore there is little incentive for the publication producing agencies to comply with the law. There is a tremendous duplication of effort, lack of bibliographic standardization, and non-compliance with the present law which we hope will be rectified later this year, once a recently appointed Governor's Task Force on State Documents makes its recommendations for improving the system of collecting, distributing, and making accessible the various State and local government publications in Maryland. (Letter from Michael S. Miller, Director, Maryland State Law Library, Annapolis, Maryland 21401, dated January 2, 1980.)

EDITORIAL COMMENT

The most recent amendments to art. 40, § 53 make these changes: 1972, ch. 582 added the McKeldin Library and the Enoch Pratt Library; 1973, ch. 340 added "an agency of the respective counties designated by their governing bodies, and the department of legislative reference of Baltimore City''; and

1979, ch. 619 changed ''State Library'' to ''State Law Library.'' The 1979 act also amended Art. 23A, § 9A and Art. 25, § 32A in the same way.

Art. 23A, § 8B on the deposit of municipal codes with the Hall of Records, State Library and State Department of Legislative Reference (originally enacted in 1960 and amended in 1966 to clarify the distinction between the state and the Baltimore departments of legislative reference) was repealed by 1976 Acts, ch. 628, § 1, effective July 1, 1976. Art. 25, § 32A, the section on county codes, was also amended by the 1966 act which amended the section on municipal codes.

RELATED LEGISLATION

Senate Joint Resolution No. 35 (1979)
Resolution No. 19
Senate Joint Resolution
A Senate Joint Resolution concerning
Task Force on Documents
FOR the purpose of requesting the Governor to create a Task Force to study and evaluate the system of collecting, distributing, and making accessible various State and local government publications and reports; and suggesting the composition of the Task Force.

WHEREAS, The General Assembly recognizes the necessity of providing better citizen access to publications and reports generated by State and local government agencies; and

WHEREAS, The existing statutory authority for the distribution of government publications is inadequate to assure widespread access to much of the printed information produced by our governmental units; and

WHEREAS, There is a great need to improve the acquisition, distribution, and preservation of these State and local documents by libraries, archives, and government agencies; and

WHEREAS, A study and evaluation of the present system of publication, public awareness, distribution, and dissemination of State and local documents would result in recommendations for increased efficiency, affecting both government agencies and citizens; now, therefore, be it

RESOLVED BY THE GENERAL ASSEMBLY OF MARYLAND, That the Governor is requested to create a Task Force on Government Publications and Reports to study possible improvements of the present system of collecting, distributing, and making accessible various State and local government documents, and be it further

RESOLVED, That the Task Force shall consist of the Governor or his designee, one member of the House of Delegates, one member of the Senate of Maryland, one representative of the Division of Library Development and

Services of the State Department of Education, one representative of each State Depository Library and Agency as specified in Article 40 Section 53 of the Annotated Code of Maryland, one representative of the Division of State Documents, and at least four members of the general public who are concerned with the quality of library services in this State; and be it further

RESOLVED, That a copy of this Resolution be sent to the Honorable Harry Hughes.

EDITORIAL COMMENT

Amendments made to the Joint Resolution during the legislative process were the addition of ''or his designee'' for the governor, and ''one representative of the Division of State Documents.''

BIBLIOGRAPHY

Litsinger, Elizabeth C. ''Collecting Maryland State Documents.'' *Between Librarians* 10:9-11 (October 1943).
Enoch Pratt Library has been collecting state documents for fifteen years. The aim is an all-inclusive collection and even more extensive bibliography, using a broad definition of documents. Acquisition methods for current and older documents are outlined. Sources checked for the bibliography are listed. The appendix gives legal provisions for Maryland document distribution.

Litsinger, Elizabeth. ''Maryland State Documents of 1950 and 1951: A Selected List.'' *Between Librarians* 18:13-15 (Spring 1952).
A list, omitting annual reports and most serial publications.

Enoch Pratt Free Library, Maryland Department. ''Maryland State Documents Mid 1953-Mid 1954.'' *Between Librarians* 21:13-16 (Winter 1954-1955).
A list of documents alphabetically arranged by personal and corporate authors.

''Maryland State Documents: A Selected List.'' *See* issues of *Maryland Libraries*, 1965-1969.

MASSACHUSETTS

MASS. ADMINISTRATIVE BULLETIN 76-5, May 12, 1976
TO: ALL AGENCY HEADS
RE: DEPOSIT OF STATE AGENCY PUBLICATIONS WITH
STATE LIBRARIAN

In the interest of freedom of information and to insure that the State Library receives all of the current publications of the agencies of the Commonwealth, agency heads are directed to give immediate attention to compliance with the following deposit rule.

DEPOSIT RULE

Every state agency receiving, issuing, or distributing a publication as defined below shall provide the State Librarian with no less than eight copies of each such publication; three of which will be made available for public consultation in the library and for permanent historical preservation by the library. The State Librarian will distribute the other copies provided to the Library of Congress and to each of the regional public libraries in the state as defined by General Laws, Chapter 78, Section 19C.

Each issuing agency shall take full cognizance of this requirement when contracting for the number of copies to be produced of any publication.

The required copies shall be forwarded to the State Librarian no later than five working days after they are received by the agency from the printer or contractor.

''Publication'' is to be defined for the purposes of this Deposit Rule as follows:

''Publication,'' any document, study, report, directory, rule, regulation, pamphlet, brochure, periodical or newsletter or other printed material regardless of its format or manner of duplication or printing paid for by funds appropriated by the General Court, issued in the name of or at the request of any agency of the Commonwealth, or produced and issued as part of a contract entered into by any agency of the Commonwealth regardless of the source of funding, excepting correspondence, blank forms, interoffice memoranda or other printed material for strictly internal office use.

/s/ John R. Buckley
John R. Buckley, Secretary of Administration

BIBLIOGRAPHY

"How to Obtain Massachusetts State Documents." *Massachusetts Library Commission Bulletin* 19:15 (1929).
Cited in both *Library Literature* and Schorr.

Chamberlin, Richard. "Introduction to United States Government, United Nations and Massachusetts State Documents." *Bay State Librarian* 56:9-11 (April 1966).
"To aid libraries in locating publications of The Commonwealth of Massachusetts, [several] serials are listed," the state checklist, the local interest list, and the *Monthly Checklist of State Publications*.

MICHIGAN

MICH. COMP. LAWS ANN. §§ 397.55, 397.56, 397.59 (West Supp. 1980-81), § 24.20 (West 1967)

397.55. Depository for state documents; permanent reference file; state system. Sec. 5. (1) The state library is designated as the depository library for state documents to preserve the public documents of this state and to make those documents available for use by the people of this state.

(2) The state library shall maintain a complete collection of copies of public documents issued or published by the state as a permanent reference file.

(3) The state library shall establish a state document depository system by which copies of public documents issued or published by the state shall be deposited in designated depository libraries. (P. A. 1895, No. 28, § 5, added by P. A. 1976, No. 367, § 1, Imd. Eff. Dec. 23, 1976.)

397.56 Public documents, furnishing by state officials and governmental units; exemptions. Sec. 6. (1) Each state official, state department, state board, state commission, and state agency which issues or publishes a public document shall furnish to the state library a minimum of 75 copies of each document issued in printed, mimeographed, or other duplicated form, which is not issued solely for use within the issuing agency. Additional copies of each public document shall be supplied upon the request of the state librarian.

(2) Publications of the various schools, colleges, divisions, and departments of the state universities and their regional campuses are exempt from the depository requirements of subsection (1), except that 2 copies of each publication shall be deposited in the state library.

(3) Publications of state university presses, directives for internal administration, intra-office and inter-office memoranda, forms, and correspondence are exempt from the depository requirements of this act. (P. A. 1895, No. 28, § 6, added by P. A. 1976, No. 367, § 1, Imd. Eff. Dec. 23, 1976.)

397.59. State library; depository public documents, distribution; designation of depository libraries; exchange system; sale and use of proceeds. Sec. 9. (1) The state library shall:

(a) Keep at least 1 copy of each public document issued or published by the state and received from a state agency as a permanent reference copy.

(b) Send 1 copy of each public document issued or published by the state and received from a state agency to the library of congress.

(c) Designate state university libraries and certain selected Michigan public, school, and college libraries in the geographical regions of the state as depository libraries to receive 1 copy of public documents issued or published by the state and received from a state agency. Selection of depository libraries shall be made by the state library and shall be based on a determination that the libraries selected will keep the documents readily accessible for use, and will render assistance for their use to the people of this state without charge.

(d) Prepare and issue quarterly, a complete list of public documents issued or published by the state during the immediately preceding quarter. The lists shall be cumulated and printed at the end of each calendar year. Copies shall be distributed by the state library to state departments, legislators, and to public and college libraries within the state.

(e) Establish a document exchange system with agencies in other states to make available selected documents published by other states for use by the people of this state.

(2) The state library may exchange the judicial decisions, statutes, journals, legislative and executive documents of Michigan, and other books placed in the care of the state library for the purpose of exchange, with the libraries of other states and the government of the United States, and of foreign countries, and with societies and institutions.

(3) The state library may sell or exchange duplicate volumes or sets of works not needed for use in the state library and apply the proceeds to the purchase of other books for the library. (Amended by P. A. 1976, No. 367, § 1, Imd. Eff. Dec. 23.)

24.20. Publications; additional copies for use and exchanges of state librarian. Sec. 20. There shall be printed of all publications, reports and documents as provided in this act, such additional copies for use and exchanges by the state library as the state librarian may in his discretion deem necessary for such purpose. (As amended P. A. 1958, No. 161, § 1, Eff. Sept. 13.)

STATE COMMENT (1973)

(Legislation): None, other than the law 24.20 requiring State departments to send copies of their publications to the State Library.

(Comment): At the present time the only legal basis for the depository mailings is the law requiring all state publications, reports, documents, be sent to the state library and disposed as the state librarian deems necessary. (Comments, 1973, when copy of legislation was sent to Documents on Documents Committee. *In* Documents on Documents Collection.)

EDITORIAL COMMENT

The 1958 amendment to 24.20 was a deletion at the end of the section which read, ''but not exceeding 200 copies of any 1 publication, and it shall be the duty of the board of state auditors to advise with the state librarian, prior to ordering the state printer to print such publications, that the proper number be ordered from the state printer and delivered to the state librarian.''

The 1976 Act (No. 367) added two sections, 397.55 and 397.56, and amended 397.59. The amendment to 397.59 was the addition of subsection (1) and the change in (2) and (3) from ''the state may'' to ''the state library may.''

MINNESOTA

MINN. STAT. ANN. §§ 3.195, 3.302, 15.18 (West 1977)

3.195. Reports to the legislature. Whenever a report to the legislature is required of a department or agency of government, it shall be made, unless otherwise specifically required by law, by the filing of one copy with the secretary of the senate, one copy with the chief clerk of the house of representatives, and ten copies with the legislative reference library. The same distribution procedure shall be followed for other reports and publications unless otherwise requested by a legislator or the legislative reference library. The legislative reference library shall monthly publish and distribute to legislators a checklist of state documents. Additional copies of the checklist sufficient for distribution to all state agencies, public, university and college libraries shall be provided by the documents section, department of administration. (Added by Laws 1974, c. 456, § 1. Amended by Laws 1976, c. 30, § 1.)

3.302. Legislative reference library. Subdivision 1. A legislative reference library is established under the jurisdiction and control of the legislative coordinating commission.

Subd. 2. The legislative reference library shall collect, index, and make available in suitable form information relative to governmental and legislative subjects which will aid members of the legislature in the performance of their duties in an efficient and economical manner. It shall maintain an adequate collection of public documents of Minnesota and other states and may enter into loan agreements with other libraries.

Subd. 3. The legislative reference library is a depository of all documents published by the state and shall receive such materials automatically without cost. As used in this chapter, "document" shall include any publication issued by the state, constitutional officers, departments, commissions, councils, bureaus, research centers, societies, or other agencies supported by state funds, or any publication prepared for the state by private individuals or organizations and issued in print, including all forms of duplicating other than by the use of carbon paper, considered to be of interest or value to the legislative reference library. Intraoffice or interoffice memos and forms and information concerning only the internal operation of an agency are not included.

Subd. 4. The legislative reference library may utilize the materials assembled to prepare studies and reports providing pertinent information regarding subjects which are or may become items of concern to members of the legislature and where warranted publish such studies and reports. (Laws 1969, c. 1130, § 2. Amended by Laws 1973, c. 598, § 3; Laws 1975, c. 271, § 6; Laws 1976, c. 30, § 2.)

15.18. Distribution of publications. Except as provided in sections 5.08, 16.02, and 648.39, when any department, agency, or official of the state issues for public distribution any book, document, journal, map, pamphlet, or report, copies thereof shall be delivered immediately as follows:

Four copies to the Minnesota Historical Society;

One copy to the general library of the University of Minnesota, and may, upon request of the librarian, deliver additional copies;

Two copies to the state library, and such additional copies as the state librarian deems necessary for exchange with other libraries, with other states, with the United States, and with governments of foreign countries;

One copy to the public library of any city of the first class;

One copy to the library of each state university as defined in Minnesota Statutes, Chapter 136. (Laws 1947, c. 365, § 1. Amended by Laws 1963, c. 179, § 1; Laws 1975, c. 321, § 2.)

STATE COMMENT

LEGAL DOCUMENTS RESPONSIBILITY

1. State Library (Supreme Court) must be maintained in the Capitol Building and need purchase only such "books, pamphlets and documents" as the justices of the court direct. (480.09, subd. 1). However, any department, agency, or official of the state, issuing for public distribution any "book, document, journal, map, pamphlet or report," must deliver two copies to the State Library, and as many more as the State Library deems necessary for exchange purposes (15.18). In addition, "All official publications of the United States and of other states and countries, which are received for the use of this state by any office thereof, shall be sent to the state library forthwith" (480.09, subd. 6). See Constitution, Art. VI, section 2.

2. Legislative Reference Library (Joint Coordinating Committee)—

"shall maintain an adequate collection of public documents of Minnesota and other states and may enter into loan agreements with other libraries." (3.302, subd. 2.)

"is a depository of all documents published by the state." (3.302, subd. 3.)

But the Legislative Reference Library is not named in section 15.18, which describes the distribution of state documents.

The Legislative Reference Library is also empowered to prepare studies and reports for the legislature and to publish them if warranted. See Chapter 456, 1974 Session laws.

3. Minnesota State Historical Society—

As of 1973, seven copies of each "book, document, journal, map, pamphlet, or report," including Minnesota Statutes and Session Laws, must be delivered to the Historical Society, five copies to be preserved by the Society and two copies to be sent to the Library of Congress. (138.03, subd. 1 [1973].) (However, Section 15.18 was not similarly amended in 1973 and calls for the delivery of only four copies to the Society.)

Any annual or biennial report issued for public distribution (unless it appears in a newspaper) by any county, city, or village, must be sent to the Historical Society upon request. (471.68, subd. 1, 2.)

The State Archives were transferred to the Historical Society in 1971 (138. 161).

"Those records preserved or appropriate for preservation as evidence of the organization, functions, policies, decisions, procedures, operations or other activities of government or because of the value of the information contained therein, when determined to have sufficient historical or other value to warrant continued preservation by the state of Minnesota and accepted for deposit in the collections of the Minnesota Historical Society, shall be known as the state archives." (138.17, subd. 1, [5] [1973].)

4. University of Minnesota Library—

"The general library of the University of Minnesota is a depository of all books, pamphlets, maps and other works published by or under the authority of the State of Minnesota." (137.04.)

5. State College Libraries—

Must receive one copy of any "book, document, journal, map, pamphlet, or report" issued for public distribution by any "department, agency, or official of the state." (15.18.) The State colleges are designated:

> Winona State College
> Mankato State College
> St. Cloud State College
> Moorhead State College
> Bemidji State College
> Southwest State College (Marshall) (136.01)

6. Commissioner of Administration—

Has the following duties:

"To provide for the printing and distribution of the capitol guidebook, official reports, and other publications of all kinds, and to supervise and control the form of such reports and publications, and make them useful and informative to the public." (16.02, subd. 13.)

"To sell all public books and documents which are subject to sale." (16.02, subd. 17.)

"The commissioner of administration shall supervise and control the making and distribution of publications of all kinds issued by the State of Minnesota and the departments and agencies thereof when not otherwise prescribed by law." (16.026, subd. 2.)

7. Chief administrative officers of public agencies—Are responsible for "preservation and care of the agency's public records, which shall include written or printed books, papers, letters, contracts, documents, maps, plans, and other records made or received pursuant to law or in connection with the transaction of public business." (15.17, subd. 2.)

Further: "Every custodian of public records shall keep them in such arrangement and condition as to make them easily accessible for convenient use." "Except as otherwise provided by law, he shall permit all public records in his custody to be inspected, examined, abstracted, or copied at reasonable time and under his supervision and regulation by any person. . . . " (15.17, subd. 4 [1973].)

8. Public libraries in cities of the first class—

Must receive one copy of any "book, document, journal, map, pamphlet, or report" issued for public distribution by any "department, agency, or official of the state." (15.18.) Libraries presently located in cities of the first class are:

> Minneapolis Public Library
> St. Paul Public Library
> Duluth Public Library

(for definition of "city of the first class" see 410.01)

9. Secretary of State—

Is to keep "all records and documents of the state not expressly required by law to be kept by other state officials." (5.01.)

10. Commissioner of Economic Development—

"shall have authority to sell, at their approximate cost to the state, such publications of the department as in his judgment should not be supplied gratis to those who wish to employ them in the conduct of their business. (Notes of Shawn Duffy, Department of Education, Library, St. Paul, Minnesota 55101, dated July 31, 1974. *In* Documents on Documents Collection.)

The Depository System as provided by law, Minnesota Statutes, chapter 15.18, is also part of Documents responsibility. At the present time forty-five copies of each publication is [*sic*] required to supply the Historical Society, University and college libraries and others as specified. (From "Documents," issued by Documents Section, rev. 7-73. *In* Documents on Documents Collection.)

EDITORIAL COMMENT

The 1976 amendment to 3.195 changed the duty of the legislative reference library from one of giving notice to legislators of each publication filed to a duty to publish a checklist for legislators. Enough copies for distribution to state agencies and public, college, and university libraries are to be provided by the documents secretary, Department of Administration.

The 1963 amendment to 15.18 changed the requirement from three copies to four copies for the Minnesota Historical Society and added the last two categories of libraries (public libraries in cities and libraries in state colleges). The 1975 amendment changed "college" to "university."

Section 3.302, enacted in 1969, was amended three times. In 1973, 3.302(1) was amended to change the control under which the legislative reference library is established from the legislative services committee to the joint coordinating committee. In 1975, the name of that committee was changed to joint coordinating commission. In 1976, an amendment added the word "automatically" to subd. 3 after the words "shall receive such materials" and deleted "in the same manner as other depositories." The 1976 amendment added the definition of "document."

BIBLIOGRAPHY

Hennen, Thomas J., Jr. "Using Minnesota Statutes, the Minnesota Code of Agency Rules and the State Register." *Minnesota Libraries* 25:180-184 (Summer 1977).
The publications listed in the title are now being "sent *free* to at least one library in each county not containing a city of the first class, thanks to a (new) law introduced by Senator Olson. . . . Since the state makes the laws and regulations, Senator Olson felt that it was the state's responsibility to provide public access to them."
"This article describes the relationships between these documents, their format, arrangement, cataloging, and processing."

Jerabek, E. (comp.). *Check List of Minnesota State Documents, 1858-1923.* Minnesota Historical Society, 1972. 216 p. (Not seen.)

Hodenfield, Jacob. "Minnesota Public Documents." *Minnesota Libraries Notes and News* 9:9-11 (1928). (Not seen.)

MISSISSIPPI

MISS. CODE ANN. §§ 25-51-1 to 7 (Supp. 1979)

CHAPTER 51. STATE DEPOSITORY FOR PUBLIC DOCUMENTS

§ 25-51-1. Designation. The Mississippi Library Commission shall be the state depository for the public records issued by any government agency for public distribution. The libraries of state agencies, public junior colleges, colleges, public universities and public libraries located in the state may also become depositories of these records, when designated as such by the director of the Mississippi Library Commission upon their written request to this effect. (Sources: Laws, 1975, ch. 347, § 1, eff. from and after July 1, 1975.)

§ 25-51-3. Agencies to furnish copies of documents. All agencies of state government shall furnish to the director of the Mississippi Library Commission sufficient copies of each public document printed, and the director of the Mississippi Library Commission shall deliver to each depository as many as two (2) copies of each document requested. These records shall be made accessible by the depository receiving them to any person desiring to examine the same. (Sources: Laws, 1975, ch. 347, § 2, eff. from and after July 1, 1975.)

§ 25-51-5. Semiannual lists of public documents. Each agency of state government shall furnish to the director of the Mississippi Library Commission semiannually a list of all its publications issued for public distribution, and the director of the Mississippi Library Commission shall make and furnish to each depository a duplicate copy of the same. (Sources: Laws, 1975, ch. 347, § 3, eff. from and after July 1, 1975.)

§ 25-51-7. Recorder of public documents. A recorder of documents shall be appointed by the director of the Mississippi Library Commission in his office, whose functions shall be to administer the provisions of this chapter under the supervision of the director of the Mississippi Library Commission. (Sources: Laws, 1975, ch. 347, § 4, eff. from and after July 1, 1975.)

EDITORIAL COMMENT

The sources for these sections as given in the 1972 MISS. CODE ANN. are: Codes 1942, § 4228-21; Laws, 1966, ch. 55, § 1 (etc.) eff. from and after passage (approved May 27, 1966).

The changes which the 1975 law made in the 1966 law were:

(1) ''Director of the Mississippi Library Commission'' was substituted for ''Secretary of State'' throughout the law;

(2) ''Mississippi Library Commission'' was substituted for ''Mississippi Research and Development Center Library'' in § 25-51-1.

(3) In § 25-51-1 the list of kinds of libraries which may become depositories was changed from ''The libraries of colleges and universities and public libraries located in the State'' to a new list;

(4) ''printed or mimeographed'' was deleted before ''public records'' in § 25-51-1 and before ''publications'' in § 25-51-5;

(5) ''as many as'' was added before ''two (2) copies'' in § 25-51-3;

(6) ''who shall be preferably a graduate librarian'' was deleted in § 25-51-7.

CONTRACT

DESIGNATION OF DEPOSITORY FOR PUBLIC DOCUMENTS

October ____, 1966

Hon. Heber Ladner
Secretary of State
New Capitol
Jackson, Mississippi
Dear Mr. Ladner:

The Library designated hereunder, through its duly constituted Librarian, hereby request[s] that said Library be constituted a _____(indicate complete or selective) Depository for _____ _____(indicate one or two copies) of Public Documents in accordance with the provisions of H. B. 125 of the Regular Session of the Legislature of 1966 in order that it may receive the Documents contemplated by said act.

_____
Library

By: _____
Librarian

APPROVED BY:_____
    SECRETARY OF STATE

BIBLIOGRAPHY

''Legislature Establishes Depository for Public Documents, Provides for Document
    Recorder.'' *Mississsippi Library News* 30:94 (September 1966).
An announcement of the signing into law of the distribution law. The recorder of documents, who will be appointed to carry out the law, will be responsible for

(1) collecting and distributing copies of state publications, (2) maintaining records and statistics on the distribution and the depository system, (3) establishing uniform entries for state agencies and their publications, (4) publishing regular and accumulative lists of state documents, and (5) providing indexes to this material. To qualify as a depository a library must receive its financial support through public funds or taxation.

"Governor of Mississippi Signed into Law House Bill 'H 125—Establish Depository for Public Documents in Research and Development Center Library and Provide for Recorder of Documents in Secretary of State's Office'." *Southeastern Librarian* 16:188 (Fall 1966).
An informal statement of the provisions of the new law; somewhat broader in scope than the actual text of the law. Title is taken from Schorr.

Gharst, Willie Dee. "Mississippi Government Publications: A Survey of Depositories." *Mississippi Library News* 38:16-17 (March 1975).
A progress report after seven years' operation, based on a questionnaire to which there was a 100 percent response from the thirty-four depository libraries. All thirty-four libraries said that a subject list was needed, and twenty-seven of those recommended LC subject headings. Problems identified are: (1) not all publications are sent to the recorder; (2) lack of adequate listing (that is, confusion in assigning numbers); (3) no subject list; (4) documents received too late; (5) semiannual list too slow; and (6) lack of staff to handle. The establishment by the Mississippi Library Association of an advisory council is recommended.

Carson, Calvin S., and Read, Dennis E. "Computer/Microform System for State Documents." *Mississippi Library News* 41:131-132 (September 1977).
A brief history of the Mississippi program established in 1966. In 1975, upon transfer of the program to Mississippi Library Commission, two problems—insufficient copies for distribution and lack of subject access in index—were resolved by microfiching documents and by a KWIC index. The KWIC index has additional subjects when needed and is the key to the microfiche (last six digits of control number are year filmed and order in which filmed.)

"Mississippi." *Documents to the People* 6:105-106 (March 1978).
Announcement of a workshop held in October 1977 on federal and state documents.

Raymond, A.L.M. "Publications of the Mississippi Legislature, 1789-1951." M.S.L.S. Thesis, Atlanta University, 1955. 123 p. (Not seen.)

MISSOURI

MO. ANN. STAT. §§ 181.100-181.140 (Vernon Supp. 1980)

181.100. State publications defined. As used in sections 181.100 to 181.140, and sections 182.140 and 182.291, RSMo, "state publications" shall include all multiple-produced publications of state agencies, regardless of format or purpose, with the exception of correspondence and interoffice memoranda. (Laws 1976, p. 674, § 2.)

181.110. Publications of state offices, indexed list of to be published, distribution—depositories of publications, designation, request. The state library shall, under the direction of the coordinating board for higher education, publish monthly an official indexed list of all printed publications of all state offices, departments, divisions, boards and commissions, whether legislative, executive or judicial, and any subdivisons of each, including state-supported institutions of higher education. The library shall also distribute such numbers of copies of such publications as it deems necessary to certain libraries, also designated by it, which shall serve as depositories for making available to the public such publications. No publications shall be distributed to any libraries unless a request is made therefor. (Laws 1976, p. 674, § 3.)

181.120. Library to distribute publications, to whom. In addition to the distribution of the publications as aforesaid, the library shall distribute two copies of each publication to the state archives for preservation and two copies to the state historical society. (Laws 1976, p. 675, § 4.)

181.130. Depository agreements permitted, when. The state library may enter into depository agreements with public libraries and college and university libraries which meet standards for depository eligibility as approved by the state library. (Laws 1976, p. 675, § 5.)

181.140. State agencies to furnish copies of publications, to whom. Every state agency, as enumerated in section 181.100, shall, upon release, deposit with the state library sufficient copies of each of its publications to meet the purposes of sections 181.100 to 181.140, and sections 182.140 and 182.291, RSMo. (Laws 1976, p. 675, § 6.)

EDITORIAL COMMENT

Section 182.140, titled Petition for library tax . . . , and section 182.291, titled City-county library, how organized . . . , both of which are mentioned in section 181.140 are not related to the depository program.

RULES AND REGULATIONS

Missouri Register. Title 6—Department of Higher Education
Division 20—State Library, Chapter 2—State Publications
Depository Library System

6CSR 20-2.010 TYPES OF DEPOSITORY LIBRARIES

PURPOSE: *The State Library has the authority to designate public, college and university libraries to act as depositories for state goverment publications. This rule defines the two types of depository designations which will be made in order to meet the varied needs of Missouri residents for state publications and to limit to a reasonable number the copies of publications to be requested from state agencies.*

(1) Depository libraries shall be of two types:

(A)   Full depositories shall receive all publications of all state agencies. The purpose of a full depository is to provide a complete research collection of state publications for the use of a major geographical area. The State Library will seek to designate at least one full depository in each of the following general areas of Missouri: northeast, northwest, southeast, southwest, central, St. Louis metropolitan area, Kansas City metropolitan area. Additional designation of full depositories may be made if justified by the needs of the residents of an area.

(B)   Partial depositories will be designated to provide ready access to state government publications of broad general interest and to publications in subject areas needed by residents in particular areas of the state. A partial depository must receive a basic core of state publications to be specified by the State Library. In addition, the State Library shall define categories of publications for selection by depository libraries. A category may be comprised of the publications of a department or division of state government or some other logical grouping of publications. Each partial depository library must select at least one category of publications to be received in addition to the core collection.

6 CSR 20-2.020 STANDARDS FOR DEPOSITORY LIBRARIES

PURPOSE: *The State Library will distribute state publications on a regular basis to the libraries designated as depositories. This rule pro-*

motes free access to the publications by all residents of the state by establishing minimum standards which libraries must meet and maintain to be eligible for depository status. It also gives the State Library power to enforce these standards.

(1) The State Library will select public, college, and university libraries to act as state publications depositories on the basis of geographic distribution, broadness of clientele served, and ability to meet the conditions specified in the following section.

(2) A depository library shall:

(A) Provide reference assistance in the use of state publications to any Missouri resident. Circulation of the publications is encouraged.

(B) Provide interlibrary loan service for state publications to any Missouri resident.

(C) Maintain sufficient hours of library service to allow convenient public access. State publications must be available for use during any hours the library is open.

(D) Inform the public frequently of the availability of state publications. The public includes the residents of the geographic area in which the library is located.

(E) Designate a professionally trained librarian to be responsible for service related to state publications, and provide adequate support staff. This librarian need not spend full time on state publications.

(F) Provide an orderly, systematic recording of receipt and subsequent arrangement of materials.

(G) Process and shelve all state publications within thirty (30) days of receipt.

(H) Provide space to house publications, with adequate provision for expansion.

(I) Dispose of publications only in accordance with policies established by the State Library. Depository publications remain the property of the State Library.

(3) The State Library shall enforce maintenance of these standards by inspections and annual surveys. A depository agreement may be terminated by the State Library for failure to comply with any of the conditions above or by a library at its own request.

CONTRACT

MISSOURI STATE PUBLICATIONS
DEPOSITORY LIBRARY AGREEMENT

This agreement made this _____ day of _____, 19_____, by and between the Missouri State Library (herein referred to as "the State Library") and the

_____Library (herein referred to as "the Depository Library".)

WHEREAS, the General Assembly of the State of Missouri in 1976 enacted House Bill 1021, establishing a depository library system for the distribution of state publications,

WHEREAS, under that legislation the State Library may enter into depository agreements with public libraries and college and university libraries; and

WHEREAS, _____Library has made application for Depository Library status and has been approved by the State Library for designation as a_____Depository Library;

(Full/Partial)

NOW THEREFORE, IT IS MUTUALLY AGREED TO AND UNDERSTOOD, that:

The State Library shall:

(1) Mail state publications obtained under the provisions of House Bill 1021 in regular shipments to the Depository Library;

(2) Provide in each shipment a shipping list showing agency, title, and Missouri classification number for each publication;

(3) Provide assistance in the organization and reference use of Missouri state publications, as requested by the Depository Library;

(4) Publish monthly an official indexed list of state agency publications;

(5) Establish policies and procedures for the disposal of depository publications.

The Depository Library shall:

(1) Provide reference assistance in the use of state publications to any Missouri resident. Circulation of the publications is encouraged.

(2) Provide interlibrary loan service for state publications to any Missouri resident.

(3) Maintain sufficient hours of library service to allow convenient public access. State publications must be available for use during any hours the library is open.

(4) Inform the public frequently of the availability of state publications. The public includes the residents of the geographic area in which the library is located.

(5) Designate a professionally trained librarian to be responsible for service related to state publications and provide adequate support staff. This librarian need not spend full time on state publications.

(6) Provide an orderly, systematic recording of receipt and subsequent arrangement of materials.

(7) Process and shelve all state publications within thirty (30) days of receipt.

(8) Provide space to house publications, with adequate provision for expansion.

(9) Dispose of publications only in accordance with policies established by the State Library. Depository publications remain the property of the State Library.

The State Library shall enforce maintenance of the above Depository Library requirements by inspections and annual surveys. A depository agreement may be terminated by the State Library for failure to comply with any of the conditions above or by a Depository Library at its own request.

IN WITNESS WHEREOF, the State Library and the Depository Library have caused this agreement to be executed on the day, month, and year first above written by their duly authorized officers or representatives.

MISSOURI STATE LIBRARY

By: Charles O'Halloran
    State Librarian

| DEPOSITORY LIBRARY | or | DEPOSITORY LIBRARY |
| (PUBLIC LIBRARY) | | (ACADEMIC LIBRARY) |

By: Library Director   By: Library Director

By: Chairman, Board of   By: University or
    Trustees   College President

APPLICATION FOR DESIGNATION AS
STATE PUBLICATIONS DEPOSITORY LIBRARY

Designation by the State Library of depository libraries for state publications is authorized by House Bill 1021 (78th General Assembly, 2nd Regular Session, effective August 13, 1976), Sections 3 and 5.

In accordance with the provisions of House Bill 1021, _____

_____ Library hereby makes application for designation as a depository library for state publications.

TYPE OF DESIGNATION DESIRED (see attached description of Types of Depository Libraries):

_____ Full _____ Partial

STANDARDS FOR DEPOSITORY LIBRARIES, approved by the Coordination Board for Higher Education September 13, 1976, provides that a library shall meet and maintain the following standards. Please place a check by each item to indicate your agreement to carry out the responsibility listed:

A depository library shall:

[Here are repeated, word for word, the duties specified in the Agreement. They are designated by capital letters and after the third one (C) is a line: "List hours of service," and after the fifth (E) are two lines: "Name of Librarian" and "Title:".]

ORGANIZATION: How do you expect to handle depository documents?

_____ Integrated into main collection

_____ Separate collection

_____ Mixture (describe:)

How do you plan to classify depository documents?

_____ Dewey   _____ Missouri Documents Classification

_____ L.C.   _____ Other (describe:)

COOPERATION: Has your library carried on any discussions with other libraries in your area as to which library/libraries should apply for full or partial depository status?

_____ Yes   _____ No   _____ Not applicable (If yours is
                                                     the only library in the area)

If so, what conclusions were reached?

AUTHORIZATION: Please attach photocopy of this application's authorization by policy-making body.

_____

(Signature)

Title: _____

Address: _____

Date: _____   _____

BIBLIOGRAPHY

Hylton, Percy H. "Missouri State Publications Need Attention." *Missouri Library Association Quarterly* 13:13-16 (March 1952).
Hylton, at the Missouri State Library, found that compilation of the 1951 document checklist was a "veritable Frankenstein," and pointed up the need for (1) a central depository, (2) a distribution plan, and (3) a regular listing. He surveyed the current situation and urged that Missouri do its share in contributing to the UNESCO/Library of Congress Bibliographical Survey and in exchanging its documents. Hylton recommends that a Missouri Library Association committee study the problem and formulate a program. In closing, he cites Huston's article on the California program.

Irvin, Charles E. "The Distribution of Missouri State Documents." *Missouri Library Association Quarterly* 13:109-112 (December 1952).
The author is in the Acquisitions Department, University of Missouri Library.
"The law concerning Missouri state documents is indefinite and ambiguous, is scattered throughout the revised statutes, and is almost impossible to find in the index to the revised statutes." There are several officers responsible for delivering copies of publications to the libraries. The Historical Society makes the greatest effort to secure the copies to which it is entitled but encounters problems because some agencies must be "prodded before they will send anything, and that is not always successful" and because there are publications the existence of which is unknown to the society.
The Historical Society gives extra copies to the university which has a mailing list and also fills miscellaneous requests. For legal materials very satisfactory exchanges, both ordinary exchanges and priced exchanges, exist. The law library of the university has some direct exchanges and some priced exchanges with a commercial dealer.
Libraries in forty-one states receive one or more official Missouri documents each year. Six of these libraries are in Missouri.

Chamberlin, Edgar W. "Do You Receive U.S. and Missouri Publications?" *Missouri Library Association Quarterly* 16:48-51 (June 1955).
The author, formerly document librarian at Kansas City Public Library, says there are seventy departments and divisions that issue publications in Missouri. He cites the biennial Missouri checklist and mentions the need for a central depository and for depositories in college and public libraries.
The column "New in Documents" appears regularly in *Show-Me Libraries*. The September 1975 issue, which outlines the features of the new Missouri Register law,

ends with the query ''Will Missouri extend the process [that is, bringing Missouri government to the people] next year with a state documents depository law?''

Atterberry, Meryl. ''Missouri Documents to the People.'' *Show-Me Libraries* 27:11-14 (January 1976).
''Buttons, posters, and displays advertised the state documents depository legislation which has been pre-filed for the 1976 session of the General Assembly'' at the Missouri Library Association Conference. Committee members from the association who may be contacted are named. The support of the governor, the secretary of state, and the director of the State Historical Society, as well as an endorsement by the Missouri Political Science Association, had been secured. The representative sponsoring the bill had been in the legislature since 1962. The article includes a statement, ''Missouri Documents to the People,'' which is ''a brief outline of the need for depository legislation and the benefits such legislation would bring to Missouri citizens.''
   ''Missouri Documents to the People'' says, ''Lack of knowledge or availability of publications is a major difficulty ... Without access to the output of agencies administering public funds, individuals can neither benefit from the information and assistance generated by state government nor expect any degree of accountability from state agencies and officials. . . . In a majority of states, libraries are utilized as a channel for dissemination of state publications.''
   The proposed legislation is outlined in detail and its cost explained. In reference to the cost, the statement says, ''The State Library has already placed a priority on state publications by devoting one full-time professional librarian and one full-time clerk to its state documents program. The monthly checklist specified in the bill is already being published. . . .''
   The concluding statement is, ''and government would be brought a giant step closer to the people.''

Atterberry, Meryl. ''Update: Missouri State Depository Law.'' *Documents to the People* 5:235, 237 (November 1977).
Distribution of Missouri publications began in January 1977 with fifty ''core list'' publications. When funding was received in June, regular weekly mailings were initiated and publications beyond the core list were added. Ten full, and seventeen partial, depositories were designated and surveyed to determine their needs.
   Part of the appropriation for the depository program was to be used for a part-time cataloger. Cataloging is to be available through OCLC, but cataloging data will also be included on shipping lists because not all depositories are OCLC members.
   A coordinated publicity effort is planned for the future, although some depositories have already ''advertised their valuable new resource locally.'' (Reprinted from *Show-Me Libraries* 28:20-21 [August 1977].)

Atterberry, Meryl. ''Missouri State Depository Documents Update.'' *Documents to the People* 6.24-25 (January 1978).
State agencies were requested to forward all publications, not just the core publications, beginning October 1. Distribution is handled by the Library Services Center of Missouri under a state-funded contract.

By January 1, a weekly shipping list should be produced which will incorporate descriptive cataloging data, Library of Congress subject headings, classification numbers, and OCLC numbers.

A list of Missouri state documents classification numbers is now available. It includes a title index. (Reprinted from *Show-Me Libraries* 29:20 [October 1977].)

Saylor, C. E. "Official Publications of the State of Missouri." M.S. Thesis, University of Illinois, 1941. 375 p. (Not seen.)

MONTANA

MONT. CODE ANN. §§ 22-1-211 to 22-1-218 (1979)

22-1-211. Definitions. As used in this part, the following definitions apply:

(1) ''Print'' includes all forms of printing and duplicating, regardless of format or purpose, with the exception of correspondence and interoffice memoranda.

(2) ''State publication'' includes any document, compilation, journal, law, resolution, bluebook, statute, code, register, pamphlet, list, book, proceedings, report, memorandum, hearing, legislative bill, leaflet, order, regulation, directory, periodical, or magazine issued in print or purchased for distribution by the state, the legislature, constitutional officers, any state department, committee, or other state agency supported wholly or in part by state funds.

(3) ''State agency'' includes every state office, officer, department, division, bureau, board, commission, and agency of the state and, where applicable, all subdivisions of each. (HISTORY: En. Sec. 1, Ch. 261, L. 1967; R. C. M. 1947, 44-132.)

22-1-212. Creation of distribution center. There is hereby created, as a division of the state library and under the direction of the state librarian, a state publications library distribution center. The center shall promote the establishment of an orderly depository library system. To this end the state library commission shall make such rules and regulations necessary to carry out the provisions of this part. (HISTORY: En. Sec. 2, Ch. 261, L. 1967; R. C. M. 1947, 44-133.)

22-1-213. State agency publications to be deposited in state library— interlibrary loan—sale publications. Every state agency shall deposit upon release at least four copies of each of its state publications with the state library for record and depository purposes. Additional copies shall also be deposited in quantities certified to the agencies by the state library as required to meet the needs of the depository library system and to provide interlibrary loan service to those libraries without depository status. Additional copies of sale publications required by the state library shall be furnished only upon reimbursement to the state agency of the full cost of such sale publications, and the state library shall also reimburse any state agency for additional publications so required where the quantity desired will necessitate additional printing or other expense to such agency. (HISTORY: En. Sec. 3, Ch. 261, L. 1967; R. C. M. 1947, 44-134.)

22-1-214. Depository libraries—eligibility. The center shall enter into depository contracts with any municipal or county free library, state college or state university library, the library of congress, the midwest interlibrary center, and other state libraries. The requirements for eligibility to contract as a depository library shall be established by the state library commission upon recommendations of the state librarian. The standards shall include and take into consideration the type of library, ability to preserve such publications and to make them available for public use, and also such geographical locations as will make the publications conveniently accessible to residents in all areas of the state. (HISTORY: En. Sec. 4, Ch. 261, L. 1967; R. C. M. 1947, 44-135.)

22-1-215. Available publications. The center shall publish and distribute regularly to contracting depository libraries and other libraries upon request a list of available state publications. (HISTORY: En. Sec. 5, Ch. 261, L. 1967; R. C. M. 1947, 44-136.)

22-1-216. Current publications. Upon request by the center, issuing state agencies shall furnish the center with a complete list of their current state publications and a copy of their mailing and/or exchange lists. (HISTORY: En. Sec. 6, Ch. 261, L. 1967; R. C. M. 1947, 44-137.)

22-1-217. No general public distribution. The center shall not engage in general public distribution of either state publications or lists of publications. (HISTORY: En. Sec. 7, Ch. 261, L. 1967; R. C. M. 1947, 44-138.)

22-1-218. Exemptions. This part shall not apply to officers of or affect the duties concerning publications distributed by:

(1) the state law library;

(2) the secretary of state in connection with his duties under 2-15-401 (13);

(3) the code commissioner in connection with his duties under Title 1, chapter 11, as amended; and

(4) the legislative council in connection with its duties under 5-11-203, as amended. (HISTORY: En. Sec. 8, Ch. 261, L. 1967; amd. Sec. 2, Ch. 3, L. 1977; R. C. M. 1947, 44-139; amd. Sec. 11, ch. 138, L. 1979.)

STATE COMMENT (1973)

The present depository law for state publications in Montana presents one major difficulty. There really is no way to be sure that the State Library receives at least "four" copies of each publication issued by various state agencies and their divisions as specified by the law. One factor contributing to this difficulty is that there is no central printing facility for the state of Montana. Thus, it is difficult to keep tab on what is coming out. Because of this fact many publications are missed. State agencies have generally been very cooperative in providing copies if we know about them. Considerable time is spent in following up leads and contacting heads of state agencies. In most cases the secretaries take care of seeing that the State Library receives copies. Because of the constant change in personnel, reminders are necessary to make sure that State Library receives copies for distribution.

The number of additional copies agencies are asked for is twenty (20), if the state agency can spare them. This number makes it possible to distribute to in-state and out-of-state depositories as well as the Library of Congress. (Commentary by Harold L. Chambers, Documents Librarian, Montana State Library, Helena, Montana 59601, prepared in 1973. *In* Documents on Documents Collection.)

EDITORIAL COMMENT

The 1977 amendment to 22-1-218 changed some section numbers, added subdivisions (3) and (4), and made minor editorial changes.

The title of the 1967 Act was: "An Act to Create a State Publications Library Distribution Center as a Division of the State Library and Amending Section 82-1916, R. C. M. 1947, Relating to Printing and Distribution of State Reports and Providing for Reimbursement for Additional Publications." The amendment to section 82-1916 made distribution to the state publications distribution center of "4 copies of each report and whatever additional copies are requested by the state library" mandatory.

The 1967 Act did not have a section providing for an appropriation.

The 1979 amendment to § 22-1-218, part of a bill affecting the legislative branch, deleted the reference to the legislative services division of the legislative council and changed a subsection number.

RULES AND REGULATIONS

STATE PUBLICATIONS LIBRARY DISTRIBUTION CENTER

RULES AND REGULATIONS

1. The Montana State Library will publish a basic list of state documents, said basic list to be revised and published annually.

2. Mail copies of the list to all depository libraries.

3. Ship documents at least once a month to all depository libraries.

4. Negotiate with state departments as to the number of copies needed for distribution to depository library.

    a.   All library inquiries, special requests, etc., concerning state documents for libraries will be channelled through the State Library.

    b.   There will be periodic revisions of number of copies needed by libraries. Each library should assume the responsibility for keeping the State Library informed as to number of copies needed.

c.   Libraries should send to the State Library names of every department on whose mailing list they are currently listed.

STATE PUBLICATIONS LIBRARY DISTRIBUTION CENTER

STANDARDS

1. There will be only one class of Depository Libraries in Montana. These will be Total Depositories. Any other library in the state may request specific state documents from the State Library, and these will be furnished whenever available.

2. Any municipal, county or district library, any community college, state college or state university library, the library of any incorporated college or university, may be designated as a depository provided that all other qualifications are met.

3. Any library designated as a depository, shall agree to the following conditions, with the understanding that failure to comply with any one condition is sufficient ground for cancellation of the contract between the State and the library:

a.   Provide space to house the publications in an approved manner with adequate provisions for expansion. State publications do not need to be maintained in a separate collection unless the receiving library prefers to do so. Housing in a vertical file rather than on shelves is acceptable for appropriate pamphlet-type materials.

b.   Provide an orderly, systematic recording of receipt of the documents.

c.   Process and shelve all state publications within 30 days after receipt of the material.

d.   Provide a professionally trained librarian to render satisfactory service without charge to qualified patrons in the use of such publications. This librarian need not spend full time on state publications.

e.   Dispose of publications only with permission of the State Librarian.

f.   Accept and maintain all publications specified as "basic items."

g.   Library rules must assure that the documents are available for public use and circulation, unless for some unusual reason it becomes necessary to restrict use.

CONTRACT

INTER-LIBRARY DEPOSITORY LIBRARY CONTRACT

This agreement made this _____ day of _____, 19_____, by and between the State Publications Library Distribution Center for the Montana State Library hereinafter called the "Center", and the _____ Library, hereinafter called the "Depository."

WITNESSETH: WHEREAS, the legislature of the State of Montana in 1967 enacted legislation codified as Chapter 261 R. C. M. creating a State Publications Library Distribution Center as a division within the State Library and

WHEREAS, under that statute the Center is authorized to enter into depository contracts with any municipal or county free library, state college or state university library, the library of any privately incorporated college or university in this state, the Library of Congress and the Center for Research Libraries, and other state libraries; and

WHEREAS, the _____ Library is desirous of entering into such an inter-library contract with the Center;

NOW, THEREFORE, IT IS MUTUALLY AGREED AND UNDERSTOOD, that

(1) The Center shall publish a basic list of documents to be revised and published annually.

(2) The Center shall send documents on permanent deposit to the Depository in monthly shipments.

(3) The Depository shall provide space to adequately house the publications in a manner approved by the Center and with adequate provision for expansion if space is needed.

(4) The Depository shall provide an orderly systematic record of receipt of all documents from the Center and all state publications shall be processed and shelved within thirty days after the receipt by it.

(5) A Depository shall provide a professionally trained librarian to provide service to patrons of the depository in the use of such publications.

(6) The Depository agrees to accept and maintain all publications specified as ''basis [sic] items'' and dispose of publications only with the permission of the Center.

(7) The Depository agrees to make the documents readily available for public use.

(8) The Depository agrees that all inquiries and special requests concerning state documents for libraries will be channelled through the Center.

(9) The Depository agrees to assume the responsibility of keeping the Center informed concerning the number of copies of specific documents of publications needed by the Depository.

(10) The Depository agrees to send to the Center the name of every (state) department from which it is currently receiving publications.

(11) The Depository agrees that title to all documents on permanent deposit with the Depository shall remain the property of the State of Montana and may not be disposed of in any manner without the written authorization of the State Library.

(12) The Depository agrees to comply with all of the rules, regulations and standards adopted by the Montana State Library Commission for depository libraries.

The contract may be terminated by either party upon six (6) months written notice to the other party that said contract is to be terminated. Upon termination of the contract the Depository shall ship all documents to the Center or to such other Depositories as may be specified by the Center.

Dated this _____ day of _____, 19_____.

MONTANA STATE PUBLICATIONS LIBRARY DISTRIBUTION CENTER

By: _____

Librarian

_____

(LIBRARY)

By: _____

Librarian

"Montana Publications Library Distribution Center." *Montana Libraries* 21:19-20
    (January 1968).
An announcement that the state library will serve as a distribution center pursuant to the
new law and that representatives of the state library had visited all the state agencies
prior to setting up service. Depository libraries are listed.

"Montana State Publications." *Montana Libraries* 22:18-23 (January 1969).
A list of publications distributed to depository libraries in 1968.

Speer, Lucille. "Progress in Availability of Montana State Documents." *Pacific
    Northwest Library Association Quarterly* 33:17-23 (July 1969).
The author, documents librarian emeritus, University of Montana, Missoula, states that

> Over the years, the availability of Montana state documents has been a two-
> pronged problem: first, the failure of many state agencies to issue reports; and
> second, the lack of a centralized distribution system for state documents.
> Legislation enacted in 1967 and 1969 legislative sessions promises amelioration of
> these problems.

The 1967 legislation is the state publications library law, enacted after four years of
studies and surveys by the State Documents Committee of the Montana Library
Association. Laws from other states were studied; state agencies were surveyed on
publication and distribution policies; and all libraries in the state were asked about the
scope and use of Montana state document collections. Only a few of the libraries were
interested in acquisition of state documents; most preferred an interlibrary loan source.
All agreed on the urgent need for a current listing of Montana documents.

The law is based on that of Washington, except that the Montana law makes
supplying of publications by state agencies mandatory, in contrast with Washington's
then permissive provision. Service to eight Montana libraries and one out-of-state
library began January 1, 1968. A total of 749 documents were distributed during the
first six months. Selective depository status is provided for by the state library which
arranges for the issuing agency to add such libraries to their mailing list. Other features
of the law are discussed, as well as the status of state document bibliography.

NEBRASKA

NEB. REV. STAT. §§ 51-411 to 51-418 (1978)

(b) NEBRASKA PUBLICATIONS CLEARINGHOUSE

51-411. Terms, defined. As used in this act, unless the context otherwise requires:

(1) Print shall include all forms of printing and duplicating, regardless of format or purpose, with the exception of correspondence and interoffice memoranda;

(2) State publications shall include any multiply-produced publications printed or purchased for distribution, by the state, the Legislature, constitutional officers, any state department, committee or other state agency supported wholly or in part by state funds;

(3) State agency shall include every state office, officer, department, division, bureau, board, commission and agency of the state, and, where applicable, all subdivisions of each including state institutions of higher education, defined as all state-supported colleges, universities, junior colleges, and vocational technical colleges; and

(4) Governmental publications shall include any publications of associations, regional organizations, intergovernmental bodies, federal agencies, boards and commissions, or other publishers that may contribute supplementary materials to support the work of the state Legislature and state agencies. (Source: Laws 1972, LB 1284, § 1.)

51-412. Nebraska Publications Clearinghouse; division of Nebraska Library Commission; created; duties. There is hereby created as a division of the Nebraska Library Commission, a Nebraska Publications Clearinghouse. The clearinghouse shall establish and operate a publications collection and depository system for the use of Nebraska citizens. To this end, the Nebraska Library Commission shall make such rules and regulations as shall be necessary to carry out the provisions of this act. (Source: Laws 1972, LB 1284, § 2.)

51-413. State agencies; publications; filing with Nebraska Publications Clearinghouse. Every state agency head or his or her appointed records officer shall notify the Nebraska Publications Clearinghouse of his or her identity. The records officer shall upon release of a state publication deposit four copies and a short summary including author, title, and subject of each of its state publications with the Nebraska Publications Clearinghouse for record purposes. One of these copies shall be forwarded by the clearinghouse to the Nebraska Historical Society for archival purposes and one to the Library of Congress. Additional copies including sale items, shall also be deposited in the Nebraska Publications Clearinghouse in quantities certified to the agencies by the clearinghouse as required to meet the needs of the Nebraska publications depository system. With the exception that the University of Nebraska Press shall only be required to deposit four copies of it publications. (Source: Laws 1972, LB 1284, § 3; Laws 1979, LB 322, § 80.)

51-414. Depository contracts; standards; establish. The Nebraska Publications Clearinghouse may enter into depository contracts with any municipal, county, or regional public library, state college or state university library, and out-of-state research libraries. The requirements for eligibility to contract as a depository library shall be established by the Nebraska Publications Clearinghouse. The standards shall include and take into consideration the type of library, ability to preserve such publications and to make them available for public use, and also such geographical locations as will make the publications conveniently accessible to residents in all areas of the state. (Source: Laws 1972, LB 1284, § 4.)

51-415. Official list of publications; publish; contents. The Nebraska Publications Clearinghouse shall publish and distribute regularly to contracting depository libraries, other libraries, state agencies and legislators, an official list of state publications with an annual cumulation. The official list shall provide a record of each agency's publishing and show author, agency, title and subject approaches. (Source: Laws 1972, LB 1284, § 5.)

51-416. Current state publications; furnish. Upon request by the Nebraska Publications Clearinghouse, records officers of state agencies shall furnish the clearinghouse with a complete list of their current state publications. (Source: Laws 1972, LB 1284, § 6.)

51-417. Distribution of state publications; restriction. The Nebraska Publications Clearinghouse shall not engage in general public distribution of either state publications or lists of publications. This act shall not affect the distribution of state publications distributed by state agencies except that the agencies must deposit in the Nebraska Publications Clearinghouse the number of copies of each of their state publications certified by the clearinghouse. (Source: Laws 1972, LB 1284, § 7.)

51-418. Interlibrary loan service; provide. The Nebraska Publications Clearinghouse shall provide access to local, state, federal and other governmental publications to state agencies and legislators and through interlibrary loan service to citizens of the state. (Source: Laws 1972, LB 1284, § 8.)

STATE COMMENT (1973)

Our depository library legislation has not been in effect long enough to make a critical assessment of it. We have yet to come to an agreement with many state agencies on what items must come to us nor have we yet established a regional depository system. To date, the law appears to be flexible enough, but as with most laws of this nature it lacks coercive powers.

The law is specific that we should receive items offered for sale or published in cooperation with other publishers. This has been very helpful. "State agency" and "publication" are very well defined by the law although some state agencies feel "state publication" is too liberally defined or interpreted.

At this point I would not attempt to propose any amendments to this legislation. It appears to be reasonably effective with no major weak points. (Letter from James M. Armour, Acting Director, Nebraska Publications Clearinghouse, Nebraska Library Commission, Lincoln, Nebraska 58509, dated April 27, 1973. *In* Documents on Documents Collection.)

STATE COMMENT (1976)

The Nebraska Publications Clearinghouse—a division of the Nebraska Library Commission—began operation July 1, 1972. Created by Legislative Bill 1284 (R. R. S. Nebraska 51-411-418), the Clearinghouse is responsible for collecting state documents, maintaining a central loan collection, establishing and supplying depositories and publishing an "official list of state publications" (Checklist).

****

The Publications Clearinghouse has been very fortunate in the high level of support it has received from the Legislature and the Governor. This has allowed for maintenance of the program and increases in staffing to match increasing workloads—even at times when other programs faced cutbacks. (Report by Susan Kling, Nebraska Library Commission, Lincoln, Nebraska 68508. *In* The State of State Documents: Past, Present, Future. Texas Legislative Reference Library, 1976, at pp. 13-14.)

EDITORIAL COMMENT

The 1972 Act has twenty-three sections. The first eight sections (set out above) added the provisions for the clearinghouse. The remaining sections amended fourteen separate sections of the Statutes to insert a requirement that eight copies of the publications mentioned in the section be sent to the clearinghouse. For example, section 9, relative to the report of the State Board of Agriculture, begins:

Sec. 9. That Section 2-105, Reissue Revised Statutes of Nebraska, 1943, be amended to read as follows:

2-105. The Secretary of State shall distribute the report as follows: ~~Five~~ *Eight copies to the Nebraska Publications Clearinghouse; five* copies thereof to each member of the Legislature and to each state officer; one copy by mail to each county clerk, ...

The final section of the 1972 Act is a standard repealing clause.

§ 51-413 was amended in 1979 to reduce the number of copies of state publications to be deposited from eight to four. The number of copies to be forwarded to the Nebraska Historical Society and to the Library of Congress was reduced from two copies for each institution to one copy for each. The University of Nebraska Press requirement of depositing four copies of its publications was not changed. Minor changes in wording included substituting ''his or her'' for ''his.''

RULES AND REGULATIONS
REVISED AUGUST 2, 1979

RULES, REGULATIONS & STANDARDS
NEBRASKA STATE DOCUMENTS DEPOSITORY SYSTEM

1. The Clearinghouse recommends that a depository library should organize its collection by the Clearinghouse number assigned to each publication. In this way, the *Nebraska State Publications Checklist* can be used as an index to the state documents collection.

2. The Clearinghouse will send a shipping list containing the title and assigned Clearinghouse number for each publication in that shipment.

3. The Clearinghouse will send shipments of documents to depositories as frequently as volume demands (normally monthly or bimonthly).

4. The Clearinghouse will provide depositories with printed forms to claim missing items from a shipment.

5. The Clearinghouse will assume the costs of mailing shipments to depositories.

6. For growth of the microfiche collection, depositories should allow 28''-30'' of drawer space per year for microfiche without microfiche jackets and 60''-63'' per year for microfiche with individual jackets.

7. The Clearinghouse staff will conduct visitations of the depositories (not more often than once per year) to check for compliance with contract provisions. Depositories will be notified before visitations occur. If a violation is found the depository will be granted a reasonable length of time to comply, and a follow-up inspection may be conducted to verify compliance.

8. The Clearinghouse will meet with personnel from each depository library to assist in setting up systematic recording procedures for documents received and to provide information and suggestions concerning maintenance and utilization of the state documents collection.

9. The depository library will appoint a staff member (one who will be largely responsible for the state documents collection) to serve as a contact person for the Clearinghouse.

10. The depository will make the state documents accessible to the public for use in the library. Circulation policies may be established by the individual depositories.

11. The depository shall take measures to publicize its state documents collection.

12. The Clearinghouse will continue to keep one hard copy and two microfiche copies of all state publications for interlibrary loan purposes.

13. The Clearinghouse will include authorization to discard any superceded publications on the shipping lists.

14. The Clearinghouse will have final authority to make selection of depository items. Recommendations of depository libraries will, however, be of prime importance in the selection process.

15. All depositories will receive the same material, subject to availability, in order of priority as established by the Clearinghouse.

16. Depositories will be expected to send a representative from their staff to attend Clearinghouse meetings on the depository system (no less than once each year).

17. The depository library will assume responsibility to replace lost depository documents and to maintain records of items which cannot be replaced.

18. The depository will return duplicate depository items received to the Clearinghouse.

19. Documents which depository libraries deem no longer valuable to their collection may be discarded with the approval of the Clearinghouse. We suggest, however, that depositories retain depository items for 5 years. The Clearinghouse and the Nebraska State Historical Society will continue to keep all items in their collections.

20. University and state college newspapers are not put on microfiche and are not sent to depository libraries. One copy of these newspapers is deposited at the Nebraska State Historical Society. One copy is deposited in the Clearinghouse collection.

BIBLIOGRAPHY

``Legislative Bills 1284 and 1284A.'' *Nebraska Library Association Quarterly* 3, no. 1:4-5 (Spring 1972).
A report that hearings had been held on the Nebraska Publications Clearinghouse bill and that the Appropriations Committee decided to sponsor the bill.

Shaffer, Dallas. ``Clearinghouse.'' *Nebraska Library Association Quarterly* 3, no. 2:4 (Summer 1972).
A news note on the passage of the depository law.

Shaffer, Dallas Y. ''State Document Legislation: Nebraska; A Case Study.'' *Government Publications Review* 1:19-27 (Fall 1973).
A detailed report on the Nebraska experience in assembling information, drafting, and working for enactment of legislation. Excerpts from the bill, and the budget request are appended.

Nebraska Library Association Quarterly 5, no. 3:21-23 (Fall 1974).
The clearinghouse has processed approximately 20,000 federal publications and 3,000 new state publications since it began operation in July 1972. A sampling (thirteen documents, annotated) of state and federal documents available on interlibrary loan is given.

''Documents.'' *Nebraska Library Association Quarterly* 6, no. 1:20-22 (Spring 1975).
A sample (nine documents, annotated) of state and federal documents available on interlibrary loan.

''Classification Abstracts: [Nebraska] Classification Number Analysis.'' *Documents to the People* 3 (no. 5): 38-43 (May 1975).
Classification numbers as used in the *Nebraska State Publications Checklist* are explained. The scheme is archival in approach.

The DOCumentor: A Government Documents Newsletter for Depository Libraries in Nebraska.
Includes news notes on state documents from time to time. Number 1 (September 1976) announced the beginning of the depository system in Nebraska, with five libraries contracting for service. The depository system was part of the original legislation enacted in 1972. The clearinghouse will continue to make all publications available through regular interlibrary loan channels.

Number 2 (December 1976) mentions a November 18 meeting of state document librarians to discuss current problems. A brief report was given on the MPLA/SWLA State Documents Pre-Conference held in Albuquerque, New Mexico, on November 10.

Number 3 reports on plans for a cumulative edition (1972-1977) of the *Checklist*.

Number 4 (October 1977) includes several notes on state documents. Most of these news notes were reprinted in *Documents to the People* 6, no. 1 (January 1978):

> ''State Documents on Microfiche'' announces the inauguration of a microfiche program for all Nebraska documents. The size of the collection, the difficulty of securing sufficient copies of publications, and the deterioration of older publications on the library's shelves influenced the decision.
>
> The project will begin with current documents and state documents depositories will receive only microfiche copies of the publications. The reduction will be 48x.
>
> ''State Document Depositories System: Information for Potential Participants'' outlines the distribution made by the Clearinghouse and reports that depositories have received more than 4,000 titles since January, 1976. Depositories are listed in the *Checklist* and publications sent to them are marked with a black dot. The depository librarians meet about twice a year.

``Nebraska State Publications Checklist'' announces that work on the Cumulative Edition of the *Checklist* is progressing well. Data processing and printing are causing some delays.

``Nebraska Documents Meeting'' reports on the May, 1977 meeting of eleven librarians who were given an explanation of the classification number and dates. The depository librarians suggested that number changes be indicated on the shipping lists, that they receive extra copies of Clearinghouse brochures on state documents for distribution, and that the Clearinghouse prepare spot radio announcements, new brochures, a decal, information on the loan policies of the depositories, and handbook for depositories.

NEVADA

NEV. REV. STAT. §§ 378.150 to 210 (1979)

STATE PUBLICATIONS DISTRIBUTION CENTER

378.150. Declaration of legislative intent. It is the intent of the legislature in enacting NRS 378.150 to 378.210, inclusive, that:

1. All state and local government publications be distributed to designated depository libraries for use by all inhabitants of the state; and

2. Designated depository libraries assume the responsibility for keeping such publications readily accessible for use and rendering assistance, without charge, to patrons using them. (Added to NRS by 1971, 499.)

378.160. Definitions. As used in NRS 378.150 to 378.210, inclusive:

1. ''Print'' means all forms of printing and duplicating other than by use of carbon paper.

2. ''State agency'' includes the legislature, constitutional officers or any department, division, bureau, board, commission or agency of the State of Nevada.

3. ''State publication'' includes any document issued in print by any state agency and which may legally be released for public distribution, but does not include:

(a) Nevada Revised Statutes;

(b) Nevada Reports;

(c) Bound volumes of the Statutes of Nevada;

(d) The Nevada Digest or Annotations to Nevada Revised Statutes prepared by the legislative counsel;

(e) Press items of the University of Nevada System which are not in the nature of public and other university items not designed for external distribution; or

(f) Correspondence and intraoffice or interoffice communications which are not of vital interest to the public; or

(g) Publications from established agencies which are required by federal and state law to be distributed to depositories which duplicate those under NRS 378.200. (Added to NRS by 1971, 499.)

378.170. State publications distribution center: Creation; rules and regulations.

1. There is hereby created within the Nevada state library a state publications distribution center.

2. The state librarian may make such rules and regulations as may be necessary to carry out the purposes of the state publications distribution center. (Added to NRS by 1971, 499.)

378.180. State, local agencies to deposit copies of publications when issued.

1. Every state agency shall, upon release, deposit a specified number of copies of each of its state publications with the state publications distribution center to meet the needs of the depository library system and to provide interlibrary loan service to those libraries without depository status. This distribution shall be required only if sufficient funds are appropriated for the printing of these materials.

2. For each item printed by the state printing and records division of the department of general services, 50 additional copies shall be authorized to be printed by the division, these to be collected by the state publications distribution center and distributed to public and university libraries within the state.

3. All city, county and regional agencies shall, upon release, deposit at least one copy of each of its publications with the state publications distribution center and a list of its publications for a calendar year. (Added to NRS by 1971, 499; A 1973, 1472.)

378. 190. Depository agreements with other libraries; standards.

1. The state publications distribution center may enter into depository agreements with any city, county, district, regional, town or university library in this state.

2. The state librarian shall establish standards for eligibility as a depository library under subsection 1. Such standards may include and take into account:

(a) The type of library;

(b) Its ability to preserve such publications and to make them available for public use; and

(c) Its geographical location in order to assure that the publications are conveniently accessible to residents in all areas of the state. (Added to NRS by 1971, 500.)

378.200. Distribution of copies of state publications.

1. After receipt of any state publications, the state publications distribution center shall distribute copies of those publications as follows:

(a) One copy to the legislative counsel bureau;

(b) Two copies to the Library of Congress; and

(c) Two copies to each depository library in this state.

2. The center shall retain sufficient copies in the Nevada state library for preservation and use by the public. The remaining copies must be used for distribution in accordance with any agreements entered into with other states for the exchange of state publications, and for loaning services to those libraries without depository status. (Added to NRS by 1971, 500; A 1973, 346; 1979, 182.)

378.210. Publication, distribution of list of state publications. The state publications distribution center shall periodically publish, and, upon request, distribute to all state agencies and contracting depository libraries a list of state publications. (Added to NRS by 1971, 500.)

STATE COMMENT

The Nevada State Library began systematically collecting State government publications and publishing a checklist (*Nevada Official Publications*) in 1953. In 1968 we began an "unofficial" depository system as a demonstration project for the Nevada legislature. In 1971 our depository legislation was passed, and while it has some loopholes and some undesirable requirements it has proved to be quite serviceable when administered and complied with in the spirit rather than the letter of the law. (Report by Joan G. Kerschner, Documents Librarian, Nevada State Library, Carson City, Nevada 89710. *In* The State of State Documents: Past, Present, Future. Texas Legislative Reference Library, 1976, at p. 15.)

EDITORIAL COMMENT

The 1973 amendment to 378.180 changed the name of the state printing agency.

The 1973 amendment to 378.200 was a change of the name of the division in 378.200 (1(a)) from "division of archives." The 1979 amendment to this section deleted the distribution to the archives unit in the secretary of state's office.

RULES AND REGULATIONS

RULES AND REGULATIONS FOR STATE
PUBLICATIONS DISTRIBUTION CENTER
Adopted January 10, 1972
Effective March 1, 1972

The following rules and regulations are promulgated for the purpose of implementing chapter 378 of NRS which provides for the establishment of a

Documents Distribution Center in the Nevada State Library, and for the distribution of state publications to depository libraries.

It is the expressed legislative intent that:

1) State and local government publications be deposited, when funds permit, with the Documents Distribution Center and then distributed to depository libraries.

2) Designated depository libraries and the Nevada State Library retain copies of publications and make them available to employees of the State of Nevada and the general public for research and reference use.

DEFINITIONS

1. "State agency" includes the legislature, constitutional officers or any department, division, bureau, board, commission or agency of the State of Nevada.

2. "State publication" includes any document issued in print by any state agency and which may legally be released for public distribution. This includes everything from lengthy technical reports to brief printed or mimeographed leaflets. It does *not* include:

a) Nevada Revised Statutes or supplements thereto;

b) Nevada reports;

c) Bound volumes of the Statutes of Nevada.

d) The Nevada Digest or Annotations to Nevada Revised Statutes supplements thereto and later case service prepared by the Legislative Counsel.

e) Items published by the University of Nevada Press which are not in the nature of public documents and other University items not designed for external distribution.

f) Correspondence and intraoffice communications which are not of vital interest to the public.

g) Publications from established agencies which are required by federal and state law to be distributed to depositories which duplicate those designated by the Documents Distribution Center.

3. "Print" means all forms of printing and duplicating other than by use of carbon paper. This is intended to include publications issued in a microform format.

AGENCIES TO DEPOSIT PUBLICATIONS

Each state agency shall, upon release, deposit at least two copies and as many additional copies, up to 50, as needed and as funds appropriated for printing will permit.

If sufficient funds have been appropriated to print fifty copies they shall be so printed and deposited with the Distribution Center unless there has been mutual agreement between the agency and the Distribution Center that a lesser number of copies will be needed for distribution.

Each agency is urged at budget preparation time to request sufficient funds to provide for the printing of 50 additional copies of its publications.

DISTRIBUTION CENTER TO DISTRIBUTE PUBLICATIONS

Upon receipt of state publications; the distribution center shall distribute copies of such publications as follows:

a) One copy to the division of archives of the office of the Secretary of State.

b) One copy to the Legislative Counsel Bureau.

c) Two copies to the Library of Congress.

d) One copy to the California State Library.

e) Two copies to each designated depository library in Nevada

University of Nevada at Reno.
University of Nevada at Las Vegas.
Washoe County Library.
Clark County Library District.
Elko County Library.

f) Two copies in the state library's permanent reference collection.

The remaining copies shall be used for exchange purposes with other states and for meeting the needs of non-depository school and public libraries in Nevada.

DISTRIBUTION CENTER TO ISSUE LISTS

The distribution center shall publish on a regular basis a list of state publications and, upon request, shall distribute such list to all state agencies and libraries in Nevada.

CITY AND COUNTY PUBLICATIONS

All city, county and regional agencies shall, upon release, deposit at least one copy of each of its publications with the state publications distribution center and a list of its publications for a calendar year.

INTERSTATE COMPACTS AND FUNCTIONS

The State Publications Distribution Center will maintain appropriate liaison with the following entities for the purpose of maintaining collections of publications, reference, and research materials concerning these multi-state cooperative functions:

a) California-Nevada Compact Commission.

b) Columbia Compact Commission.

c) Multistate Tax Commission.

d) Tahoe Regional Planning Agency.

e) Western Interstate Commission for Higher Learning.

f) Western Interstate Nuclear Board.

g) Commissioners on Uniform State Laws.

Compliance with these rules and regulations will be complete when materials have been deposited at:

Documents Distribution Center

c/o Nevada State Library

Carson City, Nevada 89701

BIBLIOGRAPHY

Gardner, Jack. "Nevada State Publications Distribution." University of Nevada, Bureau of Governmental Research. *Governmental Research Newsletter* 7:[1]-3 (November 1968).
Gardner, documents librarian of the Nevada State Library, states that "Nevada is one in a minority of states which has no legislative backing for a state publications distribution center," outlines the efforts of librarians to secure legislation, and describes the voluntary program in operation. He stresses the need to trace the history of the various state agencies and to create a permanent file of the departments and agencies of the state, based on Poulton's 1964 work and updated immediately after each legislative session. Mention is made of the Official Publications List's new format and subject index.

Kerschner, Joan. "Documents at Her Fingertips." *Nevada Government Today* (Winter 1974), p. 7.
The administrator of the Nevada State Publications Distribution Center describes the advantages of the center to government agencies, which are both producers and consumers of information as they fulfill their public service roles."

Government Documents in Nevada: A Report to the Nevada Statewide Coordination of Collection Committee. Rev. June 1975. Various paging.
The committee transmitted the report to the state librarian with a recommendation for "serious consideration of grant requests related to it." It is a revision of a report prepared February 1974, and covers all types of documents—federal, state, international, and so on.
Part I, "Overview," covers the operation of a system of nine depository libraries, priority rankings for distribution, and notation system used in each library. A chart on nondepository libraries gives the size of collection (with some descriptive notes) and the classification used.
Part II, "Evaluation," reports that all state depositories "are, for the first time this year, up and running with collections unpacked, numbered and on shelves, shelf list cards filed and a staff member assigned part time for maintenance." The problem is access by any point other than main entry. The proposed book catalog is essential. Thereafter a series of workshops is suggested. Hearings on the proposed rules and regulations need to be held and then a "concerted campaign to reeducate the state agencies."

Part III, "Plan," proposes: (1) Document book catalog (MARC format, access through author, title and subject, 1864-1975, state and local documents). Supplemented by *Nevada Official Publications*. Estimated cost—$1 per title for 6,000 titles. Appendix D is a one-page justification, emphasizing the monetary savings. (2) Publications: six different publications including update of the state agency list, an annotated bibliography for school and public libraries, a brochure, and revised procedure manual. (3) Documents workshop. The list of topics includes overview of system, rules and regulations, problems, internal procedures, and plans. (4) Agency visits are proposed after completion of the book catalog to check on titles omitted, to explain service, and to establish or reaffirm channels. (5) Regional hearings on proposed rules and regulations. After both state and federal workshops, a documents workshop for "layman librarians"—public, school and reference librarians—is planned to familiarize these librarians with all aspects of both state and federal documents.

Poulton, Helen J. *Nevada State Agencies: From Territory Through Statehood*. [Reno]: University of Nevada Press [1964] 97 p. (University of Nevada Press. Bibliographical series, no. 5.)

NEW HAMPSHIRE

N. H. REV. STAT. ANN. §§ 202-B:1 to 5 (1977)

CHAPTER 202-B. DISTRIBUTION OF PUBLIC DOCUMENTS

202-B:1.State Depository Libraries, Designated. The state librarian is authorized to designate no more than 25 public and academic libraries as state depository libraries. (Source. 1973, 140:3, eff. July 21, 1973.)

202-B:2. Copies of All State Agency Publications. Each state agency shall print 25 copies of their publications for deposit with the state librarian. Distribution to depository libraries shall be made thereafter by the state librarian, as soon as practicable. (Source. 1973, 140:3, eff. July 21, 1973.)

202-B:3. Definitions. As used in this chapter:

I. "State publication" or "publication" includes any document, compilation, code, register, pamphlet, list, book, report, memorandum [,] hearing, leaflet, order, regulation, directory [,] periodical or serial issued by state, constitutional officers, or any department, division, commission or other agency of the state in print.

II. "Print" includes all forms of duplicating other than by the use of carbon paper. (Source. 1973, 140:3, eff. July 21, 1973.)

202-B:4. Distribution Not Required. The state librarian shall not distribute copies of:

I. Joint resolutions, bills, legislative manuals, statutes, and journals as provided under RSA 20;

II. The state reporter and reports provided under RSA 505;

III. Intra-office or inter-office publications and forms. (Source. 1973, 140:3, eff. July 21, 1973.)

202-B:5. Duties of Depository Libraries. Depository libraries shall provide adequate facilities for the storage and use of the publications. They shall render reasonable service without charge to qualified patrons who desire to use the publications. They shall catalogue the publications in an acceptable fashion. (Source. 1973, 140:3, eff. July 21, 1973.)

STATE COMMENT

Now that the program is five years old, space is becoming a problem in the depository libraries. Librarians are questioning the need to retain publications for an indefinite period. (Letter from Eleanor O'Donnell, New Hampshire State Library, Concord, New Hampshire 03301, dated January 7, 1980.)

EDITORIAL COMMENT

Section 202-B:3(I) is written without a comma between ''memorandum'' and ''hearing,'' or between ''directory'' and ''periodical.''

Laws 1973, ch. 140 was titled ''An Act relative to the standardization of reports of state agencies and the distribution of state publications.'' It had 50 sections, most of them relating to the reports of individual departments. Many of these sections were amended to require *biennial* reports to the governor *and council*. The 1973 law did not include an appropriation.

BIBLIOGRAPHY

Hazelton, Philip A. ''New Hampshire State Publications.'' *North Country Libraries* 8:5 (May-June 1965).
Hazelton, law librarian at the New Hampshire State Library, comments on the ''Red Book,'' *New Hampshire Revised Statutes Annual, Directory of New Hampshire Municipal and County Officers*, and *Fiscal Facts*, and mentions other publications of interest to ''even the smallest [New Hampshire] libraries.''

Blake, T. ''Journey's End.'' *Dartmouth College Library Bulletin* 15:90-91 (April 1975).
The Dartmouth College Library which had collected New Hampshire documents for years feels that ''the chance of receiving some copies of all publications at the State Library is very much better than it was formerly,'' and because ''Dartmouth and the University of New Hampshire have a priority when there are not enough copies to go around,'' the Dartmouth Library considers itself a happy beneficiary of the depository law.

New Hampshire State Library, Concord. ''Checklist of New Hampshire's State Departments Publications.'' Suppl. of *Biennial Report . . . 1948-50*. The Library.

Brackett, T. ''New Hampshire Documents.'' *Bulletin, New Hampshire Public Library* 33:121-127 (September 1937). (Not seen.)

NEW JERSEY

N.J. STAT. ANN. §§ 52:14-25.1 to 25.2 (West 1970)

52:14-25.1. Annual or special reports; copies filed in state library. All State officers, departments and commissions or committees issuing annual reports or special reports required by law to be submitted to the Governor or to the Legislature of this State, where such reports are printed, mimeographed or otherwise mechanically reproduced, shall file with the New Jersey State Library for general reference use in said library and for exchange purposes at least 75 copies of each of such printed, mimeographed or otherwise mechanically reproduced reports, and in those cases where such reports are made in typewritten form and not subsequently printed, mimeographed or otherwise mechanically reproduced shall file in the State Library for general reference use at least one each of such typewritten reports. (Amended by L. 1957, c. 99, p. 194, § 1; L. 1967, c. 162, § 1, eff. July 25, 1967.)

52:14-25.2 Publication other than annual or special reports; copies filed in State Library. State officers, departments, commissions or committees issuing from time to time serial or other publications of a general informational character other than annual or special reports, where such publications are printed, mimeographed or otherwise mechanically reproduced for public distribution, shall file in the State Library for permanent reference use and for exchange purposes at least 75 copies of each of such publications, and in those cases where such serials or other publications are not printed, mimeographed or otherwise mechanically reproduced but are issued in typewritten form, shall file in the State Library for general reference use at least one each of such typewritten publications. (Amended by L. 1957, c. 99, p. 194, § 2; L. 1967, c. 162, § 2, eff. July 25, 1967.)

STATE COMMENT (1973)

New Jersey's document depository legislation provides 75 copies of state publications for distribution to designated depository libraries in cases where documents are printed, mimeographed or otherwise mechanically reproduced. Where reports are typewritten but not reproduced, one copy is to be filed with the State Library for reference use. Usually reports which are reproduced are no great problem, particularly those made for the Legislature since we do general distribution of materials for the Legislature. The matter of typewritten reports is harder to evaluate since it is not always possible to determine that such a report has been made unless we hear about it in one way or another.

Our collecting of all reports is a complex matter and is done in a variety of ways. We have direct contact with the Legislative Services Agency and copies of legislative reports and hearings are sent to us as soon as they are ready for distribution. Departmental reports are usually furnished either through the public information office of the various departments or through the individual office issuing the report. We also check departmental news releases and publications to learn of publications which may have been issued; we clip newspapers from various sections of the state and note the mention of any report or other publication they may mention.

It would, of course, be easier if there was one central printing office but this appears to be an impossibility. Some material which is considered as a state document is printed by private research agencies, etc. for a state agency, etc. I suppose that some sort of penalty for not submitting reports would be one way of enforcing such a regulation, but I don't think that it is really feasible.

The law is adequate for our needs. It means that the person collecting the material has to do more work than would be necessary if everything came automatically but most offices are cooperative and do supply whatever material they have available. (Report titled New Jersey Depository Legislation, dated January 16, 1973. *In* Documents on Documents Collection.)

EDITORIAL COMMENT

Section 52:14-25, an old 1907 law, provides for distribution of copies of every report, testimony, pamphlet or other publication, at the expense of the state, to all free public libraries and county historical societies.

CONTRACT

STATE OF NEW JERSEY
DEPARTMENT OF EDUCATION
Division of the State Library, Archives and History
Barbara F. Weaver, Assistant Commissioner/State Librarian

Bureau of Law, Legislative   P.O. Box 1898
and General Reference   185 West State Street
(609) 292-6294   Trenton, NJ 08625

Agreement between the New Jersey State Library, Bureau of Law, Legislative and General Reference, acting as the Primary Depository for New Jersey State Documents, and _____ acting as a Secondary Depository for New Jersey State Documents.

1.1   The _____ accepts designation as a Secondary Depository for New Jersey State Documents as offered by the New Jersey State Library and accepts the conditions for such status as agreed to in this contract.

2.1   The Primary Depository shall secure copies of State publications as specified in NJSA 52:14-25.1 and 52:14-25.2.

2.2   The Primary Depository shall ship documents to the Secondary Depositories at least once a month with shipping lists provided and the shipments numbered consecutively within the calendar year.

2.3   When the issuing agency fails to deliver to the Primary Depository enough copies to provide one copy to each Secondary Depository, the items provided will be sent to the Secondary Depositories according to a priority list developed and published by the Primary Depository.

2.4   The Primary Depository will attempt to replace items missing from shipments or missing shipments for the Secondary Depositories when claimed according to 3.3 below.

2.5   The Primary Depository shall retain forever all State publications with the exception of certain ephemeral materials such as news releases, press summaries and announcements and agency reprints of laws.

2.6   The Primary Depository will maintain both reference and circulating copies of most of the documents in its collection, thereby insuring the availability of State documents to researchers and libraries.

3.1   In exchange for the prompt procurement and free shipment of State documents, and in order to provide a local complement to the Primary Depository collection, the Secondary Depository agrees to maintain its collection for the use of the residents of New Jersey as follows.

3.2   All Secondary Depositories agree to accept and service all materials sent to them whether in paper copy or microform. The Secondary Depository may if it so desires convert microform to paper copy or convert paper copy to microform.

3.3   The Secondary Depository shall keep a record of shipments received, shall open each shipment within ten working days of receiving it, shall claim missing shipments and missing items within a shipment within a month, and shall return duplicate shipments received by mistake.

3.4   A full-time professional librarian shall be designated by the Director of the Secondary Depository to serve, as one of his/her duties, as the person with overall reponsibility for management of and reference assistance to the Secondary Depository's New Jersey Documents Collection. This person's name shall be reported to the Primary Depository by the Director of the library.

3.5   The Secondary Depository shall maintain the depository collection in as good physical condition as the other collections in the library.

3.6   The Secondary Depository shall make the depository collection available for use by the general public and shall provide reference assistance at all times that general reference assistance is available.

3.7   Beginning with shipments received two months after the date of this agreement, the Secondary Depository shall provide subject access to all newly received material. The following are several different forms of subject access any one of which is automatically acceptable to the Primary Depository. Other means of access must have the written approval of the Primary Depository.

a)   Full cataloging. including subject entries. in the main public catalog; *or*
b)   a special documents catalog that includes subject entries; *or*
c)   a special subject card file that covers all the documents; *or*
d)   pamphlet files for all materials. arranged by subjects. with a minimum of 40 different subjects; *or,*
e)   the minimum acceptable. use of the Primary Depository's subject-based classification scheme for all non-serial, non-periodical materials (call numbers will be provided on the shipping list). providing that the reference staff maintains a list of the cutter numbers and understands how to use the classification system as a subject approach.

3.8   The Secondary Depository shall assemble basic written procedures for the use of the library's staff and a brief descriptive guide to its collection of New Jersey Documents for the use of the library's patrons.

3.9   The Secondary Depository may set its own circulation policy for New Jersey Documents.

3.10   The Secondary Depositories were established to provide access to current materials. All materials received by the Secondary Depository from the Primary Depository must be retained for five years from date of receipt and then may be discarded at the option of the Secondary Depository; ephemeral items as listed in 2.5 above may be discarded when no longer of value to the Secondary Depository. Superseded lists. directories and guides may be discarded.

3.11   Those Secondary Depository libraries who choose to build strong. retrospective collections may enter into a separate "Secondary Retrospective Depository Library" agreement with the Primary Depository. These "S.R.D.L." shall be given high priority in the assignment of documents in short supply.

4.1   Because Law School Libraries are the only highly specialized libraries within this Depository Network. the following option is made available to them.

4.2   Law School Libraries may reject any materials at the time they are received if two conditions are met:
a)   There must be a non-Law School Secondary Depository within the same legal municipality so that the residents of that municipality do not lose access to a full depository; *and*
b)   The Law School Library must return to the Primary Depository at the Law School's expense at least quarterly all items it has chosen not to retain from current shipments.

4.3   This Law School Option applies only to selection at the time of receipt of shipments and does not affect any other provisions of this agreement.

5.1   The Primary Depository will make periodic inspections to insure compliance with this agreement. Libraries found to be not in compliance will be given written notice by the Assistant Commissioner/State Librarian of the areas of non-compliance.

5.2   Failure of the Secondary Depository to correct cited areas of non-compliance within 90 days of notification can result in the removal of its Secondary Depository designation upon a hearing held by the Assistant Commissioner/State Librarian at which the Secondary Depository may be heard.

5.3   The Secondary Depository can relinquish its Secondary Depository status voluntarily by making written application to the Assistant Commissioner/State Librarian.

5.4   This agreement goes into effect immediately and remains in effect indefinitely unless the depository law is changed or until replaced by a new agreement.

Barbara F. Weaver, Assistant
Commissioner/State Librarian
for the Primary Depository

Date
1/14/80

Date

STATE COMMENT

We are in the process of radically revising [the rules and regulations for our depository libraries] and hope to have the new ones agreed upon by all concerned and in operation by late Winter or early Spring, 1980. . . . Our new rules have been modelled on the Federal Depository rules. [Included here under the heading, ''Contract.''] (Letter from Robert E. Lupp, Supervisor, New Jersey Reference Section, State Library, Trenton, New Jersey 08625, dated December 31, 1979.)

BIBLIOGRAPHY

''Right-to-know Symposium and Resolution.'' *New Jersey Libraries* 10:20 (November 1977).
Discusses pending legislation on public access to unpublished government records. Government Document group recommended amendments on indexing of decisions, and so on, affecting the public and on publication of records retention schedules.

Oellrich, G. ''New Jersey State Author Headings: A Preliminary Analysis.'' M.S. Thesis, Columbia University, 1951. 57p. (Not seen.)

NEW MEXICO

N. M. STAT. ANN. §§ 18-2-4, 18-2-4.1, 18-2-7.1 (Supp. 1979)

18-2-4. Duties of the state librarian. The state librarian shall:
****

J. establish and administer a library depository and distribution system for state documents and publications. (Added by Laws 1978, ch. 140, § 1.)

18-2-4.1. State publications; copies required.

A. Unless otherwise directed by the state librarian, every state agency shall deposit twenty-five copies of all its publications intended for public distribution, when issued, with the state library depository for depository and distribution purposes, excluding those publications issued strictly for internal use and those intended for public sale.

B. The state librarian shall determine the number of copies of regularly issued publications required to meet the needs of the various libraries in the state, and shall inform the affected agencies of the exact number of copies required. (HISTORY: 1953 Comp., § 4-11-3.2, enacted by Laws 1978, ch. 140, § 2.)

18-2-7.1. Distribution system; limitation. The state library depository shall not engage in the direct distribution of state publications to the general public except in those cases where the state library does so in the course of operating as a library or a state extension service. (HISTORY: 1953 Comp., §4-11-6.1, enacted Laws 1978, ch. 140, § 3.)

STATE COMMENT (1978)

[T]he new depository law . . . is an amendment to the legislation affecting the State Library. The law was made purposely vague to avoid setting up opposition from some of the state agencies; definitions seemed to do that. Whether it was wise not to define I can't say. The bill did sail through the Legislature easily this year; perhaps members were just tired of seeing us every year. I don't consider it model legislation, however.

The State Library has hired an energetic young woman to set up a Clearinghouse for the depository system. She is working on regulations, and the New

Mexico Library Association and State Library are conducting a number of workshops in October and November to explain how it will operate. (Letter from Laura H. McGuire, Documents Librarian, Eastern New Mexico University, Portales, New Mexico 88130, dated October 11, 1978.)

EDITORIAL COMMENT

The 1978 act, in addition to enacting the two new sections (18-2-4.1 and 18-2-7.1) added subsection J to section 18-2-4 on the duties of the state librarian. The act carried a $32,000 appropriation ''for the purpose of developing and administering the state library depository and distribution system.''

A 1979 bill (House Bill 473), which called for the repeal of § 18-2-4.1, was amended to delete the repeal, thus leaving the original depository legislation in effect.

RULES AND REGULATIONS

SL Rule 79-1   February 1, 1979

STATE DOCUMENTS DEPOSITORY CLEARINGHOUSE

1. These rules are published pursuant to the New Mexico Documents Law. (NMSA 78 supp. 18-2-4.1)
2. These rules in no way amend or alter the State Rules Act and the obligations thereof. (NMSA 78 14-4-1)
3. Rules binding on the State Documents Depository Clearinghouse.
   a. CHECKLIST: New Mexico State Records Center in cooperation with the State Documents Depository Clearinghouse shall publish an official list of state publications and rules received by both agencies.
   b. LIAISON: State agencies shall be notified to provide the proper numbers of copies of state publications and rules for distribution to depository libraries. Every effort shall be made to keep up an established liaison with state agencies in order to insure that adequate numbers of copies of state publications and rules are filed.
   c. DEPOSITORY LIBRARIES: The state librarian shall designate the institutions that will be depositories for New Mexico state documents.
   d. CLASSIFICATION OF DOCUMENTS: The State Documents Depository Clearinghouse staff will assign classification numbers to all state publications and rules received from any source prior to distribution to depository libraries.
   e. DEPOSITORY SHIPMENTS: The librarian, State Documents Depository Clearinghouse will forward on a regular basis, via the most eco-

nomical means, shipments of state publications and rules to depository libraries.

f. SHIPPING LISTS: The librarian, State Documents Depository Clearinghouse will provide sufficient bibliographic information on the monthly issues of the shipping list to enable depository libraries to check in the publications and rules received.

g. STATE AGENCY LIST: The librarian, State Documents Depository Clearinghouse shall publish from time to time an updated edition or revision of the state agency author headings list.

h. INFORMATION CLEARINGHOUSE: The librarian, State Documents Depository Clearinghouse shall serve as an information clearinghouse with and among depository libraries on matters of interest such as availability of microfilm publications, discarded state publications and other matters of common interest. Such information will be added to end of the shipping list or made available in the most expedient manner.

i. DEPOSITORY LIBRARY COUNCIL: The librarian, State Documents Depository Clearinghouse shall, in consultation with the state librarian, choose depository library representatives to form a council to the clearinghouse.

j. DEPOSITORY CONTRACT: The librarian, state documents depository clearinghouse will formulate the contract to be signed by the contracting depository libraries.

k. INSPECTIONS: The librarian, state documents depository clearinghouse will make periodic inspections of all depository libraries to determine that the regulations are being carried out.

l. TRAINING: The librarian, state documents depository clearinghouse will provide basic training to all designated personnel who are named responsible for state documents in depository libraries. In addition, advanced training will be provided as needed.

m. OWNERSHIP: The New Mexico State library shall retain ownership of New Mexico State documents deposited in libraries within the state of New Mexico.

n. SALES ITEMS: Documents available only through purchase must be obtained directly from the agency of publication by the depository library, if it desires the publication.

4. Rules binding on State Agencies.
   A. DEFINITIONS:
   a. The term "State Agency" means every state office, officer[,] department, division, section, unit, service, bureau, commission, committee, and subdivision thereof of all branches of the State Government and which agencies expend appropriations of state funds.
   b. The term "publications" means any document, report, directory, bibliography, newsletter, pamphlet, brochure, periodical, or other

printed material paid for in whole or in part by funds appropriated by the State Legislature or issued at the request of a State Agency; excepting however, correspondence, inter-office memoranda, confidential publications and items for sale.

c. The term "rule" means any rule, regulation, order, standard statement of policy, including amendments thereto or repeals thereof, issued or promulgated by an agency of state government and purporting to affect one (1) or more agencies besides the agency issuing such rule or to affect persons not members or employees of such issuing agency.

B. In addition to publications, all rules and regulations promulgated by all state agencies shall be deposited with the Clearinghouse and New Mexico State Records Center.

C. PUBLICATIONS OFFICER: Each State Agency shall inform the New Mexico State Documents Clearinghouse, and New Mexico State Records Center of the person, persons or positions responsible for collecting publications and rules of that agency.

5. Rules binding on the depository libraries.

Any officially designated depository library shall agree to the following conditions, with the understanding that prolonged failure to comply with the provisions is sufficient grounds for cancellation of the contract and the removal of the privileges of the depository library status.

a. SPACE: The depository shall provide space to adequately house the publications and rules in a manner approved by the clearinghouse. (subject to inspection.)

b. RECORD OF RECEIPT: The depository shall provide an orderly systematic record of receipt of all documents from the Clearinghouse and all state publications and rules shall be processed and shelved within thirty days after receipt.

c. REFERENCE SERVICE: The depository shall provide personnel to provide service to patrons of the depository in the use of such publications and rules.

d. PUBLIC ACCESS: The depository agrees to make the documents available for public use and in the case of microforms, to provide adequate equipment for viewing them.

e. INTERLIBRARY LOAN: The depository agrees that all patrons' [requests?] concerning state documents that it cannot fill will be channelled within a reasonable amount of time through the regular New Mexico Interlibrary Loan Network.

f. CLAIMS: Publications and rules listed on a shipping list, but not received or defective copies should be claimed within thirty days of receipt of the shipping list. The exception would be insufficient copies of a publication or rule which will be indicated on the shipping list.

g. RETENTION: Retention of state documents shall be for a five year period, unless modified by the State Documents Depository Clearinghouse. Disposal of publications needs the prior approval of the State Documents Depository Clearinghouse.

h. TRAINING: Designated personnel for state documents in depository libraries shall be required to take basic training provided by the State Documents Depository Clearinghouse within nine (9) months of their appointment. In addition, the designated personnel will be responsible for attending any advanced training provided by the State Documents Depository Clearinghouse.

i. TERMINATION: The depository library may terminate its status on a six (6) month written notice to the state librarian which notice shall state the cause of termination. Upon termination of the contract, the Depository Library shall ship within a reasonable time, all documents to the Clearinghouse or to such other depositories as may be specified by the Clearinghouse.

Approved:
/s/ *Clifford Lange*
Clifford Lange
State Librarian

CONTRACT

DEPOSITORY LIBRARY CONTRACT

This agreement made this _____ day of _____, 19_____, by and between the New Mexico State Documents Depository Clearinghouse, a division of the New Mexico State Library, hereinafter called the "Clearinghouse," and the _____ hereinafter called the "Depository." The terms publication, document and state documents as used in this contract refer to the State Agency Publications deposited with the State Library Depository pursuant to Chapter 140 of the Laws of New Mexico, 1978.

WITNESSETH: WHEREAS, the legislature of the State of New Mexico in 1978 enacted legislation entitled Chaper 140 in Laws of New Mexico 1978, creating a New Mexico State Documents Depository Clearinghouse as a division within the New Mexico State Library and

WHEREAS, under that statute the Clearinghouse is authorized to enter into depository contracts with any municipal, county, or regional public library, state college or state university library, and out-of-state research libraries; and

WHEREAS: the _____ Library is desirous of entering into such an inter-library contract with the Clearinghouse;

NOW, THEREFORE IT IS MUTUALLY AGREED AND UNDERSTOOD, THAT

(1) The Clearinghouse shall regularly publish an official list of state publications;

(2) The Clearinghouse shall send documents on deposit to the Depository in regular shipments;

(3) The Clearinghouse shall provide basic training, in the use of state documents for all designated personnel who are named responsible for state documents in depository libraries. In addition advanced training will be provided as needed.

(4) The Depository shall provide space to adequately house the publications in a manner approved by the Clearinghouse (subject to inspection);

(5) The Depository shall provide an orderly systematic record of receipt of all documents from the Clearinghouse and all state publications shall be processed and shelved within thirty days after receipt;

(6) The Depository shall provide personnel to provide service to patrons of the depository in the use of such publications;

(7) The Depository agrees that designated personnel responsible for state documents shall be required to take, within nine (9) months of their appointment, basic training provided by the State Documents Depository Clearinghouse. In addition, the designated personnel will be responsible for attending any advanced training provided by the State Documents Depository Clearinghouse;

(8) The Depository agrees to make the documents available for public use and in the case of microforms, to provide adequate equipment for viewing them;

(9) The Depository agrees that all patrons' requests concerning state documents that it cannot fill will be channelled within a reasonable time through the regular New Mexico interlibrary loan network;

(10) The Depository agrees to accept and maintain one copy of all publications (microfiche or paper copies) sent to it through the state depository system. The Depository agrees that all documents on deposit with the Depository shall remain the property of the Library Division of the New Mexico Department of Educational Finance & Cultural Affairs and may not be disposed of in any manner without the written authorization of the New Mexico State Documents Depository Clearinghouse.

(11) The Depository agrees to comply with all of the rules, regulations and standards adopted by the New Mexico State Library for depository libraries.

This contract is for a five-year period, beginning _____, 19_____ and extending through _____, 19_____ and may be terminated by either party upon six (6) months written notice, which notice shall state the cause of termination. Cause of termination of contract will be failure to comply with the terms of this contract by either party or cessation of the benefit received by either party from this agreement. The continued operation of the depository system will be contingent on the availability of adequate funding of the State Library Depository System. Upon termination of the contract, the Depository shall ship, within a reasonable time, all documents deposited with it pursuant to this contract, to the Clearinghouse or to such other Depositories as may be specified by the Clearinghouse.

Dated this _____ day of _____, 19_____.

This contract may be amended or terminated by the written mutual assent of both parties involved.

_____   _____
Witness   New Mexico State Library

_____   _____
Witness   Depository Library

BIBLIOGRAPHY

Three articles on New Mexico depository legislation appeared in the New Mexico library newsletter.

McGuire, Laura. ''Upcoming State Publications Legislation.'' *New Mexico Libraries Newsletter* 3:4 (January 1975).
Announces that a state publications depository bill, the result of five years' research, will be introduced in the legislature. The legislation is needed because two-thirds of the state's publications never reach the Library of Congress, libraries must request items repeatedly, agency personnel changes often upset established arrangements, and, at the other extreme, legislators receive too many publications. The bill establishes a distribution center within the state library. ''It [the legislation] would simplify the dissemination of information by the agencies and facilitate acquisition by depository libraries.''

''State Documents Act Passes.'' *New Mexico Library Association Newsletter* 6:1+ (March 1978).
The legislative effort which began in 1973 culminated successfully in the last hour of the 1978 regular session of the legislature. The bill was identical to the one introduced in 1977 and had the same sponsor. The 1977 bill had a $25,000 appropriation. The $7,000 increase was explained by one of the documents committee chairpersons with a detailed presentation of the proposed budget. The chairperson ''noted that the system would provide increased accessibility to state documents for the general public, through accurate indexing and widespread distribution to libraries throughout the state.''

''Rep. Malry Successful in Passage of Documents Bill.'' *New Mexico Library Newsletter* 6:1 (March 1978).
Representative Malry was chairman of the House Education Committee. ''When asked about his interest, Rep. Malry replied, 'Because of the difficulty in passing the 'feed bill', I didn't do much eating. Since I couldn't eat, I read a lot.' '' Malry and his wife were invited to the New Mexico Library Association (NMLA) Conference ''to give all of the NMLA members a chance to properly thank him.''

''New Mexico Depository Library Law Passes.'' *Documents to the People* 6:143 (May 1978).
The law, passed unanimously in both House and Senate, appropriates $32,000 for staff, equipment, and supplies. Twenty-five copies can be collected for distribution, and the state library can adopt rules and regulations.

NEW YORK

N. Y. LEGIS. LAW § 47 (McKinney Supp. 1979-1980)
N. Y. STATE PRINT. & PUB. DOC. LAW § 6 (McKinney Supp.
1979-1980)
N. Y. EDUC. LAW § 250 (McKinney 1969)

LEGIS. LAW § 47. Officers and institutions entitled to receive bound volumes of journals, bills and documents.
****

2.   To the New York state library, for incorporated colleges and universities in this state, for each state and territory, and for literary and scientific exchanges to be made by the New York state library, two hundred copies of the journals, one hundred copies of the documents, and five copies of the bills. (As amended L. 1955, c. 316, § 1, eff. Oct. 1, 1955.)

STATE PRINT. & PUB. DOC. LAW § 6. Department printing.
****

3.   Every state officer, department, commission, institution and board shall, as soon as any report thereby is printed, deliver two hundred copies thereof to the state library. (As amended L. 1955, c. 316, § 3, eff. Oct. 1, 1955.)

3-a. New York state departments, agencies or authorities that produce or finance a film, audio or video tape, or other electronic information program shall, upon completion of the program, submit written notification of the program completion to the legislative library, state capitol and the gifts and exchange section of the state library.

Such notification shall include title, author and the terms of distribution.

The state gift and exchange section of the state library shall be responsible for: (I) listing the programs on the monthly and annual check lists; (II) incorporating the listing of all state and state financed films and electronic information programs into a central catalogue. (Added L. 1973, c. 1011, § 3, eff. Sept. 1, 1973.)

EDUC. LAW § 250. Duplicate department. The regents shall have charge of the preparation, publication and distribution, whether by sale, exchange or gift, of the colonial history, natural history and all other state publications not otherwise assigned by law. To guard against waste or destruction of state publications, and to provide for the completion of sets to be permanently preserved in American and foreign libraries, the regents shall maintain a duplicate department to which each state department, bureau, board or commission shall send not less than five copies of each of its publications when issued, and after completing its distribution, any remaining copies which it no longer requires. The above, with any other publications not needed in the state library, shall be the duplicate department, and rules for sale, exchange or distribution from it shall be fixed by the regents, who shall use all receipts from such exchanges or sales for expenses and for increasing the state library. (L. 1947, c. 820, eff. July 1, 1947.)

STATE COMMENT

There is no legislation establishing a State documents depository distribution program as such. The New York State Library was able to secure passage of Chapter 316, Laws of 1955 incorporated into the State Printing Law as Section 7, Subdivision 3. This law mandates the delivery of 200 copies of each printed report to the New York State Library. Using this Law as a basis, we are able to maintain a State documents distribution program. Unfortunately, during a fiscal crisis, some agencies run off mimeo copies of their report. If no contract is awarded for printing, we have to rely on the good will of the issuing agency to supply us with sufficient copies to meet our distribution needs. Although the bulk of the State publications do come without any problem, we do not receive everything without difficulty.

****

A. *Strengths*:
1. Staff performs well.
2. Variety of publications issued by State agencies allows us to exchange with most types of libraries, for example, public, college, special.
3. General goodwill of agencies in supplying publications.

B. *Weaknesses*:
1. Lack of adequate staff (evident throughout the Library)
2. Lack of sufficient administrative and Legislative support
3. Lack of guides for use by librarians interested in developing a New York State document collection.
4. Lack of a union list of State publications distributed.
5. Lack of communication between State Library and agencies issuing publications, as well as librarians using these.
6. Temporary State Commissions, etc. not required to give State Library copies of hearings, reports and other publications.

C. *Recommendations*:
    1. Develop adequate staff, guides and union lists.
    2. Law should be strengthened to require ALL State agencies to send the State Library copies of all publications authorized for printing within the Department as well as items printed by other means for a State agency.

(Letter from Henry Ilnicki, Head, Gift and Exchange, The New York State Library, Albany, New York 12224, dated July 5, 1974. *In* Documents on Documents Collection.)

EDITORIAL COMMENT

The section of the State Printing Law referred to by Ilnicki was amended and renumbered section 6 in 1976. Subdivision 3 was amended by L. 1955, c. 316, § 3, eff. Oct. 1, 1955; the number of copies was increased from 50 to 200. Subdivision 3-a of § 6 in the State Printing Law was added by L. 1973, c. 1011, § 3, eff. Sept. 1, 1973.

The 1955 amendment to the Legislative Law, § 47 reduced the number of copies of legislative documents for the state library from 200 to 100.

RULES AND REGULATIONS

PLAN FOR DEPOSITORIES OF NEW YORK STATE PUBLICATIONS

What is the purpose of this plan? The depository plan aims to make the official publications of New York State more easily accessible to the public, to increase the speed of distribution, and to eliminate the necessity for extensive correspondence. It is expected also that it will decrease the demand for the bound set of collected documents, which is no longer available for distribution.

What libraries will be included in the plan? At least one library in each county or region in New York State may be designated as a depository for New York State publications. Each depository library will be expected to serve the region in which it is located. In addition, major research and university libraries, court libraries, and certain libraries outside the State may also be so designated.

What publications will be offered? All of the documents in the numbered legislative documents series will be offered. In addition all of the annual reports of the departments, boards, and commissions will be available, even where these may not be in the legislative document series. Certain other publications will also be available.

Must a depository library take everything offered? Three types of depositories will be designated—those which will receive all documents offered (GENERAL DEPOSITORY), those which will receive only the documents in the numbered legislative document series (LD DEPOSITORY), and those which will receive only a selected list (SELECTIVE DEPOSITORY). By your response to the enclosed questions you will determine the category in which your library will be placed.

How will the depository library know what materials it will receive? Each depository library will receive a copy of the *Checklist of Official Publications of the State of New York*. This list will indicate by symbol which documents are included in the depository plan. If your library has checked the appropriate category on the enclosed selection sheet, then you will automatically receive the documents in that series.

How much will the depository library receive? Libraries which are designated as general depositories will receive materials amounting to some three or four feet of shelf space each year.

Will back documents be available? The New York State Library will be glad to help depository libraries complete back files of these documents as far as its stock permits.

Can a library dispose of depository documents? Depository documents may be disposed of at any time, PROVIDED THAT the State library is first given an opportunity to reclaim them.

FOR FURTHER INFORMATION
Write to
New York State Library
Gift and Exchange Section
Albany, New York 12224

BIBLIOGRAPHY

Yun, Jai L. "The New York State Government Documents: Their Distribution and Information Retrieval." *Government Publications Review* 3:267-270 (1976).
A system of depositories was established in 1955 when the State Printing Law prescribed that the state library of New York receive two hundred copies of legislative and departmental publications. Two hundred libraries were designated depository libraries (full or selective).

Categories of depository items include "depository documents" and "documents in the numbered *Legislative Document Series*." In the 1971 annual *Checklist*, 76 items out of 1142 (7 percent) were designated depository. The Gift and Exchange Section of the state library makes the designation of depository items, but there are inconsistencies in this designation and variations in the extent of coverage within the depository items.

Nondepository items, if designated on the *Checklist*, can be obtained from Gift and Exchange. For serials, each issue must be requested; standing orders are not acceptable.

For documents listed in the *Checklist* for September 1974 and following, a microformat is available from Research Publications, but there are disadvantages: statistics and diagrams, looseleaf documents, and reference documents all present problems. The checklist, which is the key to the microform, needs improvement. Inclusion of a title index in the checklist and inputting of cataloging data into OCLC are recent attempts at improvement.

''Classification Abstracts: Milne Library State Classification Scheme.'' *Documents to the People* 4:41-43 (November 1976).
Based on U.S. superintendent of documents along with the Arizona State Plan. For all states. Steps for processing state publications included.

Gavryck, Jacquelyn, and Knapp, Sara. ''State Secrets Made Public: The Albany Plan.''
    Library Resources & Technical Services 17:82-92 (Winter 1973).
The annotation at the beginning of the article reads:

> This article describes a simplified scheme for cataloging and classifying state and municipal documents. The plan, now in use at the State University of New York at Albany, employs a system of double Cutter numbers to designate the documents by state and then by agency. The use of consistent scheme for subject and state Cuttering makes possible both a subject and an agency approach.

This plan is for a collection of documents for *all* states.

Henrich, Frederick K., and Martino, Elizabeth. ''A Modified Archival Classification for New York State Government Publications.'' State University of New York at Buffalo, 1973. 3 p.
A statement of the assumptions, policies, procedures, and files for the classification scheme used at SUNY at Buffalo. The assumptions are (1) subject arrangement (for example, LC) involves delays and does not meet users' needs, (2) documents are records, not literature, and arise out of the activities of the agencies which produce them, and (3) a basically archival arrangement should be efficient and logical from the user's point of view. An assumption added by the author upon review of the paper in 1979 is as follows:

> The major function of a library classification is to define the physical address of the material, i.e. the place to which one must go to find it, or to which one must go to re-shelve or re-file it after it has been used. A corollary of this principle is that whatever classification symbols are chosen they need to be easily spoken and understood aurally, and easily remembered for a short period.

Sternlicht, Dorothy. ''How to Control a Runaway State Documents Collection.'' *Special Libraries* 64:561-565 (December 1973).

> This documents study was instituted to develop a structured list of New York State agencies that publish, to develop an agency classification system, and to explore a means by which subject access to Penfield Library's collection could be gained. A computer generated subject search tool—*New York (State) Documents Agency Authority File With Keyword Index*—was produced, and the ultimate purpose of the project, which was to gain bibliographic control of materials in Penfield Library's document collection, was realized.

This plan is for a collection of New York state documents. Holdings are checked on the *Checklist*.

Paulson, Peter J. ''What New York State Documents Offer Libraries.'' *The Bookmark* 21:33-36 (November 1961).
''[D]ocuments actually offer an abundant variety of subject matter, . . . some are issued in an attractive and highly readable format, and . . . many have a high current reference value.'' ''Select Subject Guide to Popular New York State Documents'' concludes the article (14 subjects).

Paulson, Peter J. ''Materials and Services Available from the Gift and Exchange Section, New York State Library.'' *In* Law Library Association of Greater New York. *Proceedings, Third Annual Institute on Law Librarianship, April 29-30, 1960.* pp. 16-20.

> Two things are required to make this treasure house accessible to all: first, a wide distribution of the documents themselves, and second, an adequate bibliography. Today the New York State Library, through its Gift and Exchange Section, attempts to provide both.
>
> Both the National Association of State Libraries (now a section of the Americn Library Association) and the National Legislative Conference have recommended that a central distribution agency for state publications be established in each state.

The author cites National Association of State Libraries, *The Role of the State Library*; National Legislative Conference, *Report of the Committee on Interstate Exchange of Legislative Service Publications* (revised October 10, 1955), and *Manual for Interstate Exchange of Legislative Service Agency Publications* (1957). Attached is: ''New York State Documents of Interest to Law Libraries.'' 7 p.

Santen, V.B. ''New York State Inventory Project.'' *American Archivist* 20:357-367 (October 1957).
A records management article. The term ''records'' refers to ''books, papers, maps, photographs, microphotographs, and other documentary materials made, acquired, or received by any State agency.'' Although this definition would encompass state documents, they are not mentioned specifically.

Douglas, Mrs. I.D. ''New York State Documents for the Reference Librarian.'' *Grosvenor Library Bulletin* 21:38-48 (December 1938-March 1939). (Not seen.)

Barron, Robert E. ''Publications in Curriculum and Media.'' *See* issues of *Bookmark*.
These publications, available to librarians in New York, are intended for professional use only and not for pupil use. They are arranged by issuing agency and then by subject.

NORTH CAROLINA

N. C. GEN. STAT. §§ 147-50 to 147-50.1 (Supp. 1979)

§ **147-50. Publications of State officials and department heads furnished to certain institutions, agencies, etc.** Every State official and every head of a State department, institution or agency issuing any printed report, bulletin, map, or other publication, shall, on request, furnish copies of such reports, bulletins, maps or other publications to the following institutions in the number set out below:

University of North Carolina at Chapel Hill	25 copies;
University of North Carolina at Charlotte	2 copies;
University of North Carolina at Greensboro	2 copies;
North Carolina State University at Raleigh	2 copies;
East Carolina University at Greenville	2 copies;
Duke University	25 copies;
Wake Forest College	2 copies;
Davidson College	2 copies;
North Carolina Supreme Court Library	2 copies;
North Carolina Central University	5 copies;
Western Carolina University	2 copies;
Appalachian State University	2 copies;
University of North Carolina at Wilmington	2 copies;
North Carolina Agricultural and Technical State University	2 copies;
Legislative Library	2 copies;

and to government officials, agencies and departments and to other educational institutions, in the discretion of the issuing official and subject to the supply available, such number as may be requested: Provided that five sets of all such reports, bulletins and publications heretofore issued, insofar as the same are available and without necessitating reprinting, shall be furnished to the North Carolina Central University. The provisions in this section shall not be interpreted to include any of the appellate division reports or advance sheets distributed by the Administrative Office of the Courts. (1941, c. 379, s. 5;

1955, c. 505, s. 7; 1967, cc. 1038, 1065; 1969, c. 608, s. 1; c. 852, s. 3; 1973, c. 476, s. 84; c. 598; c. 731, s. 2; c. 776; 1977, c. 377; 1979, c. 591, s. 1.)

§ 147-50.1. Publications of State officials and department heads deposited with Division of State Library. Every State official and every head of a State department, institution, or agency issuing any document, report, directory, statistical compendium, bibliography, map, rule, regulation, newsletter, pamphlet, brochure, periodical, or other publications shall deposit five copies with the Division of State Library of the Department of Cultural Resources. "Printed materials" are publications produced by any means, including publications issued by private bodies, such as consultant or research firms, under contract with or under the supervision of a State agency. The Division of State Library shall publish a checklist of publications received from State agencies and shall distribute the checklist without charge to all requesting libraries. The Division of State Library shall forward two of the five copies of all publications received from State agencies to the Library of Congress. The provisions of this section do not apply to the appellate division reports and advance sheets distributed by the Administrative Office of the Courts, the S.B.I. Investigative "Bulletin," or administrative materials intended only for the internal use of a State agency. (1979, c. 591, s. 2.)

EDITORIAL COMMENT

The 1977 amendment added the final sentence at the end of the paragraph. The three 1973 amendments added the last four institutions to the list of institutions.

A related section, N. C. GEN. STAT. § 121-6, provides:

Except for reports, bulletins, and other publications issued for free distribution, professional materials including books and journals published by the Department of Cultural Resources are hereby expressly excluded from provisions of G. S. 147-50. (1973, c. 476, s. 48)

This section was part of a reorganization act titled, "Executive Reorganization Act of 1973." The State Library in North Carolina is under the Department of Cultural Resources.

In 1979, an act amended G. S. 147-50 (1979 Laws, ch. 591) and enacted a new section 147-50.1. House Bill 241 was ratified on May 21, 1979 and became chapter 591 of the 1979 Laws. It deleted the Library of Congress and the Department of Cultural Resources (i.e., the Division of State Library) from the libraries entitled to request documents under § 147-50, and provided in § 147-50.1 that the state agencies shall deposit five copies of all publications with the Division of State Library. Of these, two copies are to be forwarded to the Library of Congress.

The new section also provided that the Division of State Library should issue a checklist and distribute it without charge to all requesting libraries. No appropriation was included. In fact, the act provided that passage of the bill should not obligate the General Assembly for an additional appropriation. The appellate division reports and the S. B. I. Investigative "Bulletin" were both specifically excluded. These two titles had been the subject of Attorney General's opinions.

ATTORNEY GENERAL OPINIONS

42 N. C. ATT'Y GEN. OP. 94, 11 October 1972

Subject: State Departments, Institutions and Agencies; Publications; Free Distribution on Request to Statutory List of Institutions; G. S. 147-50

Requested by: Mr. James H. Thompson
                Director
                Walter Clinton Judson Library
                University of North Carolina at Greensboro

Question: (1) Whether the University of North Carolina at Greensboro Library is entitled to receive on request at no cost two copies of any printed report, bulletin, map or other publication issued by a State department, institution or agency issuing the publication requested.

                (2) Whether publications issued by the Department of Justice, the Department of Economic and Natural Resources, the Department of Social Services, the Department of Conservation and Development, the Department of Art, Culture and History, the Department of Public Instruction and the Board of Higher Education are exempt from the requirement of G. S. 147-50 that the printed reports, bulletins, maps or other publications of State departments, institutions or agencies be furnished at no cost upon request to the University of North Carolina at Greensboro Library.

Conclusion: (1) Yes, the University of North Carolina at Greensboro Library is entitled to receive on request at no cost two copies of any printed report, bulletin, map or other publication issued by a State department, institution or agency issuing the publication requested.

                (2) No, publications issued by [the names of the departments and the board listed in (2) above are omitted] are not exempt from the requirement of G. S. 147-50.

The statute in question, G. S. 147-50, is set out verbatim: [omitted]

The statute is clear and unambiguous in its mandate to those State agencies who issue publications that they " . . . *shall*, on request, furnish . . . " to the enumerated institution the numbers specified of " . . . reports, bulletins, maps or other publication. . . . " [Emphasis added in the original.]

The statutory language "shall" is clearly mandatory in this case. The term "furnish" in this context does not contemplate the sale of the publications even at a preferred rate.

Any possible ambiguity about the mandatory nature of the requirement that the publications be furnished to the listed institutions in the number listed on request is dispelled when one notes that their obligation to furnish copies to others than the listed institutions is subject to the "discretion of the issuing official" and subject to the supply available. No such discretionary power is given the issuing authority with respect to the obligation to furnish publications to the listed institutions on request. The statutory language describing the material to be furnished, " . . . any printed report, bulletin, map, or other publication . . . " could not be more broad and all encompassing.

Granted, there may be some fiscal hardship involved for the issuing agency in having to furnish 78 free copies of their report. On the other hand, the General Assembly clearly weighed the relative hardships—those on the issuing agency to furnish the free copies as opposed to the hardship on the libraries of the State who might otherwise be compelled to allocate their limited resources so as to preclude a ready reference to State documents and publications in their institution's library. The General Assembly opted in favor of wide distribution of State financed publications by free distribution to the institutions listed in G. S. 147-50.

If a state agency issuing publications desires to be exempt from this requirement as to one or all of its publications, it should seek from the General Assembly an express exclusion for all or certain of its " . . . reports, bulletins, maps, and other publications . . . " from the purview of G. S. 147-50.

Robert Morgan, Attorney General
Sidney S. Eagles, Jr.,
Assistant Attorney General

43 N. C. ATT'Y GEN. OP. 93, 29 August 1973

Subject: State Publications; University of North Carolina at Greensboro; G. S. 147-50; Appellate Division Reports; Advance Sheets

Requested by: Mr. Robert Grey Cole, Documents Librarian
Walter Clinton Jackson Library
University of North Carolina at Greensboro

Question: Is the Library of the University of North Carolina at Greensboro entitled to receive at no cost copies of the *Advance Sheets* of the *Appellate Division Reports* under the provisions of G. S. 147-50 or 147-45 when construed in the light of G. S. 7A-6?

Conclusion: Yes. The University of North Carolina at Greensboro Library is entitled to be furnished the *Advance Sheets* of the *Appellate Division Reports* at no cost pursuant to the provisions of G. S. 147-45.

The appropriate statute involved in this controversy is G. S. 7A-6 which provides generally for sale by the Administrative Officer of the Courts of the "reports and advance sheets of the appellate division, *to the general public*, at a price not less than cost nor more than cost plus ten percent (10%), to be fixed by him in his discretion" (Emphasis added), the proceeds to go the State treasury, and a specific directive to the Administrative Officer of the Courts to furnish one copy of the *Advance Sheets* at no charge to justices and judges, solicitors, prosecutors and in greater numbers to the Supreme Court Library.

The provisions of G. S. 7A-6 relating to specific direction for free copies to each judge, etc., date back to 1967 (1967, C. 108, s. 1). The portion permitting sale of the publication to the general public was added later in the 1967 session (1967, C. 691, s. 57).

G. S. 147-50 is the general policy directive that all State departments must furnish at no cost on request copies of their "reports, bulletins, maps or other publications" to a list of named institutions. University of North Carolina at Greensboro was included in that list of 1967 (1967, C. 1065). This statute has been construed in Attorney General's Opinions to require that periodic publications analogous to the Advance Sheets, the Attorney General's Reports, be distributed at no cost to requesting institutions listed in the statute. (42 N. C. A. G. 94). The logic supporting that opinion is applicable here.

G. S. 147-45 deals with "Session Laws", "Senate and House Journals" and "Appellate Division Reports" and directs that "(and the Administrative Officer of the Courts, with respect to Appellate Division Reports) shall, at the State's expense, as soon as possible after publication, distribute such number of copies . . . as is set out. . . . " G. S. 147-45. The University of North Carolina at Greensboro is on this list of recipients. (1971 Cum. Supp. to General Statutes, Vol. 3C, p. 263).

The Governor may administratively delete from the list any named "government official, department, agency or educational institution." G. S. 147-45. However, we are not aware that the University of North Carolina at Greensboro has been administratively deleted from the applicability of G. S. 147-45.

The sole remaining basis on which free distribution of *Advance Sheets* of the *Appellate Division Reports* could be denied is that in G. S. 147-45 the General Assembly intended that only bound volumes of the Court of Appeals Reports and Supreme Court Reports and not *Advance Sheets* were to be distributed free to the listed educational institutions.

This position we find untenable in light of the language requiring distribution "as soon as possible after publication" (G. S. 147-45) and the public policy of having all State publications as widely and promptly disseminated as possible. The term "Appellate Division Reports" includes in usage and was contemplated by the General Assembly to include the *Advance Sheets* which are an integral part of the overall publication. The usefulness of the *Appellate Division Reports* to any student or citizen is substantially and materially lessened if the entire publication, including *Advance Sheets*, is not available.

Consequently, we are of the opinion that G. S. 147-45 requires distribution of one copy of the *Advance Sheets* of the *Appellate Division Reports* to the University of North Carolina at Greensboro at no cost as soon as each pamphlet is published. The language of G. S. 7A-6 does not lessen this requirement but merely specifies an additional list of court personnel to whom the publications must be made available.

Robert Morgan, Attorney General
Sidney S. Eagles, Jr.,
Assistant Attorney General

45 N. C. ATT'Y GEN. OP. 92, 7 October 1975

Subject: State Bureau of Investigation; Distribution of S. B. I. Bulletin; Publications; Public Records, G. S. 147-50, 132-1, 114-15

Requested by: Mr. Charles Dunn, Director
State Bureau of Investigation
Department of Justice

Question: Does G. S. 147-50, which requires free distribution of any publications
              of other State agencies on request, include the distribution of the S. B. I.
              Investigative "Bulletin"?
Conclusion: No. G. S. 147-50 does not require the distribution of the S. B. I.
              Investigative "Bulletin" because information contained in it is not of
              public record, but instead, is information used by law enforcement
              officers to collect and compile evidence for the trial of cases.

The statutes in question are G. S. 147-50, 132-1, 114-15. The pertinent parts of these
statutes are set below: [Omitted]

General Statute 147-50 is clear and unambiguous in its mandate to those State
agencies who issue publications that they " . . . shall on request, furnish . . . " to the
enumerated institutions the numbers specified of " . . . reports, bulletins, maps or other
publications. . . . " However, it is the opinion of this Office that the philosophy behind
this statute is one of economics. The legislative intent was to enable the various libraries
of the State to receive free copies of any State publications rather than compelling the
libraries to allocate their limited resources for the purchase of such State documents
and publications which contain information of public knowledge and record. (See 42
N. C. A. G. 94.) On the contrary, however, it was not the intent of the General
Assembly to require the distribution (free or otherwise) of information which is not of
public record, but instead, is used by various agencies in the field of law enforcement
for the purpose of gathering evidence to be used in the trial of criminal cases.

The information contained in the S. B. I. "Bulletin" pertains to suspects of crimes,
their whereabouts, activities, previous criminal involvement and any other material
which would help law enforcement agencies to fight crime. Such information is not of
public record. It is used by State and municipal law enforcement agencies in on-going
criminal investigations which by their nature must be carried on in secret in order to
insure the safety of the individual law enforcement officers involved in the investigations. The valid law enforcement interest protected by exempting the State Bureau of
Investigation "Bulletin" from public dissemination more than outweighs the small
economic savings of having copies of the "Bulletin" distributed to State libraries free
of charge or otherwise.

The S. B. I. "Bulletin" is considered an internal memorandum in that the distribution of the pamphlet is limited to law enforcement agencies. Copies are sent to the
Federal Bureau of Investigation, State Highway Patrol, State Bureau of Investigation
agents, and local police and sheriffs' departments. The Directors of Security at the large
college campuses within this State also receive copies.

The purpose of the "Bulletin" is to assist law enforcement agencies and give them an
opportunity to stay organized through close contact and communication. The close
contact and communication afforded by the S. B. I. "Bulletin" better enables the law
enforcement agencies to not only apprehend criminals but also often assists them in
preventing a continuation of their criminal acts. To disseminate this "Bulletin" could
threaten security and compromise confidential sources of information.

It was stated in an Attorney General opinion that:

If a State agency issuing publications desires to be exempt from this requirement as
to one or all of its publications, it should seek from the General Assembly an

express exclusion for all or certain of its " . . . reports, bulletins, maps, and other publications . . . " from the purview of G. S. 147-50.

It is our opinion that there exists such an express statutory exclusion for the S. B. I. 's publications of this type. G. S. 114-15 specifically excludes "all records and evidence collected and compiled by the Director of the Bureau (of Investigation) and his assistants. . . . " While it does not specifically refer to the S. B. I. "Bulletin", it is clear that *any* record or evidence compiled by the Director of the Bureau or his assistants which is used in the *investigation* of criminal cases is not to be considered a public record within the meaning of G. S. 132-1 which defines "Public records". However, it should be noted that police arrest and disposition records are subject to public examination (See 41 N. C. A. G. 407 (1971).)

G. S. 132-1 defines "Public records" as any written or printed books, papers, etc. made in pursuance of law and in the transaction of public business. Certainly, the S. B. I. "Bulletin" could be considered a public record within the meaning of the definition. However, G. S. 114-15 exempts it because each issue of the "Bulletin" contains part of the investigative files of on-going criminal investigations. Therefore, G. S. 147-50 would not apply to the S. B. I. "Bulletin" and distribution to the various State libraries would not be required.

Rufus L. Edmisten, Attorney General
T. Lawrence Pollard
Associate Attorney

BIBLIOGRAPHY

Pullen, William R. " State Document Resources of the University of North Carolina Library." *North Carolina Libraries* 13:79-82 (March 1955).
"The collection of official North Carolina publications in the North Carolina Collection in the University Library is singular in its completeness. This paper, therefore, [deals] only with the public documents of the other forty-seven states.

[T]he Library has in its holdings ninety-five per cent of all the material which is known to have been issued from the earliest date to the present time [by all the states in the categories of legislative journals, collected documents, session laws and constitutional records]. Fifty-one per cent of this is on microfilm.

This film is the product of the State Records Microfilm Project which was the joint undertaking of the Library of Congress and the University of North Carolina under the direction of William Sumner Jenkins."

Cole, Robert Grey. "North Carolina Needs an Improved Depository System for State Documents." *North Carolina Libraries* 31:35-38 (Conference Issue 1973).
Cole first outlines the current law and lists reasons why it has not been successful: first, libraries must request documents from the agencies and if a publication is not listed in the *Checklist* it is difficult to identify; and second, some agencies have maintained they were exempt from the depository library law.

Then Cole outlines an ideal state depository system: first, centralized distribution, probably in the state library; and second, a specific definition of what constitutes a state document, citing South Dakota as an example. Other elements recommended include (1) complete collection at the ``depository agency,'' (2) discretion in the ``depository agency'' on what to distribute, (3) official checklist with adequate cumulative index, (4) inclusion of public libraries, (5) standards for depository libraries, and (6) depository libraries required to furnish staff and maintenance for the collection. The North Carolina Library Association should take the lead in studying the problems and recommending legislation.

``Results of Questionnaire on State Documents Depository System Reports.'' *Docket: Newsletter of the Documents Librarians of North Carolina* no. 4 (Fall 1975).
At the third annual meeting of the documents librarians of North Carolina, Sangster Parrott reported on the questionnaire: 124 of 216 libraries responded. Thirty were willing to become depositories (eight university, five four-year college, nine two-year college, and eight public). The committee concluded that there was enough interest to request a legislative study committee, to report in 1977.

Gaines, Robert F. ``A North Carolina State Documents Depository System: An Update.'' *North Carolina Libraries* 36:21-23 (Spring 1978).
Reports analysis of Documents on Documents Collection showing that thirty-two states have depository systems and four states are working on systems. Cites the North Carolina statute, the difficulty in getting publications without charge in spite of attorney general opinions, and the weakness of bibliographical control. Reports on the Ad Hoc Committee on State Documents Depository of the North Carolina Library Association, introduction in 1977 of a bill for a study commission, which did not pass.

``North Carolina State Depository Status.'' *The Docket* 6, no. 2:3 (March 1979).
Reports the introduction of House Bill 241, amending GS 147-50 and adding GS 147-50.1. A letter from the state librarian is summarized: ``McKay does not envision a depository system statewide 'on the scale currently envisioned' to be necessary, but will support discussion by task force.'' The state librarian's letter is reproduced in full.

Thornton, M. L. ``North Carolina State Publications.'' *North Carolina Library Bulletin* 4:173-178 (1921). (Not seen.)

NORTH DAKOTA

N. D. CENT. CODE § 54-24-09 (Supp. 1979)

54-24-09. Distribution of certain state publications for certain libraries required. The state purchasing and printing agent shall arrange to deposit with the state library eight copies of all publications issued by all executive, legislative, and judicial agencies of state government intended for general public distribution. These publications shall be provided to the state library without charge. Should expense and limited supply of state publications, particularly audiovisual items, make strict compliance with the depository requirement impossible, the state library shall accept as many copies as an agency can afford to provide. However, no less than two copies shall be provided to the state library by each agency. State publications refer to any informational materials regardless of format, method of reproduction, or source, originating in or produced with the imprint of, by the authority of, or at the total or partial expense of, any state agency. The definition incorporates those publications that may or may not be financed by state funds but are released by private bodies such as research and consultant firms under contract with or supervision of any state agency. In circumstances not directly involving the state purchasing and printing agent, a state agency shall comply with the depository requirement by arranging with the necessary parties for the printing and deposit of eight copies of any state publication issued. State publications are specifically defined as public documents appearing as reports, directories, statistical compendiums, bibliographies, laws or bills, rules, regulations, newsletters, bulletins, state plans, brochures, periodicals, committee minutes, transcripts of public hearings, other printed matter, audio tapes, video tapes, films, filmstrips, or slides, but not those administrative or training materials used only within the issuing agency. As the document acquisition and distribution agency, the state library shall retain for its own use two copies of every state document received and transmit the remaining copies to the depository libraries. These shall be the libraries of the state historical board, university of North Dakota, North Dakota state university, Library of Congress, and two others to be designated by the state library. All non-depository North Dakota academic, public, and special libraries shall have the opportunity to receive state documents under an optional selection program developed by the state library. The state library shall catalog state publications and arrange for their conversion to microfilm and shall make available for distribution the same to the designated depository libraries. (Source: N. D. C. C.; S. L. 1977, ch. 492, § 1; 1979, ch. 550, § 13.)

EDITORIAL COMMENT

The 1977 Act was titled: "AN ACT to amend and re-enact section 54-24-09 of the North Dakota Century Code, relating to the distribution of state publications." A note at the beginning of the session law reads, "At the request of the State Library." The act was approved on March 12, 1977.

The 1977 Act was a complete rewriting of the section that had originally been adopted in 1965 (S. L. 1965, ch. 352, § 1). In the 1965 version, the "state departments, offices and agencies" had the duty to deposit "ten copies [a 1971 amendment (ch. 503, § 1) increased this to twelve copies] of all publications . . . whether printed, mimeographed, or duplicated in any way," except those "issued solely for use within the issuing office." The state library had the duty to send copies to five named libraries "plus five others which the state library commission shall determine." Of the five named libraries, the Minot public library and Dickinson state college are not mentioned in the 1977 Act.

The 1979 amendment changed "state library commission" to "state library."

BIBLIOGRAPHY

North Dakota, State Library Commission, Bismarck. "Publications of the State Library Commission, January 1965-September 1973." *North Dakota Library Notes* 4, no. 5 (October 1973).

North Dakota, State Library Commission, Bismarck. *Keyword Index to Publications of the State of North Dakota Received by the State Library During the Years 1965-1974.* The Library, 1975. 2 v.

OHIO

OHIO REV. CODE ANN. §§ 149.09, 149.11-12 (Anderson 1978 & Supp. 1979), § 3375.02 (Anderson 1980)

§ **149.09. Distribution of pamphlet laws.** The secretary of state shall distribute the pamphlet laws printed in accordance with section 101.52 of the Revised Code in the following manner: three copies of each pamphlet law shall be forwarded to each county law library, three copies of each pamphlet law shall be forwarded to each county auditor, two copies of each pamphlet law shall be forwarded to each library that receives publications under section 149.12 of the Revised Code, and remaining copies shall be distributed by the secretary of state on the request of interested persons. (HISTORY: 137 v S 205. Eff. 3-15-79.)

§ **149.11. Distribution of publications intended for general public use; schedules of record retention or destruction.** Any person or company, awarded a contract to print a report, pamphlet, document, or other publication intended for general public use and distribution for a department, division, bureau, board, or commission of the state government, shall print one hundred and fifty copies of such publication for delivery to the state library, subject to provisions of section 125.42 of the Revised Code.

Any department, division, bureau, board, or commission of the state government issuing a report, pamphlet, document, or other publication intended for general public use and distribution, which publication is reproduced by duplicating processes such as mimeograph, multigraph, planograph, rotaprint, or multilith, shall cause to be delivered to the state library one hundred and fifty copies of such publication, subject to the provisions of section 125.42 of the Revised Code.

The state library board shall distribute the publications so received as follows:

(A) Retain two copies in the state library;

(B) Send two copies to the document division of the library of congress;

(C) Send one copy to the Ohio historical society and to each public or college library in the state designated by the state library board to be a depository for state publications. In designating which libraries shall be depositories, the board shall select those libraries which can best preserve such publications and which are so located geographically as will make the publications conveniently accessible to residents in all areas of the state;

(D) Send one copy to each state in exchange for like publications of such state.

All copies undistributed ninety days after receipt by the state library shall be returned to the issuing agency.

The provisions of this section shall not apply to any publication of the general assembly or to the publications described in sections 149.07, 149.08, 149.09, and 149.17 of the Revised Code, except that the secretary of state shall forward to the document division of the library of congress two copies of all journals, seven copies of laws in bound form as provided for in section 149.09 of the Revised Code, and seven copies of all appropriation laws in separate form. (HISTORY: GC § 2279-1; 113 v 298; 127 v 417, § 1. Eff. 9-17-57.)

§ **149.12 [Distribution of legislative publications to libraries.]** The state library board shall forward, free of charge, one copy of each legislative bulletin, daily house and senate journal, and summary of enactments published by the legislative service commission, to the following libraries:

(A) Each library within the state that has been designated by the state library board under section 149.11 of the Revised Code as a depository for state publications;

(B) In each county containing no library described in division (A) of this section, to a public library designated by the state library board to receive the journals, bulletins, and summaries described in this section. The state library board shall designate libraries that can best preserve the publications and are so located geographically that they can make the publications conveniently accessible to the residents of the county.

The state library board shall forward the daily house and senate journals once every week while the general assembly is in session and the legislative bulletin and summary of enactments as they are published.

Each library receiving publications under this section or under section 149.09 of the Revised Code shall make these publications accessible to the public. (HISTORY: 137 v S 205. Eff. 3-15-79.)

§ **3375.02. State librarian.** The state library board shall appoint a state librarian, who shall be the secretary of said board, and under the direction and supervision of the board shall be the executive officer of the state library, with power to appoint and remove employees thereof. The state librarian shall:
****

(F) Maintain a comprehensive collection of official documents and publications of this state and a library collection and reference service to meet the reference and information needs of officers, departments, agencies of state government, and other libraries;

(G) Issue official lists of publications of the state, and other bibliographical and informational publications as appropriate;
****

(HISTORY: GC § 154-52; 109 v 105 (123); 120 v 475 (488); 122 v 166; 123 v 862 (906), § 3; 133 v S 262. Eff. 11-25-69.)

STATE COMMENT (1973)

At the present time we have not set up any official regulations regarding the keeping and storing of Ohio documents. The *Ohio Revised Code* states how many depository libraries there are to be and who they can be. Ohio law does not provide us with a means of enforcing our depository law.

Currently, Ohio has been contracting out much of the state printing. However, a considerable amount is done in-house. As anyone knows, these are just about impossible to obtain especially when the supply has been nearly exhausted and the agency refuses to reprint because of cost. (Letter from Clyde Hordusky, Documents Specialist, The State Library of Ohio, Columbus, Ohio 43215, dated June 4, 1973. *In* Documents on Documents Collection.)

EDITORIAL COMMENT

A 1979 amendment (Amended Substitute Senate Bill No. 205) refers to two pertinent sections of the Ohio law.

§ 149.09 was amended to provide that two copies of each pamphlet law should be forwarded by the secretary of state to each library that receives publications under § 149.12, thus including the depository libraries in the distribution.

§ 149.12 is a new section added in 1979 providing for distribution by the state library board to depository libraries of the daily House and Senate Journals (once a week) and the Legislative Bulletin and Summary of Enactments (as published).

§ 149.16 (not reproduced) provides that the secretary of state distribute the laws. It was amended in 1979 to add the bound House and Senate Journals to the distribution requirement.

RULES AND REGULATIONS

Ohio State Library
Application for Depository Service

The _____
   (Name of Library)

_____

(Street)   (City)   (County)   (Zip)
wishes to become a depository to receive the publications of the various departments,

divisions, bureaus, boards, commissions and other agencies of the State of Ohio in accordance with Section 149.11 of the Revised Code of Ohio.

The _____* hereby certifies that the facilities of the library are adequate to house and maintain such publications in reasonable order and to insure they will be made conveniently accessible to those residents of the state desiring access to them.

_____
(Signature)

_____
(Title)

_____
(Date)

*Insert here the name of the administrative authority of the library: Board of Trustees, President of University.

BIBLIOGRAPHY

The Ohio publications are all library tools, not descriptive articles.

Reddy, J. N. "List of Author Headings for the Official Publications of the State of Ohio, 1900-1957; With History, Subdivisions of Departments and Cross References." M.A. Thesis, Kent State University, 1958. 61 p. (Not seen.)

Gillon, E. H. "Author Headings for the Official Publications of the State of Ohio, 1803-1900." M.A.L.S. Thesis, Kent State University, 1959. 67 p. (Not seen.)

Houk, J. A. *Classification System for Ohio State Documents*. Columbus, Ohio: State Library, 1962. 27 p.
Numbers that have been assigned in alphabetical order are based on key words. The goal is to keep the classification numbers short and to maintain the alphabetical sequence.

Lester, M. A. *State Documents Classification: Ohio Edition*. Government Documents Department, Bowling Green State University, 1969. (Not seen.)

Ohio State Library. *Ohio Documents Classification Scheme*. Prepared by Joanne E. M. Tortoriello, Susan M. Correa, and Jean M. Sears. Columbus, Ohio: 1975. (Not seen.)

OKLAHOMA

OKLA. STAT. ANN. tit. 65, §§ 3-113.1 to 115; tit. 74, §§ 3104, 3106.1 (West Supp. 1979-80)

§ 3-113.1. Publications Clearinghouse—Creation—Director—Rules and regulations. The Publications Clearinghouse is hereby created as a division of the Oklahoma Department of Libraries. The Publications Clearinghouse shall be directed by the Director of the Department of Libraries. The Director shall adopt rules and regulations necessary to implement the provisions of this act. (Added by Laws 1978, c. 165, § 1.)

§ 3-113.2. Definitions. As used in this act:

1. "Agency" means any state office, officer, department, division or unit, bureau, board, commission, authority, institution, sub-state planning district, and agency of the state, and, where applicable, all subdivisions of each, including state institutions of higher education, defined as all state-supported colleges, universities, junior colleges and vocational-technical schools;

2. "Governmental publications" means any publication of associations, regional organizations, intergovernmental bodies, federal agencies, boards and commissions, or other publishers that may contribute supplementary materials to support the work of the State Legislature, state officers and state agencies;

3. "Print" means any form of printing and duplication, regardless of format or purpose, with the exception of correspondence and interoffice memoranda; and

4. "State publication" means any informational materials regardless of format, method of reproduction, or source, originating in or produced with the imprint of, by the authority of, or at the total or partial expense of, or purchased for distribution by, the state, the Legislature, constitutional officers, any state department, committee, sub-state planning district, or other state agency supported wholly or in part by state funds. The definition incorporates those publications that may or may not be financed by state funds but are released by private bodies such as research and consultant firms under a contract with and/or the supervision of any state agency; and specifically includes public documents appearing as reports, directories, statistical compendiums, bibliog-

raphies, laws or bills, rules, regulations, newsletters, bulletins, state plans, brochures, periodicals or magazines, committee minutes, transcripts of public hearings, journals, statutes, codes, pamphlets, lists, books, charts, maps, surveys, other printed matter, microfilm, microfiche and all sale items. (Added by Laws 1978, c. 165, § 2.)

§ 3-113.3. Duties of Publications Clearinghouse. The Publications Clearinghouse shall have the following duties:

1. To establish an Oklahoma government publications depository library system for the use of the citizens of the State of Oklahoma;

2. To collect state publications from every state agency and to retain and preserve permanently a minimum of four (4) copies of all such publications;

3. To enter into contracts with other libraries within the State of Oklahoma whereby the Publications Clearinghouse designates the contracting library to be a depository library for the Oklahoma Department of Libraries and agrees to distribute at least one (1) copy of every state publication deposited with the Publications Clearinghouse to such depository library, and, the contracting library agrees to receive and maintain the full and complete collection of such publications and not to dispose of any such publication without prior approval of the Publications Clearinghouse, to provide adequate facilities for the storage and use of such publications and to provide free services to its patrons in the use of such publications;

4. To determine the necessity of and to make arrangements for the conversion of state publications to microfilm or microfiche and to establish a system to assure the availability of such microfilm or microfiche for distribution to designated depository libraries;

5. To prepare and publish official lists of all state publications and to distribute them to all contracting depository libraries, other libraries within the state, and every state agency, as required by the rules and regulations. The official lists shall include the name of the publishing agency, the name of the publisher, and the title and subject matter of each publication;

6. To determine the quantity of each publication of a state agency, in excess of twenty-five (25), required to meet the needs of the Publications Clearinghouse depository library system and to notify each agency of additional required quantity;

7. To distribute copies of all state publications including annual, semiannual or biennial reports as follows:

    a. two (2) copies to the United States Library of Congress,

    b. one (1) copy to the Archives Division of the Oklahoma Department of Libraries for preservation,

    c. one (1) copy to the Center for Research Libraries,

    d. four (4) copies for the collection of state publications within the Publications Clearinghouse,

e. one (1) copy to each depository library, and

f. one (1) copy of each agency report to both the State Legislative Council and the Legislative Reference Division of the Oklahoma Department of Libraries;

8. To receive and maintain, for exchange with the official libraries of each of the other states, territories and possessions of the United States, a minimum of fifty (50) copies of all state legal publications, including bar journals, official reports of decisions, codes, opinions, rules and regulations, and one hundred ten (110) copies of statute supplements and session laws;

9. To aid in the maintenance of a law library within the Department to serve the state officers, agencies, and members of the Oklahoma Legislature; and

10. To compile and maintain a permanent record of all state publications caused to be published from and after the effective date of this act. (Added by Laws 1978, c. 165, § 3.)

§ 3-114. Deposit of state publications with Publications Clearinghouse —Failure to comply.

A. Every agency, authority, department, commission, board, institution, office or officer of the state, except institutions of higher education but specifically including any board of regents for higher education, who issue or publish, at state expense, regardless of form, any book, chart, document, facsimile, map, paper, periodical, report, serial, survey or any other type of publication, including statutes, statute supplements and session laws, shall immediately deposit a minimum of twenty-five (25) copies with the Publications Clearinghouse of the Department.

B. Upon failure of an agency to comply with this section, the Publications Clearinghouse shall forward a written notice of such failure to the chief administrative officer of the agency; such notice shall state a reasonable time, not to exceed thirty (30) days, in which the agency shall fully comply. Further failure to comply shall be reported in writing to the Speaker of the House of Representatives, the President Pro Tempore of the Senate and the Attorney General. The Attorney General shall immediately institute mandamus proceedings to secure compliance by such agency. (Laws 1967, c. 45, § 3-114. Amended by Laws 1978, c. 165, § 5.)

§ 3-115. Copies to other states, territories or possessions and The Library of Congress—Exchange agreements—Surplus publications. The Publications Clearinghouse of the Department shall retain sufficient copies for use by the Department, and shall, pursuant to exchange agreements, send copies to the official library of each of the other states, territories and possessions of the United States and The Library of Congress, and may exchange copies for the publications of other governments or organizations and may send copies upon request to other bodies or persons. The Department may sell at the fair market value or otherwise dispose of any surplus publications and any receipts shall be deposited pursuant to Section 3-107 of this title. (Laws 1967, c. 45, § 3-115. Amended by Laws 1978, c. 165, § 6.)

tit. 74, § 3104. Filing and distribution of reports. Every agency, board, department, commission or institution of the State of Oklahoma shall deposit twenty-five (25) copies of their annual, semiannual or biennial reports with the Publications Clearinghouse of the Department for distribution and depository system purposes as required by Section 3-114 of Title 65 of the Oklahoma Statutes and shall distribute such reports only to legislators and other parties specifically requesting them. The Publications Clearinghouse shall notify the members of the Legislature of the receipt of such reports. (Amended by Laws 1978, c. 165, § 10.)

tit. 74, § 3106.1. Records officers or state agencies.

A. Every state agency shall designate one (1) of its staff members or employees as the records officer for the agency and notify the Publications Clearinghouse of the identity of such records officer and of the identity of any new records officer should a change occur.

B. Each records officer of each state agency shall have the duty to provide the Publications Clearinghouse with copies of all state publications of the agency, including annual, semiannual or biennial reports, codes, rules and regulations published by the state agency, to compile and forward to the Publications Clearinghouse required lists of the state publications of the agency, and to provide other related information as may be requested by the Publications Clearinghouse for the collection of state publications and the depository library system.

C. Upon release of a state publication by an agency, the records officer shall deposit a minimum of twenty-five (25) copies of the publication with the Publications Clearinghouse for record and depository system purposes. Additional copies shall be deposited when required by the Publications Clearinghouse.

D. The records officer shall notify the Publications Clearinghouse of the production of audiotapes, videotapes, films, filmstrips, slides and other audiovisual material. Every state agency shall preserve one (1) copy of each such audiovisual publication or the records officer shall deposit one (1) copy of each such audiovisual material with the Publications Clearinghouse for preservation.

E. Every state agency, including all institutions of higher education, shall provide to the Publications Clearinghouse a complete list of its state publications, including all audiovisual publications, in accordance with the rules and regulations of the Publications Clearinghouse. (Added Laws 1978, c. 165, § 7.)

RELATED LEGISLATION

1971 Oklu. Sess. Laws S. C. Res. No. 18
CONCURRENT RESOLUTIONS
State Publications
S. C. Res. No. 18[13a]

A concurrent resolution relating to publications; expressing legislative intent that publications produced at state expense be sent to the Department of Libraries.

WHEREAS, the Department of Libraries is the main general source for the storage, accumulation and dissemination of information in all its forms; and

WHEREAS, to make the Department of Libraries effective for the purpose and functions of its creation, all material published at state expense should be on file in the Department of Libraries; and

WHEREAS, Section 3-114 of Title 65 of the Oklahoma Statutes provides for distribution of publications to the Department of Libraries.

Now, Therefore, be it resolved by the Senate of the 1st Session of the 33rd
    Oklahoma Legislature, the House of Representatives concurring therein:

Section 1. State Printing Office—Copies to Department of Libraries. It is hereby declared to be the intention of the Legislature that the State Printing Office send copies of all materials printed to the Department of Libraries.

Section 2. Material printed at state expense—Copies to Department of Libraries. It is further declared to be the intention of the Legislature that copies of all material printed at state expense by any agency, board or individual for use, distribution or sale be sent to the Department of Libraries.

Adopted by the Senate the 15th day of March, 1971.

Adopted by the House of Representatives the 22nd day of March, 1971.

13a. 65 O. S. 1971, § 3-114 note.

EDITORIAL COMMENT

The 1978 legislation (1978 Okla. Laws c. 165) consists of new and amended sections. Three new sections provide for creation of the clearinghouse, definitions, and duties of the clearinghouse. § 3-114 on deposit of publications and § 3-115 on exchanges were amended.

§ 3-114, added in 1967, was amended to include "any board of regents of higher education," to decrease the number of copies to be deposited from one hundred to twenty-five, and to delete, "unless otherwise provided by the

Director.'' The second part of the section (numbered ''B'') relates to failure to comply with the section. It is substantially the same as the 1967 version with the addition of a provision for written notice, notice to more officials and a requirement that mandamus proceedings instead of ''appropriate action'' be instituted.

§ 3-115 is substantially the same. The wording is changed, as it is in § 3-114, to refer to the clearinghouse. The authority to ''otherwise dispose of'' in addition to selling is added in the 1978 law.

A new section, tit. 74, § 3106.1, was added to provide for the appointment of records officers in each state agency. The sections on attorney general's opinions (74:20) and on annual and other reports (74:3104) were amended to provide that the clearinghouse should receive fifty copies of attorney general's opinions and twenty-five copies of reports. § 75:57 was added, providing for the clearinghouse to receive fifty copies of court reports. § 75:14, which provides for distribution of session laws and statutes to library associations, was amended to provide that the Department of Libraries receive 110 copies. Other sections of the 1978 act have less direct bearing on the clearinghouse and the depository system. The act did not include an appropriation.

RULES AND REGULATIONS

STATE OF OKLAHOMA
OKLAHOMA PUBLICATIONS CLEARINGHOUSE
OKLAHOMA DEPARTMENT OF LIBRARIES
RULES AND REGULATIONS
Adopted 10-19-78

The Department of Libraries finds that an imminent peril to the public welfare requires promulgation of the following rules and regulations because:

1. HB 1714 requires state agencies to deposit copies of their publications with the Publications Clearinghouse, and mandates corrective actions to be taken in the event of noncompliance by state agencies;

2. The Director is required by the act to promulgate rules and regulations to implement the provisions of the act; such rules and regulations are needed immediately to assist state agencies in complying with the act, in order to insure the collection, preservation, and dissemination of state government publications to the citizens of Oklahoma;

3. The possibility exists of loss of public documents and information relating to the public health, safety, and welfare, because of the inaccessibility of such documents to certain libraries.

100   GENERAL RULES

101   Authority

These rules are promulgated by the Director of the Oklahoma Department of Libraries as authorized by H.B. 1714, adopted by the 36th Oklahoma Legislature and approved by the Governor on April 10, 1978 (65 O.S. Supp. 1978, Section 3-113.1); and as required by the Administrative Procedures Act, 75 O.S. 1971, Sections 301-307, as amended.

102   Organization

The Publications Clearinghouse was created as a division of the Oklahoma Department of Libraries under the direction of the Director of the Department, who appoints a professionally trained librarian to head the division. The Clearinghouse is a division of the Oklahoma Resources Branch, which brings together all Oklahoma materials and resources of the Department, including the Archives and Records Division, the Oklahoma Publications Clearinghouse, and the Oklahoma Collection.

103   Purpose

The Publications Clearinghouse has the duty to establish an Oklahoma government publications depository library system for the use of the citizens of the State of Oklahoma.

104   Public Information, Submissions or Requests

State agencies or others seeking information about these rules and regulations or wishing to make submissions or requests are invited to contact the Clearinghouse at the following address. If further clarification is needed, the Director of the Department of Libraries should be contacted.

> Oklahoma Publications Clearinghouse
> Oklahoma Department of Libraries
> Allen Wright Memorial Library Building
> 200 N.E. 18th Street
> Oklahoma City, OK 73105
> Phone: 405/521-2502

Copies of publications deposited with the Clearinghouse may be examined at the above address from 8 a.m. to 5 p.m., Monday through Friday. Publications are loaned where sufficient copies are available, and reference assistance is provided for persons working with the collection on the premises.

105   Advisory Council

In pursuing its mission to provide citizens of the State access to state government publications, the Clearinghouse will seek the advice of an Advisory Council. Members will be appointed by the Director of the Department, and will include representatives of state agencies, depository libraries, and other interested persons. Functions of the Council shall be to advise on the selection, organization, distribution, and bibliographic control of publications; to recommend policy and procedures for the effective and efficient operation of the Clearinghouse; and to provide a forum for the exchange of information and ideas.

106   Oklahoma Gazette as Depository for Official Rules and Regulations

State law requires timely deposit of three copies of official state agency rules and regulations for registration and publication in the *Oklahoma Gazette* in accordance with the Administrative Procedures Act (75 O.S. 1971, Sections 301-306, as amended). These requirements were not changed by state law establishing the Publications Clearinghouse (H.B. 1714). Official filings of notices to adopt rules and regulations, and regulations adopted, should continue to be addressed to the *Oklahoma Gazette*, which is located in room 109 State Capitol. They should be delivered to that address if sent by messenger or interagency mail service. If filings are made by U.S. Mail, they should be addressed as follows:

>Oklahoma Gazette—Official Filing
>Oklahoma Department of Libraries
>200 N.E. 18th St.
>Oklahoma City, OK 73105
>Phone: 405/521-2502

200   DEPOSIT OF PUBLICATIONS

201   Who Shall Deposit

State agencies supported wholly or in part by state funds are required by 65 O.S. Supp. 1978, Sections 3-113.2 and 3-114 (A), to deposit copies of their state publications with the Clearinghouse immediately upon publication.

''State publications'' includes those produced by the authority of ''the state, the Legislature, constitutional officers, any state department, committee, sub-state planning district, or other state agency supported wholly or in part by state funds.'' (65 O.S. Supp. 1978, Section 3-113.2(4).)

202   State Agencies Not Required to Deposit

Institutions of higher education are not required to deposit their publications (except see rule 212), but any state board of regents for higher education is so required. (65 O.S. Supp. 1978, Section 3-114 (A).)

203   Publications Required to Be Deposited

Publications required to be deposited are those informational materials published by the authority of a state agency regardless of the source of funds which are intended for distribution to the public and which are not compiled and reproduced solely to meet the internal operating needs of the agency, its divisions, and/or units of government which have a direct relationship to the state agency in regard to its ability to carry out its responsibilities.

Materials may be in any physical format, reproduced by any method, and may deal with any subject matter; they are required to be deposited if the purpose of the compilation and reproduction is publication for distribution to the public.

See *Webster's Third New International Dictionary of the English Language, Unabridged,* for definition of *publication* and *publish*:

publication, 2a: the act or process of issuing copies (as of a book, photograph, or musical score) for general distribution to the public. . . . 2b: a published work. . . .

publish, 3d: to release (a product of creative work) for public distribution or sale. . . .

It is assumed that informational materials specifically required by Federal or State law to be disseminated to the public fall under this definition of publication and are required to be deposited with the Clearinghouse.

Materials offered to the public for sale or by paid subscription are assumed to be published for public distribution and are required to be deposited.

204   Materials Not Required to Be Deposited

The following informational materials are not required to be deposited:
   (1) Materials which are not ''state publications'' as defined in 203 above.
   (2) Correspondence and interoffice memoranda, compiled and reproduced solely to meet the internal operating needs of the agency, its divisions, and/or units of government which have a direct relationship to the agency in regard to its ability to carry out its responsibilities.
   (3) Materials which are not compiled and/or reproduced for public distribution.

(4) Audiovisual materials, including audiotapes, videotapes, films, film-strips, slides, and other audiovisual materials, except that every state agency shall preserve one copy of each such publication or the records officer shall deposit one copy of each with the Publications Clearinghouse for preservation.

"Audiovisual materials" as defined in the *A.L.A. Glossary of Library Terms*, American Library Association, 1943, are "aids to teaching through ear and eye, such as phonograph records, slides, and motion-picture films."

For the purposes of the Clearinghouse, some informational materials may or may not fall within this definition of audiovisual materials, depending on the physical format, quantity reproduced, and purpose of the reproduction. Examples are maps, works of art, photographs, building plans and specifications, and computer produced copy or microcopy. It will be necessary for the Clearinghouse to make a determination about such materials on an individual basis after consulting with the publishing agency.

205   Guidelines for Determination of Deposit Titles

To assist agencies in complying with the requirement to deposit state publications, the Clearinghouse will offer guidelines as examples of the kinds of publications which may fall within the definitions set forth in sections 203 and 204 above.

206   Number of Copies to Be Deposited

The needs of the public will be best served by distributing to all libraries in the depository library system a basic collection of state publications containing the most useful and important publications. Fewer copies of other publications may be needed to meet the needs of the depository library system.

Therefore, in the interest of economy and efficiency, the Clearinghouse with the advice of the Advisory Council, will designate a core collection to be deposited in all participating libraries, and will require state agencies to deposit 25 copies of these publications, unless more than 25 copies are needed.

For the number of copies of legal publication required to be deposited, see 207 following, and for the exception to this rule in regard to audiovisual publications, see 204 (4) above.

Other materials not designated as core collection materials may be declared surplus to the needs of the Clearinghouse and the agency will be so advised. See 208 following.

207   Legal Publications

Title 65 O.S. 1978 Supp., Section 3-113.8, requires the Clearinghouse to receive and maintain, for exchange with the official libraries of each of the other states, territories, and possessions of the United States, a minimum of fifty (50) copies of all state legal publications, including bar journals, official reports of decisions, codes, opinions, rules and regulations, and one hundred ten (110) copies of statute supplements and session laws.

Other provisions elsewhere in the statutes apply specifically to the following kinds of legal publications.

207.1   Statutes and session laws—one hundred ten (110) copies of each volume of statutes and session laws shall be furnished to the Department of Libraries for use therein and for exchange. (75 O.S. Supp. 1978, Section 14 (D).)

207.2   Attorney General Opinions—Effective January 8, 1979, fifty (50) copies of the annually published bound volumes shall be sent to the Publications Clearinghouse for purposes of exchange. (74 O.S. Supp. 1978, Section 20.)

207.3   Court Decisions—fifty (50) copies of the published volumes of the official reports of the decisions of the Supreme Court and of the Court of Criminal Appeals of the State of Oklahoma shall be deposited for exchange with the official libraries of each of the other states, territories and possessions of the United States. (75 O.S. Supp. 1978, Section 57.)

207.4   Code of Oklahoma Rules and Regulations—fifty (50) copies of any code of Oklahoma Rules and Regulations, or any supplements thereto, which may be purchased by the State of Oklahoma, shall be purchased for the Publications Clearinghouse for the use of the library and for exchange purposes. (75 O.S. Supp. 1978, Section 256 (b).)

208   Surplus Copies

The Department is authorized to dispose of any surplus publication which it receives (65 O.S. Supp. 1978, Section 3-115).

Upon request, the Clearinghouse will consult with agencies in advance of publication and insofar as is possible will designate the number of copies expected to be needed for the depository library system. The agency will not be required to deposit copies which would result in a surplus to the needs of the

Clearinghouse. If a surplus occurs after publications are deposited, the Clearinghouse will without delay offer them to the publishing agency before making other disposition.

209   Records Officer of Agency

Every state agency shall designate one of its staff members or employees as the records officer for the agency and shall notify the Publications Clearinghouse on or before the first day of January, 1979, of the identity of such records officer, and shall immediately notify the Publications Clearinghouse of any new records officer should a change occur.

The records officer of each state agency shall have the duty to provide the Publications Clearinghouse with copies of all state publications of the agency, to compile and forward to the Publications Clearinghouse required lists of the state publications of the agency, and to provide other related information as may be requested by the Publications Clearinghouse.

210   Determination Whether Rules Apply

If a state agency is in doubt whether a specific publication is required to be deposited as set forth in the above rules, or if the number of copies to be deposited is questioned, the records officer of the agency shall consult with the division head of the Publications Clearinghouse for assistance in interpreting the regulations. If the state agency is not satisfied with the determination of the head of the Publications Clearinghouse, a written request should be submitted to the Director of the Department of Libraries, who will make the final ruling.

211   Noncompliance by Agency

65 O.S. Supp. 1978, Section 3-114, provides the following procedural steps be taken in the event of noncompliance by an agency:

(1) Written notice of such noncompliance from the Director of the Department of Libraries to the chief administrative officer of the agency.
(2) Such notice shall state:
    (a) the alleged noncompliance;
    (b) a specific date on which such noncompliance must be remedied;
    (c) that further noncompliance will result in a report to the Speaker of the House of Representatives, the President Pro Tempore of the Senate, and the State Attorney General; and
    (d) that the statute requires immediate initiation of mandamus proceedings by the Attorney General upon receipt of such notice to the Attorney General to seek agency compliance.

212   Agency List of Publications

Every state agency, including all institutions of higher education, shall provide to the Publications Clearinghouse a complete list of its state publications, including all audiovisual publications, by January 31, 1979. The initial list shall include materials published from July 28, 1978 through December 31, 1978, and shall be updated by notices as materials are published or by supplements issued at least semiannually. Twenty-five copies of the list of state publications and any updates or supplements shall be mailed or delivered to the Clearinghouse no later than the 31st day of January and the 31st day of July of each year.

213   Standard Format for State Publications

To achieve bibliographic control of state government publications, that is, to assure that the identity of a publication can be ascertained in terms of the issuing authority, author, and subject matter, sufficient to distinguish it from other publications, the following information shall be included on the title page or other suitable place near the beginning of each state publication which is required to be deposited with the Publication Clearinghouse:

(1) Full name of the issuing agency, including the division or subdivision responsible for publication, and the parent body.
(2) Name of any personal author to whom credit is intended to be given.
(3) Title of the publication.
(4) Date and place of publication.
(5) Frequency of issue if a periodical, that is, weekly, monthly, etc.
(6) Volume and number of issue, if appropriate.
(7) Date, or month and year of issue, if appropriate (periodicals).

214   Publication Cost Statement

Pursuant to 74 O.S. Supp. 1978, Section 3105, agencies are required to give cost information about their publications.

Agencies are hereby required to list the following cost information on each state publication issued by them, whether the printing is accomplished by the agency internally or through an outside public or private entity.

The information shall be set forth in a separate paragraph and shall conform as nearly as practical to the following format:

This publication, printed by (*name of printing firm*) is issued by (*here list the agency, department, board, commission, or institution*) as authorized by (*cite the statute specifically authorizing the publication, and if not specifically authorized by statute, provide the name of the person or persons so authorizing).* (Number) copies have been prepared and distributed at a cost of $————.

300   DEPOSITORY LIBRARY SYSTEM

301   Goals of the Depository Library System

The goals of the depository library system shall be to preserve the record of the state's history through its government publications, and to make the important and useful publications of the State accessible to citizens statewide through a system of lending and reference libraries. The long-range objective is to provide at least one access point for the deposit and use of state government publications in each of the Oklahoma sub-state planning districts.

302   Statutory Depositories

The statutes expressly provide that the following libraries shall receive copies of state publications deposited with the Clearinghouse as shown (65 O.S. Supp. 1978, Section 3-113.3).

To receive copies of all state publications deposited with the Clearinghouse:
  (a) The United States Library of Congress, 2 copies.
  (b) The Archives Division of the Department of Libraries, 1 copy.
  (c) The Center for Research Libraries (Chicago), 1 copy.
  (d) The state publications collection within the Clearinghouse, 4 copies.

To receive one (1) copy of each agency report (annual, biennial, or semi-annual) deposited with the Clearinghouse:
  (a) The Oklahoma State Legislative Council, 1 copy.
  (b) The Legislative Reference Division of the Department of Libraries, 1 copy.

303   Other Depositories

The Clearinghouse will also contract with other libraries which wish to participate in the depository library system. Libraries may request status as "Total Depositories," or "Core Collection Depositories."

Libraries approved as "Total Depositories" will receive copies of all state publications deposited with the Clearinghouse, when there are a sufficient number of copies. Libraries approved as "Core Collection Depositories" will receive copies only of those publications designated by the Clearinghouse as core publications, including copies of state publications deposited by the substate planning district in which the participating library is located.

304   Designation of Depositories

The Director of a library in Oklahoma wishing to receive state government publications through the depository library system shall submit a written request to the Director of the Department of Libraries requesting that the library be designated a "Total Depository" Library or a "Core Collection Depository." The Director of the Department shall review applications submitted, and shall make the decision as to depository status of applicants, taking into consideration user needs, geographic coverage, the level of service to be provided, and the numbers of copies of documents available for distribution by the Clearinghouse. The Director shall execute contracts with libraries participating in the depository library system setting forth the responsibility of the Clearinghouse to distribute publications and provide other services; and the responsibility of the participating library to receive and maintain publications deposited, not to dispose of publications without prior approval of the Clearinghouse, to provide adequate facilities for the storage and use of such publications, to provide free services to patrons in the use of such publications, and to fulfill other requirements set forth by the Department in its guidelines for the depository library system. The contract shall contain provisions for termination by either party upon proper notice.

305   Procedural Guidelines for Depository Library System

The Clearinghouse shall issue guidelines for the proper maintenance, housing, and servicing of state publications by libraries participating in the depository library system, and shall delineate the respective functions and responsibilities of the Clearinghouse and the participating libraries. Guidelines shall be developed with the advice of the Advisory Council to the Publications Clearinghouse.

306   Method of Distribution of Publications

The Clearinghouse shall mail publications to libraries participating in the depository library system on a regular schedule, with postage prepaid.

307   Distribution of Legal Publications

Legal publications as described in 207 above are deposited with the Clearinghouse for purposes of exchange and use therein, but are not otherwise distributed by the Clearinghouse except to the national research centers and the law libraries. There are statutes which provide other means of public distribution for some of these. They are summarized here to assist members of the depository library system in referring patrons:

307.1   Statutes and session laws

Free copies are distributed to the following upon written application and request submitted to the Chief Clerk of the Oklahoma House of Representatives before March 1 each year, to be distributed at the discretion of the Chief Clerk. Requests for yearly supplements should state that the requesting official or agency has the last compilation of the Oklahoma Statutes because the supplement is not useful without it. Officials and others eligible to receive single copies are:

> Each state officer, including the Governor and Lieutenant Governor
> Members of the Legislature
> Chief administrative officer and his assistant of the executive departments and the state boards and commissions
> Justices of the Supreme Court and Judges of the Criminal Court of Appeals and the clerk of said courts
> Heads of the several state educational, benevolent, and penal institutions
> Judges of the district courts and district court clerks
> County treasurers
> County assessors
> District attorneys
> Sheriffs
> Members of the Oklahoma Congressional Delegation
> Libraries in counties, cities, or towns, for the benefit of the public
> County law libraries

Also

> O.U. Law Library—55 copies, with five to be kept for use therein, and 50 for exchange purposes
> O.S.U. Library—5 copies for use therein
> Department of Libraries—110 copies for use therein and for exchange

The Secretary of State may, in his discretion, furnish out of any copies of such laws as he has on hand copies to other state officers than those mentioned herein for the use of their offices.

307.2   Attorney General Opinions

The statutes (74 O.S. Supp. 1978, Section 20) provide that the Attorney General shall annually publish all of the written opinions which he promulgates, with copies to be sent as follows:

One copy of the bound volume to

> Each member of the Legislature
> Each state officer

Chairman of each board or commission

County Law Library in each county where the same shall be available to the public

Secretary of State's Office—to be kept on file and available for public inspection

Fifty copies of the bound volume to

Publications Clearinghouse for purposes of exchange

Also

The Attorney is authorized to sell surplus copies of bound volumes and individual opinions.

307.3   Court Decisions

The statutes (75 O.S. Supp. 1978, Section 57) provide that 50 copies of the published volumes of the official reports of the decisions of the Supreme Court and of the Court of Criminal Appeals of the State shall be provided to the Clearinghouse for exchange purposes. No other statutory provisions are made for distribution.

307.4   Code of Oklahoma Rules and Regulations

The statutes (75 O.S. Supp. 1978, Section 256 (b)) provide that if any Code of Oklahoma Rules and Regulations is published under this section, the publisher shall furnish 12 free copies to the Department of Libraries, three free copies to the O.U. Law Library, and one free copy to the O.S.U. Library; further the statute provides that if the state of Oklahoma should purchase any copies of such a publication, 50 unmarked copies shall be purchased for and delivered to the Publications Clearinghouse for use of the library and for exchange purposes. And further that 50 unmarked copies shall also be purchased for the University of Oklahoma Law Library to be used for the purposes of exchange.

No such Code of Oklahoma Rules and Regulations has been published as of the date of this adoption.

308   Law Materials Exchange Program

Under state law, the Publications Clearinghouse is authorized to receive and maintain, for exchange with the official libraries of each of the other states, territories and possessions of the United States, copies of all state legal publications. It is a duty of the Clearinghouse to aid in the maintenance of a law library within the Oklahoma Department of Libraries to serve the state officers, agencies, and members of the Oklahoma Legislature.

The Publications Clearinghouse will send Oklahoma law publications once each month to the official exchange libraries. Postage will be paid by the Department of Libraries.

In exchange for Oklahoma government legal publications, an official library shall send legal publications in kind for that state (or other jurisdiction) to the Department of Libraries.

Until changed by written notice, the address to which copies of such legal publications of other states and jurisdictions are to be sent is:

> Acquisitions Section
> Oklahoma Department of Libraries
> Allen Wright Memorial Library Building
> 200 N.E. 18th Street
> Oklahoma City, OK 73105

An official library shall send to the Clearinghouse a list of the titles of all legal publications available for exchange from that state (or other jurisdiction), and a list of the titles of all legal publications which it wishes to receive from the Clearinghouse.

The Publications Clearinghouse will agree to send to the official library a list of the titles of all legal publications available for exchange from Oklahoma, and a list of the titles of all legal publications which the Law Library of the Department of Libraries wishes to receive from an official library.

Written agreements will be made with a library, or libraries, in each of the other states, territories, and possessions of the United States as required for exchange of Oklahoma government legal publications.

ATTORNEY GENERAL OPINION

1969 OKLA. OP. ATT'Y. GEN., NO. 69-180
NO. 69-180
INDUSTRIAL COURT—HANDBOOKS—SALE

The Department of Libraries is not required by S. B. 155, Section 1, 32nd Oklahoma Legislature, 1st Session (1969) to pay any fee for handbooks deposited with it by the Industrial Court of Oklahoma pursuant to 65 O. S. Supp. 1968, Section 3-114.

Oklahoma Department of Libraries   May 9, 1969

The Attorney General has had under consideration your letter of April 16, 1969, wherein you relate that the Industrial Court of Oklahoma has printed a handbook of Workmen's Compensation Laws. You also state that the Industrial Court is required to deposit one hundred copies of this handbook with the Department of Libraries by virtue of 65 O. S. Supp. 1968 Section 3-114. You then ask, in effect, the following question:

Is the Department of Libraries required by S. B. 155, Section 1, 32nd Oklahoma Legislature, 1st Session (1969) to pay for the copies of this handbook so deposited with it by the Industrial Court?

Title 65 O. S. Supp. 1968, Section 3-114, provides in part: [Omitted]

The State Industrial Court states that the handbook of Workmen's Compensation Laws is published at state expense.

S.B.155, Section 1, 32nd Oklahoma Legislature, 1st Session (1969) provides in pertinent part: [Omitted]

In passing section 3-114, supra, it seems that the legislative intent was that the Department of Libraries should not be required to pay for any publications so deposited with it.

Therefore, it is the opinion of the Attorney General that your question be answered in the negative in that the Department of Libraries is not required by S. B. 155, Section 1, 32nd Oklahoma Legislature, 1st Session (1969) to pay any fee for handbooks deposited with it by the State Industrial Court pursuant to 65 O. S. Supp. 1968, Section 3-114.

GRAYSON P. VAN HORN, Assistant Attorney General

BIBLIOGRAPHY

McClure, Charles R. ''The State of Oklahoma State Documents.'' *Documents to the People* 6:231-232 (November 1978).
McClure, at the School of Library Science, University of Oklahoma, reports on the background of the recent Oklahoma legislation, the publicity after the passage of the bill, and the lessons to be learned: (1) too much publicity before passage may be detrimental, and (2) librarians must work to demonstrate the importance of the legislation and the *payoffs* for the average citizen.

Tomberlin, Irma. *State Documents Collections in Oklahoma*. For the AMIGOS Bibliographic Council. November 1977. 14 p., appendices.
A report on document responsibilities and collecting at Oklahoma Department of Libraries, the summary of a questionnaire sent to selected Oklahoma libraries (sixteen responses) and six recommendations: (1) Oklahoma Department of Libraries should be a central collection and distribution center, (2) new legislation requiring thirty-five copies of each publication, (3) checklist, (4) cataloging of documents, (5) survey of other libraries in the state, and (6) workshop.

Tomberlin, Irma. *Official Headings for Oklahoma State Publications*. Dallas: AMIGOS
     Bibliographic Council for the Oklahoma Department of Libraries, 1977. (Re-
     printed by Oklahoma Department of Libraries.) 24 p.
Headings formulated by *Anglo-American Cataloging Rules*. Not a comprehensive list
and not limited to "official" agencies.

Cramer, Rose Fulton. *Author Headings for the Official Publications of the State of
     Oklahoma*. Rev. by Carolyn C. Mohr. Chicago: American Library Association,
     1954. (Not seen.)

OREGON

OR. REV. STAT. §§ 171.215, 182.070, 357.005(j), 357.015(6) (1979)

171.215. Furnishing legislative bills, calendars and interim committee reports to State Librarian. The person responsible for distribution of legislative bills, calendars and interim committee reports issued by authority of the Legislative Assembly or of a legislative interim committee shall make available to the State Librarian for distribution and exchange purposes 50 copies of each bill and daily calendar and 125 copies of each legislative interim committee report, or such lesser number as is desired by the State Librarian. [Formerly 171.092.]

182.070. Publications of state agencies to be furnished to State Librarian. (1) Unless a greater or lesser number is agreed upon by the State Librarian and the issuer of the publication, the State Printer or, in the event the State Printer is unable to furnish the number of copies of the publication, the person responsible for distribution of a publication issued by, or by authority of a state officer, agency or institution not under the control of the State Board of Higher Education shall make available to the State Librarian for distribution and exchange purposes, 45 copies of all publications so issued in multiple form, other than interoffice memoranda or forms. The State Printer may withhold the prescribed number of copies from each printing order and forward them to the State Librarian. Cost of printing for all copies of a publication furnished to the State Librarian in compliance with this subsection shall be borne by the issuing agency.

(2) The term "publication," as used in this section, does not include:

(a) Oregon Revised Statutes or any edition thereof.

(b) Legislative bills, calendars and interim committee reports made available under ORS 171.215.

(c) Reports and publications of the Oregon Supreme Court, Oregon Court of Appeals and the Oregon Tax Court. [1953 c.527 §2; 1961 c.167 §21; 1979 c.215 §1]

357.005. State Library duties; free book loans. (1) The State Library shall be the agency of government responsible for executing the functions as set forth in ORS 357.001 and 357.003.

(2) To carry out its duties under subsection (1) of this section, the State Library may:

****

(j) Prescribe the conditions for use of state documents in depository libraries, and maintain a system of exchange of state documents with libraries outside this state. [Formerly 357.080.]

357.015. Functions of trustees. The Trustees of the State Library shall be the policy-making body for the State Library and shall:

****

(6) Designate certain libraries within the state, including the library of every nationally accredited law school, as depository libraries for state publications. [Formerly 357.230.]

EDITORIAL COMMENT

In 1961, and possibly before, the law (357.071) provided that the state library ''shall act as the official depository of Oregon State documents. . . .''

A 1971 amendment (1971 c. 185 § 1) added, ''The library of every law school within this state is designated as a depository library.''

In 1975, there was a complete revision of the library law of the state.

A 1979 amendment to ORS 182.070 (Senate Bill 246, 1979 Regular Session) changed the number of copies from twenty-five copies of technical publications and seventy-five copies of all other publications to forty-five copies of all publications The state printer is authorized to withhold the copies from each printing order. The cost of these copies is to be borne by the issuing agency. Subsection (2) was amended by adding court reports to the list of items not to be included under the term ''publication.'' The Engrossed Bill did not include an extensive definition of ''publication'' found in an earlier version of the bill.

BIBLIOGRAPHY

Moberg, Barbara. ''Oregon's Documents Depository Laws and Policies: Past and Present.'' Oregon State Library, 1965. 9 p.
This paper was ''prepared for Oregon State Library's Workshop for State Documents Depository Libraries, February 26, 1965.'' It begins with a 1905 quotation, ''People in different sections of the state should know that all state documents may be found in certain libraries,'' and traces the subsequent legislative history of depository and exchange legislation. The second half of the article outlines the present policies and mentions difficulties (learning of new titles and acquiring stock for distribution, lack of a subject index to the *Checklist*, and limited assistance possible to depository libraries).

Keefer, Mary. ''Simplified Cataloging of Federal and State Documents.'' *Library
    Resources and Technical Services* 6:262-264 (Summer 1962).
An explanation of the cataloging shortcut for Oregon documents devised by Doreen
Yorkston Portal for unbound separates. Grouping separates by year; assigning an
arbitrary series title (''General Publications'') and a series number (in square brackets);
and classifying the series by the issuing agency permit the documents to be entered in
the catalog quickly. The documents assistant can add new titles as they arrive, and by
having a separate catalog card for each year, earlier titles received can be put on an
appropriate card. Those familiar with the literature will have read of this ''Oregon
plan.''

Eaton, Katherine Girton. ''The Missing 70%: The Availability of Oregon State Docu-
    ments to Libraries.'' *Pacific Northwest Library Association Quarterly* 33:10-14
    (Fall [October] 1968).
The Oregon publication distribution system needs improvement. The term ''publication'' is broadly defined and thus causes confusion. The state librarian has authority to
request publications—and in fact sends out an annual memorandum to state agencies—
but does not always receive enough copies and does not always receive everything.
Suggestions are: (1) a coordinator of state publications could be added to the library
staff or the state printer's staff to assure that *all* state publications are made available for
review, (2) the state printer could be made responsible for *all* state publications,
(3) the cost of distribution to depository libraries could be analyzed and the value of
publications assessed, (4) Oregon needs a monthly checklist with annual cumulation,
as well as a retrospective list with annual cumulation, a retrospective list for 1925-1951,
and a union listing of holdings, and (5) the documents law should be revised to include
definitions and (if a coordinator is not possible) to impose a mandatory duty on state
agencies to supply copies.

PENNSYLVANIA

PA. STAT. ANN. tit. 24 §§ 4201, 4425 (Purdon Supp. 1980-81)

§ 4201. State library and state librarian; powers and duties. The Department of Public Instruction shall have the power, and its duty shall be—
****

(4) To receive copies of all publications of all agencies of the Commonwealth in order to maintain a definitive, organized collection of all such publications by the State Library and to provide for the distribution of such publications to other libraries. The State Librarian shall also designate selected academic or public libraries within the Commonwealth to be State government document depository libraries under the criteria and regulations approved by the Advisory Council on Library Development and, in the case of documents published pursuant to the act of July 31, 1968 (Act No. 240), known as the ``Commonwealth Documents Law,'' by the Joint Committee on Documents. (As amended 1971, Dec. 1, P. L. 578, No. 150, § 1.)

§ 4425. Libraries to receive Commonwealth publications. The Department of Property and Supplies shall, as soon as practicable after publication, forward to those libraries designated by the State Librarian as State documents depository libraries, a copy of every publication of every department, board, commission or agency of the Commonwealth. The Department of Property and Supplies shall direct each such department, board, commission or agency to supply it with the number of copies, if any, of each publication remaining after regular distribution according to existing allocations, but in no case to exceed two hundred fifty copies, and upon receipt thereof shall notify the State Librarian who shall then designate the libraries to which the publication shall be forwarded. Any public library, school library, junior college or community college library, university library or historical society library in the Commonwealth shall be eligible to receive free copies of the publications. It shall be the privilege of the state to recall any or all of the said publications in the event of the loss of their own files by fire or other casualty.

The provisions of this section shall not apply to the distribution of documents published pursuant to the Commonwealth Documents Law. The State Librarian, with the approval of the Advisory Council on Library Development, shall make recommendations from time to time to the Joint Committee on

Documents concerning criteria for the distribution to libraries of documents published pursuant to the Commonwealth Documents Law. (As amended 1971, Dec. 1, P. L. 580, No. 150, § 3.)

EDITORIAL COMMENT

§ 4201(4) formerly read, "To receive at least fifty copies of all Commonwealth publications for the documents collection and for exchange with other libraries."

§ 4425 was almost completely rewritten by the 1971 Act. It formerly required each library to send to the Department of Property and Supplies "a statement of the publications or types of publications which the library desires to receive." The last sentence, permitting recall of the publications in the event of loss, is the same.

RULES AND REGULATIONS

Pa. Code, tit. 22, §§ 143.1 to 143.8.
STATE DOCUMENT DEPOSITORIES

Authority
The provisions of this Chapter 145 issued under act of June 14, 1961, (24 P. S. § 4101 *et seq.*).

Source
The provisions of this Chapter 145 adopted April 21, 1972, 2 Pa. B. 721.

§ **143.1. Definitions.** The following words and terms, when used in this Chapter, shall have the following meanings, unless the context clearly indicates otherwise:

Depository collection—A gathering of official Commonwealth publications in a formally organized library organized either for public use under The Library Code, (24 P. S. § 4101 *et seq.*), or for academic use in a state accredited institution of higher education.

Publication—Any printed or otherwise reproduced item prepared for distribution to the public, or used within any state agency as a regulatory instrument, including but not limited to documents, pamphlets, studies, brochures, books, annual reports, codes, regulations, journals, periodicals or magazines printed by or for the Commonwealth, its legislature, its courts, its constitutional officers, or any authority, board, commission, department or other State governmental agency or issued in conjunction with, or under contract with, the

Federal government, local units of government, private individuals, institutions or corporations.

§ **143.2. Purpose.** The purpose of establishing depository collections of publications of all of the governmental agencies of this Commonwealth in selected academic and public libraries is to make the publications readily available to the citizens of the Commonwealth and to enable the selected libraries to provide information found in the publications to their clientele.

§ **143.3. Eligibility for depository collection status.**

(a) *State college and university libraries*. The main library at each state college or university shall be eligible for designation as a depository collection library.

(b) *District library centers*. Each library designated a district library center pursuant to article II, section 211, of the act of June 14, 1961, (24 P. S. § 4211), shall be eligible for designation as a depository collection library.

(c) *Regional library resource centers*. The four libraries designated as regional library resource centers pursuant to article II, section 209, of act of June 14, 1961, (24 P. S. § 4209), shall be eligible for designation as a depository collection library.

(d) *Libraries of State-related universities and colleges*. The library at each of the universities and colleges in the Commonwealth which receive annual appropriations from the state and are considered "State-related" shall be eligible for designation as a depository collection library.

(e) *U.S. Documents depository libraries*. Any library currently designated by the Superintendent of Documents as a depository for Federal documents shall be eligible for designation as a depository collection library.

(f) *Other academic libraries*. Libraries of other state accredited universities, colleges, junior or community colleges in the Commonwealth shall be eligible for designation as depository collections if the institution's total student enrollment is over 5,000 or if there are no other libraries designated under subsections (a)-(e) in the county in which the institution is located.

(g) *Other public libraries*. Other public libraries organized under the provisions of act of June 14, 1961, (24 P. S. § 4201 *et seq.*), and currently eligible to receive state aid pursuant to article III, section 303 of that act shall be eligible for designation as depository collections provided there are no other libraries in that county designated or eligible for designation under subsections (a)-(f), the library is the central library for a system of public libraries, and the library serves as an extensive regional branch reference library for a large system of libraries.

§ **143.4. Number of collections.** The state Librarian shall designate no more than 100 libraries in the Commonwealth as depository collections.

§ **143.5. Conditions for designation.** In addition to the provisions of § 143.3 of this Title (relating to eligibility for depository collection status), the libraries to be designated as depository collections shall agree to the following conditions:

(1) The publications received under the depository law must be given the same treatment or cataloging as other similar material purchased or given for the regular library collection.

(2) The depository collection library shall agree to provide free public reference and information service from the Commonwealth publications received as a depository. It shall also agree to house adequately and safely the publications until such time as disposal or return of items is authorized.

(3) The publications received must be made available for the use of any citizen of the Commonwealth whether or not that individual is a resident of the municipality in which that library is located, a registered user of the library, or an enrolled student in the institution.

(4) The publications received must be kept in the depository library's collection for at least five years except those items for which the State Librarian may authorize a shorter retention period. All publications due for disposal shall first be offered to the State Library for return before disposal is carried out.

§ 143.6. Application for depository collection status.

(a) *Automatic designation.* The State Librarian shall grant depository status to all eligible libraries falling within subsections (a)-(e) of § 143.5 of this Title (relating to eligibility for depository collection status) after receiving their agreement to the conditions outlined in § 143.5 of this Title (relating to conditions for designation).

(b) *Discretionary designation.* Eligible libraries falling within subsections (g) and (f) of § 143.5 of this Title (relating to eligibility for depository collection status) may be requested by the State Librarian to accept depository status within the given conditions in order to further the aims of the publications depository system for geographical comprehensiveness. Other libraries seeking depository status shall address their request by letter to the State Librarian. Such letters of application shall be signed by the head librarian and the board of trustees in the case of public libraries, or the head librarian and the president of the institution in the case of academic libraries. The State Librarian shall respond to the letter of application within 60 days by granting depository status or by clearly explaining by letter the ineligibility of the library for depository status.

§ 143.7. Termination of depository collection status.

(a) *Voluntary termination.* If a library decides to relinquish its status as a depository collection it shall do so by letter to the State Librarian. The letter must be signed by both the head librarian and the president of the board of trustees in the case of public libraries and the head librarian and the president of the institution in the case of academic libraries. The State Librarian will arrange to halt the shipment of Commonwealth publications to such libraries and make appropriate mutual arrangement to dispose of any unwanted state publications on deposit with the library.

(b) *Involuntary termination.* If a depository collection library does not comply with the agreed-to conditions, and, after adequate warning, refuses to comply with said conditions, the State Librarian shall terminate depository status and end the shipment of Commonwealth publications to that library. Notice of termination shall be given by a letter explaining the reasons for the termination to the head librarian with a true copy of the letter to either the president of the institution in the case of an academic library or the president of the board of trustees in the case of public library. Return to the Commonwealth of publications on deposit shall be arranged between the State Librarian and the library's head librarian.

§ 143.8. Role of the State Library.

(a) *Receiving publications.* Pursuant to sections 201 and 425 of act of June 14, 1961, (24 P. S. § 4201 *et seq.*) the State Library shall receive copies of all publications of all agencies of the Commonwealth for the maintenance of its own collection, for distribution to the depository collections, and for exchange with out-of-state libraries, the number of copies of each publication may be up to, but not exceed 250 copies.

(b) *Listing publications.* The State Library shall publish a periodic listing of Commonwealth publications received for its collection. The list shall be distributed to all public and academic libraries in the Commonwealth.

(c) *Selecting publications.* The State Library will select publications from those received for its own collection and arrange for copies of those selected to be shipped to the depository collections.

(d) *Shipping publications.* In most cases the Bureau of Publications, Department of Property and Supplies, shall be responsible for the shipment and delivery of Commonwealth publications to depository collections. When the availability of a publication becomes known to either the State Library or the Bureau of Publications, Department of Property and Supplies, the State Librarian may designate it as a depository item and request the Bureau of Publications to distribute it to the depository libraries. If the publication is not stocked by the Department of Property and Supplies, the State Library will seek to obtain a sufficient number of copies for its own collection and for distribution to the depository.

EDITORIAL COMMENT

The regulations as reproduced are the same, with minor exceptions, as those titled, "Regulations of the State Librarian for the Designation of Libraries as State Documents Depositories," which were approved by both the state librarian and the Advisory Council on Library Development on March 13, 1972. The letter of designation as a depository used by the State Library refers to the regulations as adopted by the Advisory Council.

The regulations as approved by the state librarian and the council are not reproduced. They are numbered 31-601 through 31-607 and correspond almost word for word and section by section with §§ 143.1 through 143.8 in the *Pa. Code*:

143.1 was 31-602. The *Code* added the introductory sentence and reversed the order of the two definitions.

143.2 was 31-601. The *Code* put the section on purpose after the definitions. It changed the heading of the section from "General Purpose."

143.3 was 31-603. The only substantive change occurred here. The state librarian's regulation in 31-603(g) (143.3G in the *Code*) stated that libraries would be eligible for designation if they met three numbered conditions. Although the conditions were numbered, they were not connected by "and" or "or." The *Code* substituted "provided" for "if," eliminated the numbering, and inserted "and." Thus, the *Code* states that a library must meet all three conditions. It is possible that the state librarian, by numbering the conditions, was stating them in the alternative.

143.4 was 31-604A and 143.5 was 31-604B. The state librarian's heading for 31-604 was "Number of collections and conditions for designation."

143.6 was 31-605. In subsection B, the state librarian's version numbered each of the three sentences. The first sentence of that subsection was changed from the active tense, "the State Librarian may request," to the passive, "libraries . . . may be requested."

143.7 was 31-606 and follows the state librarian's version.

143.8 was 31-607. In subsection A, the section number that was cited was changed from 420 to 425 in the *Code*. In subsection D, "shall be responsible" was changed to "will be responsible."

CONTRACT

State Library of Pennsylvania
Harrisburg, Pennsylvania

To the State Librarian, Commonwealth of Pennsylvania
    The _____

_____

accepts designation as a depository for publications issued by governmental agencies of the Commonwealth of Pennsylvania.

    The library furthermore agrees to conform with the conditions of designation set forth in the regulations adopted by the Advisory Council on Library Development on March 13, 1972.

Librarian	Date

President of the Institution or	Date
President of the Board of Trustees	

    The above named library is herewith designated as a depository for publications issued by the government agencies of the Commonwealth of Pennsylvania.

Date	State Librarian

BIBLIOGRAPHY

The Pennsylvania articles are listed in chronological order.

"Pennsylvania State Library Arrangement Scheme for Pennsylvania State Documents." *Pennsylvania Library Notes* 14:592-604 (July 1935).

Holt, Olive S. "Pennsylvania Author Headings." State College, Pa.: Library, The Pennsylvania State College, 1941. 54 p. (Pennsylvania State College Library studies, no. 3.) An issue of the Pennsylvania State College *Bulletin* 35, no. 39. (Not seen.)

Demorest. Rose. "Pennsylvania Government Documents." *Pennsylvania Library Association Bulletin* 9:3-4 (May 1953).
The author is at the Pennsylvania Room, Carnegie Library of Pittsburgh. The article begins:

> Probably a most neglected field of valuable source material for this state has been the documents issued by the various departments and bureaus. The list is a long one and complete files are difficult to find in one place. The problem remains of their lack of accessibility, the difficulty of handling them and the lack of a uniform system of distribution.

A textual discussion of important, scarce, and new Pennsylvania publications and a list of publications follow. Demorest cites Bowker and Hasse.

Hammer, Donald P. "Pennsylvania Government Publications." *Pennsylvania Library Association Bulletin* 10:8-10 (Spring 1955).
Hammer, law librarian, Pennsylvania State Library, lists thirty-eight publications from twenty-six agencies with full annotations.
"Pennsylvania state publications can be a partial solution to [the] problem [of developing] a useful up-to-date library collection with the least expenditure." He continues, "the major hindrance lies in accessibility and publicity." "The Exchange Section of the State Library is by far the best source of state documents for libraries."

Hammer, Donald P. "Pennsylvania Government Publications." *Pennsylvania Library Association Bulletin* 11:2-4 (Fall 1955).
Textual discussion of serial publications, not including annual reports and bulletins, which the author plans to discuss in future articles. He notes that all serials (except *Pennsylvania Angler*) are free and that the state library can supply individual back issues to complete files.

"Government Documents." *Pennsylvania Library Association Bulletin* 15:65-66 (Winter 1960).
"A panel on Government documents was sponsored by the College and Reference Section [of the Pennsylvania Library Association] at the annual Conference...." Speakers included representatives of a large university library (who commented on the

lack of a complete list of state documents, the late distribution of important documents and the need for a new compendium of state reorganization), of a small public library (who stated that the two types of publications most needed were ''those of a statistical nature and those concerning local Government organization''); of the Division of Research and Museum Commission (who cited important publications of the Division); of the Department of Internal Affairs (who also cited publications—statistical and local government—issued by his department), and of the New York State Library (who described the New York depository system).

Growing out of the meeting were these substantive results: Pennsylvania Library Association representatives were appointed to the Advisory Committee on Statistics and the Committee on Coordination of Municipal Research in the Department of Internal Affairs; a resolution was passed to appoint a committee on state documents in the association; and the suggestion was made that one of the first duties of this committee would be to urge every state agency to send copies of its publications to the Library of Congress.

''State Publications: Problems in Effective Use,'' by Elizabeth Ellis, Government Publications Librarian, Pennsylvania State Library, is annotated with other general articles.

Ellis, Elizabeth G., and Stewart, Robert C. *List of Basic Pennsylvania Publications for Depository Libraries*. Prelim. ed. Pennsylvania State Library, Harrisburg, Pa., 1967. 25 p. mim. (Not seen.)
Described by Stewart in his 1968 article on research resources as ''a list of 150 current State publications considered valuable for reference use and recommended for proposed depository libraries as an aid to selection and for checking holdings. The list provides complete bibliographic data for most entries with publication history of series and frequent descriptive annotations of contents.''

Stewart, R. C. ''Selected Pennsylvania Publications.'' *See* issues of *Pennsylvania Library Association Bulletin* 1967-1969. (Not seen.)

Stewart, Robert C. ''Research Resources Among Pennsylvania State Publications.'' *Pennsylvania Library Association Bulletin* 23:232-242 (May 1968).
This detailed survey of *basic state publications*, as defined in Wilcox's *Manual*, for Pennsylvania begins with constitutions and constitutional conventions and continues with legislative publications and collected documents. Stewart reports on Pennsylvania documents in microform, the bibliographic record of state publications, and a survey of Pennsylvania libraries to ascertain document acquisition methods and interest in a workshop. *See* papers from workshop in *PLA Bulletin* 25:79-123 (March 1970).

Papers presented at a workshop sponsored by the State Library, edited by Robert D. Stewart, Chairman of PLA Government Documents Committee. *Pennsylvania Library Association Bulletin* 25:79-123 (March 1970).
Ellis, Elizabeth G. ''Introduction.''
The state library survey conducted in January 1967 ''revealed that many Pennsylvania documents of basic importance were not widely available either in district library centers or in many academic libraries in Pennsylvania. The reasons for this void

include: (1) the lack of a system of depository distribution, (2) the lack of a comprehensive listing and indexing of Pennsylvania documents, and (3) the need for guidance in the acquisition, handling and use of these materials.''

The Pennsylvania Library Association Documents Committee recommended a plan for a depository system, and the state library drafted a formal proposal which was approved by the Advisory Council of Library Development. This proposal was included in the Advisory Council's legislative recommendations and the Pennsylvania Library Association's legislative program.

The state library issues a checklist, an annotated list of selected publications, and a *List of Basic Pennsylvania State Publications*. The Document Committee is compiling a union list of government serials (to include 160 Pennsylvania serial documents).

''Distribution and Acquisition of Pennsylvania State Publications.'' [1970]
This paper recommends (1) *Directory of State Publications*, (2) *Monthly Checklist of State Publications*, (3) ''Selected Pennsylvania Publications'' in the *PLA Bulletin*, and (4) Harrisburg newspapers and articles with a Harrisburg dateline in other newspapers (ask state library for help in identifying documents mentioned in news articles.)

Buber, Edward J. ''The Pennsylvania Bureau of Publications.'' [1970]
Buber is assistant director of the bureau, which ''has primary responsibility for the publication and distribution of official Pennsylvania documents in conjunction with its responsibility for the printing of all State materials.'' Pennsylvania does not have a state printer. The state publishes 1,500 titles issued by the General Assembly, the Governor's Office, twenty departments, twenty-one boards, and eleven commissions. The bureau publishes the *Directory of State Publications*.

The bureau sells all priced publications. Most free publications are available only from the issuing agency. Since 1965, 158 libraries have applied for certification. Public libraries may be certified to receive publications free.

Bordner, George W. ''The Certification Program for Documents Distribution.'' [1970]
Bordner is director of technical services at the state library. The certification program is based on a 1963 law and became effective on January 1, 1966. Each public library is given an opportunity to be certified. Initially, 125 libraries participated. Certification is approved by the state library and then by the Bureau of Publications, and is valid for two years. A list of publications needed must accompany the certificate. (This can be a marked copy of the Bureau's *Directory of State Publications*.)

There are no standing orders. The bureau ships publications held in its warehouse and forwards requests to agencies for items distributed solely by the issuing agency. If the issuing agency maintains a mailing list, publications will continue to be sent, but it may be necessary to periodically renew the request to be on the mailing list.

The state library also has a gift and exchange program.

Carter, Catherine. ''Cataloging and Classification of State Documents.'' [1970]
Catherine Carter, associate catalog librarian at the Pennsylvania State University Library, begins with the pros and cons of separate documents collections versus integrated ones. In commenting on complete cataloging and classification in an integrated collection, she says, ''Administrators should remember that documents are often

harder to catalog than books because of difficult corporate entries and because a smaller percentage of documents have Library of Congress printed cards."

Carter mentions Houk's Ohio classification scheme, which is being used as a model by the Pennsylvania State Library for the scheme it is developing. For libraries with documents from many states, she recommends consideration of the Swank scheme, which she explains. She lists as disadvantages of document classification schemes: (1) frequent name changes, mergers, and transfers of state agencies, (2) the fact that it is one more system for patrons and staff to learn, and (3) any arrangement by issuing agency affords little help to those who need a subject approach.

Substitutes for cataloging are (1) an indexed checklist (but Pennsylvania does not have one), (2) cards in catalog under all agency names, or under subjects referring the ·user to the documents department, and (3) the Oregon plan whereby monographs are given a collective title [General Publications], arranged by year and treated as though they were serials.

Full cataloging involves at least one corporate entry for each title. Carter compares the treatment of corporate entries under *Anglo-American Cataloging Rules* of 1967 and *1949 ALA Cataloging Rules*. She says, "The new code [AACR of 1967] represents a radical change of philosophy in preferring for corporate entry the form of name found on the publications of the organization." Her explanations are exceptionally clear and are well documented with examples. She says, "It is doubtful if any library patron ever understood corporate entries anyway, and the changes should not disturb him—always provided that enough added entries and cross-references are made."

Hirschmann, Agnes, and Ellis, Elizabeth, G. "Reference Use of Legislative Publica-
    tions." [1970]
Agnes Hirschmann is reference historian, Legislative Reference Bureau, Pennsylvania General Assembly. Elizabeth Ellis was formerly the head of the Government Publications Section, Pennsylvania State Library.

The paper covers "(1) background information germane to knowledge of the publications materials, (2) the definition of pertinent terms, and (3) a description of legislative publications and their use as reference materials." It includes a full statement of the steps in the legislative process.

Oller, Kathryn, and Stewart, Robert C. "Reference Use of Executive Publications."
    [1970]
Kathryn Oller is professor of library science at Drexel Institute of Technology. Robert Stewart was formerly the head of the Government Publications Section, Pennsylvania State Library.

Government publications in general are important reference sources because "(1) they are authoritative, bearing the imprint of a government agency; (2) they are primary source material on matters of government; (3) they provide up-to-date information on topics of current significance; (4) they are often the work of specialists and experts; and (5) they represent all subject areas."

"There is a serious lack of indexing of Pennsylvania State Documents. . . ." Bibliographical sources and current lists are cited.

Executive publications, useful in performing reference service, are discussed in detail by types: directories, manuals, and guides; statistical publications; maps and atlases; reports; bibliographies; compilations of sources; comprehensive works; executive budget; and rules and regulations.

''Pennsylvania State Government and Its Publications: Selected References.'' [1970]
This annotated list is divided by topics: (1) Pennsylvania government organization and functions; (2) Pennsylvania state publications; (3) state publications: manuals (here are listed the California manual, Press, and Wilcox), and (4) state publications: checklists and indexes.

Stewart, R. C. *Union List of Selected Pennsylvania Serial Documents in Pennsylvania Libraries*. Pennsylvania Library Association, 1971. 68 p. (Not seen.)

''Depository Libraries Announced.'' *Pennsylvania Library Association Bulletin* 27:
298-299 (Spring 1972).
The state librarian announced that fifty-six libraries have been designated depositories following the passage of an amendment to the Library Code setting up a state publications depository system. Requirements for designation are given, and conditions to which the libraries must agree—free reference and information service and retention of the documents for five years—are stated. The list of libraries is included.

Crowers, Clifford P. ''It's Great! Three Parts of the Federal Register System.''
Pennsylvania Library Association Bulletin 27:303-309 (November 1972).
Includes a paragraph on the *Pennsylvania Code* and *Pennsylvania Bulletin*.

Bordner, George W. ''Classification Scheme—Pennsylvania State Publications.''
Documents to the People 4:15-17 (June 1976).
The abstract says, ''Basic arrangement is alphabetical by agency, although independent agencies are at the end in a separate alphabet.'' ''P'' is used as the first letter in every instance to identify the state of Pennsylvania. Series forms are designated by numerals, and individual titles are Cuttered from the first word in the title.

LeSourd, Margaret. ''Pennsylvania Documents: A Valuable Resource.'' *Pennsylvania Library Association Bulletin* 32:4-19 (January 1977).
Documents ''are basic reference books that should be in every library.'' Five important Pennsylvania titles are described along with several popular series. *Checklist of Official Pennsylvania Publications* and *Monthly Checklist of State Publications* are both described as ''weak'' because they can list only what is received.

RHODE ISLAND

R. I. GEN. LAWS §§ 29-1-7; 29-1-8 (1968)

29-1-7. Supply of state publications. It shall be the duty of each state officer and director, upon the requisition of the state librarian, to supply the state library with a sufficient number of each publication issued from his department to enable him to carry into effect the provisions of chapters 1 and 2 of this title. (P. L. 1902, ch. 959, § 4 . . . G. L. 1956, § 29-1-7.)

29-1-8. Distribution within state of state publications. The state librarian shall distribute to the several libraries of the state, as may apply for them, copies of the laws, reports of departments and institutions, and all other books and pamphlets published by the state except such as are distributed by public law. (P. L. 1904, ch. 1148, § 1 . . . G. L. 1956, § 29-1-8.)

STATE COMMENT (1974)

We have no depository system, as such in this State at the present time. We are, however, developing one. We began when I came here in 1962 setting up files of state documents received and state documents distributed. Our control and channelling of documents has resulted in an informal depository system.

Our problem, of course, like any other State Agency in this field is in acquiring documents. We do feel that we now have the basis of a formal system, at least within this State.

As of this year we have a committee on state documents including librarians representing the various institutional libraries in the State. This committee has arranged for a consultant to come to Rhode Island the latter part of July to survey the present system and make recommendations for a formal system. (Letter from Elliott E. Andrews, State Librarian, Rhode Island State Library, Providence, Rhode Island 02903, dated June 11, 1974. *In* Documents on Documents Collection.)

EDITORIAL COMMENT

§ 29-1-7 was originally enacted in 1902 (P. L. 1902, ch. 959, § 4). § 29-1-8 was originally enacted in 1904 (P. L. 1904, ch. 1148, § 1). Neither has been amended since then.

SOUTH CAROLINA

S. C. SENATE Bill 2-203 (1972)
(*IN* DOCUMENTS ON DOCUMENTS COLLECTION)

A BILL

TO AMEND THE CODE OF LAWS OF SOUTH CAROLINA, 1962, BY ADDING SECTION 42-200.1, SO AS TO PROVIDE CERTAIN DEFINITIONS RELATING TO THE SOUTH CAROLINA STATE LIBRARY; TO AMEND THE 1962 CODE BY ADDING SECTION 42-201.1, SO AS TO PROVIDE FOR CERTAIN FUNCTIONS OF THE SOUTH CAROLINA STATE LIBRARY AND TO PROVIDE THAT SUCH LIBRARY SHALL BE THE OFFICIAL STATE DEPOSITORY OF STATE PUBLICATIONS; TO AMEND SECTION 42-204, AS AMENDED, OF THE 1962 CODE, RELATING TO THE POWERS OF THE BOARD OF DIRECTORS OF THE SOUTH CAROLINA STATE LIBRARY, SO AS TO PROVIDE ADDITIONAL POWERS; AND TO AMEND THE 1962 CODE BY ADDING SECTION 42-206, SO AS TO REQUIRE ALL STATE AGENCIES, DEPARTMENTS AND STATE-SUPPORTED COLLEGES AND UNIVERSITIES TO FORWARD TO THE SOUTH CAROLINA STATE LIBRARY TWENTY-FIVE COPIES OF EVERY STATE PUBLICATION THAT SUCH AGENCY, DEPARTMENT, COLLEGE OR UNIVERSITY PRINTS WITHIN FIFTEEN DAYS AFTER SUCH PRINTING.

Be it enacted by the General Assembly of the State of South Carolina:

SECTION 1. The 1962 Code is amended by adding Section 42-200.1 which shall read as follows:

''Section 42-200.1. The following words and phrases when used in this chapter shall, for the purpose of this chapter, have, unless the context indicates otherwise, the following meanings:

(a) 'Complete depository' is a place, usually a library, that receives at least one copy of all State publications;

(b) 'Selective depository' is a place, usually a library, that from time to time requests and receives copies of State publications;

(c) 'Depository system' is a system in which copies of all State publications are deposited in one central depository or library and copies are sent to other designated depositories or libraries;

(d) 'State publication' means any document, compilation, journal, resolution, statute, register, book, act, pamphlet, report, map, leaflet, order, regulation, directory, periodical, magazine or other similar written material excluding interoffice and intraoffice communications issued in print by the State, any State agency or department or any State-supported college or university for the use or regulation of any person; and

(e) 'Print' means all forms of duplicating other than the use of carbon paper.''

SECTION 2. The 1962 Code is amended by adding Section 42-201.1 which shall read as follows:

''Section 42-201.1. Notwithstanding any other provision of law, the South Carolina State Library shall be the official State depository of all State publications, with the responsibility for organizing such publications and for providing bibliographic control over them and shall distribute State publications to all libraries participating in a depository system established by it.

The South Carolina State Library shall also forward such publications to and receive such publications from out-of-state libraries, departments and agencies with whom the South Carolina State Library has implemented an agreement to exchange such publications; *provided*, however, that the provisions of this section shall not affect the duties of either the Legislative Council or the Code Commissioner as provided for by law.''

SECTION 3. Section 42-204 of the 1962 Code, as last amended by Act 464 of 1969, is further amended by adding the following new items:

''(9) Organize a system of complete and selective depository libraries in South Carolina for State publications to ensure that such publications are readily accessible to the citizens of the State.''

''(10) Implement agreements to exchange State publications with out-of-state libraries, departments and agencies.''

SECTION 4. The 1962 Code is amended by adding Section 42-206 which shall read as follows:

''Section 42-206. All State agencies, departments and State-supported colleges and universities shall forward to the South Carolina State Library at least twenty-five copies of every State publication that such agency, department, college or university prints or causes to be printed within fifteen days after such printing.''

SECTION 5. This act shall take effect upon approval by the Governor.

STATE COMMENT

The South Carolina State Library has endeavored since 1972 to achieve passage of State documents depository legislation. During 1979, companion bills were introduced in the House and Senate. The Senate bill passed the Senate intact and is now in the House Education and Public Works Committee.

The House bill is on the House contested calendar with three amendments awaiting further action. We hope for success in 1980. (Letter from Mary B. Toll, Documents Librarian, South Carolina State Library, Columbia, South Carolina 29211, dated January 2, 1980. *In* Documents on Documents Collection.)

EDITORIAL COMMENT

The 1972 bill was introduced on June 29, 1972 by three senators. It was referred to the Committee on Education, where it died.

The bill is almost the same as "Proposed State Document Depository Legislation" prepared by the South Carolina State Library. The differences are:

(1) Definition of "complete depository" in the state library version reads: *requests and* receives.

(2) Definition of "selective depository" in the state library version does not include "from time to time."

(3) Definition of "state publication" in the state library version does not include "journal, resolution, statutes," or "act."

(4) At the end of section 4, the state library version has an additional sentence: "The State Librarian may waive the deposition of any agency publication if: (1) The publication is of ephemeral value; (2) Less than ten copies are to be printed or; (3) The issuing agency requests a waiver."

A similar bill, H 2389, was introduced on February 1, 1979. It was referred to the Committee on Education and Public Works, which reported it out with a "do pass" recommendation. The state documents librarian said, "H 2389 did *not* pass but is in fourth place on the contested calendar and ready for a fight in January."

The 1979 bill corresponds to the South Carolina State Library version mentioned above, rather than the 1972 bill. The additional changes are: (1) a new clause is added in the definition of "state publications"—"it shall also include those publications that may or may not be financed by state funds but are released by private bodies such as research and consultant firms under contract with or supervision of any state agency"—and (2) the number of copies of a publication to be forwarded to the State Library is reduced from twenty-five to fifteen.

BIBLIOGRAPHY

Bostick, Mary. "South Carolina State Documents." *South Carolina Librarian* 15:23 (Fall 1970).

The South Carolina State Library collects South Carolina state documents to provide reference service and to ensure preservation of all South Carolina documents.

The message is that South Carolina librarians should keep the collection of state documents at the state library in mind as they serve their own users.

Smiley, W. W. "Official Publications of South Carolina." M.A. Thesis, University of Illinois, 1939. 78 p.

SOUTH DAKOTA

S. D. COMPILED LAWS ANN. §§ 14-1A-1 to 14-1A-8
(1975 & 1979 Supp.)

CHAPTER 14-1A
STATE PUBLICATIONS LIBRARY
DISTRIBUTION CENTER

14-1A-1. Definition of terms. Terms as used in this chapter, unless the context otherwise requires, mean:
  (1) ''Print,'' all forms of printing and duplicating, including audio-visual materials, regardless of format or purpose, with the exception of correspondence and interoffice memoranda;
  (2) ''State publication,'' any document, compilation, journal, law, resolution, bluebook, statute, code, register, pamphlet, list, microphotographic form, tape or disc recording, book, proceedings, report, memorandum, hearing, legislative bill, leaflet, order, regulation, directory, periodical or magazine published, issued, in print, or purchased for distribution, by the state, the Legislature, constitutional officers, any state department, committee or other state agency supported wholly or in part by public funds;
  (3) ''State agency,'' includes, but is not limited to, the Legislature, constitutional officers, and any department, division, bureau, board, commission, committee, or agency of the state of South Dakota;
  (4) ''Center,'' the state publications library distribution center. (Source: SL 1974, ch 150, § 1.)

14-1A-2. Publications distribution center created—Purpose—Rules and regulations. There is hereby created as a section of the state library, and under the direction of the state librarian, a state publications library distribution center. The center shall promote the establishment of an orderly depository library system. To this end the state library commission shall adopt rules and regulations necessary to carry out the provisions of this chapter. (Source: SL 1974, ch 150, § 2.)

14-1A-3. Deposits of state agency publications and audio-visual materials. Every state agency shall upon release, deposit at least fourteen copies of each of its state publications, with the state library for record and depository system purposes, with the exception of audio-visual materials. At least two copies of audio-visual materials shall be deposited with the state library for record and depository system purposes. (Source: SL 1907, ch 185, § 2; RC 1919, § 9923; SDC 1939, § 29.0306; SDCL, § 14-1-17; SL 1969, ch 126; 1974, ch 150, § 3.)

14-1A-4. Publications lists and mailing lists to be furnished by state agencies. Upon request by the center, each issuing state agency shall furnish the center with a complete list of its current state publications and a copy of its mailing and exchange lists. (Source: SL 1974, ch 150, § 6.)

14-1A-5. Institutions and libraries to receive copies of documents— Retention of permanent copies. The center shall assure that the university of South Dakota at Vermillion and the library of congress shall each receive two copies and that the historical resource center and the center for research libraries at Chicago shall each receive one copy of each document with the exception of audio-visual materials. The University of South Dakota at Vermillion and the historical resource center shall each retain permanently at least one copy of each document distributed by the center for the purpose of historical research. Permanent retention may be encompassed through use of microforms. (Source: SL 1974, ch 150, § 4; 1976, ch 142.)

14-1A-6. Depository library contracts—Requirements. The center shall enter into depository contracts with any municipal or county free library, state college or state university library, the library of congress and the center for research libraries, and other state libraries. The requirements for eligibility to contract as a depository library shall be established by the state library commission. The standards shall include and take into consideration the type of library, ability to preserve such publications and to make them available for public use, and also such geographical locations as will make the publications conveniently accessible to residents in all areas of the state. (Source: SL 1974, ch 150, § 4.)

14-1A-7. Distribution of state publications list. The center shall publish and distribute regularly to contracting depository libraries and other libraries upon request a list of available state publications. (Source: SL 1974, ch 150, § 5.)

14-1A-8. General public distribution prohibited. The center shall not engage in general public distribution of either state publications or lists of publications. (Source: SL 1974, ch 150, § 7.)

STATE COMMENT

South Dakota's state documents program was first authorized by the 1974 state legislature. The legislation, originally *Session Laws 1974*, Chapter 150, which created a "State Publications Library Distribution Center" within the State Library, has since been codified as SDCL 14-1A. Funding for the program was made available as of July 1, 1974, but because the State Library had just entered the Federal depository system as well, with initial depository shipments arriving in April, it was not until December 1974 that the state documents program could be implemented. (The same staff members—a clerk-typist, a library technician, and the Documents Librarian—are responsible for both the Federal and state facets of the Documents Sub-Program.)

****

The depository law states that we are to receive, besides the fourteen copies of printed publications, two copies of audio-visual materials produced by state agencies. We have not actually received any audio-visual materials as a result of the law. Microforms are not mentioned in the law, except that in a 1976 amendment there is the provision that the two depositories charged with retaining depository documents permanently for historical purposes (the University and the Historical Resource Center) may substitute microforms for the hard copy. There are no systematic projects of microforming of state documents being conducted by any of the depositories at present. (Report by Robert Newby, Documents Librarian, South Dakota State Library, Department of Education and Cultural Affairs, Pierre, South Dakota 57501. *In* The State of State Documents: Past, Present, Future. Texas Legislative Reference Library, 1976, at pp. [17]-18.)

EDITORIAL COMMENT

The 1976 amendment to 14-1A-5, in addition to providing for permanent retention of documents by two institutions in the state and permitting the use of microforms to accomplish this retention, adds the provision for the Historical Resource Center and the Center for Research Libraries to receive documents.

The title of the 1974 Act was: "An Act to amend SDCL 14-1 by adding thereto new sections related to the distribution of public documents and the establishment of a state documents depository system, and to repeal SDCL 14-1-17 through 14-1-20 inclusive." The act did not carry an appropriation. The repealed sections were titled: 14-1-17. Departmental reports furnished to legislative division—Statutes, session laws and Supreme Court reports; 14-1-18. Surplus reports of departments placed in library; 14-1-19. Miscellaneous publications from departments—Retention in library or employment in traveling libraries; and 14-1-20. Sale and exchange of duplicate publications—Use of proceeds of sale.

§ 14-1A-9, providing that distributions by the governor, secretary of state, and Bureau of Administration would not be affected by the chapter on the State Publications Distribution Center, was repealed in 1979. (SL 1979, ch 10, § 13.)

RELATED LEGISLATION

1972 S. D. Sess. Laws ch 118

(S. B. 246)
ESTABLISHING PUBLIC DOCUMENTS STUDY COMMISSION

AN ACT Entitled, An Act to establish an interim public documents study commission.

Be It Enacted by the Legislature of the State of South Dakota:

Section 1. Since free access to public documents of the state of South Dakota and its political subdivisions produced at tax expense is one of the rights of citizenship, and since no uniform system of distribution of these documents to libraries in the state is either mandated by law or practiced without legal authority, and since such a system of public document depository libraries is beneficial and essential to the right of every citizen to free access to public information, there is hereby created an interim public documents study commission.

Section 2. The commission shall be composed of the following public officials or their designates: director, university of South Dakota library, who shall be its chairman; director-secretary, state library commission; Supreme Court reporter; director, legislative research council; director, division of purchasing and printing; secretary of state; director, records management; director of policy information (crime and juvenile delinquency information center); director, central data processing division; supervisor, central printing facility; superintendent of public instruction; two school librarians to be selected by the superintendent of public instruction; commissioner of higher education; director, state historical society and representatives of the federal document depository libraries being directors thereof at: South Dakota state university, northern state college, South Dakota school of mines and technology, augustana college, black hills state college, yankton college, Rapid City public library and Sioux Falls public library.

Section 3. The commission shall initiate and complete a comprehensive study of all phases of publication and distribution of public documents on all levels of state government and including the legislative, executive and judicial branches. Such study and recommendations shall be submitted to the appropriate standing committees of the state legislature before the forty-eighth session convenes.

Approved February 9, 1972.

RULES AND REGULATIONS

S. D. Admin. Rules 24:30:06:01-07 (1974)
Chapter 24:30:06

DOCUMENTS DEPOSITORY LIBRARY SYSTEM

24:30:06:01. Standards to be met by depository libraries. The following standards shall be met by all libraries applying to the state library commission for designation as documents depository libraries under the depository library system:

(1) The library shall be administered by a librarian who possesses a master's degree in library science from a library school accredited by the American Library Association or have such a librarian on its staff to administer the depository program;

(2) The library shall be open at least fifty hours a week, including three nights and eight hours on a Saturday or a Sunday or a combination of both in each normal week.

24:30:06:02. Exceptions to standards. The only exemptions from the standards required by § 24:30:06:01 are:

(1) National research institutions where deposits of South Dakota state documents may increase the national dissemination of knowledge of the state of South Dakota; and

(2) State library agencies of this or other states or libraries maintained by this or other states for purposes of collecting and preserving the history of the state of South Dakota.

24:30:06:03. Additional requirements. In addition to meeting the standards of § 24:30:06:01, libraries not exempted by § 24:30:06:02, shall agree to:

(1) Designate an individual person by name as administrator of the depository program for purposes of direct contact from the state publications library distribution center;

(2) Make any depository item available to any citizen of South Dakota requesting such services;

(3) Assure accessibility of state documents to library users through establishment of a system or systems approved by the state publications library distribution center;

(4) Retain all state documents for a minimum period of five years with the exception of those publications which are clearly superseded by subsequent editions or which are issued at a later date in cumulated form; and

(5) Allow the state librarian, or his representative, reasonable access to the depository program for purposes of evaluation.

24:30:06:04. Selection of documents depository libraries. The state library commission shall contract for documents depository libraries from applications received from municipal or county free libraries or state college or state university libraries; provided, that no more than one contract shall be made in a model planning and development district with the exception of the district in which the state library itself shall serve as the documents depository library. If two or more libraries in a single model planning and development district apply for a documents depository library contract, the library open to the public the greatest number of hours shall be awarded the contract. If competing applications are equal in hours of opening, the library having the greatest number of the population resident in counties touched by the circumference of a circle drawn on a radius of fifty miles from the city in which the library is located shall be awarded the contract. If both conditions above are equal among competing applicants, the municipal or county free library shall be awarded the contract. The state library commission may allow exceptions to this rule upon a finding that a geographical imbalance will result from the application of this rule. Application for such exception may be made by a municipal or county free library board of trustees or by the administration of a state college or state university.

24:30:06:05. Termination of contracts. Depository contracts with libraries shall remain in effect until the library ceases to exist, terminates the contract at its own request, or has the contract revoked by the state library commission.

24:30:06:06. Termination by contracting library. A library may terminate its contract by informing the state library commission in writing at least thirty days prior to any regularly scheduled quarterly meeting of the commission.

24:30:06:07. Termination by commission. The state library commission may only revoke a contract by using the following procedure:

(1) The state librarian shall present a recommendation for revocation of a depository contract based only on written documentation that the library concerned was not meeting the standards or requirements prescribed by §§ 24:30:06:01 or 24:30:06:03. This recommendation may be made at any regular quarterly meeting of the commission;

(2) The state library commission shall act upon the recommendation of the state librarian by rejecting his recommendation or by appointing a hearing officer as provided in SDCL 1-32-6.1 and shall enter into its minutes and issue to the library involved that a recommendation for revocation of the documents depository contract has been received and that a hearing officer has been appointed and that a hearing shall be scheduled at such time as is convenient to all parties involved;

(3) Only after such hearing or forfeiture by the library in question through nonappearance after due notice may the commission revoke a depository library contract.

CONTRACT

CONTRACT

WHEREAS, the laws of the State of South Dakota provide for the South Dakota State Library to promote the establishment of an orderly depository library system for the distribution of state publications (SDCL 14-1A-2), and;

WHEREAS, to that end, the South Dakota State Library Commission is enabled to enter into depository contracts with any municipal or county free library, state college or state university library, the Library of Congress and the Center for Research Libraries, and other state libraries (SDCL 14-1A-6), be it hereby agreed that:

The South Dakota State Library Commission contracts with the Library of
_____ to serve as a depository library for South Dakota state publications.

Be it further agreed that:

1. The South Dakota State Library Commission will:
   a. Provide the Library of _____
      with depository copies of every state publication received for distribution, and
   b. Provide the Library of _____
      with regular checklists/shipping lists of state publications distributed to depository libraries, and
   c. Coordinate the state documents depository system among contracting depository libraries, and
   d. Monitor and evaluate the development of the state documents depository system.

2. The Library of _____
   will, unless it is one of those specifically exempted in section 24:30:06:02 of the rules for the documents depository library system adopted by the Commission on April 25, 1975, meet all the standards and requirements in section 24:30:06:01 and 24:30:06:03 of the aforementioned rules, to wit:
   a. Be administered by a librarian who possesses a master's degree in library science from a library school accredited by the American Library Association or have such a librarian on its staff to administer the depository program,
   b. Be open at least fifty hours a week, including three nights and eight hours on a Saturday or a Sunday or a combination of both in each normal week,
   c. Designate an individual person by name as administrator of the depository program for purposes of direct contact from the state publications library distribution center,
   d. Make any depository item available to any citizen of South Dakota requesting such services,
   e. Assure accessibility of state documents to library users through establishment of a system or systems approved by the state publications library distribution center,

    f. Retain all state documents for a minimum period of five years with the
exception of those publications which are clearly superseded by subsequent
editions or which are issued at a later date in cumulated form, and

    g. Allow the state librarian, or his representative, reasonable access to the
depository program for purposes of evaluation.

This contract is entered into this_____day of _____, 1975, by the South
Dakota State Library Commission and the Library of _____

_____
Director

_____
Library

_____
Director
South Dakota State Library

BIBLIOGRAPHY

Krueger, R. C. "South Dakota State Publications." M. A. Thesis, University of
Illinois, 1936. 180 p. (Not seen.)

Helgeson, Estella Hansine. "South Dakota State Documents." *South Dakota Library
Bulletin* 55:[51]-108 (April 1969).
A library school research report, revised after one year. Some parts are sometimes cited
separately: "Printing and Distribution of South Dakota State Documents," pp. 55-61;
"Checklist of South Dakota State Publications . . .," pp. 65-102.

    Introduction—Brief history of the territory and the state. The purpose of the paper is to
report on the distribution, organization, and recording of South Dakota documents and
to bring the 1936 Krueger bibliography up to date. Procedures in compiling the
bibliography, which is more properly a checklist, are given.

    Printing and Distribution of South Dakota State Documents—A detailed discussion
of the printing and distribution laws and practices. The report says,

> There is no well-defined system of distribution . . . as California has, although the
> librarians who are genuinely concerned about the distribution would like to have
> such a system. . . . Although there are laws designating certain libraries as deposi-
> tories, those depositories do not receive all publications. There is no up-to-date
> complete listing of South Dakota state government publications.

    Handling of the Documents in the Libraries of the State—Questionnaires were sent
out. Responses are discussed.

    Archival and Microfilm Programs—South Dakota has no legally recognized archival
depository. A microfilm program began in 1953.

    The report ends with conclusions and recommendations, the checklist, the tabulation
of the questionnaire, the questionnaire, and works cited.

Helgeson, Estella Hansine. "A Classification System for South Dakota State Publications." *South Dakota Library Bulletin* 57:185-190 (April-June 1971).

''This classification system for South Dakota state publications is adapted from the system used by the California State Library for California State publications.'' The arrangement is alphabetical by issuing agency. The complete classification scheme is given.

South Dakota. Interim Public Documents Study Commission. *Report.* Pierre, S.D.: The Commission, 1972. (ERIC ED 072 790.)
Introduction—Definitions are given for ''public documents,'' ''state public funds,'' and ''state agency.'' Excluded are local documents, problems of duplication of information in state documents, and ''records.'' The work of the commission was divided into printing and bibliographical control, and distribution.
    Chapter 1, Philosophy—Bob Carmack, the author of the report, says,

> Citizens are becoming interested in government and are exercising a basic right to know. . . .
> Free and ready access to public documents produced at public expense is ideally one of the rights of citizenship. To effect this ideal, public documents must be promptly printed, widely disseminated, systematically collected and preserved, and made available to the public.

    Chapter 2, Public Documents in Other States—Cites Casey study and Council of State Governments ''Current Checklists.''
    Chapter 3, Printing and Distribution of Public Documents in South Dakota—A survey of current practices and recommendations for appointment of person in Division of Purchasing and Printing to advise state agencies on printing, and funding of a checklist of state publications.
    Chapter 4, Proposals for Action—Includes a full outline of responsibilities for a clearinghouse/depository and a recommendation for funding.
    Appendices are : Bill authorizing the Commission, three tables from Casey, and table on cost of public printing in South Dakota.

South Dakota. Interim Public Documents Study Commission. *Guidelines for Printing and Publishing South Dakota Public Documents.* Pierre, S.D.: The Commission, 1972. 43 p. (Available from B. Carmack, University of South Dakota. Vermillion, S.D. 57069.)
A manual of minimum standards for publication of state documents. Accompanies the *Report* of the Commission.

''South Dakota Law.'' *American Libraries* 3:336 (April 1972).
Announces the passage of a bill (SB 246) providing for a government documents study commission which ''will undertake a comprehensive study of the publication and distribution of public documents on all levels of state government and will make recommendations specifically about the public distribution and deposit of state documents.''

Carmack, Bob D. ''South Dakota Public Documents: Report of a Study.'' *Government Publications Review* 1:251-256 (1974).
The study of the work of the Interim Public Documents Study Commission as told by the chairman of the commission and author of its *Report.*

TENNESSEE

TENN. CODE ANN. §§ 12-6-107 to 12-6-112 (1980)

12-6-107. Libraries as depositories for documents. The state library at Nashville, the library of the University of Tennessee, at Knoxville, the Cossitt library at Memphis, and such other libraries as the governor may at any time name are designated depositories for state documents and for all publications issued by any official of the state. [Acts 1917, ch. 42, § 1; Shan. Supp., § 1387a7; Code 1932, § 2283; T.C.A. (orig. ed.), § 12-607.]

12-6-108. Publications to be deposited. The publications and documents referred to shall include (1) The acts and journals of the legislature, the reports of the Supreme Court, and such other courts as shall have their decisions reported by the attorney-general and reporter of this state, or shall be required by any act or resolution of the legislature; (2) The periodical reports of officers of the state and any special reports that may from time to time be made by state officers or committees of the legislature or other committees provided for by law; (3) Such other reports or statements as may be published under the authority of the state, or any official thereof. [Acts 1917, ch. 42, § 4; Shan. Supp., § 1387a11; Code 1932, § 2287; T.C.A. (orig. ed.), § 12-608.]

12-6-109. Notice of publications and forwarding of copies to secretary of state. It shall be the duty of every officer of this state making any publication or in charge of the printing of any document for the state to notify the secretary of state of its publication and to send to the secretary of state such number of copies as he shall demand in accordance with the provisions of §§ 12-6-107— 12-6-112. [Acts 1917, ch. 42, § 3; Shan. Supp., § 1387a10; Code 1932, § 2286; T.C.A. (orig. ed.), § 12-609.]

12-6-110. Copies furnished each depository. The secretary of state shall keep a list of such documents and publications as are at any time issued by the state, or by any official thereof and shall notify the person in charge of the making of such publication or the issuance of such documents to furnish him with two (2) copies for each of the depositories so designated, and he shall send, at the expense of the state, two (2) copies of each document or publication to the librarian or person in charge of each of the depositories. [Acts 1917, ch. 42, § 2; Shan. Supp., § 1387a8; mod. Code 1932, § 2284; C. Supp. 1950, § 2284; T.C.A. (orig. ed.), § 12-610.]

12-6-111. Exchange copies for university. [Not reproduced.]

12-6-112. Care of depository copies. It shall be the duty of the librarian or other person in charge of each depository to give receipt for and carefully preserve all state documents and publications so received. One (1) of the two (2) copies shall be lendable on application, to the persons, if any, allowed to take other books from the library of the depository. The other copy shall not be allowed to be taken from the premises of the depository. [Acts 1917, ch. 42, § 2; Shan. Supp., § 1387a9; Code 1932, § 2285; T.C.A. (orig. ed.), § 12-612.]

12-6-113. Exchanges by state librarian. [Not reproduced.]

12-6-114. Delivery of exchange copies. [Not reproduced.]

12-6-115. Expense of exchanges. [Not reproduced.]

STATE COMMENT (1973)

The sections in the *Tennessee Code* regarding distribution and deposit of state publications are in chapter 12, 607 through 615. However, these sections, although in the Code, are not necessarily effective. The Secretary of State is charged with making a list of state publications and providing copies. This, of course, is not done. The State Library publishes an annual checklist. . . .

We have, for the past several years, considered possible legislation which would establish the State Library as the distributing agency for state publications to libraries. However, this legislation is tied to appropriations for such activity. (Letter from Kendall J. Cram, Director, Tennessee State Library, Nashville, Tennessee 37219, dated October 29, 1973. *In* Documents on Documents Collection.)

BIBLIOGRAPHY

Parsley, G. M. (comp.). "Are You Using Your State Publications?: A Selected List of
     Recent Titles." *Tennessee Libraries* 7:34-35 (January 1955).
A list of thirteen titles.

TEXAS

TEX. REV. CIV. STAT. ANN. art. 5442a (Vernon Supp. 1980)

ART. 5442a. STATE PUBLICATIONS AND DEPOSITORY LIBRARIES FOR STATE DOCUMENTS

Section. 1. In this Act:

(1) ''State publication'' means printed matter that is produced in multiple copies by the authority of or at the total or partial expense of a state agency. The term includes publications sponsored by or purchased for distribution by a state agency and publications released by private institutions, such as research and consulting firms, under contract with a state agency, but does not include correspondence, interoffice memoranda, or routine forms.

(2) ''State agency'' means any state office, officer, department, division, bureau, board, commission, legislative committee, authority, institution, sub-state planning bureau, university system or institution of higher education as defined by Section 61.003, Texas Education Code, as amended, or any of their subdivisions.

(3) ''Depository libraries'' means the Texas State Library, the Texas Legislative Reference Library, the Library of Congress, the Center for Research Libraries, and other libraries that the Texas Library and Historical Commission designates as depository libraries.

Sec. 2. The Texas Library and Historical Commission shall adopt rules to establish procedures for the distribution of state publications to depository libraries and for the retention of those publications. The commission may contract with a depository library to receive all or a part of the state publications that are distributed.

Sec. 3. (a) Each state agency shall furnish to the Texas State Library its state publications in the quantity specified by the rules of the Texas Library and Historical Commission. The commission may not require more than 75 copies of a state publication.

(b) On the printing of or the awarding of a contract for the printing of a publication, a state agency shall arrange for the required number of copies to be deposited with the Texas State Library.

Sec. 4. The Texas State Library shall:

(1) acquire, organize, and retain the state publications;

(2) collect state publications and distribute them to depository libraries;

(3) establish a microform program for the preservation and management of state publications and make available state publications in microform to depository and other libraries at a reasonable cost;

(4) periodically issue a list of all state publications that it has received to all depository libraries and to other libraries on request;

(5) catalog, classify, and index all state publications that it has received and distribute the cataloging, classification, and indexing information to depository libraries and to other libraries on request; and

(6) ensure that state publications are fully represented in regional and national automated library networks.

Sec. 5. Each state agency shall designate one or more staff persons as the agency's publications contact person and shall notify the Texas State Library of the identity of each person selected. A state agency's contact person shall furnish to the Texas State Library each month a list of all of the agency's state publications that were produced during the preceding month.

Sec. 6. If a state agency's printing is done by contract, an account for the printing may not be approved and a warrant for the printing may not be issued unless the agency first furnishes to the State Board of Control a receipt from the state librarian for the publication or a written waiver from the state librarian exempting the publication from the requirements of this Act.

Sec. 7. The state librarian may specifically exempt a publication from the requirements of this Act. (Acts 1963, 58th Leg., p. 1133, ch. 438. Secs. 2 and 3 amended by Acts 1969, 61st Leg., p. 154, ch. 55, § 10, eff. Sept. 1, 1969; Sec. 2 amended by Acts 1979, 66th Leg., p. 858, ch. 382, § 9, eff. Aug. 27, 1979. Amended by Acts 1979, 66th Leg., p. 1775, ch. 720, § 2 eff. Aug. 27, 1979.)

STATE COMMENT (1973)

The depository program for state documents, State of Texas, is very weak because of the absence of publicity. The patrons and prospective users are not aware of the availability of the materials.

Negligence on the part of the issuing agencies in furnishing quantities of their publication for distribution is the biggest hindrance to the program.

Limited liaison among the issuing agencies, the collecting and distributing agency, and the depository libraries has hindered the program. (Comments from Texas State Library, Austin, Texas, in about March 1973. *In* Documents on Documents Collection.)

STATE COMMENT (1976)

The Texas State Library has been responsible for collecting and distributing state documents since its establishment in 1909. This responsibility was formalized by legislation in 1913 and 1919. The original legislation calls for the State Library to be provided with 150 copies of "all annual, biennial and special reports of State departments, boards and institutions, findings of all investigations, bulletins, circulars, laws issued as separates, and legislative manuals." These were to be delivered to the State Library to be disposed of at the discretion of the Librarian.

****

In 1963 legislation was passed creating the state documents depository system in Texas. Under this legislation (V.A.T.S. 5442a) the State Library presently serves 50 official state depositories in Texas and 13 depositories in other states. Upon designation as a depository by the Texas Library and Historical Commission a library automatically receives copies of all publications sent to the State Library in large enough quantities for distribution. Although there is no contractual agreement involved all depositories must provide access to all documents received and service to all patrons. (Report by Dale Propp, Texas State Library, Austin, Texas 78711. *In* The State of State Documents: Past, Present, Future. Texas Legislative Reference Library, 1976, at p. 18.)

EDITORIAL COMMENT

The 1963 Act (p. 1133, ch. 438), which enacted Art. 5442, was titled: "An Act to establish depository libraries with authority in the Director and Librarian of the Texas State Library; requiring certain acts to be performed to facilitate distribution of state documents; and declaring an emergency." This act was effective on August 31, 1963.

The 1973 amendment to Art. 5442 (1973 Acts, 63rd Leg., p. 1621, ch. 583, § 1) added part (b) to the article and was effective July 15, 1973.

The 1969 amendment to Art. 5442a(2) and (3) added the legislative reference library as a depository library in (2) and as a receiving library in (3).

In 1979 Art. 5442a was amended, and Art. 5442 was repealed by an act adopted May 28 (H. B. 480).

In Art. 5442a definitions were added for "state publication," "state agency," and "depository libraries," and the old definition of "state document" was deleted.

Section 2 of that article was enacted to provide that the Texas Library and Historical Commission should adopt rules and may contract with a depository library.

Section 3 requires state agencies to furnish publications in a quantity to be specified by rules of the commission, but not more than seventy-five copies, and further requires the state agencies to arrange for the depositing of the copies with the Texas State Library.

Section 4 outlines the duties of the Texas State Library: (1) to acquire, organize, and retain state publications, (2) to collect state publications and distribute them to depository libraries, (3) to establish a microform program, (4) to issue a list, (5) to catalog, classify, and index the publications, and (6) to ensure that state publications are fully represented in regional and national automated library networks.

Section 5 requires state agencies to designate a contact person and to submit a monthly list.

Section 6 provides for receipt, or waiver, from the state librarian before approval of accounts for contract printing.

Section 7 permits the state librarian to exempt a publication from the requirements of the act.

Art. 5442 was repealed. New provisions adopted relate to publication request forms from which the agencies compile publication distribution lists. The new sections "do not apply to the distribution of information which is required by law" (which presumably includes the distribution under Art. 5442a.)

ATTORNEY GENERAL OPINION

1977 TEX. ATT'Y GEN. OP. 4356 (H-1061, September 27, 1977)

Honorable Dorman H. Winfrey
Director & Librarian
Texas State Library
Box 12927, Capitol Station
Austin, Texas 78711

Opinion No. H-1061

Re: Whether the State
Library may authorize
receipt of fewer than 150
copies of a state publication

Dear Mr. Winfrey:

You have requested our opinion concerning whether the State Library may authorize the printing of fewer than 150 copies of state publications.

Article 5442a, V.T.C.S., provides:

[the Article is quoted in full]

The statute expressly requires 150 copies "or such *additional* number as said librarian shall request." [Emphasis added in the original.] Furthermore, article 5442a, section 3 provides:

[the subsection is quoted in full]

Since the "quantity specified in article 5442" is 150 or more, in our opinion, the clear words of the Legislature require the printing of a minimum of 150 copies for the State Library, where the State Librarian requisitions a document from the Board of Control. Of course whether a document is to be requisitioned is a matter within the discretion of the State Librarian as limited by law. *See* V.T.C.S. art. 5441.

SUMMARY

The State Library may not authorize the printing and furnishing of fewer than 150 copies of state publications other than routine business forms and court reports;

where the State Librarian has requisitioned a document, at least 150 copies must be furnished.

Very truly yours,
/s/ John L. Hill
JOHN L. HILL
Attorney General of Texas

Approved:
/s/ *David M. Kendall*
DAVID M. KENDALL, First Assistant
/s/ *C. Robert Heath*
C. ROBERT HEATH, Chairman
Opinion Committee

BIBLIOGRAPHY

The number of recent articles and announcements emanating from Texas make an inverse chronology appropriate. *American Libraries* 10:217-218 (April 1979) carried an announcement of the "LC and Texas State Library Test Joint Cataloging Project." More detail on this pilot project is given in the article in *LC Information Bulletin* 38:70-72 (March 2, 1979). That article concludes, "The ALA Council has gone on record as encouraging this type of cooperative cataloging," a reference to the council resolution adopted in June 1978 (*Documents to the People* 6:207 [September 1978]).

Walton, R., and Propp, D. *Texas State Documents Depository Survey, 1977: Findings and Results.* Austin, Tex.: Texas State Publications Clearinghouse, Texas State Library, 1978. 46 p., charts (Documents Monograph Series, no. 1.)
Reports the treatment of state documents in the fifty-one official state depository libraries, by type of library and individually by library (forty-six libraries responded). No analysis or editorial comment is included. Charts on the relative importance of eleven clearinghouse (that is, distribution center) activities, current or pending, would interest other distribution center administrators. The appendices have responses from individual libraries on the checklist, the title and the subject indexes, and potential purchase of microfiche.

Propp, Dale, and Walton, Robert. *Texas State Documents: The Development of a Program.* Rev. Austin, Tex.: Texas State Publications Clearinghouse, Texas State Library, 1978. 61 p.
The "Introduction" gives the purpose: to assist those interested in learning more about the program and to facilitate staff review of the program and reassessment of goals and objectives. The program history covers the Texas State Depository System established in 1963 and the growth of the checklist from 1921 to 1977. Facsimiles of the mastheads for the checklist are reproduced.
Current programs include (1) distribution to depositories, unofficial depositories, and selecting libraries (volume is shown in graphs), (2) permanent Texas documents collection, establishd in 1974, (3) microform program being planned as a distribution device (1974 is complete and ready for use, "entry number" of monthly checklist is key to film) (4) indexing program that includes title, subject, and issuing agency indexes is

in planning stages, (5) publications include the checklists, various indexes, and "Public Documents Highlights for Texas" (bimonthly 1978-   ).

Six major goals with specific details are outlined. The program review concludes that more communication between the clearinghouse and the depository libraries is needed. Appendices give (1) list of depository libraries, (2) GODORT guidelines for minimum servicing and for checklists, and (3) Texas statutes on collection and distribution of Texas state documents.

The authors say that the program is important to agencies because agencies know that their publications are available at specific points. They can refer nondepository libraries to the state library and individuals to depository libraries. The program is supplementary to an agency's own distribution and makes publications available in a different manner. The program "insures that official reports required of state agencies are available to the public." The program is administered by the state library but is made possible through the cooperation of state agencies which produce the publications and the libraries which make them available.

Walton, Bob. "Texas State Documents Survey." *Documents to the People* 6:26 (January 1978).
During the summer of 1977, the staff of the clearinghouse conducted a three-phase review of the depository program. First, a comprehensive study of the program was made. This report, *Texas Documents: The Development of a Program*, included a history, a description of current projects, and a projection of possible future programming which could be undertaken by the state library.

A similar study of the depository libraries was undertaken by means of a questionnaire. To disseminate the results of both these undertakings, a two-day conference was held. The first day focused on various state document tools, and the second day on the areas of concern from the perspective of the depositories.

Olds, Brenda F.S. *Texas State Document Classification & Almost Compleat List of Texas State Agencies from Statehood to the Present*. Austin, Tex.: Texas State Library, 1976. 129 p. (Reference series no. 7.) (Abstracted in *Documents to the People* 4:28 [November 1976].)
Classification based on California State Library scheme. Updated monthly in "Texas State Documents." Intended to be all-inclusive; includes agencies created but never operative.

Cook, Annette F. "Texas State Documents: A Classification Scheme." M.L.S. Thesis, Texas Woman's University, 1975. 44p.
An adaptation from the superintendent of documents system. Includes a table showing states with a checklist and those with a state classification scheme, and a bibliography.

Three articles appeared in the Winter 1975 issue of *Texas Libraries*:

"Access to State Documents Improved by New Programs." *Texas Libraries* 37:180-181 (Winter 1975).
A threefold program is underway: publication of subject index to the Texas documents for 1974, microfilming of all documents, and inputting of monographs into the OCLC data base.

Fleischer, Mary Beth. "State Documents Source for Varied Information." *Texas Libraries* 37:182-188 (Winter 1975).
The librarian at the Barker Texas History Center, University of Texas at Austin, gives seven ways, with examples, in which documents can be used after their original purpose has been filled. The first two uses are (1) as background for current information and (2) to give leads to solutions to current problems.

"Texas Register to Provide Weekly Update on State." *Texas Libraries* 37:189-191 (Winter 1975).
Describes the new *Texas Register*.

Olds, Brenda F. S. "Texas State Documents: A Primer for Librarians." Austin, Tex.: Legislative Reference Library, 1975. (Reference series no. 6.)
Part One is the primer, covering the organization of Texas state government, state information sources, acquisitions (depository program, newspapers, agency mailing lists), document maintenance (integration or segregated collections), and reference service (toll-free numbers, unpublished information sources).
    Part Two is a topically arranged bibliography section with introductory comments for each topic. Individual titles are annotated.

Olds, Brenda F. S. "Texas State Documents: Survey Results." *Texas Library Journal* 50:186-191 (October 1974).
Forty-seven general quick-response questionnaires were sent to the depository libraries. Forty-three responses were received. Problems identified as most critical included, first, cataloging, and then "more inclusive collection and more access to the collection: development of reference aids (16); more aggressive acquisitions (14); development of main/subject authority file (4); development/refinement of classification scheme (4); and need for an official classification scheme (2)." Suggestions concerning the *Documents Checklist* were (1) inclusion of all documents, (2) inclusion of price, and (3) detailed annual index. The classification schemes used in Texas are explained.

"Official State Depository Libraries for Texas State Documents." *In* Texas. State Library, Austin. *Texas Public Library Statistics for 1972*. The Library, 1973. pp. 118-119.
Texas State Library and Texas Legislative Reference Library, twelve public libraries, twenty-nine public and private college and university libraries, and the Library of Congress. Names and addresses.

Brees, Mina A. "The Texas Documents Collection of the Legislative Reference Library." *Texas Library Journal* 49:259-261, 276-279 (December 1973).
The library has the largest collection of Texas documents in the nation because it has a statutory duty to collect and because appropriation acts require deposit. The broad definition that the library uses includes minutes, intraoffice press memos, and research studies contracted to a private organization. There are two hundred state agencies. Problems include handling (manila folders or notebooks are used for single sheets), lack of bibliographical data on the piece (rely on clues from the state agencies and on similar publications), and access (a classification scheme patterned on the California system is

being developed). The article continues with an explanation of the classification scheme.

''State Documents Program Serves Agencies and Libraries.'' *Texas Libraries* 34:[38]-42 (Spring 1972).
General explanation of the Texas depository program written for a general audience, including state agency personnel, librarians in general, and the library user.

Vaught, K. J. ''Author Headings for the Official Publications of Texas, 1824-1846.'' M.L.S. Thesis, University of Texas, 1955. 75 p. (Not seen.)

Rogan, O. F. ''Texas State Documents.'' *Texas Library Association News Notes* 8(4):3-6 (1932). (Not seen.)

UTAH

UTAH CODE ANN. §§ 37-5-1 to 37-5-8 (Supp. 1979)

37-5-1. Definitions. As used in this act:

(1) ''Commission'' means the state library commission established under section 37-4-3.

(2) ''Political subdivision'' means any county, city, town, school district, public transit district, redevelopment agency, special improvement or taxing district.

(3) ''State agency'' means the state, any office, department, agency, authority, commission, board, institution, hospital, college, university or other instrumentality of the state.

(4) ''State publication'' means any blue book, book, compilation, directory, document, contract and grant report, hearing memorandum, journal, law, leaflet, legislative bill, list, magazine, map, minutes, monograph, order, ordinance, pamphlet, periodical, proceeding, public memorandum, resolution, register, regulation, report, statute, audiovisual material, microphotographic form and tape or disc recording regardless of format or method of reproduction, issued or published by any state agency or political subdivision for distribution, not including correspondence, internal confidential publications, office memoranda, university press publications, and publications of the state historical society. (HISTORY: L. 1979, ch. 141, § 1.)

37-5-2. Commission to establish, operate and maintain. The commission shall establish, operate and maintain a publication collection, a bibliographic control system and depositories as provided in this act. (HISTORY: L. 1979, ch. 141, § 2.)

37-5-3. Deposit of copies of publications with commission. (1) Each state agency shall deposit with the commission copies of each state publication issued by it in such number as shall be specified by the state librarian.

(2) Each political subdivision shall deposit with the commission two copies of each state publication issued by it.

(3) The commission shall forward two copies of each state publication deposited with it by a state agency to the Library of Congress, one copy to the state archivist, at least one copy to each depository library, and retain two copies.

(4) The commission shall forward one copy of each state publication deposited with it by a political subdivision to the state archivist and retain the other copy.

(5) Each state agency shall deposit with the commission two copies of audiovisual materials, and tape or disc recordings issued by it for bibliographic listing and retention in the state library collection. Materials not deemed by the commission to be of major public interest will be listed but no copies will be required for deposit. (HISTORY: L. 1979, ch. 141, § 3.)

37-5-4. List of state agencies' state publications—Distribution. The commission shall publish a list of each state agency's state publications, which shall provide access by agency, author, title, subject and such other means as the commission may provide. The list shall be published periodically and distributed to depository libraries, state agencies, state officers, members of the legislature and other libraries selected by the commission, with at least an annual cumulation. Each state agency shall furnish the commission and the state archivist a complete list of its state publications for the previous year, annually. (HISTORY: L. 1979, ch. 141, § 4.)

37-5-5. Designation as depository library. Upon application, a library in this state may be designated as a complete or selective depository library by the commission. (HISTORY: L. 1979, ch. 141, § 5.)

37-5-6. Contract to provide facilities and service—Complete depository libraries—Selective depository libraries. To be designated as a depository library, a library must contract with the commission to provide adequate facilities for the storage and use of state publications, to render reasonable service without charge to patrons and reasonable access to state publications. A complete depository library shall receive at least one copy of all state publications issued by state agencies. A selective depository library shall receive those state publications issued by state agencies pertinent to its selection profile and those specifically requested by the library. (HISTORY: L. 1979, ch. 141, § 6.)

37-5-7. Micrographics and other copying and transmission techniques. The commission may use micrographics or other copying or transmission techniques to meet the needs of the depository system. (HISTORY: L. 1979, ch. 141, § 7.)

37-5-8. Rules and regulations—Standards. The commission may adopt rules and regulations necessary to implement and administer the provisions of this act including standards which must be met by libraries to obtain and retain a designation as a depository library. (HISTORY: L. 1979, ch. 141, § 8.)

STATE COMMENT (1973)

Code 37-4-4 of the Utah Code governs the distribution of State documents. . . . The greatest weakness in the depository library legislation is that it is difficult to enforce State Agencies to print annual reports and distribute them to the State Library as the law now reads. (Letter from Alma G. Swann, Government Reference Librarian, Utah State Library Commission, Salt Lake City, Utah 84115, dated May 3, 1973. *In* Documents on Documents Collection.)

STATE COMMENT (1976)

On July 1, 1957 the Legislature passed a law creating the State Library Commission and a State Librarian was appointed on October 15, 1957. The library laws of Utah were passed by the Legislature and became a part of the Utah Code Annotated in 1963 (U. C. A. Sec. 34-4-4). It was 1965 before the documents library and the depository system began to function with the state agencies contributing their publications and depository libraries shelving them. There are 16 depository libraries. At present there is no statute describing the conditions or responsibility of a depository library. (Report by Alma G. Swann, Documents Librarian, Utah State Library Commission, Salt Lake City, Utah 84115. *In* The State of State Documents: Past, Present, Future. Texas Legislative Reference Library, 1976, at p. 20.)

EDITORIAL COMMENT

Subsection 11 of 37-4-4 was completely rewritten in 1963 to emphasize distribution to libraries and to add the last sentence permitting omissions from the distribution.

The Utah legislation was amended in 1979 (S. B. 187). 37-4-4(11) was amended by deleting the existing wording and substituting "administer a depository library, publications collection and bibliographic information system," and eight new sections were added:

Sec. 1 defines "commission," "political subdivision," "state agency," and "state publication";

Sec. 2 provides for a publications collection, a bibliographical control system, and depositories;

Sec. 3 covers deposit of copies by state agencies, and forwarding to libraries;

Sec. 4 provides for a list of publications;

Sec. 5 provides for complete and selective depositories;

Sec. 6 provides for depository contracts;

Sec. 7 permits the use of micrographics to meet the needs of the depository system; and

Sec. 8 gives the commission the authority to adopt rules and regulations, including standards for depositories.

BIBLIOGRAPHY

Mustonen, Karlo K. ''Utah Publications Retrieval System (UPRS).'' *Agricultural Libraries Information Notes* 3:6 (September 1977).
The UPRS is a master index to Utah state publications produced in Computer Output Microfiche (COM) every ninety days. The documents are indexed at the university. The state archives produces the COM index and individual fiche copies of the documents, both of which are sent to the state library for depository distribution.

VERMONT

VT. STAT. ANN. tit. 22, §§ 603, 605 (1978)

§ 603. Appointment of state librarian; powers and duties.

****

(c) The state librarian shall distribute, in accordance with sections 1152-1163 and 1191-1193a of Title 29, and other official lists maintained by the state librarian, the acts and resolves of the general assembly, the legislative directory, the Vermont Statutes Annotated, the Vermont key number digest, the journals of the senate and house of representatives, the Vermont reports and other official reports and documents. He shall maintain records of all documents which he distributes. (Added 1969, No. 226 [Adj. Sess.], § 4, eff. March 31, 1970.)

§ 605. Duties and functions of the department of libraries. The duties and functions of the department of libraries shall be to provide, administer and maintain:

****

(2) A collection of state documents and of documents relating to other states, and local and federal governments. It shall arrange for and designate depositories of state documents which designation is to include Bailey library at the university of Vermont. The department may acquire reports and documents published by federal agencies and by other states and countries, and may arrange for the exchange of official reports and publications with federal agencies, and with governmental agencies in other states and countries. (Added 1969, No. 226 [Adj. Sess.], § 4, eff. March 31, 1970; amended 1971, No. 162 [Adj. Sess.], § 1.)

STATE COMMENT (1974)

[W]hat we have called the "Vermont Documents Depository System" has its share of problems. For example, we have struggled with the *definition* of a Vermont State Document; an insufficient number of copies of Vermont State Documents have been available for distribution; depository arrangements have been informal; etc. On the latter point, we have discussed a plan that includes the concept of *complete* depository libraries versus *selective* depository libraries. To date no concrete action has been taken to rectify the insufficiencies of the system. (Letter from Henry O. Marcy 4th, Director, Bibliographic and Reference Division, Department of Libraries, Montpelier, Vermont 03602, dated January 9, 1974. *In* Documents on Documents Collection.)

EDITORIAL COMMENT

The 1971 amendment (1971 Vt. Acts, No. 162) designated Bailey library as a depository.

BIBLIOGRAPHY

Turgeon, Lawrence J. "Vermont State Documents." *North Country Libraries* 8:3-5 (May-June 1965).
Turgeon, the state librarian in Vermont, characterizes state documents as "veritable gold mines of hard-to-find information about state government." He describes and points out the uses of the different publications of the three branches of government.

> In Vermont, by statutory mandate, the Vermont State Library is the distribution agency of all state documents. The State Librarian maintains mailing lists which make the receipt of state documents practically automatic for libraries requesting them.
> [The documents] need not be kept forever . . . we strongly recommend the discarding of the annual or biennial report type of document after two or three bienniums have passed, . . .

Turgeon's closing sentence is, "Only an informed citizenry can maintain democracy."

Hill, O. W. "Public Records Division." *Vermont Libraries* 1:11-14 (December 1970).
Archival records, state records center, and central microfilming.

Bryan, Vivian. "Materials Relating to Vermont at the Vermont Department of Libraries, Law and Documents Unit." (Guides to Major Vermont History Collections, A Bicentennial Series no. 3.) *Vermont Libraries* 5:15-18 (January-February 1976).
The Vermont State Library dates from 1825, and the Law and Documents Unit of the Department of Libraries contains a major portion of that library. It has "not only a complete set of all the session laws, compiled statutes, journals of the General Assembly, but all the annual and biennial reports of the various departments of state government. It also has numerous special reports from the different agencies (some of which are quite scarce as they were produced in limited number)."

Bryan, Vivian. "Vermont State Publications." *Vermont Libraries* 5:43-45 (March-April 1976).
A list of recent documents received by the Department of Libraries. Newsletters are not included, except for new publications.

VIRGIN ISLANDS

V. I. CODE ANN. tit. 3, § 883 (Supp. 1979)

§ 883. Depository libraries for public documents and indexes.

(a) *Statement of policy.* To effectuate the territory's public policy to make governmental information available to governmental agencies and to the general public, there are established depository libraries for specified public documents and for indexes to those public records which are not required to be deposited pursuant to this section.

(b) *Definitions.* As used in this section—

(1) "Territorial Librarian" means the Director of the Bureau of Libraries and Museums.

(2) "Depository libraries" means those libraries where, pursuant to this section, public documents and indexes shall be deposited, retained and reproduced upon demand, or made available to the general public and governmental agencies.

(3) "Governmental agency" includes the Legislature, any governmental entity, board, bureau, commission, department, agency, division, authority, office, or agent, or semi-private governmental entity receiving governmental funds for its operation in whole or in part, or any entity having bonding authority under the Virgin Islands Government in whole or in part.

(4) "Public document" means any public record, regardless of format or purpose, supported in whole or in part by public funds, for distribution by any territorial governmental agency, and which is designated for deposit pursuant to this section, but does not mean inter-office and intra-office memoranda. "Public records" includes printed or audio-visual forms of communication and their accompanying technology.

(5) "Public funds" includes cash, checks, bills, notes, drafts, stocks, bonds and all similar media of exchange which are received or disbursed under law by a governmental agency.

(6) "Publication date" means the earliest date when a copy or copies of the first publication, including preliminary drafts, advance copies, unofficial editions and confidential publications, were placed on sale, donated or exchanged, or made available to any entity outside the publishing governmental agency.

(7) "Library" means any public or private institution which maintains a media of communication collection for loan, internally or externally, including all college or university libraries, public, private or parochial school libraries.

(8) "Recognized newspaper" means any newspaper or publication accepting paid advertisements whose copies are offered for sale, by public subscription or by the copy, or whose copies are distributed without cost to the general public, issued at regular intervals, not to exceed one week.

(c) *Designation and deposit of public documents; lawful custodian for purposes of section 881.* The Territorial Librarian shall designate those public documents of a governmental agency which shall be deposited in depository libraries pursuant to this section, and shall notify the head of said agency, in writing of said designations.

(1) Each governmental agency shall be responsible for supplying the Territorial Librarian with at least two copies of each public document designated for deposit for each depository library, within five weekdays from the publication date of said public document.

(2) The Territorial Librarian shall be responsible for the subsequent distribution of at least two copies of designated public documents to each depository library within two calendar weeks from the date of receipt of said documents.

(3) For purposes of section 881 of this title, the lawful custodian of a public document designated for deposit shall be—

(A) The governmental agency until it has supplied the Territorial Librarian with the number of copies required by paragraph (1) of this subsection;

(B) The Territorial Librarian, upon receipt from the governmental agency of the number of copies of the public document required by paragraph (1) of this subsection, until deposit of said document in the depository libraries as required by paragraph (2) of this subsection;

(C) Notwithstanding subparagraph (A) or (B) of this paragraph, a depository library shall be considered a lawful custodian of all public documents in its possession.

(d) *Index to public records.* Each governmental agency shall be responsible for maintaining an index providing identifying information as to any matter issued, adopted or promulgated by said agency, after June 1, 1977, and required by section 881 of this title to be a public record and which is not designated a public document pursuant to subsection (c) of this section. Each governmental agency shall issue such an index four times a year and supply the Territorial Librarian with at least two copies for each depository library. The Territorial Librarian shall deposit at least two copies of each index in each depository library. The Territorial Library is authorized and directed to—

(1) review, at least annually, all of the records of governmental agencies to assure that indexes are being provided which are adequate to inform the general public and other governmental agencies of what information is available for inspection; and

(2) instruct and aid governmental agencies in establishing record systems which are standardized to the fullest extent possible.

Each governmental agency shall allow the Territorial Librarian access to agency records at reasonable times, upon fifteen days' notice by the Territorial Librarian to the head of said agency, and shall cooperate fully with the Territorial Librarian and his designee in determining what is an appropriate index. If the head of a governmental agency in good faith believes that the Territorial Librarian should not have access to any public record, he may seek an injunction pursuant to section 881(h) of this title, within ten days of the request by the Territorial Librarian to examine the governmental agency's records.

(e) *Quarterly checklist of public documents.* The Territorial Librarian shall issue, each fiscal year quarter, a checklist of the documents that have been sent to the depository libraries in the preceding quarter, according to the following schedule:

Period	Issue Date
July 1 to September 30	October 31
October 1 to December 31	January 31
January 1 to March 31	April 30
April 1 to June 30	July 31

Checklists shall be issued more often if needed, in the discretion of the Territorial Librarian.

Quarterly checklists shall be automatically mailed or distributed free of charge to depository libraries and to any other individual, institution, firm, library or other entity who shall request checklists, either on a single copy or subscription basis. It shall be the responsibility of the Territorial Librarian to fill such requests within a reasonable length of time.

(f) *Duplication fee.* Notwithstanding section 881(c) of this title, neither the Territorial Librarian nor a depository library shall charge any fee for examining a public document other than a reasonable fee for making a duplicate copy of the document.

(g) *Depository libraries.* The depository libraries shall include the St. Thomas Campus Library of the College of the Virgin Islands, the St. Croix Campus Library of the College of the Virgin Islands, the Enid M. Baa Library on the Island of St. Thomas, the Florence Williams Public Library on the Island of St. Croix, the Cruz Bay Public Library on the Island of St. John and any additional libraries designated as depository libraries by the Territorial Librarian.

(h) *Court records excluded*. This section shall not apply to records of the courts of the Virgin Islands. (Added May 11, 1977, No. 3975, § 1, Sess. L. 1977, p. 61.)

EDITORIAL COMMENT

Sections 2 and 3 of the 1977 Act (No. 3975) were not codified. Section 2 reads: "The Territorial Librarian is authorized to recommend to the Commissioner of Conservation and Cultural Affairs and the Governor the hiring of such personnel as are necessary to fulfill the duties of the Territorial Librarian under this Act, including the hiring of a records management officer, qualified by training and experience in records management."

Section 3 provided an appropriation of $15,000 for fiscal year 1976-1977, "to remain available until expended."

VIRGINIA

VA. CODE §§ 2.1-467.1 to 467.2, 467.7 to 467.8 (1979)

§ 2.1-467.1. Definitions. As used in §§ 2.1-467.2 through 2.1-467.8, "*agency*" includes every agency, board, commission, office, department, division, institution or other entity of any branch of the State government. "*Publication*" includes all unrestricted publications of whatever kind which are printed or reproduced in any way, published or issued by an agency of the State in full or in part at State expense. (1977, c. 672.)

§ 2.1-467.2. Agencies to furnish copies to State Library. Every agency shall furnish two copies of each of its publications at the time of issue to the Virginia State Library. The State Librarian may require an agency to deliver to the State Library not exceeding one hundred additional copies of any publication delivered to him under this section. (1977, c. 672; 1979, c.403.)

§ 2.1-467.7. State Librarian to prepare and publish catalog. The State Librarian shall prepare, publish and make available annually a catalog of publications printed by State agencies. Each such publication shall be indexed by subject, author and issuing agency. The date of publication of each listed publication shall be noted in the catalog together with information showing, in appropriate cases, that library copies only are available. To the extent such information is available, the catalog shall set forth the price charged, if any, of each publication and how and where the same may be obtained. (1977, c. 672.)

§ 2.1-467.8. Distribution of catalog. The catalog shall be made available without cost to persons indicating a continuing interest in such catalog. Copies sent out of state shall be on an exchange basis or at a price sufficient to equal the unit cost of printing and mailing; complimentary copies may be made available by the State Librarian. (1977, c. 672.)

STATE COMMENT (1980)

The Virginia State Library distributes to eleven college and university libraries, the Library of Congress and the Center for Research Libraries. The Library is trying to achieve geographical distribution of depositories. (Interview with Linda Bullock, Documents Librarian, Virginia State Library, Richmond, Virginia 23219, January 3, 1980.)

EDITORIAL COMMENT

Virginia has almost identical statutory sections at §§ 2.1-295 et seq. § 2.1-295 is the same as 2.1-467.1 except that § 467.1 adds the words "board, commission, office," and "entity of any."

§§2.1-296 and 2.1-297 were combined in 2.1-467.2. §§ 2.1-467.7 and 467.8 are identical to 2.1-301 and 302.

The 1979 amendment to § 2.1-467.2 deleted the requirement that state agencies furnish one copy of their publications to the Division of Purchases and Supply.

BIBLIOGRAPHY

A news note in *Documents to the People* 6:106 (March 1978) states:

> The State Documents Depository Committee (Deborah Carver is Chairperson) reported that after reviewing other state depository systems, the committee had developed a proposal for supporting legislation for a state documents depository system in Virginia. The committee is working with the Virginia State Library in developing cost estimates and procedures for its introduction and successful passage through the General Assembly. It is hoped that this will be accomplished during the 1978 Session. (Submitted by Sandra K. Peterson, College of William and Mary in Virginia.)

The *Shipping List*, the Virginia documents newsletter (v. 2, nos. 2-4, 1972?), had a ten-page workshop discussion on the acquisition of state documents, led by two staff members from the Virginia State Library. The role of the state library was explained, and the statement was made that the state librarian would be receptive to a depository program. An October 1977 status report announced that a subcommittee had been formed to study the prospects of a depository system. In September 1978, a later status report said that the committee had sent a questionnaire to determine library interest in a program (thirty-three of thirty-five responses were positive). Agreement was reached on the state library's position on the implementation of a state document program. Any new depository was to agree to take all documents; the State Documents Forum was to agree to lobby for any budget request that the state library found necessary. The May 1979 issue of the *Shipping List* carried an announcement of the University of Virginia key word indexes to its Virginia collection (available on COM, $3). That issue also summarized Bob Woolley's speech outlining the basic problems with state documents.

A series of articles written in 1930, none of which has been seen, are:

Corson, J. J. ''Virginia Publishes Many Documents of Importance.'' *Virginia Libraries* 2:73-77 (1930).

''Government Documents for Small Libraries in Virginia.'' *Virginia Libraries* 3:57-62 (1930).

Hall, W. L. ''Bibliography of Virginia Documents: Scope and Methods.'' *Virginia Libraries* 3:43-56 (1930). (Appeared abridged in *ALA Bulletin* 24:457-458 [1930].)

Hall, W. L. ''Some 'Lost' Virginia Documents of the Civil War Period.'' *Virginia Libraries* 3:21-23 (1930).

Robinson, M. P. ''Suitable Materials for Public Records of Virginia.'' *Virginia Libraries* 3:8-18 (1930).

Virginia Library Association, Committee on Virginia Documents. ''The Printing and Distribution of Virginia State Publications.'' *Virginia Libraries* 2:68-73 (1930).

WASHINGTON

WASH. REV. CODE ANN. §§ 40.06.010-.900 (1972 and Supp. 1980-81)

CHAPTER 40.06. STATE PUBLICATIONS DISTRIBUTION CENTER

40.06.010. Definitions. As used in this chapter:

(1) "Print" includes all forms of reproducing multiple copies, with the exception of typewritten correspondence and interoffice memoranda.

(2) "State agency" includes every state office, officer, department, division, bureau, board, commission and agency of the state, and, where applicable, all subdivisions of each.

(3) "State publication" includes annual, biennial, and special reports, state periodicals and magazines, books, pamphlets, leaflets, and all other materials, other than news releases sent exclusively to the news media, typewritten correspondence and interoffice memoranda, issued in print by the state, the legislature, constitutional officers, or any state department, committee, or other state agency supported wholly or in part by state funds. [Amended by Laws 1st Ex Sess 1977 ch 232 § 8.]

40.06.020. Center created as division of state library—Depository library system—Rules and regulations. There is hereby created as a division of the state library, and under the direction of the state librarian, a state publications distribution center. The center shall utilize the depository library system to permit citizens economical and convenient access to state publications. To this end the state library commission shall make such rules and regulations as may be deemed necessary to carry out the provisions of this chapter. [Amended by Laws 1st Ex Sess 1977 ch 232 § 9.]

40.06.030. Deposits by state agencies—Exemptions. (1) Every state agency shall promptly deposit copies of each of its state publications with the state library in quantities as certified by the state librarian as required to meet the needs of the depository library system. Upon consent of the issuing state agency such state publications as are printed by the public printer shall be delivered directly to the center.

(2) In the interest of economy and efficiency, the state librarian may specifically or by general rule exempt a given state publication or class of

publications from the requirements of this section in full or in part. [Amended by Laws 1st Ex Sess 1977 ch 232 § 10.]

40.06.040. Inter-library depository contracts (as amended by 1977 1st ex.s. c 169). The center shall enter into depository contracts with any municipal or county free library, The Evergreen State College, regional university, or state university library, the library of any privately incorporated college or university in this state, the library of congress and the midwest inter-library center, and other state libraries. The requirements for eligibility to contract as a depository library shall be established by the state library commission upon recommendations of the state librarian. The standards shall include and take into consideration the type of library, available housing and space for the publications, the number and qualifications of personnel, and availability for public use. [Amended by Laws 1st Ex Sess 1977 ch 169 § 96.]

40.06.040. Inter-library depository contracts (as amended by 1977 1st ex.s. c 232). To provide economical public access to state publications, the center may enter into depository contracts with any free public library, any state college or state university library, or, if needed, the library of any privately incorporated college or university in this state. The requirements for eligibility to contract as a depository library shall be established by the state library commission upon recommendations of the state librarian. The standards shall include and take into consideration the type of library, available housing and space for the publications, the number and qualifications of personnel, and availability for public use. The center may also contract with public, out-of-state libraries for the exchange of state and other publications on a reciprocal basis. Any state publication to be distributed to the public and the legislature shall be mailed at the lowest available postal rate. [Amended by Laws 1st Ex Sess 1977 ch 232 § 11.]

40.06.050. Center to publish list and other printed matter. The center shall publish and distribute regularly a list of available state publications, and may publish and distribute such other descriptive printed matter as will facilitate the distribution of state publications. (Legislative History: Enacted Laws 1963 ch 233 § 5 p. 1215.)

40.06.060. Agencies to furnish lists to center. Upon request by the center, issuing state agencies shall furnish the center with a complete list of its current state publications and a copy of its mailing and/or exchange lists. (Legislative History: Enacted Laws 1963 ch 233 § 6 p. 1215.)

40.06.070. Exemptions. This chapter shall not apply to nor affect the duties concerning publications distributed by, or officers of:

(1) The state law library;

(2) The statute law committee and the code reviser; and

(3) The secretary of state in connection with his duties under RCW 44.20.030 and 44.20.040. (Legislative History: Enacted Laws 1963 ch 233 § 7 p. 1215.)

40.06.900. Effective date. The effective date of this chapter shall be July 1, 1963. (Legislative History: Enacted Laws 1963 ch 233 § 8 p. 1215.)

STATE COMMENT (1973)

I am quite pleased with the State's depository library legislation. It provides enough clout so that we receive at least three [copies] of the publications for our library and more often than not the required amount for distribution to the depository libraries. During this period of short money a great many publications issued by State agencies have not been published in quantity. (Letter from Corinne B. Ackley, Documents Administrator, Washington State Library, Olympia, Washington 98504, dated May 1, 1973. *In* Documents on Documents Collection.)

EDITORIAL COMMENT

The Washington law, originally enacted in 1963, was not amended until 1977 when the first four sections were amended as part of a broad act relating to state government publications (1977 Laws, c 232). Documents librarians may be interested in this recent act which "[improves] executive management and control of state publications." It provides for consultation with the state librarian on what other printed informational material the term "state publication" might include and for deposit of copies of typewritten and limited edition publications in the state library. Only the parts which amend the State Publications Distribution Center Act are reproduced here.

The 1977 amendments to 40.06.010 were minor changes in the definition of "print," including the addition of the word "typewritten" before "correspondence." The definition of "public document" was eliminated entirely and that of "state agency" was retained with the same wording. The definition of "state publication" was amended to incorporate "annual, biennial, and special reports" (annual and biennial reports were formerly in the definition of "public document"); and to substitute "all other materials" for the enumeration of the types of publications (including document, compilation, journal, law, resolution, bluebook, statute, code, register, list, proceedings, minutes, memorandum, hearing, legislative bill, order, regulation, and directory) in the 1963 law. The exemption of news releases is new.

In 40.06.020 only the second sentence was changed in 1977. It was formerly "The center shall promote the establishment of an orderly depository library system."

40.06.030 formerly read "Every state agency *may* [emphasis added] upon release deposit at least three copies. . . . Additional copies, (as required), shall

also be deposited." The sentence providing for direct delivery to the state
library by the public printer is unchanged. 40.06.030(2) permitting the exemptions is new.

40.06.040 was amended twice in 1977. The first amendment (c 169) made
only one change: "The Evergreen State College, regional university, or state
university library" was substituted for "state college or state university library."

The second amendment (c 232) changed "municipal or county free library"
to "free public library"; inserted "or, if needed" before the provisions for
private colleges and universities; and, eliminated "the library of congress and
the midwest inter-library center, and other state libraries." The provision for
out-of-state libraries "on a reciprocal basis" is new. Also new is the final
sentence on mailing to the public and the legislature at the lowest postal rate.

RCW 1.12.025 provides that, if sections are amended more than once at the
same session, each act shall be given effect to the extent that they do not
conflict in purpose, otherwise the last filed one controls.

The duties referred to in 40.06.070 as "duties under RCW 44.20.030 and
44.20.040" relate to the temporary copies of the acts and their distribution.

RULES AND REGULATIONS

WAC 304-16-010 RULES AND REGULATIONS.

(1) The Washington state library will publish a basic list of documents at
least annually to include an author, title and subject index to the annual list.

(2) Prepare a monthly supplement to the basic list.

(3) Indicate in the monthly supplement if a publication has been sent to the
depositories, availability, etc.

(4) Ship documents at least once a week to all full depository libraries.

(5) Provide the Washington state library classification number and other
pertinent cataloguing data in each shipment as a suggested aid to other libraries
in the organization of the documents.

(6) Confirm with state departments [as specified in RCW 40.06.030] the
number of copies needed for distribution to libraries prior to publication.

(7) All library inquiries, special requests, etc., concerning state
documents for libraries will be channeled through the state library.

(8) There will be periodic revisions of number of copies needed by
libraries.

(9) Libraries should send to the state library names of every department on
whose mailing list they are currently listed.

(10) If disagreement develops on designation of a library as a depository, a
committee of arbitration will be set up by the President of the Washington
Library Association acting under instructions from the Washington Library
Association Executive Board. Any staff member of any library involved who is

also on the Washington Library Association Board will be ineligible to participate in the deliberations preparatory to the arbitration and in the arbitration
itself.

WAC 304-16-020 STANDARDS.

(1) There will be two classes of depository libraries in Washington. These
will be full and partial. Full depositories shall receive copies of all state
publications for distribution by the state library. Partial depositories shall
receive at least a core of general interest publications deemed essential to the
public interest. Any library in the state may request specific documents and, if
it is at all possible, the request will be filled.

(2) Any library designated as a depository shall meet the conditions specified in the following section:

(a) Provide space to house the publications in an approved manner with
adequate provisions for expansion. State publications do not need to be maintained in a separate collection unless the receiving library prefers to do so.
Housing in a vertical file rather than on shelves is acceptable for appropriate
pamphlet-type materials.

(b) Provide an orderly, systematic recording of receipt of the documents.

(c) Process and shelve all state publications within 30 days after receipt
of the material.

(d) Provide a professionally trained librarian to render satisfactory service without charge to qualified patrons in the use of such publications. This
librarian need not spend full time on state publications.

(e) Dispose of publications only with permission of the State Librarian.

(f) Accept and maintain all publications received as depository libraries.

(g) Library rules must assure that the documents are available for public
use and circulation, unless for some unusual reason it becomes necessary to
restrict use.

(3) There will be at least twelve full depositories in the state. Additional
depositories will be established as advisable to provide adequate public access
to Washington State publications.

(4) The State Library shall ensure that the rules, regulations and standards
are maintained.

GUIDELINES FOR THE IMPLEMENTATION OF SB 2121 RELATING TO DISTRIBUTION OF STATE PUBLICATIONS.

DEFINITIONS:

1. State agency includes "every state office, officer, department, division,
   bureau, board, commission and agency of the state, and where applicable, all subdivisions of each." [RCW 40.06.010(2).]

2. State publication includes "annual, biennial, and special reports, state periodicals and magazines, books, pamphlets, leaflets, and all other materials, (other than news releases sent exclusively to the news media, typewritten correspondence and inter-office memoranda) issued in print by the state, the legislature, constitutional officers, or any state department, committee, or other state agency supported wholly or in part by state funds." [RCW 40.06.010(3).]
3. Depository Library includes "free public library, any state college or state university library, or if needed the library of any privately incorporated college or university in this state which enters into a depository library contract with the state library. Public out-of-state libraries may also be designated depository when they contract with the state library for the exchange of state and other publications on a reciprocal basis." [RCW 40.06.040.]

    There are two types of depository libraries:

    1) Full, which will receive copies of all items distributed and 2) Selected, which receive a core of selected publications.

REQUIREMENTS:

1. Any annual, biennial, or special report required to be made by any state officer, board, agency, department, commissioner, regents, trustees, or institution to the governor or to the legislature may be typewritten and a copy shall be filed with the governor, or the governor's designee, and the legislature as the law may require. An additional copy shall be filed with the state library as a public record. [RCW 40.07.030(1).]
2. Every state agency shall deposit copies of each of its state publications with the State Library in quantities as certified by the state librarian to meet the needs of the depository library system. [RCW 40.06.030(1).]

GUIDELINES FOR DETERMINING DEPOSITORY PUBLICATION

1. A depository publication may receive distribution to either full or.selected depository libraries. Sixty copies are needed to meet the needs of full depository libraries. One hundred and twenty-five copies are needed to meet the needs of both full and selected depositories.
2. Full depository publications (i.e., materials sent only to full) are those that are necessary to keep the public informed about the activities of state government. Types of state publications to be designated full depository include but are not limited to:
    A. Annual reports/biennial reports: statements summarizing or projecting the activities of an agency, department, program for the past year(s) or subsequent

B. Revenue/Budget/Economic reports: reports describing the economic condition of the state/agency/program

C. Research reports: reports which through investigation or experimentation lead to the discovery or interpretation of facts of significant interest to Washington State, e.g., demographic, educational, geological fishery, highway forestry, etc.

D. Statistical publications: fact and figure presentations of specific programs and projects of interest to the public

E. Election material: essential to proper voting, e.g., voters' pamphlet, election results, initiatives, referendums, district maps, etc.

F. Social publications indicating the condition of the public welfare in the state: e.g., employment/unemployment, public assistance, law and justice

G. Special publications: publications on timely subjects generated by special economic or social conditions, e.g., drought information

H. Legislative reports, bills, manuals and audits

I. General informational material issued by an agency in an effort to explain a program, create further understanding of its function, and provide information about its relation to the state

J. General informational material about the state: e.g., fishing and hunting seasons, state park directories, etc.

K. Directories listing businesses, registered license holders, etc.

L. Planning publications: e.g., statewide planning publications on such subjects as law and justice, conservation, forestry, fisheries, land, etc.

M. Serial materials which provide, on a regular basis, information on any of the above categories

3. Selected depository publications are those of general interest to the public. Types of state publications to be designated selected (which shall also be distributed to full depository libraries) include:

A. Annual/biennial reports

B. Election material essential to proper voting

C. Social publications indicating the condition of the public welfare in the state

D. Economic/revenue reports indicating the condition of the economy of the state

E. Special publications on timely issues

F. Special legislative reports and the legislative manual

G. General informational material about an agency or the state: e.g., fishing and hunting seasons, state park directories, etc.

H. Serial materials which provide, on a regular basis, any of the above information

4. This category includes publications whose cost prohibits wide distribution. Publications falling into this class will be distributed to the major research centers of the state and require deposit of 15 copies.
5. No publications will be cited depository if they are:
    A. Intra-office administrative operational information (materials intended for a specific limited functional use and distributed to only one specific class and not released to the public)
    B. Inter-office memoranda
    C. Press releases sent exclusively to the news media
    D. Environmental Impact Statements, except when the plan has state-wide impact. Distribution of statements of local interest only will be handled directly by the agency to libraries in concerned areas
    E. Alumni magazines, Brochures, etc. produced by community colleges and/or universities
    F. The State Library may except a given state publication or a class of publications from distribution in the interest of economy

All documents can be sent and questions directed to:

Documents Distribution Center
Washington State Library, AJ-11
Olympia, Washington 98504
Olympia phone No. 753-4027
SCAN No. 234-4027

EDITORIAL COMMENT

SB 2121 is 1977 Laws, 1st Ex. Sess. ch 232.

WEST VIRGINIA

STATE COMMENT

1. The Act of 1905 establishing the Department of Archives and History provided for the distribution of state reports to be exchanged with *other states*. This appears in the Code of 1923 as Section 4.

2. The next provision for distribution of state documents appears in the Acts of the Legislature 1953, Chapter 63. The Department is to send 2 copies of all reports, etc. to state institutions of higher learning.

3. The above distribution program was in effect until March 1972 when Senate Bill 207 amended the code dealing with this Department and the wording changed so that it is more permissive than mandatory. It might be noted that this bill was passed by the Legislature without any consultation with anyone in the Department of Archives and History and has left us unsure and any prospect of a larger or more progressive distribution and depository program uncertain.

We have continued to distribute to the colleges and universities the documents sent to us for that purpose. Until a Director is appointed for this Department, nothing further will be done. (Notes from Department of Archives and History, Charleston, West Virginia 25305, dated December 1974. *In* Documents on Documents Collection.)

EDITORIAL COMMENT

In 1977, the powers and duties of the Department of Archives and History were transferred to the Department of Culture and History (1977 W. Va. Acts 1st Ex. Sess., c 7). The enumeration of the duties of the archives and history division, formerly in section 29-1-4, was included in 29-1-5, but the former subsection (15) was omitted.

The 1953 and 1972 legislation referred to in the "state comment" above read:

1953 W. VA. ACTS, C63

§ 2. State Historian and Archivist; Duties; Annual Report
****

It shall be the duty of each state official in the executive department of the state, board, commission and agency of the state, and the president or superintendent of each state institution to furnish the department of archives and history with a sufficient number of all state papers, public records, reports, documents and pamphlets, printed by the respective official, board, commission, agency and institution at state expense, to supply the library of every state institution of higher learning with two copies of each such publication. The state historian and archivist shall cause two copies of each such publication to be sent to each state institution of higher learning to be deposited in the library thereof.

W. VA. CODE § 29-1-4 (1976)

§ 29-1-4. POWERS AND DUTIES.

The department of archives and history and the state historian and archivist shall have the following powers and duties:
****

(15) To make agreements with the executive department and state boards, commissions and agencies, for the provision of state papers to the department and to such state institutions of higher learning as request them;
****

BIBLIOGRAPHY

Goff, Karen E. "State and State-related Publications." *West Virginia Libraries* 26:16-17 (Fall-Winter 1973).
Annotated list of five publications.

Goff, Karen E. "Bibliographic Control and Acquisition of State Documents." *West Virginia Libraries* 27:23 (Spring 1974).
Goff recommends *Monthly Checklist of State Publications, Legislative Research Checklist, Checklist of West Virginia Publications, West Virginia Blue Book,* and *Book of the States.*

Goff, Karen E. "Legislative Information." *West Virginia Libraries* 29:12 (Spring 1976).
Good explanation of publications which result from the legislative process and how to get them.

WISCONSIN

WIS. STAT. ANN. §§ 35.85(2) (b), (6), (7); 43.05(5)
and 44.06 (West 1980)

35.85 Other distribution. The department shall make the following distribution of public printing in addition to that indicated in s. 35.84:

****

(2)(b) Of every governor's message to the legislature and of every public document or circular printed at the expense of this state including, without limitation because of enumeration, the operating reports of the several departments and agencies of state government and reports publishing the results of studies by state departments and agencies, to every depository library under s. 43.05(5) the number of copies designated by the state superintendent.

****

(6) The state superintendent shall receive for his own use one copy of each document distributed under sub. (2) (b) and shall file with the department lists of public documents to be distributed to libraries designated as depositories of public documents under s. 43.05(5).

(7) There shall be delivered to the historical society 3 copies of every document reproduced at the expense of the state. The chief clerks of the legislature are responsible for the delivery of all legislative documents, and the department for all other public documents. Distribution shall also be made to the legislative reference bureau in accordance with sub. (11m).

****

43.05. General duties of division. The division shall:

****

(5) Ascertain which libraries in this state can suitably care for and advantageously use copies of the public documents printed at the expense of the state, including printing under ss. 35.28 and 35.29. The division shall designate the selected libraries as depositories of state documents and shall furnish lists of the depositories to the department of administration, to govern the distribution under s. 35.85(2) (b). All libraries designated as depositories for federal documents shall automatically be designated as depositories for state documents. The lists shall show, for each depository library, the number of copies of each printed state document it is to receive.

****

(Source: L. 1971, c. 152, § 15, eff. Dec. 17, 1971. Legislative Council Note, 1971: Restates and rearranges ss 43.10(2) and 43.14. Amended L. 1980, c. 347, § 12.)

44.06. Depository of public documents.

(1) The historical society shall be the official public documents depository for the state of Wisconsin. Three copies of all printed, mimeographed, or otherwise reproduced state publications, reports, releases and other matter published at the expense of the state shall be sent to the historical society by the department of administration in accordance with s. 35.85(7). In those instances where a given publication is not distributed by the department of administration, 3 copies shall be sent to the historical society by the department, commission or agency of origin. (HISTORY—Amended by L. 1969, c. 276, § 596, eff. Dec. 28, 1969. L. 1959, c. 516, § 4.)

(2) The director of the historical society shall file with the department of administration, and may revise, lists of state, county, municipal, federal, or other agencies to which state public printing should be distributed in accordance with interstate or international comity, with or without exchange, as provided in s. 35.86, in order to maintain or enlarge the reference collections of the society and the state. The documents so specified shall be shipped to the addresses directly from the office of the department of administration, carriage charges payable by the state. (HISTORY: Subsec. (2) amended by L. 1967, c. 29, § 4, eff. May 18, 1967. L. 1959, c. 659, § 77.)

(5) The historical society shall prepare a periodic checklist of public documents issued by the state, including all reports, circulars, bulletins and releases issued by the various state departments, boards, commissions and agencies and shall publish this list in such form and with such notes as to show the scope and purpose of such publication.

STATE COMMENT

I think our depository program within the State is realistic. The Division for Library Services determines which public and academic libraries within the State other than the Historical Society should receive depository copies. Presently 55 Wisconsin libraries are depository. The three copies which we receive are eventually added to by all the discards from State agencies. And according to the Statutes (35.86) we are permitted to engage in exchange agreements with other libraries out-of-state, but our exchange program is very limited. Administration of the State program is not centralized. We prepare the Checklist (under John Peters' editorship), and the Division of Library Services with the help of each agency distributes the actual copies on the basis of what is listed in the Checklist to the various depository libraries within the State. Outside of the State distribution is from Document Sales in the Dept. of Administration to the libraries designated by the State Historical Society.

Under 35.86 this is to 5 to 22 libraries and they receive only the Bluebook, Statutes, Laws, Opinions of the Attorney General, Report of the Public Service Commission, and the Legislative Journals. We receive on deposit material from several states e.g., California, Texas, Pennsylvania, New York, etc. Occasionally we make lists and exchange with or give to other States in an effort to weed out our stored material of Wisconsin duplicates. We also accumulate duplications from our Legislative Reference Bureau from other states. (Letter from Alice Alderman, Documents Cataloger, State Historical Society of Wisconsin, Madison, Wisconsin 53706, dated January 11, 1973. *In* Documents on Documents Collection.)

EDITORIAL COMMENT

§ 35.86, referred to above, is a section on exchanges. A 1915 attorney general's opinion interpreting this section held that public documents could be sent to "standard libraries of the country even though such libraries cannot offer documents in return" (4 Wis. Op. Att'y Gen. 459 [1915]).

The definition of "public document" in § 35.86(4), amended in 1979 to add the opinions and decisions of the transportation commission, ends with "and all serial publications distributed in quantities of 25 copies or more and consisting of 25 pages or more," a different approach to the problem of what to include within the definition.

ATTORNEY GENERAL OPINION

1915 WIS. ATT'Y GEN. OP. 459

May 28, 1959

Hon. M. M. Quaife, *Superintendent,*
State Historical Society
Madison, Wisconsin.

In your communication of the 19th inst. you ask to be advised, in effect, whether sec. 20.82, Stats., authorizes you to direct the distribution of public documents to libraries and similar institutions of other states when such libraries and other institutions are not in a position to offer a tangible equivalent in the form of similar documents.

I have considered the provisions of sec. 20.82 as affecting the situation suggested in your letter, and it seems to me that the dominant purpose of that provision of law is to prevent prodigal and wasteful distribution of public documents. I do not think it was the legislative intent to withhold the public documents of this state from the standard public libraries of the country to which the public documents of other states are usually and generally supplied. The language of the section does not express this idea as clearly as it might, but the phrase "as may accord with interstate and international comity," is of sufficient elasticity to permit of this interpretation.

An intent to withhold the public documents of this state from the large standard libraries of the country to which the public documents of other states are freely furnished should not be imputed to the legislature of this state, thus convicting it of a narrow and penurious policy as compared with the policy of its sister states. I think the phrase above quoted was intended to vest the superintendent of the state historical society with discretion in such matters, to the end that he might be generous in making such wise distribution of the public documents of the state as would accord with the usages of other states and at the same time operate as a restraint upon the theretofore extravagant and wasteful distribution thereof. I may add that Honorable L. R. Nash, revisor of statutes, who prepared the present printing law, agrees with me in this construction, and I, therefore, announce my conclusion with the greater assurance.

BIBLIOGRAPHY

The survey of Wisconsin publications on documents begins with a flurry of publishing in 1974 (Alderman, Boll, Kopischke, and Schwarz), followed by two articles in 1976 and a major series of articles in 1977. Miscellaneous articles cited in the literature are included at the end.

Alderman, Alice. *Organizing Wisconsin Public Documents: Cataloging and Classification of Documents at the State Historical Society Library*. Madison, Wis.: Department of Public Instruction, Division for Library Services, 1974. (Not seen.)
Parish annotates this item under a title beginning ''Procedures for cataloging . . . ,'' and says, ''Unique guide of cataloging rules, corporate entries, outline of agency records according to the Schellenberg theory, and Wisconsin agency codes.''

Boll, John J. ''Tame the Terror for Its Use, or What Are Wisconsin Documents?'' *Wisconsin Library Bulletin* 70:79-82 (March-April 1974).
Many definitions exist. Alton Tisdel is credited with ''the terror of librarians.'' Common elements in the definitions are ''publications *by* the government, or *for* the government, or at government expense'' [italics in original], sometimes adding, ''*for public distribution*.'' According to Boll, a broad definition is ''the only realistic one,'' and he continues, ''The use of a narrow definition would not decrease the number of items published with public money; it could only decrease the number that reach libraries easily.'' Publication expenses are ''only a tiny fraction of the total expenditure of a state government.''
    There are five types of publications, resulting from governing, operating, work (directories and research reports), helping citizens, and publicity, with many publications fitting into more than one category.
    Boll wants libraries to be able to select and receive with ease, without great expenditure of time, and with certainty that selection is being made from the total production. He favors central printing, central distribution, and realistic financial support of the bibliographical control agency.
    Boll suggests an ''automatic distribution from a central agency, not by series concept, but by subject concept and level-of-use concept.'' Several sections of the Wisconsin statutes are at the end of the article.

Kopischke, John. "State Document Depositories: Wisconsin Outlines a New Approach."
     Wisconsin Library Bulletin 70:131-133 (May-June 1974).
Kopischke begins with early laws (1901 and 1903), comments at length on implementation, and compares the Wisconsin system with the federal system, pointing out the
weaknesses of the Wisconsin system. The Bureau for Reference and Loan Services (of
which Kopischke is director) has undertaken a project to revise the Wisconsin system.
     The revision involves a new staff position, to which Kathy Schneider was appointed.
She began with in-house problems and then studied, by questionnaire, the problems of
the depository libraries. She is developing a regional approach to the depository system.
The next step is a Public Documents Advisory Board to coordinate the efforts of the four
agencies involved with public document access.

Schwarz, Philip. "Key-word Indexing of Wisconsin Public Documents." *Documents
     to the People* 2:14 (February 1974).
A KWOC (key-word-out-of-context) index was developed for the state documents
when the library was converting from Dewey to LC. A sample entry and data for
figuring costs are included. (This project was reported by the author in RQ 11:250-252
[Spring 1972].)

Alderman, Alice. "Classifying State Documents." *Documents to the People* 4:58-63
     (May 1976).
Because documents librarians are firm in the opinion that separate collections for
documents are best, they are forced to accept, choose, or devise a classification
scheme. The paper reviews what a committee, which had been collecting classification
schemes since 1973, viewed as important as to (1) the nature of classification schemes,
(2) the nature of classification schemes which deal with state documents, and (3) the
nature of state documents themselves.
     A classification scheme should be infinitely hospitable, have a quality of linearity, be
an understandable notation, and possess structure.
     Classification schemes for state documents have been designated either archival or
subject classification. A recently developed type of scheme has been recognized as
record series. The purpose of all three is to keep titles or series together on the shelves.
Both an archival scheme and a subject scheme require modification in practice.
     State documents themselves can be categorized by first drawing off the reference
documents, then the collected documents, and then dividing them along functional
lines, placing those documents acquired for their subject value in whatever collection is
appropriate.
     Alderman says, "The proper scheme for any library has to be made to serve the
library. The library should not be made to serve the scheme."

Schneider, Kathy. "Do You Know What Government Is Doing." *Wisconsin Library
     Bulletin* 72:45 (January-February 1976).
The State Depository Program Exhibit at the Wisconsin Library Association conference
displayed documents to illustrate the potential usefulness of Wisconsin documents and
to explain where and how to acquire them.
     A series of six articles (a seventh one on municipal documents by Ann Waidelich is
not included) are published in *Wisconsin Library Bulletin* 73:29-38 (January-February
1977).

Schneider, Kathy. "The Public's Right to Know: Government Must Give an Account of
      Itself."
Government accountability "means justifiable conduct and keeping the public informed
. . . the depository libraries share in the responsibility for getting information to the
public."

Crane, Elizabeth R. "Privilege vs. Responsibility: Document Depositories Are Meant
      to Serve Library Users."
The library (a public library, evidently) accepted the responsibility of depository status
because the documents are free and there is no costly acquisitions procedure. The
decision was based on the conviction that there is a need for the material and that the
library has an obligation to supply such resources. "[T]he immediacy of access
. . . makes this service valuable."
    For nondepository librarians, the selection of documents is often time-consuming
and frustrating. To receive documents with reasonable assurance that a needed publication has not been overlooked and without the necessity of selection is particularly
helpful.

Britten, Christine. "What Do You Do with Them? Put Your Documents Where Their
      Service Is."
Sample comments from this cheerful, popularly written article are: "All documents are
designed to appeal to someone, but they need an occasional spotlight to bring them out
of the shadows to their place in the sun." "Of course when documents don't appeal to
the librarian, they have little chance to appeal to the public."
    The author concludes, "Most important, let's smile when we say 'document,' and be
sure to think 'bonsai, beekeeping, canning, farming, space travel, pollution
. . . people.' Documents are for everyone."

Schultz, Carol J. "Research and Archives Plan."
The author is state documents librarian and cataloger at the Legislative Reference
Bureau. The collection has been in existence over one hundred years and serves both
archival and research purposes. The shelf arrangement is alphabetical by issuing agency
with hierarchical arrangement of divisions. Classification numbers are assigned.

Lueck, Barbara A. "Quick—a Document, Please!"
The author, documents librarian at a public library, mentions some ways of handling
documents in the library. They can be displayed after cataloging, put in the vertical file,
or be sent to the documents collection in the basement. She describes records kept.

Schneider, Kathy. "New Documents Legislation? A Wisconsin Proposal Would Ease
      and Speed Document Use."
The documents librarian of the Reference and Loan Library discusses the proposed
depository legislation. The purpose of the legislation is "to clearly identify a depository
library system, to describe a procedure for centralized document distribution to designated libraries and to define statutorily what constitutes a public document." The
legislation would also establish a permanent advisory council.
    Wisconsin has had a documents program for many years. The problem was not with
the depository libraries, but with acquiring the documents for distribution. Agencies

were unaware of their statutory obligations or were confused by the vague and contra-
dictory language of the statutes.

A documents advisory committee was set up in 1975 by the State Superintendent [of
Education] to recommend new legislation. The committee needed to decide whether to
limit itself to the depository library system or to encompass all document distribution,
and whether to recommend the repeal of all old legislation and the enactment of a new
chapter of laws.

The committee found that most people were satisfied with the intent of the law, but
that it lacked clarity. In addition, the committee believed that the law should contain
both "an expressed awareness of the need for document accessibility for all citizens"
and "a provision to restrict the extensive and haphazard free distribution of documents
that resulted in high state printing costs."

The committee held a meeting with agency printing people. After fifteen months, the
final draft was ready. The seven major provisions were: (1) to insure awareness, (2) to
encourage state agencies to distribute through the program, (3) to describe a depository
system, (4) to define public document, (5) to provide for accountability of the producers of public documents in terms of distribution, (6) to establish a permanent
advisory council, and (7) to draw existing sections together into a new chapter, "Public
Document Distribution and Sales."

Schneider, Kathy. "Wisconsin State Printing." *Wisconsin Library Bulletin* 73:142
(May-June 1977).
"Over the past few years, the staff of the Reference and Loan Library has worked
closely with the State Printing people to develop an awareness of library usage of
Wisconsin publications."

Other titles, cited in the literature but not seen, are:

Hays, F. C. "Author Headings for Current Wisconsin State Publications." *Wisconsin
Library Bulletin* 11:140-142 (May 1915).

Jackson, Ruth L. W. *Author Headings for the Official Publications of the State of
Wisconsin*. Chicago: American Library Association, 1954. 211 p.

Marshall, P. G. "Wisconsin Statutory Materials." *Law Library Journal* 35:316-324
(September 1942).
A historical account. The author refers to the constant revision system now being used
for the statutory compilation.

"State Documents." *See* issues of *Wisconsin Library Bulletin*, 1970-1973.

Whitlock, R. L. "Author Headings for the Official Publications of the State of Wisconsin." M.A. Thesis, University of Illinois, 1941. 364 p.

WYOMING

WYO. STAT. §§ 9-1-109 to 9-1-110 (1977)

§ 9-1-109. Copies of publications; deposited with state library. Each and every state officer, commission, commissioner or board of a state institution shall deposit in the state library, for its permanent file, four (4) copies of every publication which they issue. (Laws 1941, ch. 84, § 2; C. S. 1945, § 18-107; W. S. 1957, § 9-7.)

§ 9-1-110. Same; deposited with university library. Each and every state officer, commission, commissioner or board of a state institution shall deposit in the university library at Laramie at least one (1) copy of every publication and report which they issue. (Laws 1941, ch. 84, § 3; C. S. 1945, § 18-108; W. S. 1957, § 9-8.)

STATE COMMENT (1980)

As of January, 1980, there are only two provisions for depository libraries for state publications. The State Library (9-1-109) and the University (9-1-110, Wyo. Stat. 1977).

Because ''publications'' are not defined, the State Library is at the mercy of the issuing agencies to provide publications. Fortunately, most agencies have been most cooperative in providing the State Library with materials.

Pending adequate staffing, plans are to use OCLC cataloging (AACR II) to create a quarterly catalog, using the system created by the Kansas State Library.

Presently, a ''checklist'' of state publications appears in the *Outrider*, a publication of the State Library. (Letter from Jerome B. Frobom, Head, Government Publications Depository, Wyoming State Library, Cheyenne, Wyoming 82002, dated January 7, 1980.)

BIBLIOGRAPHY

Fisher, Hail. *Author Headings for the Official Publications of the State of Wyoming.* Chicago: American Library Association, 1951. 60 p. (Not seen.)

MODEL LAW

Monthly Checklist of State Publications, December 1969, p. iv.
Also included in: Council of State Governments, *1971 Suggested State Legislation*, pp. 104-105.

The following is recommended as a guide for States desiring to provide by law for furnishing the Library of Congress with copies of their official publications. Note that sections 1 and 3 are designed to provide for establishing a centralized administrative source to collect and distribute official publications. If a State already has this capability, sections 1 and 3 may be omitted. Note also that in section 2, which contains the basic provision of distributing publications to the Library of Congress, the ideal number of copies desired by the Library within each listed category is suggested in square brackets.

Be it enacted by the _____ of the State of _____:

Section 1. The _____ shall be the administrator, collector, and distributor of official State documents in printed or nearprint form. The several departments of the State government shall, upon request of the _____, supply said _____ _____ with such copies of their reports and other publications as may be necessary to effect exchange with other States for similar publications for the use of _____ or distribution to other agencies as provided herein.

Section 2. The _____ is authorized and directed to furnish the Library of Congress [five (5)] copies of the Session Laws, [five (5)] copies of Codes or Statutes, [one (1)] set(s) of Legislative Journals, [five (5)] copies of Court Reports as issued, and [two (2)] copies of all other official State publications in printed or nearprint form. Such specified numbers of copies shall be distributed to the Library of Congress before the State Printer shall certify the payment of any bill for printing or reproduction from State funds.

Section 3. The _____ shall, at his discretion, distribute publications so received to the public libraries, and other educational, scientific, literary, or art institutions of the State, which may apply to be put on the mailing list for all or a portion of the State publications; and to such libraries and other institutions outside this State with which the _____ _____ may have established exchange arrangements.

Section 4. This Act shall be in full force and effect following its approval.

INDEX

About the Author

Margaret T. Lane was formerly the administrator of the Louisiana depository program. She lobbied for the Louisiana depository legislation, was in charge of the program for twenty-six years, and, because Louisiana was one of the first states with depository legislation, helped and advised librarians in many other states. She received the Louisiana Library Association Culver Award in 1976 for distinguished library service.

Mrs. Lane now works independently on state documents projects and is currently serving as Coordinator of the State and Local Documents Task Force of the Government Documents Round Table of the American Library Association.